PEARSON BACCALAUREATE

STANDARD LEVEL

Physics

DEVELOPED SPECIFICALLY FOR THE

IB DIPLOMA

CHRIS HAMPER • KEITH ORD

PEARSON

Pearson Education Limited is a company incorporated in England and Wales, having its registered office at Edinburgh Gate, Harlow, Essex, CM20 2JE. Registered company number: 872828

www.pearsonbaccalaureate.com

Text © Pearson Education Limited 2007

First published 2007

13 12 11
10 9 8 7 6 5

ISBN 978 0 435994 47 1

Edited by Maggie Rumble and Alexandra Clayton
Designed by Tony Richardson
Typeset by Tech-Set Ltd
Original illustrations © Pearson Education Limited 2007
Illustrated by Tech-Set Ltd
Cover design by Tony Richardson
Printed and bound in China (SWTC)

Acknowledgements
The authors and publisher would like to thank the following individuals and organisations for permission to reproduce photographs:
© Alamy Images pp 16 (Craig Holmes), 37 (Imagebroker), 38 (The Print Collector), 137-bottom (Tetra), 293 (Mary Evans Picture Library), 295 (Pictorial Press Ltd), 366-top (SciencePhotos), 366-bottom (M Shields Photos), 368, 385-bottom; © Chris Hamper p 279; © Mike Baldwin (Cornered) p 418-top; © Brand X Pictures p 176; © Corbis pp. 19 (EPA/Ahmad Yusni), 397, 404; © Digital Vision pp.70, 148, 179-bottom, 418-bottom, 421-top; © Getty Images pp 92, 116, 129, 235, 281, 387-top, 414-bottom right (PhotoDisc), (StockDisc); © Pearson Ltd pp 103, 366-margin (Trevor Clifford), 276 (Gareth Boden), 398, 421-bottom (Tudor Photography); © iStockPhoto.com pp 83 (Paul Piebinga), 415-bottom right (Lise Gagne); © NASA p.26 (Johnson Space Center); © Omegatron p 282; © Pasco p 127; © Photos.com p 416; © Punchstock p 195 (Fancy); © Science Photo Library pp 1, 190, 273 (Detlev Van Ravenswaay), 2 (SLAC), 24 (TRL Ltd), 27, 106, 191, 380, 386, 415-top (Sheila Terry), 32, 53, 97, 226, 247-top (Edward Kinsman), 51, 63 (Charles D Winters), 52, 151, 251, 384 (Mehau Kulyk), 56 (Dr Arthur Tucker), 58 (John Beatty), 80, 82, 96, 107, 137-top, 220, 234, 304 (Andrew Lambert Photography), 85 (FS Westmoreland), 86, 193 (Martin Bond), 93 (Alex Bartel), 95 (Erich Schrempp), 98, 215, 218, 385-top (David Parker), 99 (Pasquale Sorrentino), 109 (David R Frazier), 147, 414-bottom left (Dr Matk J Winter), 156 (C.T.R. Wilson), 159-top (Maria Platt-Evans), 159-bottom (Philippe Psaila), 161 (Prof. K. Seddon & Dr T Evans, Queens Univ. Belfast), 163 (Seymour), 172 (Maximillion Stock Ltd), 179-top (Simon Fraser), 183, 414-top (Ria Novosti), 188 (EFDA-JET), 192 (Bernhard Edmaier), 207 (John Chumack), 209 (Dr Juerg Alean), 217 (Annabella Bluesky), 230 (Andrew Syred), 239 (Volker Steger), 245 (Omikron), 246 (Dr David Wexler, Coloured by Dr Jeremy Burgess), 247-bottom (Physics Dept., Imperial College), 252, 269 (Christian Darkin), 264 (Dr Tony Brain), 270 (Dr Jeremy Burgess), 277 (Thomas Porett), 288 (Library of Congress), 292 (Colin Cuthbert), 311 (Goronwy Tudor Jones, University of Birmingham), 317 (Leonard Lessin), 299 (CERN), 326-top (David Nunek), 326-bottom (Canada-France-Hawaii Telescope), 327, 334-top (Mark Garlick), 328-top (Maddox, Sutherland, Efstathiou & Loveday), 328-bottom (Ron Sandford), 333 (National Optical Astronomy Observation), 334-bottom (G Bacon, NASA, ESA, STSci), 345 (Laguna Design), 351 (David May Jones), 387-bottom (R Mesna, Fundamental Photo), 389 (Coneyl Jay), 420-top (B McNamara (University of Waterloo), NASA, ESA, STSci), 420-bottom (KH Kjeldsen), 89 (David Weintraub), 155, 157, 257, 259, 377, 415-bottom left, 417; © Windows to the Universe p.334-top.

Cover photograph of fibre optic cable reproduced with kind permission of © Getty Images / PhotoDisc and of particle tracks reproduced with kind permission of © Science Photo Library.

Every effort has been made to contact copyright holders of material reproduced in this book. Any omissions will be rectified in subsequent printings if notice is given to the publishers.

The assessment statements and various examination questions have been reproduced from IBO documents and past examination papers. Our thanks go to the International Baccalaureate Organization for permission to reproduce its intellectual copyright.

This material has been developed independently by the publisher and the content is in no way connected with nor endorsed by the International Baccalaureate Organization.

There are links to relevant websites in this book. In order to ensure that the links are up-to-date, that the links work, and that the sites are not inadvertently linked to sites that could be considered offensive, we have made the links available on our website at www.heinemann.co.uk/hotlinks. When you access the site, the express code is 4266S (S for Secondary).

Contents

Introduction   vi

1: Physics and physical measurement   1

    1.1 The realm of physics   1

    1.2 Measurement and uncertainties   3

    1.3 Vectors and scalars   10

2: Mechanics   15

    2.1 Kinematics   15

    2.2 Forces and dynamics   25

    2.3 Work, energy and power   33

    2.4 Uniform circular motion   40

3: Thermal physics   50

    3.1 Thermal concepts   50

    3.2 Thermal properties of matter   55

    3.3 Kinetic model of an ideal gas   62

4: Simple harmonic motion and waves   70

    4.1 Kinematics of simple harmonic motion   70

    4.2 Energy changes during simple harmonic motion (SHM)   78

    4.3 Forced oscillations and resonance   80

    4.4 Wave characteristics   85

    4.5 Wave properties   92

5: Electrical currents   103

    5.1 Electric potential difference, current and resistance   103

    5.2 Electric circuits   110

6: Fields and forces   127

    6.1 Gravitational force and field   127

    6.2 Electric force and field   132

    6.3 Magnetic force and field   137

7: Atomic and nuclear physics   144

    7.1 The atom   144

    7.2 Nuclear structure   149

    7.3 Radioactive decay   154

    7.4 Half-life   160

    7.5 Nuclear reactions   162

Contents

8: Energy, power and climate change — 169

8.1 Energy degradation and power generation — 169

8.2 World energy sources — 173

8.3 Fossil fuel power production — 177

8.4 Nuclear power — 181

8.5 Solar power — 189

8.6 Hydroelectric power — 191

8.7 Wind power — 194

8.8 Wave power — 196

8.9 The greenhouse effect — 198

8.10 Global warming — 205

8.11 What might happen and what can be done? — 209

9: Sight and wave phenomena — 215

9.1 The eye and sight — 215

9.2 Standing (stationary) waves — 219

9.3 The Doppler effect — 223

9.4 Diffraction — 226

9.5 Resolution — 228

9.6 Polarization — 231

10: Quantum physics and nuclear physics — 239

10.1 Quantum physics — 239

10.2 Nuclear physics — 254

11: Digital technology — 263

11.1 Analogue and digital signals — 263

11.2 Data capture; digital imaging — 275

11.3 Electronics — 281

11.4 The mobile phone system — 288

12: Relativity and particle physics — 293

12.1 Introduction to relativity — 293

12.2 Concepts and postulates of special relativity — 295

12.3 Relativistic kinematics — 297

12.4 Description and classification of particles — 303

12.5 Fundamental interactions — 306

12.6 Quarks — 314

12.7 Feynmann diagrams — 318

13: Astrophysics   325

    13.1 Introduction to the universe   325

    13.2 Stellar radiation and stellar types   329

    13.3 Stellar distances   337

    13.4 Cosmology   343

14: Radio communication   351

    14.1 Radio communication   351

    14.2 Digital signals   359

    14.3 Optic fibre transmission   367

    14.4 Channels of communication   372

15: Electromagnetic waves   380

    15.1 The nature of EM waves and light sources 380

    15.2 Two-source interference of waves   390

    15.3 Diffraction grating   394

    15.4 Lenses and image formation   396

    15.5 Optical instruments   402

    15.6 Aberrations   409

16: Theory of knowledge   414

Internal assessment   424

Extended essay   430

Answers   433

Index   441

Introduction

Welcome to your new course! This book is designed to act as a comprehensive course book, covering both the core material and all the options you might take while studying for the IB Diploma in Physics at Standard Level. It will also help you to prepare for your examinations in a thorough and methodical way.

Content

As you will see when you look at the table of contents, there is a chapter for each of the core topics, and for each of the options you might choose to take. Within each chapter, there are numbered exercises for you to practise and apply the knowledge that you have gained. They will also help you to assess your progress. Sometimes, there are worked examples that show you how to tackle a particularly tricky or awkward question.

Worked example

A mass on a spring is oscillating with a frequency 0.2 Hz and amplitude 3.0 cm. What is the displacement of the mass 10.66 s after it is released from the top?

Solution

$$x = x_0 \cos \omega t. \qquad \text{Since this is SHM}$$

where x = displacement

$\qquad x_o$ = amplitude = 3 cm

$\qquad \omega$ = angular velocity = $2\pi f = 2\pi \times 0.2$

$\qquad\quad = 0.4\pi$ Hz

$\qquad t$ = time = 10.66 s

$\qquad x = 0.03 \times \cos(0.4\pi \times 10.66).$ Substituting into the formula.

$\qquad x = 0.02$ m

$\qquad\quad = \mathbf{2\ cm}$

At the end of each chapter, there are practice questions taken from past exam papers. Towards the end of the book, just before the index, you will find pages with numerical answers to all the exercises and practice questions that have been included. The answers are grouped into Exercises and Practice questions for each chapter.

After the options chapters, you will find a Theory of Knowledge chapter, which should stimulate wider research and the consideration of moral and ethical issues in the field of physics.

Finally, there are two short chapters offering advice on internal assessment and on writing extended essays.

Information boxes

Throughout the book you will see a number of coloured boxes interspersed through each chapter. Each of these boxes provides different information and stimulus as follows.

Assessment statements
4.1.1   Describe examples of oscillations.
4.1.2   Define the terms *displacement*, *amplitude*, *frequency*, *period* and *phase difference*.

You will find a box like this at the start of each section in each chapter. They are the numbered objectives for the section you are about to read and they set out what content and aspects of learning are covered in that section.

When we say light is a wave we mean it has the same properties as a wave. Does this mean it actually *is* a wave?

In addition to the Theory of Knowledge chapter, there are ToK boxes throughout the book. These boxes are there to stimulate thought and consideration of any ToK issues as they arise and in context. Often they will just contain a question to stimulate your own thoughts and discussion.

Light and sound
Both light and sound are disturbances that spread out, so can be thought of as waves. Light can be polarized (for example, by Polaroid sunglasses) but sound cannot. This is one way to tell that light is transverse and sound is longitudinal.

These boxes contain interesting information which will add to your wider knowledge but which does not fit within the main body of the text.

Since waves in a string do not spread out, they cannot diffract or refract. You would have to observe the 2D equivalent, waves in a rubber sheet, to see this.

These facts are drawn out of the main text and are highlighted. This makes them useful for quick reference and they also enable you to identify the core learning points within a section.

The acceleration due to gravity is slightly lower off the coast of India and slightly higher in the South Pacific, owning to the nature of the rocks in the Earth's crust.

These boxes indicate examples of internationalism within the area of study. The information in these boxes gives you the chance to think about how biology fits into the global landscape. They also cover environmental and political issues raised by your subject.

● **Examiner's hint:** In an exam do not say that energy is 'lost' but instead say it has been changed or converted to other forms.

These boxes can be found alongside questions, exercises and worked examples and they provide insight into how to answer a question in order to achieve the highest marks in an examination. They also identify common pitfalls when answering such questions and suggest approaches that examiners like to see.

To see a simple spreadsheet model for the Earth (without the greenhouse effect), visit, www.heinemann.co.uk/hotlinks, enter the express code 4266S and click on Weblink 8.9. Here you will also find a lot of information about climate change and details of the other simulations they are running.

These boxes direct you to the Heinemann website, which in turn will take you to the relevant website(s). On the web pages you will find background information to support the topic, video simulations and the like.

Now you are ready to start. Good luck with your studies!

1 Physics and physical measurement

The realm of physics

Assessment statements

1.1.1 State and compare quantities to the nearest order of magnitude.
1.1.2 State the ranges of magnitude of distances, masses and times that occur in the universe, from the smallest to the largest.
1.1.3 State ratios of quantities as different orders of magnitude.
1.1.4 Estimate approximate values of everyday quantities to one or two significant figures and/or to the nearest order of magnitude.

Range of magnitudes of quantities in our universe

Physics seeks to explain the universe itself, from the very large to the very small. At the large end, the size of the visible universe is thought to be around 10^{25} m, and the age of the universe some 10^{18} s. The total mass of the universe is estimated to be 10^{50} kg.

 How do we know all this is true? What if there is more than one universe?

A planet was recently discovered in the constellation Libra (about 20 light years from Earth) that has all the right conditions to support alien life. This artist's impression shows us how it might look.

Some physicists think that there are still undiscovered particles whose size is around the Planck length.

What are the reasons for there being a lower limit for length? Why should there be a lower limit for time?

The diameter of an atom is about 10^{-10} m, and of a nucleus 10^{-15} m. The smallest particles may be the quarks, probably less than 10^{-18} m in size, but there is a much smaller fundamental unit of length, called the Planck length, which is around 10^{-35} m.

There are good reasons for believing that this is a lower limit for length, and we accept the speed of light in a vacuum to be an upper limit for speed ($3 \times 10^8 \, \text{m s}^{-1}$). This enables us to calculate an approximate theoretical lower limit for time:

$$\text{time} = \frac{\text{distance}}{\text{speed}}$$

$$= \frac{10^{-35} \, \text{m}}{10^8 \, \text{m s}^{-1}} = 10^{-43} \, \text{s}.$$

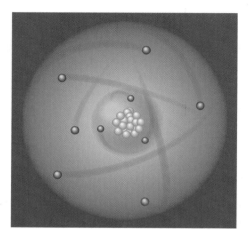

Figure 1.1 The exact position of electrons in an atom is uncertain; we can only say where there is a high probability of finding them.

Rest mass is the mass of a particle when at rest; the mass increases if the particle moves fast enough.

If the quarks are truly fundamental, then their mass would give us a lower limit. Quarks hide themselves inside protons and neutrons so it is not easy to measure them. Our best guess is that the mass of the lightest quark, called the *up quark*, is around 10^{-30} kg, and this is also the approximate rest mass of the electron.

Production and decay of bottom quarks. There are six types of quarks called *up, down, charm, strange, top* and *bottom*.

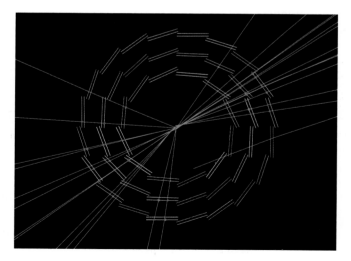

If we can split an atom why can't we split an electron?

You need to be able to state ratios of quantities as differences of orders of magnitude. For example, the approximate ratio of the diameter of an atom to its nucleus is:

$$\frac{10^{-10} \, \text{m}}{10^{-15} \, \text{m}} = 10^5$$

10^5 is known as a difference of five orders of magnitude.

This is not a small ratio; it means that if the atom were as big as a football pitch, then the nucleus would be about the size of a pea on the centre circle. This implies that most of the atoms of all matter consist of entirely empty space.

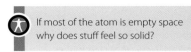 If most of the atom is empty space why does stuff feel so solid?

Another example is that the ratio of the rest mass of the proton to the rest mass of the electron is of the order:

$$\frac{1.67 \times 10^{-27} \text{ kg}}{9.11 \times 10^{-31} \text{ kg}} \approx 2 \times 10^3$$

You should be able to do these estimations without using a calculator.

Exercise

1 The diameter of a proton is of the order of magnitude of
   A 10^{-12} m.   B 10^{-15} m.   C 10^{-18} m   D 10^{-21} m.

You also need to be able to estimate approximate values of everyday quantities to one or two significant figures.

For example, estimate the answers to the following:

How high is a two-storey house in metres?

What is the diameter of the pupil of your eye?

How many times does your heart beat in an hour when you are relaxed?

What is the weight of an apple in newtons?

What is the mass of the air in your bedroom?

What pressure do you exert on the ground when standing on one foot?

There is help with these estimates at the end of the chapter.

1.2 Measurement and uncertainties

Assessment statements

1.2.1   State the fundamental units in the SI system.
1.2.2   Distinguish between fundamental and derived units and give examples of derived units.
1.2.3   Convert between different units of quantities.
1.2.4   State units in the accepted SI format.
1.2.5   State values in scientific notation and in multiples of units with appropriate prefixes.
1.2.6   Describe and give examples of random and systematic errors.
1.2.7   Distinguish between precision and accuracy.
1.2.8   Explain how the effects of random errors may be reduced.
1.2.9   Calculate quantities and results of calculations to the appropriate number of significant figures.
1.2.10   State uncertainties as absolute, fractional and percentage uncertainties.
1.2.11   Determine the uncertainties in results.
1.2.12   Identify uncertainties as error bars in graphs.
1.2.13   State random uncertainty as an uncertainty range ($\pm$) and represent it graphically as an 'error bar'.
1.2.14   Determine the uncertainties in the slope and intercepts of a straight line graph.

The SI system of fundamental and derived units

If you want to measure something, you have to use a unit. For example, it is useless to say that a person's mass is 10, 60, 140 or 600 if we do not know whether it is measured in kilograms or some other unit such as stones or pounds. In the old days, units were rather random; your mass might be measured in stones, but your height would not be measured in sticks, but in feet.

Soon after the French Revolution, the International System of units was developed. They are called the SI units because SI stands for Système International.

There are seven base, or fundamental, SI units and they are listed in the table below.

Name	Symbol	Concept
metre or meter	m	length
kilogram	kg	mass
second	s	second
ampere	A	electric current
kelvin	K	temperature
mole	mol	amount of matter
candela	cd	intensity of light

Mechanics is the study of matter, motion, forces and energy. With combinations of the first three base units (metre, kilogram and second), we can develop all the other units of mechanics.

$$\text{density} = \frac{\text{mass}}{\text{volume}} \; \text{kg m}^{-3}$$

$$\text{speed} = \frac{\text{distance}}{\text{time}} \; \text{m s}^{-1}$$

As the concepts become more complex, we give them new units. The derived SI units you will need to know are as follows:

Name	Symbol	Concept	Broken down into base SI units
newton	N	force or weight	kg m s^{-2}
joule	J	energy or work	$\text{kg m}^2\,\text{s}^{-2}$
watt	W	power	$\text{kg m}^2\,\text{s}^{-3}$
pascal	Pa	pressure	$\text{kg m}^{-1}\,\text{s}^{-2}$
hertz	Hz	frequency	s^{-1}
coulomb	C	electric charge	As
volt	V	potential difference	$\text{kg m}^2\,\text{s}^{-3}\,\text{A}^{-1}$
ohm	Ω	resistance	$\text{kg m}^2\,\text{s}^{-3}\,\text{A}^{-2}$
tesla	T	magnetic field strength	$\text{kg s}^{-2}\,\text{A}^{-1}$
weber	Wb	magnetic flux	$\text{kg m}^2\,\text{s}^{-2}\,\text{A}^{-1}$
becquerel	Bq	radioactivity	s^{-1}

Worked examples

1 Give units for the following expressed as (i) the derived unit (ii) base SI units:

   (a) force

   (b) kinetic energy.

2 Check if these equations work by substituting units into them.

   (a) power = work/time or energy/time

   (b) power = force × velocity

● **Examiner's hint:**
force = mass × acceleration.

● **Examiner's hint:**
kinetic energy = $\frac{1}{2}mv^2$

Solutions

1 (a) (i) N   (ii) kg × (m s^{-2}) or kg m s^{-2}

   (b) (i) J   (ii) kg (m s^{-1})^2 or kg m^2 s^{-2}

2 (a) W : J s^{-1} or W : (kg m^2 s^{-2}) s^{-1} or W : kg m^2 s^{-3}

   (b) W : N × (m s^{-1}) or W : (kg m s^{-2}) × (m s^{-1}) or W : kg m^2 s^{-3}

Exercises

2 Which **one** of the following units is a unit of energy?
   A   eV   B   W s^{-1} C   W m^{-1} D   N m s^{-1}

3 Which **one** of the following lists a derived unit and a fundamental unit?

A	ampere	second
B	coulomb	kilogram
C	coulomb	newton
D	metre	kilogram

In addition to the above, there are also a few important units that are not technically SI, including:

Name	Symbol	Concept
litre	l	volume
minute, hour, year, etc.	min, h, y, etc.	time
kilowatt-hour	kWh	energy
electronvolt	eV	energy
degrees celsius	°C	temperature
decibel	dB	loudness
unified atomic mass unit	u	mass of nucleon

Worked example

Convert these units to SI:.

(a) year   (b) °C   (c) kWh   (d) eV

Solution

(a) 1 year $= 1 \times 365$ days $\times 24$ hours $\times 60$ minutes $\times 60$ seconds

$$\approx 3.15 \times 10^7 \text{ s}$$

● **Examiner's hint:** The size of one degree Celsius is the same as one Kelvin — the difference is where they start, or the zero point. The conversion involves adding or subtracting 273. Since absolute zero or 0 K is equal to -273 °C, temperature in °C = temperature in K $-$ 273.

(b) Here are some common conversions:

$$0 \text{ K} = -273 \text{ °C}$$
$$273 \text{ K} = 0 \text{ °C}$$
$$300 \text{ K} = 27 \text{ °C}$$
$$373 \text{ K} = 100 \text{ °C}$$

● **Examiner's hint:** To change kilowatt-hours to joules involves using the equation:
     energy = power × time.
1 kW = 1000 W
and 1 hour = 60 × 60 seconds.

(c) 1 kWh (energy) $= 1000$ W (power) $\times 3600$ s (time)

$$= 3\,600\,000 \text{ J}$$
$$= 3.6 \times 10^6 \text{ J}$$

● **Examiner's hint:** The electronvolt is defined as the energy gained by an electron accelerated through a potential difference of one volt. So the electronvolt is equal to the charge on an electron multiplied by one volt.

(d) electrical energy = electric charge × potential difference

$$1 \text{ eV} = 1.6 \times 10^{-19} \text{ C} \times 1 \text{ V}$$
$$= 1.6 \times 10^{-19} \text{ J}$$

The SI units can be modified by the use of prefixes such as *milli* as in millimetre (mm) and *kilo* as in kilometre (km). The number conversions on the prefixes are always the same; *milli* always means one thousandth or 10^{-3} and *kilo* always means one thousand or 10^3.

These are the most common SI prefixes:

Prefix	Abbreviation	Value
tera	T	10^{12}
giga	G	10^9
mega	M	10^6
kilo	k	10^3
centi	c	10^{-2}
milli	m	10^{-3}
micro	μ	10^{-6}
nano	n	10^{-9}
pico	p	10^{-12}
femto	f	10^{-15}

Exercises

4   Change 2 360 000 J to scientific notation and to MJ.

5   A popular radio station has a frequency of 1 090 000 Hz. Change this to scientific notation and to MHz.

6   The average wavelength of white light is 5.0×10^{-7} m. What would this be in nanometres?

7   The time taken for light to cross a room is about 1×10^{-8} seconds. Change this into microseconds.

Uncertainty and error in measurement

Even when we try to measure things very accurately, it is never possible to be absolutely certain that the measurement is perfect.

The errors that occur in measurement can be divided into two types, *random* and *systematic*. If readings of a measurement are above and below the true value with equal probability, then the errors are random. Usually random errors are caused by the person making the measurement; for example, the error due to a person's reaction time is a random error.

Systematic errors are due to the system or apparatus being used. Systematic errors can often be detected by repeating the measurement using a different method or different apparatus and comparing the results. A zero offset, an instrument not reading exactly zero at the beginning of the experiment, is an example of a systematic error. You will learn more about errors as you do your practical work in the laboratory.

Random errors can be reduced by repeating the measurement many times and taking the average, but this process will not affect systematic errors. When you write up your practical work you need to discuss the errors that have occurred in the experiment. For example: *What difference did friction and air resistance make? How accurate were the measurements of length, mass and time? Were the errors random or systematic?*

Another distinction in measuring things is between *precision* and *accuracy*. Imagine a game of darts where a person has three attempts to hit the bull's-eye. If all three darts hit the double twenty, then it was a precise attempt, but not accurate. If the three darts are evenly spaced just outside and around the bull's-eye, then the throw was accurate, but not precise enough. If the darts all miss the board entirely then the throw was neither precise nor accurate. Only if all three darts hit the bull's-eye can the throws be described as both precise and accurate!

What conditions would be necessary to enable something to be measured with total accuracy?

Examples of random errors:
- changes in experimental conditions, such as temperature, pressure or humidity
- a different person reading the instrument
- malfunction of a piece of apparatus.

Examples of systematic errors:
- an observer consistently making the same mistake
- apparatus calibrated incorrectly
- energy converted to heat due to friction on a pulley.

Figure 1.2 All the players try to hit the bull's eye with their three darts, but only the last result is both precise and accurate.

precise,
not accurate

accurate,
not precise

neither precise
nor accurate

both accurate
and precise

It is the same with measurements; they can be precise, accurate, neither or both. If there have been a large number of measurements made of a particular quantity, we can show these four possibilities on graphs like this:

Figure 1.3 Here is another way of looking at the difference between precision and accuracy, showing the distribution of a large number of measurements of the same quantity around the correct value of the quantity.

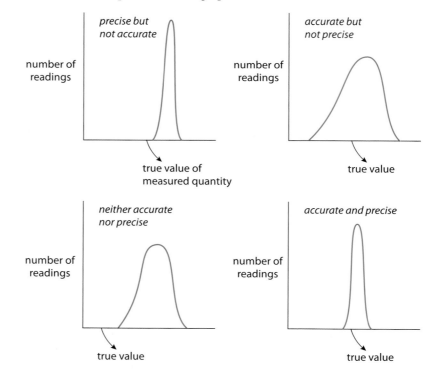

If you are describing a person you have just met to your best friend, which is more important — accuracy, precision or some other quality?

Significant figures

When measuring something, in addition to a unit, it is important to think about the number of significant figures or digits we are going to use.

For example, when measuring the width and length of a piece of A4 paper with a 30 cm ruler, what sort of results would be sensible?

Measurements (cm)	Number of significant figures	Sensible?
$21 \times 30 \pm 1$	2	yes
$21.0 \times 29.7 \pm 0.1$	3	maybe
$21.03 \times 29.68 \pm 0.01$	4	no

With a 30 cm ruler it is not possible to guarantee a measurement of 0.01 cm or 0.1 mm so these numbers are not significant.

This is what the above measurements of width would tell us:

Measurements (cm)	Number of significant figures	Value probably between (cm)
21 ± 1	2	20–22
21.0 ± 0.1	3	20.9–21.1
21.03 ± 0.01	4	21.02–21.04

The number of significant figures in any answer or result should not be more than that of the least precise value that has been used in the calculation.

Worked example

Calculate the area of a piece of A4 paper, dimensions 21 cm $\times$ 29.7 cm. Give your answer to the appropriate number of significant figures.

Solution

$21 \times 29.7 = 623.7$

$\quad$ Area $= 620 \text{ cm}^2$

$\quad\quad\quad = \mathbf{6.2 \times 10^2\,cm^2}$

● **Examiner's hint:** The least precise input value, 21 cm, only has 2 significant figures.

● **Examiner's hint:** Because we are using scientific notation, there is no doubt that we are giving the area to 2 significant figures.

Exercise

8   When a voltage V of 12.2 V is applied to a DC motor, the current I in the motor is 0.20 A. Which **one** of the following is the output power VI of the motor given to the correct appropriate number of significant digits?

A.   2 W   B.   2.4 W   C.   2.40 W   D.   2.44 W

Uncertainties in calculated results

If we use a stopwatch to measure the time taken for a ball to fall a short distance, there will inevitably be errors or uncertainties due to reaction time. For example, if the measured time is 1.0 s, then the uncertainty could reasonably be $\pm$ 0.1 s. Here the uncertainty, or plus or minus value, is called an *absolute uncertainty*. Absolute uncertainties have a magnitude, or size, and a unit as appropriate.

There are two other ways we could show this uncertainty, either as a fraction or as a percentage. As a fraction, an uncertainty of $\pm$ 0.1 s in 1.0 s would be $\frac{1}{10}$ and as a percentage it would be 10%.

These uncertainties increase if the measurements are combined in calculations or through equations. In an experiment to find the acceleration due to gravity, the errors measuring both time and distance would influence the final result.

If the measurements are to be combined by addition or subtraction, then the easiest way is to add absolute uncertainties. If the measurements are to be combined using multiplication, division or by using powers like x^2, then the best method is to add percentage uncertainties. If there is a square root relationship, then the percentage uncertainty is halved.

Uncertainties in graphs

When you hand in your lab reports, you must always show uncertainty values at the top of your data tables as $\pm$ a sensible value. On your graphs, these are represented as *error bars*. The error bars must be drawn so that their length on the scale of the graph is the same as the uncertainty in the data table. Error bars can be on either or both axes, depending on how accurate the measurements are. The best-fit line must pass through all the error bars. If it does not pass through a point, then that point is called an outlier and this should be discussed in the evaluation of the experiment.

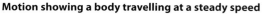

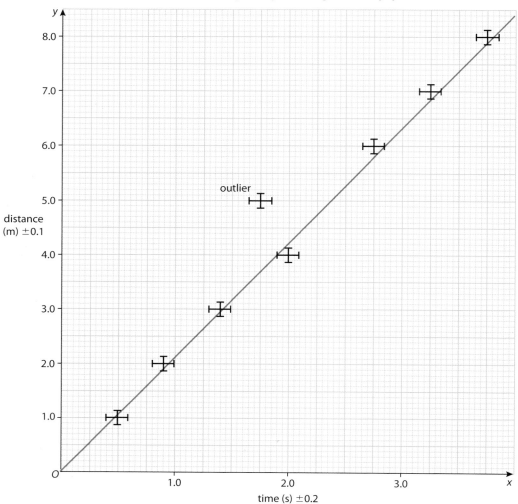

Motion showing a body travelling at a steady speed

1.3 Vectors and scalars

Assessment statements

1.3.1 Distinguish between vector and scalar quantities, and give examples of each.
1.3.2 Determine the sum or difference of two vectors by a graphical method.
1.3.3 Resolve vectors into perpendicular components along chosen axes.

Scalars are measurements that have size, or magnitude. A scalar almost always needs a unit. *Vectors* have magnitude and also have a direction. For example, a Boeing 747 can fly at a speed of 885 km h^{-1} or 246 m s^{-1}. This is the speed and is a scalar quantity. If the plane flies from London to New York at 246 m s^{-1} then this is called its velocity and is a vector, because it tells us the direction. Clearly, flying from London to New York is not the same as flying from New York to London; the speed can be the same but the velocity is different. Direction can be crucially important.

Here is another example of the difference between a vector and a scalar. Suppose you walk three metres to the east and then four metres towards the north.

The distance you have travelled is seven metres but your *displacement*, the distance between where you started and where you ended up, is only five metres. Because displacement is a vector, we also need to say that the five metres had been moved in a certain direction north of east.

Here are some common examples:

Scalar	Vector
Distance	Displacement
Speed	Velocity
Temperature	Acceleration
Mass	Weight
All types of energy	All forces
Work	Momentum
Pressure	All field strengths

A vector is usually represented by a bold italicized symbol, for example *F* for force.

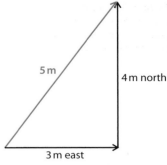

distance walked = 7 m
displacement = 5 m (north of east)

Figure 1.5 Distance is a scalar, and in this case, the distance travelled is 3 m + 4 m = 7 m. Displacement is a vector, and here it is the hypotenuse of the triangle (5 m).

Exercises

9 Which **one** of the following is a scalar quantity?
   A   Pressure   B   Impulse
   C   Magnetic field strength   D   Weight

10 Which **one** of the following is a vector quantity?
   A   Electric power   B   Electrical resistance
   C   Electric field   D   Electric potential difference

Free body diagrams

(a) Book resting on a table:

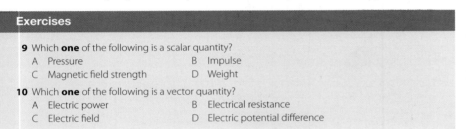

weight = normal force

(b) Car travelling at constant *velocity* to the left:

weight = normal forces
driving force = resistive forces

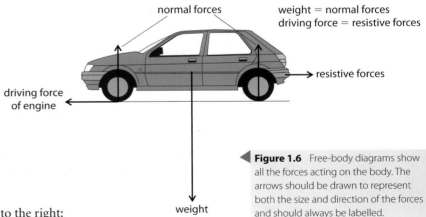

Figure 1.6 Free-body diagrams show all the forces acting on the body. The arrows should be drawn to represent both the size and direction of the forces and should always be labelled.

(c) Aeroplane in level flight *accelerating* to the right:

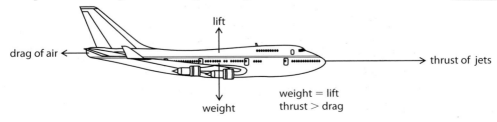

weight = lift
thrust > drag

Figure 1.7 When the vectors are parallel, the resultant is found by simple addition or subtraction.

If two or more forces are acting at the same point in space, you need to be able to calculate the resultant, or total effective force, of the combination. **The resultant is the single force that has the same effect as the combination.**

(a)

2 N → ← 3 N

resultant = 1 N to left

(b)

2 N → 3 N →

resultant = 5 N to right

(c)

3 N →
3 N → ← 6 N

resultant = zero

If they are not parallel, the easiest way to determine the resultant is by the parallelogram law. This says that **the resultant of two vectors acting at a point is given by the diagonal of the parallelogram they form.**

Figure 1.8 We can use a graphical method to find the resultant accurately.

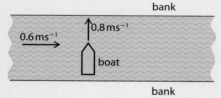

6 N   resultant

60°   10 N

magnitude of resultant = 14 N

Exercise

● **Examiner's hint:** You can do this by scale drawing using graph paper.

11 The diagram below shows a boat that is about to cross a river in a direction perpendicular to the bank at a speed of 0.8 m s^{-1}. The current flows at 0.6 m s^{-1} in the direction shown.

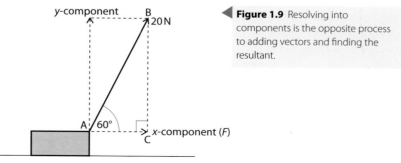

bank

0.6 ms^{-1} 0.8 ms^{-1}

boat

bank

The magnitude of the displacement of the boat 5 seconds after leaving the bank is

A   3 m.   B   4 m.   C   5 m.   D   7 m.

You also need to be able to resolve, or split, vectors into components or parts. A component of a vector shows the effect in a particular direction. Usually we resolve vectors into an x-component and a y-component.

Worked example

A force of 20 N pulls a box on a bench at an angle of 60° to the horizontal. What is the magnitude of the force F parallel to the bench?

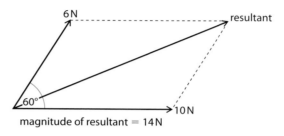

y-component   B
                      20 N

A   60°
          x-component (F)
        C

Figure 1.9 Resolving into components is the opposite process to adding vectors and finding the resultant.

Solution

The string will tend to pull the box along the bench but it will also tend to pull it upwards.

$$\text{cosine } 60° = \frac{\text{adjacent}}{\text{hypotenuse}} = \frac{F}{20}$$

$$F = 20 \text{ N} \times \cos 60° = \mathbf{10 \text{ N}}$$

● **Examiner's hint:** In the right-angled triangle ABC, the x-component (F) is adjacent to the 60° angle while the 20 N force is the hypotenuse.

Exercise

12 A force of 35 N pulls a brick on a level surface at an angle of 40° to the horizontal. The frictional force opposing the motion is 6.8N. What is the resultant force F parallel to the bench?

● **Examiner's hint:** Here is an example of how **not** to answer a basic question: Find x.

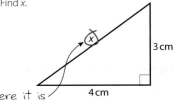

Practice questions

1 Which one of the following contains three fundamental units?

A	Metre	Kilogram	Coulomb
B	Second	Ampere	Newton
C	Kilogram	Ampere	Kelvin
D	Kelvin	Coulomb	Second

2 The resistive force F acting on a sphere of radius r moving at speed v through a liquid is given by

$$F = cvr$$

where c is a constant. Which of the following is a correct unit for c?

A N

B $N\,s^{-1}$

C $N\,m^2\,s^{-1}$

D $N\,m^{-2}\,s$

3 Which of the following is *not* a unit of energy?

A $W\,s$

B $W\,s^{-1}$

C $k\,Wh$

D $kg\,m^2\,s^{-2}$

4 The power P dissipated in a resistor R in which there is a current I is given by

$$P = I^2 R$$

The uncertainty in the value of the resistance is $\pm 10\%$ and the uncertainty in the value of the current is $\pm 3\%$. The best estimate for the uncertainty of the power dissipated is

A $\pm 6\%$

B $\pm 9\%$

C $\pm 16\%$

D $\pm 19\%$

Here are some ideas to help you with the estimates on page 3:

1 *How high is a two floor house in metres?*

First we could think about how high a normal room is. When you stand up how far is your head from the ceiling? Most adults are between 1.5 m and 2.0 m tall, so the height of a room must be above 2.0 m and probably below 2.5 m. If we multiply by two and add in some more for the floors and the roof then a sensible value could be 7 or 8 m.

2 *What is the diameter of the pupil of your eye?*

This would change with the brightness of the light, but even if it were really dark it is unlikely to be above half a centimetre or 5.0 mm. In bright sunshine maybe it could go down to 1.0 mm so a good estimate would be between these two diameters.

3 *How many times does your heart beat in an hour when you are relaxed?*

You can easily measure your pulse in a minute. When you are relaxed it will most probably be between 60 and 80 beats per minute. To get a value for an hour we must multiply by 60, and this gives a number between 3600 and 4800. As an order of magnitude or 'ball park figure' this would be 10^3.

4 *What is the weight of an apple in newtons?*

Apples come in different sizes but if you buy a kilogram how many do you get? If the number is somewhere between 5 and 15 that would give an average mass for each apple of around 100g which translates to a weight of approximately 1 N.

5 *What is the mass of the air in your bedroom?*

If air is that heavy then why don't we feel it?

To estimate this you need to know the approximate density of air, which is 1.3 kg m^{-3}. Then you need an estimate of the volume of your bedroom, for example 4 m $\times$ 3 m $\times$ 2.5 m, which would give 30 m^3. Then mass = density $\times$ volume would give around 40 kg; maybe more than expected.

6 *What pressure do you exert on the ground standing on one foot?*

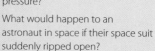

How does the pressure exerted by one foot compare to blood pressure and atmospheric pressure?

What would happen to an astronaut in space if their space suit suddenly ripped open?

For this we would use the equation pressure $= \dfrac{\text{force}}{\text{area}}$. The force would be your weight; if your mass is 60 kg then your weight would be 600 N. If we take average values for the length and width of your foot as 30 cm and 10 cm, change them to 0.3 m and 0.1 m, and multiply, then the area is 0.03 m^2. Dividing 600 N by 0.03 m^2 gives an answer of 20 000 Pa.

You need to practise these kinds of estimations without a calculator.

Mechanics

2

2.1 Kinematics

What is kinematics?

Kinematics is the study of motion. As we have already seen, distance is a scalar and displacement is a vector quantity. Distance travelled is a simple measure of length while **displacement is defined as the distance travelled in a particular direction from a specified origin.**

When we want to describe how fast something is moving we say that:

$$\text{speed} = \frac{\text{distance}}{\text{time}}$$

$$\text{velocity} = \frac{\text{displacement}}{\text{time}}$$

These simple equations can be used for two situations; firstly when the body is moving at a constant speed, and secondly in order to find the average speed. In the second case we need to know the total distance and the total time.

Worked example

Calculate your average speed if your journey to school takes half an hour and the distance is 10 km.

Solution

$$\text{speed} = \frac{10\,\text{km}}{0.5\,\text{h}}$$

$$= 20\,\text{km h}^{-1}$$

● **Examiner's hint:** Speed $= \frac{\text{distance}}{\text{time}}$

This works even though your car or bus has to slow down, speed up and sometimes stop according to the traffic conditions.

If your vehicle is changing speed, or direction, it must be changing velocity, which means that it is accelerating. **Acceleration is defined as the change in velocity per unit time**. Acceleration a can be written as:

$$a = \frac{\Delta v}{\Delta t}$$

where Δv is change in velocity and Δt is change in time.

Worked example

A car starts from rest and accelerates steadily to a speed of 40 m s^{-1} in a time of 5.0 s. Find the magnitude of the acceleration of the car.

Solution

$$a = \frac{40 \text{ m s}^{-1}}{5.0 \text{ s}}$$

$$= \textbf{8.0 m s}^{-2}$$

The units of velocity and acceleration are different, and you must always be careful to measure speed and velocity in **m s^{-1}** but acceleration in **m s^{-2}**.

If a ball is rolling down a slope, its speed will be increasing. We can find the *average speed* of the ball by dividing the total distance by the total time, as seen earlier. Another way to describe the motion is by using the *instantaneous speed* of the ball; the speed at any instant in time. You can find this by drawing a distance–time graph of the motion and measuring the tangent at a particular instant – we will see how this works later on in this chapter.

The equations for uniformly accelerated motion

If speed or velocity is changing at a steady rate, then the acceleration is constant. In these situations we can use the equations of uniformly accelerated motion, which we will call the *suvat* equations. These are a set of equations with five variables as follows:

s	distance	(m)
u	initial velocity	(m s^{-1})
v	final velocity	(m s^{-1})
a	acceleration	(m s^{-2})
t	time	(s)

It is essential that you remember that 's' in these equations stands for distance travelled, and not for speed.

There are four *suvat* equations and their power is that if we know any three of the five variables, by using the equations carefully, we can solve for the other two unknown quantities.

These are the equations:

$$v = u + at$$
$$s = \frac{u + v}{2}t$$
$$s = ut + \tfrac{1}{2}at^2$$
$$v^2 = u^2 + 2as$$

Worked examples

1 A ball is thrown vertically upwards with an initial velocity of 20 m s^{-1}. Taking the acceleration due to gravity as 10 m s^{-2} and neglecting air resistance, find:
   (a) the time taken to return to the thrower's hand
   (b) the maximum height reached.

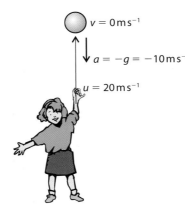

$v = 0\,\text{m}\,\text{s}^{-1}$

$a = -g = -10\,\text{m}\,\text{s}^{-2}$

$u = 20\,\text{m}\,\text{s}^{-1}$

Figure 2.1 The maximum speed will be reached just after the ball leaves the girl's hand.

Solution
(a) $s = ?$
     $u = 20$ m s^{-1}
     $v = 0$
     $a = -10$ m s^{-2}
     $t = ?$

$$v = u + at$$

$$0 = 20 - 10t$$
$$10t = 20$$
$$t = 2\ s$$

Time to return to the thrower's hand will be twice this = **4 s.**

(b) $s = ?$
     $u = 20$ m s^{-1}
     $v = 0$
     $a = -10$ m s^{-2}
     $t = 2$ s

$$s = \frac{u + v}{2}t$$
$$s = \frac{20 + 0}{2} \times 2$$
$$s = \textbf{20 m}$$

● **Examiner's hint:** Always write down the equation you are using, sometimes you can get a mark for just writing down the correct equation.

● **Examiner's hint:** Next plug in the numbers and solve for the unknown.

● **Examiner's hint:** To find the maximum height we again list the variables for the motion upwards.

● **Examiner's hint:** Choose an equation and write it down.

● **Examiner's hint:** First list the *suvat* variables.

Then choose the best equation, the one with the relevant variables.

In this case the final velocity, when the ball reaches the maximum height, will be zero.

The acceleration will be negative, if we consider the ball travelling upwards, because it will be slowing down.

 This type of problem involving gravity is always symmetrical; the distance, time and speed going up are the same as those coming back down.

2 A stone is dropped into the sea from a cliff 45 m high. Taking the acceleration due to gravity as 10 m s^{-2} and neglecting air resistance find:
   (a) the speed of the stone when it hits the sea
   (b) the time taken to reach the sea.

● **Examiner's hint:** This time the initial speed is zero and the acceleration is positive. Again we list the variables:

(a) $s = 45 \text{ m}$
$u = 0$
$v = ?$
$a = 10 \text{ m s}^{-2}$
$t = ?$

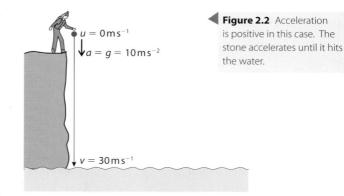

Figure 2.2 Acceleration is positive in this case. The stone accelerates until it hits the water.

$$v^2 = u^2 + 2as$$
$$v^2 = 0 + (2 \times 10 \times 45)$$
$$= 900$$
$$v = \textbf{30 m s}^{-1}$$

(b) $s = 45 \text{ m}$
$u = 0$
$v = 30 \text{ m s}^{-1}$
$a = 10 \text{ m s}^{-2}$
$t = ?$

● **Examiner's hint:** To find the time in this case we could use any of the other three equations.

$$s = ut + \tfrac{1}{2}at^2$$
$$45 = 0 + (0.5 \times 10 \; t^2)$$
$$45 = 5t^2$$
$$t^2 = 9$$
$$t = \textbf{3 s}$$

Try this last problem for yourself using the other two equations to make sure you get the same value for the time taken.

In the two examples above, the acceleration of the bodies was g, the acceleration due to gravity. This varies from place to place on the Earth's surface, but is often taken as 9.81 m s^{-2}, or approximated to 10 m s^{-2}.

The *suvat* equations work for any situation where the acceleration of the body is constant, and you must learn to spot the type of problem where the *suvat* equations will provide the solution.

To view an animation of motion in 2D, visit heinemann.co.uk/hotlinks, enter the express code 4266S and click on the Weblink 2.1.

Exercises

1   In an experiment a small steel ball is filmed and timed as it falls, from rest, next to a metre ruler. Calculate the time taken for the ball to fall
    (a) from the zero mark to the 90 cm mark on the ruler
    (b) from the 90 cm mark to the end of the ruler.
    Neglect air resistance and take $g = 9.8 \text{ m s}^{-2}$.

2   A car is travelling at 20 m s^{-1} when a dog runs out into the road. If the driver's reaction time is 0.40 s and the car decelerates steadily at a rate of 20 m s^{-2}, calculate the minimum distance travelled before the car can come to rest.

In the real world, bodies do not fall in a vacuum — they experience the effects of *air resistance*. As long as the body is small and hard, and the height is not too great, then we can ignore these effects. Otherwise air resistance or drag becomes important; obviously the motion of a falling body such as a feather or a leaf will be significantly changed by the air through which it falls. If a feather or a leaf were to fall in a vacuum they would drop just like a stone.

 The acceleration due to gravity is slightly lower off the coast of India and slightly higher in the South Pacific, owning to the nature of the rocks in the Earth's crust.

Imagine what happens to the speed of a skydiver who jumps out of a plane, falls free for a while and finally opens a parachute.

Initially the skydiver's speed is low, so the air resistance is much smaller than the weight, and the skydiver accelerates. As the speed increases, the air resistance increases until a point is reached when the drag force is equal and opposite to the weight. Then the skydiver will fall at a constant, maximum speed called the *terminal velocity*. When the parachute opens, the air resistance increases significantly and a new, slower terminal velocity is reached, enabling a safe landing.

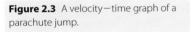

Figure 2.3 A velocity–time graph of a parachute jump.

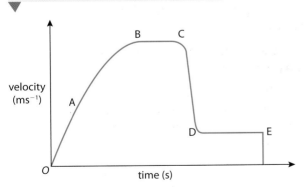

● **Examiner's hint:** When you are asked to *sketch* a graph, you should draw a pair of labelled axes with units, and a line showing the trend. You do not have to show numbers on a sketch graph but you should draw it clearly with a ruler and pencil.

From O to A, the velocity is low and acceleration fairly constant.

From A to B, air resistance becomes greater as the velocity increases so the *rate* of acceleration decreases.

From B to C, acceleration is zero, the skydiver is falling at constant terminal velocity.

At C, the parachute opens and velocity rapidly decreases.

From D to E, a new, lower, terminal velocity is reached.

At E, the skydiver lands on the ground.

 For a person in free fall, terminal velocity is about $180 \, km \, h^{-1}$ or $50 \, m \, s^{-1}$, similar to a speeding car.

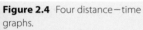

To view an animation of the lunar lander, visit Heinemann.co.uk/hotlinks, enter the express code 4266S and click on Weblink 2.2.

 In 1944, the plane in which Nicholas Alkemade was flying, was set on fire and his parachute destroyed. Nicholas chose to jump without a parachute rather than stay in the burning plane. Although he fell nearly 6000 m, he was extremely lucky because he blacked out, landing relaxed, through pine trees and into snow. He suffered only minor sprains, cuts and bruises and survived until 1987!

Graphing motion

We have already seen some examples of motion graphs, but now we will look at them in more detail. Note that time always goes on the x-axis.

Distance or displacement vs time

Figure 2.4 Four distance–time graphs.
The car shown in these graphs is:
1. at rest, not moving
2. moving at a constant speed
3. accelerating
4. decelerating

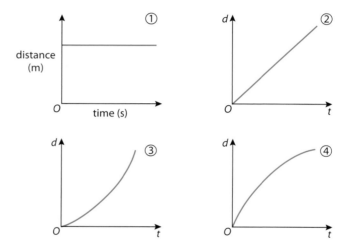

The next graph shows *displacement* against time; remember that displacement is a vector quantity. The way we show the difference between scalars and vectors on a graph is to draw the scalar above the x-axis only, and the vector both above and below.

Figure 2.5 Displacement–time graph.
O–A   constant velocity forwards
A–B   decelerating
B–C   stopped
C–D   accelerating and changing direction
D–E   constant velocity back to starting point
E–F   constant velocity backwards
F–G   decelerating
G–H   stopped
H–I   accelerating and again changing direction
I–J   constant velocity back to starting point

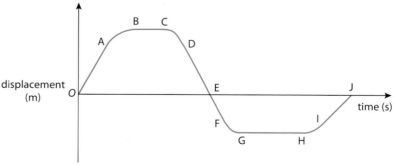

The slope or gradient of a distance–time graph gives the speed, while **for a displacement–time graph the gradient gives the velocity.** In Figure 2.5 above, the car is travelling at constant velocity from O to A because the gradient is constant. From A to B, the velocity is decreasing because the gradient is decreasing; in other words the car is decelerating.

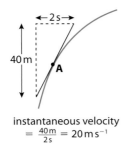

instantaneous velocity
$= \frac{40\,\text{m}}{2\,\text{s}} = 20\,\text{m s}^{-1}$

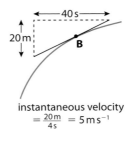

instantaneous velocity
$= \frac{20\,\text{m}}{4\,\text{s}} = 5\,\text{m s}^{-1}$

Figure 2.6 The instantaneous velocity is found by by measuring the slope of the tangent to the curve.

A The tangent line is steep at this point indicating a high instantaneous velocity.

B Because the curve has flattened out at this point, the tangent is less steep and the instantaneous velocity is lower.

Velocity vs time

It is vitally important that you do not mix up the various different types of motion graph. The next ones we will consider are speed and velocity against time. Try and describe what is happening to a car moving as follows:

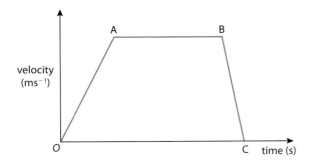

Figure 2.7 Velocity–time graph.

The car starts from rest when the speed is zero, and then from O to A its speed increases at a steady rate. This is known as *constant acceleration*. Then from A to B the car is *not stopped*, but is moving at *constant speed*. From B to C we have constant deceleration and finally the car again comes to rest. As long as the car is travelling in a straight line in the same direction, this graph would be exactly the same with either speed or velocity on the y-axis.

The gradient of a velocity–time graph gives the acceleration. So in Figure 2.7 above from O to A the acceleration is constant because the gradient is constant; the graph is a straight line. From A to B the gradient is zero because the rise, or Δy term is zero; so the acceleration is zero. From B to C the gradient is steeper than from O to A and this tells us that the rate of deceleration was more rapid than the rate of acceleration.

Now we will analyse the same graph using numbers.

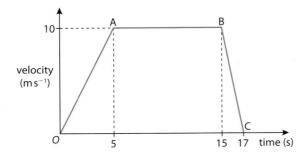

The slope or gradient of a graph
$= \frac{\text{rise}}{\text{run}} = \frac{y_2 - y_1}{x_2 - x_1} = \frac{\Delta y}{\Delta x}$

Figure 2.8 Finding distance travelled from a velocity–time graph.

O–A   constant acceleration
$$= \frac{10\,\text{m s}^{-1}}{5\,\text{s}} = 2\,\text{m s}^{-2}$$

A–B   constant maximum, velocity of $10\,\text{m s}^{-1}$ for $10\,\text{s}$

B–C   constant deceleration
$$= \frac{10\,\text{m s}^{-1}}{2\,\text{s}} = 5\,\text{m s}^{-2}$$

The area under a velocity–time graph gives the displacement. In this case the area is the sum of a triangle, a rectangle and a smaller triangle. Remember that **the area of a triangle is half the base times the height.**

$$\text{Displacement} = (\tfrac{1}{2} \times 5\,\text{s} \times 10\,\text{m s}^{-1}) + (10\,\text{s} \times 10\,\text{m s}^{-1}) + (\tfrac{1}{2} \times 2\,\text{s} \times 10\,\text{m s}^{-1})$$
$$= 25\,\text{m} + 100\,\text{m} + 10\,\text{m}$$
$$= \mathbf{135\,m}$$

You need to be able to sketch and label these types of graph for various situations.

Exercises

3 A girl throws a ball up in the air and then catches it. Sketch a speed–time graph and then a velocity–time graph for the motion of the ball.

4 A ball is dropped onto the floor and bounces twice. Sketch a velocity–time graph and then a speed–time graph for the motion of the ball.

Acceleration vs time

The last type of motion graph we are going to look at is acceleration against time. If the acceleration is uniform or constant, then these graphs will be simply vertical and horizontal straight lines. An acceleration–time graph for the car in Figure 2.8 would look like this:

Figure 2.9 Acceleration–time graph
O–A constant acceleration of 2 m s^{-2} for 5 s
A–B zero acceleration for 10 s
B–C constant negative acceleration or deceleration of 5 m s^{-2} for 2 s

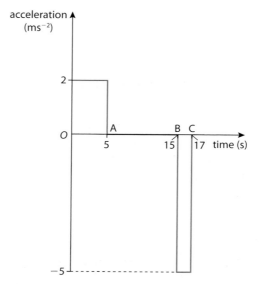

The area under an acceleration–time graph gives the change in velocity.

So from O to A, the change in velocity = the area of the rectangle
$$= (5\,\text{s} \times 2\,\text{m s}^{-2})$$
$$= 10\,\text{m s}^{-1}$$

From A to B, the area under the graph is zero, so the change in velocity is zero.

You can check for yourself that the area from B to C is 10 m s^{-1} in the opposite direction, and that this all fits with the data in Figure 2.8.

If the acceleration is not constant, we cannot use the *suvat* equations to solve the problems. The area under the graph will still tell us the change in velocity, however, as shown in the next example.

Worked example

Find the change in velocity of a body that accelerates as shown in the graph below.

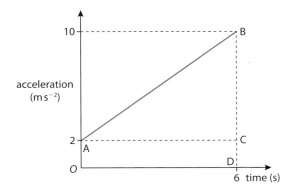

Figure 2.10 Acceleration–time graph. The change in velocity is the area of triangle ABC plus area of rectangle OACD.

Solution

Change in velocity = $(\frac{1}{2} \times 6 \text{ s} \times 8 \text{ m s}^{-2}) + (6 \text{ s} \times 2 \text{ m s}^{-2})$

$\qquad\qquad\qquad = 24 \text{ m s}^{-1} + 12 \text{ m s}^{-1}$

$\qquad\qquad\qquad = \textbf{36 m s}^{-1}$

To view *The moving man* simulation, visit Heinemann.co.uk/hotlinks, enter the express code 4266S and click on the Weblink 2.3.

Relative velocity

Imagine you are riding in a train travelling at 140 km h^{-1}. Another train overtakes you at a speed of 150 km h^{-1}. It looks like the other train is moving quite slowly. This is because *relative* to you, the speed of the other train is only 10 km h^{-1}.

Think about the following scenario; Diego is standing on the platform and Maria, on a train, passes through. We can talk about the relative motion in two ways; the motion of Maria relative to Diego, or the motion of Diego relative to Maria. The magnitude, or speed, will be the same but the direction will clearly be different.

Maria is on the train travelling to the right with a constant velocity 7 m s^{-1}

7 m s^{-1}

Diego is on the platform

Figure 2.11 Relative velocity.
The velocity of Maria, relative to Diego is 7 m s^{-1} to the right.
The velocity of Diego relative to Maria is 7 m s^{-1} to the left.

Head-on car collisions are likely to have serious consequences. One reason is that the relative speeds will add up, and so the resulting damage will also increase.

So far we have been looking at relative motion in one dimension. To understand how it works in two dimensions, imagine you are in a car driving down a long straight road. A bird is flying at right angles to the road and you can see it out of the window.

at 90° to the road

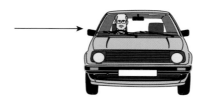

car driving along
a straight road
at constant velocity

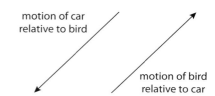

motion of car
relative to bird

motion of bird
relative to car

Figure 2.12 The motion of the bird relative to the car is different from the motion of the car relative to the bird.

You will learn a lot more about relative motion if you study Option D which includes Einstein's theory of Special Relativity.

Practical hints on drawing graphs

When you are asked to sketch or plot a motion graph, think about the following points:

1 Is this a graph of distance, displacement, speed, velocity or acceleration? They are all usually sketched against time but they are all different graphs!

2 Is this a scalar or a vector graph? In other words do you need to draw it just above the line, or both above and below?

3 Remember to label the axes with both the name and the unit; sometimes you will get a mark for just doing that alone.

4 Does the graph start from the origin (the zero-zero point)?

5 Is the graph going to be a straight line or a smooth curve?

6 Make sure you plot the graph with a sensible scale; use numbers like 2, 4 and 5, not numbers like 3 and 7.

7 Aim for your graph to fill at least half the available space.

8 Measure the gradient or tangent over at least half the space.

9 Link what you need to find to the gradient, intercept or area under the graph.

10 Always remember the equation of a straight line is of the form $y = mx + c$ and link it whenever possible to any graph you come across.

Much of this applies to other types of physics graphs, not just motion graphs.

2.2 Forces and dynamics

Force, weight and mass

In simple terms a force is a pull or a push. Force is a vector quantity and is measured in newtons. There are many different types of force, including

- friction
- normal or supporting or contact force
- tension and compression
- air resistance or drag
- upthrust or buoyancy
- lift
- thrust
- weight.

Figure 2.13 Force can be a pull or a push.

Weight is the pull of gravity on a body. Assuming that the body is on the surface of the earth, it is directed towards the centre of the earth. Usually we call this direction 'down'.

Strictly speaking, weight and mass are not the same thing. *Weight* is a vector measured in newtons, and *mass* is a scalar measured in kilograms. Mass can be described as the amount of matter in a body.

In everyday speech, weight and mass are taken to mean the same, but in physics, we need to remember that there is a difference.

 If you went to the moon, your mass would not change, but your weight would decrease because the pull of gravity is less on the moon.

Astronauts on the moon were able to take giant steps because their weight was less (although their mass hadn't changed).

Weight is related to mass in a simple way:

$$W = mg$$

W is the weight measured in N
m is the mass measured in kg
g is the acceleration due to gravity measured in m s^{-2}

Worked example

What is the weight of a 1.0 kg mass on the surface of the earth where $g = 9.8$ m s^{-2}?

Solution

$$W = mg$$
$$W = 1.0 \, \text{kg} \times 9.8 \, \text{m s}^{-2}$$
$$= 9.8 \, \text{N}$$

If a body is in *translational equilibrium*, it means that the forces acting on the body, in all three dimensions, are balanced.

Balanced forces

Here, *translating* means moving from one place to another in a straight line. If a body is in translational equilibrium then it will not be accelerating. This is the basic idea described in Newton's first law.

We have already seen some free-body diagrams in Chapter 1, but here are some more examples.

The helium balloon is at rest, so must be in translational equilibrium.

$$\text{upthrust} = \text{weight} + \text{tension}$$

The weight of the balloon will be small but cannot be zero. If the string breaks, then the tension becomes zero and the balloon will accelerate upwards.

Figure 2.14 Notice that the direction of the tension in the string must be downwards to balance the forces.

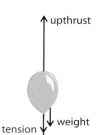

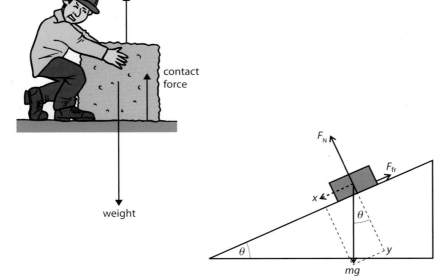

pulling force

contact force

weight

Figure 2.15 If the person pulls harder and just succeeds in lifting the block, then the contact force becomes zero and the pulling force is equal to the weight.

F_N

F_{fr}

x

θ

mg

y

Figure 2.16 Inclined plane — the weight is resolved into x and y components, parallel and perpendicular to the incline. The three forces acting on the block are mg (the weight), F_N anf F_{fr}

The free-body diagram must show only the three real forces acting on the block. Since the block is accelerating, the forces are not balanced down the incline.

$$x > F_{fr}$$
$$y = F_N$$

where F_{fr} is the frictional force and F_N is the normal (or perpendicular) force.

Using geometry, you can see that the angle of the incline is equal to the angle between the weight vector and the y-component. This is because there are 180° in a triangle and the normal force is at 90° to the incline.

Using trigonometry, we can then deduce that:

$$\sin \theta = \frac{x}{mg}$$
$$x = mg \sin \theta$$
$$\cos \theta = \frac{y}{mg}$$
$$y = mg \cos \theta$$

Newton's laws of motion

 The last recorded outbreak of the Black Death in England was in 1665. In those days people thought that the plague would remain local, so they returned to their villages, often spreading the infection. In 1665 Isaac Newton was a young Cambridge professor, working on some problems regarding the physics of motion. The plague forced him into isolation at his family home in Woolsthorpe and he worked alone there for eighteen months. During this time he made several completely original contributions to mathematics and science, effectively inventing calculus and revolutionizing our ideas about gravitation and light.

Isaac Newton

Constant velocity means two things, constant speed and constant direction; in other words constant speed in a straight line.

Aristotle (384–322 BC) was one of the most important of the ancient Greek philosophers and he tutored Alexander the Great. Aristotle thought that a heavy object would fall more quickly than a light one, and that a force was necessary for an object to move.

Galileo (1564–1642) was born in Pisa, Italy and in many ways was the founder of modern physics. Galileo thought that a heavy object and a light object should fall at the same rate and that a body could move forever if no force were acting.

Who was right, Aristotle or Galileo?

If two variables are directly proportional to each other it means that if one increases, the other will increase in proportion, or at the same rate. A graph of the two variables will be a straight line through the origin.

Newton's first law states that a body will either remain at rest, or move with constant velocity, unless acted on by an unbalanced force.

We have already seen how this law works, and it is simply common sense that something does not start to move unless there is resultant force acting on it. More difficult to understand is the idea that a body can be in equilibrium, even though it is moving. It can be difficult to accept that a body can move without a force being exerted, as this goes against both common sense and the teaching of Aristotle.

Newton's second law states that the rate of change of momentum of a body is proportional to the applied force and takes place in the direction in which the force acts. This law tells us what happens when an unbalanced force acts and is expressed in the most important equation of basic mechanics:

$$F = ma$$

F is the resultant or unbalanced force measured in N

m is the mass measured in kg

a is the acceleration measured in m s^{-2}

Note that the earlier definition of weight is a special case of this general law.

For a constant mass, this means that force is directly proportional to acceleration.

If we take a constant out of a simple equation, then we get a relationship that is directly proportional. For example if:

$$y = mx$$

and m is a constant, then

$$y \propto x$$

Conversely if two things are directly proportional to each other and we put in a constant then we get an equality or equation. For example if:

$$F \propto x$$

and k is a constant, then

$$F = kx$$

Worked example

Find the acceleration of a block of mass 500 g pulled across a table with a force of 12 N, if there is a frictional force of 6 N.

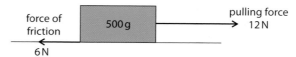

Figure 2.17 The resultant force = 6 N to the right.

Solution

$$F = ma$$

$$a = \frac{F}{m}$$

$$a = \frac{6\,\text{N}}{0.5\,\text{kg}}$$

$$a = 12\ \text{m s}^{-2} \quad \text{to the right.}$$

The force in Newton's second law is always the resultant or unbalanced force.

Practical hints on calculations

The basic method for numerical physics problems is not complicated.

1   Choose the correct equation

2   Usually you can find the equations in the Data Booklet but sometimes you simply have to memorise them.

3 Make sure you know what the symbols (letters) stand for.
4 When solving the problem, always write down the equation you are using —
   sometimes you will get a mark for just writing the equation.
5 Plug in the numbers.
6 Make sure the units are consistent; if not, change them all to SI units.
7 Give your final answer to the correct number of significant figures and make
   sure you have included the correct unit.
8 Before you move on, ask yourself whether the answer you have given is sensible
   and realistic.

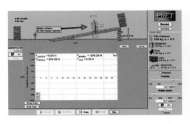

To view a simulation of forces in one dimension – The ramp, visit Heinemann.co.uk/hotlinks, enter the express code 4266S and click on the Weblink 2.4.

Exercises

5 A train of mass 1.5×10^5 kg is travelling at 40 m s^{-1} when the brakes are applied and it decelerates steadily. The train travels a distance of 250 m before coming to a halt.
   (a) Calculate the deceleration of the train.
   (b) Find the average braking force.

6 A large helium balloon is attached to the ground by two fixing ropes. Each rope makes an angle of 50° with the ground. There is a force F vertically upwards of 2.15×10^3 N. The total mass of the balloon and its basket is 1.95×10^2 kg.
   (a) State the magnitude of the resultant force when it is attached to the ground.
   (b) Calculate the tension in *either* of the fixing ropes.
   (c) The fixing ropes are released and the balloon accelerates upwards. Calculate the magnitude of this initial acceleration.
   (d) The balloon reaches a terminal velocity 10 s after take-off. The upward force F remains constant. Describe how the magnitude of the air resistance on the balloon varies during the first 10 s of its flight.

Momentum and impulse

The momentum of a body is a property that depends on its mass and its velocity.
Linear momentum is defined as the product of mass and velocity. Linear simply means *in a straight line*.

Note that the definition refers to velocity, not speed.

$$\text{momentum} = \text{mass} \times \text{velocity}$$
$$p = mv$$

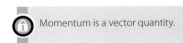

Momentum is a vector quantity.

p is the momentum measured in kg m s^{-1}
m is the mass measured in kg
v is the velocity measured in m s^{-1}

Given that mass usually remains constant, this is often written:

$$p = m\Delta v$$

Worked example

Find the momentum of a car of mass 600 kg travelling at a constant velocity of 72 km h^{-1}.

Solution

$$72 \text{ km h}^{-1} = \frac{72 \times 1000}{(60 \times 60)} \text{ m s}^{-1}$$
$$= 20 \text{ m s}^{-1}$$
$$p = mv$$
$$p = 600 \text{ kg} \times 20 \text{ m s}^{-1}$$
$$p = \mathbf{12\,000 \text{ kg m s}^{-1}}$$

● **Examiner's hint:** The velocity is not given in SI units so we must convert.

Conservation of momentum

Momentum is important for solving problems involving collisions and explosions. We say that momentum is *conserved* in these interactions. This means that the total momentum before an event is equal to the total momentum after the event.

Worked example

A ball of mass 1.0 kg is dropped and hits the floor with a velocity of 8 m s⁻¹. It bounces back with a velocity of 6 m s⁻¹. Find the change of momentum.

Figure 2.18

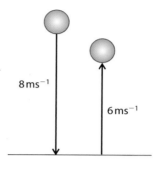

$8\,\text{ms}^{-1}$

$6\,\text{ms}^{-1}$

Solution

The change in momentum = final momentum − initial momentum

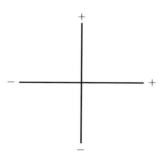

For a vector problem like this, we must use a convention for direction. Usually we take the directions up or to the right as positive and down or to the left as negative.

Figure 2.19 Vector quadrant.

$$\Delta p = mv - mu$$

$$\Delta p = (1.0\ \text{kg} \times +6\ \text{m s}^{-1}) - (1.0\ \text{kg} \times -8\ \text{m s}^{-1})$$

$$\Delta p = 6\ \text{kg m s}^{-1} + 8\ \text{kg m s}^{-1}$$

$$\Delta p = \mathbf{14\ kg\,m\,s^{-1}}$$

This idea can be expressed as a problem-solving equation in different ways:

$$m_1v_1 = m_2v_2$$

$$m_1v_1 = m_2v_2 + m_3v_3$$

$$m_1v_1 + m_2v_2 = m_3v_3$$

The law of conservation of linear momentum states that the total momentum remains constant in any interaction, providing there is no external force.

The version we choose depends on the problem, whether it is a collision or explosion and whether the two bodies stick together after the collision.

Worked example

A car of mass 600 kg travelling at 20 m s^{-1} collides head on with a truck of mass 2400 kg. If both vehicles come to rest immediately after the crash what was the velocity of the truck?

Solution

$$m_1v_1 + m_2v_2 = m_3v_3$$

$$(600 \text{ kg} \times 20 \text{ m s}^{-1}) + (2400 \text{ kg} \times -v_2) = (3000 \text{ kg} \times 0 \text{ m s}^{-1})$$
$$12\,000 \text{ kg m s}^{-1} - 2400v_2 = 0$$
$$v_2 = \frac{12\,000}{2400}$$
$$v_2 = 5 \text{ m s}^{-1}$$

● **Examiner's hint:** Since the bodies involved stick together after the collision, use this equation.

● **Examiner's hint:** The final velocity, v_3, is zero, and we will take the direction of motion of the car as positive.

Impulse

The change in momentum of a body is also known as the *impulse*.
Impulse is defined as the product of a force and the time during which it acts.

$$\text{Impulse} = F\Delta t = m\Delta v$$

The unit for impulse is Ns and this can also be used as a unit of momentum.

Imagine what happens if a girl kicks a football and a boy kicks a brick of the same mass, say 500 g. Both the ball and the brick are accelerated from rest to a velocity of 10 m s^{-1}.

The difference is that the brick is harder than the ball so the girl's foot is in contact with the ball for a longer time interval. If the girl's foot is in contact with the ball for 0.2 s then we can calculate the force exerted like this:

$$F\Delta t = m\Delta v$$
$$F \times 0.2 \text{ s} = 0.5 \text{ kg} \times 10 \text{ m s}^{-1}$$
$$F = \frac{5}{0.2}$$
$$F = 25 \text{ N}$$

If the boy's foot is in contact with the brick for 0.01 s then the force would be much greater:

$$F\Delta t = m\Delta v$$
$$F \times 0.01 \text{ s} = 0.5 \text{ kg} \times 10 \text{ m s}^{-1}$$
$$F = \frac{5}{0.01}$$
$$F = 500 \text{ N}$$

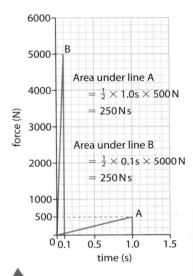

This graph shows a simplified version of the forces exerted on a person involved in a car crash. Line A shows the force exerted by the steering wheel on a driver wearing a seat belt. Line B shows the force if the driver were not wearing a seat belt. In both cases, the impulse, or change in momentum, seen as the area under the graph, is the same. Clearly, the greater force, shown in Line B, will be more damaging to the driver.

Figure 2.20 It is not a good idea to kick a brick. For the same change in momentum, if the time of contact is smaller, the force will be greater. We say that the time is inversely proportional to the force.

Remember that Newton's second law is:

$$F = ma$$

As we saw earlier in the chapter:

$$a = \frac{\Delta v}{\Delta t}$$

Substituting for a in the second law gives:

$$F = \frac{m\Delta v}{\Delta t}$$

Knowing that:

$$m\Delta v = p$$

We can re-write Newton's second law as:

$$F = \frac{\Delta p}{\Delta t}$$

Notice this can be rearranged to give the impulse equation:

$$F\Delta t = \Delta p = m\Delta v$$

In words we say that **impulse is the change in momentum** while **force is the rate of change of momentum.**

Newton's third law of motion

Newton's third law states that if body A exerts a force on body B, then body B exerts an equal and opposite force on body A.

Clearly there must always be two different bodies involved in the third law. An easy way to demonstrate this is with two spring balances.

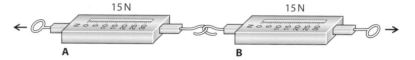

Figure 2.21 Two spring balances. The reading on A will always be the same as the reading on B.

There are examples of third law pairs of forces all around us; here are just a few examples.

- When you kick a football (or a brick), your foot exerts a force on the ball and the ball exerts an equal and opposite force on your foot. The ball moves, hopefully towards the goal, and you can feel the force on your foot.
- When a cannon is fired, the cannon ball moves forward but the ball exerts an equal and opposite force on the cannon, so it recoils.
- If you play tennis, your racket exerts a force on the ball and the ball exerts an equal and opposite force on your racket.
- The Earth exerts a force on the Moon and the Moon exerts an equal and opposite force on the Earth. We know the Earth pulls the Moon because it remains in orbit around us and we know the Moon pulls on the Earth because it influences the tides in the oceans.

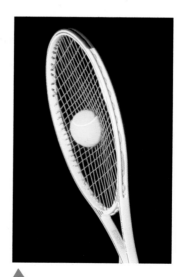

The photo shows the racket strings being stretched and deformed.

Education is not the same in every country and depends on differences in language, politics, culture and religion, among many other things. In all educational systems there is however, agreement in the validity of the ideas behind Newton's three laws of motion.

2.3 Work, energy and power

Physical work

Sometimes in science we use words in a different sense to the way they are normally used in the English language. Although a word often looks, sounds and is spelt the same, it sometimes has a different meaning in physics. One example is the definition of *work* in the study of physics.

Work is defined as the force times the distance moved in the direction of the force.

This means that if there is no movement in the direction of the force, then no work is done. If your car is stuck in the mud or the sand, you can push it as hard as you like, and get completely exhausted, but if you do not move it then you have done no work (on the car)!

Work is a scalar quantity and is measured in joules. It is independent of the mass of the body being moved and the path taken. It only depends on the magnitude of the force and the distance moved in the direction of the force.

The equation for work is:

$$W = Fs\cos\theta$$

W is the work measured in J
F is the force measured in N
s is the distance moved measured in m
θ is the angle between the applied force and the direction of motion

Worked example

A force of 40 N acting at 60° to the horizontal pulls a block of mass 10 kg a distance of 2.0 m across a smooth surface. How much work is done?

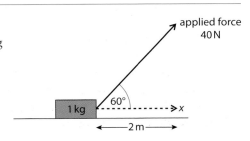

applied force
40 N

◀ **Figure 2.22** Work done pulling a block.

Solution

The size of the mass makes no difference to the work done.

If the surface is smooth, there is no friction, so the resultant force in the *x*-direction is the *x*-component of the 40 N force.

Since the *x*-component is adjacent to 60° angle:

$$\cos 60° = \frac{x}{40}$$
$$x = 40 \cos 60° \, N$$
$$W = Fs\cos\theta$$
$$W = 40 \cos 60° \, N \times 2 \, m$$
$$W = \mathbf{40 \, J}$$

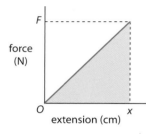

F ⋯⋯⋯⋯

force (N)

O extension (cm) x

Figure 2.23 A graph of force against extension for a stretched spring.

The gradient $k = \frac{F}{x}$

$F = kx$

k is the spring constant.

When a series of weights are hung on a spring causing it to stretch, work is done. The force is the *weight* and the distance moved is the *extension* of the spring. As long as the spring is not stretched beyond a certain point, called the *elastic limit*, then the force is directly proportional to the extension. A graph of force against extension is a straight line through the origin.

The work done by this non–constant force is found from the area under the graph.

$$\text{work done} = \tfrac{1}{2} \times x \times F$$
$$W = \tfrac{1}{2}x \times kx$$
$$W = \tfrac{1}{2}kx^2$$

In physics, energy and work are very closely linked; in some senses they are the same thing. Both are scalar quantities and both are measured in joules. If you have energy, you can do work.

In general, we say that:

Energy is defined as the ability to do work.

$$\text{work done} = \text{energy converted}$$
$$W = \Delta E$$

When work is done, energy is converted or changed to different types. In the case of the spring being stretched, the work done increases the elastic potential energy of the spring.

$$\text{elastic potential energy} = \tfrac{1}{2} \, kx^2$$

Kinetic energy

● **Examiner's hint:** Kinetic energy is often abbreviated to KE or E_k.

Kinetic energy (E_k) is the energy a body has because it is moving. The word *kinetic* refers to motion.

Imagine a block of mass m accelerated from rest by a resultant force, F. After travelling a distance s the mass has an acceleration a.

● **Examiner's hint:** Sometimes in an exam you will be asked to derive an equation, such as the kinetic energy derivation here. Many students find this difficult and there is really only one way to improve your skills. You simply have to practise and repeat them with the book closed and then practise some more!

The work done, $W = Fs$
but from Newton's second law $F = ma$
so that $W = mas$ (substituting for F)
From the *suvat* equations, $v = u^2 + 2as$
since $u = 0$ then $v^2 = 2as$
$as = \tfrac{1}{2}v^2$
Since $W = mas = \Delta E$
and the energy converted is kinetic energy
kinetic energy $= mas = m \times \tfrac{1}{2} v^2$
$E_k = \tfrac{1}{2}mv^2$

Worked example

Find the kinetic energy of a truck of mass 4000 kg travelling at a speed of 30 m s^{-1}

Solution

$$E_k = \tfrac{1}{2}mv^2$$

$$E_k = \tfrac{1}{2} \times 4000 \text{ kg} \times (30 \text{ m s}^{-1})^2$$

$$E_k = \mathbf{1.8 \times 10^6 \text{ J}}$$

Potential energy

Gravitational potential energy (E_p) is the energy a body has because of its position, in particular, its vertical height relative to a given point.

Now imagine a mass m lifted a vertical height h. Here work is being done against the pull of gravity.

the work done, $W = Fs$

here the force is the weight $= mg$

and the distance is the height h

so the work $W = mgh$

The work is increasing the gravitational potential energy of the mass.

$$W = \Delta E_p$$

$$\Delta E_p = \mathbf{mg\Delta h}$$

● **Examiner's hint:** Potential energy is often abbreviated to PE or E_p.

Worked example

The Leaning Tower of Pisa is 56 m high.
(a) Find the gravitational potential energy of a 10 kg cannon ball at the top of the tower.

(b) If the cannon ball is dropped from the top of the tower, what will be its speed when it hits the ground?
(Neglect air resistance and take g = 10 m s^{-2})

Solution
(a)

$$\Delta E_p = mg\Delta h$$

$$\Delta E_p = 10 \text{ kg} \times 10 \text{ m s}^{-2} \times 56 \text{ m}$$

$$\Delta E_p = \mathbf{5600 \text{ J}}$$

(b)

$$\Delta E_p = E_k$$

$$5600 \text{ J} = \tfrac{1}{2}mv^2$$

$$5600 \text{ J} = \tfrac{1}{2} \times 10 \text{ kg} \times v^2$$

$$v^2 = \frac{5600}{5}$$

$$v = \mathbf{33 \text{ m s}^{-1}}$$

● **Examiner's hint:** We could solve this using the *suvat* equations, but if air resistance is neglected, all the gravitational potential energy will be changed to kinetic energy.

There is a famous story about Galileo dropping cannon balls of different weights from the top of the Leaning Tower of Pisa to demonstrate that heavy objects and lighter objects fall at the same rate. This story may or may not be true.

To view a more recent version of Galileo's experiment, visit Heinemann.co.uk/hotlinks, enter the express code 4266S and click on Weblink 2.5.

Conservation of energy

The idea of one form of energy changing into another is summarised in a very important principle or law of physics, the principle conservation of energy.

We usually classify energy as the following forms:

1 Kinetic energy

2 Gravitational potential energy

3 Elastic potential energy

4 Thermal or heat energy

5 Light energy

6 Sound energy

7 Chemical energy

8 Electrical energy

9 Magnetic energy

10 Nuclear energy

In any given transformation, some of the energy is almost inevitably changed to heat.

There are energy changes happening all around us all of the time. Here are a few examples to think about.

- A bouncing ball

The gravitational potential energy is changed to kinetic energy and back again with each bounce. While the ball is in contact with the ground, some energy is stored as elastic potential energy. Eventually the ball comes to rest and all the energy has become low grade heat.

- An aeroplane taking off

As fuel is burned in the engines, chemical energy is converted to heat, light and sound. The plane accelerates down the runway and its kinetic energy increases. There will be heat energy due to friction between the tyres and the runway. As the plane takes off and climbs into the sky, its gravitational potential energy increases.

- A nuclear power station

Nuclear energy from the uranium fuel changes to thermal energy that is used to boil water. The kinetic energy of the steam molecules drives turbines, and as the kinetic energy of the turbines increases, it interacts with magnetic energy to give electrical energy.

- A laptop computer

The electrical energy form the mains or chemical energy from the battery is changed to light on the screen and sound through the speakers. There is kinetic energy in the fan, magnetic energy in the motors, and plenty of heat is generated.

- A human body

Most of the chemical energy from our food is changed to heat to keep us alive. Some is changed to kinetic energy as we move, or gravitational potential energy if we climb stairs. There is also elastic potential energy in our muscles, sound energy when we talk and electrical energy in our nerves and brain.

The principle of conservation of energy states that energy cannot be created or destroyed; only changed from one form to another.

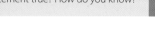

All of the energy on Earth has come originally from the Sun. Is this statement true? How do you know?

- **Examiner's hint:** In an exam do not say that energy is 'lost' but instead say it has been changed or converted to other forms.

There is a useful relationship between kinetic energy and momentum which will help you to solve numerical problems.

$$E_k = \tfrac{1}{2}\, mv^2 = \frac{mv^2}{2}$$

Multiplying top and bottom by m gives $\qquad E_k = \dfrac{m^2 v^2}{2m}$

Momentum $\qquad\qquad\qquad\qquad\qquad p = mv$

Squaring gives $\qquad\qquad\qquad\qquad p^2 = m^2 v^2$

Finally substituting in the above equation $\qquad E_k = \dfrac{p^2}{2m}$

Collisions

When we looked at momentum earlier, we mentioned that it was important for collisions. Now we must distinguish between two different types of collisions. When *elastic collisions* occur, momentum is conserved and kinetic energy is also conserved. This means that no energy is changed to heat in an elastic collision. In fact there is really no such thing as a perfectly elastic collision, although, of course, some collisions are more elastic than others. After an elastic collision the bodies always move separately.

During *inelastic collisions*, momentum is conserved, but kinetic energy is not conserved. In other words, some of the kinetic energy is converted to heat and other forms of energy. After an inelastic collision the bodies may stick together.

Kinetic energy can sometimes increase, for example, if there is an input of chemical energy from a fuel or explosive material.

Power

Power is a measure of how fast work is done or how quickly energy is converted. Power is a scalar quantity.

$$\text{power} = \frac{\text{energy or work}}{\text{time}}$$

If the energy or work is measured in joules and the time in seconds, then the power will be measured in watts (W).

$$1\,\text{W} = 1\,\text{J s}^{-1}$$

A 100 W light bulb converts electrical energy to heat and light at the rate of 100 J every second.

Sometimes you will see power given in kW or even MW.

◀ Billiard ball collisions are highly elastic because the balls are so hard. In a perfectly elastic collision, one ball could stop, and the other move off with the same speed as the first. In practice, this cannot happen because some of the kinetic energy changes to heat and sound.

 Particle physicists believe some collisions between sub-atomic particles are perfectly elastic.

● **Examiner's hint:** In exam questions about collisions and explosions, especially multiple-choice, assume that momentum is always conserved.

 Power is defined as the rate of doing work.

Worked example

Calculate the power of a worker in a supermarket who stacks shelves 1.5 m high with cartons of orange juice, each of mass 6.0 kg, at the rate of 30 cartons per minute.

Solution

$$\text{power} = \frac{\text{work}}{\text{time}}$$

$$\text{power} = \frac{Fs}{t}$$

$$\text{power} = \frac{(30 \times 60\,\text{N}) \times 1.5\,\text{m}}{60\,\text{s}}$$

$$\text{power} = \mathbf{45\,W}$$

This engraving shows a steam engine designed by James Watt.

James Watt (1736–1819) was a Scotsman whose work on the steam engine was a major influence on the Industrial Revolution.

From the days of Aristotle, through the time of Galileo, Newton, Watt and Joule right up until Einstein in the early 20th century, scientists worked mostly alone. Nowadays, scientists often work in multinational teams. These teams may make important discoveries in fields such as particle physics, or work on solving the great global problems like HIV/Aids and global warming.

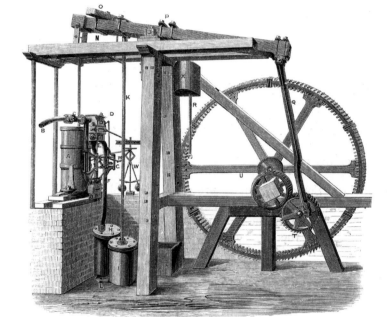

There is another way to calculate power.

$$\text{power} = \frac{Fs}{t} = F \times \frac{s}{t} = Fv$$

In other words, power is equal to force times velocity, providing the velocity is constant.

Efficiency

Efficiency is a ratio of how much work, energy or power we get out of a system compared to how much is put in.

One of the most efficient devices is the electric transformer. They can be over 99% efficient because, since there are no moving parts, there are no energy losses due to friction or air resistance.

$$\text{efficiency} = \frac{\text{useful output}}{\text{total input}}$$

Since it is a ratio, there is no unit, and we can express efficiency as a percentage by multiplying by 100%.

No real machine or system can ever be 100% efficient, because there will always be some energy changed to heat due to friction, air resistance or other causes.

Worked example

A car engine has an efficiency of 20% and produces an average of 25 kJ of useful work per second. How much energy is converted to heat per second?

Solution

$$\text{efficiency} = \frac{\text{useful output}}{\text{total input}}$$

$$0.2 = \frac{25\,000\,\text{J}}{\text{total input}}$$

$$\text{total input} = \frac{25\,000}{0.2} = 125\,000\,\text{J}$$

If the total input is 125 kJ, and 25 kJ of useful work are obtained then the heat produced must be:

$$125\,\text{kJ} - 25\,\text{kJ} = \textbf{100 kJ}$$

● **Examiner's hint:** The efficiency is 20% which equals 0.2.

● **Examiner's hint:** 25 kJ = 25 000 J.

Exercises

7 This question is about driving a metal bar into the ground.
Large metal bars can be driven into the ground using a heavy falling object.

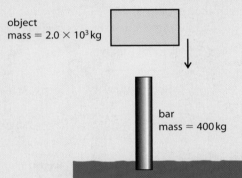

object
mass = 2.0×10^3 kg

bar
mass = 400 kg

In the situation shown, the object has a mass 2.0×10^3 kg and the metal bar has a mass of 400 kg. The object strikes the bar at a speed of $6.0\,\text{m s}^{-1}$. It comes to rest on the bar without bouncing. As a result of the collision, the bar is driven into the ground to a depth of 0.75 m.
(a) Determine the speed of the bar immediately after the object strikes it.
(b) Determine the average frictional force exerted by the ground on the bar.

8. This question is about estimating energy changes for an escalator (moving staircase).
The diagram below represents an escalator. People step on to it at point A and step off at point B.
(a) The escalator is 30 m long and makes an angle of 40° with the horizontal. At full capacity, 48 people step on at point A and step off at point B every minute.
  (i) Calculate the potential energy gained by a person of weight 7.0×10^2 N in moving from A to B.
  (ii) Estimate the energy supplied by the escalator motor to the people every minute when the escalator is working at full capacity.
  (iii) State **one** assumption that you have made to obtain your answer to (ii).
The escalator is driven by an electric motor that has an efficiency of 70 %.
(b) Using your answer to (a) (ii), calculate the minimum input power required by the motor to drive the escalator.

Uniform circular motion

Assessment statements
2.4.1 Draw a vector diagram to illustrate that the acceleration of a particle moving with constant speed in a circle is directed towards the centre of the circle.
2.4.2 Apply the expression for centripetal acceleration.
2.4.3 Identify the force producing circular motion in various situations.
2.4.4 Solve problems involving circular motion.

Motion in a circle

If a body is travelling in a circular path, then it is constantly changing direction; at no point is it travelling in a straight line. Even if it is travelling at constant or uniform speed, a body that is moving round a circle must be changing velocity. This is because velocity is a vector and a change in velocity can be a change of speed or direction.

If the velocity of the body is changing, then, by definition the body must be accelerating. This type of acceleration is called *centripetal acceleration*. The word *centripetal* means *centre-seeking* and the direction of the acceleration is always *towards the centre of the circle.*

Figure 2.25 A particle moving in a circle. The instantaneous velocity, *v*, is the tangent to the circle. The direction of the centripetal force will be in the same direction as the centripetal acceleration.

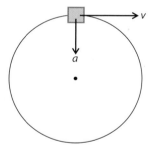

The equation for centripetal acceleration is:
$$a = \frac{v^2}{r}$$

a   centripetal acceleration   m s^{-2}
v   speed   m s^{-1}
r   radius of the circle   m

Since the body moves with constant speed we can use the simple equation:
$$\text{speed} = \frac{\text{distance}}{\text{time}}$$

If the body goes round the entire circle once, then this can be written:
$$v = \frac{2\pi r}{T}$$

$2\pi r$ is the circumference of a circle.
T is the period (or time period) and is the **time taken for one complete revolution.**

If we square this equation it becomes:
$$v^2 = \frac{4\pi^2 r^2}{T^2}$$

Substituting for v^2 in the centripetal acceleration and cancelling one of the r terms gives:

$$a = \frac{4\pi^2 r}{T^2}$$

If a body is accelerating, we know from Newton's second law that it must be being acted on by an unbalanced force. The force causing the centripetal acceleration is called the *centripetal force*. The direction of the centripetal force is also towards the centre of the circle; this is logical because bodies accelerate in the direction of the resultant force.

To understand this, think about a car driving round a circular track. If the friction is too low, for example, if the car skids on a patch of ice, then the car will fly off at a tangent.

> The centripetal force is simply an extra name we give to a force that is already there; it is not a new or different force.

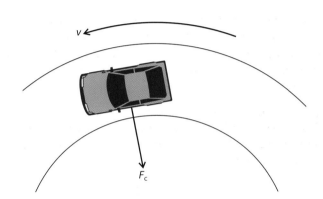

◀ **Figure 2.26** There must be friction between the car tyres and the road to keep the car going round.

The friction is the force that turns the car into the bends and it is directed towards the center of the circle. **The friction here is the centripetal force.**

In the same way, when the Moon orbits the Earth there is a centripetal force from the Moon towards the centre of the Earth. In this case the force is gravitational. If you whirl a rubber bung or a stone tied to a piece of string around your head, then the centripetal force that keeps the stone turning is the tension in the string. If the string breaks and the tension becomes zero, the bung or stone flies off in a straight line.

● **Examiner's hint:** If you are asked to draw the force on a body moving in a circle, always draw it pointing towards the centre of the circle. Do not be tempted to add another arrow pointing outwards to balance the forces; they are not balanced because the body is accelerating.

If the equation for centripetal acceleration is:

$$a = \frac{v^2}{r}$$

and we know that $$F = ma$$

we can substitute for a to give:

$$F = \frac{mv^2}{r}$$

This is the equation for centripetal force.

Worked example

A ball of mass 50 g tied to the end of a piece of string is whirled by a student in a horizontal circle of radius 1.2 m at constant speed. The ball makes 1.5 revolutions per second.
(a) Find the acceleration of the ball.
(b) Find the force that the student must exert on the string.

Solution

(a)

$$\text{speed} = \frac{\text{distance}}{\text{time}}$$

$$v = \frac{1.5 \times 2\pi \times 1.2 \text{ m}}{1.0 \text{ s}}$$

$$v = 11.3 \text{ m s}^{-1}$$

$$a = \frac{v^2}{r}$$

$$a = \frac{(11.3 \text{ m s}^{-1})^2}{1.2 \text{ m}}$$

$$= \mathbf{107 \text{ m s}^{-2}}$$

(b)

$$F = \frac{mv^2}{r}$$

$$= \frac{0.050 \text{ kg} \times (11.3 \text{ m s}^{-1})^2}{1.2 \text{ m}}$$

$$= \mathbf{5.3 \text{ N}}$$

● **Examiner's hint:** Since the ball is moving in a circle, the acceleration will be centripetal.

Exercises

9   An aircraft accelerates from rest along a horizontal straight runway and then takes off. The mass of the aircraft is 8.0×10^3 kg.
   (a) The average resultant force on the aircraft while travelling along the runway is 70 kN. The speed of the aircraft just as it lifts off is 75 m s^{-1}. Estimate the distance travelled along the runway.
   (b) The aircraft climbs to a height of 1250 m. Calculate the potential energy gained during the climb.
   (c) When approaching its destination, the pilot puts the aircraft into a holding pattern. This means the aircraft flies at a constant speed of 90 m s^{-1} in a horizontal circle, and the radius of the circle is 500 m.
     For the aircraft in the holding pattern,
      (i) calculate the magnitude of the resultant force on the aircraft
      (ii) state the direction of the resultant force.

10   A geostationary satellite, for example a communications satellite, orbits the Earth with a time period of 24 hours. If the distance from the satellite to the centre of the Earth is 4.2×10^7 m, calculate the acceleration of the satellite.

Practice questions

1   A ball, initially at rest, takes time t to fall through a vertical distance h. If air resistance is ignored, the time taken for the ball to fall from rest through a vertical distance $9h$ is
   A $3t$
   B $5t$
   C $9t$
   D $10t$

2   A raindrop falling through air reaches a terminal velocity before hitting the ground. At terminal velocity, the frictional force on the raindrop is
   A   zero.
   B   less than the weight of the raindrop.
   C   greater than the weight of the raindrop.
   D   equal to the weight of the raindrop.

3 An athlete runs round a circular track at constant speed. Which **one** of the following graphs best represents the variation with time t of the magnitude d of the **displacement** of the athlete from the starting position during one lap of the track?

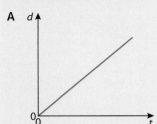

A

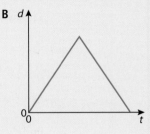

B

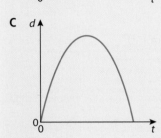

C

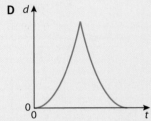

D

4 A ball is dropped from rest at time $t = 0$ on to a horizontal surface from which it rebounds. The graph shows the variation of time t with **speed** v of the ball.

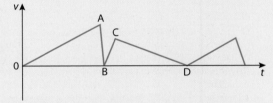

Which one of the following best represents the point at which the ball just loses contact with the surface after the first bounce?

A

B

C

D

5 Juan is standing on the platform at a railway station. A train passes through the station with speed 20 m s^{-1} in the direction shown measured relative to the platform. Carmen is walking along one of the carriages of the train with a speed of 2.0 m s^{-1} measured relative to the carriage in the direction shown. Velocity is measured as positive in the direction shown on the diagram.

The velocity of Carmen relative to Juan is

A -22 m s^{-1}

B -18 m s^{-1}

C $+18$ m s^{-1}

D $+22$ m s^{-1}

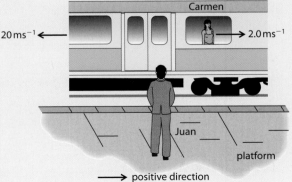

6 The graph below shows the variation with time of the distance moved by a car along a straight road. During which time interval does the car have its greatest acceleration?

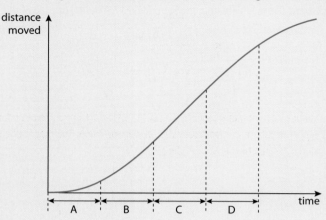

7 The variation with time t of the speed v of a car moving along a straight road is shown below.

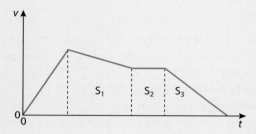

Which area, S_1, S_2 or S_3, or combination of areas, represents the total distance moved by the car during the time that its speed is reducing?

A S_1

B S_3

C $S_1 + S_3$

D $S_1 + S_2 + S_3$

8 When a body is accelerating, the resultant force acting on it is equal to its

A change of momentum.

B rate of change of momentum.

C acceleration per unit of mass.

D rate of change of kinetic energy.

9 A ball of mass m, travelling in a direction at right angles to a vertical wall, strikes the wall with a speed v_1. It rebounds at right angles to the wall with a speed v_2. The ball is in contact with the wall for a time Δt. The magnitude of the force that the ball exerts on the wall is

A $\dfrac{m(v_1 + v_2)}{\Delta t}$

D $m(v_1 + v_2)\Delta t$

B $\dfrac{m(v_1 - v_2)}{\Delta t}$

C $m(v_1 - v_2)\Delta t$

10 A sphere of mass m strikes a vertical wall and bounces off it, as shown below.

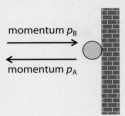

momentum p_B

momentum p_A

The magnitude of the momentum of the sphere just before impact is p_B and just after impact is p_A. The sphere is in contact with the wall for time t. The magnitude of the average force exerted by the wall on the sphere is

A $\dfrac{(p_B - p_A)}{t}$

B $\dfrac{(p_B - p_A)}{t}$

C $\dfrac{(p_B - p_A)}{mt}$

D $\dfrac{(p_B + p_A)}{mt}$

11 A truck collides head on with a less massive car moving in the opposite direction to the truck. During the collision, the average force exerted by the truck on the car is F_T and the average force exerted by the car on the truck is F_C. Which **one** of the following statements is correct?

A F_T will always be greater in magnitude than F_C.

B F_T will always be equal in magnitude to F_C.

C F_T will be greater in magnitude than F_C only when the speed of the car is less than the speed of the truck.

D F_T will be equal in magnitude to F_C only when the speed of the truck is equal to the speed of the car.

12 A small boat in still water is given an initial horizontal push to get it moving. The boat gradually slows down. Which of the following statements is true for the forces acting on the boat as it slows down?

A There is a forward force that diminishes with time.

B There is a backward force that diminishes with time.

C There is a forward force and a backward force both of which diminish with time.

D There is a forward force and a backward force that are always equal and opposite.

13 The graph below shows the variation with displacement d of the force F applied by a spring on a cart.
The work done by the force in moving the cart through a distance of 2 cm is

A 10×10^{-2} J

B 7×10^{-2} J

C 5×10^{-2} J

D 2.5×10^{-2} J

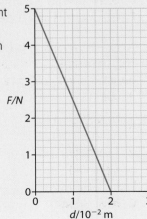

14 Which **one** of the following is a true statement about energy?
   A   Energy is destroyed due to frictional forces.
   B   Energy is a measure of the ability to do work.
   C   More energy is available when there is a larger power.
   D   Energy and power both measure the same quantity.

15 An electric train develops a power of 1.0 MW when travelling at a constant speed of 50 m s^{-1}. The net resistive force acting on the train is
   A   50 MN
   B   200 kN
   C   20 kN
   D   200 N

16 Which of the following quantities is/are conserved in an inelastic collision in an isolated system of two objects?

	Linear momentum of system	Kinetic energy of system
A	Yes	Yes
B	Yes	No
C	No	Yes
D	No	No

17 The diagram below represents energy transfers in an engine.

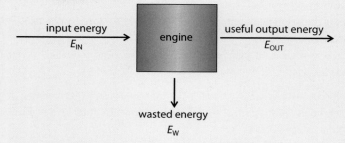

The efficiency of the engine is given by the expression

   A $\dfrac{E_W}{E_{IN}}$

   B $\dfrac{E_W}{E_{OUT}}$

   C $\dfrac{E_{OUT}}{E_{IN}}$

   D $\dfrac{E_{OUT}}{E_W}$

18 A machine lifts an object of weight 1.5×10^3 N to a height of 10 m. The machine has an overall efficiency of 20%. The work done by the machine in raising the object is
   A 3.0×10^3 J
   B 1.2×10^4 J
   C 1.8×10^4 J
   D 7.5×10^4 J.

19 An electric motor, with an input power of 250 W, produces 200 W of mechanical power. The efficiency of the motor is

A   20%.

B   25%.

C   55%.

D   80%.

20 A stone of mass m is attached to a string and moves round in a horizontal circle of radius R at constant speed V. The work done by the pull of the string on the stone in one complete revolution is

A   zero

B $2\pi mV^2$

C $\dfrac{2\pi mV^2}{R}$

D $\dfrac{2\pi mV^2}{R}$

21 Two objects X and Y are moving away from the point P. The diagram below shows the velocity vectors of the two objects.

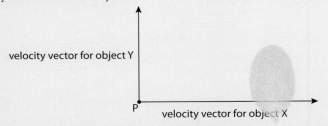

velocity vector for object Y

P   velocity vector for object X

Which of the following velocity vectors best represents the velocity of object X relative to object Y?

A   B   C   D

22 This question is about throwing a stone from a cliff.

Antonia stands at the edge of a vertical cliff and throws a stone vertically upwards.

The stone leaves Antonia's hand with speed $v = 8.0\,\text{m s}^{-1}$.

The acceleration of free fall g is $10\,\text{m s}^{-2}$ and all distance measurements are taken from the point where the stone leaves Antonia's hand.

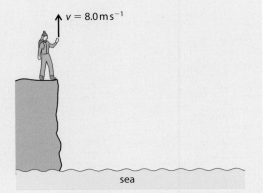

$v = 8.0\,\text{m s}^{-1}$

sea

(a) Ignoring air resistance, calculate

    (i) the maximum height reached by the stone.

    (ii) the time taken by the stone to reach its maximum height.

The time between the stone leaving Antonia's hand and hitting the sea is 3.0 s.

(b) Determine the height of the cliff.

23 This question is about the collision between two railway trucks (carts).

(a) Define *linear momentum*.

In the diagram on the right, truck A is moving along a horizontal track. It collides with a stationary truck B, and on collision, the two join together. Immediately before the collision, truck A is moving with speed 5.0 m s⁻¹. Immediately after collision, the speed of the trucks is *v*.

The mass of truck A is 800 kg and the mass of truck B is 1200 kg.

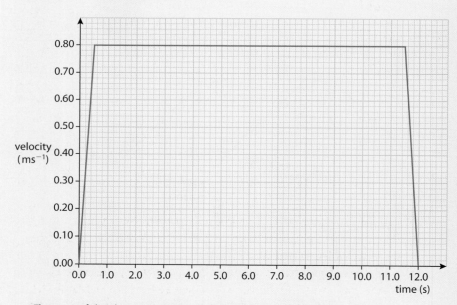

immediately before collision

immediately after collision

(b) (i) Calculate the speed *v* immediately after the collision.

(ii) Calculate the total kinetic energy lost during the collision.

24 An elevator (lift) starts from rest on the ground floor and comes to rest at a higher floor. Its motion is controlled by an electric motor. A simplified graph of the variation of the elevator's velocity with time is shown below.

The mass of the elevator is 250 kg. Use this information to calculate

(a) the acceleration of the elevator during the first 0.50 s

(b) the total distance travelled by the elevator

(c) the minimum work required to raise the elevator to the higher floor

(d) the minimum average power required to raise the elevator to the higher floor

(e) the efficiency of the electric motor that lifts the elevator, given that the input power to the motor is 5.0 kW.

25 This question is about momentum and the kinematics of a proposed journey to Jupiter.

(a) State the law of conservation of momentum.

A solar propulsion engine uses solar power to ionize atoms of xenon and to accelerate them. As a result of the acceleration process, the ions are ejected from the spaceship with a speed of $3.0 \times 10^4 \, m\,s^{-1}$.

xenon ions
speed = $3.0 \times 10^4 \, m\,s^{-1}$

spaceship
mass = $5.4 \times 10^2 \, kg$

(b) The mass (nucleon) number of the xenon used is 131. Deduce that the mass of one ion of xenon is $2.2 \times 10^{-25} \, kg$.

(c) The original mass of the fuel is 81 kg. Deduce that, if the engine ejects 7.7×10^{18} xenon ions every second, the fuel will last for 1.5 years. (1 year = $3.2 \times 10^7 \, s$)

(d) The mass of the spaceship is $5.4 \times 10^2 \, kg$. Deduce that the initial acceleration of the spaceship is $8.2 \times 10^{-5} \, m\,s^{-2}$.

The graph below shows the variation with time t of the acceleration a of the spaceship. The solar propulsion engine is switched on at time $t = 0$ when the speed of the spaceship is $1.2 \times 10^3 \, m\,s^{-1}$.

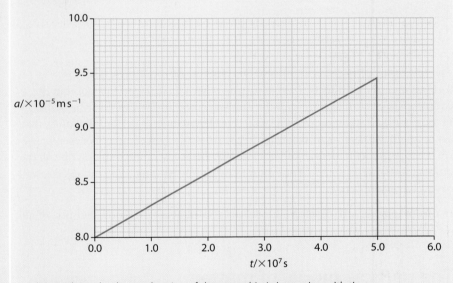

(e) Explain why the acceleration of the spaceship is increasing with time.

(f) Using data from the graph, calculate the speed of the spaceship at the time when the xenon fuel has all been used.

(g) The distance of the spaceship from Earth when the solar propulsion engine is switched on is very small compared to the distance from Earth to Jupiter. The fuel runs out when the spaceship is a distance of $4.7 \times 10^{11} \, m$ from Jupiter. Estimate the total time that it would take the spaceship to travel from Earth to Jupiter.

3 Thermal physics

3.1 Thermal concepts

Assessment statements
3.1.1 State that temperature determines the direction of thermal energy transfer between two objects.
3.1.2 State the relation between the Kelvin and Celsius scales of temperature.
3.1.3 State that the internal energy of a substance is the total potential energy and random kinetic energy of the molecules of the substance.
3.1.4 Explain and distinguish between the macroscopic concepts of temperature, internal energy and thermal energy (heat).
3.1.5 Define the mole and molar mass.
3.1.6 Define the Avogadro constant.

The role of the physicist is to observe our physical surroundings, take measurements and think of ways to explain what we see. Up to this point in the course we have been dealing with the motion of bodies. We can describe bodies in terms of their mass and volume, and if we know their speed and the forces that act on them, we can calculate where they will be at any given time. We even know what happens if two hit each other. However, this is not enough to describe all the differences between objects. For example, by simply holding different objects, we can feel that some are hot and some are cold.

In this chapter we will develop a model to explain these differences, but first of all we need to know what is inside matter.

The particle model of matter

Ancient Greek philosophers spent a lot of time thinking about what would happen if they took a piece of cheese and kept cutting it in half.

Figure 3.1 Can we keep cutting the cheese for ever?

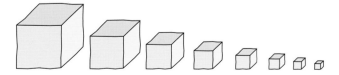

They didn't think it was possible to keep halving it for ever, so they suggested that there must exist a smallest part – this they called the *atom*.

Atoms are too small to see (about 10^{-10} m in diameter) but we can think of them as very small perfectly elastic balls. This means that when they collide, both momentum and kinetic energy are conserved.

Elements and compounds

We might ask: 'If everything is made of atoms, why isn't everything the same?' The answer is that there are many different types of atom.

 hydrogen atom gold atom

There are 117 different types of atom, and a material made of just one type of atom is called an *element*. There are, however, many more than 117 different types of material. The other types of matter are made of atoms that have joined together to form molecules. Materials made from molecules that contain more than one type of atom are called *compounds*.

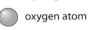 hydrogen atom

oxygen atom

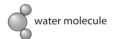 water molecule

Figure 3.2 Gold is made of gold atoms and hydrogen is made of hydrogen atoms.

This is a good example of how models are used in physics. Here we are modelling something that we can't see, the atom, using a familiar object, a rubber ball.

Figure 3.3 Water is an example of a compound.

The mole

When buying apples, you can ask for 5 kg of apples, or, say, 10 apples — both are a measure of amount. It's the same with matter — you can express amount in terms of either mass or number of particles.

A mole of any material contains 6.022×10^{23} atoms or molecules; this number is known as *Avogadro's number*.

Although all moles have the same number of particles, they don't all have the same mass. A mole of carbon has a mass of 12 g and a mole of neon has a mass of 20 g — this is because a neon atom has more mass than a carbon atom.

Moles of different compounds.

The three states of matter

From observations we know that there are three types, or *states* of matter: *solid*, *liquid* and *gas*. If the particle model is correct, then we can use it to explain why the three states are different.

Solid Fixed shape and volume

Liquid No fixed shape but fixed volume

Gas No fixed shape or volume

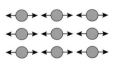

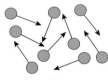

Molecules held in position by a force. Vibrate but don't move around.

Force between molecules not so strong so molecules can move around.

No force between molecules (ideally).

Figure 3.4 The particle model explains the differences between solids, liquids and gases. (The arrows represent velocity vectors.)

 We can't prove that this model is true — we can only provide evidence that supports it.

Ice, water and steam.

Worked example

1 If a mole of carbon has a mass of 12 g, how many atoms of carbon are there in 2 g?

2 The density of iron is 7874 kg m^{-3} and the mass of a mole of iron is 55.85 g. What is the volume of 1 mole of iron?

Solution

1 One mole contains 6.022×10^{23} atoms.

2 g is $\frac{1}{6}$ of a mole so contains $\frac{1}{6} \times 6.022 \times 10^{23}$ atoms = **1.004×10^{23} atoms**

2
$$\text{density} = \frac{\text{mass}}{\text{volume}}$$

$$\text{volume} = \frac{\text{mass}}{\text{density}}$$

$$\text{Volume of 1 mole} = \frac{0.05585}{7874}\,\text{m}^3$$

$$= 7.093 \times 10^{-6}\,\text{m}^3$$

$$= \textbf{7.09 cm}^3$$

• **Examiner's hint:** Be careful with the units. Do all calculations using m^3.

Exercises

1 The mass of 1 mole of copper is 63.54 g and its density 8920 kg m^{-3}
   (a) What is the volume of 1 mole of copper?
   (b) How many atoms does one mole of copper contain?
   (c) How much volume does one atom of copper occupy?

2 If the density of aluminium is 2700 kg m^{-3} and the volume of 1 mole is 10 cm^3, what is the mass of one mole of aluminium?

Internal energy

In the Chapter 2, Mechanics, you met the concepts of energy and work. Use these concepts to consider the following:

Figure 3.5 A wooden block is pulled along a rough horizontal surface at a constant velocity.

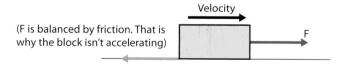

(F is balanced by friction. That is why the block isn't accelerating)

Velocity

F

To a view a simulation showing how friction can increase temperature, visit Heinemann.co.uk/hotlinks, enter the express code 4266S and click on Weblink 3.1.

Is any work being done on the block by force F?

Is energy being transferred to the block?

Is the KE of the block increasing?

Is the PE of the block increasing?

Where is the energy going?

You will have realised that since work is done, energy is given to the block, but its PE and KE are not increasing. Since energy is conserved, the energy must be going somewhere. It is going inside the block as internal energy. We can explain what is happening using the particle model.

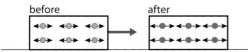

before   after

Molecules vibrate faster and are slightly further apart.

 Figure 3.6 Molecules gain internal energy.

When we do work on an object, it enables the molecules to move faster (increasing KE) and move apart (increasing PE). We say that the *internal energy* of the object has increased.

In a solid, this means increasing the KE and PE of the molecules; in a gas it is just the KE. This is because there are no forces between the molecules of a gas, so it doesn't require any work to pull them apart.

Worked example

1 A car of mass 1000 kg is travelling at 30 m s^{-1}. If the brakes are applied, how much heat energy is transferred to the brakes?

This thermogram of a car shows how the wheels have become hot owing to friction between the road and the tyres, and the brakes pads and discs.

Solution

When the car is moving it has kinetic energy. This must be transferred to the brakes when the car stops.

$KE = \frac{1}{2}mv^2$

$\quad = \frac{1}{2} \times 1000 \times 30^2 \, J$

$\quad = 450 \, kJ$

So thermal energy transferred to the brakes $= 450 \, kJ$

Exercises

3 A block of metal, mass 10 kg, is dropped from a height of 40 m.
   (a) How much energy does the block have before it is dropped?
   (b) How much heat energy do the block and floor gain when it hits the floor?

4 If the car in Example 1 was travelling at 60 m s^{-1}, how much heat energy would the brakes receive?

Temperature

If we now pick a block up, after dragging it, we will notice something has changed. It has got hot; doing work on the block has made it hot. *Hotness* and *coldness* are the ways we perceive differences between objects. In physics, we use temperature to measure this difference more precisely.

 It is important to realise the difference between perception and physical measurement.

Temperature (T) is a measure of how hot or cold an object is, and it is temperature that determines the direction of heat flow.

Temperature is a *scalar* quantity, and is measured in degrees Celsius (°C) or kelvin (K).

0 °C is equivalent to 273 K.
100 °C is equivalent to 373 K.

At normal atmospheric pressure, pure water boils at 100 °C and freezes at 0 °C. Room temperature is about 20 °C.

During the first part of this chapter, we will measure temperature in Celsius. However when dealing with gases, we will use kelvin — this is because the Kelvin scale is based on the properties of a gas.

To convert from Celsius to Kelvin, simply add 273.

Thermometers

Temperature cannot be measured directly, so we have to find something that changes when the temperature changes. The most common thermometer consists of a small amount of alcohol in a thin glass tube. As temperature increases, the volume of the alcohol increases, so it rises up the tube. When we measure temperature, we are really measuring the length of the alcohol column, but the scale is calibrated to give the temperature in °C.

Temperature and the particle model

Figure 3.7 Temperature is related to kinetic energy.

Cold – molecules vibrate a bit.

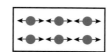

Hot – molecules vibrate faster and are slightly further apart.

From the previous model, we can see that the particles in a hot body move faster than those in a cold one. The temperature is related to the average KE of the particles.

Heat transfer

Pulling a block of wood along a rough surface is not the only way to increase its temperature. We can make a cold body hot by placing it next to a hot body. We know that if the cold body gets hot, then it must have received energy — this is heat or *thermal* energy.

We are often more interested in preventing heat flow than causing it. Placing an insulating layer (e.g. woollen cloth) between the hot and cold bodies will reduce the rate of heat flow.

Thermal equilibrium

Figure 3.8 Heat flows from the hot body to the cold body until they are at the same temperature.

before

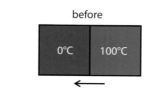

Heat flows from the hot to the cold.

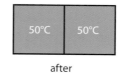

after

At this point no more heat will flow — this is called *thermal equilibrium*.

3.2 Thermal properties of matter

Assessment statements
3.2.1 Define *specific heat capacity* and *thermal capacity*.
3.2.2 Solve problems involving specific heat capacities and thermal capacities.
3.2.3 Explain the physical differences between the solid, liquid and gaseous phases in terms of molecular structure and particle motion.
3.2.4 Describe and explain the process of phase changes in terms of molecular behaviour.
3.2.5 Explain in terms of molecular behaviour why temperature does not change during a phase change.
3.2.6 Distinguish between evaporation and boiling.
3.2.7 Define *specific latent heat*.
3.2.8 Solve problems involving specific latent heats.

Thermal capacity

If heat is added to a body, its temperature rises, but the actual increase in temperature depends on the body.

The *thermal capacity* (C) of a body is the amount of heat needed to raise its temperature by 1°C. Unit: $J\,°C^{-1}$

If the temperature of a body increases by an amount ΔT when quantity of heat Q is added, then the thermal capacity is given by the equation:

$$C = \frac{Q}{\Delta T}$$

 This doesn't only apply when things are given heat, but also when they lose heat.

Worked example

1 If the thermal capacity of a quantity of water is $5000\,J\,°C^{-1}$, how much heat is required to raise its temperature from $20\,°C$ to $100\,°C$?

2 How much heat is lost from a block of metal of thermal capacity $800\,J\,°C^{-1}$ when it cools down from $60\,°C$ to $20\,°C$?

Solution

1 Thermal capacity $Q = \dfrac{Q}{\Delta T}$ From definition

     So $Q = C\Delta T$ Rearranging

     Therefore $Q = 5000 \times (100 - 20)\,J$

     So the heat required $Q = \mathbf{400\,kJ}$

2 Thermal capacity, $C = \dfrac{Q}{\Delta T}$ From definition

     So $Q = C\Delta T$ Rearranging

     Therefore $Q = 800 \times (60 - 20)\,J$

     So the heat lost $Q = \mathbf{32\,kJ}$

5 The thermal capacity of a 60 kg human is 210 kJ °C⁻¹. How much heat is lost from a body if its temperature drops by 2 °C?

6 The temperature of a room is 10 °C. In 1 hour the room is heated to 20 °C by a 1 kW electric heater.
   (a) How much heat is delivered to the room?
   (b) What is the thermal capacity of the room?
   (c) Does all this heat go to heat the room?

• **Examiner's hint:** Remember, power is energy per unit time.

Specific heat capacity (c)

The thermal capacity depends on the size of the object and what it is made of. The *specific heat capacity* depends only on the material. Raising the temperature of l kg of water requires more heat than raising 1kg of steel by the same amount, so the specific heat capacity of water is higher than that of steel.

The specific heat capacity of a material is the amount of heat required to raise the temperature of 1kg of the material by 1°C. Unit: $J\,kg^{-1}\,°C^{-1}$

If a quantity of heat Q is required to raise the temperature of a mass m of material by ΔT then the specific heat capacity (c) of that material is given by the following equation:

$$c = \frac{Q}{m\Delta T}$$

The specific heat capacity of water is quite high, so it takes a lot of energy to heat up the water for a shower.

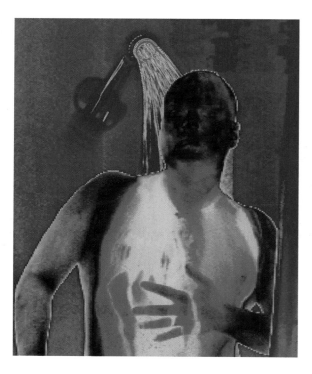

Worked example

1 The specific heat capacity of water is 4200 J kg⁻¹°C⁻¹. How much heat will be required to heat 300 g of water from 20 °C to 60 °C?

2 A metal block of mass 1.5 kg loses 20 kJ of heat. As this happens, its temperature drops from 60 °C to 45 °C. What is the specific heat capacity of the metal?

Solution

1 Specific heat capacity, $c = \dfrac{Q}{m\Delta T}$ From definition

So $\qquad\qquad\qquad\qquad Q = cm\Delta T$ Rearranging

Therefore $\qquad\qquad\quad Q = 4200 \times 0.3 \times 40$ Note: Convert g to kg

$\qquad\qquad\qquad\qquad\quad Q = \mathbf{50.4\,kJ}$

2 Specific heat capacity, $c = \dfrac{Q}{m\Delta T}$ From definition

So $\qquad\qquad\qquad\qquad c = 20\,000/1.5(60-45)$ Rearranging

$\qquad\qquad\qquad\qquad\quad c = \mathbf{888.9\,J\,kg^{-1}\,{}^{\circ}C^{-1}}$

Exercises

Use the data in the table to solve the problems:

Substance	Specific heat capacity ($J\,kg^{-1}\,{}^{\circ}C^{-1}$)
Water	4200
Copper	380
Aluminium	900
Steel	440

7 How much heat is required to raise the temperature of 250 g of copper from 20 °C to 160 °C?

8 The density of water is 1000 kg m^{-3}.
 (a) What is the mass of 1 litre of water?
 (b) How much energy will it take to raise the temperature of 1 litre of water from 20 °C to 100 °C?
 (c) A water heater has a power rating of 1 kW. How many seconds will this heater take to boil 1 litre of water?

9 A 500 g piece of aluminium is heated with a 500 W heater for 10 minutes.
 (a) How much energy will be given to the aluminium in this time?
 (b) If the temperature of the aluminium was 20°C at the beginning, what will its temperature be after 10 minutes?

10 A car of mass 1500 kg travelling at 20 m s^{-1} brakes suddenly and comes to a stop.
 (a) How much KE does the car lose?
 (b) If 75% of the energy is given to the front brakes, how much energy will they receive?
 (c) The brakes are made out of steel and have a total mass of 10 kg. By how much will their temperature rise?

11 The water comes out of a showerhead at a temperature of 50 °C at a rate of 8 litres per minute.
 (a) If you take a shower lasting 10 minutes, how many kg of water have you used?
 (b) If the water must be heated from 10 °C, how much energy is needed to heat the water?

Change of state

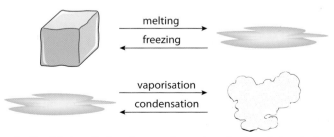

Figure 3.9 When matter changes from liquid to gas, or solid to liquid, it is changing state.

When water boils, this is called a *change of state* (or *change of phase*). As this happens, the temperature of the water doesn't change — it stays at 100 °C. In fact, we find that whenever the state of a material changes, the temperature stays the same. We can explain this in terms of the particle model.

Figure 3.10 Molecules gain PE when the state changes.

Solid molecules have KE since they are vibrating.

Liquid molecules are now free to move about but have the same KE as before.

When matter changes state, the energy is needed to enable the molecules to move more freely. To understand this, consider the example below.

Figure 3.11 A ball-in-a-box model of change of state.

Ball has KE as it is moving in the box.

Ball now has KE + PE.

Ball now has same KE as before but also has PE and is free to move around.

An iceberg melts as it floats into warmer water.

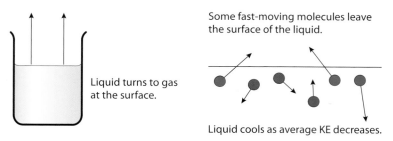

Boiling and evaporation

These are two different processes by which liquids can change to gases.

Boiling takes place throughout the liquid and always at the same temperature. *Evaporation* takes place only at the surface of the liquid and can happen at all temperatures.

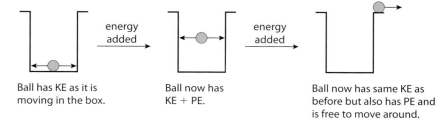

Figure 3.12 A microscopic model of evaporation.

Liquid turns to gas at the surface.

Some fast-moving molecules leave the surface of the liquid.

Liquid cools as average KE decreases.

When a liquid evaporates, the fastest-moving particles leave the surface. This means that the average kinetic energy of the remaining particles is lower, resulting in a drop in temperature.

The rate of evaporation can be increased by:

- Increasing the surface area; this increases the number of molecules near the surface, giving more of them a chance to escape.
- Blowing across the surface. After molecules have left the surface they form a small 'vapour cloud' above the liquid. If this is blown away, it allows further molecules to leave the surface more easily.
- Raising the temperature; this increases the kinetic energy of the liquid molecules, enabling more to escape.

 People sweat to increase the rate at which they lose heat. When you get hot, sweat comes out of your skin onto the surface of your body. When the sweat evaporates, it cools you down. In a sauna there is so much water vapour in the air that the sweat doesn't evaporate.

Specific latent heat (L)

The *specific latent heat* of a material is the amount of heat required to change the state of 1kg of the material without change of temperature.

Unit: $J\,kg^{-1}$

Latent means *hidden*. This name is used because when matter changes state, the heat added does not cause the temperature to rise, but seems to disappear.

If it takes an amount of energy Q to change the state of a mass m of a substance, then the specific latent heat of that substance is given by the equation:

$$L = \frac{Q}{m}$$

 Solid→liquid
Specific latent heat of fusion

Liquid→gas
Specific latent heat of vaporization

Worked example

1 The specific latent heat of fusion of water is $3.35 \times 10^5\,J\,kg^{-1}$. How much energy is required to change 500 g of ice into water?
2 The amount of heat released when 100 g of steam turns to water is $2.27 \times 10^5\,J$. What is the specific latent heat of vaporization of water?

Solution

1 The latent heat of fusion, $L_f = \dfrac{Q}{m}$ From definition

So $Q = mL$ Rearranging

Therefore $Q = 0.5 \times 3.35 \times 10^5\,J$

So the heat required, $Q = \mathbf{1.675 \times 10^5 J}$

2 The specific latent heat of vaporization, $L = \dfrac{Q}{m}$ From definition

Therefore $L = 2.27 \times 10^5/0.1\,J\,kg^{-1}$

So the specific latent heat of vaporization, $L = \mathbf{2.27 \times 10^6\,J\,kg^{-1}}$

 This equation $\left(L = \frac{Q}{m}\right)$ can also be used to calculate the heat lost when a substance changes from gas to liquid, or liquid to solid.

Exercises

Latent heats of water

Latent heat of vaporization	$2.27 \times 10^6\,J\,kg^{-1}$
Latent heat of fusion	$3.35 \times 10^5\,J\,kg^{-1}$

Use the data about water in the table to solve the following problems.

12 If the mass of water in a cloud is 1million kg, how much energy will be released if the cloud turns from water to ice?

13 A water boiler has a power rating of 800 W. How long will it take to turn 400 g of boiling water into steam?

14 The ice covering a 1000 m² lake is 2 cm thick.
   (a) If the density of ice is 920 kg m⁻³, what is the mass of the ice on the lake?
   (b) How much energy is required to melt the ice?
   (c) If the sun melts the ice in 5 hours, what is the power delivered to the lake?
   (d) How much power does the sun deliver per m²?

Graphical representation of heating

The increase of the temperature of a body can be represented by a temperature–time graph. Observing this graph can give us a lot of information about the heating process.

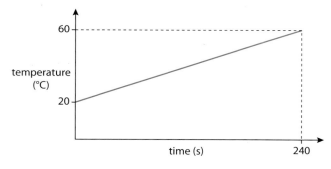

From this graph we can calculate the amount of heat given to the water per unit time (power).

$$\text{The gradient of the graph} = \frac{\text{temperature rise}}{\text{time}} = \frac{\Delta T}{t}$$

We know from the definition of specific heat capacity that

$$\text{heat added} = mc\Delta T$$

$$\text{The rate of adding heat} = P = \frac{mc\Delta T}{t}$$

So $P = mc \times gradient$

$$\text{The gradient of this line} = \frac{(60 - 20)}{240} \,°C\,s^{-1} = 0.167\,°C\,s^{-1}$$

So the power delivered $= 4200 \times 0.167\,W = 700\,W$

If we continue to heat this water it will begin to boil.

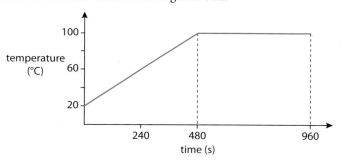

If we assume that the heater is giving heat to the water at the same rate, then we can calculate how much heat was given to the water whilst it was boiling.

Power of the heater $= 700\,W$

Time of boiling $= 480\,s$

Energy supplied $= \text{power} \times \text{time} = 700 \times 480\,J = 3.36 \times 10^5\,J$

From this we can calculate how much water must have turned to steam.

Heat added to change state $= \text{mass} \times \text{latent heat of vaporization}$,

where latent heat of vaporization of water $= 2.27 \times 10^6\,J\,kg^{-1}$.

$$\text{Mass changed to steam} = \frac{3.36 \times 10^5}{2.27 \times 10^6} = 0.15\,kg$$

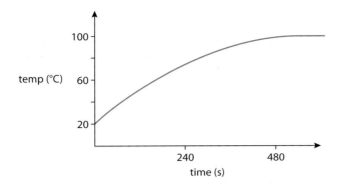

Figure 3.15 Heat loss.

When boiling a kettle, heat is continually being lost to the room. The amount of heat loss is proportional to the temperature of the kettle. For this reason, a graph of temperature against time is actually a curve, as shown in Figure 3.15.

The fact that the gradient decreases, tells us that the amount of heat given to the water gets less with time. This is because as it gets hotter, more and more of the heat is lost to the room.

Measuring thermal quantities by the method of mixtures

The method of mixtures can be used to measure the specific heat capacity and specific latent heat of substances.

Specific heat capacity of a metal

A metal sample is first heated to a known temperature. The most convenient way of doing this is to place it in boiling water for a few minutes; after this time it will be at 100 °C. The hot metal is then quickly moved to an insulated cup containing a known mass of cold water. The hot metal will cause the temperature of the cold water to rise; the rise in temperature is measured with a thermometer. Some example temperatures and masses are given in Figure 3.16.

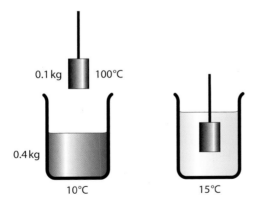

Figure 3.16 Measuring the specific heat capacity of a metal.

As the specific heat capacity of water is 4180 J kg^{-1} °C^{-1}, we can calculate the specific heat capacity of the metal.

ΔT for the metal $= 100 - 15 = 85$ °C

and ΔT for the water $= 15 - 10 = 5$ °C

Applying the formula $Q = mc\Delta T$ we get

$(mc\Delta T)_{\text{metal}} = 0.1 \times c \times 85 = 8.5c$

$(mc\Delta T)_{\text{water}} = 0.4 \times 4180 \times 5 = 8360$

If no heat is lost, then the heat transferred from the metal $=$ heat transferred to the water

$8.5c = 8360$

$c_{\text{metal}} = 983$ J kg^{-1} °C^{-1}

Latent heat of vaporization of water

To measure the latent heat of vaporization, steam is passed into cold water. Some of the steam condenses in the water, causing the water temperature to rise. The heat from the steam = the heat to the water.

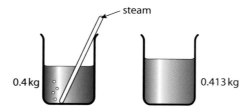

steam

Figure 3.17 By measuring the rise in temperature, the specific latent heat can be calculated.

In Figure 3.17, 13 g of steam have condensed in the water, raising its temperature by 20 °C. The steam condenses then cools down from 100 °C to 30 °C.

Heat from steam $= ml_{steam} + mc\Delta T_{water}$

$0.013 \times L + 0.013 \times 4.18 \times 10^3 \times 70 = 0.013L + 3803.8$

Heat transferred to cold water $= mc\Delta T_{water} = 0.4 \times 4.18 \times 10^3 \times 20$

$$= 33\,440\,J$$

Since heat from steam = heat to water

$0.013L + 3803.8 = 33\,440$

So $L = \dfrac{33\,440 - 3803.8}{0.013}$

$L = 2.28 \times 10^6\,J\,kg^{-1}$

Heat loss

In both of these experiments, some of the heat coming from the hot source can be lost to the surroundings. To reduce heat loss, the temperatures can be adjusted, so you could start the experiment below room temperature and end the same amount above (e.g. if room temp is 20 °C, then you can start at 10 °C and end at 30 °C).

Transfer of water

In the specific heat capacity experiment, droplets of hot water may be transferred with the metal block. This would add extra energy to the water, causing the temperature to rise a little bit too high. In the latent heat experiment, droplets of water sometimes condense in the tube – since they have already condensed, they don't give so much heat to the water.

3.3 Kinetic model of an ideal gas

Assessment statements

3.2.9   Define *pressure*.

3.2.10   State the assumptions of the kinetic model of an ideal gas.

3.2.11   State that temperature is a measure of the average random kinetic energy of the molecules of an ideal gas.

3.2.12   Explain the macroscopic behaviour of an ideal gas in terms of a molecular model.

The ideal gas

Of the three states of matter, the gaseous state has the simplest model; this is because the forces between the molecules of a gas are very small, so they are able to move freely. We can therefore use what we know about the motion of particles learnt in the mechanics section to study gases in more detail.

According to our simple model, a gas is made up of a large number of perfectly elastic, tiny spheres moving in random motion.

This model makes some assumptions:

- The molecules are perfectly elastic.
- The molecules are spheres.
- The molecules are identical.
- There are no forces between the molecules – this means that the molecules move with constant velocity between collisions.
- The molecules are very small, that is, their total volume is much smaller than the volume of the gas.

Some of these assumptions are not true for all gases, especially when the gas is compressed (when the molecules are so close together that they experience a force between them). The gas then behaves as a liquid. However, to keep things simple, we will only consider gases that behave like our model. We call these gases ideal gases.

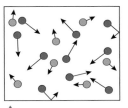

Figure 3.18 Simple model of a gas in a box. In reality the molecules have a range of velocities, not just two.

Nitrogen becomes a liquid at low temperatures.

Temperature of a gas

From our general particle model of matter, we know that the temperature of a gas is directly related to the average KE of the molecules. If the temperature increases, then the speed of the particles will increase.

Figure 3.19 The molecules in a hot gas have a higher average KE.

200 K   300 K

Pressure of a gas

Let us apply what we know about particles to one molecule of a gas. Consider a single gas molecule in a box. According to the model, this is like a perfectly elastic sphere bouncing off the sides

We can see that this particle keeps hitting the walls of the container. Each time it does this, its direction, and therefore its velocity, changes.

Newton's first law of motion says that if a particle isn't at rest or moving with a constant velocity then it must be experiencing an unbalanced force. The particle is therefore experiencing an unbalanced force.

Newton's second law says that the size of this force is equal to the rate of change of momentum, so the force will be greater if the particle travels with a greater speed, or hits the sides more often.

Newton's third law says that if body A exerts a force on body B, then body B will exert an equal and opposite force on A. The wall exerts a force on the particle, so the particle must exert a force on the wall.

If we now add more molecules (as in Figure 3.21) then the particles exert a continuous force, F, on the walls of the container. If the walls have a total area A, then since

$$\text{pressure} = \frac{\text{force}}{\text{area}}$$

we can say that the pressure exerted on the walls is F/A — in other words, the particles exert a pressure on the container.

It is important to realise that we have been talking about the gas model, not the actual gas. The model predicts that the gas should exert a pressure on the walls of its container and it does.

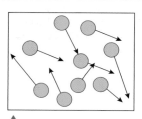

Figure 3.20 A rubber ball bouncing around a box.

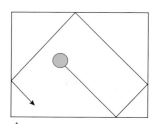

Figure 3.21 Many rubber balls bouncing around a box.

The atmosphere also exerts a pressure; this changes from day to day but is approximately 100 kPa.

1 pascal = 1 Pa = 1 N m^{-2}

Figure 3.22 A gas in a piston can be used to vary the properties of a gas.

Properties of a gas

We can now use the particle model to explain why a gas behaves as it does.

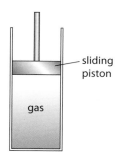

sliding piston

gas

If you push on the piston you can feel the gas push back.

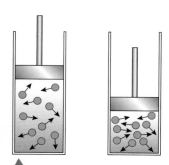

Figure 3.23 The volume of a gas is reduced.

Pressure and volume

If the volume is reduced, the particles hit the walls more often, since the walls are closer together. The force exerted by the molecules is equal to the rate of change of momentum; this will increase if the hits are more frequent, resulting in an increased pressure.

Pressure and temperature

 Slow moving molecules of cold gas.

 Fast moving molecules of hot gas.

Increase in temperature increases the speed of the molecules. When the molecules hit the walls, their change of momentum will be greater and they will hit the walls more often. The result is a greater rate of change of momentum and hence a larger force. This results in an increase in pressure.

Doing work on a gas

When you push the piston of a pump, it collides with the molecules, giving them energy (rather like a tennis racket hitting a ball). You are doing work on the gas. The increase in kinetic energy results in an increase in temperature and pressure. This is why the temperature of a bicycle pump increases when you pump up the tyres.

Gas does work

When a gas expands, it has to push away the surrounding air. In pushing the air away, the gas does work, and doing this work requires energy. This energy comes from the kinetic energy of the molecules, resulting in a reduction in temperature. This is why an aerosol feels cold when you spray it; the gas expands as it comes out of the canister.

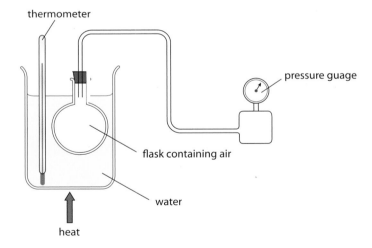

Figure 3.24 The temperature of a gas is increased.

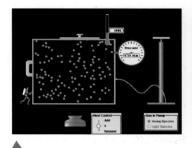

To understand how pressure, temperature and volume of a gas are related, visit heinemann.co.uk/hotlinks, enter the express code 4266S and click on Weblink 3.2.

Figure 3.25 The pressure of a fixed volume of gas can be measured as the temperature is changed.

Absolute zero and the Kelvin scale

From our particle model of matter, we accept that temperature is related to the average KE of the molecules. This implies that there is a lowest possible temperature when the average KE is zero, in other words, when the molecules stop moving. This temperature is called *absolute zero*.

When dealing with gases we will always use the Kelvin scale since this is directly related to the properties of a gas.

Figure 3.26 A graph of the pressure of a fixed volume of gas against temperature in Celsius.

● **Examiner's hint:** Since you don't have to know any equations relating to gases, there won't be any mathematical problems on the exam. However, you could be asked to use the kinetic model to explain why a gas behaves as it does.

In the section on temperature and thermometers, it was mentioned that to measure temperature, we need a quantity that varies with temperature, like the length of a mercury column. The problem with this is that as temperature goes down, the length gets shorter but the length of the column can never be zero — so at very low temperatures, the scale wouldn't work. It would be better if we based the temperature scale on something that was actually zero at the lowest possible temperature, e.g. the pressure of a fixed mass of gas with a constant volume. This scale is called the Kelvin scale.

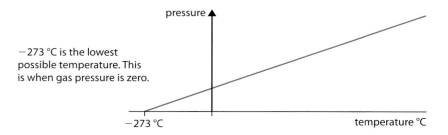

−273 °C is the lowest possible temperature. This is when gas pressure is zero.

Worked example

1 Explain why a balloon gets bigger when you blow it up.
2 Use the kinetic model to explain why a solid doesn't exert pressure in the same way that a gas does.

Solution

1 When you blow into a balloon, you are increasing the number of air molecules inside it. Increasing the number of molecules means that the number of air molecules hitting the sides of the balloon per second increases, resulting in an increase in pressure, which stretches the rubber of the balloon.

2 A gas is made of molecules that move about freely. If a gas is enclosed in a container, the gas molecules collide with the walls of the container. It is these collisions that result in the gas pressure. A solid is made of molecules that are not free to move about and therefore do not collide with the walls of the container.

Practice questions

1 This question is about the change of phase (state) of ice.

A quantity of crushed ice is removed from a freezer and placed in a calorimeter. Thermal energy is supplied to the ice at a constant rate. To ensure that all the ice is at the same temperature, it is continually stirred. The temperature of the contents of the calorimeter is recorded every 15 seconds.

The graph at the top of the next page shows the variation with time t of the temperature θ of the contents of the calorimeter. (Uncertainties in the measured quantities are not shown.)

(a) On the graph, mark with an X, the data point on the graph at which all the ice has just melted. (1)

(b) Explain, with reference to the energy of the molecules, the constant temperature region of the graph. (3)

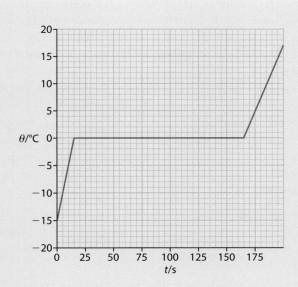

The mass of the ice is 0.25 kg and the specific heat capacity of water is 4200 J kg^{-1} K^{-1}.

(c) Use these data and data from the graph to
    (i) deduce that energy is supplied to the ice at the rate of about 530W   (3)
    (ii) determine the specific heat capacity of ice   (3)
    (iii) determine the specific latent heat of fusion of ice.   (2)

Specific heat capacity of ice $= 2.1 \times 10^3$ J kg^{-1} K^{-1}
Specific heat capacity of water $= 4.2 \times 10^3$ J kg^{-1} K^{-1}
Specific latent heat of fusion of ice $= 3.3 \times 10^5$ J kg^{-1}

2 This question is about thermal physics.
  (a) Explain why, when a liquid evaporates, the liquid cools unless thermal energy is
    supplied to it.   (3)
  (b) State two factors that cause an increase in the rate of evaporation of a liquid.   (2)
  (c) A mass of 350 g of water at a temperature of 25 °C is placed in a refrigerator that
    extracts thermal energy from the water at a rate of 86W.
    Calculate the time taken for the water to become ice at −5.0 °C.   (3)

3 Explain, in terms of the behaviour of the molecules of an ideal gas, why the pressure of
the gas rises when it is heated at constant volume.   (3)

4 This question is about the phase (state) changes of the element lead.
A sample of lead has a mass of 0.50 kg and a temperature of 27 °C. Energy is supplied
to the lead at the rate of 1.5 kW. After 0.2 minutes of heating it reaches its melting
point temperature of 327 °C. After heating for a further 3 minutes, all the lead has
become liquid.
  (a) Assuming that all the energy goes into heating the lead, calculate a value for the
    (i) specific heat capacity of lead   (3)
    (ii) latent heat of fusion of lead.   (2)
  (b) Energy continues to be supplied to the lead. Sketch a graph to show how the
    temperature of the lead varies with time from the start of heating to some 5
    minutes after the time when all the lead has become liquid. Indicate on the graph
    the time at which it starts to melt and the time when it has become liquid.   (2)
(You are not expected to have accurate scales; this is just a sketch graph.)

5 This question is about modelling the thermal processes involved when a person is running.

When running, a person generates thermal energy but maintains approximately constant temperature.

(a) Explain what *thermal energy* and *temperature* mean. Distinguish between the two concepts. (4)

The following simple model may be used to estimate the rise in temperature of a runner, assuming no thermal energy is lost.

A closed container holds 70 kg of water, representing the mass of the runner. The water is heated at a rate of 1200 W for 30 minutes. This represents the energy generation in the runner.

(b) **(i)** Show that the thermal energy generated by the heater is 2.2×10^6 J. (2)

(ii) Calculate the temperature rise of the water, assuming no energy losses from the water. (3)

The specific heat capacity of water is 4200 J kg^{-1} K^{-1}.

(c) The temperature rise calculated in **(b)** would be dangerous for the runner. Outline three mechanisms, other than evaporation, by which the container in the model would transfer energy to its surroundings. (6)

(d) A further process by which energy is lost from the runner is the evaporation of sweat.

(i) Describe, in terms of molecular behaviour, why evaporation causes cooling. (3)

(ii) Percentage of generated energy lost by sweating: 50%

Specific latent heat of vaporization of sweat: 2.26×10^6 J kg^{-1}

Using the information above, and your answer to (b) (i), estimate the mass of sweat evaporated from the runner. (3)

(iii) State and explain two factors that affect the rate of evaporation of sweat from the skin of the runner. (4)

6 A gas is contained in a cylinder fitted with a piston as shown below.

When the gas is compressed rapidly by the piston, its temperature rises because the molecules of the gas

A   are squeezed closer together.

B   collide with each other more frequently.

C   collide with the walls of the container more frequently.

D   gain energy from the moving piston. (1)

7 The Kelvin temperature of an ideal gas is a measure of the

A   average speed of the molecules.

B   average momentum of the molecules.

C   average kinetic energy of the molecules.

D   average potential energy of the molecules. (1)

8 The temperature of an ideal gas is reduced. Which one of the following statements is true?

A The molecules collide with the walls of the container less frequently.

B The molecules collide with each other more frequently.

C The time of contact between the molecules and the wall is reduced.

D The time of contact between molecules is increased. (1)

9 When a gas in a cylinder is compressed at constant temperature by a piston, the pressure of the gas increases. Consider the following three statements.

I The rate at which the molecules collide with the piston increases.

II The average speed of the molecules increases.

III The molecules collide with each other more often.

Which statement(s) correctly explain the increase in pressure?

A I only

B II only

C I and II only

D I and III only (1)

4 Simple harmonic motion and waves

4.1 Kinematics of simple harmonic motion

Assessment statements

4.1.1 Describe examples of oscillations.
4.1.2 Define the terms *displacement*, *amplitude*, *frequency*, *period* and *phase difference*.
4.1.3 Define *simple harmonic motion* (SHM) and state the defining equation as $a = -\omega^2 x$.
4.1.4 Solve problems using the defining equation for SHM.
4.1.5 Apply the equations $v = v_0 \sin \omega t$, $v = v_0 \cos \omega t$, $v = \pm\omega\sqrt{(x_0{}^2 - x^2)}$, $x = x_0 \cos \omega t$ and $x = x_0 \sin \omega t$ as solutions to the defining equation for SHM.
4.1.6 Solve problems, both graphically and by calculation, for acceleration, velocity and displacement during SHM.

A swing is an example of oscillatory motion.
▼

Oscillations

In this section we will derive a mathematical model for an oscillating or vibrating body. There are many different examples of naturally occurring oscillations but they don't all have the same type of motion. We are going to consider the simplest form of oscillation; simple harmonic motion. The most common example of this is a pendulum (Figure 4.1). Before we start to model this motion, we need to define some new terms and quantities.

Figure 4.1 The simple pendulum swings from A to B and back.

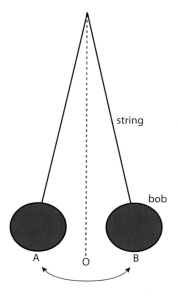

string

bob

A   O   B

Cycle

One cycle is defined as one complete oscillation of the pendulum. The term *cycle* is also used to describe circular motion; one cycle is one complete circle or 2π radians.

Equilibrium position

The equilibrium position is the position where the pendulum bob would rest if not disturbed – this is position O.

Amplitude (x_o)

The amplitude is defined as the maximum displacement from the equilibrium position, this is distance OB or OA.

Unit: metre

Time period (T)

The time period is the time taken for one complete cycle.

Unit: second

Frequency (*f*)

The frequency is the number of cycles that the pendulum makes per unit time. This is equal to 1/time period.

Unit: s^{-1} or hertz (Hz)

Angular frequency (ω)

The angular frequency is found by multiplying *f* by 2π ($\omega = 2\pi f$). This quantity is normally used when describing circular motion. An angular frequency of 2π rads s^{-1} means that a body makes one revolution per second. However, it is also used to describe an oscillation, 2π being equivalent to one complete cycle.

Unit: s^{-1} or hertz (Hz)

> **Measuring time period**
>
> To reduce the uncertainties when measuring the time period of an oscillation, it is best to measure the time for many oscillations e.g. 10. The time period is found by dividing this time by the number of oscillations.

Worked example

A pendulum completes 10 swings in 8 s. What is the angular frequency?

Solution

There are 10 swings in 8 seconds, so each swing takes 0.8 s.

Time period = 0.8 s.

$\text{Frequency} = \dfrac{1}{T} = \dfrac{1}{0.8} = 1.25\,\text{Hz}$

Angular frequency $\omega = 2\pi f = 2\pi \times 1.25 = \mathbf{7.8\ rad\ s^{-1}}$

Analysing oscillations

To make a model of oscillatory motion, we will analyse two different oscillations and see if there are any similarities.

The pendulum

Figure 4.2 As the angle increases, the horizontal component of tension increases, but is always pointing towards the centre.

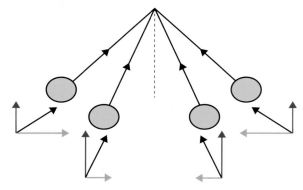

When a pendulum bob is pushed to one side and released, it will swing back down. The reason for this can be understood by drawing the forces acting on the bob. In Figure 4.2, we can see that when the string makes an angle to the vertical, the tension has a component in the horizontal direction; this component causes the bob to accelerate back towards the middle. As the bob swings down, the angle of the string gets smaller, and the horizontal component decreases. The horizontal acceleration of the bob is proportional to the horizontal force, so we can therefore deduce that the acceleration is proportional to the displacement from the lowest point.

When the ball reaches the lowest position, it is travelling at its maximum speed. It passes through this position and continues to swing up on the other side. The horizontal component of the tension is now acting in the other direction. This is in the *opposite* direction to the motion so will slow the bob down. We can conclude that no matter where the bob is, its acceleration is always directed towards O.

Mass on a spring

Figure 4.3 The tension increases as the spring is stretched. The resultant (red) increases with increased distance from the centre and is always directed towards the centre.

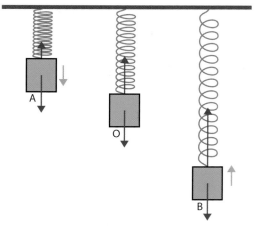

If a mass hanging on the end of a spring is lifted up and released, it will bounce up and down as in Figure 4.3. The forces acting on the mass are *weight* and the *tension in the spring*. The weight is always the same but the tension depends on how far the spring is stretched. (When you stretch a spring, the tension is proportional to the extension).

At A, the spring is short, so the tension will be small; the weight will therefore be bigger than the tension, so the resultant force will be downwards.

As the mass passes through the middle point, the forces will be balanced.

At B, the spring is stretched, so the tension is large; the tension will therefore be greater than the weight, so the resultant force will be upwards.

Again we can see that the acceleration is proportional to the displacement from the central point and always directed towards it.

This type of motion is called *simple harmonic motion* or SHM.

SHM
The acceleration is proportional to the distance from a fixed point. The acceleration is always directed towards a fixed point.

Exercises

1   State whether the following are examples of simple harmonic motion.

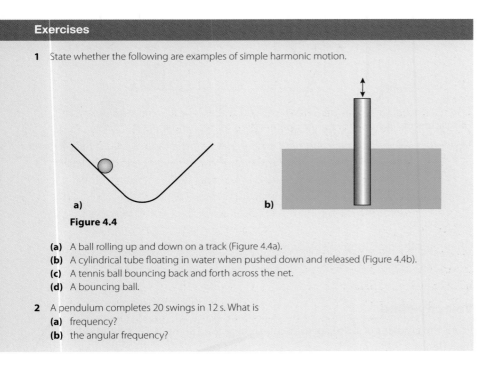

a)

b)

Figure 4.4

  (a) A ball rolling up and down on a track (Figure 4.4a).
  (b) A cylindrical tube floating in water when pushed down and released (Figure 4.4b).
  (c) A tennis ball bouncing back and forth across the net.
  (d) A bouncing ball.

2   A pendulum completes 20 swings in 12 s. What is
  (a) frequency?
  (b) the angular frequency?

Graphical treatment

To analyse the oscillation further, we can plot graphs for the motion. In this example, we will consider a mass on a spring, but we could choose any simple harmonic motion.

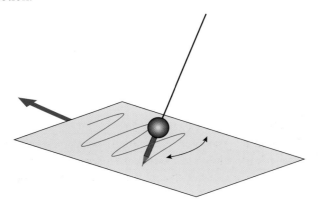

Figure 4.5 You can plot a displacement–time graph by attaching a pen to a pendulum and moving paper beneath it at a constant velocity.

To see how the equation fits the graph we can put some numbers into the equation.

In this example, the time period $= 4\,s$

Therefore $f = \frac{1}{4} = 0.25\,Hz$

Angular frequency $= 2\pi f = 0.5\pi$

So displacement $= 2\cos(0.5\pi t)$

Calculating displacement at different times gives:

$t = 1\,s\ y = 2\cos(\pi/2) = 0\,cm$

$t = 2\,s\ y = 2\cos(\pi) = -2\,cm$

$t = 3\,s\ y = 2\cos(3\pi/2) = 0\,cm$

$t = 4\,s\ y = 2\cos(2\pi) = 2\,cm$

Displacement – time

As before, O is the equilibrium position and we will take this to be our position of zero displacement. Above this is positive displacement and below is negative.

At A, the mass has maximum positive displacement from O.

At O, the mass has zero displacement from O.

At B, the mass has maximum negative displacement from O.

We can see that the shape of this displacement – time graph is a cosine curve.

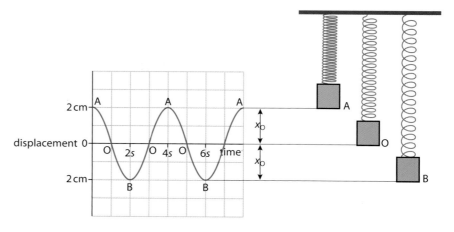

Figure 4.6 Displacement–time graph.

The equation of this line is $x = x_o \cos\omega t$,

where x_o is the maximum displacement and ω is the angular frequency.

Velocity–time

From the gradient of the displacement–time graph (Figure 4.6), we can calculate the velocity.

At A, gradient $= 0$ so velocity is zero.

At O, gradient is negative and maximum, so velocity is down and maximum.

At B, gradient $= 0$ so velocity is zero.

Figure 4.7 Velocity–time graph.

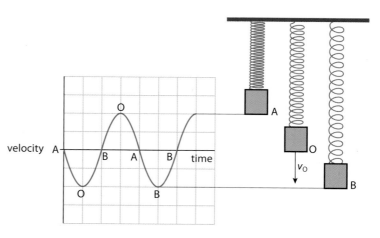

The equation of this line is $v = -v_o \sin\omega t$ where v_o is the maximum velocity.

Acceleration–time

From the gradient of the velocity–time graph (Figure 4.7) we can calculate the acceleration.

At A, the gradient is maximum and negative so acceleration is maximum and downwards.

At O, the gradient is zero so acceleration is zero.

At B, the gradient is maximum and positive so the acceleration is maximum and upwards.

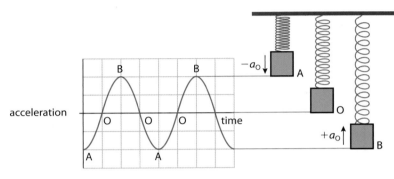

◀ **Figure 4.8** Acceleration–time graph.

The equation of this line is $a = -a_0 \cos \omega t$ where a_0 is this maximum acceleration. So $x = x_0 \cos \omega t$ and $a = -a_0 \cos \omega t$

When displacement increases, acceleration increases proportionally but in a nrgative sense; in other words: $a \propto - x$

We have confirmed that the acceleration of the body is directly proportional to the displacement of the body and always directed towards a fixed point.

Worked example

A mass on a spring is oscillating with a frequency 0.2 Hz and amplitude 3.0 cm. What is the displacement of the mass 10.66 s after it is released from the top?

Solution

$x = x_0 \cos \omega t.$ Since this is SHM

where $x = $ displacement

$x_0 = $ amplitude $= 3$ cm

$\omega = $ angular velocity $= 2\pi f = 2\pi \times 0.2$

$= 0.4\pi$ Hz

$t = $ time $= 10.66$ s

$x = 0.03 \times \cos(0.4\pi \times 10.66).$ Substituting into the formula.

$x = 0.02$ m

$= 2$ cm

 Radians
When calculating cos ωt, you must have your calculator set on radians.

Exercises

3 For the same mass on a spring in Example 1, calculate the displacement after 1.55 s.

4 Draw a displacement time sketch graph for this motion.

5 A long pendulum has time period 10 s. If the bob is displaced 2 m from the equilibrium position and released, how long will it take to move 1 m?

6 As a mass on a spring travels upwards through the equilibrium position, its velocity is 0.5 m s^{-1}. If the frequency of the pendulum is 1 Hz what will the velocity of the bob be after 0.5 s?

SHM and circular motion

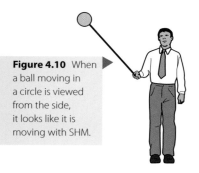

Figure 4.9 A short time after the ball starts moving, the radius makes an angle θ with the horizontal.

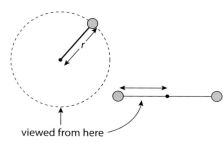

Figure 4.10 When a ball moving in a circle is viewed from the side, it looks like it is moving with SHM.

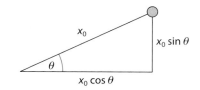

viewed from here

If we analyse the motion of the ball in Figure 4.9, we find that it is also SHM. The ball is travelling in a circle of radius x_o with a constant speed v. The ball takes a time T to complete one revolution.

Let us consider the horizontal component of motion. We can write equations for this component.

Displacement

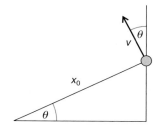

Figure 4.11 From the triangle we can see that *the horizontal displacement $x = x_o \cos \theta$.*

Velocity

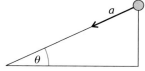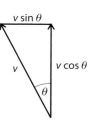

Figure 4.12 Horizontal velocity vectors.

Speed, $v = \dfrac{\text{distance}}{\text{time}}$

$= \dfrac{\text{circumference}}{\text{time period}}$

$= \dfrac{2\pi r}{T}$

But $\dfrac{2\pi}{T} = \omega$

So speed $= \omega r$

Centripetal acceleration $= \dfrac{v^2}{r}$

$= \dfrac{\omega^2 r^2}{r}$

$= \omega^2 r$

The horizontal velocity $= -v \sin \theta$

But for circular motion $v = \omega r$ so in this case $v = \omega x_o$

So horizontal velocity $= -\omega x_o \sin \theta$

Acceleration

When bodies travel in a circle, they have an acceleration towards the centre (the centripetal acceleration) $a = \omega^2 r$. In this case, acceleration is $\omega^2 x_o$ since the radius is x_o.

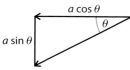

Figure 4.13 Horizontal acceleration vectors.

Horizontal component of acceleration $= -a \cos \theta$

But $a = \omega^2 x_o$

So horizontal acceleration $= -\omega^2 x_o \cos \theta$

Now we have found that the displacement $x = x_o \cos \theta$

So acceleration $= -\omega^2 x$

So the horizontal acceleration is proportional to the displacement, and is always directed towards the centre. In other words, the horizontal component of the motion is SHM. We have also found out that the constant of proportionality is ω^2.

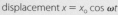

If you have done differentiation in maths then you will understand that if

displacement $x = x_o \cos \omega t$

then velocity $\dfrac{dx}{dt} = -x_o \omega \sin \omega t$

and acceleration, $\dfrac{d^2x}{dt^2} = -x_o \omega^2 \cos \omega t$

This implies that $a = -\omega^2 x$

This is a much shorter way of deriving this result!

Now we have concluded that this motion is SHM we can use the equations that we have derived to model all simple harmonic motions.

Equations for SHM

Displacement $= x_0 \cos \omega t$ (1)

Velocity $= -\omega x_0 \sin \omega t$ (2)

Acceleration $= -\omega^2 x_0 \cos \omega t$ (3)

We also know that $a = -\omega^2 x$

From Pythagoras, $1 = \sin^2 \theta + \cos^2 \theta$

So, $\sin \theta = \sqrt{1 - \cos^2 \theta}$ Rearranging

Therefore $\sin \omega t = \sqrt{1 - \cos^2 \omega t}$ Substituting for $\theta = \omega t$

Multiplying by ω gives $\omega x_0 \sin \omega t = \omega x_0 \sqrt{1 - \cos^2 \omega t}$

$\omega x_0 \sin \omega t = \omega \sqrt{x_0^2 - x_0^2 \cos^2 \omega t}$ Taking x_0 into the square root

But from equation (1) $x_0^2 \cos^2 \omega t = x^2$

So $v = \omega \sqrt{x_0^2 - x^2}$ Substituting.

The maximum velocity is when the displacement is 0 so $x = 0$

Maximum velocity $= \omega x$

Worked example

1. A pendulum is swinging with a frequency of 0.5 Hz. What is the size and direction of the acceleration when the pendulum has a displacement of 2 cm to the right?

2. A pendulum bob is swinging with SHM at a frequency of 1Hz and amplitude 3 cm. At what position will the bob be moving with maximum velocity and what is the size of the velocity?

Solution

1. Assuming the pendulum is swinging with SHM, then we can use the equation $a = \omega^2 x$ to calculate the acceleration.

   $\omega = 2\pi f = 2\pi \times 0.5 = \pi$

   $a = -\pi^2 \times 0.02 = \mathbf{-0.197\ m\ s^{-2}}$ Since $-$ve direction is to the left.

2. $v = \omega \sqrt{x_0^2 - x^2}$ Since the motion is SHM.

   This is maximum when $x = 0$ This is when the pendulum swings through the central position.

   The maximum value $= \omega x_0$ where $\omega = 2\pi f = 2 \times \pi \times 1 = 2\pi\ \text{rad s}^{-1}$

   Maximum $v = 2\pi \times 0.03 = \mathbf{0.188\ m\ s^{-1}}$

> **Summary**
> If a body oscillating with SHM has an angular frequency $\omega = 2\pi f$ and amplitude x_0 then its displacement (x), velocity (v) and acceleration (a) at any given time can be found from the following equations:
> $x = x_0 \cos \omega t$
> $v = -x_0 \omega \sin \omega t$
> $a = -\omega^2 x_0 \cos \omega t$
> In addition, at a given displacement x, the velocity and acceleration can be found from the following equations:
> $v = \omega \sqrt{x_0^2 - x^2}$
> Maximum velocity $= \omega \times 0$
> $a = -\omega^2 x$

> **The real pendulum**
> The pendulum is a classic example of SHM. However it is only SHM if the swings are very small (less than 10°). This is worth remembering if you ever do an experiment with a real pendulum.

Exercises

7. A long pendulum swings with a time period of 5 s and an amplitude of 2 m.
   (a) What is the maximum velocity of the pendulum?
   (b) What is the maximum acceleration of the pendulum?

8. A mass on a spring oscillates with amplitude 5 cm and frequency 2 Hz. The mass is released from its highest point. Calculate the velocity of the mass after it has travelled 1cm.

9. A body oscillates with SHM of time period 2 s. What is the amplitude of the oscillation if its velocity is 1 m s^{-1} as it passes through the equilibrium position?

4.2   Energy changes during simple harmonic motion (SHM)

At the top of the swing the mass has maximum PE and minimum KE.

At the bottom of the swing the mass has maximum KE and minimum PE.

Figure 4.14 In the simple pendulum, energy is changing from one form to another as it moves.

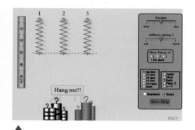

To view the PhET *Masses and springs* simulation, visit heinemann.co.uk/ hotlinks, enter the express code 4266S and click on Weblink 4.1.

Assessment statements

4.2.1   Describe the interchange between kinetic energy and potential energy during SHM.

4.2.2   Apply the expression $E_K = \frac{1}{2}m\omega^2(x_0^2 - x^2)$ for the kinetic energy of a particle undergoing SHM, $E_T = m\omega^2x_0^2$ for the total energy and $E_P = \frac{1}{2}m\omega^2x^2$ for the potential energy.

4.2.3   Solve problems, both graphically and by calculation, involving energy changes during SHM.

If we once again consider the simple pendulum, we can see that its energy changes as it swings.

Kinetic energy

We have already shown that the velocity of the mass is given by the equation

$$v = \omega\sqrt{x_0^2 - x^2}$$

From definition, $KE = \frac{1}{2}mv^2$

Substituting: $KE = \frac{1}{2}m\omega^2(x_0^2 - x^2)$

KE is a maximum at the bottom of the swing where $x = 0$.

So $KE_{max} = \frac{1}{2}m\omega^2x_0^2$

At this point the PE is zero.

Total energy

The total energy at any moment in time is given by:

total energy = KE + PE

So at the bottom of the swing:

total energy $= \frac{1}{2}m\omega^2x_0^2 + 0 = \frac{1}{2}m\omega^2x_0^2$

Since no work is done on the system, according to the law of conservation of energy, the total energy must be constant.

So total energy $= \frac{1}{2}m\omega^2x_0^2$

Potential energy

Potential energy at any moment = total energy − KE

So $PE = \frac{1}{2}m\omega^2x_0^2 - \frac{1}{2}m\omega^2(x_0^2 - x^2)$

$PE = \frac{1}{2}m\omega^2x^2$

Solving problems graphically

Kinetic energy

From previous examples we know that the velocity, $v = -v_0 \sin \omega t$

So $\frac{1}{2}mv^2 = \frac{1}{2}mv_0{}^2 \sin^2 \omega t$

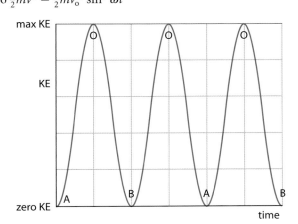
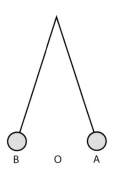

Figure 4.15 The graph of KE vs time is a sin² curve.

Potential energy

The graph of PE can be found from $\text{PE} = \frac{1}{2}m\omega^2 x^2$

Since $x = x_0 \cos \omega t$

$\text{PE} = \frac{1}{2}m\omega^2 x_0^2 \cos^2 \omega t = \frac{1}{2}mv_0^2 \cos^2 \omega t$

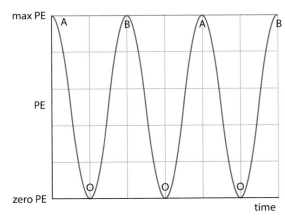

Figure 4.16 The graph of PE vs time is a cos² curve.

Total energy

If these two graphs are added together it gives a constant value, the total energy. (This might remind you of Pythagoras: $1 = \cos^2\theta + \sin^2\theta$.)

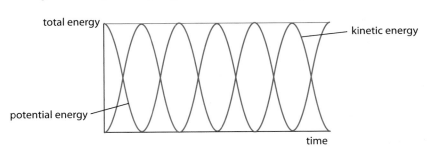

Figure 4.17 Total energy vs time.

Worked example

1 A pendulum bob of mass 200 g is oscillating with amplitude 3 cm and frequency 0.5 Hz. How much KE will the bob have as it passes through the origin?

Solution

1 $KE_{max} = \frac{1}{2}m\omega^2x_o^2$ ● **Examiner's hint:** Since the bob has SHM.

where $x_o = 0.03$ m and $\omega = 2\pi f = 2\pi \times 0.5 = \pi$

$KE_{max} = \frac{1}{2} \times 0.2 \times \pi^2 \times (0.03)^2 = \mathbf{8.9 \times 10^{-4} J}$

(4.3) Forced oscillations and resonance

Assessment statements

4.3.1 State what is meant by *damping*.
4.3.2 Describe examples of damping.
4.3.3 State what is meant by *natural frequency of vibration* and *forced oscillations*.
4.3.4 Describe graphically the variation with forced frequency of the amplitude of vibration of an object close to its natural frequency of vibration.
4.3.5 State what is meant by *resonance*.
4.3.6 Describe examples of resonance where the effect is useful and where it should be avoided.

Damping

When deriving the equations for KE and PE, we assumed that no energy was lost. In real oscillating systems there is always friction and sometimes also air resistance. The system has to do work against these forces resulting in a loss of energy. This effect is called *damping*.

The suspension of a car. The damper is the red telescopic part.

A car suspension system has many springs between the body and the wheels. Their purpose is to absorb shock caused by bumps in the road.

The car is therefore an oscillating system that would oscillate up and down every time the car went over a bump. As this would be rather unpleasant for the passengers, the oscillations are damped by dampers (wrongly known as shock absorbers).

Light damping

If the opposing forces are small, the result is a gradual loss of total energy. This means that the amplitude of the motion gets slowly less with time. For example, a mass on a spring hanging in the air would have a little damping due to air resistance.

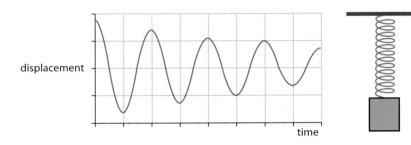

Figure 4.18 Reduction in amplitude due to light damping.

Frequency of damped harmonic motion
You can see from the graph that the frequency does not change as the amplitude gets less. As the motion slows down, the distance travelled gets less, so the time for each cycle remains the same.

If the mass is suspended in water, the damping is greater, resulting in a more rapid loss of energy.

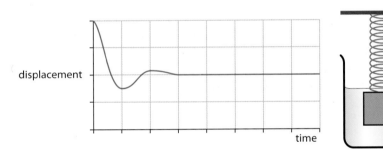

Figure 4.19 Reduction in amplitude due to heavier damping.

Critical damping

Critical damping occurs if the resistive force is so big that the system returns to its equilibrium position without passing through it. This would be the case if the mass were suspended in a thicker liquid such as honey.

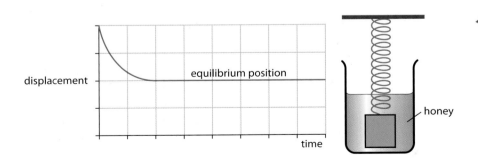

Figure 4.20 Reduction in amplitude due to critical damping.

Resonance

In all of the previous examples, a system has been displaced and released, causing an oscillation. The frequency of this oscillation is called the *natural frequency*. If a system is forced to oscillate at a frequency other than the natural frequency, this is called a *forced oscillation*.

Resonance is an increase in amplitude that occurs when an oscillating system is forced to oscillate at its own natural frequency.

For example, when you hit a wine glass with your finger, it vibrates.If you sing at the same frequency, your voice can cause the wine glass to resonate. Sing loud enough and the wine glass will shatter (not many people can do this).

It's possible to shatter a wine glass if you sing at its natural frequency.

If a spring is pulled down and released, then it will oscillate at its own natural frequency. If the support is oscillated, then the system will be forced to vibrate at another frequency. If the driving frequency is the same as the natural frequency, then resonance occurs.

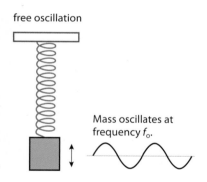

free oscillation

Mass oscillates at frequency f_o.

forced oscillation

System driven at frequency f causes mass to oscillate.

resonance

System driven at frequency f_o causes large amplitude oscillation.

Figure 4.21 The effect of varying driving frequency.

Resonance curve

A graph of the amplitude of oscillation against the driving frequency is called a resonance curve. The sharpness of the peak is affected by the amount of damping in the system.

The radio tuner
When you tune your radio, you are adjusting an electric circuit so that it resonates with the signal of a particular frequency. If the resonance curve for the circuit were not sharp, you would be able to tune into the station over a wide range of frequencies, and would be likely to get interference from other stations.

Figure 4.22 Graph of amplitude vs frequency for different levels of damping.

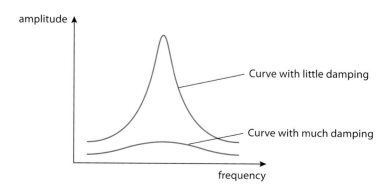

amplitude

Curve with little damping

Curve with much damping

frequency

Phase

If we take two identical pendulum bobs, displace each bob to the right and release them at the same time, then each will have the same displacement at the same time. We say the oscillations are *in phase*. If one is pulled to the left and the other to the right, then they are *out of phase*.

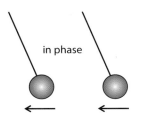

in phase   out of phase

Figure 4.23 The pendulum bobs are in phase when they swing together.

This can be represented graphically:

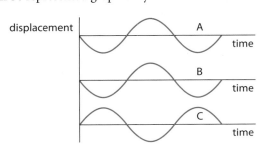

displacement

A and B represent motions that are in phase.

B and C represent motions that are out of phase.

Figure 4.24 Displacement–time graphs for bodies in and out of phase.

Riding a horse
When riding a horse it is important to stay in phase with the horse. If you are out of phase, then you will be coming down when the horse is going up, resulting in an uncomfortable experience. If the horse goes up and down too fast, then it can be very difficult to stay in phase. A mechanical horse is more difficult to ride; you can only accelerate downwards at $9.8\,\mathrm{m\,s^{-2}}$, so if the horse accelerates down too fast then you can't keep up with it.

Phase difference

The phase difference is represented by an angle (usually in radians). We can see from the previous graphs that if two oscillations are completely out of phase then the graphs are displaced by an angle π. We say the *phase difference* is π.

When juggling balls (or oranges) they go up and down at different times — they are out of phase.

Worked example

A ball is sitting on a platform oscillating with amplitude 1cm at a frequency of 1 Hz. As the frequency is increased, the ball starts to lose contact with the platform. At what frequency does this take place?

Solution

The ball will lose contact when the acceleration of the platform is greater than $9.8\,\mathrm{m\,s^{-2}}$.

Using the formula $a = -\omega^2 x_o$

$$\omega = \sqrt{9.8/0.01} = 31.3 \text{ rads s}^{-1}$$

$$f = \frac{\omega}{2\pi} = 5\,\text{Hz}$$

Experimental measurement of oscillations

The frequency at which a child oscillates on a swing is low enough to measure using a stopwatch (although to be accurate, you should use some sort of marker, so you can easily judge when the child has made a complete cycle). Higher frequency oscillations are not possible to measure in this way but can be measured using electronic sensors. Here are some examples of how you could make those measurements.

Photo gate

A photo gate sends a signal to a computer each time something passes through it. If a vibrating object passes through the gate each cycle then the computer can calculate the time period of the oscillation.

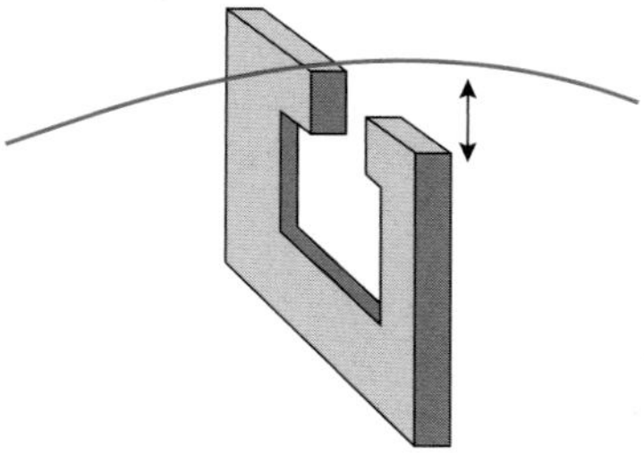

Figure 4.25 A photo gate is used to measure the time period of a vibrating elastic string.

The computer will record the time from when the string passes down through the gate until it passes through on its way back up again. The time period is twice this value. Depending on the software used, it may be possible for the computer to calculate and display the frequency.

Force sensor

When a pendulum swings, the tension in the string varies with time. A force sensor can be used to measure the tension, enabling you to plot a graph of tension *vs* time on the computer. The frequency is calculated from the graph.

Figure 4.26 The maximum force gets less as the amplitude gets less.

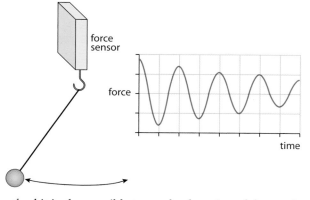

With this method it is also possible to see the damping of the motion.

Position sensor

To measure an oscillation using a position sensor, the oscillating body must move backwards and forwards (or up and down) in front of the sensor. The sensor sends out a sound that is reflected off the object back to the sensor. By measuring the time taken for the sound to reflect back from the object, the computer can calculate the distance between the sensor and the object. This method has the advantage of not disturbing the motion, but the object must be big enough for the sensor to detect it.

Wave characteristics

4.4

Assessment statements

4.4.1 Describe a wave pulse and a continuous progressive (travelling) wave.
4.4.2 State that progressive (travelling) waves transfer energy.
4.4.3 Describe and give examples of transverse and of longitudinal waves.
4.4.4 Describe waves in two dimensions, including the concepts of wavefronts and of rays.
4.4.5 Describe the terms *crest*, *trough*, *compression* and *rarefaction*.
4.4.6 Define the terms *displacement*, *amplitude*, *frequency*, *period*, *wavelength*, *wave speed* and *intensity*.
4.4.7 Draw and explain displacement–time graphs and displacement – position graphs for transverse and for longitudinal waves.
4.4.8 Derive and apply the relationship between wave speed, wavelength and frequency.
4.4.9 State that all electromagnetic waves travel with the same speed in free space, and recall the orders of magnitude of the wavelengths of the principal radiations in the electromagnetic spectrum.

The word *wave* was originally used to describe the way that a water surface behaves when it is disturbed. We use the same model to explain sound, light and many other physical phenomena. This is because they have some similar properties to water waves, so let's first examine the way water waves spread out.

If a stone is thrown into a pool of water, it disturbs the surface. The disturbance spreads out or *propagates* across the surface, and this disturbance is called a *wave*. Observing water waves, we can see that they have certain basic properties (in other words, they do certain things).

Reflection

If a water wave hits a wall, the waves reflect.

◀ Sea waves reflect off a cliff.

Refraction

When sea waves approach a beach, they change direction because of the difference in height of different parts of the sea floor. This causes the waves to bend.

Interference

When two waves cross each other, they can add together creating an extra big wave.

Diffraction

When water waves pass through a small opening, the waves spread out.

Anything that reflects, refracts, interferes and diffracts can also be called a wave.

Waves change direction as they approach a beach.

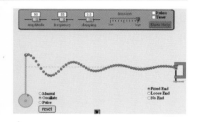

To view the PhET *Waves on a string* simulation, visit heinemann.co.uk/hotlinks, enter the express code 4266S and click on Weblink 4.2.

One-dimensional waves

The next step is to derive a model for wave motion and use it to help us understand why waves behave in the way that they do. However, since water waves are two-dimensional, they are not the easiest waves to start with. We will begin by looking at two examples of one-dimensional waves: waves in a string and waves in a spring.

Wave pulse in a string

If a string held between two people is displaced (flicked), a disturbance can be seen to travel from one end to the other. This is called a *wave pulse*.

Figure 4.27 A wave pulse.

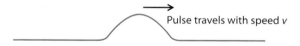
Pulse travels with speed *v*

We can see that the pulse travels with a certain speed — this is called the *wave speed*.

Wave speed is the distance travelled by the wave profile per unit time.

Note: No part of the string actually moves in the direction of the wave velocity — in fact, each particle in the string moves at right angles to the direction of wave velocity.

Reflection of a wave pulse

If the pulse meets a fixed end (e.g a wall), it exerts an upward force on the wall. The wall being pushed up, pushes back down on the string sending an inverted reflected pulse back along the string.

Figure 4.28 A reflected pulse.

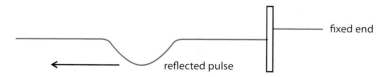
fixed end

reflected pulse

Interference of wave pulses

If two pulses are sent along a string from each end, they will cross each other in the middle of a string.

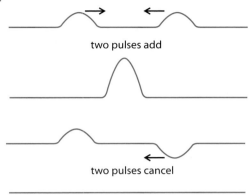

two pulses add

two pulses cancel

Figure 4.29 The resultant wave is the sum of the individual waves.

 Since waves in a string do not spread out, they cannot diffract or refract. You would have to observe the 2D equivalent, waves in a rubber sheet, to see this.

Transfer of energy

It can be seen that as the string is lifted up it is given PE. This PE is transferred along the string. A wave can therefore be thought of as a transfer of energy. There is in fact so much energy transferred by waves in the sea that they can be used to produce electricity.

Continuous waves in a string

wave direction ⟶

Figure 4.30 The 'sine shape' or profile moves along the string with the wave speed.

If the end of a string is moved up and down with simple harmonic motion, of frequency *f*, a series of pulses moves along the string in the shape of a sine curve, as in Figure 4.30.

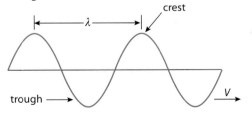

crest

λ

trough ⟶

V

Figure 4.31 The quantities used to define a wave.

Amplitude (*A*)
The maximum displacement of the string from the equilibrium position.

Wave speed (*v*)
The distance travelled by the wave profile per unit time.

Wavelength (λ)
The distance between two consecutive crests or any two consecutive points that are in phase.

Frequency (*f*)
The number of complete cycles that pass a point per unit time.

Period (*T*)
Time taken for 1 complete wave to pass a fixed point ($T = 1/f$)

Phase
The phase is a quantity that tells us whether parts of a wave go up and down at the same time or not.

Transverse waves

direction of disturbance

wave direction

direction of disturbance

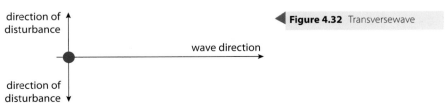

Figure 4.32 Transversewave

A wave in a string is an example of a transverse wave. The direction of disturbance is perpendicular to the direction that the wave profile moves.

Stringed instruments

When you pluck the string of a guitar, a wave reflects backwards and forwards along the string. The vibrating string creates the sound that you hear. The pitch of the note is related to the frequency of the string (high pitch = high frequency).

- Why are the low notes thick strings?
  The speed of the wave is inversely related to the mass per unit length of the string. Thick strings have a greater mass per unit length, so the wave will travel more slowly in a thick string. If we rearrange the formula $v = f\lambda$, we find that $f = \frac{v}{\lambda}$ so reducing the wave speed will reduce the frequency of the wave.
- Why does shortening the string make the note higher?
  Shortening the string reduces the wavelength of the wave. According to the formula $f = \frac{v}{\lambda}$, reducing the wavelength will increase the frequency.
- Why does tightening the string make the note higher?
  The wave speed is directly related to the tension in the string. Increasing tension increases the wave speed, which, according to the formula $f = \frac{v}{\lambda}$, will increase the frequency of the wave.

Worked example

1 The A string of a guitar vibrates at 110 Hz. If the wavelength is 153 cm, what is the velocity of the wave in the string?

2 A wave in the ocean has a period of 10 s and a wavelength of 200 m. What is the wave speed?

Solution

1 $v = f\lambda$
   $f = 110 \text{ Hz}$ and $\lambda = 1.53 \text{ m}$ ● **Examiner's hint:** Change cm to m.
   $v = 110 \times 1.53 \text{ m s}^{-1}$
     $= \mathbf{168.3 \text{ m s}^{-1}}$

2 $T = 10 \text{ s}$
   $f = 1/T \text{ Hz}$
     $= 0.1 \text{ Hz}$
   $v = f\lambda$
   $v = 0.1 \times 200 \text{ m s}^{-1}$
     $= \mathbf{20 \text{ m s}^{-1}}$

$v = f\lambda$

If the frequency is f then the time for the wave to progress one cycle is $1/f$. In this time the wave has moved forward a distance equal to one wavelength (λ).

$\text{Velocity} = \frac{\text{distance}}{\text{time}}$

$v = \frac{\lambda}{1/f} = f\lambda$

Waves in a spring

If a long soft spring (a slinky) is stretched and one end moved back and forth, a compression can be seen to travel along it. Although this may not look like a wave, it *is* transferring energy from one end to the other and so fits the definition.

Figure 4.33 The difference between a compression wave in a spring and the transverse wave in a string is the direction of disturbance.

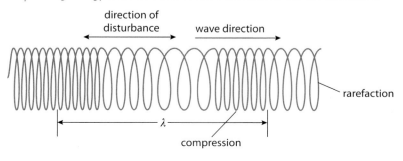

direction of
disturbance   wave direction

rarefaction

λ

compression

Longitudinal waves

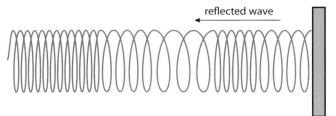

Figure 4.34 Longitudinal wave.

A compression wave in a slinky is an example of a longitudinal wave. In a longitudinal wave, the disturbance is parallel to the direction of the wave.

Reflection

When the wave in a spring meets a fixed end, it will reflect.

Figure 4.35 A wave in a spring is reflected off a wall.

> **Earthquake waves**
> An earthquake is caused when parts of the earth's crust move against each other. This disturbance causes both longitudinal and transverse waves to spread around the earth.
>
> **Transverse wave**
> When an earthquake occurs the ground shakes up and down.
>
> **Longitudinal wave**
> The movement in the earth's crust compresses the rock.

Interference

Although not easy to observe, when two longitudinal waves meet, the displacements superpose in the same way as transverse waves.

Polarization

A wave is polarized if the displacement is only in one direction.

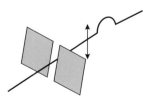

> **Light and sound**
> Both light and sound are disturbances that spread out, so can be thought of as waves. Light can be polarized (for example, by Polaroid sunglasses) but sound cannot. This is one way to tell that light is transverse and sound is longitudinal.

Figure 4.36 A string wave can be polarized by passing through a narrow slit.

The string can only move up and down so a wave in this string will be polarized. To test if the wave is polarized we can place another slit on the string; the wave only passes if the slits are parallel. Only transverse waves can be polarized, so this property can be used to tell if a wave is transverse or longitudinal.

Graphical representation of a wave

There are two ways we can represent a wave graphically, either by drawing a displacement–time graph for one point on the wave, or a displacement–position graph for each point along the wave.

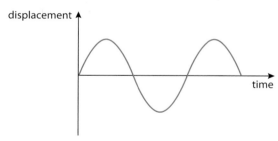

Displacement–time

Consider point A on the transverse wave in Figure 4.37.

Point A is moving up and down with SHM as the wave passes. At present, it is at a minimum of displacement. As the wave progresses past A, this point will move up and then down.

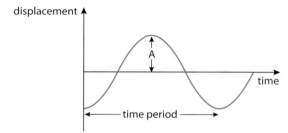

We can also draw a graph for point B. This point starts with zero displacement then goes up.

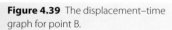

Displacement–position

To draw a displacement–position graph, we must measure the displacement of all the points on the wave at one moment in time.

Fig 4.40 shows the graph at the same time as the snapshot was taken. The position is measured from point O.

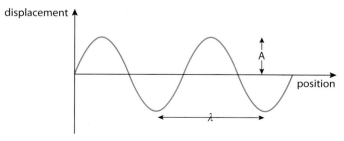

This is just like a snapshot of the wave – however, depending on the scale of the axis, it might not look quite like the wave.

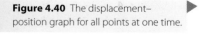

Longitudinal waves

We can also draw graphs for a longitudinal wave. Consider a chain of balls connected with springs. If the red ball on the left were moved back and forth with SHM, it would send a longitudinal wave along the chain.

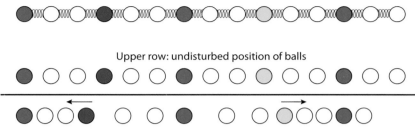

Figure 4.41 A line of balls joined by springs.

Upper row: undisturbed position of balls

Figure 4.42 A snapshot taken as a wave passes through the chain.

Lower row: position of balls at an instant as wave passes

Each ball simply moves back and forth with SHM. Ball A is at present displaced to the left. This ball has negative displacement.

Displacement–time

We can draw a displacement–time graph for ball A starting at the time of the snapshot.

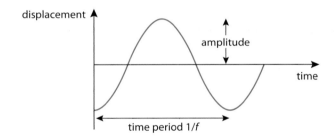

Figure 4.43 The displacement time graph for point A.

Displacement–position

To draw a displacement–position graph, we must compare the position of each ball with its original position.

The red balls have not moved, so their displacement is 0.

The blue balls have moved to the left, so their displacement is negative.

The yellow ball has moved to the right, so its displacement is positive.

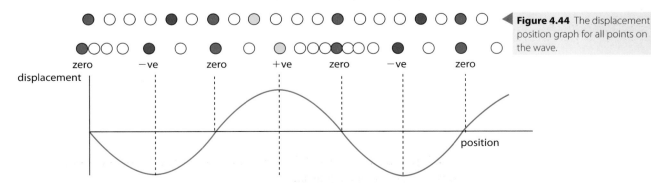

Figure 4.44 The displacement position graph for all points on the wave.

Superposition of one-dimensional waves

When two waves are incident along the same string, we can find the resultant wave by adding the individual displacements.

Figure 4.45 Superposition of waves.

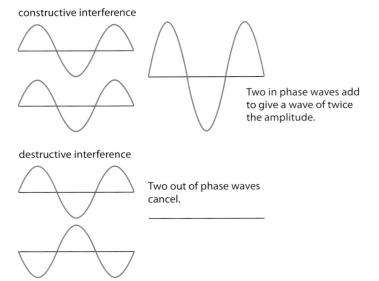

constructive interference

Two in phase waves add to give a wave of twice the amplitude.

destructive interference

Two out of phase waves cancel.

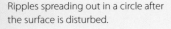

4.5 Wave properties

Assessment statements

4.5.1 Describe the reflection and transmission of waves at a boundary between two media.
4.5.2 State and apply Snell's law.
4.5.3 Explain and discuss qualitatively the diffraction of waves at apertures and obstacles.
4.5.4 Describe examples of diffraction.
4.5.5 State the principle of superposition and explain what is meant by constructive interference and by destructive interference.
4.5.6 State and apply the conditions for constructive and for destructive interference in terms of path difference and phase difference.
4.5.7 Apply the principle of superposition to determine the resultant of two waves

Ripples spreading out in a circle after the surface is disturbed.

Two-dimensional waves

We will now use water waves to model the motion of waves in 2D. If a disturbance is made by a point object in the middle of a tank of water, ripples spread out in circles across the tank. We will use pictures from a computer simulation to show the effect more clearly.

Wavefront

This is a line joining points that are in phase. The straight or circular lines that you can see in the photos are wavefronts.

Rays

Rays are lines drawn to show the direction of the waves — they are always at right angles to the wavefront.

Circular wavefronts

A circular wavefront is produced by a point disturbance. The rays are radial, as they are perpendicular to the wavefronts.

Plane wavefront

Plane wavefronts are produced by an extended disturbance e.g. a long piece of wood dipped into the water, or a point that is so far away that the circles it produces look like straight lines.

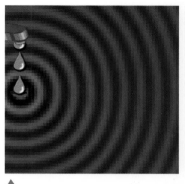

To view the PHet simulation *Wave interference*, visit heinemann.co.uk/hotlinks, enter the express code 4266S and click on Weblink 4.3.

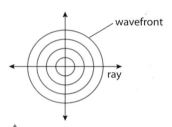

Figure 4.46 A circular wavefront spreading out from a point.

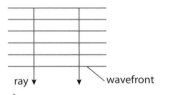

Figure 4.47 Parallel plane wavefronts.

A plane wavefront moves towards the beach.

Reflection

When a wave hits a barrier, it is reflected.

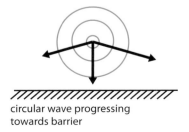

circular wave progressing towards barrier

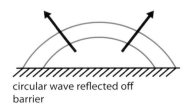

circular wave reflected off barrier

Figure 4.48 Reflection of a circular wavefront.

Notice how the reflected wave appears to originate from somewhere on the other side of the barrier. This is just the same as the appearance of an image of yourself behind a mirror.

Figure 4.49 A plane wavefront is reflected at the same angle that it comes in at.

incident and reflected waves

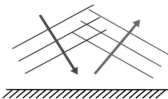

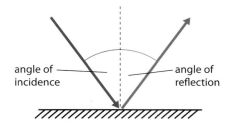

angle of incidence — angle of reflection

Rather than measuring the angle that the wavefront makes, it is more convenient to measure the angles that the rays make with a line drawn at 90° to the barrier. This line is called the *normal*.

The laws of reflection

The laws of reflection describe how waves are reflected from barriers.
- The angle of incidence = the angle of reflection.
- The incident and reflected rays are in the same plane as the normal.

Change of medium

Whenever a wave travels from one medium to another, part of the wave is reflected and part transmitted. An example of this is when light hits a glass window: most passes through but a fraction is reflected. So you see a reflection of yourself in the window and someone standing on the other side of the window can see you. The part of the wave that passes through the window is called the *transmitted* part.

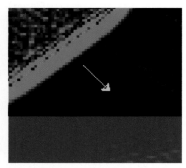

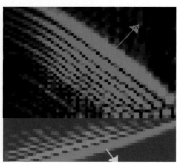

To view screenshots showing the reflected and transmitted wave, visit heinemann.co.uk/hotlinks, enter the express code 4266S and click on Weblink 4.4.

Refraction

When a wave passes from one medium to another, its velocity changes. For example, when a water wave passes from deep water into shallow water, it slows down. If the wave hits the boundary between the media at an angle, then the wave also changes direction.

Figure 4.50 Refraction is the change of direction when a wave passes from one medium to another.

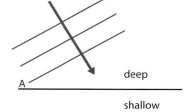

deep

shallow

A

incident

deep

shallow

refracted wave

Point A on the incident wave hits the boundary first, so this part of the wave then progresses into the shallow water more slowly. The rest of the wave in the deep water is still travelling fast so catches up with the slow moving part, causing the wavefront to change direction. This is simpler to see if we just draw the rays.

Figure 4.51 Angles of incidence and refraction.

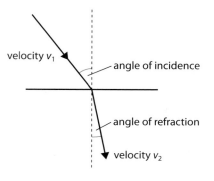

velocity v_1

angle of incidence

angle of refraction

velocity v_2

Snell's law

Snell's law relates the angles of incidence and refraction to the ratio of the velocity of the wave in the different media. The ratio of the sine of the angle of incidence to the sine of the angle of refraction is equal to the ratio of the velocities of the wave in the different media.

$$\frac{\sin i}{\sin r} = \frac{v_1}{v_2}$$

As can be seen from the example of the bent straw in the photo, light refracts when it passes from one medium to another. The ratio of the velocity of light in the two media is called the *refractive index*.

Light reflected off the straw is refracted as it comes out of the water causing the straw to appear bent.

Worked example

A water wave travelling at 20 m s^{-1} enters a shallow region where its velocity is 15 m s^{-1} (Figure 4.52). If the angle of incidence of the water wave to the shallow region is 50°, what is the angle of refraction?

▶ **Figure 4.52** Always draw a diagram.

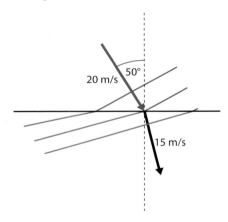

Refractive index
When light travelling in air is refracted by an optical medium, the ratio *sin i/sin r* is called the refractive index of the medium. If the refractive index is large it means that the light is refracted by a large angle.

Material	Refractive index
Water	1.33
Glass	1.50
Diamond	2.42

Solution

$$\frac{\sin i}{\sin r} = \frac{v_1}{v_2} = \frac{20}{15}$$

so $\sin r = \dfrac{\sin 50°}{1.33} = 0.576$ ● **Examiner's hint:** Applying Snell's law.

$r = 35.2°$

Exercises

Use the refractive indices in the table to solve the following problems.

10 Light travelling through the air is incident on the surface of a pool of water at an angle of 40°. Calculate the angle of refraction.

11 Calculate the angle of refraction if a beam of light is incident on the surface of a diamond at an angle of 40°.

12 If the velocity of light in air is 3 × 10^8 m s^{-1}, calculate its velocity in glass.

Diffraction

Diffraction takes place when a wave passes through a small opening. If the opening is very small, then the wave behaves just like a point source as shown below.

Figure 4.53 If the opening is a bit bigger then the effect is not so great.

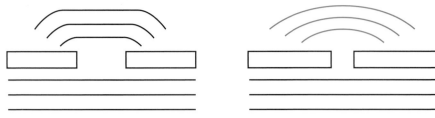

Water waves diffracting through two different sized openings. The waves are diffracted more through the narrower opening.

Interference

When two-dimensional waves interfere, the phase difference between the two waves is different in different places. This means that in some places the waves add and in other places they cancel. This can be seen in the picture below. This shows two sources producing waves of the same frequency.

Figure 4.54 How phase difference is related to path difference.

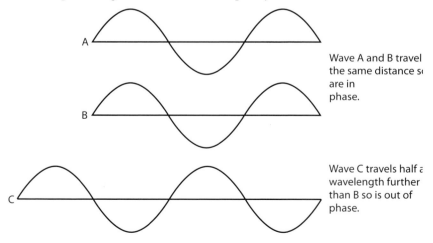

Wave A and B travel the same distance so are in phase.

Wave C travels half a wavelength further than B so is out of phase.

If the path difference is a whole number of wavelengths, then the waves are *in phase*.

If the path difference is an odd number of ½ wavelengths then the waves are *out of phase*.

The effect of interference in two dimensions can be seen in Figure 4.55.

Identical waves from A and B spread out across the surface. At X, the waves from A and B have travelled the same distance, so are in phase and add together. At Y, the wave from B has travelled half a wavelength more then the wave from A, so the waves are out of phase and cancel out.

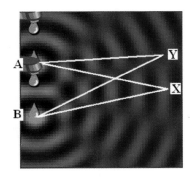

Figure 4.55 Interference effects seen in the PhET simulation. To view this, visit heinmann.co.uk/hotlinks, enter the express code 4266S and click on Weblink 4.5.

Worked example

Figure 4.56 A diagram always helps, no matter how silly it is.

Two boys playing in a pool make identical waves that travel towards each other. The boys are 10 m apart and the waves have a wavelength 2 m. Their little sister is swimming from one boy to the other. When she is 4 m from the first boy, will she be in a big wave or a small wave?

Solution
The waves from the boys will interfere when they meet, if the girl is 4 m from the first boy, then she must be 6 m from the other. This is a path difference of 2 m, one whole wavelength. The waves are therefore in phase and will add.

Examples of waves

Light
It is worth having a more detailed look at the wave properties of light. We have seen examples of how light reflects and refracts, and if light is a wave, then it must also interfere and diffract.

- Diffraction of light

We have seen that if a wave passes through an opening that is about the same size as its wavelength then it will spread out. If a beam of light passes through a narrow slit (close to the wavelength of light − around 500 nm), it will spread out.

- Interference of light

Waves only interfere if they have the same frequency and similar amplitude. If we take a source of light and split it into two we can create two identical (or *coherent*) wave sources,. If the waves from these sources overlap, then areas of bright and dark are created, where the waves interfere constructively and destructively.

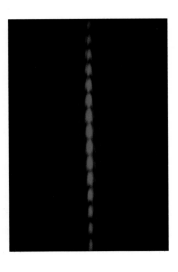

The combined effect of diffraction and interference cause this pattern of dots when laser light passes through a pair of narrow slits.

• Polarization

Figure 4.57 The light passes through Polaroid 1 and 2, which have the same alignment, but not 3.

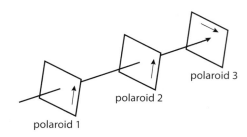

polaroid 3

polaroid 2

polaroid 1

When light passes through polaroid sunglasses, it becomes polarized in one direction. We can test to see if the light is polarized by taking a second piece of polaroid and rotating it in front of the sunglasses. As we rotate the polaroid we find that the polarized light can only pass when the second piece is in the same orientation as the first.

• Wavelength and amplitude of light

Light is an electromagnetic (EM) wave; that is a propagation of transverse disturbance in an electric and magnetic field. Unlike the other types of waves considered here, EM waves can travel through a vacuum. As with all waves, light waves have wavelength and amplitude. The wavelength of light can vary from 400 nm to 800 nm, with different wavelengths having different colours. White light is made up of all colours mixed together, but if white light is passed through a prism, the different colours are split up, forming a spectrum. This happens because each wavelength refracts by a different amount, and therefore a different angle. This is what happens when a rainbow is formed.

White light can be split up into its component colours by passing it through a prism.

Visible light is just one small part of the complete EM spectrum. The full range of wavelength is from 10^{-14}m to 10^4m. Each part of the spectrum has different properties and a different name, as illustrated in the diagram below.

When we say light is a wave we mean it has the same properties as a wave. Does this mean it actually *is* a wave?

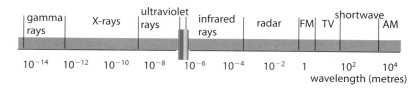

gamma rays	X-rays	ultraviolet rays		infrared rays	radar	FM	TV	shortwave	AM

10^{-14} 10^{-12} 10^{-10} 10^{-8} 10^{-6} 10^{-4} 10^{-2} 1 10^2 10^4

wavelength (metres)

The amplitude of light is related to its brightness. The brightness of light is how we perceive light. The physical quantity that measures it is the light *intensity*. This is proportional to the square of the amplitude.

The speed of EM waves in a vacuum is $2.99 \times 10^8 \, \text{m s}^{-1}$.

Sound

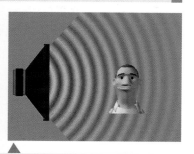

To view the Phet sound waves simulation, visit heinmann.co.uk/hotlinks, enter the express code 4266S and click on Weblink 4.6.

• Reflection

If you shout in front of a cliff, the sound reflects back as an echo. In fact any wall is a good reflector of sound, so when speaking in a room, the sound is reflected off all the surfaces This is why your voice sounds different in a room and outside.

- Refraction

When sound passes from warm air into cold air, it refracts. This is why sounds carry well on a still night.

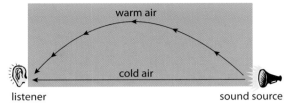

Figure 4.58 Sound refracts through layers of air.

The sound travels to the listener by two paths, one direct and one by refraction through the layers of air. This results in an extra loud sound.

- Diffraction and interference

Because sound reflects so well off all surfaces, it is very difficult to do sound experiments in the laboratory. This makes it difficult to observe sound diffracting and interfering.

A room with no echo is called an anechoic chamber, and these rooms are used for experimenting with sound waves.

Sound spreads out when passing through small openings, around obstacles and through doorways. However, the effects are often owing to multiple reflections rather than diffraction.

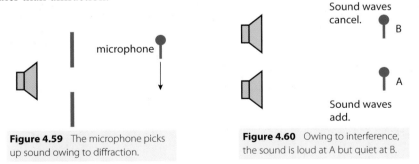

Figure 4.59 The microphone picks up sound owing to diffraction.

Figure 4.60 Owing to interference, the sound is loud at A but quiet at B.

Sound waves cancel.

B

A

Sound waves add.

Sound
Sound is created when the pressure of air is is varied. This change in pressure spreads out as a longitudinal wave. When a sound wave meets a microphone, it causes it to vibrate. The microphone then changes this vibration to an electrical signal that can be used to plot a graph. The graph that we see is a displacement–time graph.

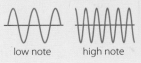

low note   high note

Sound has the properties of a wave, so that means we can use our wave theory to model sound. Sound is a propagation of disturbance in air pressure. Sound is an example of a longitudinal wave. The speed of sound in air is $330\ \mathrm{m\,s^{-1}}$.

- Frequency and amplitude of sound

Different frequency sound waves have different pitch (that is, a high note has a high frequency). The loudness of a sound is related to the amplitude of the wave.

Practice questions

1 This question is about sound waves.

A sound wave of frequency 660 Hz passes through air. The variation of particle displacement with distance along the wave at one instant of time is shown below.

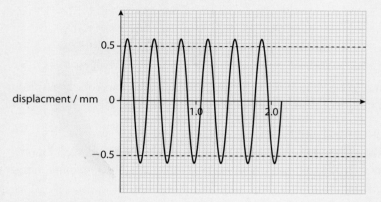

(a) State whether this wave is an example of a longitudinal or a transverse wave. (1)

(b) Using data from the above graph, deduce for this sound wave,
    (i) the wavelength. (1)
    (ii) the amplitude. (1)
    (iii) the speed. (2)

2 This question is about waves and wave properties.

(a) By making reference to waves, distinguish between a *ray* and a *wavefront*. (3)

The following diagram shows three wavefronts incident on a boundary between medium I and medium R. Wavefront CD is shown crossing the boundary. Wavefront EF is incomplete.

(b)

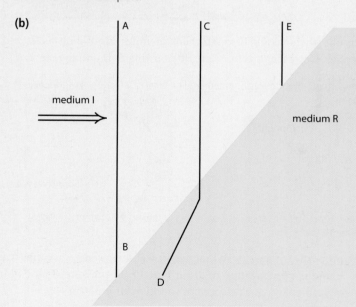

    (i) On the diagram above, draw a line to complete the wavefront EF. (1)
    (ii) Explain in which medium, I or R, the wave has the higher speed. (3)

The graph below shows the variation with time t of the velocity v of one particle of the medium through which the wave is travelling.

(c)

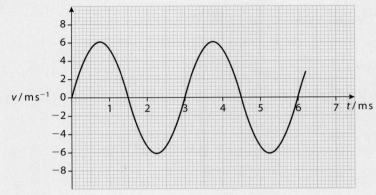

    (i) Explain how it can be deduced from the graph that the particle is oscillating. (2)

    (ii) Determine the frequency of oscillation of the particle. (2)

    (iii) Mark on the graph with the letter M one time at which the particle is at maximum displacement. (1)

    (iv) Estimate the area between the curve and the x-axis from the time $t = 0$ to the time $t = 1.5\,\mathrm{m\,s}$.

    (v) Suggest what the area in c(iv) represents. (3)

3 This question is about waves and wave motion.

  (a) **(i)** Define what is meant by the *speed of a wave*. (2)

      (ii) Light is emitted from a candle flame. Explain why, in this situation, it is correct to refer to the 'speed of the emitted light', rather than its velocity. (2)

  (b) **(i)** Define, by reference to wave motion, what is meant by *displacement*. (2)

      (ii) By reference to displacement, describe the difference between a longitudinal wave and a transverse wave. (3)

The centre of an earthquake produces both longitudinal waves (P waves) and transverse waves (S waves). The graph below shows the variation with time t of the distance d moved by the two types of wave.

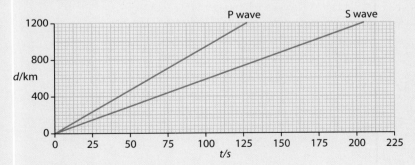

  (c) Use the graph to determine the speed of

      (i) the P waves. (1)

      (ii) the S waves. (1)

(d) The waves from an earthquake close to the Earth's surface are detected at three laboratories L_1, L_2 and L_3. The laboratories are at the corners of a triangle so that each is separated from the others by a distance of 900 km, as shown in the diagram below. (2)

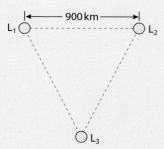

The records of the variation with time of the vibrations produced by the earthquake as detected at the three laboratories are shown below. All three records were started at the same time.

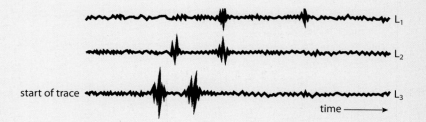

On each record, one pulse is made by the S wave and the other by the P wave. The separation of the two pulses is referred to as the S-P interval.

    (i) On the trace produced by laboratory L_2, identify, by reference to your answers in **(c)**, the pulse due to the P wave (label the pulse P). (1)

    (ii) Using evidence from the records of the earthquake, state which laboratory was closest to the site of the earthquake. (1)

    (iii) State **three** separate pieces of evidence for your statement in **(d)(ii)**. (3)

    (iv) The S-P intervals are 68s, 42s and 27s for laboratories L_1, L_2 and L_3 respectively. Use the graph, or otherwise, to determine the distance of the earthquake from each laboratory. Explain your working.

    (v) Mark on the diagram a possible site of the earthquake.

5 Electrical currents

5.1 Electric potential difference, current and resistance

Assessment statements

5.1.1 Define electric potential difference.
5.1.2 Determine the change in potential energy when a charge moves between two points at different potentials.
5.1.3 Define the electronvolt.
5.1.4 Solve problems involving electric potential difference.
5.1.5 Define electric current.
5.1.6 Define resistance.
5.1.7 Apply the equation for resistance in the form $R = \rho l/A$ where ρ is the resistivity of the material of the resistor.
5.1.8 State Ohm's law.
5.1.9 Compare ohmic and non-ohmic behaviour.
5.1.10 Derive and apply expressions for electrical power dissipation in resistors.
5.1.11 Solve problems involving potential difference, current and resistance.

In this chapter we will develop the theory behind electric circuits, but first we need to understand how the individual components work.

The battery

All electrical devices convert electrical energy into other forms; an MP3 player produces sound, a torch produces light and an electric motor produces mechanical energy. In cordless devices (ones that don't plug into the mains) the source of this energy is the battery.

All electrical appliances convert electrical energy into other forms.

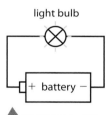

light bulb

Figure 5.1 This simple circuit consists of a battery and a light bulb. The battery has two ends, one is positive (+) and the other is negative (−). To make a circuit, the bulb must be connected as shown .

Inside the battery, chemicals react with each other to convert chemical energy into electrical energy.

When the light bulb is connected across the ends of the battery, it gets hot and starts to glow, giving out energy in the form of light and heat. This energy comes from the battery. To make the bulb light up, we must make a complete circuit. If this circuit is broken, the bulb goes out. It seems like something is flowing through the wire; we call the flow *current* and the thing that is flowing we call *charge*.

 To build your own circuits and test the theories in this chapter, visit www.heinemann.co.uk/hotlinks, enter the express code 4266S and click on the Weblink 5.1.

Water analogy

To explain the observations, we can use an analogy.

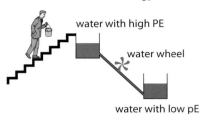

water with high PE

water wheel

water with low pE

Figure 5.2 Water flow is similar to the flow of electricity.

Figure 5.2 shows a man carrying water up the stairs and pouring it into a tank. The water flows from this tank through a pipe into a lower one. As it flows, the water turns a water wheel. The water wheel turns a grindstone that rubs against a hard surface producing heat.

Energy explanation

We can explain what is happening using the principle of conservation of energy. As the man carries the water up the stairs he does work on the water, increasing its potential energy(PE). When the water flows downhill into the lower tank, it loses PE. This energy is given to the water wheel, which turns the grindstone, producing heat. So we can say that the work done by the man is the same as the heat produced at the grindstone.

Figure 5.3 Energy changes.

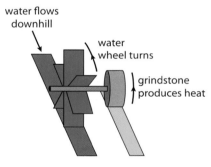

water flows downhill

water wheel turns

grindstone produces heat

Charge

Unlike with water, we cannot see charge flowing through the wire. We will find out later (Chapter 6) that there are two types of charge (+ and −) but to make things simple we will just consider + charge. The unit of charge is the coulomb (C).

Electrical potential energy

To make the water flow through the pipe, the man did work on the water to raise its potential energy. In the electrical circuit, the battery does work to increase the electrical potential energy of the charges. The charges on the + end of the battery have a higher potential energy than the ones on the − end, so charge flows from + to − outside the cell.

Current

Current is the flow of charge, and since charges at the + end of the battery have higher PE than those at the − end, the current flows from + to −.

The unit of current is the amp (A).

The amp is a scalar quantity.

$$\text{Current} = \frac{\text{charge}}{\text{time}}$$

1 amp = 1 coulomb per second.

The complete picture

The battery takes charges and puts them in a position of high potential at the + end. If a bulb is connected between the ends of the battery, this charge flows from the position of high potential to a position of low potential. The potential energy is converted to heat and light.

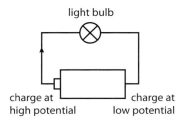

Microscopic model

Metals allow charge to flow because they contain small negatively charged particles called *electrons*. Since the electrons are negative, they flow from low potential to high potential. Trying to imagine something flowing uphill is not very easy, so we will stick with positive charges flowing downhill. This is not a problem but we must always remember that electrons flow in the opposite direction to conventional current.

The electron is a small particle responsible for carrying charge in conductors.
Charge $= -1.6 \times 10^{-19}$ C
Electrons are negative so flow in the opposite direction to conventional current.

Energy transformation in a battery

Since energy is conserved, the energy given to the charges must come from somewhere − in fact, the battery converts chemical energy to electrical PE. The chemicals in the battery contain charges that are all mixed up. When these chemicals react, the charges are rearranged so that there are more + charges at the + end of the battery. After the reaction, the chemicals have less energy, as the chemical energy has been converted to electrical PE.

We consider current to flow in the opposite direction to the way that electrons actually flow. Does it matter that our model is actually completely backwards?

The PhET simulation 'Battery voltage' shows how the charges are rearranged. The little people represent chemical energy. To view this, visit www.heinemann.co.uk/hotlinks, enter the express code 4266S and click on the Weblink 5.2.

Potential difference

If we move a + charge from the negative end of the battery to the positive end, we need to do work. This is because the charge has a higher potential energy at the positive end than the negative end. The amount of work done per unit charge is defined as the potential difference (p.d.) between the plates or terminals.

The unit of p.d. is the volt. The volt is a scalar quantity. 1 volt = 1 joule per coulomb.

The p.d. between A and B is defined as the amount of work done per unit charge in taking a small +ve test charge from A to B.

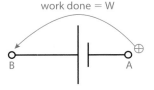

Conductors and insulators

A *conductor* is a material that allows charge to flow through it. An *insulator* doesn't. All metals are good conductors of electricity, but plastics are insulators.

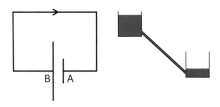

The metal core of the cable conducts electricity; the plastic cover is an insulator.

Worked examples

1 If a current of 10 A flows for 15 s, how much charge flows?

2 How much energy is lost when +5 C of charge flows from the +ve terminal to the −ve terminal of a 9 V battery?

Solutions

1 Current I = charge per unit time = $\dfrac{Q}{t}$

    $Q = It$

      $= 10 \times 15$ C

      $= 150$ C

2 Energy to move 1 C = 9 J

   Energy to move 5 C = 5×9 J = 45 J

● **Examiner's hint:** From definition of p.d., the energy lost per unit charge moving from one terminal to the other is $9\,\text{J}\,\text{C}^{-1}$.

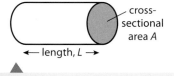

Figure 5.8 Dimensions of a conductor.

cross-sectional area A

← length, L →

Resistance

The rate at which charge can flow through a conductor depends on the size and material of the conductor. A conductor that does not let much current flow for a given p.d. is said to have a high resistance.

Resistance (R) is related to: cross-sectional area (A), length (L) and the material.

$$R \propto \frac{L}{A}$$

The constant of proportionality is called the *resistivity* (ρ).

So
$$R = \rho\frac{L}{A}$$

The unit of resistance is the ohm (Ω).

This means that more current flows through a short fat conductor than a long thin one.

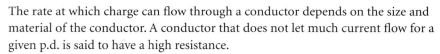

Resistivity

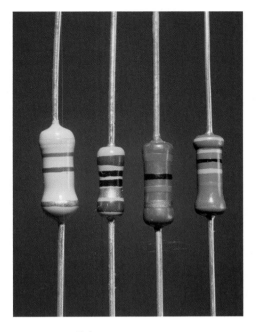

A resistor is a component with a known resistance. You can work out the resistance from the colours.

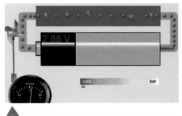

To try the battery-resistance circuit, visit www.heinemann.co.uk/hotlinks, enter the express code 4266S and click on Weblink 5.3.

By rearranging $R = \rho\dfrac{L}{A}$ we get $\rho = \dfrac{RA}{L}$ (units Ωm).

From this we can deduce that if the length of a sample of material is 1m and the cross-sectional area is $1m^2$, then $\rho = R$. You can probably imagine that the resistance of such a large piece of metal will be very small – that's why the values of resistivity are so low (e.g. for copper $\rho = 1.72 \times 10^{-8}\,\Omega$m).

Microscopic model of resistance

As mentioned earlier, it is actually the negative charges called *free electrons* that move. As they move through the metal, they give energy to the metal atoms, causing the temperature of the metal to increase.

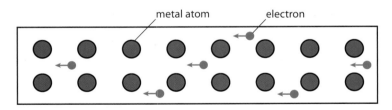

metal atom   electron

◀ **Figure 5.11** Electrons move through metal, giving energy to atoms.

Worked example

The resistivity of copper is $1.72 \times 10^{-8}\,\Omega$m. What is the resistance of a 1 m length of 2 mm diameter copper wire?

Solution
Cross-sectional area $= \pi\,(0.001)^2$

$\qquad\qquad\qquad = 3.14 \times 10^{-6}\,m^2$

$R = \rho\dfrac{L}{A}$

$\quad = 1.72 \times 10^{-8} \times \dfrac{1}{3.14 \times 10^{-6}}\ \Omega$

$\quad = 0.0055\ \Omega$

● **Examiner's hint:**
Area $= \pi r^2$ where radius $= \frac{1}{2} \times 2\,mm = 0.001\,m$.

Ohm's law

Ohm's law relates the current flowing through a conductor with the potential difference across it.

Figure 5.12 We can now make a simple circuit with a battery and a resistor.

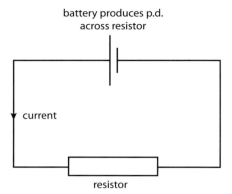

battery produces p.d. across resistor

current

resistor

The current flowing through an ohmic conductor is directly proportional to the potential difference across it, provided temperature and other physical conditions remain constant.

Figure 5.13 Doubling p.d. doubles the current.

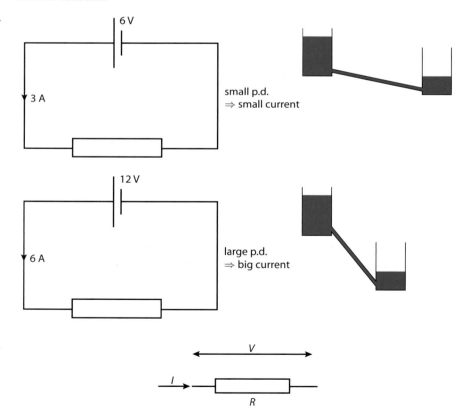

6 V

3 A

small p.d.
⇒ small current

12 V

6 A

large p.d.
⇒ big current

Figure 5.14 V, I and R

V

I

R

If the p.d. across a conductor is V and the current flowing through it is I, then according to Ohm's law:

$$V \propto I$$

The constant of proportionality is the resistance, R.

So:

$$V = IR$$

Worked example

If the p.d. across a 3 Ω resistance is 9 V what current will flow?

Solution

$V = IR$ From Ohm's law.

$I = \dfrac{V}{R}$ Rearranging.

$I = \dfrac{9}{3}$ A

$= 3$ A

The water behind this dam has a high potential energy but because the hole is small only a small current of water can flow out. This is equivalent to a high resistance leading to a small current.

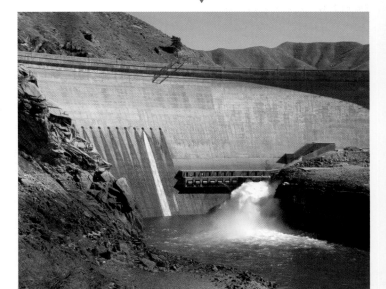

Graphical treatment

Ohmic conductor

Since $V \propto I$ for an ohmic conductor, a graph of I against V will be a straight line.

In this example, resistance $= \dfrac{V}{I} = 2\,\Omega$

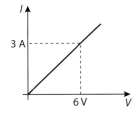

Figure 5.15 *I-V* for an ohmic conductor

> Note: The resistance is found by taking the ratio V/I – this is the same as $\dfrac{1}{\text{gradient}}$.

Non-ohmic conductors

Not all conductors obey Ohm's law. *I-V* graphs for these conductors will not be straight. A light bulb filament is an example of a non-ohmic conductor.

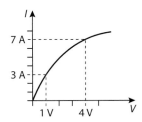

Figure 5.16 This *I-V* graph for a light bulb shows that the resistance has increased.

> Why do we plot *V* on the *x*-axis? To produce an *I-V* graph, the current through the resistor is measured as the p.d. is changed. The variable that is changed is called the independent variable, the variable that changes is the dependent variable. The independent variable is generally plotted on the *x*-axis; that's why we plot *I* against *V*. So if an *I-V* graph gets steeper it means that the resistance is getting lower.

In this example, the resistance at the start is $\tfrac{1}{3}\,\Omega$ $(0.33\,\Omega)$ and at the end it is $\tfrac{4}{7}\,\Omega$ $(0.57\,\Omega)$.

The reason for this is that when the light bulb gets hot, the metal atoms vibrate more. This means that there are more collisions between the electrons and metal atoms, leading to an increase in resistance.

1. If a p.d. of 9 V causes a current of 3 mA to flow through a wire, what is the resistance of the wire?
2. A current of 1 μA flows through a 300 kΩ resistor. What is the p.d. across the resistor?
3. If the p.d. across a 600 Ω resistor is 12 V, how much current flows?
4. Below is a table of the p.d. and current through a device called a thermistor.

p.d. (volts)	Current (milliamps)
1.0	0.01
10	0.1
25	1.0

Calculate the resistance at different potential differences.

5.2 Electric circuits

Assessment statements
5.2.1   Define electromotive force (emf).
5.2.2   Describe the concept of internal resistance.
5.2.3   Apply the equations for resistors in series and in parallel.
5.2.4   Draw circuit diagrams.
5.2.5   Describe the use of ideal ammeters and ideal voltmeters.
5.2.6   Describe a potential divider.
5.2.7   Explain the use of sensors in potential divider circuits.
5.2.8   Solve problems involving electric circuits.

The simple circuit – an energy view

We can now consider the energy changes that take place as current flows around the simple circuit.

Figure 5.17 The shopping centre analogy.
The energy changes of the charges that flow round an electric circuit are similar to the energy changes as you walk around a multi-storey shopping centre. The escalator gives you potential energy as it takes you up.
When you come down the stairs your potential energy gets less. This energy is given to the stairs; as your feet hit each step, the step gets hot.

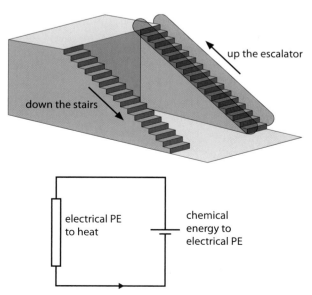

The cell uses chemical energy to place the charges in a position of high potential. As the charges flow through the resistor, this potential energy is converted to heat, so the resistor gets hot. These changes in energy are defined by the following terms:

- Emf (ε)

The emf of a cell is the amount of chemical energy converted to electrical energy, per unit charge. The unit is the volt (V).

- Potential difference (p.d. or V)

The p.d. across a resistance is the amount of electrical energy converted to heat, per unit charge. The unit is the volt (V).

Both of these quantities are energy per unit charge, but emf specifically applies to cells, batteries, generators and any other device that gives the charges potential energy. (One volt is the same as one joule per coulomb.)

Applying the law of conservation of energy

Since energy cannot be created or destroyed, the energy converted from chemical to electrical in the cell must be equal to the amount converted from electrical to heat in the resistor.

From Ohm's law, $V = IR$

Worked examples

1 If the emf of a battery is 9 V, how much energy is converted from chemical to electrical when 2 C of charge flow?

2 What is the p.d. across a resistor if 24 J of heat are produced when a current of 2 A flows through it for 10 s?

Solutions

1 emf = energy converted from chemical to electrical per unit charge.
So energy converted = 2×9 J
$= 18$ J

2 2A for 10 s = 2×10 C = 20 C of charge.
If 20 C of charge flows, then the energy per unit charge = $\frac{24}{20}$ V = 1.2 V

To look at the simulations on the PhET website, visit www.heinemann.co.uk/hotlinks, enter the express code 4266S and click on the Website 5.4.
'Battery voltage' shows how the battery changes chemical energy to electrical potential energy by moving the charges.
'Battery-resistor current' shows how the electrical energy is converted to heat in the resistor.
Note: these simulations show the movement of electrons, not conventional current.

- **Examiner's hint:** If the amount of charge = 2 C then energy converted = 2 × emf
- **Examiner's hint:** Current is charge flowing per unit time.
- **Examiner's hint:** From the definition, p.d. = energy converted from electrical to heat per unit charge.

Internal resistance of cells

All cells are made of materials that have resistance. The resistance of the cell is called the *internal resistance.*

If a cell with internal resistance is connected to a resistor, current will flow from the cell. As current flows through the internal resistance, some energy is converted from electrical to heat inside the cell (so the cell gets hot). This means that there is less energy to be converted to heat in the resistor. The p.d. across the resistor is therefore less than the emf of the cell.

The shopping centre analogy is an example of how we use models to visualize things that we can't see. It is much easier to understand the changes in height as you walk around the shops than the changes of energy as electrons flow around a circuit.

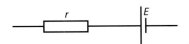

Figure 5.18 The symbol for a cell includes a resistor *r* next to the cell to show internal resistance.

Figure 5.19 Internal resistance acts
like a small step down.

Figure 5.19 Internal resistance acts
like a small step down.

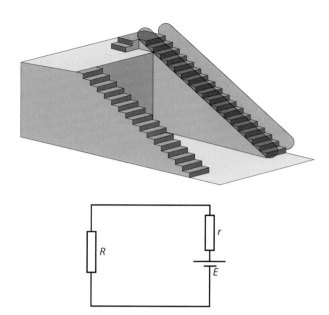

Shopping centre analogy
In the shopping centre analogy
you can see that the elevator still
lifts you up to the same level but
you must come down a few steps
as soon as you step off it.
In the electrical circuit the emf is
still the same but the charges lose
some energy before they leave the
battery.

Applying Ohm's law to the internal resistance, the p.d. across it will be Ir.

From the law of conservation of energy, when a certain charge flows, the amount
of energy converted from chemical to electrical equals the amount converted from
electrical to heat.

$$\varepsilon = IR + Ir$$

Rearranging this formula, we can get an equation for the current from the battery.

$$I = \frac{\varepsilon}{R + r}$$

If the resistance connected to
the battery is very small, then the
current will be large. This means
that most of the electrical energy
is converted to heat inside the
battery so the battery gets very
hot. This is why you shouldn't
connect a wire between the ends
of a battery. You can try this with
the *PhET* circuit construction kit,
but don't try it with a real battery.

Worked example

A battery of emf 9 V with an internal resistance 1 Ω is connected to a 2 Ω resistor,
as shown in Figure 5.20.

How much current will flow?

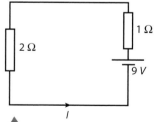

Solution

$$I = \frac{\varepsilon}{R + r}$$

$$I = \frac{9}{2 + 1}\,A$$

$$= 3\,A$$

What is the p.d. across the 2 Ω resistor?

$V = IR$

$V = 3 \times 2\,V$

$= 6\,V$

Figure 5.20 Always start by drawing a
circuit showing the quantities you know
and labelling the ones you want to find.

● **Examiner's hint:** The
current through the resistor
is 3 A.

Exercises

5 A current of 0.5 A flows when a battery of emf 6 V is connected to an 11 Ω resistor. What is
the internal resistance of the battery?

6 A 12 V battery with internal resistance 1 Ω is connected to a 23 Ω resistor. What is the p.d.
across the 23 Ω resistor?

Electrical power

Electrical power is the rate at which energy is changed from one form to another.

Power delivered

In a perfect battery, the power is the amount of chemical energy converted to electrical energy per unit time.

If the emf of a battery is ε, then if a charge Q flows, the amount of energy converted from chemical to electrical is εQ.

If this charge flows in a time t then the power delivered $= \varepsilon Q/t$

But $Q/t =$ the current, I

So the power delivered $= \varepsilon I$

In a real battery, the actual power delivered will be a bit less, since there will be some power dissipated in the internal resistance.

Power dissipated

The power dissipated in the resistor is the amount of electrical energy converted to heat per unit time.

Consider a resistance R with a p.d. V across it. If a charge q flows in time t then the current, $I = q/t$

The p.d., V, is defined as the energy converted to heat per unit charge so, the energy converted to heat in this case $= Vq$

Power is the energy used per unit time so $P = Vq/t$

but $q/t = I$ so $P = VI$

Kilowatt-hours
The electrical energy used at home is measured in kilowatt-hours. This is the amount of energy used by a 1 kilowatt heater switched on for 1 hour. When the electricity bill comes, you have to pay for each kilowatt-hour of energy that you have used.
Since $1\,W = 1\,J\,s^{-1}$
1 kilowatt-hour $= 1000 \times 60 \times 60$ J
$1\,kWh = 3.6 \times 10^6$ J

Worked examples

1 If a current of 2 A flows through a resistor that has a p.d. of 4 V across it, how much power is dissipated?

2 What power will be dissipated when a current of 4 A flows through a resistance of 55 Ω?

Solutions

1 $P = VI$ where $V = 4$ V and $I = 2$ A   First we need to find out the p.d. across the resistor

   $P = 4 \times 2$ W

   $\quad = 8$ W

2 Using Ohm's law $V = IR$

   $\quad = 4 \times 55$ V

   $\quad = 220$ V

   $P = VI$

   $\quad = 220 \times 4$ W

   $\quad = 880$ W

Alternative ways of writing $P = VI$

In Example 2, we had to calculate the p.d. before finding the power. It would be convenient if we could solve this problem in one step. We can write alternative forms of the equation by substituting for I and V from Ohm's law.

We have shown that power $P = VI$

But from Ohm's law $V = IR$

If we substitute for V we get $P = IR \times I = I^2R$

We can also substitute for $I = V/R$

Power $= V \times I = V \times V/R = V^2/R$

Power
$P = VI$
$P = I^2R$
$P = V^2/R$

Exercises

7 5 A flows through a 20 Ω resistor.
   (a) How much electrical energy is converted to heat per second?
   (b) If the current flows for 1 minute, how much energy is released?
8 If a battery has an internal resistance of 0.5 Ω, how much power will be dissipated in the battery when 0.25 A flows?
9 A current of 0.5 A flows from a battery of emf 9 V. If the power delivered is 4 W, how much power is dissipated in the internal resistance?

Electric kettle (water boiler)

An electric kettle transfers the heat produced when current flows through a wire element to the water inside the kettle.

Worked example

A current of 3 A flows through an electric kettle connected to the 220 V mains. What is the power of the kettle and how long will it take to boil 1 litre of water?

Solution

The power of the kettle $= VI = 220 \times 3 = 660\,\text{W}$

To calculate energy needed to boil the water, we use the formula

heat required = mass $\times$ specific heat capacity $\times$ temperature change.

The specific heat capacity of water is $4180\,\text{J}\,\text{kg}^{-1}\,^\circ\text{C}^{-1}$

The mass of 1 litre of water is 1 kg, so if we assume that the water was at room temperature, 20°C, then to raise it to 100°C the energy required is:
$1 \times 4180 \times 80 = 334\,400\,\text{J}$

$$\text{power} = \text{energy/time so the time taken} = \frac{\text{energy}}{\text{power}}$$

$$= \frac{334\,400}{660}$$

$$\text{Time} = 506.67\,\text{s}$$

$$= 8\text{ minutes } 27\text{ seconds}$$

The light bulb

If the power dissipated in a wire is large, then a lot of heat is produced per second. When heat is added quickly, the wire doesn't have time to lose this heat to the surroundings. The result is that the temperature of the wire increases, and if the temperature is high enough, the wire will begin to glow, giving out light. Only about 10% of the energy dissipated in a light bulb is converted to light - the rest is heat.

The electric motor

A motor converts electrical energy to mechanical energy; this could be in the form of potential energy, if something is lifted by the motor, or kinetic energy, if the motor is accelerating something like a car.

Worked example

An electric motor is used to lift 10 kg through 3 m in 5 seconds. If the p.d. across the motor is 12 V, how much current flows (assuming no energy is lost)?

Solution

Work done by the motor $= mgh$
$$= 10 \times 10 \times 3\,\text{J}$$
$$= 300\,\text{J}$$

$$\text{Power} = \frac{\text{work done}}{\text{time}}$$
$$= \frac{300}{5}\,\text{W}$$
$$= 60\,\text{W}$$

Electrical power, $P = IV$ so $I = P/V$
$$= \frac{60}{12}\,\text{A}$$
$$= 5\,\text{A}$$

Exercises

10 An electric car of mass 1000 kg uses twenty-five 12 V batteries connected together to create a p.d. of 300 V. The car accelerates from rest to a speed of 30 m s^{-1} in 12 seconds.
   (a) What is the final kinetic energy of the car?
   (b) What is the power of the car?
   (c) How much electrical current flows from the battery?
   What assumptions have you made in calculating a) to c)?

11 A light bulb for use with the 220 V mains is rated at 100 W.
   (a) What current will flow through the bulb?
   (b) If the bulb converts 20% of the energy to light, how much light energy is produced per second?

12 A 1 kW electric heater is connected to the 220 V mains and left on for 5 hours.
   (a) How much current will flow through the heater?
   (b) How much energy will the heater release?

Combinations of components

In practical situations, resistors and cells are often joined together in combinations e.g. fairy lights, flashlight batteries.

There are many ways of connecting a number of components – we will consider two simple arrangements, series and parallel.

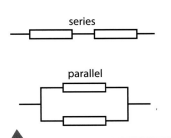

Figure 5.21 Two simple combinations of resistors.

Resistors in series

In a series circuit the same current flows through each resistor.

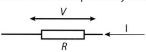
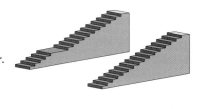

Figure 5.22 Two resistors in series are similar to two flights of stairs.

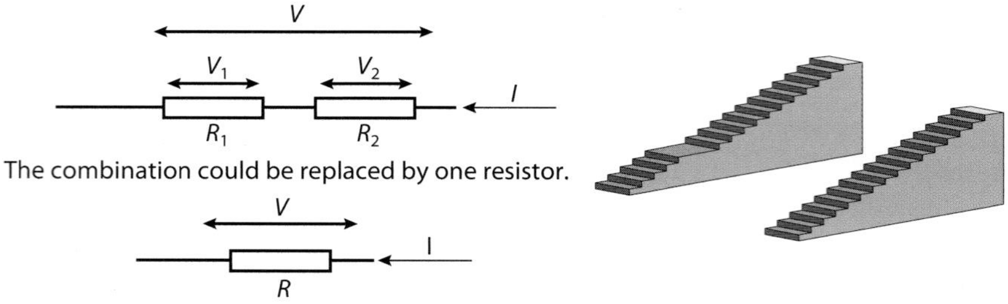

The combination could be replaced by one resistor.

Applying the law of conservation of energy, the p.d. across R_1 plus the p.d. across R_2 must be equal to the p.d. across the combination.

$$V_1 + V_2 = V$$

Applying Ohm's law to each resistor: $IR_1 + IR_2 = IR$

Dividing by I: $R_1 + R_2 = R$

Worked example

What is the total resistance of a 4Ω and an 8Ω resistor in series?

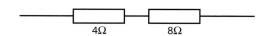

4Ω 8Ω

Figure 5.23

Solution

Total resistance $= R_1 + R_2$
$= 4 + 8\ \Omega$
$= 12\ \Omega$

These coloured lights are connected in series – if you take one out they all go out.

Resistors in parallel

In a parallel circuit the current splits in two.

Figure 5.24 Resistors in parallel are similar to stairs side by side.

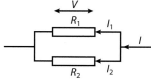

The combination could be replaced by one resistor.

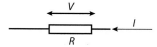

Applying the law of conservation of charge, we know that the current going into a junction must equal the current coming out.

$$I = I_1 + I_2$$

Applying Ohm's law to each resistor gives: $\dfrac{V}{R} = \dfrac{V}{R_1} + \dfrac{V}{R_2}$

Dividing by V: $\dfrac{1}{R} = \dfrac{1}{R_1} + \dfrac{1}{R_2}$

Worked examples

1 What is the total resistance of a 4 Ω and an 8 Ω resistor in parallel?

2 What is the total resistance of two 8 Ω resistors in parallel?

Solutions

1 Using $\dfrac{1}{R} = \dfrac{1}{R_1} + \dfrac{1}{R_2}$

$$\dfrac{1}{R} = \dfrac{1}{4} + \dfrac{1}{8}$$

$$= \dfrac{2+1}{8} = \dfrac{3}{8}$$

so $R = \dfrac{8}{3}\,\Omega$

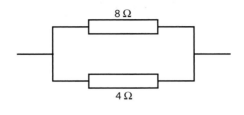

Figure 5.25

2 Using $\dfrac{1}{R} = \dfrac{1}{R_1} + \dfrac{1}{R_2}$

$$\dfrac{1}{R} = \dfrac{1}{8} + \dfrac{1}{8} = \dfrac{2}{8}$$

$$R = \dfrac{8}{2}\,\Omega$$

$$= 4\,\Omega$$

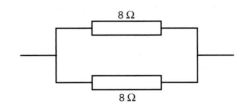

Figure 5.26 The total resistance of two equal resistors in parallel is half the resistance of one of them.

Multiple combinations

When there are many resistors, the total is found by splitting the circuit into small units of parallel and series resistors; for example in the circuit shown in Figure 5.27.

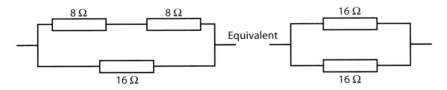

Figure 5.27 Equivalent circuits.

The two 8 Ω resistors at the top are equivalent to one 16 Ω resistor.

This gives two 16 Ω resistors in parallel, a total of 8 Ω.

Exercises

Calculate the total resistance for the circuits in Figure 5.28.

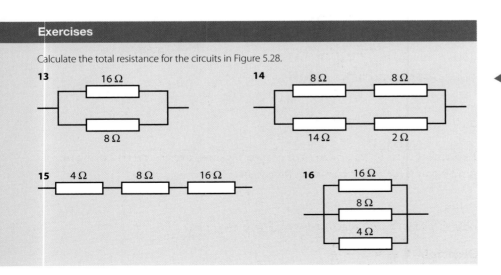

Figure 5.28

Cells in series

Cells are very often added in series to produce a larger p.d.

Figure 5.29 Cells in series are similar to two flights of escalators.

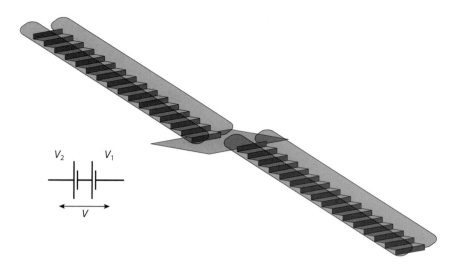

The p.d. of cells in series simply add

$$V = V_1 + V_2$$

Worked example

Two 12 V batteries are connected in series to a 10 Ω resistor. If each battery has an internal resistance of 1 Ω, how much current will flow?

The three resistors are in series (it looks like the 10 Ω is in parallel with the 1 Ω resistors, but they are in series because the same current flows through them all).

Solution

The total p.d. for two batteries in series $= 12 + 12 = 24$V

Figure 5.30 The circuit for Example 1.

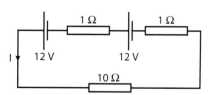

Total resistance $= 1 + 1 + 10 = 12\,\Omega$.

Applying Ohm's law, $\quad I = \dfrac{V}{R}$

$$= \dfrac{24}{12}\,\text{A}$$

$$= 2\,\text{A}$$

Electrical measurement

Measurement of potential difference

P.d. can be measured using a voltmeter. There are two main types of voltmeter, digital and analogue.

P.d. is the difference in potential between two points. To measure the p.d. between A and B, one lead of the voltmeter must be connected to A, the other to B.

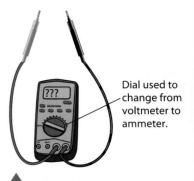

Dial used to change from voltmeter to ammeter.

Figure 5.31 A multimeter is a common instrument that can measure both p.d. and current. It can also measure resistance.

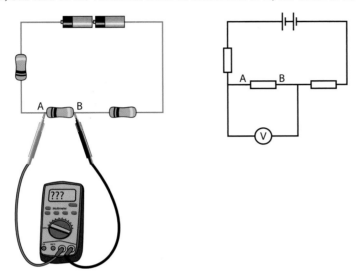

Figure 5.32 A voltmeter is connected from A to B.

An ideal voltmeter has infinitely high resistance so that it does not take any current from the circuit.

Measurement of current

To measure the current flowing through a resistor, the ammeter must be connected so that the same current will flow through the ammeter as flows through the resistor. This means disconnecting one of the wires and connecting the ammeter.

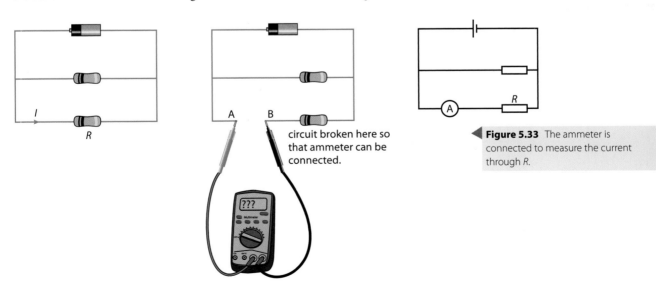

circuit broken here so that ammeter can be connected.

Figure 5.33 The ammeter is connected to measure the current through R.

An ideal ammeter has zero resistance so that it doesn't change the current in the circuit.

Worked example

Calculate the current and potential difference measured by the meters in the circuit in Figure 5.34. Assume the battery has no internal resistance and that the meters are ideal.

Solution

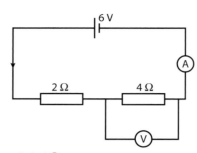

Figure 5.34

Total resistance $= 2 + 4\,\Omega$

$= 6\,\Omega$ The two resistors are in series.

$I = \dfrac{V}{R}$ Applying Ohm's law, to find the current.

$= \dfrac{6}{6}\,A$

$= 1A$

So ammeter reading $= 1A$

$V = IR$ Applying Ohm's law to the 4 Ω resistor.

$= 1 \times 4\,V$

$= 4\,V$

So the voltmeter reads 4 V.

Exercises

Find the ammeter and voltmeter readings in the circuits in Figure 5.35. All meters are ideal and the batteries have no internal resistance. (You can build them in the Phet 'circuit construction kit' to see whether your answers agree.)

Figure 5.35

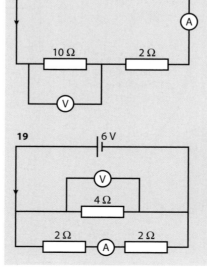

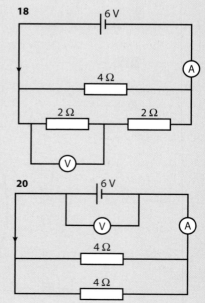

Electrical sensors

An electrical sensor is a device whose electrical properties change with changing physical conditions.

Thermistor

A thermistor is made from a semiconducting material whose resistance decreases as temperature increases. As the thermistor gets hotter, more charge carriers are released, so the current can flow more easily.

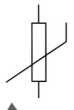

Figure 5.36 A thermistor.

Light sensor (LDR)

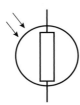

Figure 5.37 An LDR.

A light sensor or light dependent resistor (LDR) is also a semiconducting device, but, unlike the thermistor, it is light that releases more charge carriers, resulting in a lower resistance.

Strain gauge

A strain gauge is a thin metal wire. If it is stretched, its length increases and its cross-sectional area gets smaller. This results in an increase in resistance.

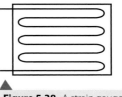

Figure 5.38 A strain gauge.

Use of sensors

The resistance of all three sensors varies with some physical property. However, it would be much more useful if the devices gave a changing p.d. rather than a changing resistance. To convert the changing resistance to a changing p.d., we use a potential divider.

The potential divider

The battery creates a p.d. across the resistors equal to V_{in}

From Ohm's law we know that the current in the circuit $I = \dfrac{V}{R}$

Since the total resistance is $R_1 + R_2$

The current $I = \dfrac{V_{in}}{(R_1 + R_2)}$ Equation (1)

The p.d. across $R_2 = V_{out}$

Applying Ohm's law to R_2 gives

$V_{out} = IR_2$

Substituting from equation (1) gives

$V_{out} = V_{in} \dfrac{R_2}{R_1 + R_2}$

This is the potential divider formula.

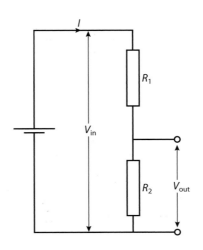

Figure 5.39 A potential divider circuit consists of two series resistors.

Worked example

Calculate the output voltage for the potential divider in Figure 5.40.

Figure 5.40 ▶

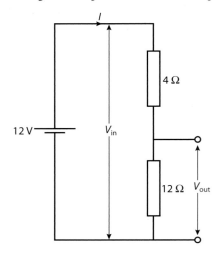

Solution

Using the potential divider formula

$$V_{out} = V_{in} \frac{R_2}{R_1 + R_2}$$

$$V_{out} = 12\frac{12}{4 + 12} = 9\,\text{V}$$

Using the potential divider with sensors

Automatic light switch

Figure 5.41 An LDR and a potential divider can be used to operate an automatic light switch. ▶

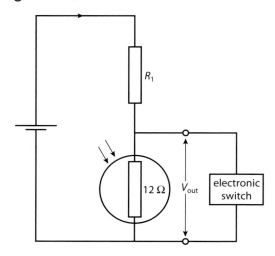

When light stops shining on the LDR, its resistance increases, resulting in an increase in V_{out}. The increase in V_{out} in turn activates the electronic switch that puts on the lights. The electronic switch needs a minimum p.d. to activate it, so it doesn't switch on the lights until V_{out} is big enough.

The important point here is that the electronic switch needs a p.d. to activate it, hence the need for a potential divider.

Worked example

The battery in Figure 5.41 has an emf of 12 V and no internal resistance. The p.d. required to activate the switch is 5 V. Find the value of R_1 that will cause the lights to turn on when the resistance of the LDR rises to 200 kΩ.

Solution

$V_{in} = 12\,V$

$R_2 = 200\,k\Omega$

$V_{out} = 5\,V$

Rearranging the potential divider equation $V_{out} = V_{in}\dfrac{R_2}{R_1 + R_2}$

gives $R_1 = R_2\dfrac{V_{in} - V_{out}}{V_{out}}$

$$= 200\,k\Omega \times \frac{(12-5)}{5}$$

$$= 280\,k\Omega$$

The fire alarm

When the thermistor gets hot, its resistance decreases, resulting in an increased current through R_2, which in turn leads to an increase in V_{out}. The increase in V_{out} activates an electronic switch that rings a bell.

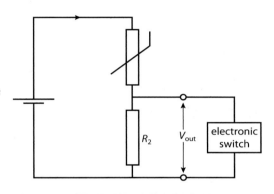

Figure 5.42 The fire alarm bell must ring if the thermistor gets hot.

Exercises

21 Assume that the circuit in Figure 5.42 has a 12V battery and a switch that activates when the p.d. is 5V. Calculate the value of R_2, if the bell rings when the resistance of the thermistor drops to 1 kΩ?

Using a strain gauge

A strain gauge can be used to detect whether parts of a building are stretching. For example, a strain gauge stuck to the underside of a bridge will be stretched if the bridge bends when a heavy truck crosses it. If the strain gauge is connected in a potential divider circuit, the V_{out} can be used to measure how much the bridge stretches.

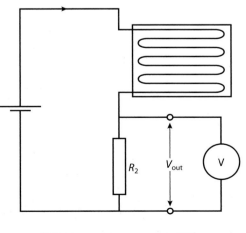

Figure 5.43 Strain gauge circuit.

Strain gauge
stuck here

Figure 5.44 As the bridge bends, the strain gauge gets longer.

Practice questions

1   This question is about electrical energy and associated phenomena.

A cell of electromotive force (emf) E and internal resistance r is connected in series with a resistor R, as shown below. The cell supplies 8.1×10^3 J of energy when 5.8×10^3 C of charge moves completely round the circuit. The current in the circuit is constant.

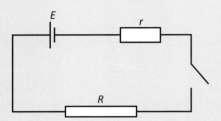

    (i)   Calculate the emf E of the cell.   (2)

   (ii)   The resistor R has resistance 6.0 Ω. The potential difference between its terminals is 1.2 V. Determine the internal resistance r of the cell.   (3)

  (iii)   Calculate the total energy transfer in the resistor R.   (2)

  (iv)   Describe, in terms of a simple model of electrical conduction, the mechanism by which the energy transfer in the resistor R takes place.   (5)

2   This question is about a filament lamp.

   (a)   On the axes below, draw a sketch graph to show the variation with potential difference V of the current I in a typical filament lamp (the I–V characteristic). (Note: this is a sketch graph; you do not need to add any values to the axes).   (1)

   (b)   **(i)**   Explain how the resistance of the filament is determined from the graph.   (1)

         (ii)   Explain whether the graph you have sketched indicates ohmic behaviour or non-ohmic behaviour.   (1)

        A filament lamp operates at maximum brightness when connected to a 6.0 V supply. At maximum brightness, the current in the filament is 120 mA.

   (c)   **(i)**   Calculate the resistance of the filament when it is operating at maximum brightness.   (1)

         (ii)   You have available a 24 V supply and a collection of resistors of a suitable power rating and with different values of resistance. Calculate the resistance of the resistor that is required to be connected in series with the supply such that the voltage across the filament lamp will be 6.0 V.   (2)

3 This question is about electric circuits.

Susan sets up the circuit below in order to measure the current-voltage (*I-V*) characteristic of a small filament lamp.

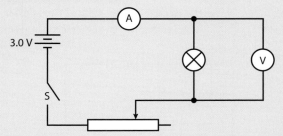

The supply is a battery that has an emf of 3.0 V and the ammeter and voltmeter are considered to be ideal. The lamp is labelled by the manufacturer as '3 Volts, 0.6 Watts'.

(a) **(i)** Explain what information this labelling provides about the normal operation of the lamp. (2)

   (ii) Calculate the current in the filament of the lamp when it is operating at normal brightness. (2)

Susan sets the variable resistor to its maximum value of resistance. She then closes the switch S and records the following readings.

Ammeter reading = 0.18 A   Voltmeter reading = 0.60 V

She then sets the variable resistor to its zero value of resistance and records the following readings.

Ammeter reading = 0.20 A   Voltmeter reading = 2.6 V

(b) **(i)** Explain why, by changing the value of the resistance of the variable resistance, the potential difference across the lamp cannot be reduced to zero or be increased to 3.0 V. (2)

   (ii) Determine the internal resistance of the battery. (3)

(c) Calculate the resistance of the filament when the reading on the voltmeter is

   (i) 0.60 V. (1)

   (ii) 2.6 V. (1)

(d) Explain why there is a difference between your answers to **(c) (i)** and **(c) (ii)**. (2)

(e) Using the axes as in question 2, draw a sketch-graph of the *I-V* characteristic of the filament of the lamp. (Note: this is a sketch-graph; you do not need to add any values to the axis.) (1)

The diagram below shows an alternative circuit for varying the potential difference across the lamp.

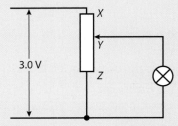

The potential divider *XZ* has a potential of 3.0 V across it. When the contact is at the position *Y*, the resistance of *XY* equals the resistance of *YZ* which equals 12 Ω. The resistance of the lamp is 4 Ω.

(f) Calculate the potential difference across the lamp. (4)

4 This question is about emf and internal resistance.

A dry cell has an emf E and internal resistance r and is connected to an external circuit. There is a current I in the circuit when the potential difference across the terminals of the cell is V.

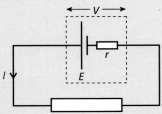

(a) State expressions, in terms of E, V, r and I where appropriate, for
  (i) the total power supplied by the cell.   (1)
  (ii) the power dissipated in the cell.   (1)
  (iii) the power dissipated in the external circuit.   (1)

(b) Use your answers to **(a)** to derive a relationship between V, E, I and r.   (2)
The graph below shows the variation of V with I for the dry cell.

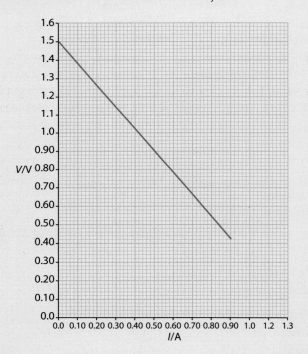

(c) Draw the circuit that could be used to obtain the data from which the graph was plotted.   (3)

(d) Use the graph, explaining your answers, to
  (i) determine the emf E of the cell.   (2)
  (ii) determine the current in the external circuit when the resistance R of the external circuit is very small.   (2)
  (iii) deduce that the internal restance r of the cell is about 1.2Ω.   (1)

(e) The maximum power dissipated in the external circuit occurs when the resistance of the external circuit has the same value as the internal resistance of the cell. Calculate the maximum power dissipation in the external circuit.   (3)

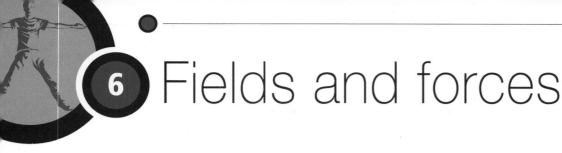

6 Fields and forces

6.1 Gravitational force and field

Assessment statements

6.1.1 State Newton's universal law of gravitation.
6.1.2 Define *gravitational field strength*.
6.1.3 Determine the gravitational field due to one or more point masses.
6.1.4 Derive an expression for gravitational field strength at the surface of a planet, assuming that all its mass is concentrated at its centre.

Gravitational force and field

We have all seen how an object falls to the ground when released. Newton was certainly not the first person to realize that an apple falls to the ground when dropped from a tree. However, he did recognize that the force that pulls the apple to the ground is the same as the force that holds the Earth in its orbit around the Sun; this was not obvious - after all, the apple moves in a straight line and the Earth moves in a circle. In this chapter we will see how these forces are connected.

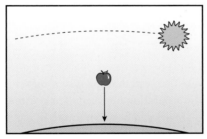

Figure 6.1 The apple drops and the Sun seems to move in a circle, but it is gravity that makes both things happen.

Newton's universal law of gravitation

Newton extended his ideas further to say that every single particle of mass in the universe exerts a force on every other particle of mass. In other words, everything in the universe is attracted to everything else. So there is a force between the end of your nose and a lump of rock on the Moon.

 Was it reasonable for Newton to think that his law applied to the whole universe?

The modern equivalent of the apparatus used by Cavendish to measure G in 1798.

Newton's universal law of gravitation states that:

every single point mass attracts every other point mass with a force that is directly proportional to the product of their masses and inversely proportional to the square of their separation.

Figure 6.2 The gravitational force between two point masses.

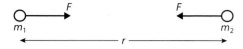

If two point masses with mass m_1 and m_2 are separated by a distance r then the force, F, experienced by each will be given by:

$$F \propto \frac{m_1 m_2}{r^2}$$

The constant of proportionality is the universal gravitational constant G.

$$G = 6.6742 \times 10^{-11} \, \text{m}^3 \, \text{kg}^{-1} \, \text{s}^{-2}$$

Therefore the equation is

$$F = G \frac{m_1 m_2}{r^2}$$

Spheres of mass

Figure 6.3 Forces between two spheres. Even though these bodies don't have the same mass, the force on them is the same size. This is due to Newton's third law – if mass m_1 exerts a force on mass m_2 then m_2 will exert an equal and opposite force on m_1.

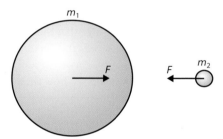

By working out the total force between every particle of one sphere and every particle of another, Newton deduced that spheres of mass follow the same law, where the separation is the separation between their centres. Every object has a centre of mass where the gravity can be taken to act. In regularly-shaped bodies, this is the centre of the object.

How fast does the apple drop?

If we apply Newton's universal law to the apple on the surface of the Earth, we find that it will experience a force given by

$$F = G \frac{m_1 m_2}{r^2}$$

where:

m_1 = mass of the Earth = $5.97 \times 10^{24} \, \text{kg}$

m_2 = mass of the apple = $250 \, \text{g}$

r = radius of the Earth = $6378 \, \text{km}$ (at the equator)

So $F = 2.43 \, \text{N}$

From Newton's 2nd law we know that $F = ma$.

So the acceleration (a) of the apple = $\frac{2.43}{0.25} \, \text{m s}^{-2}$

$a = 9.79 \, \text{m s}^{-2}$

This is very close to the average value for the acceleration of free fall on the Earth's surface. It is not exactly the same, since 9.82 m s^{-2} is an average for the whole Earth, the radius of the Earth being maximum at the equator.

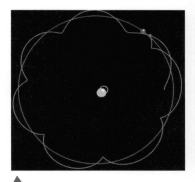

Exercise

1 The mass of the Moon is 7.35×10^{22} kg and the radius 1.74×10^3 km. What is the acceleration due to gravity on the Moon's surface?

How often does the Earth go around the Sun?

Applying Newton's universal law, we find that the force experienced by the Earth is given by:

$$F = G \frac{m_1 m_2}{r^2}$$

where

m_1 = mass of the Sun = 1.99×10^{30} kg

m_2 = mass of the Earth = 5.97×10^{24} kg

r = distance between the Sun and Earth = 1.49×10^{11} m

So $F = 3.56 \times 10^{22}$ N

▲ To build your own solar system with the 'solar system' simulation from PhET, visit www.heinemann.co.uk/hotlinks, enter the express code 4266S and click on Weblink 6.1.

◀ The planets orbit the Sun.

We know that the Earth travels in an elliptical orbit around the Sun, but we can take this to be a circular orbit for the purposes of this calculation. From our knowledge of circular motion we know that the force acting on the Earth towards the centre of the circle is the centripetal force given by the equation $F = mv^2/r$

 Here the law is used to make predictions that can be tested by experiment.

So the velocity $v = \sqrt{\dfrac{Fr}{m}}$

$$= 29\ 846 \text{ m s}^{-1}$$

The circumference of the orbit = $2\pi r = 9.38 \times 10^{11}$ m

Time taken for 1 orbit $= \dfrac{9.38 \times 10^{11}}{29\ 846}$

$$= 3.14 \times 10^7 \text{ s}$$

This is equal to 1 year.

This agrees with observation. Newton's law has therefore predicted two correct results.

Gravitational field

The fact that both the apple and the Earth experience a force without being in contact makes gravity a bit different from the other forces we have come across. To model this situation, we introduce the idea of a *field*. A field is simply a region of space where something is to be found. A potato field, for example, is a region where you find potatoes. A gravitational field is a region where you find gravity. More precisely, gravitational field is defined as a region of space where a mass experiences a force because of its mass.

So there is a gravitational field in your classroom since masses experience a force in it.

Gravitational field strength (*g*)

This gives a measure of how much force a body will experience in the field. It is defined as the force per unit mass experienced by a small test mass placed in the field.

So if a test mass, *m*, experiences a force *F* at some point in space, then the field strength, *g*, at that point is given by $g = F/m$.

g is measured in $N\,kg^{-1}$, and is a vector quantity.

Note: The reason a small test mass is used is because a big mass might change the field that you are trying to measure.

Gravitational field around a spherical object

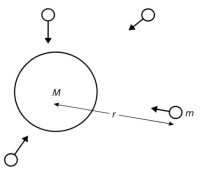

The force experienced by the mass, *m* is given by;

$$F = G\frac{Mm}{r^2}$$

So the field strength at this point in space, $g = F/m$

So
$$g = G\frac{M}{r^2}$$

Field strength on the Earth's surface:
Substituting *M* = mass of the Earth
$= 5.97 \times 10^{24}\,kg$
r = radius of the Earth = 6367 km
gives $g = Gm_1M/r^2$
$= 9.82\,N\,kg^{-1}$
This is the same as the acceleration due to gravity, which is what you might expect, since Newton's 2nd law says $a = F/m$.

Figure 6.4 The region surrounding *M* is a gravitational field since all the test masses experience a force.

Exercises

2 The mass of Jupiter is 1.89×10^{27} kg and the radius 71 492 km.
What is the gravitational field strength on the surface of Jupiter?

3 What is the gravitational field strength at a distance of 1000 km from the surface of the Earth?

Field lines

Field lines are drawn in the direction that a mass would accelerate if placed in the field – they are used to help us visualize the field.

The field lines for a spherical mass are shown in Figure 6.5.

The arrows give the direction of the field.

The field strength (g) is given by the density of the lines.

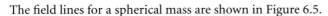

Figure 6.5 Field lines for a sphere of mass.

Gravitational field close to the Earth

When we are doing experiments close to the Earth, in the classroom for example, we assume that the gravitational field is uniform. This means that wherever you put a mass in the classroom it is always pulled downwards with the same force. We say that the field is *uniform*.

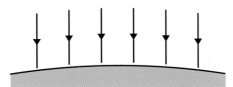

Figure 6.6 Regularly spaced parallel field lines imply that the field is uniform.

Addition of field

Since field strength is a vector, when we add field strengths caused by several bodies, we must remember to add them vectorially.

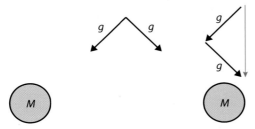

Figure 6.7 Vector addition of field strength.

In this example, the angle between the vectors is 90°. This means that we can use Pythagoras to find the resultant.

$$g = \sqrt{g_1^2 + g_2^2}$$

Worked example

Calculate the gravitational field strength at points A and B in Figure 6.8.

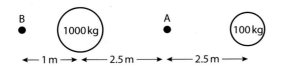

Figure 6.8

Solution

The gravitational field strength at A is equal to the sum of the field due to the two masses.

Field strength due to large mass = $G \times 1000/2.5^2 = 1.07 \times 10^{-8}\,\mathrm{N\,kg^{-1}}$

Field strength due to small mass = $G \times 100/2.5^2 = 1.07 \times 10^{-9}\,\mathrm{N\,kg^{-1}}$

Field strength = $1.07 \times 10^{-8} - 1.07 \times 10^{-9}$

$\quad\quad\quad\quad\quad = 9.63 \times 10^{-9}\,\mathrm{N\,kg^{-1}}$

● **Examiner's hint:** Since field strength g is a vector, the resultant field strength equals the vector sum.

Exercises

4 Calculate the gravitational field strength at point B.

5 Calculate the gravitational field strength at A if the big mass were changed for a 100 kg mass.

6.2 Electric force and field

Assessment statements

6.2.1 State that there are two types of electric charge.

6.2.2 State and apply the law of conservation of charge.

6.2.3 Describe and explain the difference in the electrical properties of conductors and insulators.

6.2.4 State Coulomb's law.

6.2.5 Define *electric field strength*.

6.2.6 Determine the *electric field strength* due to one or more point charges.

6.2.7 Draw the electric field patterns for different charge configurations.

Electric force

So far we have dealt with many forces; for example, friction, tension, upthrust, normal force, air resistance and gravitational force. If we rub a balloon on a woolen pullover, we find that the balloon is attracted to the wool of the pullover – this cannot be explained in terms of any of the forces we have already considered, so we need to develop a new model to explain what is happening. First we need to investigate the effect.

This is another example of how models are used in physics.

Consider a balloon and a woollen pullover – if the balloon is rubbed on the pullover, we find that it is attracted to the pullover. However, if we rub two balloons on the pullover, the balloons repel each other.

Whatever is causing this effect must have two different types, since there are two different forces. We call this force the *electric force*.

Figure 6.9 Balloons are attracted to the wool but repel each other.

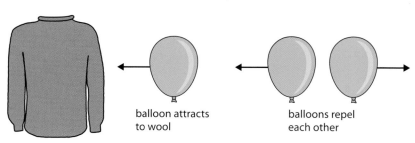

balloon attracts to wool

balloons repel each other

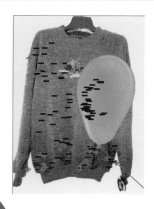

You can try this with real balloons or, to use the simulation 'Balloons and static electricity', visit www.heinemann.co.uk/hotlinks, enter the express code 4266S and click on Weblink 6.2.

Charge

The balloon and pullover must have some property that is causing this force. We call this property *charge*. There must be two types of charge, traditionally called positive (+ve) and negative(−ve). To explain what happens, we can say that, when rubbed, the balloon gains −ve charge and the pullover gains +ve charge. If like charges repel and unlike charges attract, then we can explain why the balloons repel and the balloon and pullover attract.

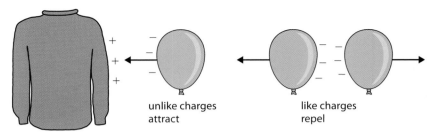

Figure 6.10 The force is due to charges.

unlike charges
attract

like charges
repel

Here +ve and −ve numbers are used to represent something that they were not designed to represent.

The unit of charge is the coulomb (C).

Conservation of charge

If we experiment further, we find that if we rub the balloon more, then the force between the balloons is greater. We also find that if we add +ve charge to an equal −ve charge, the charges cancel.

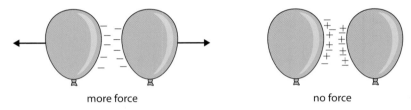

Figure 6.11 Charges cancel each other out.

more force

no force

We can add and take away charge but we cannot destroy it.

The law of conservation of charge states that charge can neither be created nor destroyed.

Electric field

We can see that there are certain similarities with the electric force and gravitational force; they both act without the bodies touching each other. We used the concept of a field to model gravitation and we can use the same idea here.

Electric field is defined as a region of space where a charged object experiences a force due to its charge.

Field lines

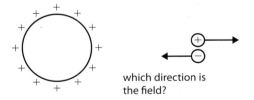

which direction is the field?

Figure 6.12 Field is in the direction in which a +ve charge would accelerate.

Field lines can be used to show the direction and strength of the field. However, because there are two types of charge, the direction of the force could be one of two possibilities.

It has been decided that we should take the direction of the field to be the direction that a small +ve charge would accelerate if placed in the field. So we will always consider what would happen if +ve charges are moved around in the field. The field lines will therefore be as shown in Figures 6.13 to 6.15.

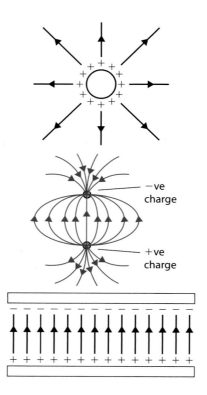

Figure 6.13 Field lines close to a sphere of charge.

Figure 6.14 Field due to a dipole.

−ve charge

+ve charge

Figure 6.15 A uniform field.

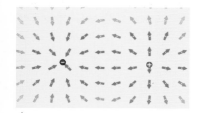

In the PhET simulation 'Charges and fields' you can investigate the force experienced by a small charge as it is moved around an electric field. To try this, visit www.heinemann.co.uk/hotlinks, enter the express code 4266S and click on Weblink 6.3.

Coulomb's law

In a gravitational field, the force between masses is given by Newton's law, and the equivalent for an electric field is Coulomb's law.

Coulomb's law states that the force experienced by two point charges is directly proportional to the product of their charge and inversely proportional to the square of their separation.

The force experienced by two charges Q_1 and Q_2 separated by a distance r in a vacuum is given by the formula

$$F = k\frac{Q_1 Q_2}{r^2}$$

The constant of proportionality $k = 9 \times 10^9 \ \text{Nm}^2\,\text{C}^{-2}$

Note: Similarly to gravitational fields, Coulomb's law also applies to spheres of charge, the separation being the distance between the centres of the spheres.

Electric field strength (*E*)

The electric field strength is a measure of the force that a +ve charge will experience if placed at a point in the field. It is defined as the force per unit charge experienced by a small +ve test charge placed in the field.

So if a small +ve charge q experiences a force F in the field, then the field strength at that point is given by $E = F/q$. The unit of field strength is NC^{-1}, and it is a vector quantity.

Worked examples

A 5 μC point charge is place 20 cm from a 10 μC point charge.

1   Calculate the force experienced by the 5μC charge.

2   What is the force on the 10 μC charge?

3   What is the field strength 20 cm from the 10 μC charge?

Solutions

1 Using the equation $F = \dfrac{kQ_1Q_2}{r^2}$

$Q_1 = 5 \times 10^{-6}\,\text{C}$, $Q_2 = 10 \times 10^{-6}\,\text{C}$ and $r = 0.20\,\text{m}$

$$F = \dfrac{9 \times 10^9 \times 5 \times 10^{-6} \times 10 \times 10^{-6}}{0.20^2}\,\text{N}$$

$$= 11.25\,\text{N}$$

2 According to Newton's third law, the force on the $10\,\mu\text{C}$ charge is the same as the $5\,\mu\text{C}$.

3 Force per unit charge $= \dfrac{11.25}{5 \times 10^{-6}}$

$E = 2.25 \times 10^6\,\text{N\,C}^{-1}$

● **Examiner's hint:** Field strength is defined as the force per unit charge so if the force on a $5\,\mu\text{C}$ charge is 11.25 N, the field strength E is equal to 11.25 N divided by $5\,\mu\text{C}$.

Exercises

6 If the charge on a 10 cm radius metal sphere is $2\,\mu\text{C}$, calculate
   (a) the field strength on the surface of the sphere
   (b) the field strength 10 cm from the surface of the sphere
   (c) the force experienced by a $0.1\,\mu\text{C}$ charge placed 10 cm from the surface of the sphere.
7 A small sphere of mass 0.01 kg and charge $0.2\,\mu\text{C}$ is placed at a point in an electric field where the field strength is $0.5\,\text{N\,C}^{-1}$.
   (a) What force will the small sphere experience?
   (b) If no other forces act, what is the acceleration of the sphere?

● **Examiner's hint:** When solving field problems you always assume one of the charges is in the field of the other. E.g in Example 1 the $5\,\mu\text{c}$ charge is in the field of the $10\,\mu\text{c}$ charge. Don't worry about the fact that the $5\,\mu\text{C}$ charge also creates a field – that's not the field you are interested in.

Electric field strength in a uniform field

A uniform field can be created between two parallel plates of equal and opposite charge as shown in Figure 6.16. The field lines are parallel and equally spaced. If a test charge is placed in different positions between the plates, it experiences the same force.

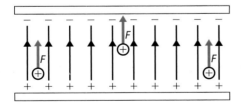

Figure 6.16 In a uniform field the force on a charge q is the same everywhere.

So if a test charge q is placed in the field above, then $E = F/q$ everywhere between the two charged plates.

Worked example

If a charge of $4\,\mu\text{C}$ is placed in a uniform field of field strength $2\,\text{N\,C}^{-1}$ what force will it experience?

Solution

$F = EQ$ Rearranging the formula $E = F/Q$

$\quad = 2 \times 4 \times 10^{-6}\,\text{N}$

$\quad = 8\,\mu\text{N}$

Electric field strength close to a sphere of charge

Figure 6.17

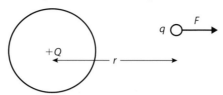

From definition: $E = F/q$

From Coulomb's law: $F = k\dfrac{Qq}{r^2}$

Substituting: $E = k\dfrac{Q}{r^2}$

Addition of field strength

Field strength is a vector, so when the field from two negatively charged bodies act at a point, the field strengths must be added vectorially. In Figure 6.18, the resultant field at two points A and B is calculated. At A the fields act in the same line but at B a triangle must be drawn to find the resultant.

Figure 6.18 Since both charges are negative, the field strength is directed towards the charges. Since they are at right angles to each other, Pythagoras can be used to sum these vectors.

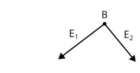

E_3 is the field due to the charge on the left, E_4 is due to the charge on the right. E_3 is bigger than E_4 because the charge on the left is closer.

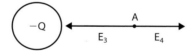

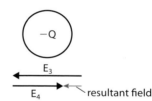

Worked example

Figure 6.19

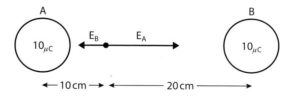

Two $+10\ \mu C$ charges are separated by 30 cm. What is the field strength between the charges 10 cm from A?

Solution

Field strength due to A, $E_A = \dfrac{9 \times 10^9 \times 10 \times 10^{-6}}{0.1^2}$

$= 9 \times 10^6\ \text{N C}^{-1}$

$E_B = \dfrac{9 \times 10^9 \times 10 \times 10^{-6}}{0.2^2}$

$= 2.25 \times 10^6\ \text{N C}^{-1}$

Resultant field strength $= (9 - 2.25) \times 10^6\ \text{N C}^{-1}$

$= 6.75 \times 10^6\ \text{N C}^{-1}$

6.3 Magnetic force and field

Assessment statements
6.3.1   State that moving charges give rise to magnetic fields.
6.3.2   Draw magnetic field patterns due to currents.
6.3.3   Determine the direction of the force on a current-carrying conductor in a magnetic field.
6.3.4   Determine the direction of the force on a charge moving in a magnetic field.
6.3.5   Define the magnitude and direction of a magnetic field.
6.3.6   Solve problems involving magnetic forces, fields and currents.

What is a magnet?

We all know that magnets are the things that stick notes to fridge doors, but do we understand the forces that cause magnets to behave in this way?

Magnetic poles

 The north-seeking pole (red) always points to the north.

▲ Not all magnets are man-made; certain rocks (for example, this piece of magnetite) are naturally magnetic.

There is evidence in ancient Greek and Chinese writing, that people knew about magnets more than 2600 years ago. We do not know who discovered the first magnet, but since antiquity it was known that if a small piece of magnetite was suspended on a string and held close to another larger piece, the small one experienced a turning force, causing it to rotate. It was also found that if the small rock was held on its own, it would always turn to point toward the North Pole. The end of the rock that pointed north was named the *north-seeking pole*, the other end was named the *south-seeking pole*.

Every magnet has two poles (north and south) – they are therefore called *dipoles*. It is not possible to have a single magnetic pole or monopole. This is not the same as electricity where you can have a dipole or monopoles. If you cut a magnet in half, each half will have both poles.

Figure 6.20 Magnets are dipoles.

magnetic dipoles

electric dipole and monopoles

Unlike poles attract

If we take two magnets and hold them next to each other, we find that the magnets will turn so that the S and N poles come together.

Figure 6.21 Magnets experience a turning force causing unlike poles to come together.

Figure 6.22 The north-seeking pole of a compass points north.

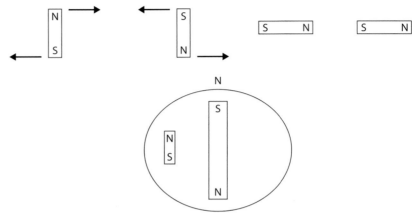

We can therefore conclude that the reason that a small magnet points toward the North Pole of the Earth is because there is a south magnetic pole there. This can be a bit confusing, but remember that the proper name for the pole of the magnet is north-seeking pole.

Magnetic field

Magnetism is similar to gravitational force and electric force in that as the effect is felt even though the magnets do not touch each other; we can therefore use the concept of field to model magnetism. However, magnetism isn't quite the same; we described both gravitational and electric fields in terms of the force experienced by a small mass or charge. A small magnet placed in a field does not accelerate – it rotates, and therefore magnetic field is defined as a region of space where a small test magnet experiences a turning force.

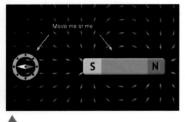

To plot magnetic fields on the PhET 'Faraday's electromagnetic lab', visit www.heinemann.co.uk/hotlinks, enter the express code 4266S and click on Weblink 6.4.

Figure 6.23 The small magnet is caused to turn, so must be in a magnetic field.

Since a small magnet rotates if held above the Earth, we can therefore conclude that the Earth has a magnetic field.

Magnetic field lines

In practice, a small compass can be used as our test magnet. Magnetic field lines are drawn to show the direction that the N pole of a small compass would point if placed in the field.

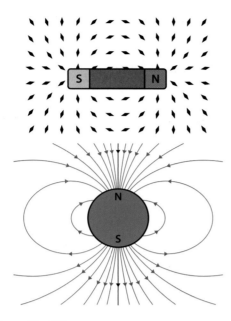

Figure 6.24 If the whole field were covered in small magnets, then they would show the direction of the field lines.

Figure 6.25 The Earth's magnetic field.

Magnetic flux density (*B*)

From what we know about fields, the strength of a field is related to the density of field lines. This tells us that the magnetic field is strongest close to the poles. The magnetic flux density is the quantity that is used to measure how strong the field is – however it is not quite the same as field strength as used in gravitational and electric fields.

The unit of magnetic flux density is the tesla (T) and it is a vector quantity.

> **_B_ field**
> Since the letter *B* is used to denote flux density, the magnetic field is often called a *B field*.

Field caused by currents

Figure 6.26 The field due to a long straight wire carrying a current is in the form of concentric circles.

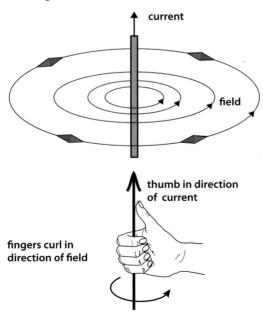

If a small compass is placed close to a straight wire carrying an electric current., then it experiences a turning force that makes it always point around the wire. The region around the wire is therefore a magnetic field. This leads us to believe that magnetic fields are caused by moving charges.

Field inside a coil

When a current goes around a circular loop, the magnetic field forms circles.

Figure 6.27 The direction of the field can be found by applying the right-hand grip rule to the wire. The circles formed by each bit of the loop add together in the middle to give a stronger field.

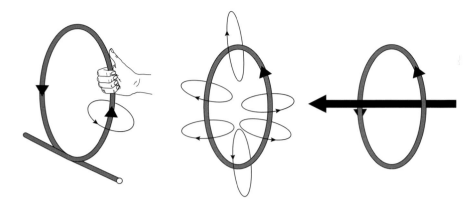

The field inside a solenoid

Figure 6.28 The direction of the field in a solenoid can be found using the grip rule on one coil.

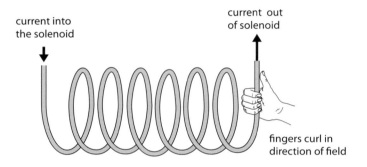

The resulting field pattern is like that of a bar magnet but the lines continue through the centre.

Figure 6.29 The field inside a solenoid.

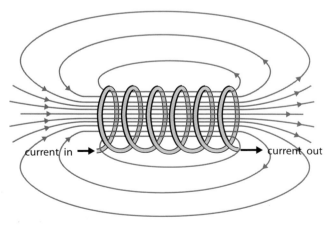

Force on a current-carrying conductor

We have seen that when a small magnet is placed in a magnetic field, each end experiences a force that causes it to turn. If a straight wire is placed in a magnetic field, it also experiences a force. However, in the case of a wire, the direction of the force does not cause rotation – the force is in fact perpendicular to the direction of both current and field.

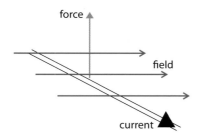

Figure 6.30 Force, field and current are at right angles to each other.

The size of this force is dependent on:

- how strong the field is – flux density B
- how much current is flowing through the wire – I
- the length of the wire – l

If B is measured in tesla, I in amps and l in metres,

$$F = BIl$$

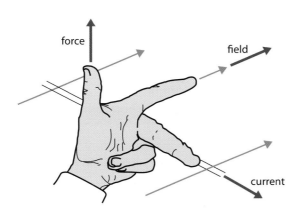

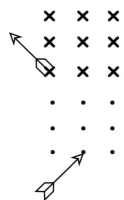

Worked example

What is the force experienced by a 30cm long straight wire carrying a 2 A current, placed in a perpendicular magnetic field of flux density 6 μT?

Solution

$B = 6\,\mu\text{T}$

$I = 2\,\text{A}$

$l = 0.3\,\text{m}$

$F = 6 \times 10^{-6} \times 2 \times 0.3\,\mu\text{N}$

$\quad = 3.6\,\mu\text{N}$

● **Examiner's hint:** Use the formula $F = B \times I \times l$

Exercises

8 A straight wire of length 0.5 m carries a current of 2 A in a north – south direction. If the wire is placed in a magnetic field of 20 μT directed vertically downwards
(a) what is the size of the force on the wire?
(b) what is the direction of the force on the wire?

9 A vertical wire of length 1m carries a current of 0.5 A upwards. If the wire is placed in a magnetic field of strength 10 μT directed towards the N geographic pole
(a) what is the size of the force on the wire?
(b) what is the direction of the force on the wire?

Charges in magnetic fields

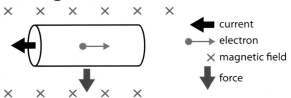

Figure 6.33 The force experienced by each electron is in the downward direction. Remember the electrons flow in the opposite direction to the conventional current.

The force on each charge q moving with velocity v perpendicular to a field B is given by the formula $F = Bqv$.

Figure 6.34 Wherever you apply Fleming's left hand rule, the force is always towards the centre.

From the microscopic model of electrical current, we believe that the current is made up of charged particles (electrons) moving through the metal. Each electron experiences a force as it travels through the magnetic field; the sum of all these forces gives the total force on the wire. If a free charge moves through a magnetic field, then it will also experience a force. The direction of the force is always perpendicular to the direction of motion, and this results in a circular path.

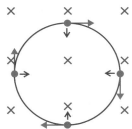

Practice Exercises

1. This question is about gravitation and orbital motion.
   (a) Define gravitational field strength at a point in a gravitational field. (2)

   The diagram below shows three points above a planet. The arrow represents the gravitational field strength at point A.

   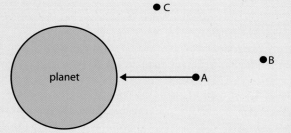

   (b) Draw arrows to represent the gravitational field strength at point B and point C. (2)
   A spacecraft is in a circular orbit around the planet as shown in the diagram below. The radius of the orbit is 7500 km.

   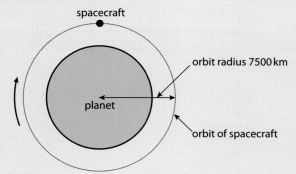

(c) For the spacecraft in the position shown, draw and label arrows representing

    (i) the velocity (label this arrow V).   (1)

    (ii) the acceleration (label this arrow A).   (1)

    The speed of the spacecraft is 6.5 km s⁻¹.

(d) Deduce the value of the magnitude of the gravitational field strength at a point in the spacecraft's orbit.   (3)

2 This question is about gravitation and ocean tides.

  (a) State Newton's law of universal gravitation.   (2)

  (b) Use the following information to deduce that the gravitational field strength at the surface of the Earth is approximately 10 N kg⁻¹.

    Mass of the Earth $= 6.0 \times 10^{24}$ kg

    Radius of the Earth $= 6400$ km   (2)

The Moon's gravitational field affects the gravitational field at the surface of the Earth. A high tide occurs at the point where the resultant gravitational field due to the Moon and to the Earth is a minimum.

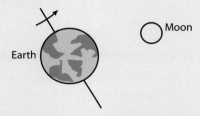

  (c)   **(i)** On the diagram, label, using the letter P, the point on the Earth's surface that experiences the greatest gravitational attraction due to the Moon. Explain your answer.   (2)

      (ii) On the diagram label, using the letter H, the location of a high tide. Explain your answer.   (2)

      (iii) Suggest **two** reasons why high tides occur at different times of the day in different locations.   (2)

3 This question is about gravitational fields.

  (a) Define *gravitational field strength*.   (2)

The gravitational field strength at the surface of Jupiter is 25 N kg⁻¹ and the radius of Jupiter is 7.1×10^7 m.

  (b)   **(i)** Derive an expression for the gravitational field strength at the surface of a planet in terms of its mass M, its radius R and the gravitational constant G. (2)

      (ii) Use your expression in **(b) (i)** above to estimate the mass of Jupiter.   (2)

7 Atomic and nuclear physics

7.1 The atom

Assessment statements
7.1.1 Describe a model of the atom that features a small nucleus surrounded by electrons.
7.1.2 Outline the evidence that supports a nuclear model of the atom.
7.1.3 Outline one limitation of the simple model of the nuclear atom.
7.1.4 Outline evidence for the existence of atomic energy levels.

The historical development of atomic theory

The electron is a fundamental particle with
charge -1.6×10^{-19} C and mass 9.1×10^{-31} kg.

We already know that matter is made up of particles (atoms), and we have used this model to explain the thermal properties of matter. We also know that matter contains charges which we used to explain the electrical properties of matter. Since matter contains charge and matter is made of atoms, it seems logical that atoms contain charge. But how is this charge arranged?

There are many possible ways that charge could be put into the atom, but since atoms are not themselves charged, they must have equal amounts of positive and negative charge. Maybe the atom is half positive and half negative?

What does it mean when we say we know these things? Do we know that this is true or is it just the model that's true?

Figure 7.1 This model could have been used until Thomson proposed the raisin bun model.

Figure 7.2 Thomson suggested that a more likely model was that the atom was like a raisin bun, with negative raisins in a positive bun.

The discovery of the electron in 1897 by J.J. Thomson led to the development of a new model.

Rutherford's model

In 1909, under the direction of Ernest Rutherford, Geiger and Marsden performed an experiment which proved that this model could not be correct either. They fired very small, fast moving particles called *alpha particles* at a very thin gold foil. If the raisin bun model were true, then this would be equivalent to firing bullets at a wall made of raisin buns. You would expect the bullets to either pass through or get stuck, but not bounce back. However, some of the alpha particles did bounce back (although most passed through).

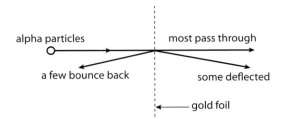

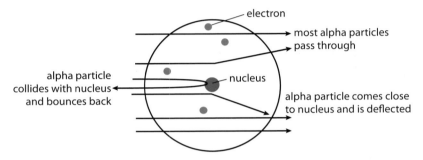

Figure 7.3
Figure 7.3 The Geiger–Marsden experiment showed that atoms are mostly empty space.

The ones that bounced back implied that the alpha particles had a head-on collision with a heavier particle; whatever this was had to be very small, since very few hit it head on. This small heavy object must also be positive, causing the positive alpha particles to be pushed away.

Sizes and masses
Diameter of nucleus = 10^{-15} m
Diameter of atom = 10^{-10} m
Mass of nucleus = 10^{-27} kg
Mass of electron = 9×10^{-31} kg
Charge of electron = -1.6×10^{-19} C

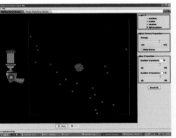

Figure 7.4 The results are explained in terms of the Rutherford model.

So the Rutherford model says that the atom contains a small, heavy positive nucleus, surrounded by negatively charged electrons. The most surprising thing about this model is that the atom is mostly empty space!

The PhET simulation 'Rutherford scattering' shows the scattering of alpha particles by atoms in the plum pudding and Rutherford models. To view this, visit www.heinemann.co.uk/hotlinks, and enter the express code 4266S and click on Weblink 7.1.

Bohr's model

In 1913 Niels Bohr developed this model, suggesting that the electrons could be orbiting the nucleus like the planets orbiting the Sun. We know from studying circular motion that for a body to move in a circle, it must experience a force directed towards the centre (centripetal force). This force is provided by the electrostatic attraction between the electrons and nucleus.

Figure 7.5 The Bohr atom

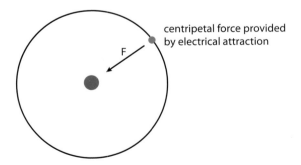

This is a good example of how physical models are adapted to take into consideration new experimental evidence.

Bohr's model also explained the connection between the atom and light. According to this model, the electrons could only exist in certain orbits. The radius of the orbit was dependent on the energy of the electrons: high energy electrons had large orbits. When the electrons changed from a high to a low energy orbit, energy was emitted in the form of light. The frequency of the emitted light was found to be proportional to the change of energy of the electron.

$$hf = E_2 - E_1$$

where h = Planck's constant = 6.6×10^{-34} m^2 kg s^{-1}

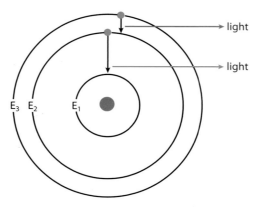

Figure 7.6 Light is emitted when an electron changes energy level.

So since blue light has the highest frequency, it must come from the greatest energy changes. If the electrons in an atom can only have certain values, then the light it produces can only have certain wavelengths. If this light is split into a spectrum (a rainbow) then it would be made up of a set of lines, one line for each wavelength, unlike a normal (continuous) rainbow.

Figure 7.7 A line spectrum and continuous spectrum.

The PhET simulation 'Neon lights and other discharge tubes' shows the emission of EM radiation by a gas. To view this, visit www.heinemann.co.uk/hotlinks, enter the express code 4266S and click on Weblink 7.2.

Line spectrum for hydrogen

The Bohr model predicts that hydrogen atoms have a certain set of possible orbits. When the electron changes from one orbit to another, it gives out different frequencies of light. If the light from hydrogen atoms is analyzed, it is found to be made up of all the frequencies predicted by the model.

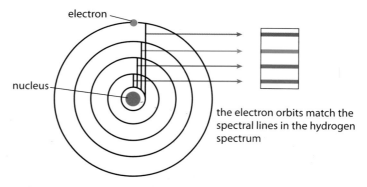

Figure 7.8 Electron level changes and corresponding wavelengths.

the electron orbits match the spectral lines in the hydrogen spectrum

To view emission and absorption spectra of elements in the periodic table, visit www.heinemann.co.uk/hotlinks, enter the express code 42665 and click on weblink 7.3.

The problem with this model was that it only worked for hydrogen. There is also another problem; if the electrons orbit the nucleus, they must be accelerating. Accelerating charges continuously give out electromagnetic radiation, resulting in a loss of energy. As the electrons lose energy they will spiral into the nucleus. This doesn't happen.

The modern model

The model we now accept is that there is a nucleus at the centre of the atom and the electrons do exist in certain energy levels, but they don't simply orbit the nucleus. The position of the electrons is given by wave equations, resulting in some interesting patterns (see photo below).

◀ Computer representation of electron energy levels.

A simple model is the *energy level model*. This model is not a picture of the atom but just represents the possible energy of the electrons.

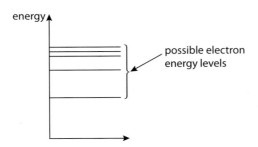

energy

possible electron energy levels

◀ **Figure 7.9** Electron energy levels.

As with the Bohr model, a change in energy level results in emission of light. According to classical wave theory, the energy of a wave is related to its amplitude, not its frequency. The modern theory of the atom makes us change the way we think about light.

The photon

Light undergoes reflection, refraction, diffraction and interference. These are wave properties, and we can therefore model light in terms of a wave and define its wavelength, frequency and amplitude. However, if light is produced each time an electron changes from a high energy to a low energy, then it would appear that light is not a continuous wave but is made up of packets. These packets are called *photons*. Each photon has a frequency that is proportional to the change in energy of the electron.

According to the law of conservation of energy, this means that each photon has an energy hf.

$$\Delta E = hf$$

A beam of light is therefore made up of a large number of photons emitted each time an electron changes its energy. The brighter the light the more photons there are in the beam.

Figure 7.10 A photon is emitted each time an electron drops an energy level.

The Aurora Borealis is caused when atoms in the air are given energy by cosmic radiation. They give out light when the electrons lose this energy.

The energy of an electron

Using the formula $\Delta E = hf$, we can calculate the energy change required to produce a photon of red light of wavelength 700 nm.

$$f = \frac{c}{\lambda}$$
$$= \frac{3 \times 10^8}{700 \times 10^{-9}}$$
$$= 429 \times 10^{12} \, \text{Hz}$$
$$\Delta E = hf$$
$$= 6.6 \times 10^{-34} \times 429 \times 10^{12}$$
$$= 2.8 \times 10^{-19} \, \text{J}$$

We can compare this energy to the energy given to an electron by a 1 V battery. Remember that potential difference V is defined as work done per unit charge ($V = W/q$) so the change in PE when an electron moves through a potential difference V will be $V \times$ the charge of the electron ($W = Vq$).

So for 1V the energy change $= 1 \times 1.6 \times 10^{-19}$ J. We call this quantity the *electronvolt*.

The electronvolt
The amount of energy gained by an electron accelerated through a potential difference of 1 V.
$1 \, \text{eV} = 1.6 \times 10^{-19} \text{J}$

To convert from joules to eV simply divide by 1.6×10^{-19}

Because electron energies are so small, it is more convenient to use the unit electronvolt than the joule.

The energy of the electron in this example is 2.8×10^{-19} J. This is $1.75 \times 1.6 \times 10^{-19}$ J, in other words 1.75 eV

It is strange to think that if you put the probes of a voltmeter into the atom you would measure potential differences of several volts.

Ionization

Ionization occurs when one or more of the electrons are completely removed from an atom, leaving a charged particle called an *ion*. This can happen if the atom absorbs a high-energy photon or the electron could be 'knocked off' by a fast moving particle like an alpha. These interactions are quite different; when a photon interacts with an atom, it is absorbed but when an alpha interacts it 'bounces off'.

Absorption of light

A photon of light can only be absorbed by an atom if it has exactly the right amount of energy to excite an electron from one energy to another. If light containing all wavelengths (white light) is passed through a gas, then the photons with the right energy to excite electrons will be absorbed. The spectrum of the light that comes out will have lines missing. This is called an *absorption spectrum* and is further evidence for the existence of electron energy levels.

Comparing energies in eV

- The average KE of an atom in air at 20°C is about 0.02 eV
  a red light photon is 1.75 eV
  a blue light photon is 3.1 eV.
- The energy released by one molecule in a chemical reaction is typically 50 eV.
- The energy released by one atom of fuel in a nuclear reaction is 200 MeV.

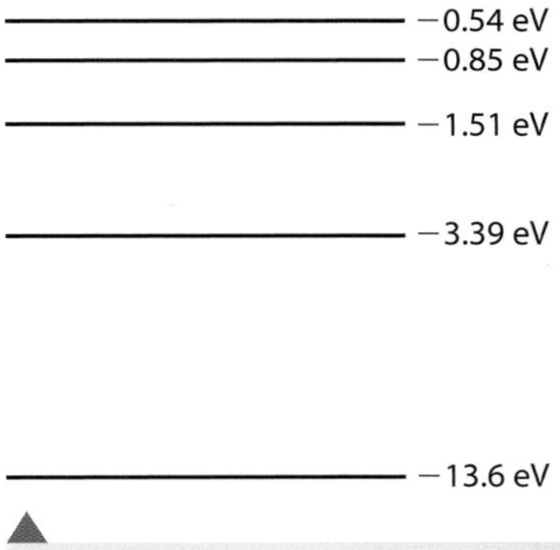

−0.54 eV
−0.85 eV
−1.51 eV
−3.39 eV
−13.6 eV

Figure 7.11

Exercises

Use the energy level diagram of Figure 7.11 to answer the following questions.

1 How many possible energy transitions are there in this atom?
2 Calculate the maximum energy (in eV) that could be released, and the frequency of the photon emitted.
3 Calculate the minimum energy that could be released and the frequency of the associated photon.
4 How much energy would be required to completely remove an electron that was in the lowest energy level? Calculate the frequency of the photon that would have enough energy to do this.

7.2 Nuclear structure

Assessment statements

7.1.5 Explain the terms *nuclide*, *isotope* and *nucleon*.
7.1.6 Define nucleon number A.
7.1.7 Describe the interactions in a nucleus.
7.3.3 Define the term *unified atomic mass unit*.
7.3.4 Apply the Einstein mass–energy equivalence relationship.
7.3.5 Define the concepts of mass defect, binding energy and binding energy per nucleon.
7.3.6 Draw and annotate a graph showing the variation with nucleon number of the binding energy per nucleon.
7.3.7 Solve problems involving mass defect and binding energy.

Masses and charges

Proton mass $= 1.672 \times 10^{-27}$ kg
Neutron mass $= 1.675 \times 10^{-27}$ kg

Proton charge $= +1.6 \times 10^{-19}$ C
Neutron charge $= 0$

Mass of the nucleus

By measuring the masses of all known nuclei it was discovered that they all have a mass that is a multiple of the same number. This led to the idea that the nucleus is made up of smaller particles. In the same way, if you measured the mass of many boxes of apples and found that the mass of every box was a multiple of 100 g, you may conclude that the mass of each apple was 100 g.

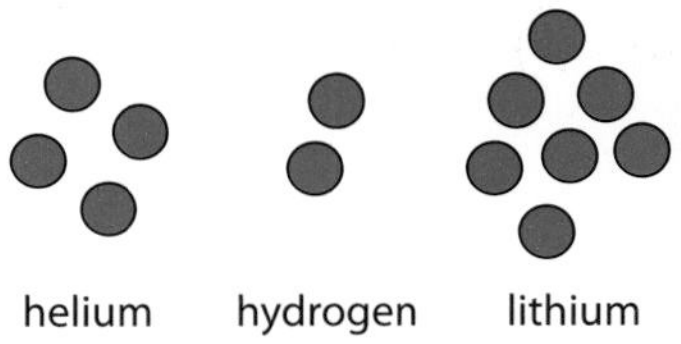

helium
hydrogen
lithium

Figure 7.12 Some different sized nuclei.

Figure 7.13 Nuclei showing protons and neutrons.

Charge of the nucleus

It is also possible to measure the charge of all known nuclei. Each nucleus is found to have a charge that is a multiple of the charge on the electron but positive. It would be reasonable to think that each of the particles in the nucleus must have a positive charge, but that makes the charge too big. It is therefore suggested that there are two types of particles in the nucleus, protons with positive charge and neutrons with no charge.

helium   hydrogen   lithium

Some quantities and terms related to the nucleus

- Nucleon
The name given to the particles of the nucleus (proton, neutron).

- Nuclide
A combination of protons and neutrons that from a nucleus.

- Symbol for a nucleus
A nuclide can be represented by a symbol that gives details of its constituents.

- Isotopes
Nuclei with the same number of protons but different numbers of neutrons (as shown in Figure 7.14).

- Nucleon number (A)
The number of protons plus neutrons in the nucleus (e.g. lithium-7). This will be different for different isotopes of the same element.

- Proton number (Z)
The number of protons in the nucleus (e.g. for lithium this is 3). This is always the same for a given element.

- Neutron number (N)
The number of neutrons in a nucleus.

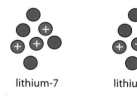

lithium-7   lithium-6

Figure 7.14 Two isotopes of lithium.

The nuclear force (strong force)

If a metal wire is heated it will readily emit electrons. However, you would have to heat it to temperatures approaching the temperature of the Sun before any neutrons or protons broke free. The fact that it requires a lot of energy to pull the nucleus apart implies that the force holding the nucleons together is a very strong force. It is therefore not surprising that when particles do come out of the nucleus, they have very high energy. We know that protons are positive, so they must repel each other. However, the nuclear force is so much bigger than the electric force that the nucleons are not pushed apart.

Although the nuclear force is strong, different nuclei do not attract each other. This means that the force must be very short range, unlike the electric force that extends forever.

Since protons repel each other, we might expect that the nuclear force would be stronger between protons than between neutrons. If this were the case, then nuclides with more neutrons would be pulled together more tightly than those with a lot of protons. But since all nuclei have the same density, this is not the case.

So the nuclear force is very strong, short range and the same for all nucleons.

Exercises

5 How many protons and neutrons are there in the following nuclei?

(a) $^{35}_{17}$Cl

(b) $^{58}_{28}$Ni

(c) $^{204}_{82}$Pb

6 Calculate the charge in coulombs and mass in kg of a $^{54}_{26}$Fe nucleus.

7 An isotope of uranium (U) has 92 protons and 143 neutrons. Write the nuclear symbol for this isotope.

8 Describe the structure of another isotope of uranium, having the symbol $^{238}_{92}$U.

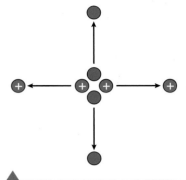

Figure 7.15 Work must be done to pull a nucleus apart; if a nucleus is put together then energy must be released.

Binding energy

The binding energy is defined as the amount of work required to pull apart the constituents of a nucleus.

If work is done, then energy must have been transferred to the nucleons. However, they aren't moving so haven't any KE, and they aren't in a field, so don't have PE.

Where has the energy gone?

Einstein solved this problem with his famous equation

$$E = mc^2$$

The energy has been converted into mass. This would imply that the mass of the particles when they are apart is greater than when they are together. If a nucleus has a large binding energy then it will require a lot of work to pull it apart – we say it is stable.

We measure nuclear energies in MeV. 1 MeV is the KE an electron would gain if accelerated through a p.d. of 1 000 000 V.

$E = mc^2$ is probably the most famous formula in the world – and Albert Einstein, definitely the most famous physicist.

The binding energy curve

It is possible to calculate the binding energy (BE) of a nucleus by finding the difference between the mass of the nucleus and the mass of the parts – this is called the *mass defect*. We can then plot a graph of BE/nucleon against nucleon number for all known nuclei. The result is shown below.

Figure 7.16 Graph of BE/nucleon vs nucleon number.

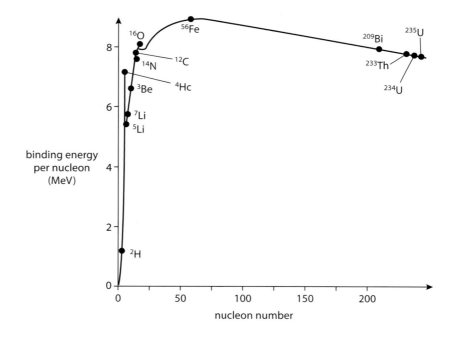

From this chart we can see that some nuclei are more stable than others. Iron is in fact the most stable, which is why there is so much of it. In nuclei where there are a lot of protons the electric repulsion tends to push them apart. This means that large nuclei are less stable, and there are no nuclei that have more than about 300 nucleons.

Figure 7.17 To lift a ball out of the bottom of a bowl we need to do work. This is just like the BE of the nucleus. When the ball is in the bowl, it does not have this energy – it is what was lost when it rolled to the bottom.

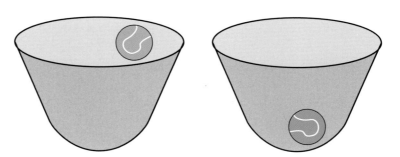

We have found that all physical systems will, if possible, reach a position of lowest possible energy. So, if possible, a nucleus will change into one with lower energy – this means that a nucleus will change to one with more BE. Remember, BE is released when the nucleus is formed, so changing to a higher BE means energy is released.

Figure 7.18 A section of the BE curve.

As we can see from the section of the graph shown in Figure 7.18, ^{233}Th has a higher BE than ^{235}U. It would therefore be energetically favourable for ^{235}U to change into ^{233}Th. However this may not be possible.

Nuclear masses			
Z	Symbol	A	Mass (u)
1	H	1	1.0078
1	D	2	2.0141
2	He	3	3.0160
3	Li	6	6.0151
4	Be	9	9.0122
7	N	14	14.0031
17	Cl	35	34.9689
26	Fe	54	53.9396
28	Ni	58	57.9353
36	Kr	78	77.9204
38	Sr	84	83.9134
56	Ba	130	129.9063
82	Pb	204	203.9730
86	Rn	211	210.9906
88	Ra	223	223.0185
92	U	233	233.0396

 Database
For a fully searchable database of all nuclides , visit www.heinemann.co.uk/hotlinks, enter the express code 4266S and click on Weblink 7.4. Click on the element in the periodic table to find nuclear data.

The table gives a selection of nuclear masses measured in u. With these values it is possible to calculate the binding energy of the nucleus.

Worked example

Calculate the binding energy of iron (Fe).

Nucleon	Mass (u)
Proton	1.00782
Neutron	1.00866

Solution

From the table we can see that the iron nucleus is made of 26 protons and $(54 - 26) = 28$ neutrons.

The total mass of the nucleons that make up iron is therefore:

$26 \times$ mass of a proton $+ 28 \times$ mass of a neutron $= 54.4458\,\text{u}$

But from the table, the mass of iron is $53.9396\,\text{u}$

The difference between these two values is $0.5062\,\text{u}$

This is equivalent to an energy of $0.5064 \times 931.5\,\text{MeV}$

$\text{BE} = 471.5\,\text{MeV}$

Since there are 54 nucleons in iron then the binding energy per nucleon is

$\frac{471.5}{54} = \textbf{8.7 MeV/nucleon}$

Remember: 1u is equivalent to 931.5 MeV.

7.3 Radioactive decay

Assessment statements
7.2.1 Describe the phenomenon of natural radioactive decay.
7.2.2 Describe the properties of α- and β-particles and γ-radiation.
7.2.3 Describe the ionizing properties of α- and β-particles and γ-radiation.
7.2.4 Outline the biological effects of ionizing radiation.
7.2.5 Explain why some nuclei are stable while others are unstable.

The nucleus can lose energy by emitting radiation. There are three types of ionizing radiation: alpha, beta and gamma. Alpha and beta emissions result in a change in the number of protons and neutrons. Gamma is a form of electromagnetic radiation, similar to X-rays. When a nucleus changes in this way it is said to *decay*.

Figure 7.19 A nucleus can emit radiation only if the result is an increase in binding energy.

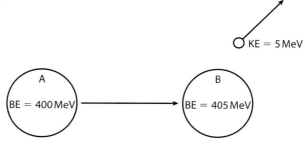

If nucleus A were made from nucleons, 400 MeV of energy would be released, but making B would release 405 MeV. Therefore if A changes to B, 5 MeV of energy must be released. This excess energy is given to the particle emitted.

Alpha radiation (α)

Figure 7.20 An alpha particle is a helium nucleus (2 protons + 2 neutrons).

Alpha particles have energies of about 5 MeV. To knock an electron out of an atom requires about 10 eV, so alpha particles can ionize a lot of atoms before they lose all their KE. This property makes them very easy to detect using a Geiger-Muller tube, photographic paper or cloud chamber. It also makes them harmful since ionizing atoms of human tissue causes damage to the cells similar to burning.

Due to their high reactivity and ionization, alpha particles have a range of only a few centimetres in air and cannot penetrate paper.

Cloud chamber track of an alpha particle. These are like mini vapour trails. The red lines are some of the electrons that the alpha has knocked off atoms in the chamber.

Effect on nucleus

When a nucleus emits an alpha particle it loses 2 protons and 2 neutrons. The reaction can be represented by a nuclear equation. Radium decays into radon when it emits an alpha particle.

$$^{226}_{88}\text{Ra} \rightarrow ^{222}_{86}\text{Rn} + ^{4}_{2}\text{He}$$

4 nucleons are emitted, so the nucleon number is reduced by 4.
2 protons are emitted, so the proton number is reduced by 2.

Energy released

When radium changes to radon the BE is increased. This leads to a drop in total mass, this mass having been converted to energy.

Mass of radium > (mass of radon + mass of alpha)

Energy released = $\{\text{mass}_{Ra} - (\text{mass}_{Rn} + \text{mass}_{alpha})\}c^2$

$\text{mass}_{Ra} = 226.0254\,\text{u}$

$\text{mass}_{Rn} = 222.0176\,\text{u}$

$\text{mass}_{He} = 4.002602\,\text{u}$

Change in mass = 0.005198 u

This is equivalent to energy of $0.005198 \times 931.5\,\text{MeV}$

Energy released = 4.84 MeV

Alpha energy

Since an alpha particle, when ejected, is much smaller than the parent nucleus, it receives almost all of the energy released in the form of KE. Since the same amount of energy is released by all decays, all alpha particles have the same energy.

Properties of alpha radiation	
Range in air	~5 cm
Penetration	stopped by paper
Ionizing ability	very high
Detection	GM tube, cloud chamber, photographic paper

Beta minus (β−)

Beta minus particles are electrons. They are exactly the same as the electrons outside the nucleus but they are formed when a neutron changes to a proton. When this happens an antineutrino is also produced.

Figure 7.21 Beta minus decay.

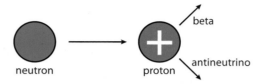

neutron — proton — beta / antineutrino

It appears that a neutron must be made of a proton with an electron stuck to it, but this isn't the case. Electrons cannot exist within the nucleus. One reason is that electrons are not affected by the strong force that holds the nucleons together, and the electric attraction between proton and electron is not strong enough to hold the electrons in place. During beta decay, the neutron changes into the proton and electron, rather like the frog that changes to a prince in the fairy tale.

Beta particles are not as heavy as alphas and although they travel with high speed they are not as effective at knocking electrons off atoms. As a result they are not as ionizing, although they do produce enough ions to be detected by a GM tube, cloud chamber or photographic plate. Since betas are not as reactive or ionizing as alphas, they pass through more matter and have a longer range in air.

A cloud chamber image of a beta track — notice it is much thinner than the alpha tracks.

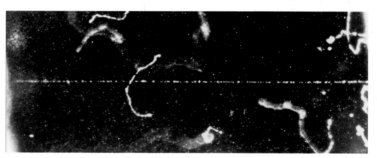

Properties of beta radiation	
Range in air	~30 cm
Penetration	~1 mm aluminium
Ionizing ability	not very
Detection	GM tube, cloud chamber, photographic paper

The neutrino

As beta particles do not all have the same energy, there must be a third particle in this reaction. This particle is the antineutrino which is the antiparticle of the neutrino. Neutrinos remained undetected for many years because they are so unreactive. In fact they can pass through thousands of kilometres of lead without interacting with an atom. They are not uncommon either; billions pass through us every second.

Neutrinos have no charge and a very small mass (almost nothing).

Effect on nucleus

When a nucleus emits a beta particle, it loses 1 neutron and gains 1 proton.
Carbon-14 decays into nitrogen-14 when it emits a beta particle.

$$^{14}_{6}\text{C} \rightarrow {}^{14}_{7}\text{N} + e^- + \bar{\nu}$$

Exercises

11 $^{45}_{20}$Ca (calcium) decays into Sc (scandium) by emitting a β-particle. How many protons and neutrons does Sc have?

12 Cs (caesium) decays into $^{137}_{56}$Ba (barium) by emitting a β-particle. How many protons and neutrons does Cs have?

Antimatter
It is also possible for a proton to change into a neutron and a positive electron plus a neutrino. The positron is in some way the opposite of an electron — it is called an *antiparticle*. The antineutrino $\bar{\nu}$ is also the antiparticle of the neutrino. Every particle has an antiparticle. Atoms made of negative positrons and positive electrons are called *antimatter*.

Gamma radiation (γ)

Gamma radiation is electromagnetic radiation, so when it is emitted there is no change in the particles of the nucleus – they just lose energy. Each time a nucleus decays, a photon is emitted. As we have seen, the energy released from nuclear reactions is very high, so the energy of each gamma photon is also high. The frequency of a photon is related to its energy by the formula $E = hf$. This means that the frequency of gamma photons is very high. Their high energy also means that if they are absorbed by atomic electrons, they give the electrons enough energy to leave the atom. In other words they are ionizing – which means they can be detected with a GM tube, photographic paper or a cloud chamber. As they pass easily through human tissue, gamma rays have many medical applications.

A cloud chamber photograph of a gamma radiation produced by a cosmic ray.

Gamma energy

Gamma photons are often emitted when a nucleus is left in an excited state after emitting another form of radiation e.g. beta.

Consider the following example of beta decay

$$^{12}_{5}\text{B} \rightarrow {}^{12}_{6}\text{C} + \beta^- + \bar{\nu}$$

The BE of ^{12}B is 79 MeV and the BE of ^{12}C is 92 MeV

The energy released during this decay is therefore:

$$92 - 79 = 13 \text{ MeV}$$

This can result in a maximum β energy of 13 MeV.

Alternatively, only 10 MeV could be given to the β leaving the nucleus in an excited state. The extra energy could then be released as a gamma photon of energy 3 MeV.

Decay chains

Radioactive nuclei often decay into other nuclei that are also radioactive; these in turn decay, forming what is known as a *decay chain*. An example of a decay chain is the uranium-235 series that starts with plutonium and ends with lead. The table below includes the isotopes at the start of this series.

Table of nuclear masses			
Z	Symbol	A	Mass (u)
94	Pu	239	239.052156
92	U	235	235.043923
91	Pa	231	231.035883
90	Th	231	231.036304
90	Th	227	227.027704
89	Ac	227	227.027752

Note:

For the alpha decays in the following exercises, you will also need to know that the mass of an alpha particle is 4.002602 u. But you don't need to include the mass of the beta since it is already taken into account. This is because the masses are actually atomic masses, which include the electrons in a neutral atom. If you add up the electrons, you will discover that there is already an extra one on the left of the equation.

Exercises

13 State whether the following are α or β-decays.
   (a) $^{239}Pu \rightarrow {}^{235}U$
   (b) $^{235}U \rightarrow {}^{231}Th$
   (c) $^{231}Th \rightarrow {}^{231}Pa$

14 In each of the examples above, use the information in the table to calculate the energy released.

Nuclear radiation and health

Alpha and beta particles have energies measured in MeV. To ionize an atom requires about 10 MeV, so each particle can ionize 10^5 atoms before they have run out of energy. When radiation ionizes atoms that are part of a living cell, it can affect the ability of the cell to carry out its function or even cause the cell wall to be ruptured. If a large number of cells that are part of a vital organ are affected then this can lead to death. In minor cases the effect is similar to a burn. The amount of harm that radiation can cause is dependent on the number and energy of the particles. When a gamma photon is absorbed, the whole photon is absorbed so one photon can ionize only one atom. However, the emitted electron has so much energy that it can ionize further atoms, leading to damage similar to that caused by alpha and beta.

Very high dose

- Can affect the central nervous system, leading to loss of coordination and death within two or three days.

Medium dose

- Can damage the stomach and intestine, resulting in sickness and diarrhoea and possibly death within weeks.

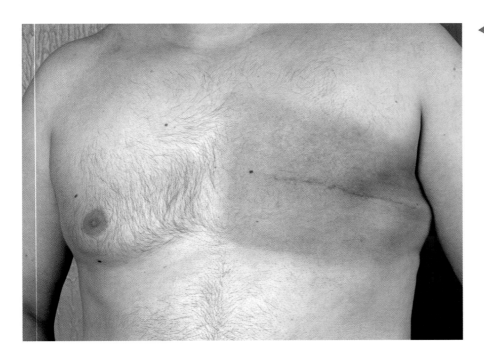

Low dose

- Loss of hair, bleeding and diarrhoea.

Safe dose

- All ionizing radiation is potentially harmful so there is no point below which it becomes totally safe. However, at very low levels the risk is small and can be outweighed by the benefits gained when, for example, an X-ray is taken of a broken leg.

 A lot of the data about the effect of radiation comes from studying the victims of the atom bombs dropped on Japan in the Second World War. Is it ethically correct to use this data?

Long term

- There is some evidence that after exposure to radiation, the probability of getting cancer or having a child with a genetic mutation increases.

Cancer

Rapidly dividing cancer cells are very susceptible to the effects of radiation and are more easily killed than normal cells. In radiotherapy, nuclear radiation is used to cure cancer by killing the cancerous cells.

Protection against radiation

There are two ways that we can reduce the effect of nuclear radiation: distance and shielding. Alpha and beta radiation have a very short range in air, so will not be dangerous a few metres from the source. The number of gamma photons decreases proportional to $\frac{1}{r^2}$ (where r is the distance from the source), so the further away you are, the safer you will be. Although alpha is the most ionizing radiation, it can be stopped by a sheet of paper (although this means that alpha is the most harmful if ingested). Beta and gamma are more penetrating, so need a thick lead shield to provide protection.

A suit designed to protect the wearer from radiation.

(7.4) Half-life

Assessment statements

7.2.6 State that radioactive decay is a random and spontaneous process and that the rate of decay decreases exponentially with time.

7.2.7 Define the term *radioactive half-life*.

7.2.8 Determine the half-life of a nuclide from a decay curve.

7.2.9 Solve radioactive decay problems involving integral numbers of half-lives.

A nucleus that can decay into another is said to be unstable; the more energy released, the more unstable the nucleus is.

It is not possible to say exactly when an unstable nucleus will decay, but if you compare two nuclei, then the one that is most unstable is most likely to decay first. It is like watching two leaves on a tree – you don't know which will fall first, but the brown crinkly one will probably fall before the green one. Staying with the tree analogy, it is also the case that the number of leaves that fall in an hour will be greater if there are more leaves on the tree. In the same way, the number of decays per unit time of an amount of unstable material is proportional to the number of nuclei.

To view a simulation of random decay, visit www.heinemann.co.uk/hotlinks, enter the express code 4266S and click on Weblink 7.5.

Rate of decay ∝ number of nuclei.

The exponential decay curve

If we start with 100 unstable nuclei, then as time progresses and the nuclei decay, the number of nuclei remaining decreases. As this happens, the rate of decay also decreases. If we plot a graph of the number of nuclei against time, the gradient (rate of decay) starts steep but gets less steep with time.

Figure 7.22 The shape of the decay curve is an exponential.

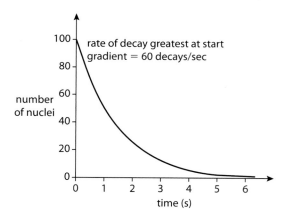

This curve tends towards zero but will never get there (it's an asymptote), so it is impossible to say at what time the last nucleus will decay. However, we can say how long it will take for *half* of the nuclei to decay – this is called the *half-life*.

An artist's impression of nuclei randomly emitting alpha particles.

Half-life

The half-life is defined as the time taken for half of the nuclei in a sample to decay.

In Figure 7.23, you can see that the time taken for the original 100 nuclei to decay to 50 is 1 second. The half-life of this material is therefore 1 second. You can also see that after each further second the number of nuclei keeps on halving.

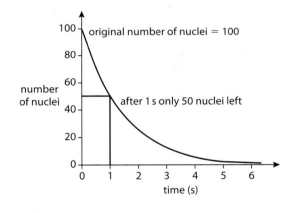

Figure 7.23 Decay curve showing half-life.

Activity

It is not very easy to count the number of undecayed nuclei in a sample – it is much easier to measure the radiation. Since the rate of decay is proportional to the number of nuclei, a graph of the rate of particle emission against time will have the same shape.

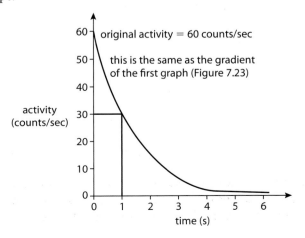

Figure 7.24 Activity *vs* time.

Becquerel (Bq)
The becquerel is the unit of activity, measured as counts per second.

Carbon dating
There are two isotopes of carbon in the atmosphere: ^{14}C and ^{12}C. ^{12}C is stable but ^{14}C is radioactive with a half-life of 5000 years. However, it is made as quickly as it decays, so the ratio of ^{14}C to ^{12}C is always the same. As plants grow, they continuously absorb carbon from the atmosphere, so the ratio of ^{14}C to ^{12}C is also constant in them. When plants die, the ^{14}C decays, so by measuring the ratio of ^{14}C to ^{12}C, the age of a piece of dead organic matter can be found.

Worked examples

Cobalt-60 decays by beta emission and has a half-life of approximately 5 years. If a sample of cobalt-60 emits 40 beta particles per second, how many will the same sample be emitting in 15 years time?

Solution

After 5 years the activity will be 20/sec.

After another 5 years it will be 10/sec.

Finally after a further 5 years it will emit 5 particles/sec.

Exercises

15 ^{17}N decays into ^{17}O with a half-life of 4 s. How much ^{17}N will remain after 16 s, if you start with 200 g?

16 ^{11}Be decays into ^{11}B with a half-life of 14 s. If the ^{11}Be emits 100 particles per second, how many particles will it emit after 42 s?

17 A sample of dead wood contains $\frac{1}{16}$ of the amount of ^{14}C that it contained when alive. If the half-life of ^{14}C is 5000 years how old is the sample?

7.5 Nuclear reactions

Assessment statements
7.3.1 Describe and give an example of an artificial (induced) transmutation.
7.3.2 Construct and complete nuclear equations.
7.3.8 Describe the processes of nuclear fission and nuclear fusion.
7.3.9 Apply the graph in 7.3.6 to account for the energy release in the processes of fission and fusion.
7.3.10 State that nuclear fusion is the main source of the Sun's energy.
7.3.11 Solve problems involving fission and fusion reactions.

Transmutation

We have seen how nuclei can change from one form to another by emitting radioactive particles. It is also possible to change a nucleus by adding nucleons. These changes or transmutations can occur naturally, as in the production of nitrogen from carbon in the atmosphere, or can be artificially initiated by bombarding a target material with high-energy particles.

Transmutation of nitrogen into carbon

Nuclide/particle	Mass (u)
^{14}N	14.0031
neutron	1.008664
^{14}C	14.003241
proton	1.007825

$$^{14}_{7}N + ^{1}_{0}n \rightarrow ^{14}_{6}C + ^{1}_{1}p$$

In this reaction, a nitrogen nucleus absorbs a neutron and gives out a proton.

Note: In all nuclear reactions, the nucleon number and proton number must balance.

Comparing the masses before and after the reaction:

Initial mass − final mass = 0.000698 u

This loss of mass must have been converted to the KE of the proton.

$E = 931.5 \times 0.000698 = 0.65$ MeV

Remember: 1 u = 931.5 MeV.

Exercises

18 In the following transmutations, fill in the missing nucleon and proton numbers
   (a) $^{4}_{2}He + ^{16}_{8}O \rightarrow ^{?}_{9}F + ^{1}_{1}H + ^{?}_{0}n$
   (b) $^{4}_{2}He + ^{121}_{51}Sb \rightarrow ^{?}_{?}I + 2^{1}_{0}n$
   (c) $^{2}_{1}H + ^{17}_{7}N \rightarrow ^{?}_{8}O + ^{1}_{0}n$
   (d) $^{31}_{15}P \rightarrow ^{?}_{15}P + ^{1}_{0}n + \gamma$

19 (a) Using the table, calculate the change in mass in Question 18 (a).

Nuclide/particle	Mass (u)
^{4}He	4.002 603
^{16}O	15.994 914
^{18}F	18.998 403
^{1}H	1.007 825
neutron	1.008 664

   You will notice that this is a negative number, which means that energy is required to make it happen. This energy is supplied by a particle accelerator used to accelerate the helium nucleus.

   (b) From your previous answer calculate the KE of the He nucleus.

Nuclear fusion

Nuclear fusion is the joining up of two small nuclei to form one big one.

If we look at the BE/nucleon *vs* nucleon number curve on page 164, we see that the line initially rises steeply. If you were to add two $^{2}_{1}H$ nuclei to get one $^{4}_{2}He$ nucleus, then the He nucleus would have more BE per nucleon.

An artist's impression of the fusion of ^{2}H and ^{3}H to form ^{4}He. ▶

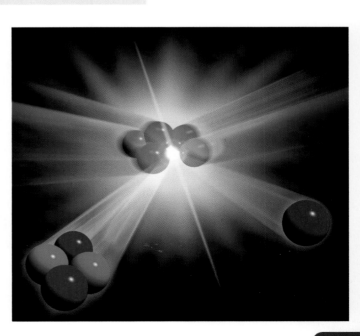

Figure 7.25 BE/nucleon *vs* nucleon number curve, showing fusion possibility.

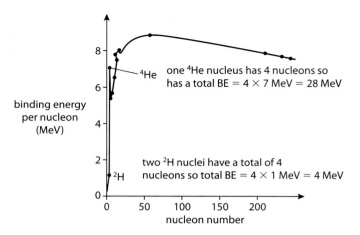

one ^{4}He nucleus has 4 nucleons so has a total BE = 4×7 MeV = 28 MeV

two ^{2}H nuclei have a total of 4 nucleons so total BE = 4×1 MeV = 4 MeV

If we add up the total BE for the helium nucleus, it has 24MeV more BE than the two hydrogen nuclei. This means that 24MeV would have to be released; this could be by the emission of gamma radiation.

Nuclide	Mass in u
^{1}H	1.007825
^{2}H	2.014 101
^{3}H	3.016 049
^{3}He	3.016 029
^{4}He	4.002 603
^{0}n	1.008 664

Worked example

Calculate the energy released by the following reaction:

$$^2_1\text{H} + ^3_1\text{H} \rightarrow ^4_2\text{He} + ^1_0\text{n}$$

Solution

If the masses are added, we find that the mass of the original nuclei is greater than the mass of the final ones. This mass has been converted to energy.

Mass difference = 0.018883 u

1u is equivalent to 931.5 MeV so energy released = 17.6 MeV

Each small nucleus has a positive charge so they will repel each other. To make the nuclei come close enough for the strong force to pull them together, they must be thrown together with very high velocity. For this to take place, the matter must either be heated to temperatures as high as the core of the Sun (about 13 million kelvin) or the particles must be thrown together in a particle accelerator.

The fusion reaction produces a lot of energy per unit mass of fuel and much research has been carried out to build a fusion reactor. You can read more about this in Chapter 8.

It wouldn't be possible to conserve both KE and momentum if two fast moving nuclei collided and fused together. That's why all the reactions result in two particles not one big one.

20 Use the data in the table on page 164 to calculate the change in mass and hence the energy released in the following examples of fusion reactions:

(a) $_1^2H + _1^2H \rightarrow _2^3He + _0^1n$

(b) $_1^2H + _1^2H \rightarrow _1^3H + _1^1p$

(c) $_1^2H + _2^3He \rightarrow _2^4He + _1^1p$

Nuclear fission

Looking at the right-hand side of the graph we see that if one large nucleus is split into two smaller ones, then the total BE would again be increased. This reaction forms the basis of the nuclear reactor that you will learn more about in Chapter 8.

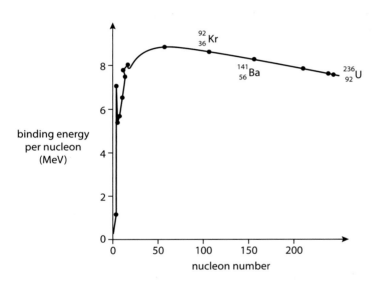

Figure 7.26 BE/nucleon *vs* nucleon number curve showing fission possibility.

Worked example

Find the energy released if uranium-236 splits into krypton-92 and barium-141.

Solution

BE of $^{236}U = 236 \times 7$

$= 1652\,\text{MeV}$

BE of $^{141}Ba = 141 \times 8$

$= 1128\,\text{MeV}$

BE of $^{92}Kr = 92 \times 8.2$

$= 754.4\,\text{MeV}$

Gain in BE $= (1128 + 754.4) - 1652$

$= 230.4\,\text{MeV}$

Since this leads to a release of energy, this process is possible.

● **Examiner's hint:** Use the graph to find the BE per nucleon.

Exercises

	Table of nuclear masses		
Z	Symbol	A	Mass (u)
92	U	233	233.039628
92	U	236	236.045563
42	Mo	100	99.907476
50	Sn	126	125.907653
56	Ba	138	137.905233
36	Kr	86	85.910615
0	n	1	1.008664

● **Examiner's hint:** To answer these questions you must find the difference in mass between the original nucleus and the products. To convert to MeV, simply multiply by 931.5.

Use the table above to answer the following questions.

21 If ^{236}U splits into ^{100}Mo and ^{126}Sn, how many neutrons will be produced? Calculate the energy released in this reaction.

22 ^{233}U splits into ^{138}Ba and ^{86}Kr plus 9 neutrons. Calculate the energy released when this takes place.

Practice questions

1 This question is about nuclear reactions.

(a) Complete the table below, by placing a tick (✔) in the relevant columns, to show how an increase in each of the following properties affects the rate of decay of a sample of radioactive material.

Property	Effect on rate of decay		
	increase	decrease	stays the same
temperature of sample			
pressure on sample			
amount of sample			

(2)

Radium-226 ($^{226}_{88}$Ra) undergoes natural radioactive decay to disintegrate spontaneously with the emission of an alpha particle (α-particle) to form radon (Rn). The masses of the particles involved in the reaction are

radium: 226.0254 u
radon: 222.0176 u
α-particle: 4.0026 u

(b) (i) Complete the nuclear reaction equation below for this reaction.

$$^{226}_{88}\text{Ra} \rightarrow \,^{......}_{......}...... + \,^{......}_{......}\text{Rn}$$

(2)

(ii) Calculate the energy released in the reaction. (3)

(c) The radium nucleus was stationary before the reaction.
(i) Explain, in terms of the momentum of the particles, why the radon nucleus and the α-particle move off in opposite directions after the reaction. (3)
(ii) The speed of the radon nucleus after the reaction is v_R and that of the α-particle is v_α. Show that the ratio $\frac{v_\alpha}{v_R}$ is equal to 55.5. (3)
(iii) Using the ratio given in (ii) above, deduce that the kinetic energy of the radon nucleus is much less than the kinetic energy of the α-particle. (3)

(d) Not all of the energy of the reaction is released as kinetic energy of the α-particle and of the radon nucleus. Suggest **one** other form in which the energy is released. (1)

Another type of nuclear reaction is a fusion reaction. This reaction is the main source of the Sun's radiant energy.

(e) **(i)** State what is meant by a *fusion reaction*.

(ii) Explain why the temperature and pressure of the gases in the Sun's core must both be very high for it to produce its radiant energy.

High temperature:

High pressure: (5)

(Total 25 marks)

2 This question is about nuclear reactions.

(a) **(i)** Distinguish between *fission* and *radioactive decay*. (4)

A nucleus of uranium-235 ($^{235}_{92}$U) may absorb a neutron and then undergo fission to produce nuclei of strontium-90 ($^{90}_{38}$Sr) and xenon-142 ($^{142}_{54}$Xe) and some neutrons. The strontium-90 and the xenon-142 nuclei both undergo radioactive decay with the emission of β^- particles.

(ii) Write down the nuclear equation for this fission reaction. (2)

(iii) State the effect, if any, on the mass number (nucleon number) and on the atomic number (proton number) of a nucleus when the nucleus undergoes β^- decay.

Mass number:

Atomic number: (2)

The uranium-235 nucleus is stationary at the time that the fission reaction occurs. In this fission reaction, 198 MeV of energy is released. Of this total energy, 102 MeV and 65 MeV are the kinetic energies of the strontium-90 and xenon-142 nuclei respectively.

(b) **(i)** Calculate the magnitude of the momentum of the strontium-90 nucleus. (4)

(ii) Explain why the magnitude of the momentum of the strontium-90 nucleus is not exactly equal in magnitude to that of the xenon-142 nucleus. (2)

On the diagram right, the circle represents the position of a uranium-235 nucleus before fission. The momentum of the strontium-90 nucleus after fission is represented by the arrow.

strontium-90

(iii) On the diagram above, draw an arrow to represent the momentum of the xenon-142 nucleus after the fission. (2)

(c) In a fission reactor for the generation of electrical energy, 25% of the total energy released in a fission reaction is converted into electrical energy.

(i) Using the data in (b), calculate the electrical energy, in joules, produced as a result of nuclear fission of one nucleus. (2)

(ii) The specific heat capacity of water is 4.2×10^3 J kg^{-1}. Calculate the energy required to raise the temperature of 250 g of water from 20 °C to its boiling point (100°C). (3)

(iii) Using your answer to (c)(i), determine the mass of uranium-235 that must be fissioned in order to supply the amount of energy calculated in (c)(ii). The mass of a uranium-235 atom is 3.9×10^{-25} kg. (4)

(Total 25 marks)

3 This question is about nuclear binding energy.

  (a) **(i)** Define *nucleon*.   (1)

        (ii) Define *nuclear binding energy of a nucleus*.   (1)

The axes below show values of nucleon number A (horizontal axis) and average binding energy per nucleon E (vertical axis). (Binding energy is taken to be a positive quantity).

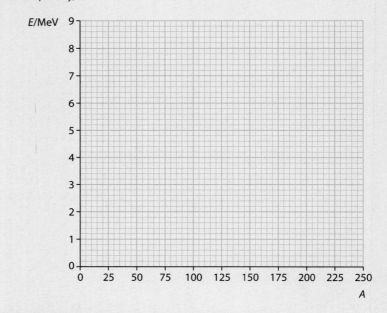

  (b) Mark on the E axis above, the approximate position of

    (i) the isotope $^{56}_{26}\text{Fe}$ (label this F).   (1)

    (ii) the isotope $^{2}_{1}\text{H}$ (label this H).   (1)

    (iii) the isotope $^{238}_{92}\text{U}$ (label this U).   (1)

  (c) Using the grid in part (a), draw a graph to show the variation with nucleon number A of the average binding energy per nucleon E.   (2)

  (d) Use the following data to deduce that the binding energy per nucleon of the isotope $^{3}_{2}\text{He}$ is 2.2 MeV.

$$\text{nuclear mass of } {}^{3}_{2}\text{He} = 3.01603\,\text{u}$$
$$\text{mass of proton} \quad = 1.00728\,\text{u}$$
$$\text{mass of neutron} \quad = 1.00867\,\text{u} \qquad (3)$$

In the nuclear reaction

$$^{2}_{1}\text{H} + {}^{2}_{1}\text{H} \rightarrow {}^{3}_{2}\text{He} + {}^{1}_{0}\text{n}$$

energy is released.

  (e) **(i)** State the name of this type of reaction.   (1)

    (ii) Use your graph in (c) to explain why energy is released in this reaction.   (2)

                                       (Total 13 marks)

8 Energy, power and climate change

Energy degradation and power generation

Assessment statements

8.1.1 State that thermal energy may be completely converted to work in a single process, but that continuous conversion of this energy into work requires a cyclical process and the transfer of some energy from the system.

8.1.2 Explain what is meant by degraded energy.

8.1.3 Construct and analyse energy flow diagrams (Sankey diagrams) and identify where the energy is degraded.

8.1.4 Outline the principal mechanisms involved in the production of electrical power.

In this section we will look at how we use energy. You already know from the law of conservation of energy that energy cannot be created nor destroyed. So we cannot make energy, we can only change it from one form to another. There are only two ways to transfer energy from one body to another – either by doing work or by transfering thermal energy. Before looking at the different ways that we utilize sources of energy, we will consider the basic physical principles behind converting the energy possessed by different sources into useful work.

Fuels

When we think of sources of energy we often think of fuels such as coal, oil and nuclear fuel. A fuel is a substance that can release energy by changing its chemical or nuclear structure. For example, when a piece of coal burns it is changing its chemical structure. As far as we need to know that means that the atoms are changing their positions; this leads to a reduction in their PE and hence an increase in their KE. The average KE is related to the temperature of the material so the coal gets hot. This is obviously great if we need heat but if we want to use the energy to turn the wheels of a machine we need an engine – coal can't do work on its own. There are many different types of engine but they all work on the same physical principles. To demonstrate this we will consider a very simple but rather impractical engine that uses a hot air balloon.

The hot air balloon engine

Figure 8.1 shows the hot air balloon engine; it might never have been made but it would work. The hot air in the balloon is less dense than the surrounding cold air so the balloon floats up in the same way that a cork will float to the top of a bowl of water. As the balloon rises, a rope attached to it turns the reel, producing

Figure 8.1 Underneath the balloon is a flame which when lit heats the air in the balloon and this drives the engine.

mechanical energy, so the balloon is doing work on the reel. The heat produced by the burning fuel is being converted to energy that could be used to turn a machine or drive a car.

The problem is that once the rope has all been used up the machine will stop. To make a continuous process you have to get the balloon down and to do that it has to lose thermal energy. If the balloon loses thermal energy and cools down it will fall back to the ground and the process can be repeated. This is true for all engines; they can only work if some thermal energy is transferred to the surroundings. You may think that if you could catch this energy then you could use it again and create a machine that kept on going forever without requiring any input of energy, a perpetual motion machine, but this is not possible.

The second law of thermodynamics

For many years scientists tried to make engines that would turn thermal energy into useful work without loss of heat. Eventually they decided that their failure was not due to bad experimental method but that it simply wasn't possible. A law was written to take this into account.

It is impossible to take heat from a hot object and use it all to do work without losing some to the surroundings.

The reason for this is all to do with the nature of matter and the way it behaves in our universe. We have seen that matter is made up of molecules and if you transfer thermal energy to a body then the molecules start to move faster. If we take the example of a block (whose temperature is 0 K) falling to the ground as in Figure 8.2, then we start with the PE of the block held above the ground and end up with thermal energy when it hits the ground. If we compare the molecules before and after, then we see that before, all the molecules had about the same energy due to their position above the ground, but afterwards the energy is spread out between the molecules in the ground and the block. Whenever energy is transferred it always spreads out, and once it spreads out you can't get it back. This is why engines cannot convert heat completely to do work and also why it is not possible to make a perpetual motion machine: energy is always lost to the surroundings.

Figure 8.2 As time progresses the energy from the dropped block spreads further and further through the ground.

before drop (same energy throughout block)

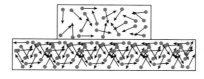

after drop (energy is spread)

Degradation of energy

We can see from the example above that energy becomes more spread out or disordered. This is called the *degradation of energy*. Thermal energy is the most degraded form of energy and we have seen that to convert thermal energy into mechanical energy we must always transfer some of the thermal energy to the cold surroundings. Once energy becomes thermal energy we can never get it all back.

All energy eventually turns to heat. Taking this to extremes means that the end of the universe will be when everything is at the same temperature; it will then be impossible to do any work.

gravitational PE
elastic PE
electric PE
kinetic energy (KE)

→ heat

Examples of energy transfer

There are many examples of devices that transfer energy from one form to another. According to the second law, energy transfer must always lead to some thermal energy being transferred to the surroundings. Let us test this with a few examples:

Light bulb – Converts electrical energy to light + heat.

Electric motor – Converts electrical energy to mechanical + heat.

Battery – Converts chemical energy to electrical + heat

Car engine – Converts chemical energy to mechanical + heat

Solar cell – Converts light to electrical + heat

Sankey diagrams

Sankey diagrams are used to visualize the flow of something, for instance the flow of water down a river or the flow of energy as it changes from one form to another. In the rest of this chapter Sankey diagrams will be used to represent different ways of producing useful energy. Here are some examples:

Figure 8.4 Sankey diagram for a car engine.

The car engine

A car engine converts the chemical energy in petrol to the KE of the car plus heat. The Sankey diagram shows 200 MJ of chemical energy in the petrol coming into the car and changing to 80 MJ of mechanical energy and 120 MJ of heat.

mechanical energy: 80 MJ

petrol: 200 MJ

heat: 120 MJ

Electric motor

An electric motor uses the energy flow from a battery to drive the motor.

In Sankey diagrams the widths of the elements are proportional to the amount of energy flowing. This can be quite difficult to draw properly for complex systems but is made easier using computer programs such as e!sankey.

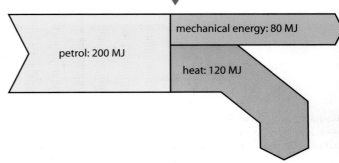

chemical: 100 J | battery | electrical: 90 J | motor | mechanical: 70 J

heat: 10 J

heat: 20 J

Figure 8.5 Sankey diagram for an electric motor.

Exercises

1 Draw a Sankey diagram for an electric light bulb.
2 Draw a Sankey diagram for a bicycle dynamo producing the electricity to illuminate a light from mechanical energy.

Generating electricity

Electricity is a very useful form of energy because it can be sent from one place to another through wires. Taking the example of heating a house; it is possible to heat a house using coal; however coal must first be transported from the coal mine to the house. This uses up a lot of energy, since trucks must be driven to each house every time they need more. It is much better to use the coal to produce electricity and send that electricity to the house through wires. Electricity can be produced from many different types of energy, and all of these methods make use of a generator to convert mechanical energy to electrical energy.

Electrical generator

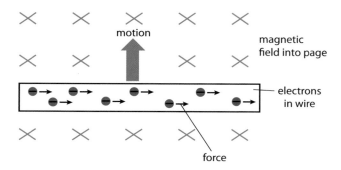

Figure 8.6 As electrons move upwards with the wire they will experience a force to the right (use Fleming's left hand rule but remember the electrons move opposite to current flow so current is downwards).

The coils of an electricity generator. Magnets fitted to a cylinder rotate inside the coils causing electricity to be induced.

The way that the current changes direction is difficult to imagine, but to see an animation, visit www.heinemann.co.uk/hotlinks, enter the express code 4266S and click on Weblink 8.1.
This makes it very clear.

In Chapter 6 you learnt about the connection between electricity and magnetism: if a charged object moves in a magnetic field it experiences a *force*. Wires contain charged objects, electrons, so if a wire moves in a magnetic field, the electrons inside it experience a force causing them to move to one end of the wire. This causes a potential difference along the wire which can be used to create current in a circuit. We say that current has been induced in the wire.

A generator uses the same principle, but instead of the wire moving in a straight line, a coil rotates in the field. As the coil rotates, its sides are sometimes moving up and sometimes down through the field. This results in a current that keeps changing direction, called an *alternating current* or AC for short. To prevent the wires from getting twisted when the coil rotates, there must be sliding contacts between the coil and circuit. However, friction between these sliding components will eventually wear away the contacts. An alternative arrangement is for the magnets to rotate inside the coils, this also results in an alternating current but has no sliding parts.

8.2 World energy sources

Assessment statements
8.2.1 Identify different world energy sources.
8.2.2 Outline and distinguish between renewable and non-renewable energy sources.
8.2.3 Define the *energy density* of a fuel.
8.2.4 Discuss how choice of fuel is influenced by its energy density.
8.2.5 State the relative proportions of world use of the different energy sources that are available.
8.2.6 Discuss the relative advantages and disadvantages of various energy sources.

Sources of energy

In this section we will look at the different sources of energy available on Earth that can be turned into useful work. From the principles of physics that we have just been looking at, we know that energy transfer always leads to the degradation of energy, so, if we want to do useful work, the energy source must be in a form that can be degraded or spread out. If we take the example of a room where everything is at the same temperature, then there is no way that we can make the energy more spread out than it is. However, if there is a red hot piece of coal in the middle of the room we can use the flow of energy from the coal to the room to power an engine. As this happens, the energy will become spread out in the room. So, sources of energy are either things that are hot like a volcano or the Sun, or things that contain ordered energy like the PE of the water in a reservoir or the chemical energy of coal.

Fuels

As mentioned before, a fuel is a substance that can release energy by changing its chemical or nuclear structure. There are several different sources of fuel available on Earth.

Coal

Coal is composed of plants that died millions of years ago. They were then covered by layers of sand and mud that squashed them into the hard black substance we call coal. For that reason it is called a fossil fuel. Whilst living, plants are able to convert the Sun's energy into plant matter by a process known as *photosynthesis*. In physics terms, the plant is reorganizing the atoms from the air plus some from the ground to make the large molecules that the plant is made of. This process requires energy and that energy comes from the Sun. To release the energy in coal, we have to burn it. This is problematic since it leads to the emission of carbon dioxide, one of the contributors to global warming.

Another problem with coal is that it has to be dug up from the ground. This was traditionally done by digging a deep hole until the coal was reached and then taking it out through the same hole (mining). With today's large machinery it is often cheaper to uncover the coal by removing all the rock above it (open cast mining), but this has a large environmental impact.

 Energy density
The value of different fuels can be measured by their energy density. This is the amount of energy that can be extracted per kg of fuel. A fuel with high energy density costs less to transport than one with a low energy density. A comparison of different energy densities is given in Table 8.1.

There is only a certain amount of coal in the ground and since it takes a long time to turn a tree into coal, the rate at which it is being used is much greater than the rate of production. Coal is, therefore, classified as a non-renewable source of energy. One day it will all be used up. However there is still a lot of coal left in the ground. In 2006 it was estimated that there was about 1×10^{15} kg of coal left, enough to meet world needs for 155 years.

Oil and gas

Although it was coal that fuelled the industrial revolution, since the 1950s oil has overtaken coal as the most important source of energy. Oil is another fossil fuel, formed from microscopic organisms that sank to the bottom of the sea when they died. Over a long period of time this organic matter was covered in sand that turned to rock and it was pressed into oil and gas. Oil and gas are easier to extract than coal since they are fluid and can be pumped up from where they lie underground. Sometimes extraction is not simple since a lot of oil reserves are in rock that is at the bottom of the sea. However, as technology has advanced, the methods of extracting oil have become more and more ingenious and it is now possible to drill for many kilometres and even go sideways from a platform that is floating in water many kilometres deep.

Like coal, oil is non-renewable and has to be burned to turn its stored energy into heat that can be used to power an engine. This makes oil another source of greenhouse gases.

It is not possible to say how much oil there is left in the Earth because technology does not yet enable accurate predictions of how much remains in the known deposits. The information is also clouded by false claims. However, based only on statistics that were 90% sure, the estimate in 2003 was around 1×10^{14} litres.

Barrels
Oil is usually measured in barrels. One barrel is equivalent to 159 litres.

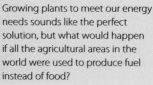

Growing plants to meet our energy needs sounds like the perfect solution, but what would happen if all the agricultural areas in the world were used to produce fuel instead of food?

Wood and biomass

The reserves of fossil fuels are not renewable so one day will run out. Living plants convert sunlight plus carbon dioxide into plant matter, so can also be used as fuel. Wood is the most obvious example of this and has been used for heating and cooking since the time of primitive man. Sugarcane and many plants that produce oils can also be used to produce what is called biofuel that can be used to run cars. It is possible to run a diesel car on the fat that you use to fry food in the kitchen. Food waste can also be used to produce fuel as can cow manure; however these are not high grade fuels.

These fuels have to be burned so that their energy can be used, which means that they also contribute to global warming. However, whilst the plants were growing, they were absorbing carbon dioxide and reducing the overall greenhouse effect.

Nuclear fuel

Unlike the other fuels mentioned above, the energy in nuclear fuel does not come from the Sun. Nuclear fuels are materials that have unstable nuclei, and when these nuclei split they give out energy. This was explained in Chapter 7. Nuclear fuel is a non-renewable resource and although it does not have to be burned and therefore does not contribute to the greenhouse effect, it gives rise to waste materials that are highly radioactive and therefore difficult to dispose of. Like coal, nuclear fuels such as uranium have to be extracted from the ground and then purified before use.

Fusion fuel

Although a test power plant has been successfully put into operation, *nuclear fusion* is not used for the commercial production of energy. The fuel is *hydrogen* that can be extracted from water. Although not renewable, there is a lot of water on the planet and only a little hydrogen is needed to produce a lot of energy (as can be seen from its energy density in Table 8.1).

Fuel	Energy density (MJ kg^{-1})
Fusion fuel	300 000 000
Uranium 235	90 000 000
Petrol	46.9
Diesel	45.8
Biodiesel	42.2
Crude oil	41.9
Coal	32.5
Sugar	17.0
Wood	17.0
Cow dung	15.5
Household waste	10

 Table 1 The energy density of materials shows the most suitable for use as fuels.

Other sources of energy derived from the Sun

Several of the fuels mentioned convert the energy radiated from the Sun into a material that can be burned. However, there are other ways that we can utilize the Sun's energy that are all renewable and produce no greenhouse gases.

Solar energy

The most obvious way of using the Sun's energy is to collect it directly. This can be done using mirrors to focus the radiation into a point. Once we have created a hot spot, the energy can be used to power an engine that can do work. Alternatively, the Sun's radiation can be turned directly into electricity using a photovoltaic cell. Using the Sun's energy in this way is only possible in countries where there is a lot of sunlight.

Hydroelectric power

The Sun heats water in the sea and turns it into water vapour; this vapour produces clouds which lead to rain. When water rains onto a mountain the water has a high PE. This energy can be made to do work as the water runs down the mountain; this is the principle of the hydro electric power station.

Wind power

When the Sun heats the atmosphere it causes the air to become less dense and move upwards. These air movements combined with the rotation of the Earth cause winds. The KE in moving air can be used to turn a turbine and produce electricity.

Wave power

The movement of the air can become very strong leading to storms; if these occur over the sea, then the water will be disturbed, leading to the production of waves. As waves spread out, so their energy spreads out, arriving at beaches all around the world. This energy can be used to power turbines and produce electricity. With present-day technology it is now becoming viable to use wave power for some isolated communities in areas of rough sea.

Sources of energy not derived from the Sun

Tidal power

Although the Sun has some influence on the tides they are mainly caused by the Moon. The reason for the tides is that the surface and bottom of the oceans are different distances from the Moon, so experience a different gravitational force, this causes the ocean to bulge outward on parts of the Earth that are closest and furthest away from the Moon. As the Earth rotates, these bulges travel round the Earth, causing the tides. This movement of water can be used to drive turbines and produce electricity.

Geothermal energy

In certain areas of the world parts of the Earth's crust move against each other, the friction between the rocks creates heat. When water runs into cracks in these rocks, it turns to steam and forms geysers on the Earth's surface. This explosive energy can be used to produce electricity.

Old Faithful, a geyser in the Yellowstone National Park, USA gives water some PE. ▶

Worldwide consumption of energy

The following graphs show what percentages of the different energy sources are used worldwide. They take into account all use of fuel, including transport. The amount of energy used depends on how much time you measure the consumption for, and for that reason the units used are watts (joules/second).

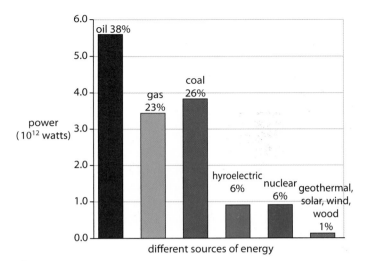

Figure 8.7 Worldwide usage of different sources of energy.

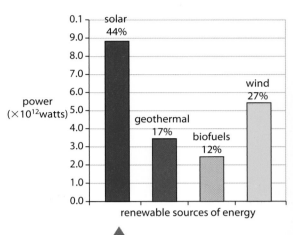

Figure 8.8 Worldwide usage of renewable sources of energy.

Worldwide consumption of electrical energy

Figure 8.9 shows the percentage of different fuels that are used to produce electricity alone.

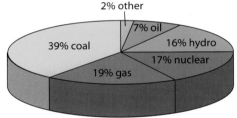

Figure 8.9 The percentage of different fuels used to produce electricity.

8.3 Fossil fuel power production

Assessment statements

8.3.1 Outline the historical and geographical reasons for the widespread use of fossil fuels.

8.3.2 Discuss the energy density of fossil fuels with respect to the demands of power stations.

8.3.3 Discuss the relative advantages and disadvantages associated with the transportation and storage of fossil fuels.

8.3.4 State the overall efficiency of power stations fuelled by different fossil fuels.

8.3.5 Describe the environmental problems associated with the recovery of fossil fuels and their use in power stations.

History of coal and oil from a physics perspective

It is known that coal has been used since the bronze age some 4000 years ago. In those days it was possible to find lumps of coal on the ground; however, early man did not have the same energy needs that we have today, so for them wood was a much more convenient source of fuel since it could be found almost anywhere. As technology advanced it became possible to extract coal from the ground by mining. However, this was a difficult and dangerous job and even though coal produced more heat than wood, it didn't become a major energy source until the industrial revolution.

In many developing countries wood is still the main source of fuel used in heating and cooking.

The invention of the steam engine

Although drawings of an early steam engine date back to the first century, they did not make a big impact until 1769 when James Watt invented a steam engine that could turn a wheel. Up to that point, steam engines had been able to move a beam up and down but the pistons did not move smoothly enough to turn a wheel. Suddenly, the possibility for powered transport became a reality and the first steam trains were on the tracks by the early 1800s. It is, of course, possible to use wood to power a steam engine but the energy density of wood is only half the energy density of coal, which means that twice as much wood is needed to do the same amount of work. This presents the biggest problem when the steam engine is used for transport, since all the fuel needs to be carried along with the engine.

Energy use of a steam train

Let us take as an example a steam engine with a power of 6000 horse power. Horse power is the unit used for measuring engine energy and 1 h.p. is equivalent to 0.75 kW.

The power of the engine is therefore $0.75 \times 6000 = 4500\,\text{kW}$

The engine will use 4500 kJ each second.

So energy used in 5 hours $= 5 \times 60 \times 60 \times 4500 \times 10^3$

$= 81 \times 10^9\,\text{J}$

The energy density of wood is $17\,\text{MJ}\,\text{kg}^{-1}$, so to produce this amount of energy will require $\dfrac{81 \times 10^9}{17 \times 10^6} = 4765\,\text{kg}$ of wood

The energy density of coal is about twice as much as wood so only half the mass of coal would be needed (2223.5 kg)

Coal is also about twice as dense which means the volume of each kg of coal is only half that of wood. The volume of coal needed would therefore be a quarter of the volume of wood. The difference is increased by the fact that wood has a very irregular shape so a pile of wood takes up a lot more space than a pile of coal.

● **Examiner's hint:** To simplify this example the efficiency of the engine has been ignored. In reality, the efficiency of a steam engine was only about 12%. This means that the amount of fuel required was about eight times more than calculated here.

The industrial revolution

The invention of the steam engine led to the possibility of the mechanization of industry and the ability to transport goods and raw materials around the world. This whole mechanization was dependent on coal as a source of energy, and since it was more economical to use the coal near its source, industrial cities grew around areas where coal could be found.

Oil (petroleum)

Oil has also been used for thousands of years but when crude oil comes out of the ground it is a thick sticky substance. Until the development of the technology to drill into the deposits and extract it with pipes, it was more difficult to utilize than coal, even though it does have a higher energy density. In 1852 when Ignacy Łukasiewicz invented a method of refining crude oil to make kerosene (a much cleaner fuel with an even higher energy density of 43.1 MJ kg^{-1}), it became possible to inject the fuel inside the piston of the engine instead of heating it from the outside. The internal combustion engine revolutionized transport; not only did it use fuel with a higher energy density but was about twice as efficient. There is also another advantage of using oil as a fuel – since it is liquid it can be easily pumped from an oil well to the place of use through pipes, with no need for costly transport. However, the fluid nature of oil does lead to one major problem: if a tanker carrying oil spills its load, the oil spreads over a large area. This has led to many environmental disasters over the past 100 years.

Generation of electricity

Until the late 1800s, the main source of household heating in industrialized countries was coal, and the main form of lighting was gas, kerosene or candles. To transport all of these fuels meant using a lot of energy and a lot of time. The way to make electricity from moving a wire in a magnetic field was discovered by Michael Faraday in 1831, but it wasn't until 1866, when Werner Siemens invented the dynamo, that electricity generation on a big scale became a possibility. When in 1884 Sir Charles Pearson invented the steam turbine, all the pieces of the jigsaw could be fitted together. Suddenly, electricity was the easiest way to transfer energy from one place to another.

Cleaning up after oil spilled from a tanker is washed up on a beach.

Exercises

3 When a car is driving at 80 km/h it is doing work against air resistance at a rate of 40 kW.
  (a) How far will the car travel in 1 hour?
  (b) How much work does the car do against air resistance in 1hour?
  (c) If the engine of a modern diesel car is 75% efficient, how much energy must the car get from the fuel?
  (d) If the energy density of diesel is 45.8 MJ kg^{-1}, how many kg of diesel will the car use?
  (e) If the density of diesel is 0.9 kg/litre, how many litres will the car use?
  (f) Calculate the litres of fuel used per kilometre.

The coal-fired power station

Cooling towers are a common sight near power stations. They are used to cool down the steam coming out of the turbine. This waste heat could be used to heat the houses nearby. This would increase the efficiency of the power station up to 70%.

Figure 8.10 represents a typical coal-fired power station. The heat from the furnace boils water in the boiler that turns into steam and powers the turbine, the turbine turns a generator and produces electricity. When the steam comes out of the turbine it is cooled, causing it to condense, and this water is then returned to the boiler.

Figure 8.10 In a coal-fired power station the coal is made into dust and blown into a furnace. This produces a lot of smoke that must be cleaned before it is released into the atmosphere.

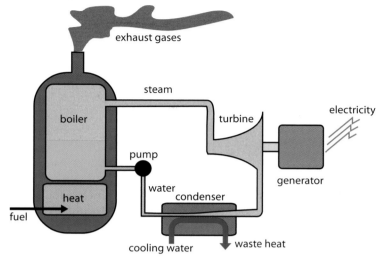

The overall efficiency of a coal-fired power station is around 40% as not all of the chemical energy from the coal gets converted to electricity. The exhaust gases from the original burning take some of the heat, as does the heat given out when the steam from the turbine condenses. There is also some friction in the components of the turbine and generator.

Figure 8.11 Sankey diagram for energy flow in a coal-fired power station.

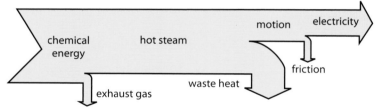

Oil-fired power station

This is the same as a coal-fired set up but oil is burnt to produce the energy needed to boil the water. Oil is a cleaner fuel than coal and is easier to transport. Using modern drilling technology, it is also much easier to get out of the ground than coal, which still has to be mined.

Exercises

4   A coal-fired power station gives out 1000 MW of power.
  (a) How many joules will be produced in one day?
  (b) If the efficiency is 40%, how much energy goes in?
  (c) The energy density of coal is 32.5 MJ kg^{-1}. How many kg are used?
  (d) How many rail trucks containing 100 tonnes each are delivered per day?

Gas-fired power station

Using gas is more efficient than using coal because there can be two stages of energy use. First, the burning gas is blasted through a turbine then the heat produced by the burning can be used to boil water and power a steam turbine as in Figure 8.13.

Power stations producing electricity from gas can be up to 59% efficient but if the wasted heat is used to heat houses, the overall efficiency can be as high as 80%.

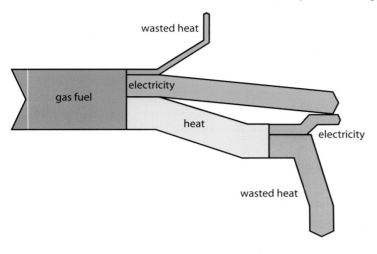

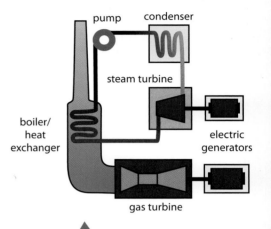

Figure 8.13 The gas-fired power station has two stages of energy use.

8.4 Nuclear power

Assessment statements

8.4.1 Describe how neutrons produced in a fission reaction may be used to initiate further fission reactions (chain reaction).

8.4.2 Distinguish between controlled nuclear fission (power production) and uncontrolled nuclear fission (nuclear weapons).

8.4.3 Describe what is meant by fuel enrichment.

8.4.4 Describe the main energy transformations that take place in a nuclear power station.

8.4.5 Discuss the role of the moderator and the control rods in the production of controlled fission in a thermal fission reactor.

8.4.6 Discuss the role of the heat exchanger in a fission reactor.

8.4.7 Describe how neutron capture by a nucleus of uranium-238 (^{238}U) results in the production of a nucleus of plutonium-239 (^{239}Pu).

8.4.8 Describe the importance of plutonium-239 (^{239}Pu) as a nuclear fuel.

8.4.9 Discuss safety issues and risks associated with the production of nuclear power.

8.4.10 Outline the problems associated with producing nuclear power using nuclear fusion.

8.4.11 Solve problems on the production of nuclear power.

The fission reaction

In Chapter 7 you learnt about *nuclear fission*; this is when a big nucleus such as ^{236}U splits into two smaller nuclei, resulting in a loss of mass and hence a release of energy.

Here is the example:

^{236}U (uranium) splits into ^{92}Kr (krypton) and ^{142}Ba (barium).

Table 2 Nuclear masses of elements with big nuclei.

Z	Symbol	A	Mass (U)
92	U	236	236.045563
56	Ba	142	141.916361
36	Kr	92	91.926270
0	n	1	1.008664

First we can use the data from Table 8.2 and calculate that if this reaction takes place the number of protons balances: $56 + 36 = 92$. But the masses don't balance: $142 + 92 = 234$.

Since the mass of ^{236}U (uranium) was 236 and not 234, two neutrons were emitted in this reaction.

The amount of energy released can be found from the change of mass:

$$236.045\,563 - (141.916361 + 91.926\,270 + (2 \times 1.008\,664)) = 0.185\,604\,u$$

This is equivalent to $931.5 \times 0.185\,604\,MeV = 172.8\,MeV$

To convert this to joules we must remember that 1 eV is the energy gained by an electron accelerated through a potential difference of 1 V.

$$E = Vq = 1 \times 1.6 \times 10^{-19}\,J$$

So, the energy released $= 172.8 \times 10^6 \times 1.6 \times 10^{-19}\,J = 2.76 \times 10^{-11}\,J$.

This energy is given to the fission fragments as KE.

One mole of uranium has a mass of 236 g and contains Avogadro's number of atoms. If a whole mole of uranium split then the energy released would be $16.5 \times 10^{12}\,J$. That is about $63 \times 10^{12}\,J$ per kg. This is a lot more energy per kg than coal.

● **Examiner's hint:** This calculation is based on all the nuclei in a pure sample of ^{236}U undergoing fission. The fuel used in a nuclear reactor only contains 3% of ^{235}U which is converted to ^{236}U by absorbing a neutron, and not all of this undergoes fission.

The chain reaction

To split a ^{236}U nucleus requires some energy because the nucleons are held together by a strong force. This energy can be supplied by adding a neutron to a ^{235}U nucleus. This actually increases the binding energy of the nucleus, but because the nucleus cannot get rid of this energy, it splits in two. As a result there are too many neutrons and some are released. These neutrons can be captured by more ^{236}U nuclei, and so on, leading to a chain reaction.

Figure 8.14 A chain reaction from nuclear fission.

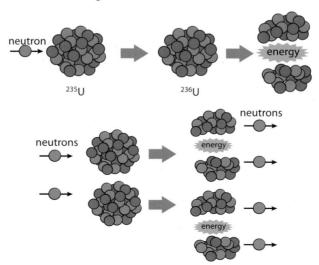

Moderation of neutrons

The chain reaction can only occur if the neutrons are moving slowly – otherwise they will pass straight through the nucleus. In fact their KE should be about 1 eV. We calculated earlier that when the nucleus splits it releases about 170 million eV, and although most of this is given to the fission fragments, the neutrons receive a lot more than 1 eV. To make a chain reaction these neutrons need to be slowed down – this is done by introducing some nuclei in between the ^{235}U nuclei. When the neutrons hit these nuclei they lose energy and slow down.

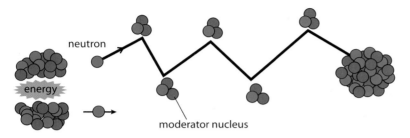

Figure 8.15 A neutron slows down as it collides with moderator nuclei.

Critical mass

Another critical factor that determines whether a chain reaction can take place is the size of the piece of uranium. If it is too small, then before the neutrons have travelled far enough to be slowed down they will have left the reacting piece of uranium. The minimum mass required for a chain reaction is called the *critical mass*.

Nuclear fuel

Uranium is taken out of the ground in the form of uranium ore and processed into a metal that is more than one and a half times as dense as lead. Natural uranium is made up of several different isotopes but 99.3% of it is ^{238}U. This is a weak alpha emitter but is not able to undergo fission; in fact, it absorbs neutrons but doesn't split, so it actually prevents a chain reaction taking place. The isotope ^{235}U is the one useful as a nuclear fuel, but this makes up only 0.7% of the metal. So, before uranium can be used as a fuel the percentage of ^{235}U must be increased in a process called *enrichment*. Uranium used to fuel a nuclear reactor has 3% of the isotope ^{235}U. The ^{238}U that is removed to increase the proportion of remaining ^{235}U is depleted uranium, a heavy, tough metal that is used for making radiation shielding and weapons, particularly armour-piercing ammunition.

For use in a nuclear reactor the fuel is made into small cylinders that are stacked together to make rods (fuel rods). There are many different designs of rod but they are typically 1 cm in diameter and several metres in length. The fuel rods are bundled together making a *fuel bundle*. A reactor will contain many of these bundles.

Pellets of nuclear fuel are stacked into tubes that are bundled together before being put into the reactor.

Plutonium (Pu)

When ^{238}U absorbs a neutron it turns into ^{239}U and this decays by giving out β radiation to form ^{239}Np (neptunium), which in turn decays again by β radiation to ^{239}Pu. Plutonium also undergoes fission and can be used as a fuel or in the manufacture of nuclear weapons. In this way, as the ^{235}U fuel is used up, it actually makes ^{239}Pu. This can be extracted and used for subsequent energy production (or bombs).

Controlling the rate of reaction

The neutrons are the key to making the chain reaction and they are also the key to controlling it. If more than one neutron from each fission goes on to make another fission then the reaction will accelerate; if less than one then it will slow down.

Loss of control: the atom bomb

The atom bomb, or fission bomb, is an out-of-control reaction. This is easy to achieve: if enough ^{235}U is mixed with a moderator, the reaction will go out of control. To stop this happening before the bomb is dropped, the uranium fuel plus moderator is kept in two halves, each half is smaller than the critical mass but when they are put together, a chain reaction starts in the combined piece. The rate of reaction required for an explosion is much greater than for a nuclear reactor, therefore the percentage of ^{235}U in the fuel must be much greater. It is possible to make a bomb with 20% of isotope ^{235}U but 85% is considered 'weapons grade'. The amount of this material required to make an atom bomb would be about the size of a soft drinks can.

Control in a nuclear reactor

The rate of reaction in a nuclear reactor is limited by the fact that the fuel contains a high proportion of ^{238}U, which absorbs neutrons. Since this cannot easily be altered it cannot be used to slow the reaction down if it goes too fast. This is done by introducing rods of a neutron-absorbing material, such as boron, in between the fuel rods.

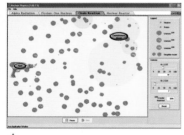

The PhET simulation 'Nuclear Physics' shows what happens when the ratio of ^{235}U to ^{236}U is changed as well as showing the effect of the control rods. To try this, visit www.heinemann.co.uk/hotlinks, enter the express code 4266S and click on Weblink 8.2.

Exercises

5 Write the nuclear equation for:
   (a) ^{238}U changing to ^{239}U
   (b) ^{239}U changing to ^{239}Np
   (c) ^{239}Np changing to ^{239}Pu.

The nuclear power station

There are many different designs of nuclear reactor but they all have a nuclear reaction at the core. The energy released when the nuclei split is given to the fission fragments (although about 10 MeV is given to neutrinos that escape). As you know from Chapter 3, the temperature of a body is related to the average KE of the atoms; this means that the temperature of the fuel increases. The hot fuel can then be used to boil water and drive a turbine as in the coal-fired power station.

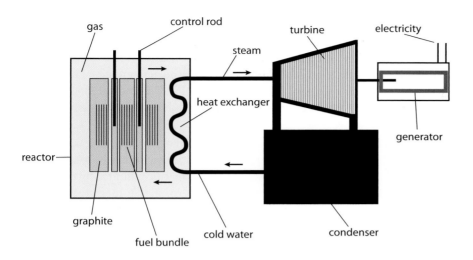

gas
control rod
turbine
electricity
steam
heat exchanger
generator
reactor
graphite
fuel bundle
cold water
condenser

Figure 8.16 An advanced gas-cooled reactor (AGR).

The nuclear reactor is the part that produces heat and contains the fuel rods surrounded by a graphite moderator (yellow). The control rods can be raised and lowered to control the rate of reaction. The nuclear reactor is housed in a pressure vessel in which a gas is circulating (blue). This picks up heat from the fuel rods and transfers it to water in the heat exchanger. This water turns to steam and turns the turbine. The steam cools down and turns back to water in the condenser and is recirculated.

Nuclear submarines
The mechanical energy can also be used directly instead of being used to make electricity. This is particularly useful for powering submarines since the reactor does not use up oxygen and only needs refuelling every 10 years or more.

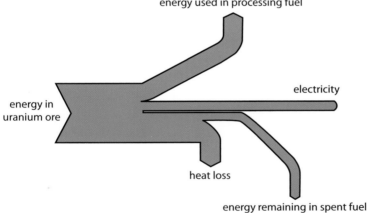

energy used in processing fuel

electricity

energy in uranium ore

heat loss

energy remaining in spent fuel

Figure 8.17 Sankey diagram for a nuclear reactor.

Wasted energy
The efficiency of the nuclear reactor is not as high as might be expected. Firstly, the fuel has to be enriched, which takes a lot of energy. Then, it is not possible to get all the energy from the fuel because when the amount of ^{235}U falls below a certain value a chain reaction can no longer be sustained.

Problems with nuclear energy

As with all forms of large scale energy production, there are problems associated with producing power from nuclear energy.

Extraction of uranium

There are several ways of getting uranium out of the ground and none are problem free. Open-cast mining creates environmental damage and underground mining is dangerous for the workers who operate the machines, especially due to the radioactive nature of the rock. Both methods also leave piles of radioactive waste material (tailings). An alternative method involves 'leaching' where solvents are used to dissolve the uranium, which is then pumped out of the ground. However, this can lead to contamination of groundwater.

Meltdown

If the nuclear reaction is not controlled properly it can overheat and the fuel rods can melt: this is called *meltdown*. When this happens the fuel cannot be removed and may cause the pressure vessel to burst, sending radioactive material into the atmosphere. A similar situation occurred in Chernobyl, Ukraine in 1986. However, it is not possible for the reactor to blow up as an atom bomb, since the fuel is not of a high enough grade.

Meltdown can be caused by a malfunction in the cooling system or a leak in the pressure vessel. It would result in severe damage to the reactor maybe leading to complete shutdown. Further damage outside the reactor is limited by the containment building, an airtight steel construction covered in concrete which, not only prevents dangerous material leaking out, but will withstand a missile attack from the outside. Improved reactor design and construction coupled with computer monitoring of possible points of weakness has reduced the possibility of any failure of the structure that might lead to meltdown.

Waste

There are two types of waste associated with nuclear power:

Low level waste

The extraction of uranium from the ground, the process of fuel enrichment and the transfer of heat from the fuel rods all leave some traces of radioactive material that must be carefully disposed of. The amount of radiation given off by this material is not great, but it must be disposed of in places away from human contact for 100–500 years.

Old reactors are another form of low level waste. They cannot simply be knocked down and recycled since most of the parts will have become radioactive. Instead, they must be left untouched for many years before demolition, or they can be encased in concrete.

High level waste

The biggest problem faced by the nuclear power industry is the disposal of spent fuel rods. Some of the isotopes they contain have a half-life of thousands of years so need to be placed in safe storage for a very long time. In the case of plutonium it would not be considered safe for at least 240 000 years. There have been many suggestions: sending it to the Sun; putting it at the bottom of the sea; burying it in the icecap; or dropping it into a very deep hole. For the moment, most of it is dealt with in one of two ways:
- stored under water at the site of the reactor for several years to cool off, then sealed in steel cylinders.
- reprocessed to separate the plutonium and any remaining useful uranium from the fission fragments. This results in waste that is high in concentrations of the very radioactive fission fragments, but the half-life of these fragments is much shorter than either uranium or plutonium, so the need for very long term storage is reduced.

Making weapons from fuel

The fuel used in nuclear reactors does not have enough ^{235}U to be used in the manufacture of atom bombs. However, the same technology used to enrich the uranium to make it into fuel could be used to produce weapons grade uranium. It is, however, plutonium that is the most used isotope in the construction of atomic weapons and this can be obtained by reprocessing the spent fuel rods.

Benefits of fission

No CO_2

The greatest benefit of nuclear power production is that it does not produce any CO_2 or other 'greenhouse gases' and so does not add to global warming.

Sustainability

Although the amount of uranium known to be in the ground would only last about 100 years if used at the same rate as today, the fact that the fission process creates plutonium, which can also be used as a fuel, extends the potential to over 2000 years. Plutonium is, however, a more dangerous fuel to handle than uranium as it is highly radioactive (decaying by alpha emission).

It is also possible to use fuels other than uranium and plutonium.

 There seem to be a lot of problems associated with the production of energy from nuclear fuel. However, these problems are not insoluble. Scientists found the way of producing the energy, so surely they can find the solutions to these problems.

Exercises

6 Barium-142 ($^{142}_{56}$Ba) is a possible product of the fission of uranium-236. It decays by β- decay to lanthanum (La) with a half-life of 11 months.
   (a) Write the equation for the decay of barium.
   (b) Estimate how long will it take for the activity of the barium in a sample of radioactive waste to fall to $\frac{1}{1000}$ of its original value.

7 Plutonium-239 splits into zirconium-96 and xenon-136. Use the table to answer the following questions.

Isotope	Mass (U)
^{239}Pu	239.052158
^{96}Zr	95.908275
^{136}Xe	135.907213
neutron	1.008664

   (a) How many neutrons will be emitted?
   (b) Write the nuclear equation for the reaction.
   (c) How much energy is released when the fission takes place?
   (d) What is the mass of 1 mole of plutonium?
   (e) How many atoms are there in 1 kg of plutonium?
   (f) How much energy in eV is released if 1 kg of plutonium undergoes fission?
   (g) Convert the answer to part f) into joules.

8 A sample of nuclear fuel contains 3% ^{235}U. If the energy density of ^{235}U is 9×10^{13} J kg^{-1}, how much energy will 1 kg of fuel release?

9 An individual uses around 10 000 kWh of energy in a year.
   (a) How many joules is this?
   (b) From your answer to Q8, calculate how much nuclear fuel this amounts to.

Fusion

As you learnt in Chapter 7, *fusion* is the fusing together of light nuclei to form larger ones. The larger nuclei have lower mass than the sum and the difference in mass is converted to energy. It certainly works as a way of producing energy – after all this is the way the Sun produces its energy.

In the 1950s fusion was thought to be the energy source of the future and all that had to be done was to solve the technical problems of confinement and sustaining the reaction, then all the energy needs of the world would be satisfied. Fifty years later these problems have still not been solved.

The fusion reactor

Experimental reactors have come very close to producing more energy than the amount of energy put in, although a commercial fusion reactor has yet to be built. The fuel of the fusion reactor is a *plasma*. This is gas in which the electrons and nuclei are separate, but if the plasma is made hot enough, the nuclei can collide with each other fast enough to overcome their electric repulsion and fuse together. The first problem is to find a way to contain plasma with a temperature of 100 million K.

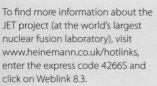

Inside the tokamak the moving charges themselves cause a magnetic field which, together with an external field produced by more magnets, holds the particles away from the walls.

To find more information about the JET project (at the world's largest nuclear fusion laboratory), visit www.heinemann.co.uk/hotlinks, enter the express code 4266S and click on Weblink 8.3.

Magnetic confinement

The way that the hot plasma is confined is by using a magnetic field. In Chapter 6 you learnt about how charged particles travel in a circle when moving perpendicular to a magnetic field. By using specially shaped magnets the plasma can be made to travel around the inside of a doughnut-shaped ring – a *tokamak*. The process is difficult to control and relies on fast computers to adjust the different magnetic fields.

Heating the plasma

Since plasma contains charged particles, it can be given energy in the same way as giving energy to electrons in a wire. Earlier in this chapter you saw how current is induced in a generator by moving a coil through a magnetic field. In the tokamak instead of moving the wire through the field, the field is changed in such a way as to make the charges move faster around the doughnut.

Burning plasma

When you burn wood on a fire you only need to light it once and the burning wood sets fire to any new wood. It wouldn't be good if you had to light the fire every time a new piece of wood was added; however, this is the problem with fusion reactors so far. The energy comes in bursts: each time new plasma is added, the input of energy needed to raise the temperature sufficiently for the nuclei to fuse is huge.

The fusion bomb

The complete theory of how a fusion bomb works is a military secret. Who owns knowledge?

The fusion bomb, or hydrogen bomb, uses a conventional fission bomb to create enough heat and at the same time compress nuclei so they fuse together. This gives out a huge amount of energy but it is not controllable.

The Sun

The Sun is often described as a burning ball of gas. By measuring the spectrum of the light that is emitted by the Sun we know that it is made of helium and hydrogen. It does not burn in the way that coal burns, but the thermal energy is generated by a fusion reaction. The temperature of the outer part of the Sun, the bit we see, is only 6000 K and not hot enough for fusion to take place. The fusion reaction takes place in the much hotter and denser core (Figure 8.18).

How do we know the temperature of the Sun?
The outer part of the Sun gives out light and its the temperature can be calculated from the wavelength of this light. However, this method can't be used for the core, but if we assume that the energy is coming from a fusion reaction, it is possible to calculate the temperature that must be achieved for this reaction to take place.

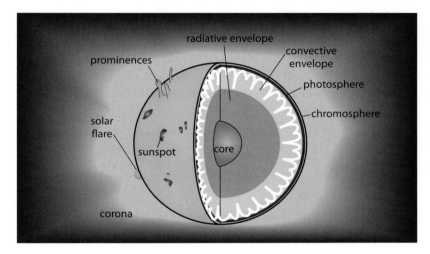

Figure 8.18 The layers and parts of the Sun.

The core

The core of the Sun is a very dense ball of plasma at an estimated temperature of 15million K (if it wasn't this hot it would collapse due to the gravitational force pulling all the particles together). The fusion reaction is the only energy source that we know of that could produce enough energy to maintain this temperature. It has several stages that take place over a long period of time (Figure 8.19).

Figure 8.19 The energy from the proton-proton chain of the fusion reaction in the core of the Sun radiates through the other layers.

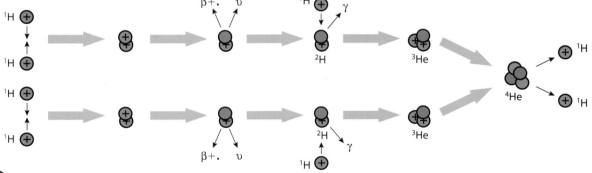

(8.5) Solar power

Assessment statements

8.4.12 Distinguish between a photovoltaic cell and a solar heating panel.

8.4.13 Outline reasons for seasonal and regional variations in the solar power incident per unit area of the Earth's surface.

8.4.14 Solve problems involving specific applications of photovoltaic cells and solar heating panels.

Energy from the Sun

The energy in the form of electromagnetic radiation that is emitted from the Sun in each second is 3.90×10^{26} J. This energy spreads out, and by the time it reaches the Earth, the energy is spread out over a sphere with a radius equal to the Earth's orbital radius of 1.5×10^{11} m. The power per m², or intensity, is therefore:

$$\frac{3.90 \times 10^{26}}{4\pi \times (1.5 \times 10^{11})^2} = 1380 \text{ W m}^{-2}$$

This is called the *solar constant*.

The amount that reaches the surface of the Earth depends upon how much atmosphere it has to travel through.

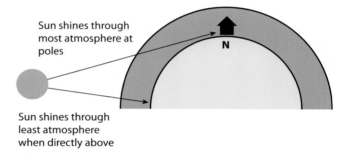

Sun shines through most atmosphere at poles

N

Sun shines through least atmosphere when directly above

Figure 8.20 Variation of Sun's intensity with latitude. ▶

Figure 8.20 shows how the intensity varies with latitude. It is also less intense when rising and setting.

When the Sun's radiation lands on the Earth's surface it is either absorbed, causing the surface to get hot, or it is reflected. The amount absorbed depends on the colour of the object. Black/dull objects absorb more radiation than white/shiny ones. So we should use black objects to collect the Sun's radiation.

There are two common ways of using the Sun's energy: either to heat something or to make electricity.

The solar heating panel

A solar heating panel can be used for central heating or for making hot water for household use. They are placed on the roofs of houses (Figure 8.21).

Figure 8.21 A solar heating panel allows radiation from the Sun to enter but prevents the radiation from the warm pipes escaping. This is called the greenhouse effect. ▶

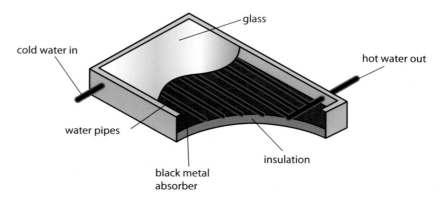

glass

cold water in

hot water out

water pipes

insulation

black metal absorber

Solar radiation enters the panel through the glass cover, is absorbed by a black metal plate which gets hot and in turn makes the water hot by conduction. Water is continuously circulated so that, as the water gets hot, it flows out and more cold water flows in.

Photovoltaic cell (solar cell)

The photovoltaic cell converts solar radiation into electrical energy. In simple terms, the semiconductors in a photovoltaic cell release electrons when photons of light are absorbed. If different types of semiconductor are placed together then this creates an electrical field that will cause these freed electrons to flow in an external circuit. It's a bit like a battery but light energy rather than chemical energy is converted to electrical energy. The potential difference (pd) and current produced by a single photovoltaic cell is only small, so many cells are usually connected together and can be used to produce power commercially.

 Positioning of solar panels
Solar panels are positioned so that they absorb maximum sunlight in the middle of the day. On the Equator the Sun is directly overhead at midday so the panels are placed horizontally, but in other countries the position of the Sun changes with the seasons, so a compromise has to be made. In countries with bad weather (lots of clouds) the position is not so important because the sunlight does not come from one direction (it is said to be diffuse).

The position of solar panels depends on the amount and direction of sunlight as well as the design of the building and other considerations. Solar heating panels on top of houses in Antalya.

Exercises

10 A 4 m² solar heating panel is positioned in a place where the intensity of the Sun is 1000 W m⁻².
   (a) What is the power incident on the panel?
   (b) If it is 50% efficient, how much energy is absorbed per second?
   (c) If 1 litre (1 kg) of water flows through the system in 1 minute, by how much will its temperature increase? (Specific heat capacity of water = 4 200 J kg⁻¹ °C⁻¹)

11 A photovoltaic cell of 1 cm² is placed in a position where the intensity of the Sun is 1000 W m⁻².
   (a) If it is 15% efficient, what is the power absorbed?
   (b) If the potential difference across the cell is 0.5 V, how much current is produced? (Remember Power = IV)
   (c) If 10 of these cells were placed in series, what would the total potential difference be?
   (d) If 10 of these cells were placed in parallel, what would the current be?
   (e) How many of these cells would you need to produce 100 W?

12 Draw a Sankey diagram for a photovoltaic cell.

 ## 8.6 Hydroelectric power

Assessment statements
8.4.15 Distinguish between different hydroelectric schemes.
8.4.16 Describe the main energy transformations that take place in hydroelectric schemes.
8.4.17 Solve problems involving hydroelectric schemes.

Energy from water

It may not be obvious at first, but the energy converted into electrical energy by hydroelectric power stations comes originally from the Sun. Heat from the Sun turns water into water vapour, forming clouds. The clouds are blown over the land and the water vapour turns back into water as rain falls. Rain water falling on high ground has PE that can be converted into electricity (see Figure 8.22). Some countries like Norway have many natural lakes high in the mountains and the energy can be utilized by simply drilling into the bottom of the lake. In other countries rivers have to be dammed.

The Hoover Dam in Colorado can generate 1.5×10^9 watts.

The energy stored in a lake at altitude is gravitational PE. This can be calculated from the equation: $PE = mgh$ where h is the height difference between the outlet from the lake and the turbine. Since not all of the water in the lake is the same height, the average height is used (this is assuming the lake is rectangular in cross section).

Figure 8.22 The main components in a hydroelectric power station.

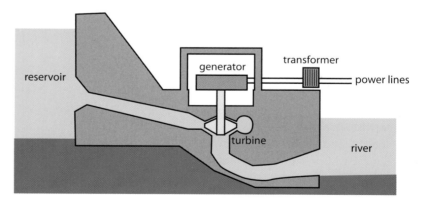

Worked example

Figure 8.23

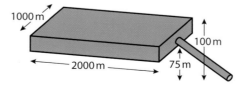

Calculate the total energy stored and power generated if water flows from the lake at a rate of 1 m³ per second.

Solution

The average height above the turbine is

$$\frac{(100 + 75)}{2} = 87.5\,\text{m}$$

Volume of the lake $= 2000 \times 1000 \times 25 = 5 \times 10^7\,\text{m}^3$

Mass of the lake $=$ volume $\times$ density $= 5 \times 10^7 \times 1000$

$= 5 \times 10^{10}\,\text{kg}$

PE $= mgh = 5 \times 10^{10} \times 9.8 \times 87.5 = \mathbf{4.29 \times 10^{13}\,J}$

If the water flows at a rate of 1 m³ per second then 1000 kg falls 87.5 m per second

So the energy lost by the water $= 1000 \times 9.8 \times 87.5 = 875\,000\,\text{J}\,\text{s}^{-1}$

Power = 875 kW

Pumped storage schemes

Most countries produce electricity from a variety of sources such as burning fossil fuel, nuclear power and hydroelectric power. At night when demand is low, it is possible to turn off the hydroelectric power, but if you put out the fire in a coal-fired station it takes a long time to get hot again. The excess power produced from coal-fired power stations can be used to pump water up into a reservoir which can be used to drive the turbines in the daytime. In the long run, this reduces the amount of fossil fuel that needs to be burnt.

Run-of-the-river power stations

One of the big problems with hydroelectric power in countries without mountain lakes is the need to dam river valleys to create a difference in height to drive the turbines. Run-of-the-river power stations use water that has been diverted from a fast-flowing river without damming the river.

Small is good

Whenever electrical energy is produced it must be transmitted through wires to the place where it will be used. However, passing current through wires results in energy loss because the wires get hot. To reduce this loss, it is quite common for factories that are dependent on large amounts of electrical power, e.g. the production of aluminium, to be sited next to power stations. An alternative approach is to build small-scale power stations near to where people live.

Tidal power

Where there is a big difference between high and low tide, the tidal flow can be used to drive turbines and produce hydroelectric power. One way to do this is to build a dam or barrage across a river estuary. The water is held back as it flows in and out of the estuary and then released to drive turbines. An alternative is to fix turbines to the bottom of the estuary and allow the free flowing water to turn them.

The tidal barrage at Rance in France. After water has flowed into the estuary on the incoming sea tide it is held back and then released through 24 turbines producing 240 MW. The tidal range is up to 13.5 m.

Exercises

13 The Hoover Dam is 221 m high with an area of 694 km².
  (a) Estimate the mass of water in the dam.
  (b) How much PE is stored in this water?
  (c) The Hoover Dam can produce 1.5×10^9 W of electricity. If the power station is 80% efficient how much PE must be lost per second from the water to produce this power?
  (d) What mass of water must flow though the turbines each second to produce this power?

14 A mountain hut has 4×50 W light bulbs, a 1 kW electric heater and a 2 kW cooker.
  (a) Calculate the total power consumed if all appliances are in use.
  (b) Outside the hut is a 5 m high waterfall. The owner is interested in building a small hydro generator. How many kg of water must flow per second to generate enough power? (Assume 100% efficiency.)

8.7 Wind power

Assessment statements
8.4.18 Outline the basic features of a wind generator.
8.4.19 Determine the power that may be delivered by a wind generator, assuming that the wind KE is completely converted into mechanical KE, and explain why this is impossible.
8.4.20 Solve problems involving wind power.

Wind

Using the wind as a source of energy is nothing new; it is over a thousand years since their first known use in Persia was recorded. In those days windmills were used to grind (or mill) corn (hence the name); now they are used to generate electricity. The energy in the wind originates from the Sun. In simple terms the Sun heats the air which becomes less dense and rises, leaving an area of low pressure close to the Earth. Surrounding air will move into this low pressure area and this air movement is the wind. The rotation of the Earth causes this moving air to move in a circular pattern, causing the weather systems that we are familiar with.

Here we have only touched on the basic physical principles behind wind production. The complete picture is far more complicated. In fact, to apply our kinetic model of a gas to the movements of air around the world would be rather pointless. In these situations a systems approach is much simpler.

Coastal winds

Coastal areas are particularly windy due to the different rates of heating of the land and the sea. During the day, when the Sun is shining, the land and sea absorb energy and get hot. The sea has a bigger specific heat capacity than the land so the temperature of the sea does not rise by as much as the temperature of the land ($Q = mc\Delta T$). The result is that the air above the land rises and this causes a low pressure that allows the air above the sea to flow in. At night the reverse happens, when the land cools down more quickly than the sea.

Figure 8.24 Flow of coastal winds during the day

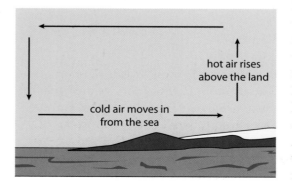

Katabatic winds

A katabatic wind is formed when a high pressure is caused by cold air pressing down at the top of a mountain, resulting in air flowing downhill. An example of this regularly takes place when cold air from the Alps and Massif Central areas in France descend towards the Mediterranean coast. Funnelling by the Rhone valley causes the air to speed up as it reaches the sea, causing a strong wind called the Mistral.

The wind turbine

Wind turbines are rather like a fan or the propeller of an aeroplane, except they are moved by the air rather than making the air move. These large turbines are often grouped together in wind farms.

Energy calculation for a wind turbine

Wind has energy in the form of KE. This enables the wind to do work against the turbine which turns a generator creating electrical energy. To calculate how much energy there is in the wind, we consider a cylinder of air with a radius the same as the radius of the turbine as shown in Figure 8.25.

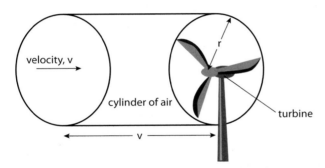

If the velocity of air is v then in 1 s it will move a distance v. The volume of air passing by the turbine per second is therefore $v \times \pi r^2$ where r is the length of one of the turbine blades.

The mass of this cylinder of air, $m = \rho v \pi r^2$ where ρ is the density of air.

The KE of this air $= \frac{1}{2}mv^2 = \frac{1}{2}\rho v \pi r^2 v^2 = \frac{1}{2}\rho \pi r^2 v^3$.

Since this is the KE of air moving past the turbine per second it gives us the power in the wind.

The wind doesn't stop after passing the turbine so not all of this energy is turned into electricity. The maximum theoretical percentage of the wind's energy that can be extracted using a turbine is 59%.

Windy places

The best place to put a wind turbine is obviously in a windy place. However, wind speed isn't the only consideration. It is also important that the wind is fairly regular so that the turbine doesn't have to keep changing its orientation. Another factor is how easy it is to lay power lines to the turbine and how easy it is to build the turbine in that position. The main problems associated with wind power are that the turbines often need to be built in areas of natural beauty and that they are unreliable – when the wind stops they produce no electricity.

A wind turbine with the generator on top of the tower in order to reduce the number of moving parts and hence energy loss due to friction.

Figure 8.25 Energy from air approaching a wind turbine

 Wind power in Denmark
Denmark produces 20% of its electricity from wind power. This is because Denmark has a long flat windy coastline that is ideal for building wind farms.

To find more information about wind power in Denmark, visit www.heinemann.co.uk/hotlinks, enter the express code 4266S and click on Weblink 8.4.

Exercises

15 A turbine with a turbine blade length of 54 m is operated in a wind of speed 10 m s⁻¹. The density of air is 1.2 kg m⁻³.

(a) How much power is in the wind passing through the turbine?
(b) How much electrical power can be generated if the turbine is 20% efficient?
(c) If the wind speed increased to 15 m s⁻¹, how much power would be produced?

8.8   Wave power

Assessment statements

8.4.21   Describe the principle of operation of an oscillating water column (OWC) ocean-wave energy converter.
8.4.22   Determine the power per unit length of a wavefront, assuming a rectangular profile for the wave.
8.4.23   Solve problems involving wave power.

Waves

If you have ever watched waves crashing into a beach on a stormy day you will have realised that there is a lot of energy transmitted in water waves. Waves in the sea are caused by winds disturbing the surface of the water; these winds can be local, in which case the waves tend to be small and with a short wavelength. The big powerful rolling waves favoured by surfers originate way out in the deep ocean. The weather map in Figure 8.26 shows the typical situation that would cause big waves to arrive at the surfing beaches of western Europe.

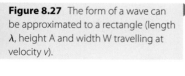

Figure 8.26 In this weather map the low pressure system in the middle of the Atlantic is a storm. This will create waves that travel towards Europe. The amount of energy carried by the waves is directly related to the duration of the storm.

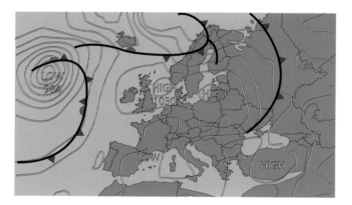

Power in a water wave

Calculating the power in a wave is quite difficult but we can make an estimate if we simplify the situation. The energy in a wave alternates between PE as the water is lifted up, and KE as it falls.

Figure 8.27 The form of a wave can be approximated to a rectangle (length λ, height A and width W travelling at velocity *v*).

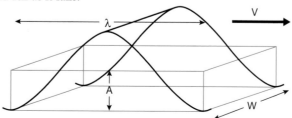

The PE of this mass of water is given by PE = mgh

where h = the average height of the wave = $\dfrac{A}{2}$

so PE = $\dfrac{mgA}{2}$

But if the density of water = ρ

then $m = \rho \times$ volume = $\rho \times \lambda AW$

so PE = $\dfrac{\rho \lambda AWgA}{2} = \dfrac{\rho \lambda WgA^2}{2}$

Power = energy per unit time, so if the waves arrive every T seconds then

power = $\dfrac{\rho \lambda WgA^2}{2T}$

But $\dfrac{\lambda}{T}$ = wave velocity, v

so power = $\dfrac{\rho v WgA^2}{2}$

The power per unit length of wavefront is therefore $\dfrac{\rho vgA^2}{2}$

Generating electricity from water waves

The oscillating water column

The principle of the oscillating water column is shown in Figure 8.28 and consists of a column that is half full of water, such that when a wave approaches it pushes water up the column. This compresses the air that occupies the top half, pushing it through a turbine which drives an electric generator. The turbine is specially designed so that it also turns when the water drops back down the column, pulling air into the chamber.

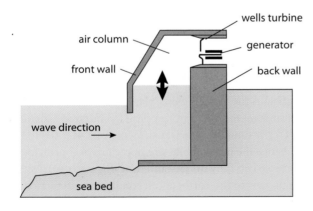

wells turbine
air column
generator
front wall
back wall
wave direction
sea bed

Figure 8.28 The main components of an oscillating water column generator.

Pelamis

The pelamis is named after a sea snake because that's what it looks like. Each pelamis is made of four sections with a total length of 150 m. Each section is hinged, and when a wave passes it bends. The bending drives pumps that move fluid back and forth, powering electrical generators. A pelamis can generate 750 kW of electricity.

To find out more about wave power, visit www.heinemann.co.uk/hotlinks, enter the express code 4266S and click on Weblink 8.5.

Figure 8.29 The four sections of a single pelamis.

16 Waves of amplitude of 1 m roll onto a beach at a rate of one every 12 s. If the wavelength of the waves is 120 m, calculate
  (a) the velocity of the waves
  (b) how much power there is per metre along the shore
  (c) the power along a 2 km length of beach.

The greenhouse effect

Assessment statements
8.5.1   Calculate the intensity of the Sun's radiation incident on a planet.
8.5.2   Define *albedo*.
8.5.3   State factors that determine a planet's albedo.
8.5.4   Describe the greenhouse effect.
8.5.5   Identify the main greenhouse gases and their sources.
8.5.6   Explain the molecular mechanisms by which greenhouse gases absorb infrared radiation.
8.5.7   Analyse absorption graphs to compare the relative effects of different greenhouse gases.
8.5.8   Outline the nature of black-body radiation.
8.5.9   Draw and annotate a graph of the emission spectra of black bodies at different temperatures.
8.5.10   State the Stefan-Boltzmann law and apply it to compare emission rates from different surfaces.
8.5.11   Apply the concept of emissivity to compare the emission rates from the different surfaces.
8.5.12   Define surface heat capacity C_s.
8.5.13   Solve problems on the greenhouse effect and the heating of planets using a simple energy balance climate model.

The greenhouse effect is the warming of a planet due its atmosphere allowing in ultraviolet radiation from the Sun, but trapping the infrared radiation emitted by the warm Earth. This is similar to the way that the glass of a greenhouse warms the plants inside, hence the name. There are many physical principles that need to be explained before we can fully understand how this effect works: firstly, how the energy from the Sun gets to the Earth; and secondly, the interaction between this energy and the atmosphere.

Solar radiation

As explained in an earlier section, the Sun radiates 3.9×10^{26} joules per second. This energy spreads out in a sphere. By the time it reaches the Earth at a distance of 1.5×10^{11} m, the power per m^2 (or intensity) is $\dfrac{3.9 \times 10^{26}}{4\pi \times (1.5 \times 10^{11})^2} = 1380\,\text{W m}^{-2}$

The intensity of radiation at each planet is related to its distance from the Sun: Mercury, the closest planet, receives more power per m^2 than Neptune, the furthest.

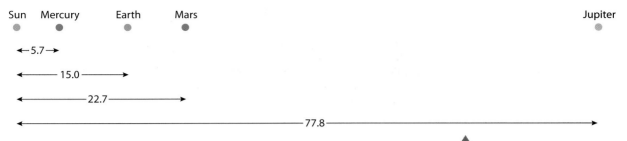

Sun   Mercury   Earth   Mars   Jupiter

←5.7→

←——— 15.0 ———→

←———— 22.7 ————→

←———————————— 77.8 ————————————→

Figure 8.30 The solar system with planet orbits drawn to scale. The size of the planets and the Sun are not to scale – they would be much smaller. The units are 10^{10} m.

Exercises

17 Calculate the intensity of the Sun's radiation on the surface of
(a) Mercury
(b) Jupiter.

Interaction between light and matter

Exciting electrons

The light that comes from the Sun is made up of photons of many different wavelengths. When a photon interacts with an atom, it can give energy to the atom by exciting one of its electrons into a higher energy level, as explained in Chapter 7. This can only happen if the energy of the photon is exactly the same as the energy needed to excite the electron, and when it happens the photon disappears. This can be reversed, and an electron that has been excited into a higher energy level can give a photon back out again, when the electron goes back to its original energy level. This is what happens when light is scattered by the atmosphere.

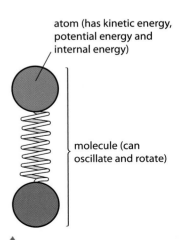

Figure 8.31 Different wavelengths excite electrons to different energy levels.

Ionization

If the photon is of high frequency and therefore high energy (remember $E = hf$) then an absorbed photon can cause an electron to be ejected from an atom. This is called *ionization*. When this happens the energy of the photon doesn't have to be an exact value, just big enough to get the electron away from the atom.

Excitation of molecules

In previous chapters we have mainly been interested in individual atoms rather than molecules. However, to understand the greenhouse effect we must look at how molecules can absorb a photon. A molecule is made of several atoms held together by the electromagnetic force. A simple model would be two balls joined together with a spring as in Figure 8.32. According to what you have learnt in this course, a single ball can only have three types of energy, kinetic due to its movement, potential due to its position and, thirdly, internal energy. If you consider the balls in the figure, they can also be made to oscillate or rotate. If the frequency of oscillation of a molecule is the same as the frequency of a photon, then the molecule can absorb the photon. This causes the molecules to move more and hence have a higher temperature. This is an example of resonance. The frequencies that cause this sort of vibration tend to be quite low, in the infrared region of the spectrum.

atom (has kinetic energy, potential energy and internal energy)

molecule (can oscillate and rotate)

Figure 8.32 A simple model of atoms in a molecule.

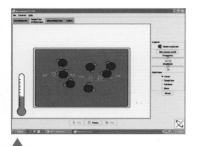

The PhET simulation 'Microwaves' shows how water molecules are excited by microwave radiation. To view, visit www.heinemann.co.uk/hotlinks, enter the express code 4266S and click on Weblink 8.6.

Interaction with solids

When dealing with electron energy levels in Chapter 7, we were considering individual atoms. However, a solid is made up of many atoms that interact with each other. When this happens the electrons no longer have to exist in special (discrete) energy levels but they can have many different energies, and these different energies form bands. This means that solids can absorb many different wavelengths of light rather than just a few special ones. Another consequence of this structure is that it is easier for the energy absorbed by the electrons to be passed on to the atoms, resulting in an increased temperature. When the molecules of a solid are given energy, they can vibrate and give out low frequency radiation. So when light is absorbed, it causes a solid to get hot, resulting in the emission of infrared radiation.

Albedo

When electromagnetic radiation is incident on a surface it is either absorbed, causing the surface to get hot, or it is reflected. The ratio of reflected to incident radiation is called the *albedo*. The albedo for snow is high (90%) since it reflects most of the radiation incident on it, whereas a dark forest has a low albedo of around 10%. The average for the planet Earth including its atmosphere is 30%.

Black body radiation

Figure 8.33 A continuous spectrum from a solid and the line spectrum for the gas hydrogen.

As mentioned previously, due to their atomic structure, solids can absorb many different wavelengths of radiation: for the same reason, if a solid is heated it will emit a wide range of frequencies. If we observe the spectrum of light from a solid we see it is continuous because it is made up of many wavelengths. The spectrum from a low pressure gas, on the other hand, consists of just a few lines as in Figure 8.33.

A black object is an object that absorbs all wavelengths, and if heated, it will emit all wavelengths, too. However, not all frequencies will be equally intense. The spectrum for light emitted from a black body is shown in Figure 8.34. The peak of this graph represents the most intense part of the spectrum; this is dependent on the temperature of the body (T). The hotter it is the shorter wavelength this will be. This wavelength (λ_{max}) can be calculated from Wien's displacement law:

$$\lambda_{max} = \frac{b}{T} \text{ where } b = 2.89 \times 10^{-3} \text{ mK}$$

Figure 8.34 The intensity distribution for a black body at different temperatures.

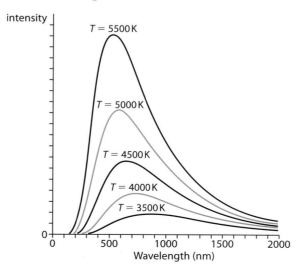

Red hot
When a rod of metal is heated to around 1000 K it starts to glow red. Although the most intense part of the spectrum is not in the visible region, there is enough visible red light to make the rod glow.

Stefan-Boltzmann Law

From the graph in Figure 8.34 we can see that as the temperature of a black body increases, the intensity of the radiation also increases. In other words, the amount of energy emitted from the surface increases. The Stefan-Boltzmann Law relates the power emitted per unit area to the temperature of the surface with the equation:

Power per unit area $= \sigma T^4$ where $\sigma = 5.67 \times 10^{-8}\,\text{W m}^{-2}\,\text{K}^{-4}$

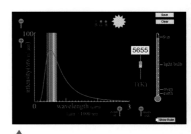

Exercises

18 Calculate the amount of energy in one photon of light of wavelength 600 nm.
The Sun is a hot dense gas so can be treated like a black body.
19 The temperature of surface of the Sun is 6000 K. Use Wien's displacement law to calculate the most intense wavelength in the spectrum of emitted radiation.
20 Use the Stefan-Boltzmann Law to calculate the power per m^2 emitted from the Sun.
21 The Sun's radius is 7×10^8 m. Use your answer to Question 20 to calculate the total energy radiated by the Sun per second.

The PhET simulation, 'Black body', will help you to see how the temperature of a body affects the radiation emitted. To view this, visit www.heinemann.co.uk/hotlinks, enter the express code 4266S and click on Weblink 8.7.

Radiation from the Sun

As calculated in Question 19, the spectrum of electromagnetic radiation from the Sun has a maximum intensity around 480 nm. This is the wavelength of blue light as seen in the spectrum shown in Figure 8.33. This means that the visible part of the spectrum is right on the peak of the intensity curve – it is no surprise therefore that this is the part we have evolved to see.

Temperature of the Earth with no atmosphere

Energy comes from the Sun to the Earth; this warms up the Earth and the Earth radiates some energy back into space. As the temperature of the Earth increases, it will radiate more and more until the amount of energy radiated = amount of energy absorbed, at which point the temperature will stay constant.

If we ignore the atmosphere we can calculate how hot the Earth should be. We know that the energy incident on the Earth per second is 1360 W m^{-2}. As the Earth only catches radiation on one side at a time, we can simplify this as a disc of radius 6400 km. The energy incident on the whole Earth per second is

$$1360 \times \pi \times (6.4 \times 10^6)^2 = 1.75 \times 10^{17}\,\text{W}$$

But the average albedo of the Earth is 30%. This means that 70% is absorbed, therefore:

$$\text{absorbed energy per second} = 1.23 \times 10^{17}\,\text{W}$$

To calculate the heat radiated by the planet, we have to consider the complete area of the sphere: if the temperature is T then (using Stefan-Boltzmann) the radiated energy per second is:

$$(5.67 \times 10^{-8} \times T^4) \times 4\pi r^2 = 2.9 \times 10^7 \times T^4$$

When this equals the heat absorbed, the temperature will stay constant so:

$$2.9 \times 10^7 \times T^4 = 1.23 \times 10^{17}$$

This gives a value of $T = 255$ K ($-18°$ C)

This is quite a lot colder than the Earth actually is, because the Earth's atmosphere absorbs some of the radiation radiated by the Earth. This is the greenhouse effect.

Emmisivity (e)

The reason that the temperature in the previous example was too low was that the Earth does not radiate as well as a black body.

The emmisivity, e, of the Earth tells us how it compares to a black body; it is the ratio of the energy radiated by a body to the energy radiated by a black body of the same temperature.

The average temperature of the Earth is 288 K. From the previous calculation we know that if the Earth was a black body it would radiate

$$2.9 \times 10^7 \times 288^4 \, \text{W} = 1.99 \times 10^{17} \, \text{W}$$

But we know that since this is the stable temperature then the Earth must be radiating $1.23 \times 10^{17} \, \text{W}$ (the same as the radiation from the Sun) so the emmisivity is $\frac{1.23}{1.99} = 0.6$

Absorption by the atmosphere

Before the radiation from the Sun lands on the surface of the Earth it first has to pass through the atmosphere. The atmosphere is in layers, the outer layers containing ozone (a form of oxygen whose molecules are made of three oxygen atoms, O_3). This absorbs the higher-energy parts of the spectrum, ultraviolet and X-rays. If it were not for this layer, these harmful rays would reach the Earth. As the radiation passes through the lower layers, infrared radiation is absorbed by water vapour and carbon dioxide. These gases have molecules that can be excited by the frequency equal to that of infrared photons.

Figure 8.35 The solar spectrum showing all wavelengths emitted by the Sun.

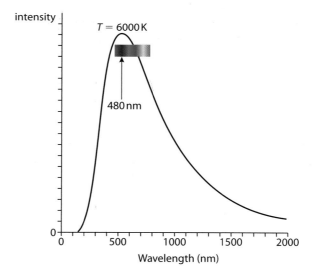

Absorption spectroscopy

The amount of different wavelengths absorbed by each gas can be found by measuring the intensity of light of known wavelength passing into and out of the gas. Figure 8.36 shows the absorption spectra for three different gases showing how ozone absorbs UV, and how carbon dioxide and water absorb IR. Notice that none of these gases absorb visible light.

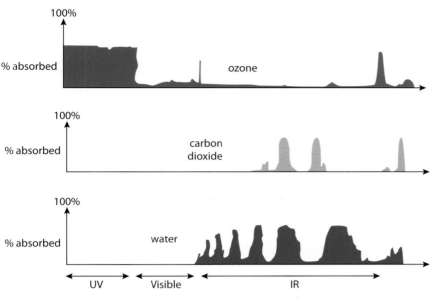

Figure 8.36 Absorption spectra for ozone, carbon dioxide and water.

ozone

carbon dioxide

water

UV Visible IR

Absorption by the ground

When solar radiation lands on the ground, some of it is reflected straight back, depending on the albedo of the ground. Since this radiation is the same as the radiation that has just made it through the atmosphere, it goes back through the atmosphere without being absorbed. The remaining radiation (mostly visible light) is absorbed and this increases the temperature of the ground. Since the ground is not very hot, then according to Wien's Law, the wavelength of the emitted radiation will be in the IR region.

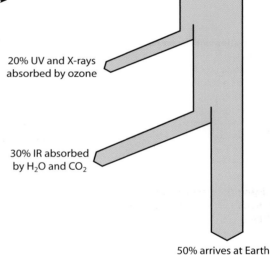

radiation from Sun

20% UV and X-rays absorbed by ozone

30% IR absorbed by H_2O and CO_2

50% arrives at Earth

Figure 8.37 Sankey diagram showing solar radiation absorbed by the atmosphere.

Surface heat capacity

The temperature increase of the ground can be calculated from the surface heat capacity (C_s). This is the amount of heat required to raise the temperature of 1 m^2 of the ground by 1 K. For the Earth this is 4×10^8 J km^{-2}.

To see how the greenhouse gases contribute to the warming of planet Earth, visit www.heinemann.co.uk/hotlinks. enter the express code 4266S and click on Weblink 8.8.

The greenhouse effect

The IR radiation radiated from the ground travels upwards through the atmosphere and as it does it is absorbed by CO_2 and H_2O. As a result, these molecules become excited, raising the temperature of the atmosphere. They themselves can then radiate IR radiation in all directions, some of which goes back to the Earth. We have seen that the temperature of the Earth is determined by the point at which the radiation leaving the Earth is equal to that arriving. By reducing the amount leaving, the temperature at which this balance will be achieved will be higher.

Sankey diagrams

We have calculated already that by the time it gets to the Earth the intensity of the Sun's radiation is 1380 W m^{-2}. However, the Earth is a sphere, so the power received per unit area will be different at different places (less at the poles than at the equator). The average value is taken here to be 342 W m^{-2}.

To understand the energy flow diagram for the complete greenhouse effect let us first consider the flow diagram with no greenhouse gases (Figure 8.38).

Figure 8.38 Sankey diagram for energy flow without greenhouse gases. The amount of radiation absorbed by the ground equals the amount being radiated.

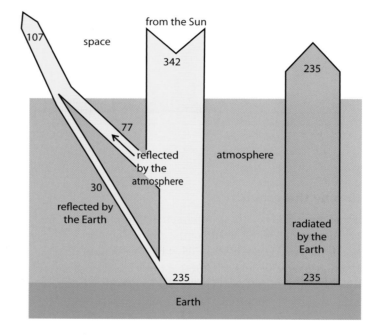

Energy flow with greenhouse gases

Here we can see that 342 W m^{-2} still enter and leave but now the Earth is radiating more energy. This energy is recirculated by the greenhouse gases. 519 W m^{-2} are absorbed by the gases and 519 W m^{-2} are given out while 324 W m^{-2} of this do not leave the atmosphere.

But we know that due to the greenhouse effect, the Earth is hotter than in this model and so emits more radiation.

Figure 8.39 Sankey diagram for energy flow for the Earth and greenhouse gases in the atmosphere. The 102 W m^{-2} wiggly line represents energy that is partly lost by convection and partly used when water in the sea turns to water vapour.

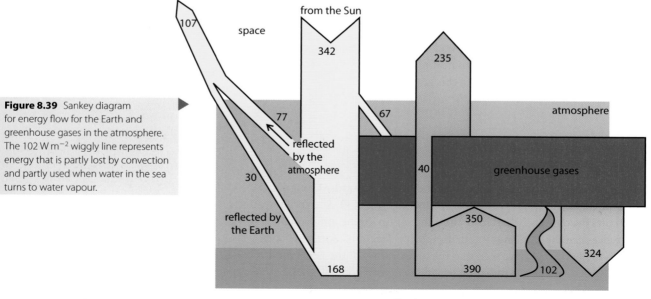

8.10 Global warming

We can see from our model of the greenhouse effect that the temperature of the
Earth depends on several factors. For example, if the amount of radiation coming
from the Sun were to increase then there would be more energy reaching the
Earth. This would cause the temperature of the Earth to increase until equilibrium
is restored; this is called *global warming.*

Models for global warming

The factors affecting the temperature of the planet are very complex and
interrelated. Physicists use their knowledge to make mathematical models so that
they can predict the outcome of changing variables. However, this problem is
rather more difficult than an ideal gas or any other system considered so far in this
course, and the equations are equally difficult to solve. To solve these equations,
physicists make computer models and program computers to do the millions
of calculations required. To show how these are built up, we will consider an
analogous situation.

Sand analogy

It is difficult to imagine what is happening to all the energy flowing in and out of
the Earth. To make this easier to visualize, we can consider an analogous situation
such as loading sand onto a truck.

Imagine you are filling a truck with sand. As you put sand onto the truck someone
else takes off a fixed percentage of the complete load. As the amount on the
truck increases, they take off more until they take off as much as you put on – an
equilibrium is reached.

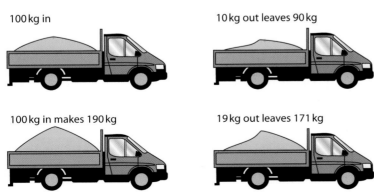

100 kg in

10 kg out leaves 90 kg

100 kg in makes 190 kg

19 kg out leaves 171 kg

Figure 8.40 In the sand analogy, if
100 kg are put in each minute and
10% is taken out each minute then the
outcome would be as shown.

To find out how the load varies until equilibrium is reached we have to do a lot of calculations, or we can use a spreadsheet to do it for us (See Figure 8.41). Once the data has been entered into a spreadsheet it is a simple matter of copying the formula down in as many rows as you want. If you do this, then make sure you copy row 3 not row 2, since row 2 only contains zeros. If this is copied down to 100 minutes you will see that equilibrium has been reached when the load contains 900 kg, as every time another 100 kg is added, 100 kg will be taken out. Once you have made this model it is very easy to change the variables to see what would happen. You can try adding more sand by changing column D or taking more out by changing the factor 0.1 in column E.

Figure 8.41 shows how the sand analogy would be put into a spreadsheet and how the results can be displayed as a graph of load against time.

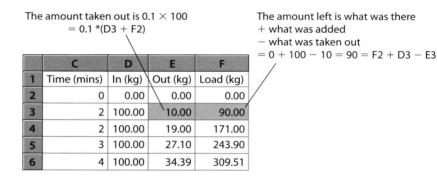

The amount taken out is 0.1×100
$= 0.1 *(D3 + F2)$

The amount left is what was there
$+$ what was added
$-$ what was taken out
$= 0 + 100 - 10 = 90 = F2 + D3 - E3$

	C	D	E	F
1	Time (mins)	In (kg)	Out (kg)	Load (kg)
2	0	0.00	0.00	0.00
3	2	100.00	10.00	90.00
4	2	100.00	19.00	171.00
5	3	100.00	27.10	243.90
6	4	100.00	34.39	309.51

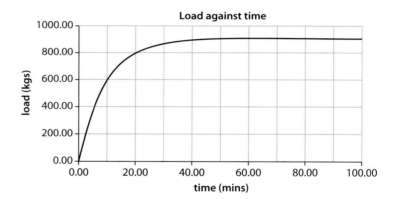

Global warming is not as simple as the sand model but it's the same principle.

Modelling global warming

The energy flow for the Earth and atmosphere is rather more complicated than the sand analogy. One complication is the greenhouse effect, which would be like putting some of the sand back into the truck. Computer simulations that model the climate of the Earth must take all factors into consideration, and that takes a lot more computer power than even the fastest home computer. One concerned group, 'Climate prediction', have been doing calculations on thousands of private computers in homes and schools all around the world to gain the power needed to run their computer model.

 To see a simple spreadsheet model for the Earth (without the greenhouse effect), visit www.heinemann.co.uk/hotlinks, enter the express code 4266S and click on Weblink 8.9. Here you will also find a lot of information about climate change and details of the other simulations they are running.

Exercises

22 Try making the spreadsheet model as above. See what happens if you change the variables.

Causes of global warming

By analysing the energy flow diagram in Figure 8.38 we can see that there are several ways that the temperature of the Earth could increase.

The radiation from the Sun

The radiation from the Sun is not constant. If the amount of radiation incident on the Earth increases, then its temperature would increase. There are several factors that affect this:

Solar flares/sunspots

Sunspots are black spots on the surface of the Sun that can be seen if you look at the Sun through a sufficiently dark filter. The spots are cool areas. However, when there are a lot of sunspots, the Sun emits more energy due to the increased temperature of the gas surrounding the spot. The number of sunspots varies on an 11-year cycle.

Earth's orbit

The Earth's orbit is not circular but elliptical; this means that the distance between the Earth and the Sun is not constant. There are also other variations due to the change of angle of the Earth's axis in relation to the Sun. These are called Milankovitch cycles.

Enhanced greenhouse effect

If the amount of greenhouse gases in the atmosphere is increased, then the amount of radiation absorbed by the atmosphere increases. The amount of energy leaving the Earth is reduced and the temperature of the Earth would rise until equilibrium was restored.

The greenhouse gases include water, carbon dioxide, methane and nitrous oxide. Water is the biggest contributor to the greenhouse effect, with carbon dioxide second. Methane has a much bigger effect, but there isn't so much of it in the atmosphere.

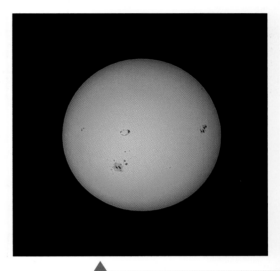

The increase in temperature as a result of many sunspots together leads to solar flares, jets of gas flying out from the Sun's surface like huge flames.

Greenhouse gases
There are many gases that contribute to the greenhouse effect and the complete picture of their combined contribution is very complicated and out of the scope of this book. To simplify matters we will only deal with CO_2 since this is the major contributor.

Ice cores

For hundreds of thousands of years the ice of Antarctica has been growing. Each year a new layer is added on top of the old, so that the ice that is there now is made up of thousands of layers, each layer representing a year's growth (like the rings of a tree). By drilling into the ice with a hollow drill it is possible to extract samples (ice cores) that were laid down thousands of years ago. From the concentration of the different isotopes of hydrogen in the water it is possible to determine the temperature of the layers: more heavy isotopes means the temperature was colder. These layers of ice also contain bubbles of air that have been trapped since the ice was laid down; from these bubbles we can find how the composition of the atmosphere has changed since the ice was formed. If we compare the temperature of the Earth with the concentration of CO_2 we get an interesting result, as shown in Figure 8.42. Comparing these two graphs we can see that when the concentration of CO_2 increases, so does the temperature.

Figure 8.42 Data from the Vostok Antarctic ice core can be explained using the greenhouse gas model, however this piece of evidence alone is not enough to say that temperature depends on CO_2 concentration.

If the results from the ice core were a class practical, then you would devise an experiment to test the hypothesis that, when the concentration of CO_2 increases so does the temperature (making sure that the variables were controlled). It's of course not possible to experiment with the amount of CO_2 in the atmosphere so computer simulations may be used instead.

The temperature scale is the difference in temperature between the temperature calculated from the hydrogen isotopes in the ice core and the average temperature now.
To find data from the ice cores, visit www.heinemann.co.uk/hotlinks, enter the express code 4266S and click on the Weblink 8.10.

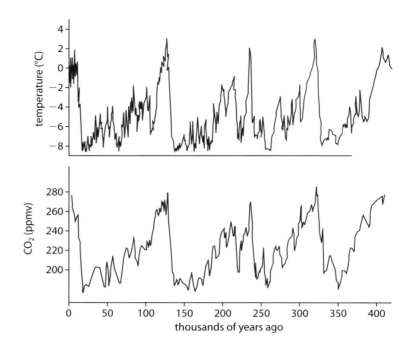

More recent data

From measurements of the average temperature of the Earth and the amount of CO_2 in the atmosphere, it can be seen that there could be a relationship between the two. The graphs in Figure 8.43 show both have risen in the past 50 years. Notice there is regular yearly variation in CO_2, the maximum coming after the northern hemisphere winter; this is because during the summer, plants absorb CO_2 from the atmosphere.

Figure 8.43 Graphs to show the temperature anomaly (difference between the measured temperature and the average temperature) and CO_2 concentration measured since 1960.

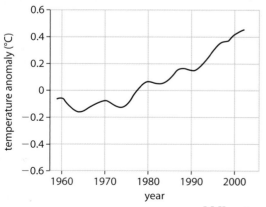

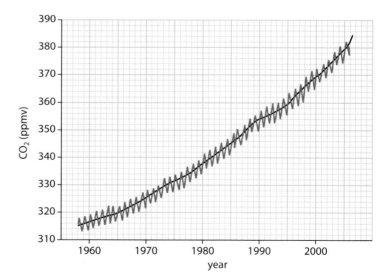

What causes the change in CO_2?

It is widely believed that the increase in CO_2 is due to human activity, mainly because of the burning of fossil fuels which produces the gas, and deforestation which removes plants that would normally absorb the gas. This hypothesis is supported by the increased use of fossil fuels during the past 50 years (see Figure 8.44).

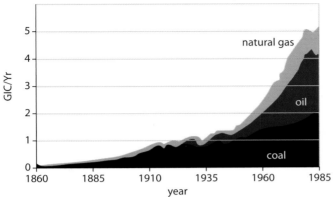
Growth in fossil fuel consumption

natural gas

oil

coal

Figure 8.44 The exponential increase in fossil fuel consumption has contributed to the increase in CO_2 in the atmosphere.

8.11 What might happen and what can be done?

Assessment statements

8.6.6 Define *coefficient of volume expansion*.

8.6.7 State one possible effect of the enhanced greenhouse effect

8.6.8 Outline possible reasons for a predicted rise in mean sea-level.

8.6.9 Identify climate change as an outcome of the enhanced greenhouse effect.

8.6.10 Solve problems related to the enhanced greenhouse effect.

8.6.11 Identify some possible solutions to reduce the enhanced greenhouse effect.

8.6.12 Discuss international efforts to reduce the enhanced greenhouse effect.

The Steigletscher glacier in Switzerland photographed in 1994 (top) and 2006 (bottom). Glaciers are shrinking like this all round the world.

To find out what would happen if the average temperature of the Earth were to increase, we can look at what has happened during the past 50 years, especially global warming in recent years, or we can use computer simulations.

Rise in sea level

As the temperature of a liquid increases, it expands. The relationship between the increase in volume (ΔV) and the temperature change (ΔT) is given by the formula

$$\Delta V = \beta V_o \Delta T$$

where β = coefficient of volume expansion

V_o = the original volume

If this is applied to water, then we can conclude that if the average temperature of the oceans increases then they will expand. This has already been happening; over the past 100 years sea level has risen by 20 cm. Trying to predict what will happen as the sea temperature increases is complicated by the anomalous expansion of water. Unlike a lot of other liquids, water does not expand uniformly, in fact from 0 °C to 4 °C water actually contracts and then from 4 °C upwards it expands. Trying to calculate what happens as different bodies of water expand and contract is very difficult, but most models predict some rise in sea level.

Another factor that could cause the sea level to rise is the melting of the ice caps. This is the ice that covers the land masses of Antarctica, Greenland and the glaciers in mountainous regions. It doesn't include the Arctic since this ice is floating. Floating ice displaces its own mass of water so when it melts it makes no difference. If the ice caps melt and the water runs into the sea, then it could make the sea level rise so much that some countries could disappear under water.

Albedo

Melting ice caps have dual impact. We have discussed the way that the amount of radiation reflected off the Earth is an important factor in determining the Earth's temperature. The ice caps are white and therefore reflect a high amount of radiation (their albedo is high). If they melt, then the amount of reflected radiation would be reduced, causing the temperature to rise further; this is called *positive feedback*.

Change in the weather

The other obvious consequence of the enhanced greenhouse effect is a change in the weather. What would happen is, again, difficult to predict but most models agree that countries near the equator will get hotter and countries in the northern hemisphere will get wetter.

Solutions

To reduce the enhanced greenhouse effect, the levels of greenhouse gases must be reduced, or at the very least, the rate at which they are increasing must be slowed down. There are several ways that this can be achieved:

1 **Greater efficiency of power production**
   In recent years the efficiency of power plants has been increasing significantly. According to the second law of thermodynamics, they can never be 100% efficient but some of the older less efficient ones could be replaced. This would mean that to produce the same amount of power would require less fuel, resulting in reduced CO_2 emission.

2 **Replacing the use of coal and oil with natural gas**
   Gas-fired power stations are more efficient than oil and gas and produce less CO_2.

3 **Use of combined heating and power systems (CHP)**
   Using the excess heat from the power station to heat homes would result in a more efficient use of fuel.

4 **Increased use of renewable energy sources and nuclear power**
  Replacing fossil fuel burning power stations with alternative forms such as wave power, solar power and wind power would reduce CO_2 emissions.

5 **Use of hybrid vehicles**
  A large amount of the oil used today is used for transport, and even without global warming, there will be a problem when the oil runs out. Cars that run on electricity or a combination of electricity and petrol (hybrid) are already in production. Aeroplanes will also have to use a different fuel.

6 **Carbon dioxide capture and storage**
  A different way of reducing greenhouse gases is to remove CO_2 from the waste gases of power stations and store it underground.

An international problem

Global warming is an international problem, and if any solution is going to work then it must be a joint international solution. Before working on the solution the international community had to agree on pinpointing the problem and it was to this end that the Intergovernmental Panel on Climate Change (IPCC) was formed.

IPCC

In 1988 the World Meteorological Organisation (WMO) and the United Nations Environmental Programme (UNEP) established the IPCC, the panel of which was open to all members of the UN and WMO. Its role was not to carry out research but to assess all the available information relating to human induced climate change.

An excerpt from the first report of Working Group I in 1990 states:
"The experts concluded that they are certain that emissions from human activities are substantially increasing the atmospheric concentrations of greenhouse gases and that this will enhance the greenhouse effect and result in an additional warming of the Earth's surface."

Kyoto Protocol

In 1997 the Kyoto Protocol was open for signature: countries ratifying this treaty committed to reduce their greenhouse gas emissions by given percentages. By May 2007, 177 countries had signed and ratified.

Asia-Pacific Partnership on Clean Development and Climate (APPCDC)

This is a non-treaty agreement between six countries that account for 50% of the greenhouse emissions. The countries involved agreed to cooperate on the development and transfer of technology with the aim of reducing greenhouse emissions.

 To access the websites of the IPCC, the UN and the Asia-Pacific Partnership, visit www.heinemann.co.uk/hotlinks, enter the express code 4266S and click on Weblinks 8.11, 8.12 and 8.13.

Practice questions

1 This question is about energy sources.

(a) Fossil fuels are being produced continuously on Earth and yet they are classed as being non-renewable. Outline why fossil fuels are classed as non-renewable. (2)

(b) Some energy consultants suggest that the solution to the problem of carbon dioxide pollution is to use nuclear energy for the generation of electrical energy. Identify **two** disadvantages of the use of nuclear fission when compared to the burning of fossil fuels for the generation of electrical energy. (2)

(Total 4 marks)

2 This question is about solar energy.

(a) By reference to energy transformations, distinguish between a solar panel and a solar cell. (2)

Some students carry out an investigation on a solar panel. They measure the output temperature of the water for different solar input powers and for different rates of extraction of thermal energy. The results are shown below.

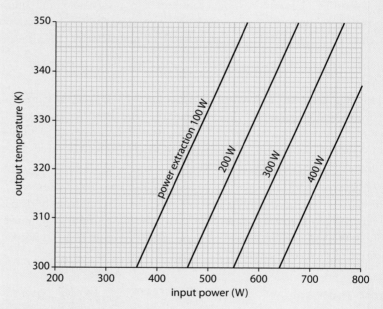

(b) Use the data from the graph to answer the following.

(i) The solar panel is to provide water at 340 K whilst extracting energy at a rate of 300 W when the intensity of the sunlight incident normally on the panel is 800 W m^{-2}. Calculate the effective surface area of the panel that is required. (2)

(ii) Deduce the overall efficiency of the panel for an input power of 500 W at an output temperature of 320 K. (3)

(Total 7 marks)

3 This question is about the production of electrical energy.

(a) Outline the principal energy transfers involved in the production of electrical energy from thermal energy in a coal fired power station. (2)

(b) State and explain whether the energy sources used in the following power stations are renewable **or** non-renewable.

(i) Coal fired (1)

(ii) Nuclear (1)

(c) The core of some nuclear reactors contains a moderator and control rods. Explain the function of these components.

    (i) The moderator (2)

    (ii) The control rods (2)

(d) Discuss **one** advantage of a nuclear power station as opposed to a coal-fired power station. (2)

(Total 10 marks)

4 This question is about wind energy.

It is required to design wind turbines for a wind farm for which the following information is available.

Total required annual electrical energy output from the wind farm = 120 TJ

Maximum number of turbines for which there is space on the farm = 20

Average annual wind speed at the site = 9.0 m s^{-1}

(a) Deduce that the average power output required from one turbine is 0.19 MW. (3)

(b) Estimate the blade radius of the wind turbine that will give a power output of 0.19 MW. (Density of air = 1.2 kg m^{-3}) (3)

(c) State **one** reason why your answer to (b) is only an estimate. (1)

(d) Discuss briefly **one** disadvantage of generating power from wind energy. (2)

(Total 9 marks)

5 This question is about the production of nuclear energy and its transfer to electrical energy.

(a) When a neutron "collides" with a nucleus of uranium-235 (U) the following reaction can occur.

$$^{235}_{92}\text{U} + {}^{1}_{0}\text{n} \rightarrow {}^{144}_{56}\text{Ba} + {}^{90}_{36}\text{Kr} + 2{}^{1}_{0}\text{n}$$

    (i) State the name given to this type of nuclear reaction. (1)

    (ii) Energy is liberated in this reaction. In what form does this energy appear? (1)

(b) Describe how the neutrons produced in this reaction may initiate a chain reaction. (1)

The purpose of a nuclear power station is to produce electrical energy from nuclear energy. The diagram below is a schematic representation of the principle components of a nuclear reactor "pile" used in a certain type of nuclear power station.

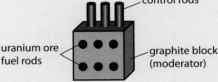

control rods

uranium ore fuel rods

graphite block (moderator)

The function of the moderator is to slow down neutrons produced in a reaction such as that described in part (a) above.

(c) **(i)** Explain why it is necessary to slow down the neutrons. (3)

    (ii) Explain the function of the control rods. (2)

(d) Describe briefly how the energy produced by the nuclear reactions is extracted from the reactor pile and then transferred to electrical energy. (4)

(Total 12 marks)

6 This question is about nuclear power and thermodynamics.

(a) A fission reaction taking place in the core of a nuclear power reactor is

$$^{1}_{0}\text{n} + {}^{235}_{92}\text{U} \rightarrow {}^{144}_{56}\text{Ba} + {}^{89}_{36}\text{Kr} + 3{}^{1}_{0}\text{n}.$$

    (i) State **one** form in which energy is released in this reaction. (1)

    (ii) Explain why, for fission reactions to be maintained, the mass of the uranium fuel must be above a certain minimum amount. (2)

(iii) The neutrons produced in the fission reaction are fast moving. In order for a neutron to fission U-235 the neutron must be slow moving. Name the part of the nuclear reactor in which neutrons are slowed down. (1)

(iv) In a particular reactor approximately 8.0×10^{19} fissions per second take place. Deduce the mass of U-235 that undergoes fission per year. (3)

(b) The thermal power from the reactor is 2400 MW and this is used to drive (operate) a heat engine. The mechanical power output of the heat engine is used to drive a generator. The generator is 75 % efficient and produces 600 MW of electrical power. This is represented by the energy flow diagram below.

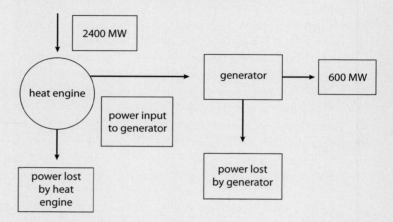

(i) Calculate the power input to the generator. (1)

(ii) Calculate the power lost from the generator. (1)

(iii) Calculate the power lost by the heat engine. (1)

(iv) State the name of the law of physics which prohibits **all** of the 2400 MW of input thermal power from being converted into mechanical power. (1)

(vi) The heat engine operates in a Carnot cycle with a low temperature reservoir of 300K. Calculate the temperature of the hot reservoir. (2)

(Total 14 marks)

7 This question is about wind power.

(a) A wind turbine produces 15 kW of electric power at a wind speed v.

(i) Assuming a constant efficiency for the wind turbine, determine the power output of the turbine for a wind speed of $2v$. (2)

(ii) Suggest **two** reasons why all the kinetic energy of the incident wind cannot be converted into mechanical energy in the turbine. (2)

(b) State and explain **one** advantage of using wind power to generate electrical energy as compared to using fossil fuels. (2)

(Total 6 marks)

9 Sight and wave phenomena (Option A)

The eye and sight

Assessment statements
A.1.1 Describe the basic structure of the human eye.
A.1.2 State and explain the process of depth of vision and accommodation.
A.1.3 State that the retina contains rods and cones, and describe the variation in density across the surface of the retina.
A.1.4 Describe the function of the rods and of the cones in photopic and scotopic vision.
A.1.5 Describe colour mixing of light by addition and subtraction.
A.1.6 Discuss the effect of light and dark, and colour, on the perception of objects.

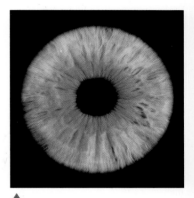

The coloured part of the eye is called the *iris* and it consists of a ring of muscle fibres that contract and relax to alter the amount of light entering the eye through the pupil.

When the human eye is viewed from the front, the pupil looks black. In fact it is a circular hole in the centre of the iris, and the black colour comes from a layer inside the eye that prevents internal reflections. If the intensity of incident light is high, then the iris reduces the size of the pupil; in low intensity light, the pupil dilates to allow more light to enter.

The front of the eye is covered with a layer of transparent skin called the *cornea*. The lens and the cornea both play a part in focusing light onto the retina at the back of the eye. The retina is the light-sensitive layer and it sends messages to the brain through the optic nerve.

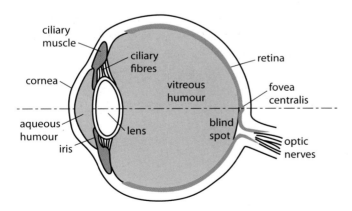

Figure 9.1 The human eye. The humours are transparent jellies that nourish the eye and keep its shape. The blind spot is where the optic nerve exits the eye and there is no retina. The fovea is directly opposite the centre of the lens and is sometimes called the yellow spot.

The lens in our eyes can change shape to enable us to focus on both near and far objects.

This process is called *accommodation*. When we look at a distant object, the ciliary muscles relax and the taut fibres make the lens longer and thinner. When we focus on something close to our eyes, the ciliary muscles contract and the lens changes shape to become shorter and thicker.

 Modern laser surgery can reshape the cornea to correct many defects of vision and remove the need for glasses or contact lenses.

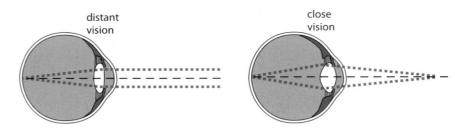

Figure 9.2 Rays of light from a distant object arrive at the eye effectively parallel, and so need less refraction than rays from an object close to the eye.

distant vision   close vision

The near point is defined as the position where an object can be seen most clearly. As you are reading this page you are automatically holding it at your near point. If you hold it closer to your eyes it will appear blurred and if you hold it further away the writing will appear smaller and so more difficult to read.

The range over which the eye can focus is from the *near point* to the *far point*. For a normal eye, the far point is at infinity; we focus on the far point when the ciliary muscles are completely relaxed and the eye is not accommodating. The near point varies from person to person but is taken to be 25 centimetres.

Depth of vision

Depth of vision is the ability to see things in three dimensions. It is the perception of depth that enables us to judge how far away things are, and this is crucially important when playing ball games or driving a car.

Using only one eye we can get some information about depth of vision. This is based on our previous experience and from cues we get from relative sizes of objects, perspective and relative motion between objects.

If the image from an object falls on the blind spot, it cannot be detected by the brain. With two eyes one compensates for the other, so we do not lose sight of things.

With two eyes we are able to obtain two images of the same thing and the brain is then able to judge distances and motion far more accurately. This is particularly important for nearby objects; for things that are far away there will not be a big difference in the images received by each eye.

Colour vision

The retina contains two types of receptor cells called *rods* and *cones*. The rods detect motion, enable us to see in low light intensity and are responsible for peripheral vision (seeing things from the corner of our eyes). The cones are responsible for colour vision and also visual acuity. We need good visual acuity for reading the very small letters at the bottom of opticians' charts.

The fovea or yellow spot, located in the centre of the retina, consists entirely of cones. This is the part of the retina where our vision is most acute. Just a few degrees from the fovea, the concentration of rods is at a maximum and the rods spread out all around the rest of the retina with a gradually decreasing concentration.

People in different parts of the world literally see things differently. The indigenous peoples of the Australian and Kalahari deserts have been found to have exceptional long distance vision; useful when scanning the horizon for moving animals. People who have spent their whole life in the rainforest have been found to lack depth perspective. When they see animals at a distance on the plains, they simply assume that the animals are very small; they have no other means of making a judgement.

Figure 9.3 Variation in density of rods and cones across the retina. The diagram shows high density of cones in the fovea but low density elsewhere. There are no rods in the fovea but they are highly dense in other parts of the retina.

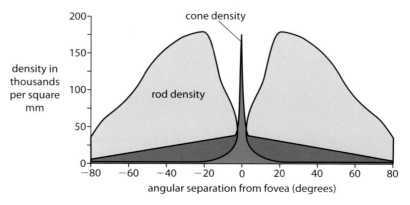

In each eye we have about 120 million rods but only about 6 million cones.

Experiments show that we have three types of cones in our retina. They are known as *blue*, *green* and *red* or as S, M and L which stands for short, medium and long, referring to the wavelength of light to which they are most sensitive.

There is overlap between the wavelengths to which each of the three types of cone responds and this enables the brain to perceive the full spectrum of colours. You can see from the diagram that both green and red cones respond to yellow light, but the blue cones do not respond to yellow or red light.

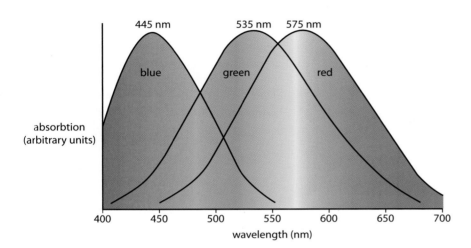

People who are colour-blind have difficulty in distinguishing between different colours. The most common type is red-green colour-blindness and is inherited. It stems from problems in the green and red cones and involves an inability to properly distinguish between reds, yellows and greens. There are other types of colour blindness but they are quite rare.

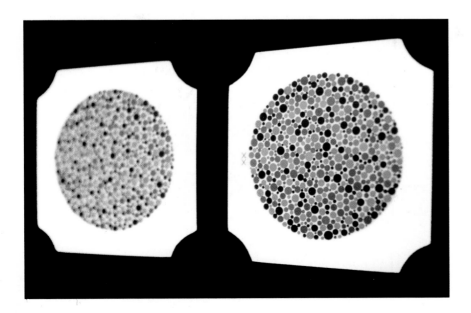

Photopic vision refers to colour vision under normal lighting and is the function of the cones. Scotopic vision refers to our ability to see in dim light, it is completely lacking in colour and is the function of the rods.

Figure 9.4 Spectral response curves for cones: each of the three types of cone responds to a different region of the visible spectrum.

Only 2% of our 6 million cones are for seeing blue, but since we appear to see equally well in the short end of the visible spectrum, the blue cones must be more sensitive.

● **Examiner's hint:** You need to be able to sketch and interpret this type of graph.

Some apes also have been found to have three types of cones, so they see colours in a similar way to us. Other animals see things very differently; the vision of bees extends into the ultraviolet region of the electromagnetic spectrum, while some snakes can see infrared. Sharks are apparently unable to detect any colours.

Figure 9.5 This is an example of a test used to see if people are colour-blind. A person with normal colour vision will be able to trace both the orange and red lines. A person who is colour-blind will find one line easier to follow than the other.

Colour mixing of light

White light is a mixture of all the colours of the visible spectrum. A prism can separate the colours by a process called *dispersion*.

If three projectors are arranged to shine red, green and blue light of the correct intensity onto a screen, the result will appear white. It is for this reason that these colours are called *primary colours*.

Mixing the three primary colours in pairs gives us the three secondary colours.

Colours of light can be subtracted by absorption using filters. The colour of light that is transmitted by the filter is the same as the colour of the filter itself. For example, if white light is shone through a red filter, then all the wavelengths will be absorbed except for red; only red light will be transmitted.

▲
The white light is dispersed into the colours of the spectrum because different colours of light travel at different speeds in glass.

Figure 9.6 Adding red to green makes yellow. Adding red to blue makes magenta. Adding blue to green makes cyan. Adding all three together makes white. This is called additive colour mixing.

 Red, green and blue are the primary colours of light.

 Yellow, magenta and cyan are the secondary colours of light.

Figure 9.7 If a second green or blue filter is placed after the red filter, it will block the red light and then no light will be visible.

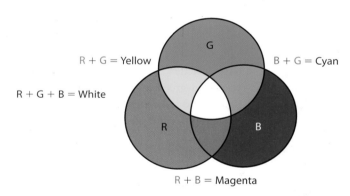

R + G = Yellow

R + G + B = White

B + G = Cyan

G

R

B

R + B = Magenta

filter layer

incoming light

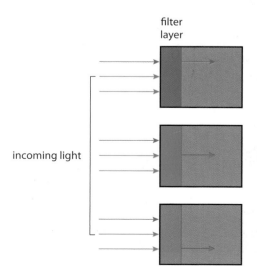

When white light passes through filters of the secondary colours, the wavelengths absorbed depend on the make up of the secondary colour. For example, magenta is made up of red and blue, so magenta transmits red and blue.

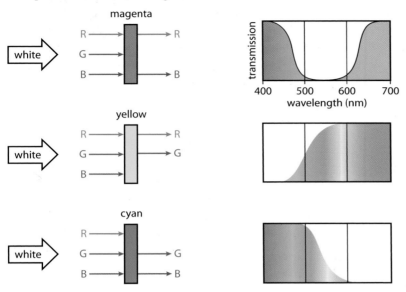

Figure 9.8 If another secondary filter is placed after the first one, then one primary colour will still be transmitted.

To view a fun simulation 'Color vision and filters', visit www.heinemann.co.uk/hotlinks, enter the express code 4266S and click on Weblink 9.1.

Perception

Information collected by the eye is sent to the brain for processing. There is so much information coming in all the time that the brain must select what is relevant. Perception involves collection, selection and also organization and interpretation of the sensory input.

Light, shade and colour are used by artists, designers and architects to deliberately influence, and even alter, our perception of reality. For example, deep shadow in a painting, or in a church, can give the impression of massiveness.

Blue is perceived as a cold colour, orange and red glow can give the impression of warmth. A room can be made to appear bigger and lighter by the careful placing of mirrors and it can be made to appear higher by a light-coloured ceiling.

Sense perception is one of the ways of knowing. To what extent do our eyes give us knowledge of the world as it really is?

Exercises

1 Explain the process of accommodation in the human eye.

2 Distinguish between photopic and scotopic vision.

3 Sketch and label a graph to show the spectral response of cones in the human eye.

9.2 Standing (stationary) waves

Assessment statements

A.2.1 Describe the nature of standing (stationary) waves.

A.2.2 Explain the formation of one-dimensional standing waves.

A.2.3 Discuss the modes of vibration of strings and air in open and in closed pipes.

A.2.4 Compare standing waves and travelling waves.

A.2.5 Solve problems involving standing waves.

In Chapter 4 we looked at continuous, travelling waves and saw that they transfer energy without transferring matter. If two waves that are travelling in opposite directions meet, and the conditions are right, then they will superpose and interfere to set up a standing wave.

Standing waves can occur in many different situations but the two that we will be concerned with here are in strings and in columns of air inside pipes.

◀ The standing wave is a result of interference between two waves travelling in opposite directions, in this case circular waves reflecting from the edges of the cup and the centre of the cup.

A standing wave results when two waves of the same frequency and speed, and nearly the same amplitude, travelling in opposite directions, meet and superpose.

Waves in strings

All stringed instruments such as the guitar, the piano and the violin, use the principles of waves in strings. The speed of these waves depends on the tension in the string and the mass per unit length (how thick or heavy the string is).

The most common way for standing waves in strings to be formed is by reflection of a travelling wave at a boundary. The reflected wave will be flipped over; it will undergo a phase inversion, and interfere with the incoming wave.

Figure 9.9 Since the reflection is at a fixed end there is a total or 180° phase inversion and the reflected wave superposes with the incident wave. ▶

incident wave

reflected wave

resultant wave

When we play most musical instruments we are making use of standing waves in strings or in columns of air.

At either end of a standing wave in a string, there will always be a *node*, where there is no movement. For the lowest frequency mode, known as the *fundamental frequency*, there will be an *antinode* in the middle where the amplitude is the largest.

A node is a position of minimum displacement and an antinode is a position of maximum displacement.

Figure 9.10 There is a node at each end, so the number of antinodes is always one less than the number of nodes. ▶

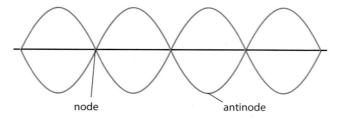

node   antinode

To view the simulation 'Waves on a string', visit www.heinemann.co.uk/hotlinks, enter the express code 4266S and click on Weblink 9.2.

We will now look in detail at the harmonics of standing waves on strings. The two fixed ends determine the length of the string and control the *boundary conditions* of the waves.

The fundamental frequency is also known as the *first harmonic*. In this case the length of the string will be half the wavelength:

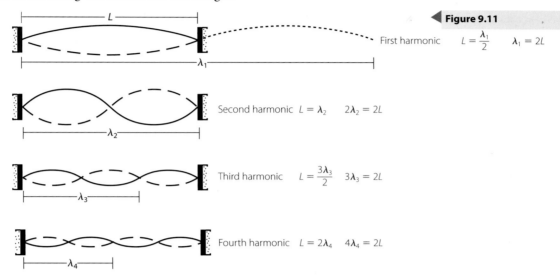

◀ **Figure 9.11**

First harmonic $\quad L = \frac{\lambda_1}{2} \qquad \lambda_1 = 2L$

Second harmonic $\quad L = \lambda_2 \qquad 2\lambda_2 = 2L$

Third harmonic $\quad L = \frac{3\lambda_3}{2} \qquad 3\lambda_3 = 2L$

Fourth harmonic $\quad L = 2\lambda_4 \qquad 4\lambda_4 = 2L$

We can write this as a general equation:

$$n\lambda = 2L \qquad \text{where } n \text{ is any integer.}$$

As $v = f\lambda$ we can also write: $\qquad f_n = \dfrac{v}{\lambda_n} = \dfrac{nv}{2L}$

f_n is the frequency of the nth harmonic in hertz (Hz)
v is the speed of the wave in m s^{-1}

Waves in pipes

Here we are looking at sound waves travelling in columns of air. Obviously the waves move at the speed of sound, which is around 340 m s^{-1}. The ideas here are those that control the wind instruments, such as the pipe organ and the bagpipes.

There are two different types of pipe, open at one end and open at both ends. A closed pipe must have a node at the closed end and an antinode at the open end.

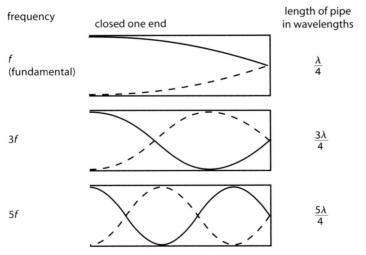

frequency

closed one end

length of pipe in wavelengths

f (fundamental) $\qquad \dfrac{\lambda}{4}$

$3f \qquad \dfrac{3\lambda}{4}$

$5f \qquad \dfrac{5\lambda}{4}$

◀ **Figure 9.12**

For the fundamental or first harmonic, the length of the pipe $\qquad L = \dfrac{\lambda}{4}$

For the next harmonic, the length of the pipe $\qquad L = \dfrac{3\lambda}{4}$

For the next harmonic, the length of the pipe $\qquad L = \dfrac{5\lambda}{4}$

We can write this as a general equation:

$n\lambda = 4L$ where n is an *odd* integer 1, 3, 5 etc; the even harmonics are missing.

We can also write: $\qquad f_n = \dfrac{nv}{4L}$

An open pipe must have an antinode at both ends.

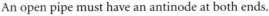

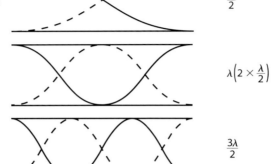

Figure 9.13
For the fundamental or first harmonic,
the length of the pipe $L = \frac{\lambda}{2}$

For the next harmonic,
the length of the pipe $L = \lambda$

For the next harmonic,
the length of the pipe $L = \frac{3\lambda}{2}$

To try a simple simulation showing harmonics in pipes and on strings, visit www.heinemann.co.uk/hotlinks, enter the express code 4266S and click on Weblink 9.3.

Note that the harmonics are the same as the strings, and so we can write

$$n\lambda = 2L \quad \text{where } n \text{ is any integer}$$

f_n is the frequency of the nth harmonic in hertz (Hz)

$$f_n = \frac{nv}{2L}$$

v is the speed of the wave in m s^{-1}

Travelling waves and standing waves

1 Travelling waves transfer energy and standing waves do not.
2 All points on a travelling wave have the same amplitude but all points on standing waves have different amplitudes.

● **Examiner's hint:** If you remember the positions of the nodes and antinodes and practise the diagrams you do not need to memorize the equations; they are fairly easy to figure out if you draw the diagrams correctly.

Worked example

Find the fundamental frequency of an open pipe of length 85 cm. The speed of sound in air $= 340$ m s^{-1}.

Solution

If the pipe is open for the fundamental frequency:

$$L = \frac{\lambda}{2}$$

$$\begin{aligned}
\lambda &= 2 \times L \\
&= 2 \times 85\,\text{cm} \\
&= 170\,\text{cm} \\
&= 1.7\,\text{m}
\end{aligned}$$

$$v = f\lambda \quad f = \frac{v}{\lambda} = \frac{340\,\text{m s}^{-1}}{1.7\,\text{m}}$$

$$f = \mathbf{200\ Hz}$$

Exercises

4 By reference to energy transfer and the amplitude of vibration of particles in a wave, distinguish between a travelling wave and a standing wave.
A stretched string is fixed at both ends and then plucked at its centre. The diagram right illustrates the vibrating string. The distance between the fixed points is 120 cm.
(a) Find the wavelength of the standing wave.
(b) The frequency of vibration of the string is 250 Hz. Determine the speed of the wave on the string.

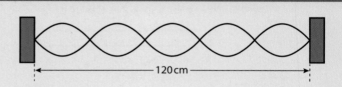

— 120 cm —

5 A tube that is open at both ends is placed in a deep tank of water, as shown right. A tuning fork of frequency 256 Hz is sounded continuously above the tube. The tube is slowly raised out of the water and, at one position of the tube, a maximum loudness of sound is heard.
(a) Explain the formation of a standing wave in the tube.
(b) The tube is gradually raised from a position of maximum loudness until the next position of maximum loudness is reached. The length of the tube above the water surface is increased by 65.0 cm. Calculate the speed of sound in the tube.

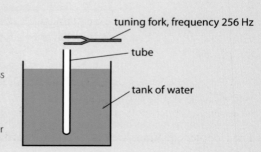

tuning fork, frequency 256 Hz

tube

tank of water

9.3 The Doppler effect

Assessment statements

A.3.1 Describe what is meant by the Doppler effect.
A.3.2 Explain the Doppler effect by reference to wavefront diagrams for moving-detector and moving-source situations.
A.3.3 Apply the Doppler effect equations for sound.
A.3.4 Solve problems on the Doppler effect for sound.
A.3.5 Solve problems on the Doppler effect for electromagnetic waves using the approximation
$$\Delta f = \frac{v}{c} f$$
A.3.6 Outline an example in which the Doppler effect is used to measure speed.

 The Doppler effect is a result of relative motion between the source of waves and the observer. The result is a difference between the observed frequency and the actual frequency.

In general, if a source of waves is moving towards us, the frequency of the waves is shifted upwards. If the source is emitting sound waves, we hear a higher frequency than the actual frequency.

The effect is commonly observed as a car or a train approaches while emitting a sound wave. This is because the wavefronts bunch up and the wavelength seems to be shortened, which increases the observed frequency.

Conversely, when a source of waves is moving away from us, the wavefronts are more spaced out, and the wavelength seems to be increased, which decreases the observed frequency.

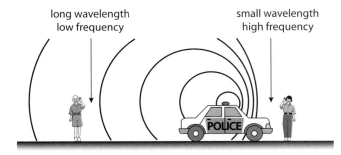

long wavelength
low frequency

small wavelength
high frequency

Figure 9.14 This shows a moving –source situation where the wavefronts are bunched up closer together in front of the car. The observer on the right will hear the frequency of the sound, Doppler-shifted upwards.

The wavefronts emitted are all are circular; in three dimensions they are spherical. The Doppler effect does not change this fact, it is just that the centre of the circle moves as the source of the sound moves.

If the car were to remain stationary, and the observer on the right moved towards the car, the effect would be exactly the same. It is the relative motion that is important, though of course the relative speed makes a difference to the scale of the effect.

Note that the speed of sound itself does not change as the frequency and wavelength are Doppler shifted. If the observer is moving towards the source however, the *apparent* speed of the waves will be greater.

The Doppler equations are not straightforward but the good news is that you do not have to derive them!

 The Doppler effect provides evidence for the Big Bang model, describing the origins of the universe. This is because measurements of the radiation reaching us from the stars show us that, in every direction, nearly all the stars are moving away from the Earth. Logically, the stars must have all been much closer together at any earlier point in time, and the extension of the logic is the beginning of space and time!

 Many people believe that the universe was created by a 'Higher Being'. Is this view in conflict with physics?

For a moving source:

$$f' = f\left(\frac{v}{v \pm u_s}\right)$$

f'	is the shifted frequency	Hz
f	is the actual frequency	Hz
v	is the speed of the wave	m s^{-1}
u_s	is the speed of the source	m s^{-1}

The $\pm$ sign depends on the direction of motion of the source. If the source is moving towards the observer, then the frequency is shifted up, so the sign is negative. If the source is moving away from the observer, then the frequency is shifted down, so the sign is positive.

For a moving observer:

$$f' = f\left(\frac{v \pm u_o}{v}\right)$$

f'	is the shifted frequency	Hz
f	is the actual frequency	Hz
v	is the speed of the wave	m s^{-1}
u_o	is the speed of the observer	m s^{-1}

If the observer is moving towards the source, then the frequency is shifted up, so the sign is positive. If the observer is moving away from the source, then the frequency is shifted down, so the sign is negative.

To view a simulation, visit www.heinemann.co.uk/hotlinks, enter the express code 4266S and click on Weblink 9.4.

Although the Doppler effect is most easy to observe with sound waves, it is an effect common to all waves. We have already mentioned the measurements made on radiation reaching us from the stars, and this radiation consists of electromagnetic waves.

All electromagnetic waves travel at the speed of light and this is an upper limit for speed – nothing can go faster. In fact, the only things that can approach the speed of light are subatomic particles; normal bodies travel at very much slower speeds.

As long as $v \ll c$ we can solve problems on the Doppler effect for electromagnetic waves using the approximation:

$$\Delta f = \frac{v}{c} f$$

Δf	is the shift in frequency	Hz
v	is the speed of the body	m s^{-1}
c	is the speed of light	m s^{-1}
f	is the frequency of the radiation	Hz

Police radar speed traps work by using the Doppler effect.

The police direct microwaves of known frequency at a car that is thought to be speeding. The microwaves reflect back from the car and are Doppler shifted. The speed of the car can then be found using the equation:

$$v = \frac{c\Delta f}{2f}$$

v	is the speed of the car	m s^{-1}
c	is the speed of light	m s^{-1}
Δf	is the shift in frequency	Hz
f	is the frequency of the microwaves	Hz

Normally the police do not actually have to use the equation themselves; the speed trap will read off the speed of the car automatically.

This equation can also be written in the form:

$$\Delta\lambda = \frac{v}{c}\lambda$$

Where λ is the wavelength of the radiation.

Worked examples

1. A car is moving at a speed of $34\,\mathrm{m\,s^{-1}}$ towards a stationary source of sound emitting a note with a constant frequency of 5.0 kHz. What frequency will be observed by the people in the car? The speed of sound in air $= 340\,\mathrm{m\,s^{-1}}$.

2. A star is moving away from the Earth at a speed of $3.0 \times 10^5\,\mathrm{m\,s^{-1}}$. If the light emitted from the star has a frequency of 6.0×10^{14} Hz, find the frequency shift observed on Earth.

Solutions

1. The observer is moving and the source is stationary so we use:

$$f' = f\left(\frac{v \pm u_o}{v}\right)$$

The observer is moving towards the source so the sign is positive:

$$f' = \left(\frac{5000\,\mathrm{Hz}\ 340\,\mathrm{m\,s^{-1}} + 34\,\mathrm{m\,s^{-1}}}{340\,\mathrm{m\,s^{-1}}}\right)$$
$$= \mathbf{5500\ Hz}$$

2. $\Delta f = \dfrac{v}{c}f$

$$\Delta f = \frac{3.0 \times 10^5\,\mathrm{m\,s^{-1}}}{3.0 \times 10^8\,\mathrm{m\,s^{-1}}} \times 6.0 \times 10^{14}\,\mathrm{Hz}$$

$$\Delta f = 6.0 \times 10^{11}\,\mathrm{Hz}$$

Exercises

6. Waves of frequency **f** and speed **c** are emitted by a stationary source of sound. An observer moves along a straight line towards the source at a constant speed **v**.
   State, in terms of **f, c** and **v**, an expression for
   (a) the wavelength of the sound detected by the observer

   (b) the apparent speed of the wave as measured by the observer.

7. A car is initially at rest with its radio playing music. There is a musical note of frequency 440 Hz spreading out form the car. The speed of sound in air is $330\,\mathrm{m\,s^{-1}}$.
   (a) Calculate the
      (i) distance between the wavefronts
      (ii) frequency of the note as heard by an observer standing some distance in front of the car

   (b) The car now moves at constant speed, **v**, towards the observer with the radio still playing. At what speed are the wavefronts progressing towards the observer?

   (c) If the speed of the car is $8.00\,\mathrm{m\,s^{-1}}$, calculate
      (i) the distance between the wavefronts that approach the observer
      (ii) the frequency of the note as heard by the observer.

8. A star is moving away from the Earth at a speed of $3.0 \times 10^5\,\mathrm{m\,s^{-1}}$. If the light emitted from the star has a frequency of 6.0×10^{14} Hz, find the wavelength shift observed on Earth.

9.4 Diffraction

Diffraction at a single slit

We saw in Chapter 4 that waves are diffracted when passing through slits. This is most noticeable if the size of the slit is approximately the same as the wavelength.

Light from a green laser at 532 nm is transmitted through a single slit to show the diffraction pattern. The central bright spot is much more intense and wider than the other bright spots.

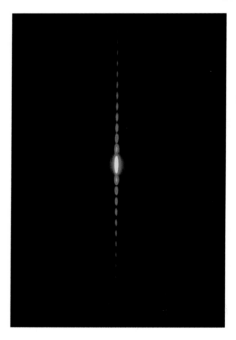

Visible light has very small wavelengths so it will be diffracted only by very narrow slits. In order to observe diffraction and interference, the light sources must be *coherent*. This means that there is a constant frequency and constant phase difference.

Figure 9.15 shows the intensity of the light diffracted against the angular position.

The reason why the central maximum is so much brighter and wider than the subsidiary maxima is that all the light interferes constructively at the centre. The angular positions of the minima are multiples of $\theta = \dfrac{\lambda}{b}$.

Figure 9.15 Single slit diffraction pattern.
In the centre of the pattern is a very bright spot called a maximum. The intensity here is much higher than the other maxima.

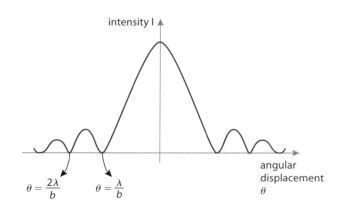

Derivation of the formula $\theta = \dfrac{\lambda}{b}$

In Figure 9.16, θ is the angular position of the first minimum. Light at a minimum interferes destructively, having arrived out of phase.

This means the path difference $\qquad$ AN $= \dfrac{\lambda}{2}$

The slit has width b and is divided into $2n$ equal parts.

This means the width of each part $\quad = \dfrac{b}{2n}$

$$\text{AB} = \dfrac{b}{2n}$$

$$\sin \theta = \dfrac{\text{AN}}{\text{AB}}$$

$$\text{AN} = \text{AB} \sin \theta = \dfrac{\lambda}{2}$$

$$\dfrac{b}{2n} \sin \theta = \dfrac{\lambda}{2}$$

Given that $n = 1$ $\qquad b \sin \theta = \lambda$

The small angle approximation tells us $\sin \theta \approx \theta$

$$b\theta = \lambda$$

$$\theta = \dfrac{\lambda}{b}$$

θ	is the angular position of the first minimum	radians
λ	is the wavelength of the light	m
b	is the width of the slit	m

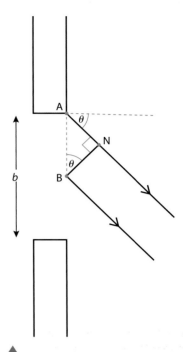

Figure 9.16

● **Examiner's hint:** The small angle approximation works if the angles are in radians. Remember $360° = 2\pi$ rad. Make sure your calculator is always in the correct mode for the problem you are trying to solve; you need to be able to switch easily between degrees and radians.

● **Examiner's hint:** You need to be able to derive this equation.

Worked example

Light of wavelength 500 nm is diffracted by a single slit 0.05 mm wide. Find the angular position of the first minimum.

Solution

We need to be careful with the units here:

$$\theta = \dfrac{\lambda}{b}$$

$$\theta = \dfrac{500 \times 10^{-9}\ m}{0.05 \times 10^{-3}\ m}$$

$$\theta = 0.01\ \text{rad}$$

 To try an applet showing single slit diffraction, visit www.heinemann.co.uk/hotlinks, enter the express code 4266S and click on Weblink 9.5.

Exercises

9 When light with a wavelength of 440 nm is diffracted through a single slit, the angular position of the first minimum is found to be 0.02 rad. Calculate the width of the slit.

9.5 Resolution

> **Assessment statements**
> A.5.1　Sketch the variation with angle of diffraction of the relative intensity of light emitted by two point sources that has been diffracted at a single slit.
> A.5.2　State the Rayleigh criterion for images of two sources to be just resolved.
> A.5.3　Describe the significance of resolution in the development of devices such as CDs and DVDs, the electron microscope and radio telescopes.
> A.5.4　Solve problems involving resolution.

Optical resolution refers to the ability of an optical system to distinguish detail. Initially we are particularly interested in the ability of a system to determine whether an image is formed by one single object, or by two different objects that are close together.

This issue applies particularly to stars viewed through telescopes but also to cells viewed through microscopes. Indeed when we look at car headlights in the distance and cannot tell if they are separate or not, it is due to the resolving power of our eyes.

Light from a distant star passes through the lens of a telescope and is diffracted around the aperture.

Lenses are circular and so they produce circular diffraction patterns. These patterns consist of a central bright disc, called *Airy's disc*, surrounded by a series of less intense rings.

◀ The bright circle in the middle contains over 90% of the diffracted light.

The Rayleigh criterion states that two images are just resolvable when the maximum intensity of the central pattern of one object falls on the first minimum of the other.

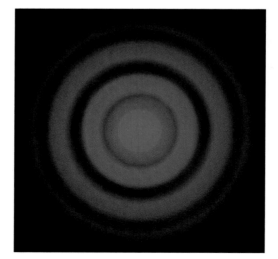

Whether or not two images can be resolved depends on how close to each other their diffraction patterns are formed. The condition for resolution is known as the *Rayleigh criterion*.

Two things limit the ability of a system to produce distinct images of two points; lens aberration and diffraction.

The Rayleigh criterion is explained in Figure 9.17. The graphs show the intensity of the diffraction patterns against distance.

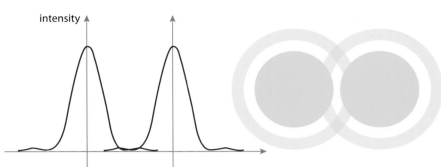

These two sources are clearly resolvable, as their Airy disks do not overlap.

Figure 9.17 The overlapping diffraction patterns from two sources.

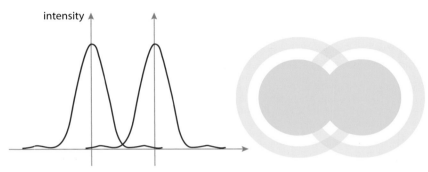

These two sources are just resolvable, the maximum of one falls on the first minimum of the other.

● **Hint:** You need to be able to sketch these three graphs.

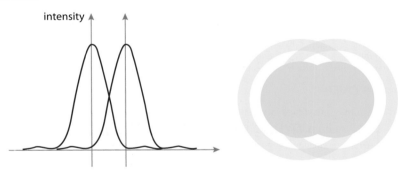

These two sources are not resolvable.

A circular aperture is not uniform like a rectangular slit. Its width varies from zero to a maximum diameter = b.

The **average** width of a circle $= \dfrac{b}{1.22}$

For this reason, the equation for solving problems involving resolution and the Rayleigh criterion is:

$$\theta = 1.22 \frac{\lambda}{b}$$

To view a simulation, visit www.heinemann.co.uk/hotlinks, enter the express code 4266S and click on Weblink 9.6.

θ	is the angle subtended by the two sources at the lens	rad
λ	is the wavelength of the light	m
b	is the diameter of the lens	m

Two objects that can only just be resolved need to have an angular separation θ (in radians) of $1.22 \frac{\lambda}{b}$.

Worked example

A spy satellite is orbiting 180 km above the surface of the Earth. If the diameter of the lens is 45 cm, find the smallest distance on the ground that can be resolved by the camera on the satellite. Take the wavelength of light to be 500 nm.

Solution

We need to be careful with the units:

$$\theta = 1.22 \frac{\lambda}{b}$$

$$\theta = 1.22 \frac{500 \times 10^{-9}\,\text{m}}{0.45\,\text{m}}$$

$$\theta = 1.36 \times 10^{-6}\,\text{rad}$$

$$\theta = \frac{s}{r} \quad (s \text{ is the arc and } r \text{ is the radius of a circle})$$

$$s = r \times \theta$$

$$= 180 \times 10^{3}\,\text{m} \times 1.36 \times 10^{-6}\,\text{rad}$$

$$\mathbf{= 0.24\ m}$$

Exercises

10 A student looks at two distant point sources of light. The wavelength of each source is 590 nm. The angular separation between these two sources is 3.6×10^{-4} radians subtended at the eye. At the eye, images of the two sources are formed on the retina.
   (a) State the Rayleigh criterion for the two images on the retina to be just resolved.
   (b) Estimate the diameter of the circular aperture of the eye.
   (c) Use your estimate in (b) to determine whether the student can resolve these two sources. Explain your answer.

Resolution and technology

Resolution or resolving power has had great significance in recent technological development.

CDs and DVDs

Music CDs have data tracks around 5×10^{-7} m wide, with pits and bumps just over 1×10^{-7} m high. DVDs and HD DVDs use similar technology, but with different formats and smaller tracks and pits, so they can store much more data. The data is read by a laser and the beam must be focused perfectly by a lens in order that the information can be resolved. The dimensions of the tracks and pits are of the order of the wavelengths of visible light.

Micrograph of the pits that encode information on the surface of a DVD (digital versatile disc). These pits are read by a focused laser as the disc rotates.

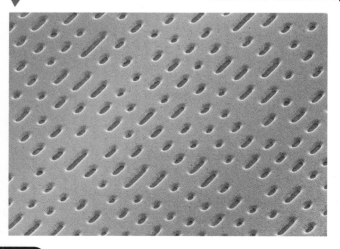

Electron microscopes

In order to resolve below the limits imposed by the wavelength of visible light, the wave properties of electrons are used in electron microscopes.

In a transmission electron microscope a high voltage electron beam carries information about the structure of the object to the imaging system, where it is magnified by electromagnetic lenses and detected by a CCD.

A scanning electron microscope detects information from secondary electrons emitted from the surface of an object due to excitation by the primary electron beam.

The wavelengths associated with electrons are very much shorter than those of visible light so there is greater magnification and better resolution of detail.

9.6 Polarization

Assessment statements

A.6.1   Describe what is meant by *polarized light*.
A.6.2   Describe polarization by reflection.
A.6.3   State and apply Brewster's law.
A.6.4   Explain the terms polarizer and analyser.
A.6.5   Calculate the intensity of a transmitted beam of polarized light using Malus' law.
A.6.6   Describe what is meant by an *optically active* substance.
A.6.7   Describe the use of polarization in the determination of the concentration of certain solutions.
A.6.8   Outline qualitatively how polarization may be used in stress analysis.
A.6.9   Outline qualitatively the action of liquid-crystal displays (LCDs).
A.6.10   Solve problems involving the polarization of light.

Radio telescopes are used in the search for extraterrestrial intelligence. They are large dishes that collect data in the radio frequency range of the electromagnetic spectrum. To increase their resolution they are combined in large arrays.

The electromagnetic nature of light

The speed of light can be found from the electric and magnetic constants.

$$c = \sqrt{\frac{1}{\varepsilon_o \mu_o}}$$

c is the speed of light in a vacuum $m\,s^{-1}$
ε_o is the permittivity of free space $C^2N^{-1}m^{-2}$
μ_o is the permeability of free space TmA^{-1}

This is very good evidence that light is electromagnetic in nature. The fact that light can be shown to undergo diffraction and interference provides evidence that light behaves as a wave.

The vibrations of light waves can be considered as oscillating, mutually perpendicular electric and magnetic fields. The fields have the same frequency and are in phase. The oscillations are perpendicular to the direction of travel; light is a *transverse wave*.

The fact that light can be polarized provides evidence that it is a transverse wave.

One way of polarizing light is by passing it through a filter known as a *polaroid*.

Light can also be shown to have a particle nature; we say it has a dual nature, rather like a split personality!

Light waves in which the oscillations occur in only one plane is known as *polarized* or *plane-polarized* light. The process of transforming natural light into polarized light is called *polarization*.

◀ **Figure 9.18** The polaroid only transmits oscillations in one plane.

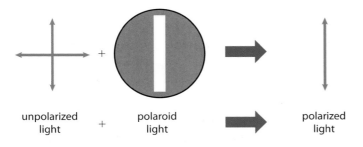

unpolarized light   +   polaroid light   polarized light

Polarization by reflection

When natural light is incident on the surface of a stretch of calm water, some light will enter the water and be refracted, and some light will be reflected.

The incident ray is travelling in air ($n = 1$) so we can write:

$$n\,(\text{water}) = \frac{\sin i}{\sin r}$$

Only transverse waves can be polarized; longitudinal waves cannot be polarized.

Some animals can see the polarization of light and obtain navigational cues from the direction of the plane polarization.

n is the refractive index of water

$\sin i$ is the sine of the angle of incidence

$\sin r$ is the sine of the angle of refraction

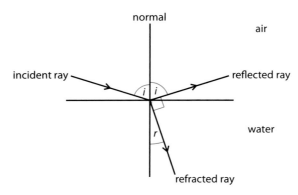

Since the reflected ray and the refracted ray are at 90° and the straight line down the normal is 180°:

$$i + r = 90°$$
$$r = 90° - i$$

From the above equation:

$$n = \frac{\sin i}{\sin(90 - i)}$$

$$n = \frac{\sin i}{\cos i}$$

$$n = \tan i$$

The angle here is known as the *polarizing angle* or the *Brewster angle*.

$$n = \tan \Phi$$

n is the refractive index of the medium

Φ is the Brewster angle

Whenever light is reflected it is partially plane polarized; natural light is also partially polarized when it is scattered on passing through the atmosphere.

The reflected glare off the surface of a lake is partially polarized light that was incident at an angle too large to be refracted. This glare usually prevents us from seeing anything below the surface of the water.

Polaroid sunglasses use selective absorption in the polarizing material of the lenses to reduce glare.

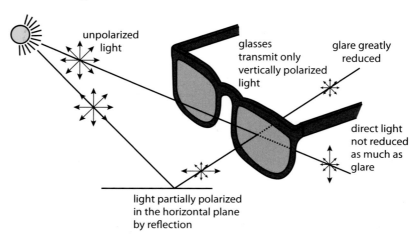

Polaroid combinations

If two sheets of polarizing material, or polaroids, are arranged so that they are mutually perpendicular then no light can pass through the combination. This is because the first one transmits light in only one plane, and this plane is blocked or absorbed by the second one. Such a combination is said to be crossed.

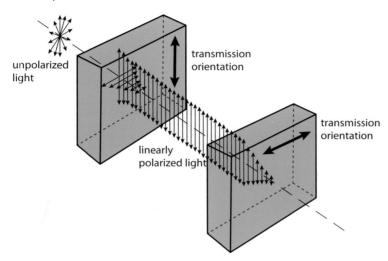

Figure 9.21 Natural light passes through the first polaroid and plane polarized light is incident on the second polaroid. The orientation of the second polaroid is at 90° so no light is transmitted.

The second polaroid is called the *analyser* because it determines both whether the light is polarized and also the plane of the polarization.

If the analyser is not perpendicular to the polarizer, but orientated at an angle θ, then the intensity of the transmitted light is given by Malus' law.

In this situation, the first polaroid is called the *polarizer* and the second one is called the *analyser*.

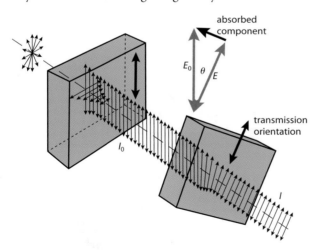

Figure 9.22 When the analyser is rotated, the component perpendicular to its transmission plane is absorbed.

Some of the light incident on the analyser is absorbed and some is transmitted, the amount depending on the angle. The intensity of the light is reduced by the combination.

Malus' law can be expressed as an equation:

$$I = I_o\cos^2\theta$$

I is the transmitted intensity   candela (cd) or W m^{-2}

I_o is the incident intensity   cd or W m^{-2}

θ is the angle between the two polaroids

The candela is a fundamental SI unit and measures the intensity of light.

Optically active substances

A material that rotates the plane of incident plane polarized light is said to be *optically active*. Some substances rotate the plane in the clockwise direction and some rotate it in the anticlockwise direction.

Optical activity is used in the sugar industry to measure the concentrations of syrup.

Some naturally occurring substances show optical activity when they are in solution. Examples include quartz and simple sugars like glucose and fructose. The amount of optical activity depends on the concentration of the solution.

In the photographs you can see how this looks in practice using the fruit sugar fructose.

▶ Optical activity of fructose demonstrated by using polarized light. Optically active compounds rotate light waves that pass through them. This can only be seen under polarized light. Different angles produce different colours - here the angle is 75°.

▶ Polarized light passes through the fructose, and then through another polarizing filter. The second filter shows fructose's optical activity strengthening one of the colours of the light. The colour depends on the relative angles of the filters, here 50°.

Some transparent materials become optically active under stress, and so polarization can be used in *stress analysis*. The colours become visible when the stressed material is viewed placed between two crossed polaroids.

Engineers can use the idea by making a model of a structure from a transparent material. For example, if engineers are designing a bridge, they can construct a scale model and subject it to the kinds of stress that are anticipated in real life.

An analysis of the coloured patterns can help them modify and improve the design and maybe prevent expensive mistakes.

Liquid-crystal displays (LCDs)

LCD's are made of arrays of pixels between crossed polaroids. When a voltage is applied across electrodes, the resulting electric field moves the liquid crystal molecules in the pixels. In one of the most common type of LCD, the liquid crystals twist and untwist according to the strength of the field.

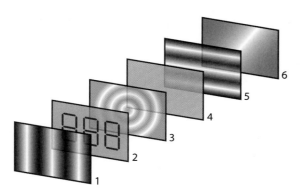

◀ Figure 9.23
1. Vertical filter polarizes the light as it enters.
2. Glass substrate with electrodes. The shapes of these electrodes will determine the dark shapes that appear when the LCD is turned on or off.
3. Twisted liquid crystals.
4. Glass substrate with common electrode film.
5. Horizontal filter film to block/allow through light.
6. Reflective surface to send light back to viewer.

There is a reflector at the back of the display and when no voltage is applied to the electrodes, light simply reflects straight back. When the display is switched on, the liquid crystal molecules untwist and block the light.

Worked examples

1 Find the angle of incidence at which natural light can be reflected plane polarized from the surface of a lake. The refractive index of water is 1.33.

2 Natural, unpolarized light of intensity 6.0 W m^{-2} is incident on two polaroids orientated at 60° to each other. Find the intensity of light that will be transmitted.

Solutions

1 We will use the Brewster equation:

$$n = \tan \Phi$$

$$1.33 = \tan \Phi$$

$$\Phi = \tan^{-1}(1.33)$$

$$\boldsymbol{\Phi = 53.1°}$$

2 The first polaroid will absorb half the incident intensity, so 3.0 W m^{-2} will be incident on the second polaroid.

To find how much is transmitted we must use Malus' law:

$$I = I_o \cos^2 \theta$$

$$I = 3.0 \text{ W m}^{-2} \cos(60)^2$$

$$I = 3.0 \times 0.25$$

$$\boldsymbol{I = 0.75 \text{ W m}^{-2}}$$

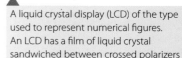

A liquid crystal display (LCD) of the type used to represent numerical figures. An LCD has a film of liquid crystal sandwiched between crossed polarizers and set on top of a mirror.

LCDs are truly global and have impacted on all our lives; they are all around us. LCDs are found in our watches, digital clocks, calculators, laptops and flat screen televisions. We see them in the displays of our microwave ovens, CD players and mobile phones.

Exercises

11 (a) A ray of unpolarized light is incident on two sheets of Polaroid, but an observer behind the second sheet cannot see any light. Explain this observation.

(b) One of the sheets of polaroid is held stationary while the other is rotated about its axis through 360°. Sketch a graph to show the variation of intensity (as seen by the observer) against the angle of rotation from zero to 360°.

12 At what angle should the axes of two polaroids be placed so the intensity of incident unpolarized light is reduced *in total* by 75%?

Practice questions

1 This question is about standing waves in pipes.
The diagram below shows two pipes of the same length. Pipe A is open at both ends and pipe B is closed at one end.

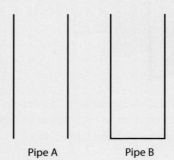

Pipe A   Pipe B

(a) **(i)** On the diagrams above, draw lines to represent the waveforms of the fundamental (first harmonic) resonant note for each pipe.

(ii) On each diagram, label the position of the nodes with the letter N and the position of the antinodes with the letter A.

The frequency of the fundamental note for pipe A is 512 Hz.

(b) **(i)** Calculate the length of the pipe A. (Speed of sound in air = 325 m s^{-1})

(ii) Suggest why organ pipes designed to emit low frequency fundamental notes (*e.g.* frequency $\approx$ 32 Hz) are often closed at one end.

2 This question is about the Doppler effect.
The diagram below shows wavefronts produced by a stationary wave source S. The spacing of the wavefronts is equal to the wavelength of the waves. The wavefronts travel with speed *V*.

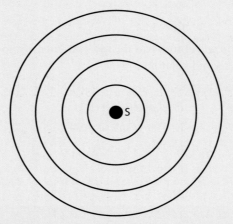

(a) The source S now moves to the right with speed $\frac{1}{2}V$. In the space below, draw *four* successive wavefronts to show the pattern of waves produced by the moving source.

(b) The Sun rotates about its centre. The light from one edge of the Sun, as seen by a stationary observer, shows a Doppler shift of 0.004 nm for light of wavelength 600.000 nm.
Assuming that the Doppler formula for sound may be used for light, estimate the linear speed of a point on the surface of the Sun due to its rotation.

3 The two point sources shown in the diagram below (not to scale) emit light of the same frequency. The light is incident on a rectangular, narrow slit and after passing through the slit, is brought to a focus on the screen.

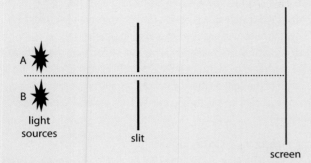

Source B is covered.

(a) Using the axes below, draw a sketch graph to show how the intensity *I* of the light from A varies with distance along the screen. Label the curve you have drawn A.

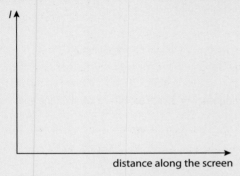

Source B is now uncovered. The images of A and B on the screen are just resolved.

(b) Using the same axes as in (a), draw a sketch graph to show how the intensity *I* of the light from B varies with distance along the screen. Label this curve B.

The bright star Sirius A is accompanied by a much fainter star, Sirius B. The mean distance of the stars from Earth is 8.1×10^{16} m. Under ideal atmospheric conditions, a telescope with an objective lens of diameter 25 cm can just resolve the stars as two separate images.

(c) Assuming that the average wavelength emitted by the stars is 500 nm, estimate the apparent, linear separation of the two stars.

4 In an experiment, monochromatic light of wavelength 400 nm is incident on a single slit of width 1600 nm. Bright and dark fringes are viewed on a screen and the angular positions of the maxima and minima are measured.

(a) Calculate the first two angles at which the intensity of the light is at a *minimum*.

(b) Sketch a graph to show how the intensity of the light varies as a function of angle up to 30°.

5 This question is about resolution.

(a) State the name of the wave phenomenon that limits the resolution of any optical instrument.

(b) Explain with the aid of a diagram, the Rayleigh criterion.

6 Yasmin looks at a particular star with her naked eye and she sees the star as a point of light. When she looks at the star through a telescope she sees that there are two points of light. The star Yasmin is looking at is actually two stars close together.

  (a) Explain, assuming Yasmin's eyes are functioning normally,

  (i) why she is unable to distinguish the two stars with her naked eye

  (ii) how the telescope enables her to distinguish the stars.

  (b) The system that Yasmin is observing is 4.2×10^{16} m from the Earth and the two stars are separated by a distance of 2.6×10^{11} m. Assuming that the average wavelength of the light emitted by the stars is 500 nm, estimate the diameter of the objective lens of a telescope that will just enable the two stars to be distinguished.

7 This question is about the polarization of light.

  (a) Joe looks into a pond on a bright day. Explain why he will get a clearer view of the bottom of he pond if wears polaroid sunglasses than if he were to wear ordinary sunglasses.

  (b) At what angle to the normal should Joe look in order to see the bottom of the pond most clearly? (Refractive index of water = 1.3)

10 Quantum physics and nuclear physics (Option B)

10.1 Quantum physics

Assessment statements
B.1.1 Describe the photoelectric effect.
B.1.2 Describe the concept of the photon and use it to explain the photoelectric effect.
B.1.3 Describe and explain an experiment to test the Einstein model.
B.1.4 Solve problems involving the photoelectric effect.
B.1.5 Describe the de Broglie hypothesis and the concept of matter waves.
B.1.6 Outline an experiment to verify the de Broglie hypothesis.
B.1.7 Solve problems involving matter waves.
B.1.8 Outline a laboratory procedure for producing and observing atomic spectra.
B.1.9 Explain how atomic spectra provide evidence for the quantization of energy in atoms.
B.1.10 Calculate wavelengths of spectral lines from energy level differences and vice versa.
B.1.11 Explain the origin of atomic energy levels in terms of the "electron in a box" model.
B.1.12 Outline the Schrödinger model of the hydrogen atom.
B.1.13 Outline the Heisenberg uncertainty principle with regard to position–momentum and time-energy.

The quantum nature of radiation

There is a famous physics experiment called *Young's two slits*, because it is generally believed to have been performed by Thomas Young in Cambridge, England in 1801. It shows that light undergoes diffraction and interference. Because these are classic wave properties, the experiment provides compelling evidence for the wave nature of light.

Although earlier theories, including that of Newton, had described light as a stream of corpuscles, or particles, few people in the late 19th century doubted that light was a wave.

The photoelectric effect

From around 1840 onwards, scientists had been conducting experiments which seemed to show that, when they shone a light on a metal surface, there was some kind of electrical reaction. In 1887 Heinrich Hertz

Hallwachs' electroscope. This device was used in an 1888 experiment by the German physicist Wilhelm Hallwachs. Light passing through the square hole in the black screen illuminates a round copper plate. Below is a charged electroscope; the thread is deflected to one side. If the light is of sufficient energy, the electroscope will lose its charge and the thread will drop. This is because the light is causing electrons to be emitted from the copper plate.

published the results of his work on this effect but he did not attempt to explain it. The famous and well-respected physicist J.J. Thomson explained the effect by hypothesizing that, when light was incident, electrons were being emitted from the metal surface.

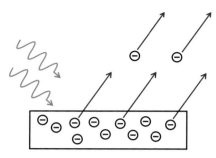

Figure 10.1 In order for photoelectrons to be emitted from a metal surface, sufficient energy must be gained from the incoming radiation.

The electrons emitted were called *photoelectrons,* and if the experimental set-up was right, they could cause a small electric current to flow. The phenomenon was called the *photoelectric effect.* The photoelectric effect is caused by electrons in the surface of the metal absorbing sufficient energy from incoming radiation to overcome the attractive electrostatic (or coulomb) force of the protons in the nucleus.

The experiments were conducted carefully and repeated many times and the results were surprising. Whether or not photoelectrons were emitted depended on the colour, or, more accurately, the frequency of the incident light. Sometimes the experimenters used electromagnetic radiation of higher frequency than visible light, such as ultra-violet, and this seemed to be more effective with some metals.

The reasons wave theory could not account for the photoelectric effect are:

1 There was no explanation for the existence of the threshold frequency.
2 There was no reason why the *frequency* should affect the kinetic energy of the photoelectrons.
3 According to wave theory, increasing the *intensity* should increase the kinetic energy of the photoelectrons.
4 If the light is of low intensity, wave theory predicts that it would take some time for an electron to absorb sufficient energy to escape.

For a given metal there was a particular frequency below which no photoemission occurred and this came to be known as the *threshold frequency.* Increasing the frequency of the incident radiation above the threshold frequency was found to increase the kinetic energy of the photoelectrons.

Increasing the intensity, or brightness, of the incident light had no effect on the kinetic energy of the photoelectrons, but it was discovered that the number of electrons emitted was directly proportional to the intensity.

In addition it was found that the emission of photoelectrons started *immediately* the metal surface was irradiated.

The reason these results were so surprising was that they could not be explained by classical wave theory, and of course, at the time, light was believed to have an exclusively wave nature.

Einstein published his paper on the photoelectric effect on 1905. He proposed that radiation could be considered as quanta or little packets of light and these later came to be known as *photons.*

Here is a fundamental change in the way we think about light. Previously there had been no doubt about the wave nature of light but now it seems light also behaves as a particle. A change like this is called a *paradigm shift.*

According to Einstein, when a photon collided with an electron in the surface of a metal it could either rebound or transfer all its energy to the electron. This explained why the number of electrons emitted was directly proportional to the intensity of the light, since intensity is a measure of the number of incident photons.

Einstein used Planck's equation to explain other features of the photoelectric effect. Planck had shown in 1901 that the energy distribution of a spectrum could be explained by assuming that the radiation was emitted as discrete, separate units or *quanta* of energy.

Einstein reasoned that the energy of the incident photons needed to be sufficient to overcome the binding coulomb attraction of the nucleus to cause photoemission. If there were surplus incoming energy this could be converted to kinetic energy of the photoelectrons.

Assuming that the energy of the photons was given by Planck's equation, then this explained the threshold frequency. The light had to have a frequency, and thus energy, high enough to separate the electrons from the nucleus before any photoelectric current could be detected.

The amount of energy needed to overcome the attractive force of the nucleus on the electron is called the *work function*. This is a constant for any given metal. If the frequency of the incoming photon is the threshold frequency, then there will be just sufficient energy to remove the electron from the atom. This situation is summarised in the following equation.

$$E = hf_o = \Phi$$

E	is the energy of the incident photon	J
h	is Planck's constant	Js
f_o	is the threshold frequency	Hz
Φ	is the work function	J

Planck's equation is:
$$E = hf$$
E is a quantum of energy   J

h is a constant known as Planck's constant $= 6.63 \times 10^{-34}$ Js

f is the frequency of the radiation   Hz

If we take out the constant, the equation tells us that the energy of light is directly proportional to the frequency.

Max Planck (1858–1947) was a very talented musician but preferred to study physics.

Worked example

In an experiment to investigate the photoelectric effect, electrons are emitted from a metal surface when the wavelength of the incident radiation reaches 300 nm. Find the work function of the metal.

Solution

First we calculate the threshold frequency using the equation:

$$c = f_o \lambda$$

c is the speed of light

λ is the wavelength of the incident light

$$f_o = \frac{c}{\lambda}$$

$$f_o = \frac{3 \times 10^8 \text{ m s}^{-1}}{3 \times 10^7 \text{ m}}$$

$$f_o = 1.0 \times 10^{15} \text{ Hz}$$

Then we can calculate the work function:

$$\Phi = hf_o$$

$$\Phi = 6.6 \times 10^{-34} \text{ Js} \times 1.0 \times 10^{15} \text{ Hz}$$

$$\boldsymbol{\Phi = 6.6 \times 10^{-19} \text{ J}}$$

Of course, if the work function is greater than the energy of the photon then no photoemission can occur. If the energy of the photon is greater than the work function then we can apply Einstein's photoelectric equation:

$$hf = hf_o + E_{max}$$

Einstein's photoelectric equation is:
$$hf = hf_o + E_{max}$$

hf is the energy of the incident photon   J

hf_o is the energy required to separate the electron from the nucleus   J

E_{max} is the maximum kinetic energy of the photoelectrons   J

Some ten years after Einstein published his ideas about the photoelectric effect, the great experimenter Robert Millikan performed experiments to test the Einstein model. He shone monochromatic light of a large range of frequencies onto various metal surfaces in an evacuated chamber.

The electrons emitted were collected and flowed through a meter to show a current. Millikan then applied a positive voltage or potential to the target metal until the photoemission was stopped and the current dropped to zero. This potential is called the *stopping potential*. Here is a simplified diagram of the apparatus.

Figure 10.2 Millikan's photoelectric effect experiment.

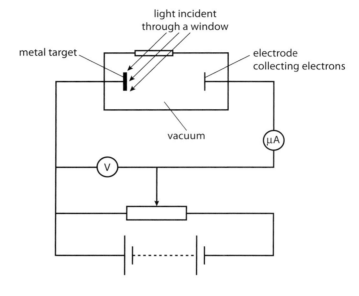

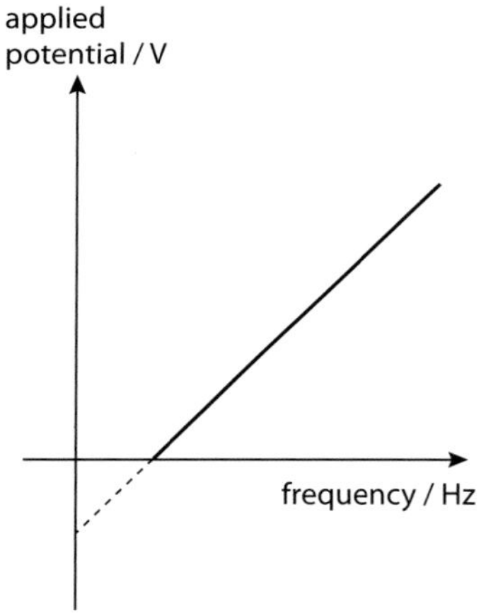

applied potential / V

frequency / Hz

When the current dropped to zero it meant that the there was sufficient electrical energy to reduce the kinetic energy of the electrons to zero. This idea can be expressed in the equation:

$$eV = E_{max}$$

eV	is the electrical energy	J
e	is the charge on the electron	C
V	is the stopping potential	V
E_{max}	is the maximum kinetic energy of the photoelectrons	J

Einstein's photoelectric equation can be re-written as:

$$hf = hf_o + eV$$

Experimental results give a graph as shown in Figure 10.3.

Remembering that $\Phi = hf_o$, then we can write the equation in the form:

$$hf = \Phi + eV$$

Rearranging:

$$eV = hf - \Phi$$

Dividing by e:

$$V = \frac{hf}{e} - \frac{\Phi}{e}$$

Because the graph is a straight line it has the general form:

$$y = mx + c$$

V is on the y-axis and f on the x-axis so the gradient is $\frac{h}{e}$ and the y-intercept is negative.

Figure 10.3 The gradient of this graph is $\frac{h}{e}$ the y-intercept is $-\frac{\phi}{e}$ and the x-intercept is f_o.

To try the simulation 'The photo-electric effect', visit www.heinemann.co.uk/hotlinks, enter the express code 4266S and click on Weblink 10.1.

1 Light is incident on a clean metal surface in a vacuum. The maximum kinetic energy KE_{max} of the electrons ejected from the surface is measured for different values of the frequency f of the incident light.

The measurements are shown in Figure 10.4.

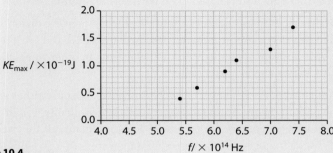

$KE_{max} / \times 10^{-19} J$

$f/ \times 10^{14}$ Hz

Figure 10.4

(a) Draw a line of best fit for the plotted data points.

(b) Use the graph to determine
   (i) the Planck constant
   (ii) the minimum energy required to eject an electron from the surface of the metal (the **work function**).

(c) Explain briefly how Einstein's photoelectric theory accounts for the fact that no electrons are emitted from the surface of this metal if the frequency of the incident light is less than a certain value.

2 In order to demonstrate the photoelectric effect, the apparatus shown in Figure 10.5 is used.

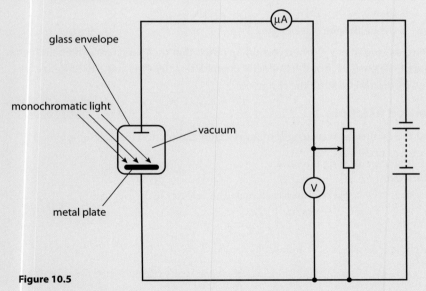

Figure 10.5

Monochromatic light is incident on the metal plate. The potentiometer is adjusted to give the minimum voltage at which there is zero reading on the microammeter.

(a) State and explain what change, if any, will occur in the reading of the microammeter when
   (i) the intensity of the incident light is increased but the frequency remains unchanged
   (ii) the frequency of the light is increased at constant intensity.

(b) For light of wavelength 540 nm, the minimum reading on the voltmeter for zero current is 1.9 V.
   (i) State the connection between photon energy and the energy of the emitted electron.
   (ii) Hence calculate the work function of the surface of the metal plate.

Light has existed since the beginning of time. Does it really matter whether we call it a wave or a particle?

The wave-particle duality is not as strange as it seems; think about the following analogy. When you look at a good map you will see lots of information. There will be lines showing the roads in different colours and there will be lines showing the contours of the land, the altitude relative to sea level. Both of these sets of lines are accurate descriptions of the reality of the local geography, but neither is complete without the other.

The de Broglie hypothesis states that any particle of matter with momentum p, has an associated wavelength λ.

In 1927 de Broglie's theory was proved experimentally with the measurement of the wavelength of the electron. This wave-particle duality was used by Schrödinger in his formulation of quantum mechanics. In 1929 de Broglie received the Nobel prize for physics.

The wave nature of matter

As the implications of the photoelectric effect became apparent, physicists were forced to reassess their thinking about the nature of light. On the one hand the Young's two slits experiment had apparently shown that light had a wave nature. The fact that light could be polarized even indicated the type of wave; transverse. Now it seemed that light also behaved like a particle, the photon.

When repeatable experiments do not support the theory, then the theory must change, and in this case a compromise was reached. It is called the *wave-particle duality* and what it means is that light has a dual nature. In other words, light can behave both as a wave and as a particle.

In order to understand the results of any experiment we must use either wave theory or the photon theory, but not both. In some senses, duality was already inherent in Planck's equation, $E = hf$, because E in the equation is the energy of a particle and f is the frequency of the corresponding wave.

Louis de Broglie felt that nature should be symmetrical, and so he reasoned, writing in 1924, that if light had a particle nature, then particles should also have a wave nature.

This wavelength of particles is called the *de Broglie wavelength* and the waves are often called *matter waves*. In fact they are not mechanical or electromagnetic waves but mathematical constructs related to the probability of finding the particle in a particular place.

The de Broglie equation is:
$$p = \frac{h}{\lambda}$$

p	is the momentum of the particle	Ns
h	is Planck's constant	Js
λ	is the de Broglie wavelength	m

Remembering that $p = mv$, it should be noted that the mass here is the relativistic mass of the particle, but if its velocity is much less than the velocity of light ($v \ll c$), then we can use the rest mass.

Worked example

Find the de Broglie wavelength of an electron accelerated through a potential difference of 30 V.

Solution

We use energy conservation to calculate the velocity if the electron:

$$eV = \tfrac{1}{2} mv^2$$

$$v = \sqrt{\frac{2eV}{m}}$$

$$= \sqrt{\frac{2 \times 1.6 \times 10^{-19}\,\text{C} \times 30\,\text{V}}{9.1 \times 10^{-31}\,\text{kg}}}$$

$$3.2 \times 10^6\,\text{m s}^{-1}$$

Then we can calculate the de Broglie wavelength:

$$p = \frac{h}{\lambda}$$

$$\lambda = \frac{h}{p}$$

$$= \frac{6.6 \times 10^{-34}\,\text{Js}}{9.1 \times 10^{-31}\,\text{kg} \times 3.2 \times 10^6\,\text{m s}^{-1}}$$

$$= 2.3 \times 10^{-10}\,\text{m}$$

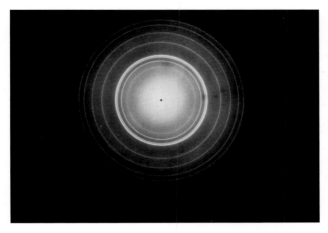

In this photograph, electrons have produced the pattern of rings associated with diffraction. Diffraction occurs when a wave passes through an aperture similar in size to its wavelength. But electrons are particles, so should not exhibit the same phenomenon unless they can also behave like waves.

In 1927 Davisson and Germer confirmed the de Broglie hypothesis experimentally by showing that electrons could be diffracted. They fired a beam of electrons, accelerated by an electron gun, at a crystal of nickel, which functioned as a diffraction grating.

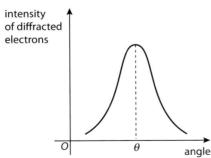

Figure 10.6 The beam from an electron gun is scattered by the crystal. Regularly spaced nickel atoms in the lattice act like a diffraction grating.

Davisson and Germer observed maxima of intensity at particular angles depending on the accelerating voltage.

Figure 10.7 The graph shows the distribution of intensity, or number of electrons in the scattered beam, against the angle.

They analyzed the data using the diffraction equation:

$$d \sin\theta = n\lambda$$

where d is the spacing of the atoms.

Electron microscopes are practical applications of the de Broglie hypothesis; they are based on the idea that electrons have a shorter wavelength than visible light, and this is why they are able to see deeper into matter than light microscopes.

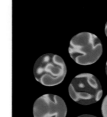

To try a simulation of Davisson-Germer: 'Electron Diffraction', visit www.heinemann.co.uk/hotlinks, enter the express code 4266S and click Weblink 10.2.

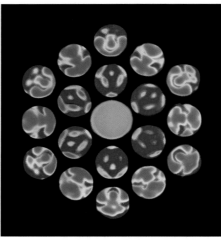

The values they obtained experimentally for λ agreed with those predicted by the de Broglie equation. Their experiments confirmed Louis de Broglie's hypothesis that electrons have a dual nature; they can behave both as particles and as waves.

Electron diffraction pattern of a particle in an alloy of 90% titanium and 10% nickel. This alloy is used in the aerospace industry and in medical operations like hip replacements.

Exercises

3 **(a)** Explain what is meant by the *de Broglie wavelength* of a particle.
   (b) Calculate the de Broglie wavelength of an electron that has been accelerated from rest through a potential difference of 5.0 kV.

4 An experiment is carried out in which a beam of electrons is scattered from a single nickel crystal. A schematic diagram of the apparatus is shown below.

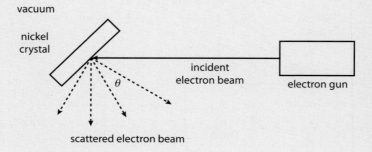

The electrons are accelerated in the electron gun by a potential difference of 75 V.
(a) Determine the wavelength associated with the electrons as predicted by the de Broglie hypothesis.

The number n of electrons scattered per second through an angle θ is measured. The graph below shows the variation with angle θ of n.

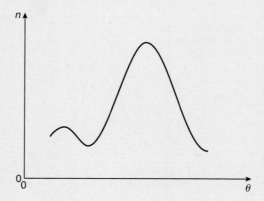

(b) Suggest how the shape of this graph supports the de Broglie hypothesis.

Atomic spectra and atomic energy states

In Chapter 7 we introduced the ideas of atomic energy levels and emission and absorption spectra. If an atom gains energy, in the form of either heat or electrical energy, its electrons will become excited and rise to a higher energy level. Later the electrons will drop back to a lower energy level, emitting energy in the form of electromagnetic radiation or photons.

The energy emitted forms a spectrum with colours, or frequencies, that are characteristic of the element.

The element helium was named from the Greek word for the Sun, Helios, after the gas was discovered in a spectrum emitted from the Sun.

Observing atomic spectra

Line spectra can be observed in the laboratory using a *spectroscope* or a *spectrometer*. Sometimes these names are used interchangeably but the word spectroscope is usually used for a small tube, like a miniature telescope, containing a diffraction grating.

When light is viewed through the spectroscope, correctly focused, a characteristic spectrum is observed. If the light is from a neon or sodium lamp, then we see an *emission spectrum* with coloured lines on a black background.

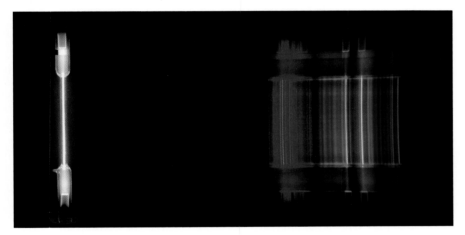

The spectra of neon gas observed through a diffraction grating. Each coloured line corresponds to a specific energy of photons released by electrons jumping down to different energy levels.

For any particular element the emission and absorption spectra are the same, but the emission spectrum consists of coloured lines on a black background, while the absorption spectrum consists of black lines on a coloured background.

If we view light from the Sun through the spectroscope, we see a continuous spectrum with a number of black lines. This is called an *absorption spectrum* and the lines are called *absorption lines*. Atoms can absorb light at the same frequencies they emit light. The missing lines are caused by absorption both by the cooler outer atmosphere of the Sun and by the atmosphere of the Earth.

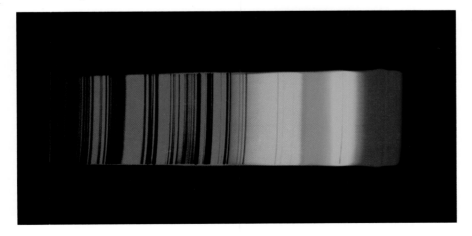

In this solar spectrum, the dark absorption lines are the result of photons of specific energy, and therefore frequency, being absorbed by elements in the atmosphere, so that they do not reach Earth. The faint line at the red end of the spectrum is one of the hydrogen lines. The line in the yellow part is due to a pair of sodium lines.

Figure 10.8 A spectrometer. The wavelength of the light can be accurately measured using the diffraction grating equation:
$$d \sin\theta = n\lambda.$$

The spectrometer

A more sophisticated way of observing an atomic spectrum involves using a spectrometer; a piece of apparatus with a moveable eyepiece on a turntable. Light from the source enters through a slit into the collimator; a device which transmits a parallel beam. The light then passes through a diffraction grating before being viewed through the eyepiece.

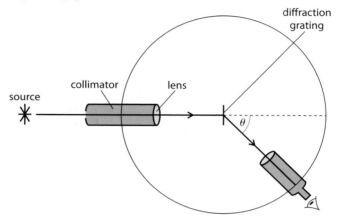

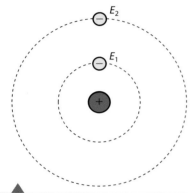

Figure 10.9 If the electron at energy level E_1 absorbs energy, it can move up to energy level E_2.

When it drops back again, it emits the absorbed energy as an electromagnetic wave where:
$$E_2 - E_1 = hf$$
and f is the frequency of the wave.

According to the Bohr model of the atom the energies of electrons can only have certain permitted values called *energy levels*.

If the electron gains energy it can be promoted to a higher energy level. Some time later it will drop back to a lower level and emit the energy as electromagnetic radiation. The electrons move between quantized states.

The energy levels are characteristic of elements, and the lines on atomic emission spectra show the electromagnetic radiation emitted by electrons dropping back to lower energy levels. Atomic spectra provide evidence for the quantization of energy in atoms.

The values of the energy levels are negative and usually given in electronvolts. The numbers of the energy levels are called *quantum numbers*. The lowest energy level, called the *ground state*, is when the quantum number $n = 1$. If the electron gains enough energy to totally escape the electrostatic force of the nucleus, it reaches $n = \infty$ and the atom becomes ionized.

Figure 10.10 Energy levels of hydrogen. The values of the energy levels are shown on the left and the quantum numbers are shown on the right.

If the electron absorbs enough energy to reach $n = \infty$ then the value rises to zero.

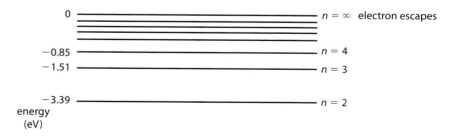

If an electron has absorbed sufficient energy to rise from the ground state to level $n = 3$ it can return to level $n = 1$ in two ways:

directly from $n = 3 \rightarrow n = 1$

or from $n = 3 \rightarrow n = 2 \rightarrow n = 1$

There are three possible transitions here:

$n = 3 \rightarrow n = 1$

$n = 3 \rightarrow n = 2$

$n = 2 \rightarrow n = 1$

Each transition involves the emission of a different colour of light corresponding to the lines of the emission spectrum. The transition from $n = 3 \rightarrow n = 1$ has the greatest energy difference and so the electromagnetic radiation emitted will have the greatest frequency, according to the equation $\Delta E = hf$. Note that because the frequency is the greatest, the wavelength will be the smallest.

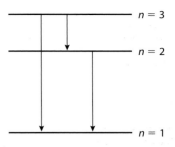

Figure 10.11 The difference in energy as the electron drops back between $n = 3$ and $n = 1$ is the clearly the largest. This means the electromagnetic radiation emitted as a result will be the most energetic of these three transitions.

Worked example

Find the wavelength of light in the hydrogen spectrum corresponding to a transition from $n = 2$ to $n = 1$.

Solution

As always, first we write down the equation we need:

$$\Delta E = E_2 - E_1 = hf$$

Using values from Figure 10.10:

$$\Delta E = (-3.39\,\text{eV}) - (-13.6\,\text{eV}) = 10.21\,\text{eV}$$

This must be converted to SI units:

$$10.21\,\text{eV} \times 1.6 \times 10^{-19}\,\text{C} = 1.63 \times 10^{-18}\,\text{J}$$

Now we can calculate the frequency:

$$f = \frac{\Delta E}{h}$$

$$= \frac{1.63 \times 10^{-18}\,\text{J}}{6.63 \times 10^{-34}\,\text{J}}$$

$$= 2.46 \times 10^{15}\,\text{Hz}$$

Then the wavelength

$$\lambda = \frac{c}{f}$$

$$= \frac{3.0 \times 10^{8}\,\text{m s}^{-1}}{2.46 \times 10^{15}\,\text{Hz}}$$

$$= 1.22 \times 10^{-7}\,\text{m}$$

This is equal to 122 nm and is below the visible wavelengths of light; it would be in the ultra-violet region of the electromagnetic spectrum.

These types of calculations agree with the observed values for hydrogen and provide evidence for the Bohr model and for the existence of energy levels. For more complex atoms, the frequency values calculated do not agree with the observed frequencies.

 In science when the theory only works for simple situations, then it needs to be replaced by a better, more successful, theory.

5   Diagram **(a)** below shows part of the emission line spectrum of atomic hydrogen. The wavelengths of the principal lines in the visible region of the spectrum are shown. Diagram **(b)** shows some of the principal energy levels of atomic hydrogen.

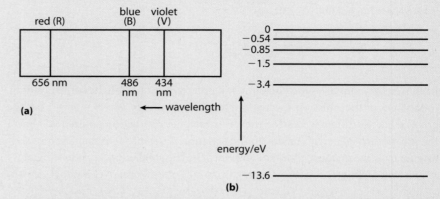

(a) Show, by calculation, that the energy of a photon of red light of wavelength 656 nm is 1.9 eV.
(b) On part (b), draw arrows to represent
    (i) the electron transition that gives rise to the red line (label this arrow R).
    (ii) a possible electron transition that gives rise to the blue line (label this arrow B).

The *electron in a box* model

Imagine an electron trapped in a thin, flat box, reflecting and undergoing interference back and forth in one dimension. The *electron in a box* model assumes that the de Broglie waves associated with the electron will be standing waves.

From wave theory the wavelengths of standing waves can be found like this:

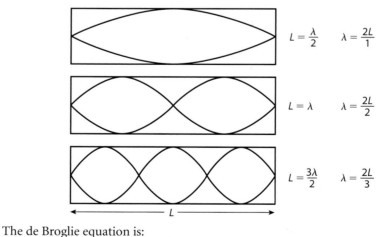

Figure 10.12 The general equation for the wavelength is
$\lambda = \frac{2L}{n}$ where L is the length of the box and n is a positive integer.

The de Broglie equation is:

$$p = \frac{h}{\lambda}$$

and if

$$\lambda = \frac{2L}{n}$$

this becomes

$$p = h \times \frac{1}{\lambda}$$

$$= h \times \frac{n}{2L}$$

$$= \frac{nh}{2L}$$

Remember from Chapter 2 that the kinetic energy of the electrons E_k can be found by:

$$E_k = \frac{p^2}{2m}$$

substituting for p

$$E_k = \left(\frac{nh}{2L}\right)^2 \times \frac{1}{2m}$$

$$= \frac{n^2 h^2}{4L^2} \times \frac{1}{2m}$$

$$= \frac{n^2 h^2}{8mL^2}$$

The Schrödinger model

In 1926, two years after de Broglie proposed his hypothesis, Erwin Schrödinger, an Austrian physicist, published a paper on wave mechanics. In this paper he used a wave equation to describe matter waves. The equation is called the *Schrödinger equation*, and his model of the atom is known as the *Schrödinger model*.

The Schrödinger model assumes that electrons may be described by mathematical wave functions. In the equation, the wave function Ψ (psi) is the amplitude of the matter wave. The term Ψ^2 relates to the *probability* of finding an electron in a particular place at a particular time.

In this model, the electrons have undefined positions, but in the hydrogen atom, for example, there is a greater probability that it will be close to the nucleus. When the model is used to plot 3-dimensional probability regions for hydrogen, we get a sphere that is denser in the centre. Of course, for more complex atoms the plots are more intricate.

These probability regions are sometimes called *electron clouds*. The model is better than the Bohr model because it works for larger atoms and not just for hydrogen.

● **Examiner's hint:** It would be wise to practise this derivation because it is specifically mentioned in the syllabus.

 To see how the Schrödinger model is compared to earlier models, visit www.heinemann.co.uk/hotlinks, enter the express code 4266S and click on Weblink 10.4.

A two-dimensional representation of the hydrogen atom. The most likely place to find the electron is close to the nucleus so the cloud is denser there. More complex atoms have more elaborate clouds or orbitals.

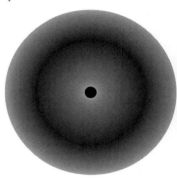

Schrödinger's cat. In this hypothetical situation, the cat is thought to be both alive and dead until observed. This is because a quantum event (the decay of a radioactive particle) is set up to trigger the release of a lethal poison that kills the cat. According to quantum physics, the unstable particle exists in an intermediate 'probabilistic' state until it is observed. Schrödinger devised this experiment to demonstrate the bizarre philosophical implications of quantum theory.

The Heisenberg uncertainty principle

Newtonian mechanics is deterministic. This means that if we know the exact position and momentum of a particle at any given time, we can apply Newton's laws to determine its exact position and momentum at any time in the future.

With the advent of wave-particle duality and quantum mechanics, things became less certain. There are inevitable limits on precision that lead to uncertainty, and we can only know the *probability* of a particle being in a certain place *or* having a particular momentum.

This is not the same as the uncertainties in measurements you make in the laboratory. In experimental measurement there are random and systematic errors due to the person making the measurements and the apparatus used. What quantum mechanics theory tells us is that even with perfect apparatus and perfect observation, in the particle world there is still going to be uncertainty.

There is fundamental uncertainty in the universe according to Heisenberg's uncertainty principle. Einstein expressed his lack of satisfaction with such interpretations of quantum theory by saying: "God does not play dice".

The very act of attempting to locate a particle may change its position or condition. In fact this is not as strange as it initially sounds. If you are in a completely dark room trying to locate a table tennis ball somewhere on the floor using only the sense of touch, when you locate the ball you will probably disturb its position. If you are attempting to measure the temperature of a small beaker of hot water, the act of inserting a thermometer will alter the very property you are trying to measure.

These examples are taken from our experience of the everyday world. Clearly we have no direct experience of the interactions of microscopic particles, so we should not be too surprised if their behaviour does not always match our common-sense expectations.

The Heisenberg uncertainty principle states that the simultaneous measurement of the position and momentum of a particle will always have some uncertainty.

Werner Heisenberg was a German physicist and a colleague of Niels Bohr. He was one of the creators of quantum mechanics for which he received the Nobel Prize in 1932. By 1927 he had already proposed his famous uncertainty principle.

In fact, the more certain we are about the position of the particle, the less certain we are about its momentum, and vice versa. The two quantities are linked by the following relationship:

$$\Delta x \Delta p \geq \frac{h}{4\pi}$$

Δx is the uncertainty in the position
Δp is the uncertainty in the momentum
h is Planck's constant

Worked example

The velocity of an electron is measured to be $1.0 \times 10^6 \, \mathrm{m \, s^{-1}} \pm 0.01 \times 10^6 \, \mathrm{m \, s^{-1}}$. Find the maximum precision that can be given in a simultaneous measurement of its position.

Solution

The uncertainty in the velocity
$$= \frac{0.01 \times 10^6 \, \mathrm{m \, s^{-1}}}{1.0 \times 10^6 \, \mathrm{m \, s^{-1}}} \times 100\% = 1.0\%$$

The momentum of the electron $\quad p = mv$

$$= 9.1 \times 10^{-31} \, \mathrm{kg} \times 1.0 \times 10^6 \, \mathrm{m \, s^{-1}}$$

$$= 9.1 \times 10^{-25} \, \mathrm{kg \, m \, s^{-1}}$$

The uncertainty in the measurement of the momentum

$$= 1.0\% \times 9.1 \times 10^{-25} \, \mathrm{kg \, m \, s^{-1}}$$

$$= 9.1 \times 10^{-27} \, \mathrm{kg \, m \, s^{-1}}$$

From the uncertainty principle:
$$\Delta x \Delta p \geq \frac{h}{4\pi}$$

So the best position measurement for the electron will have an uncertainty given by:
$$\Delta x = \frac{h}{\Delta p 4\pi}$$

$$x = \frac{6.6 \times 10^{-34} \, \mathrm{Js}}{9.1 \times 10^{-27} \, \mathrm{kg \, m \, s^{-1}} \times 4\pi}$$

$$= 5.8 \times 10^{-9} \, \mathrm{m}$$

Remember that the de Broglie equation is:
$$p = \frac{h}{\lambda}$$

What this means for the uncertainty principle is that, if the de Broglie wavelength of a particle is known precisely, then we can calculate its momentum exactly, but then we would have no knowledge about its position.

There is another aspect to the uncertainty principle concerning the uncertainty in the energy of a particle. This idea is expressed in the relationship:
$$\Delta E \Delta t \geq \frac{h}{4\pi}$$

ΔE is the uncertainty in the energy

Δt is the uncertainty in the time interval

h is Planck's constant

This tells us that, if a particle remains in a certain state for a long time, then it can have a well-defined energy, but if it remains in that state for a short time interval, then the uncertainty in its energy will be larger.

Heisenberg was the director of the German project to develop an atomic bomb during World War II. After the war there was some speculation that he had deliberately slowed down the project for moral reasons.

The uncertainty principle revolutionized science. According to Newtonian physics, if you knew the initial state of a system precisely, you could predict the behaviour of the system far into the future. The uncertainty principle removed that comfort zone, and this also had profound implications for other disciplines, including philosophy and politics.

10.2 Nuclear physics

Assessment statements

B.2.1 Explain how the radii of nuclei may be estimated from charged particle scattering experiments.

B.2.2 Describe how the masses of nuclei may be determined using a Bainbridge mass spectrometer.

B.2.3 Describe one piece of evidence for the existence of nuclear energy levels.

B.2.4 Describe $\beta+$ decay, including the existence of the neutrino.

B.2.5 State the radioactive decay law as an exponential function and define the decay constant.

B.2.6 Derive the relationship between decay constant and half-life.

B.2.7 Outline methods for measuring the half-life of an isotope.

B.2.8 Solve problems involving radioactive half-life.

In Chapter 7 we looked at an experiment in which a very thin piece of gold foil was bombarded with alpha particles. The charged alpha particles were scattered owing to the repulsive coulomb force of the gold nucleus. These experiments were mostly carried out by Geiger and Marsden under the direction of Lord Rutherford. They provided evidence for the existence of the nucleus.

Rutherford was once quoted as saying 'A theory that you can't explain to a bartender is probably no damn good'.

If an alpha particle was travelling directly towards the centre of the gold nucleus it would be repelled straight back. Although this happened rarely, it was a total surprise to the experimenters. Rutherford said that it was as surprising as a large shell from a gun bouncing back from a piece of tissue paper.

Figure 10.13 The closer the alpha particles come to the gold nucleus, the stronger the repulsive force and the greater the angle of deflection. The particle that is on a line of direct approach will be repelled back in the direction from which it came.

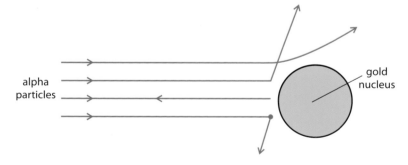

To try a good simulation of this experiment, visit, www.heinemann.co.uk/hotlinks, enter the express code 4266S and click on Weblink 10.5.

The particle that is repelled straight back will have to come to rest for a short time before it changes direction. Rutherford realised that he could use the idea of energy conservation in this situation to estimate the size of the nucleus. At the instant that the alpha particle is at rest, its kinetic energy will be exactly balanced by the electric potential energy due to the repulsive electrostatic force.

Worked example

In an alpha-particle scattering experiment, an alpha particle of kinetic energy 7.7 MeV is repelled straight back from a thin gold foil. Find the distance of closest approach of the particle. (The proton number of gold is 79.)

Solution

First we will change the kinetic energy into SI units:

$$E_k = 7.7 \times 10^6 \, \text{eV} \times 1.6 \times 10^{-19} \, \text{C}$$

$$= 1.23 \times 10^{-12} \, \text{J}$$

The energy conservation equation is:

$$E_k = E_p = \frac{kq_1 q_2}{r}$$

Rearranging to find r, the distance of closest approach:

$$r = \frac{kq_1 q_2}{E_k}$$

$$= \frac{(9.0 \times 10^9) \times (2 \times 1.6 \times 10^{-19}) \times (79 \times 1.6 \times 10^{-19})}{1.23 \times 10^{-12}}$$

$$= 3.0 \times 10^{-14} \, \text{m}$$

The mass spectrometer

The masses of the nuclei of isotopes can be found using a piece of apparatus called a mass spectrometer. These different nuclear mass values provide evidence for the existence of isotopes.

The basic components of the mass spectrometer are a source of ions, a means of accelerating the ions and selecting them by velocity, a magnetic deflector and a detector.

A velocity selector works by using crossed electric and magnetic fields. What this means is that the fields are arranged to be mutually perpendicular so the forces exerted are balanced; the electric force on the ions is equal and opposite to the magnetic force. The idea is shown in the diagram.

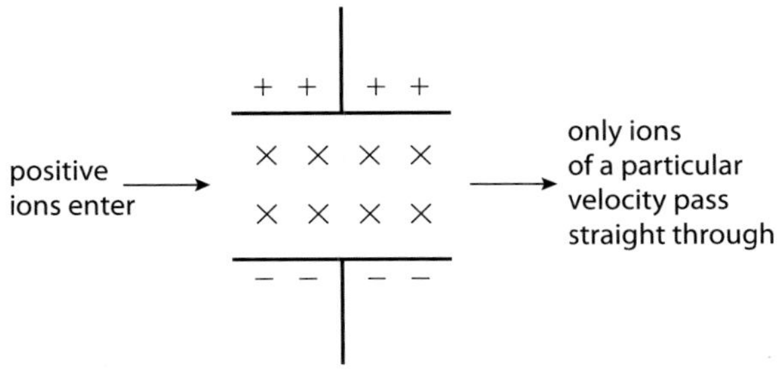

Isotopes are different forms of the same element that have the same number of protons in the nucleus, but different numbers of neutrons. They have the same number of electrons (so are chemically identical) but because the mass of the nucleus if different, they have different physical properties.

positive ions enter →   + + | + +
                         × × × ×
                         × × × ×
                         − − | − −

→ only ions of a particular velocity pass straight through

◀ **Figure 10.14** Positive ions enter from the left and the electric force tends to push them down. The magnetic field is into the page so the magnetic force pushes them up. Ions of a particular velocity are selected and pass straight through.

Note it is the forces that are equal, not the fields.

$$\text{electric force} = \text{magnetic force}$$

$$Eq = qvB$$

$$v = \frac{E}{B}$$

The next diagram represents the mass spectrometer schematically; you do not need to know all the experimental details. Electrons are emitted from the hot filament and collide with atoms of the gas to create positive ions. The positive ions are accelerated, pass through the velocity selector and are collimated by a slit.

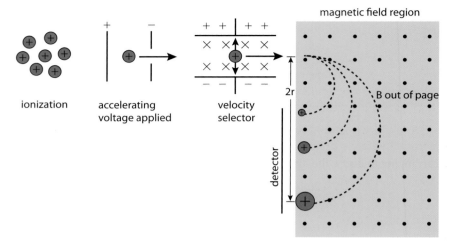

Figure 10.15 In the mass spectrometer region there is a magnetic field directed out of the page. This field deflects the positive ions downwards and they move in semicircular paths. The radius of the path depends on the mass of the ion.

The ions enter the mass spectrometer region which is evacuated. After deflection they strike a photographic detector. The magnetic force is centripetal, the ions move in semi-circular paths. This is described in the equation:

$$qvB = \frac{mv^2}{r}$$

$$qBr = mv$$

The charge q, the magnetic field strength B and the velocity v are all constant. So the equation simplifies to:

$$r \propto m$$

The radius of the path is directly proportional to the mass of the ion; the isotopes with the most neutrons will be detected at the bottom of the photographic plate.

Nuclear energy levels

We have already seen that there are three different types of radioactive emission from the nucleus; alpha, beta and gamma. While the energy of beta emission forms a continuous spectrum, the energies of both alpha and gamma are discrete or quantized and have only certain values.

Figure 10.16 The energy of alpha particles produced by the decay of a nucleus has discrete values while the beta energy spectra are continuous.

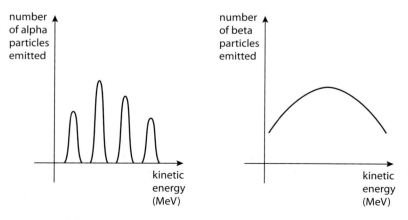

The existence of discrete nuclear energy levels provides evidence that the nucleus, like the atom, is a quantum system.

Radioactive decay

The neutrino

The experiments that showed a continuous spectrum of energy for beta decay appeared to contradict the principle of conservation of energy. The beta particles emitted had less kinetic energy than predicted; the calculations showed that some energy was lost, or went missing, during beta decay.

In 1930 Wolfgang Pauli suggested a hypothesis to preserve the conservation laws. He postulated that there was a new particle, very hard to detect, that was carrying away the missing kinetic energy and momentum.

The particle was named the *neutrino* by Enrico Fermi; it is electrically neutral and was initially thought to have zero mass, travelling at the speed of light. We now believe it does have mass but that it is too small to measure.

Due to their lack of charge, their high speed, low mass and the fact that they pass through matter essentially unnoticed, neutrinos proved difficult to detect. It was not until 1956 that experiments finally provided conclusive evidence for their existence.

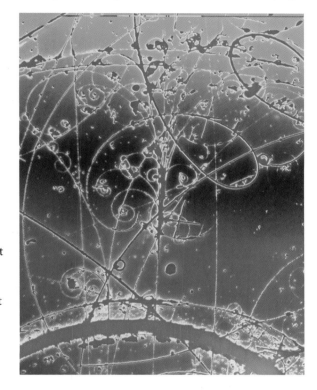

At the time the problem was serious enough to force scientists to question the very idea of energy conservation.

The word *neutrino* means 'little neutral one' in Italian. It is estimated that each person on Earth has over 50,000,000,000,000 neutrinos passing through their body every second.

Neutrino interactions in a bubble chamber. The neutrino enters the bubble chamber at the bottom of the picture, but does not leave a track itself because it is electrically neutral. It interacts with a proton in the liquid filling the bubble chamber, producing a spray of other particles that travel up the picture. Most of the tracks visible are the characteristic spirals of electrons and positrons.

Beta decay

There are two types of beta decay, negative and positive. In negative beta decay a neutron is converted to a proton, an electron and an antineutrino. The electron is emitted as a beta particle; an antineutrino is the antimatter version of a neutrino.

Here is the equation for negative beta decay and an example using carbon-14. The symbol for a neutrino is the Greek letter ν and to show that it is an antiparticle we draw a bar over it:

$$n \rightarrow p^+ + \beta^- + \bar{\nu}$$

$$^{14}_{6}\text{C} \rightarrow {}^{14}_{7}\text{N} + {}^{0}_{-1}\beta + \bar{\nu}$$

In positive beta decay, a proton is converted to a neutron, a positron and a neutrino. A positron is the antimatter version of an electron.

Here is the equation for positive beta decay and an example using carbon-11:

$$p^+ \rightarrow n + \beta^+ + \nu$$

$$^{11}_{6}\text{C} \rightarrow {}^{11}_{5}\text{B} + {}^{0}_{+1}\beta + \nu$$

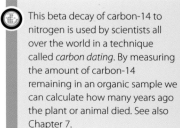

This beta decay of carbon-14 to nitrogen is used by scientists all over the world in a technique called *carbon dating*. By measuring the amount of carbon-14 remaining in an organic sample we can calculate how many years ago the plant or animal died. See also Chapter 7.

The decay constant

The activity of a radioactive isotope is defined as the number of disintegrations per unit time. This can be expressed as an equation:

$$A = -\frac{\Delta N}{\Delta t}$$

A is the activity in becquerel (Bq)

ΔN is the number of disintegrations

Δt is the time interval in seconds

The minus sign shows that the number of disintegrations is decreasing.

The activity will obviously depend on the number of atoms in the sample, N.

$$A \propto N$$

We can convert this to an equation by introducing a constant:

$$A = \lambda N$$

λ is the decay constant s^{-1}

The decay constant is defined as the probability of a nucleus decaying per unit time.

Radioactive decay is a random process. This means we cannot predict exactly when an individual nucleus will decay. The number of atoms, in even a small sample, is so enormous, however, that we can make predictions about the number decaying in a given time interval.

The number of atoms remaining in a radioactive sample decreases exponentially with time. The time taken for the activity, or number of atoms remaining, to fall by half is called the *half-life*, $T_{\frac{1}{2}}$. The average rate of decay is always exponential, no matter how long the half-life, and it is independent of any physical or chemical changes.

Figure 10.17 The original number of atoms decreases to one half in one half-life, and to one quarter in two half-lives etc.

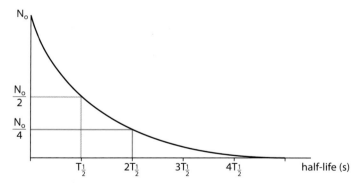

The equation of this curve is:

$$N = N_o e^{-\lambda t}$$

N_o is the original number of atoms in the sample

N is the number of atoms remaining after time t

λ is the decay constant

e is the mathematical constant on which natural logs are based

This equation is known as the radioactive decay law.

We can combine the equations:

$$A = \lambda N = \lambda N_o e^{-\lambda t}$$

The relationship between decay constant and half-life

From the radioactive decay law:

$$N = N_o e^{-\lambda t}$$

$$\frac{N}{N_o} = e^{-\lambda t}$$

$$\frac{N_o}{N} = e^{\lambda t}$$

When the time is equal to the half-life, N will be equal to half N_o.

$$\text{If } t = T_{\frac{1}{2}} \text{ then } N = \frac{N_o}{2}$$

$$\frac{N_o}{N} = 2$$

$$2 = e^{\lambda T_{\frac{1}{2}}}$$

Taking natural logs of both sides:

$$\ln 2 = \lambda T_{\frac{1}{2}}$$

$$T_{\frac{1}{2}} = \frac{\ln 2}{\lambda}$$

Measuring half-life

● **Examiner's hint:** It would be wise to learn this derivation because it is specifically mentioned in the syllabus.

Henri Becquerel discovered radioactivity when crystals containing uranium formed an image on a photographic plate in a closed drawer of his desk. He passed the problem for further investigation to one of his students, Marie Curie.

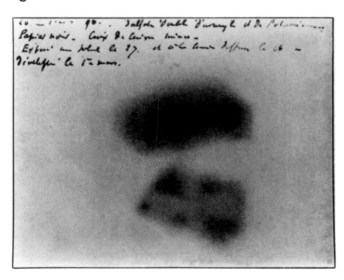

This photograph led to the discovery of radioactivity by Henri Becquerel. The dark patches show where he put crystals of a uranium salt on a photographic plate; his comments are above. Becquerel realised that he had found a new form of radiation.

For an isotope with a short half-life, first the background count rate is measured using a Geiger counter or a sensor. The background radiation comes from the rocks and also from space. Then the count rate from the source is measured at regular fixed intervals, over a period of time. The background count rate is subtracted from each measurement to find the actual count rate from the source.

A graph of the count rate of the source against time is plotted. From the exponential curve, the time taken for the count rate to fall by half is measured. This is repeated for the time to fall to a quarter and an eighth, and the average gives best value for the half-life.

For an isotope with a long half-life the best method is to plot the activity against time on semi-log graph paper. The gradient of this graph gives the decay constant and then the equation $T_{\frac{1}{2}} = \frac{\ln 2}{\lambda}$ gives the half-life.

Worked example

A sample of radioactive isotope originally contains 1.0×10^{24} atoms and it has a half-life of 6.0 hours. Find:
a) the decay constant
b) the initial activity
c) the number of atoms remaining after 12 hours
d) the number of atoms remaining after 30 minutes.

Solution

a) $T_{\frac{1}{2}} = \dfrac{\ln 2}{\lambda}$ $\lambda = \dfrac{\ln 2}{T_{\frac{1}{2}}}$

$$\lambda = \frac{\ln 2}{(6.0 \times 3600 \text{ s})}$$

$$\lambda = 3.2 \times 10^{-5}\,\text{s}^{-1}$$

b) $A = \lambda N$

$A = 3.2 \times 10^{-5}\,\text{s}^{-1} \times 1.0 \times 10^{24}$

$A = (-)\,3.2 \times 10^{19}\,\text{Bq}$

c) 12 hours is two half-lives so the number remaining:

$N = \frac{1}{4} \times 1.0 \times 10^{24}$

$N = 2.5 \times 10^{23}$ **atoms**

d) $N = N_o e^{-\lambda t}$

$N = 1.0 \times 10^{24}\, e^{(-3.2 \times 10^{-5} \times 30 \times 60)}$

$N = 9.4 \times 10^{23}$ **atoms**

Exercises

6 A nucleus of the nuclide $^{40}_{19}\text{K}$ (potassium-40) decays to a stable nucleus of the nuclide $^{40}_{18}\text{Ar}$ (argon-40).
(a) State the names of the *two* particles emitted in this decay.
(b) A sample of the isotope potassium-40 initially contains 1.5×10^{16} atoms. On average, 16 nuclei in this sample of the isotope undergo radioactive decay every minute. Deduce that the decay constant for potassium-40 is $1.8 \times 10^{-17}\,\text{s}^{-1}$.
(c) Determine the half-life of potassium-40.

7 Cerium-145 is a radioactive isotope with a half-life of 3.0 minutes. It emits β-particles and also antineutrinos.
(a) Give **one** reason why the existence of the neutrino was postulated in order to explain β-decay.
(b) Determine the probability for the decay of a cerium-145 nucleus in a time of 1.0 minute.
(c) Determine the time taken for the activity of a particular sample of cerium-145 to be reduced to a fraction $\frac{1}{10}$ of its initial activity.

Practice questions

1 (a) The element helium was first identified from the *absorption spectrum* of the Sun.
    (i) Explain what is meant by the term *absorption spectrum*.
    (ii) Outline how this spectrum may be experimentally observed.
(b) One of the wavelengths in the absorption spectrum of helium occurs at 588 nm.
    (i) Show that the energy of a photon of wavelength 588 nm is 3.38×10^{-19} J.

(ii) The diagram below represents some of the energy levels of the helium atom. Use the information in the diagram to explain how absorption at 588 nm arises.

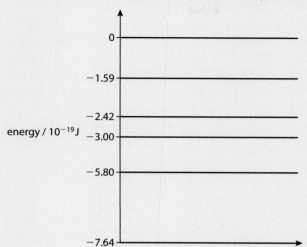

Two different models have been developed to explain the existence of **atomic** energy levels. The **Bohr model** and the **Schrödinger model** are both able to predict the principal wavelengths present in the spectrum of atomic hydrogen.

(c) Outline

  (i) the Bohr model, and

  (ii) the Schrödinger model.

2 (a) State *one* aspect of the photoelectric effect that *cannot* be explained by the wave model of light. Describe how the photon model provides an explanation for this aspect.

Light is incident on a metal surface in a vacuum. The graph below shows the variation of the maximum kinetic energy E_{max} of the electrons emitted from the surface with the frequency f of the incident light.

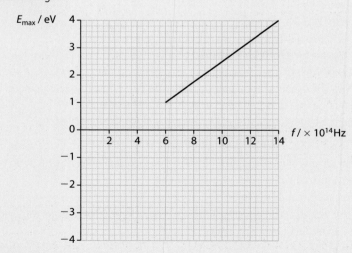

(b) Use data from the graph to determine

  (i) the threshold frequency.

  (ii) a value of the Planck constant

  (iii) the work function of the surface.

3 Photoelectric emission takes place when ultra-violet light is incident on zinc but it does not take place when visible light is incident on zinc. However, photoelectric emission does take place when visible light is incident on potassium.

(a) Explain what is meant by *photoelectric emission*.

The work function of zinc is 4.2 eV.

(b) (i) Explain whether the work function for potassium is greater **or** less than 4.2 eV.

(ii) Ultra-violet light of wavelength 210 nm is incident on a zinc surface. Calculate the maximum kinetic energy, in eV, of a moving electron emitted from the surface.

4 A beam of singly ionized atoms moving at speed v enters a region of magnetic field strength B as shown below.

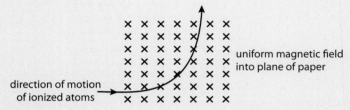

direction of motion of ionized atoms

uniform magnetic field into plane of paper

The magnetic field is directed into the plane of the paper. The ions follow a circular path.

(a) Deduce that the radius r of the circular path is given by

$$r = \frac{mv}{Bq}$$

where m and q are the mass and charge respectively of the ions.

In one particular experiment, the beam contains singly ionized neon atoms all moving at the same speed. On entering the magnetic field, the beam divides in two. The path of the ions of mass 20 u has radius 15.0 cm.

(b) Calculate in terms of u, the mass of the ions having a path of radius 16.5 cm.

(c) State the number of protons and neutrons in each type of neon ion.

5 A sample of cobalt-60 has an activity of 3.0×10^5 Bq. The half-life of cobalt-60 is 5.3 years.

(a) Define *half-life*.

(b) Determine the decay constant of cobalt-60.

(c) Calculate the time taken for the activity of the cobalt-60 to be reduced to 1.0×10^5 Bq.

6 A nucleus of the radioactive isotope potassium-40 decays into a stable nucleus of argon-40.

(a) Complete the equation below for the decay of a potassium-40 nucleus.

$$^{40}_{19}\text{K} \longrightarrow \, ^{40}_{18}\text{Ar} +$$

A certain sample of rocks contains 1.2×10^{-6} g of potassium-40 and 7.0×10^{-6} g of trapped argon-40 gas.

(b) Assuming that all the argon originated from the decay of potassium-40 and that none has escaped from the rocks, calculate what mass of potassium was present when the rocks were first formed.

The half-life of potassium-40 is 1.3×10^9 years.

(c) Determine

(i) the decay constant of potassium-40

(ii) the age of the rocks.

11 Digital technology
(Option C)

11.1 Analogue and digital signals

Assessment statements

C.1.1 Solve problems involving the conversion between binary numbers and decimal numbers.

C.1.2 Describe different means of storage of information in both analogue and digital forms.

C.1.3 Explain how interference of light is used to recover information stored on a CD.

C.1.4 Calculate an appropriate depth for a pit from the wavelength of the laser light.

C.1.5 Solve problems on CDs and DVDs related to data storage capacity.

C.1.6 Discuss the advantage of the storage of information in digital rather than analogue form.

C.1.7 Discuss the implications for society of ever-increasing capability of data storage.

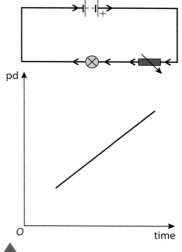

Figure 11.1 An analogue signal.

In this topic we will be learning about the physical principle behind the operation of many of today's digital devices, the digital camera, data storage on CD and DVD and the mobile phone system. Before starting this section you will need to have covered the basic electricity and waves sections in the core chapters.

Electrical signals

When dealing with electronic appliances we will often refer to a *signal*. A signal is the transfer of information from one place to another. For example, if you wave your hand to a friend, that is a signal from one person to another. An electrical signal is when information is sent via a changing electric field; a simple example would be if the switch in Figure 11.1 is opened and closed so that a changing electric field is sent to a light bulb.

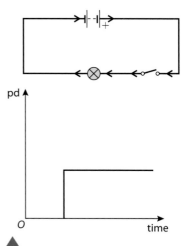

Figure 11.2 A digital signal.

Analogue signal

An analogue signal is a continuously varying signal. For example, in the circuit shown in Figure 11.1, the current changes from a minimum to a maximum as the resistance is decreased, causing the bulb get progressively brighter. The change in potential difference (pd) is an analogue signal.

Digital signal

A digital signal is not a continuously varying signal but one that changes from one value to another. If we consider the circuit in Figure 11.2 the bulb is off but if the switch is closed the bulb will suddenly glow bright. This step from low potential to high is a digital signal.

Transmitting sound

A more complicated signal could be sent using a microphone. The change in pressure caused when you speak makes a part inside the microphone vibrate, resulting in a changing pd. The pd across the microphone varies in exactly the same way as the pressure of the sound wave. A graph of pd against time would therefore have the same shape as a graph of displacement against time

This signal can then be fed to an amplifier which increases the pd. If the pd is now connected across a loudspeaker, the loudspeaker will reproduce the original sound but louder.

The electrical signal between microphone and speaker is an analogue signal because it is a continuously varying signal.

Figure 11.3 Graph1 shows the displacement of the microphone and Graph 2 the pd produced.

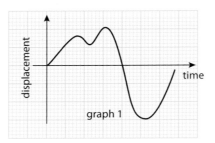
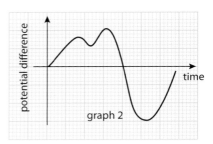

Recording an analogue signal

A sound can be stored on a vinyl record or an audio tape. These are both examples of analogue recording.

Vinyl record (LP)

The grooves in a vinyl record have the same shape as a graph of the original sound.

A record is a disc made of plastic (vinyl) that has a thin groove cut in it by a needle that moves from side to side at the same frequency as the sound. If you look at the groove under a microscope it looks like a graph of the sound wave. The record is played on a turntable with a needle resting in the groove. As the record rotates the needle is made to vibrate by the wavy groove at the same frequency as the original sound. The needle is connected to a device that turns this vibration back into an electrical signal, which can then be amplified and transmitted to a loudspeaker. The groove in the record spirals inwards so the needle moves through the groove faster when it is playing music on the edge of the LP. This means that the wavy groove is more squashed in the centre of the record than at the outer edge.

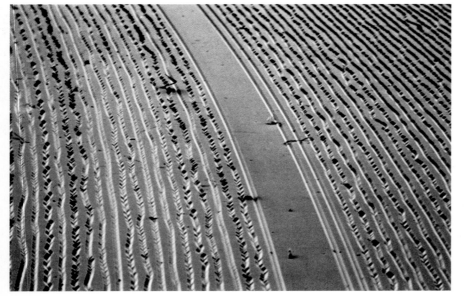

Audio tape

Audio tape is a magnetic tape wound between two spools in a cassette. It is reeled past an electromagnet which varies its magnetic field at the same rate as the signal. The result is that the tape gains a magnetic field that varies continuously at the same rate as the signal.

Digital devices

Many of today's electronic devices are said to be digital, e.g. computers, MP3 players and some telephones. These devices contain a microprocessor that can perform many functions. For example, an MP3 player not only plays music but tells you the name of the track and the artist. A DVD player can give subtitles in many different languages and a computer can do amazing things to a photograph. The microprocessor contains millions of tiny switches that can be either on or off. When they are on they give out a signal and when off there's no output. They are able to process digital signals.

Digital electronics

To understand the significance of using digital signals we will have a look at some simple digital electronics; you will do a bit more of this later in this chapter.

Logic gates

Digital circuits, for example the microprocessor in a computer, are made up of logic gates; these give out different signals depending on the input. There are two main types of gate: the AND gate and the OR gate (see Figures 11.5 and 11.6)

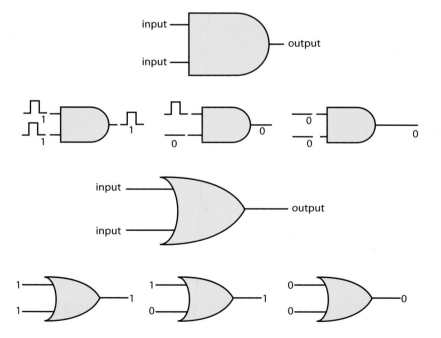

By using combinations of different types of logic gates, many processes can be performed that are much more complicated than simply switching lights on and off, for example making an MP3 player play the right track when you press certain buttons. Logic gates are simple devices and they only work with simple digital

> We say that the audio tape stores an analogue signal – in other words, it is continuously varying. In fact, it cannot be continuously varying since the tape is not continuous; it is made of molecules.

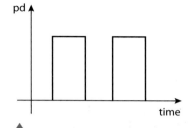

Figure 11.4 A digital signal can be represented mathematically by a series of 1s and 0s. The high part of the signal is a 1 and the low a 0.

Figure 11.5 The AND gate symbol. An AND gate has two inputs and one output. It only gives an output if there is a signal on each input. It could be used to switch on a light, for example, only if two switches are closed.

Figure 11.6 The OR gate symbol. This gate gives an output if there is a signal on one input or the other. It could be used to switch on a light when either one or both switches are closed.

signals that are made of 1s and 0s. This may not seem very useful until you realise that all numbers can be made out of a series of 1s and 0s. This is called the *binary system*.

Binary numbers

Our normal system of numbers is called the *decimal system*. In this system we can use 10 symbols (0–9) to represent any number. The way it works is that we group units, tens, hundreds and so on. So 365 is 3 hundreds, 6 tens and 5 units. Units, tens and hundreds are all powers of 10: 10^0, 10^1, 10^2 etc. We can represent this in Table 1.

Table 1 The decimal system of numbers.

Power of 10	3	2	1	0
	1000	100	10	1
	thousands	hundreds	tens	units

The base of our number system doesn't have to be 10. We can use any number. If we use 2, this is called the binary system, as represented in Table 2.

Table 2 The binary system of numbers.

Power of 2	3	2	1	0
	8	4	2	1
	eights	fours	twos	ones

In this system the number 7 would be one 4, one 2 and one 1. See Table 3 for the numbers 1–10 in binary. With 4 digits we can count from 0 to 15, with 8 digits we can count to 255.

Table 3

decimal	binary
1	00000001
2	00000010
3	00000011
4	00000100
5	00000101
6	00000110
7	00000111
8	00001000
9	00001001
10	00001010

Bit (b)
Each 1 or 0 is called a binary digit or 'bit'.

Byte (B)
A byte is 8 binary digits. 8 digits can represent any number from 0 to 256.

Exercises

1 Convert the following numbers into 8-digit binary:
   (a) 7   **(b)** 14   **(c)** 16   **(d)** 67   **(e)** 125

2 Convert the following 6-bit binary numbers to base 10 numbers:
   (a) 000111   **(b)** 100100   **(c)** 110011   **(d)** 111111

ASCII code

It is not at all obvious that a computer uses 1s and 0s to perform its functions. After all, we don't communicate with a computer in this way, we type letters on a keyboard. What the computer does is to convert each letter into an 8-bit binary code. This is called the ASCII code, which stands for American Standard Code for Information Interchange. A small part of it is shown in Table 4 where each letter is 8 bits, or 1byte, of information. You can test this by typing the word *computer* into a notepad document and saving it on your computer. If you look at the properties of this file you will see that it has a file size of 8 bytes with one byte for each letter. If you do the same exercise in MS Word you will find the file size is much bigger because of all the formatting.

ASCII code	
A	0100 0001
B	0100 0010
C	0100 0011
D	0100 0100
E	0100 0101

Table 4 The ASCII code uses 8 bits to represent each character.

 Why don't we communicate in binary language?

 Chinese has tens of thousands of characters so each one cannot be represented by one byte of code. Two bytes are used instead, giving about 64 000 possible combinations.

Exercises

3 Write the word BAD in ASCII code.

4 If you typed the letter A once every second into a notepad document, how long would it take you to fill a 200 GB hard drive?

Analogue to digital conversion

We have seen that a digital signal is more versatile than an analogue signal. It would, therefore, be a great advantage if we could change analogue signals, such as music, into digital signals. This can be done using an analogue to digital converter or ADC.

Sampling an analogue signal

The first stage in converting an analogue signal to a digital one is to measure the voltage at regular intervals to create a pulse amplitude modulated (PAM) signal. This is called *sampling*. Consider the signal in Figure 11.7. The first sample is rough but if the sampling rate is increased then the digital signal begins to look like the original analogue sample.

Sampling rate
The sampling rate is the rate at which a digital signal is measured. If the sampling rate is higher, the digital signal will be closer to the original sound.

Figure 11.7 An analogue signal is sampled at twice a second and then four times a second.

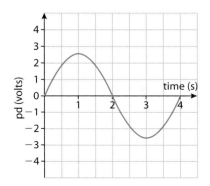
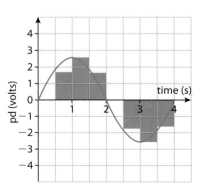
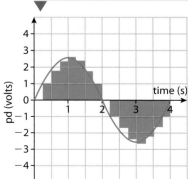

Nyquist frequency

The Nyquist theory states that to record a certain frequency the sampling rate must be at least twice the frequency. This is so that at least one point on each peak and trough is recorded per cycle. Sound is often sampled at a rate of 40 000 Hz so the highest frequency that can be recorded is 20 000 Hz, which is the highest frequency that humans can hear.

Exercises

5   Figure 11.8 shows a graph of the varying pd from a microphone. Convert this signal to a digital signal by measuring the pd at a sampling rate of 200 Hz. Round off all of the pds to the nearest whole volt. Draw a graph showing the digital signal.

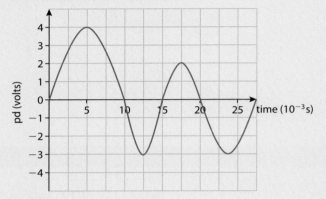

Figure 11.8

Does this sampling rate give a true representation of the signal?

6   Repeat with a sampling rate of 400 Hz.

7   To measure the variation of a 50 Hz AC signal using a digital device, what is the minimum sampling rate you should use?

Changing to binary

PAM signals cannot be processed by a microprocessor until they are converted to the binary system. To change a PAM signal to binary we must split the pd into different levels which can then be converted to a binary number. The number of levels depends upon how many bits we are going to use to represent the number.

Figure 11.9 The pd of the example digital signal is split into **a)** 6 levels for a 3-bit digital conversion and **b)** 12 levels for a 4 bit-digital conversion.

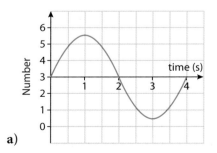

a)

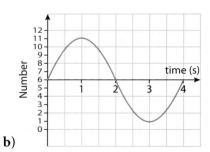

b)

Number of bits

If we consider the signal in Figure 11.7 we see that it goes from about $-3\,\text{V}$ to $+3\,\text{V}$. This range can most easily be represented by the numbers 0–6, each number representing a different voltage, as in Figure 11.9 . If we convert these numbers to binary they can be represented by 3 bits. If we sample this signal at a sampling rate of 1 Hz then we reach the values given in Table 5.

For 3-bit digital conversion		
Time	Number	Binary
0	3	011
1	6	110
2	3	011
3	0	000
4	3	011

◀ **Table 5** Binary values for an analogue signal for 3-bit digital conversion.

For 4-bit digital conversion		
Time	Number	Binary
0	6	0110
1	11	1011
2	6	0110
3	1	0001
4	6	0110

◀ **Table 6** Binary values for an analogue signal for 4-bit digital conversion.

The complete signal for the 3-bit conversion is 011110011000011. This string of 1s and 0s can be turned back into the original signal as long as we know how many bits were being used in the original conversion.

In the process of converting the pd to a number we have had to round off the values, for example at 1 second the number is between 5 and 6 when using levels 1–6 for 3 bits. It would be better if we had more levels but this would require more bits. With 4 bits we can represent numbers from 0–15, and this would enable us to split the voltage range into 12 numbers, as in Figure 11.9. This would give the values in Table 6.

So, to record the signal accurately we need a high sampling rate and a large number of bits. A typical MP3 player samples 16 bits at a rate of 44.1 kHz. This means that the signal can be split into 65 536 levels. This sounds very impressive, but remember the original analogue signal was continuous, you could say it had an infinite number of levels.

▲ A computer hard drive stores information in microscopic magnets that can either point in an up or down direction.

Exercises

8 Convert the data in the 12-level graph (Figure 11.9 b)) to 4-bit binary with a sampling rate of 2 Hz. Present your data in a table similar to Table 6.

9 The following string of 1s and 0s is 3-bit binary data sampled at 2 Hz. Turn this data into a table giving time and a number representing the pd. Use this data to draw the signal.
011100101100011000

Digital storage

A digital storage device, such as a computer hard drive or a CD, stores a series of 1s and 0s.

Compact disc (CD)

An electron microscope image of the pits that form the spiralling track on a CD.

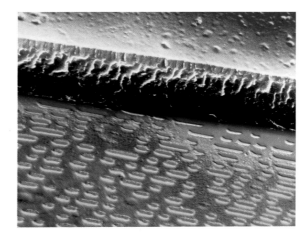

Construction

A CD is a 12 cm plastic disc. Information is stored on it in the form of a spiralling track of small pits that are pressed into the plastic. To make the pits readable with a laser they are sprayed with a thin film of aluminium before being filled with an acrylic layer and a label. The result when viewed from the readable side is a shiny disc covered in microscopic bumps that spiral outwards from the centre in a 5 km long track.

Figure 11.10 A diagram of a CD showing the dimensions and layers.

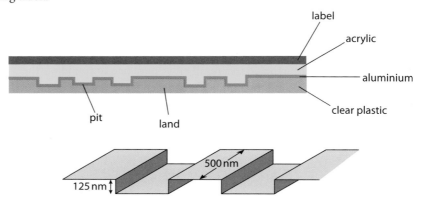

Reading the CD

The shiny bumps or pits are read using a laser. When it shines on the step at the edge of a pit, part of the beam reflects off the pit and part off the land. The height of the pit (125 nm) is $\frac{1}{4}$ of the wavelength of the laser light. (The laser light has a wavelength of 780 nm but when it passes into the plastic it slows down resulting in a decrease of the wavelength to 500 nm).

 The bumps are called pits because they are small holes in the plastic disc. When they are filled with aluminium, they form bumps. The lands are the parts in between.

After reflection the two beams meet at a sensor located in the pickup. At this point the beam reflected off the bottom of the disc has travelled $\frac{1}{2}$ a wavelength further than the wave reflected off the top of the pit. The two waves are, therefore, out of phase and interfere destructively.

The sensor produces an emf that is proportional to the amount of light it receives. When the destructive interference occurs the emf goes down.

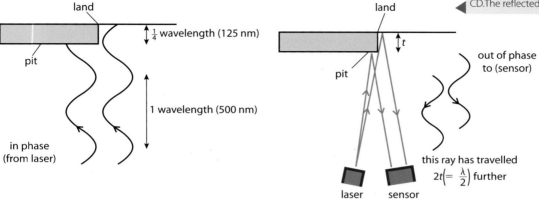

Figure 11.11 Two rays of laser light reflected off the edge of a pit on a CD. The reflected rays are out of phase.

Worked example

If the laser light used had a wavelength of 600 nm in plastic, what depth of pit would the CD have?

Solution
To achieve destructive interference, the path difference between light from the top of the pit and bottom of a land should be $\frac{1}{2}\lambda$. Since the light travels there and back the pit height must therefore be $\frac{1}{4}\lambda = \frac{600}{4} = 150$ nm.

Tracking

When a CD is put into a CD player, it spins at about 700 rpm and the laser and sensor are moved slowly outwards, following the spiralling path of pits. The sensor samples at 44 100 times per second, which means that about every 23 μs a reading is taken. Whenever there is a change from a pit to a land, the laser blinks. This is represented by a 1 and if there is no blink then this is represented by a 0.

It is important that the laser reads the pits at a constant rate, otherwise it might miss some information or record more 'no blinks' than actually exist. If the CD rotated at a constant rate, the velocity would increase as the laser moved to the outer edge, so the CD slows down as the laser moves outwards. A CD can store 700 MB of information.

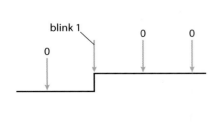

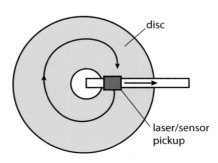

Figure 11.12 The laser tracks outwards. If the signal changes it's a 1 and if there's no change it is a 0.

Worked example

If the CD rotates at a rate of 500 rpm when the pickup is 2 cm from the centre, how fast should it rotate when it is 4 cm from the centre?

Solution

We know from circular motion that the speed of a rotating body is given by:

$v = \omega r$ where $\omega = 2\pi f$

so $v = 2\pi f r$

If v is constant this means that $f \propto \frac{1}{r}$ so if the radius is doubled the frequency is halved to 250 rpm.

Digital video disc (DVD)

A DVD operates on the same physical principle but has a much higher storage capacity. This is achieved in several ways

Laser

The laser used to read a DVD has a wavelength of 640 nm, which means that smaller pits can be read.

Track

Each pit is about $\frac{1}{2}$ the size of the pits on a CD. In addition, the track spirals are twice as close, making the track length twice as long as that of a CD with twice as many pits on it.

Layers

It is possible to double the information on a disc by having two layers of pits. The top layer is coated with a semi-reflective coating enabling light to also pass through to read the bottom layer.

On a double sided double layer DVD it is possible to store 17 GB of data, a lot more than the 700 MB of a typical CD.

How many bytes?
1 page of writing 10^6
1 metre book shelf of books 10^{10}
1 floor of a library 10^{13}
All books published in a year 10^{15}.

Exercises

10 The track on a CD is 5 km long and is made up of a series of pits and lands that are a minimum of 0.83 µm long.
   (a) How many pits are there on the CD track (remember each pit is followed by a land)?
   (b) Each short pit has two edges so represents 2 bits of data. How many bits are there on a CD?
   (c) How many bytes of data are there on a CD?

11 A CD can store 74 minutes of stereo music.
   (a) If 16 bits are recorded at 44 000 samples per second, how many bits are recorded in 74 minutes?
   (b) The music is stereo so there are 2 channels. How many bits must the CD contain?
   (c) How many bytes is that?

Comparing analogue and digital storage

There will always be a difference between an analogue signal and its digital equivalent. However, we must remember that when an analogue signal like a piece of music is stored on an analogue storage device such as an LP or audio tape, it will not be exactly the same as the original sound: the electronics needed to move the needle to cut the groove in an LP will make small changes to the signal. It is true that an analogue storage device does store more data than a digital device, although there is a point beyond which it is not possible to hear the difference between a digital recording and an analogue recording. However, once the information is stored, there are many advantages to storing digitally.

Processing data

A computer is a powerful tool that can process digital information. A clear advantage of storing data digitally is that you can use a computer to change it. For example, digital photographs can be enhanced or completely changed using Adobe Photoshop; a singer's voice can be edited to sing in tune; video clips can be joined and edited together.

A digitally manipulated photograph of Einstein.

All of these functions can be carried out on analogue data but the processes require specially made, expensive equipment. The reason that it is cheaper to process a digital signal is that the components do not have to be very precise, as the 1s and 0s can be represented by a high and a low potential, respectively. The high potential can vary but will still be high and therefore recognised as a 1, but changing an analogue signal by the same amount will make it unrecognisable.

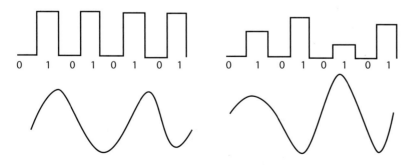

Figure 11.13 Even though the digital signal is changed the data is the same, unlike the analogue signal that is now very different.

Accessing data

One major advantage of an MP3 or CD player over either a tape recorder or record player is the possibility of jumping from track to track. The analogue data on an audio tape is stored in sequence, so to get to the last track on an album you have to wind the tape to the end. This is not a problem with a digital device where the data is stored like folders in a filing cabinet. This form of storage also makes it possible to combine different sorts of data, such as the language of the subtitles on a DVD.

Figure 11.14 The loudness is related to the magnetic field strength in an analogue tape but this has no relevance in a digital tape.

Corruption of data

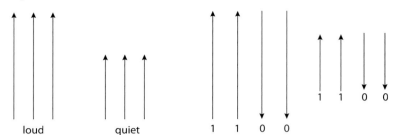

Over a period of time the storage medium can deteriorate or become damaged leading to a corruption of the data. We have seen that both the audio tape and the computer hard drive use magnetic fields to store data. A piece of music sounds as it does because of variations in the frequency and loudness of the sound. These are recorded on an audio tape as variations in the strength and orientation of microscopic magnets, so that in a loud sound there would be a strong field and in a quiet sound a weak field (see Figure 11.14). If the magnets deteriorate with time then the strength of the field will be smaller and hence the loudness recorded will be less. We have seen that when an ADC converts a sound to a digital signal the information about loudness and frequency is recorded as a series of 1s and 0s which are recorded by the orientation of magnets. If these magnets deteriorate, the signal will not change.

Storing text

We have seen that it is possible to convert text to binary data using ASCII code and this can be stored on a hard drive, CD or other storage device. The small size of these devices makes it possible to store large amounts of data in a small space.

Retrieving damaged data

When data is converted to digital form and stored on a CD or other device then extra information is also stored, so that it is possible for the laser reader to recognize whether some of the data has been changed or damaged.

Social implications of digital data storage

In 1830, when Carl Friedrich Gauss first produced a binary electrical signal, he would have had no idea of the far-reaching social implications of his work. Today we are in the middle of the digital revolution, with new applications of digital technology arriving in the shops each week. We still don't really have any idea of the social implications for the future; however, we can see some of the effects of these advancements over the past 20 years.

Home entertainment

Switching from analog to digital storage for music and video has made it possible to produce cheap but high quality music and video playback machines for home entertainment. Via the internet, it is now possible to download and store music and films without payment. This has resulted in lower attendance at cinemas and a whole new branch of the law to deal with illegal copying.

Digital video has also made it possible to edit and produce high quality home videos: this is good news for families but also has negative aspects.

A word of warning

In 1975 the data from the *Viking* Lander Mission to Mars was stored on digital tape. Unfortunately, in recent years these were found to have deteriorated and the formatting used was unreadable. Luckily there were paper copies.

In 1986 the BBC stored data for their Doomsday Project on a laser disc. This method of storage is now obsolete.

Personal information

Because digital storage of information takes up so little space it is now possible to keep and use every piece of information about any individual. The essays you write at school can now be stored and published when you become a famous author. Every time you send an email or do an internet search, the information can be stored and used ... either for you or against you. Once information is in a digital form it can also be processed in many ways; for example it is possible to use face recognition software to recognize faces in a crowd.

 Advances in science and technology often have far-reaching consequences. Who should decide whether a piece of research that might have social implications should be carried out or not?

11.2 Data capture; digital imaging

Assessment statements

C.2.1   Define capacitance.
C.2.2   Describe the structure of a charge-coupled device (CCD).
C.2.3   Explain how incident light causes charge to build up within a pixel.
C.2.4   Outline how the image on a CCD is digitized.
C.2.5   Define quantum efficiency of a pixel.
C.2.6   Define magnification.
C.2.7   State that two points on an object may be just resolved on a CCD if the images of the points are at least two pixels apart.
C.2.8   Discuss the effects of quantum efficiency, magnification and resolution on the quality of the processed image.
C.2.9   Describe a range of practical uses of a CCD, and list some advantages compared with the use of film.
C.2.10 Outline how the image stored in a CCD is retrieved.
C.2.11 Solve problems involving the use of CCDs.

In the previous section we were mainly concerned with the storage of music and text. In this section we will look at how images can be turned into digital form so they can be manipulated and stored. It is quite possible that many readers have never used a film camera, so before we consider digital devices we should look at the workings of a simple film camera.

The film camera

A camera uses a convex lens to focus light from an image onto a film.

Lens

A convex lens refracts the light so that rays coming from an object will cross over on the film. This is called *focusing* as shown in Figure 11.15.

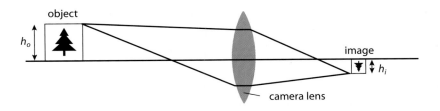

◀ **Figure 11.15** The optics of a simple film camera. . If you were to look at the film you would see a small upside down version of the object, this is called an image.

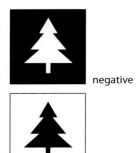

negative

positive

Figure 11.16

A digital camera showing the flash card used for digital storage. CCD was invented when it was found out that certain computer memory chips were light sensitive.

Film

A photographic film comes in a roll, which has to be loaded into the back of a camera. The film has to inserted into the camera so that it is not exposed to light until you take a picture. The film is a plastic sheet covered with grains of a photosensitive chemical, such as silver bromide. When you take a picture, a shutter is opened and this allows light to fall on the film. When photons land on a grain, it changes the chemical nature some of the atoms in the grain and records the image. As the film is dipped into a liquid, known as developer, the grain turns black. Since all the light areas on the image are now recorded as black dots, the picture will be a reverse of the original image. This is called a *negative* (see Figure 11.16). The developing process has to be repeated a second time to convert the negative to an image that looks like the object. This whole procedure takes some time to be performed and needs specialist equipment. Anyone who has used a digital camera will already see some of the advantages.

The digital camera

The optics of a digital camera are exactly the same as the film camera but instead of a film, the digital camera has a charge coupled device, or CCD, to record the image. This converts the image into a digital signal that can be then be stored on a digital storage device such as a CD. To understand its operation, we must first run through some basic physical principles that have not been covered in the core chapters of this course.

Capacitance

A CCD is a small slice of silicon that has been divided into many tiny squares. Each square acts as a capacitor that stores charge released from the silicon when light shines on it. A capacitor is an electrical component that stores charge. In its simplest form it is made out of two parallel plates separated by a small air gap. If a pd is applied to the capacitor, then charge flows onto the plates, as in Figure 11.17. The charge can't flow round the circuit because of the air gap so it collects on the plates.

Figure 11.17 A capacitor charged by a battery stores charge. Even if the battery is now disconnected, the charge remains on the capacitor plates. We say the capacitor is charged.

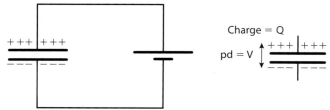

Charge = Q

pd = V

The photodiode

In a CCD, the capacitors are not charged by a battery but store charge when light shines on them. Instead of air inside the capacitors there is silicon that has been impregnated with some impurity. When a photon of light is absorbed by a silicon atom, an electron becomes excited into a higher energy level. In silicon, this results in the electrons being able to move around the material freely and allowing them to collect on the capacitor plates. This arrangement is called a *photodiode*. Electrons are also liberated due to thermal energy – this is called *thermionic emission* and can cause problems, as we shall see later on.

Capacitance
When a capacitor is charged there is a pd between the plates. The size of the pd is proportional to the amount of stored charge.

$$\text{Capacitance} = \frac{\text{charge}}{\text{potential}}$$

$$C = \frac{Q}{V}$$

Unit: farad

Exercises

12 What will be the potential difference between the plates of a 15 μF capacitor if there is a charge of 5 μC on the plates?

13 The capacitance of the photodiodes in a typical CCD is about 100 μF. What charge will cause a pd of 1 V across it?

14 What is the charge of 50 electrons? If there are 50 electrons stored on a 100 nF photodiode what will the pd across it be?

The CCD array of photodiodes

The CCD is a two-dimensional (2D) array of photodiodes that have been created on a thin wafer of silicon. The wafer has many layers; a simplified version is shown in Figure 11.18.

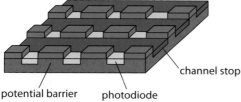

channel stop

potential barrier   photodiode

Figure 11.18 The layers of a CCD. If a photon of light lands on a photodiode, it causes an electron to be freed from a silicon atom (the photoelectric effect). This electron is trapped by the channel stop (an insulating strip) and a potential barrier created by adding impurities to the silicon. The photodiode therefore acts like a capacitor, storing charge.

Pixels

When light is focused onto the CCD by the camera lens, an image of the object is projected onto the CCD. This causes electrons to be stored in each photodiode; the number of electrons stored depends on the intensity of the light. In this way the image is recorded. However, not all the information from the light can be recorded, only the light that falls on the photodiodes. The picture has been turned into millions of small squares, or *pixels*. The number of pixels on the CCD is often quoted in camera adverts; a 6-mega pixel camera has 6 million photodiodes on its CCD chip.

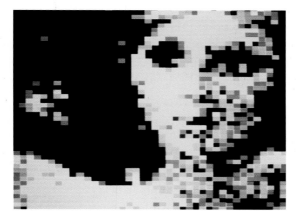

Artists also use pixels. Here a painting of a face is made out of small squares.

Reading the data

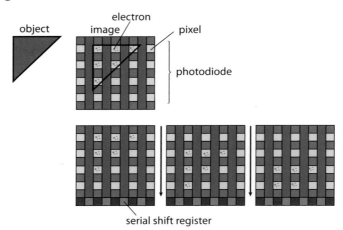

Figure 11.19 A pixelated image of a triangle on a CCD chip. Notice how the number of electrons stored depends on the amount of light landing on the pixel. The electrons are moved down to the serial register where they are read line by line.

serial shift register

The data is now stored as charge on the 2D grid of the CCD. To turn this into a digital signal we need a single line of 1s and 0s. This is achieved by applying a potential difference across the chip: this moves all the electrons down one row. The end row is called the *serial register*; this is a row of photodiodes that have wires connected to them enabling the pd between their top and bottom to be measured. This pd is proportional to the amount of charge stored (remember that $Q = CV$). As each row is moved down (clocked) the pds are measured and converted to a binary number by an analogue-to-digital converter. After measurement, the charge is removed from the row. The whole process is rather like counting the eggs in an egg box by tilting the box so that the eggs roll into the end row. After the eggs are counted they are removed and another row of eggs rolls down (see Figure 11.19).

Terms and quantities related to digital imaging

Magnification (M)

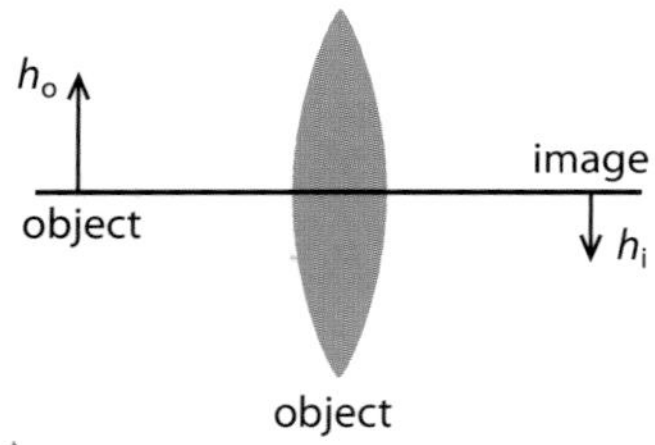

Magnification is the ratio of the height of the image and the height of the object $\left(\dfrac{h_i}{h_o}\right)$. If the image on the CCD is very small then only a small number of photodiodes will be illuminated, and this will result in a poor quality image. The size of the image on the CCD depends on the size of the CCD. The most common sizes of CCD range from 6 mm to 16 mm (diagonal measurement). If a large format CCD is used, then the image can be big and will be made up of more pixels.

Quantum efficiency

The quantum efficiency of a photosensitive device is defined as the ratio of the number of photons absorbed to the number of electrons freed, as a percentage. If 5 photons hit a photodiode and 3 electrons are freed then:

$$\text{quantum efficiency} = \tfrac{3}{5} \times 100\% = 60\%$$

If quantum efficiency is low, then some parts of the image will be lost.

Lenslets

If light falls on the gaps between the photodiodes, the photons will not cause any emission of electrons. To make all the photons land in the right area, small lenses are attached on top of each photodiode.

Figure 11.20

15 What is the height of a 6 mm CCD?
If each pixel is a square of 10 μm side, how many pixels will a 6 mm CCD have?

16 A picture of a 10 m high tree is to be taken with a camera containing a 6 mm CCD. What is the magnification of the camera if the tree just fits on the CCD?

17 **(a)** If 10^{10} photons enter the camera and land on the CCD of a 5 megapixel camera, how many photons land on each photodiode?
(b) If the quantum efficiency is 70%, how many electrons are liberated in each photodiode?

18 If the rate of reading each pixel in the serial register is 5 MHz, how long will it take to read all the pixels in a 1 megapixel CCD?

19 A video camera takes 30 pictures per second. If rate of reading pixels is 5 MHz, how many pixels can the camera have?

Resolution

Resolution of an image defines the amount of detail that an image contains. You can see someone surfing in the first photo, but if the image is enlarged the person is bigger but you can't see much detail. This is because the resolution is not good enough.

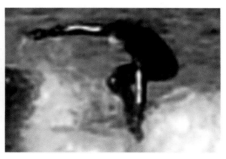

A surfing scene taken on a 5 megapixel camera and an enlarged view of the surfer showing the limit of resolution. The words on the arm of the wetsuit say 'second skin' but the resolution is not good enough for you to read them.

The final image quality is determined by a combination of magnification, size of CCD and quantum efficiency.

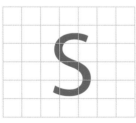
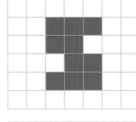

Figure 11.21 The letter S represented by 12 pixels and the same letter represented by 170 pixels.

Magnification

If the final image is very small, then all the points will be very close together. This means that it is possible for two points on the image to fall on the same photogate. These will not be distinguishable on the final picture. A large CCD will mean that the magnification can be greater, resulting in a higher resolution image.

Quantum efficiency

If the quantum efficiency is low, then not all of the incident photons will be recorded. This will result in a loss of detail, particularly in the dark areas. The quantum efficiency is different for different colours, leading to some coloured parts of objects appearing less bright.

Colour

A colour filter is fixed over the CCD in order to record colour. The pixels are grouped in three for the primary colours (red, blue and green). These three can be thought of as one pixel and they record the intensity of these three different colours of light. From this information it is possible to calculate the colour of this area of the image.

Video

A video digital camera also uses a CCD to turn the image into a digital signal. To get a moving image, the camera must take around 30 pictures per second. This means that the information from the CCD must be read very quickly. This limits the number of pixels possible and will affect the resolution, as pixels are grouped into three for a colour image. To achieve a high resolution colour image, three CCDs are used, one for each colour. This is achieved by splitting the light beam into three directions as it passes through the camera and passing each through a different colour filter. Each CCD records a different colour and they are then put together to make the final image.

Comparing digital photography with film

When digital photography was first introduced the quality of pictures was very poor. This was due to the large size of the photodiodes compared to the grain size of the photographic film. However, improvements in the CCD has meant that the photodiode size is comparable to the grain size, resulting in images with high resolution, similar to those achieved with a traditional camera. In fact, due to the much better quantum efficiency of the CCD (70%) compared to film grains (2%) the resolution can be much better.

The most obvious advantage of digital photography is the instant results; no more waiting for photographs to return from the printers. Another advantage of using a digital camera is that you can delete pictures that you don't want to print or keep. This could also be seen as a disadvantage, as the tendency is to delete all but the best records, whereas the chances of a wider variety of photographs is more likely from records of the past.

As with all digital signals, a big advantage of digital photography is the possibility of being able to use a computer to manipulate the data. Using programs, such as Adobe Photoshop, it is possible to change faces, remove buildings, and even see what people will look like when they are old.

Other uses of CCDs

The main use for CCDs is in digital photography and video, however there are many other possible applications.

X-ray machines

Since the photodiodes are sensitive to X-rays as well as light, they can be used in X-ray machines, thus replacing the need for film that has to be processed. An advantage of the digital image is that it can be sent to different parts of the hospital and even enhanced with colour. If you have had an X-ray recently it may well have been digital; however, the machine may have used a reusable phosphor plate that has to be scanned by a reader rather than a CCD.

Astronomy

CCDs are now commonly attached to the eyepiece of telescopes to replace the traditional film camera. This is particularly useful with remote telescopes, such as the Hubble telescope that has to send its pictures to astronomers on the Earth. The digital signal is rather easier to send than a roll of film. The CCD of a camera used in astronomy must have high quantum efficiency.

One problem with using the CCD in applications where light intensity is very low is that at normal room temperatures electrons can be excited by thermal energy. This means that even if you take a picture with the lens cap on, some electrons will be excited and the picture won't be completely black. This is not a problem when using the camera in normal daylight but can cause problems for astronomers. However, there are two ways that this can be solved. One is to cool the CCDs down to around $-80\,°C$, and another is to remove this background light digitally. This can be simply achieved by subtracting the data collected from a photograph taken without light from the photograph of the stars.

A digital photograph from a telescope alongside the same stars but with lower quantum efficiency. The less bright stars have disappeared.

 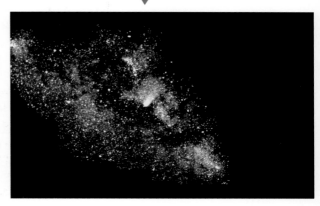

11.3 Electronics

Assessment statements

C.3.1 State the properties of an ideal operational amplifier (op-amp).
C.3.2 Draw circuit diagrams for both inverting and non-inverting amplifiers (with a single input) incorporating operational amplifiers.
C.3.3 Derive an expression for the gain of an inverting amplifier and for a non-inverting amplifier.
C.3.4 Describe the use of an operational amplifier circuit as a comparator.
C.3.5 Describe the use of a Schmitt trigger for the reshaping of digital pulses.
C.3.6 Solve problems involving circuits incorporating operational amplifiers.

The operational amplifier

An amplifier is a device that takes a signal and makes it bigger. For example, an MP3 player gives out a very small pd that produces sound you can hear using headphones but not in your whole room. If you connect the signal from the MP3 player to an amplifier, then the signal can be made big enough to drive a large pair of speakers. The amplifier needs energy from a supply, such as the mains, to power the speakers. However, an operational amplifier, or op amp, can be made to do more than amplify. It can be wired in different ways to carry out functions that are the basis of many devices used in digital electronics.

Op amp chips. ▶

The actual op amp is a small black rectangle called a *chip*. It has 8 numbered connecting legs although we will only use 5 of them. Inside the chip is a complicated circuit with many transistors and resistors etched onto a thin piece of silicon. Fortunately, you do not have to understand all the internal parts; we are only concerned with what happens to the output when we change the input.

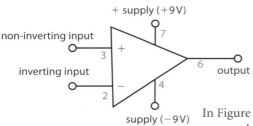

In Figure 11.22, the inputs show where the signal is fed into the amp and the output shows where the amplified signal comes out. In this diagram the supply is shown to be 9 V. This is the maximum value that the output can be.

Open loop gain

If a very small pd is applied between the inputs, a large potential is created on the output. The ratio $\dfrac{V_0}{(V_+ - V_-)}$ is called the *open loop gain* of the amplifier. This is typically about 1 000 000 .

This would mean that if the pd between the input terminals were 0.01 V, then the output potential would be 10 000 V. This is not possible since the supply voltage (9 V) can not be exceeded.

In an ideal op amp, the open loop gain is infinite.

Inverting and non-inverting

If V+ is bigger than V− the output is +9 V since both are +ve. The +ve terminal is called non-inverting.

If V− is bigger than V+ the output is −9 V since these have opposite signs. The −ve terminal is called the inverting input.

Figure 11.22 The op amp symbol. The numbers show how the 5 terminals of the op amp are connected inside to the legs on the chip.

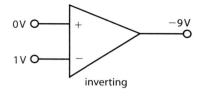
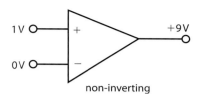

Figure 11.23 Inverting and non-inverting amplifiers (note: supply not shown).

Input impedance

This is effectively the resistance that would be measured if a meter were placed across the input terminals. For an ideal op amp this is infinite, therefore no current flows into the inputs.

Output impedance

The output of the op amp is like a 9 V battery: it can be used to power loudspeakers, light bulbs and other devices. The output impedance is equivalent to the internal resistance of the battery. In an ideal op amp this is zero. This means that it can deliver a lot of current. To get a current to flow through a load resistor there must be a pd across it; this is achieved by connecting the resistor between the output and a wire at 0 V. This is called an *earth*.

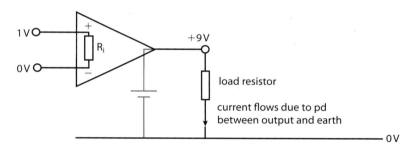

Figure 11.24 The input impedance is represented by R_i. The output impedance is like a battery with zero internal resistance.

The ideal op amp

The ideal op amp can be summarised as having:
- infinite input impedance
- infinite gain
- zero output impedance.

No op amp is really like this but this assumption makes it easier to understand how the following applications work.

Exercises

20 An op amp with an open loop gain of 1 000 000 is connected to a 9 V source. What will the output be if:
  (a) the potential of the non-inverting input is 5 μV?
  (b) the potential of the non-inverting input is 5 V?
  (c) the potential of the inverting input is 5 V?

Amplifiers

Using an op amp on its own is not very useful for amplifying music. If the open loop gain is 1 000 000, then once the signal goes above 0.000 009 V the output will be a constant 9 V. An amplifier must be able to produce a signal that is the same shape as the input but with larger amplitude.

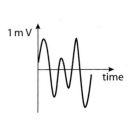

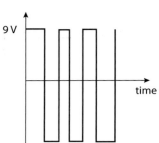

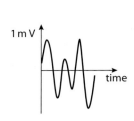

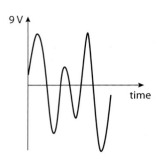

Figure 11.25 Comparison of a signal amplified open loop and a signal properly amplified.

Simplifications
You may wonder how there can be an output if the two inputs are equal.
Well of course there wouldn't be, this is a simplification to enable us to be able to calculate the gain.

The non-inverting amplifier

Consider the circuit for a non-inverting amp shown in Figure 11.26. We know that if the difference between V+ and V− is more than $9\,\mu V$ the output will be a constant 9 V. Therefore, we can say that the two inputs are about the same:

$$V_+ = V_- = V_{input}$$

This means that the potential in the middle of R_1 and R_2 is also V_{input}

If the current through this combination is I, then applying Ohm's law to the combination R_1 and R_2 gives $I = \dfrac{V_{output}}{R_1 + R_2}$

And to R_2 alone $I = \dfrac{V_{input}}{R_2}$

Equating gives $\dfrac{V_{output}}{R_1 + R_2} = \dfrac{V_{input}}{R_2}$

So $\dfrac{V_{output}}{V_{input}} = \dfrac{R_1}{R_2} + \dfrac{R_2}{R_2} = 1 + \dfrac{R_1}{R_2}$

This is the gain of the amplifier.

Figure 11.26 A non-inverting op amp. ▶

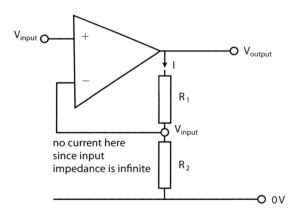

Exercises

21 Referring to the non-inverting amplifier in Figure 11.26 (the supply is 9 V):
If $R_1 = 10\,k\Omega$ and $R_2 = 1\,k\Omega$:
(a) What is the gain of the amplifier?
(b) If the input is 0.5 V what will the output be?
(c) Calculate the current through R_1.
(d) What is the pd across R_1?

The inverting amplifier

Now consider an amplifier that gives an inverted signal as shown in Figure 11.27. Again the difference between V_+ and V_- must be very small, so let's say they are equal. Since V+ is connected to earth then V_+ and V_- are equal to 0 V.

$V_+ = V_- = 0$

The potential at a point between R_1 and R_2 is therefore also 0 V.

Applying Ohm's law to R_1 gives $I = \dfrac{V_{input}}{R_2}$

Applying Ohm's law to R_2 gives $I = \dfrac{V_{output}}{R_1}$

Equating gives $I = \dfrac{V_{input}}{R_2} = \dfrac{V_{output}}{R_1}$

$\dfrac{V_{output}}{V_{input}} = \dfrac{R_1}{R_2}$

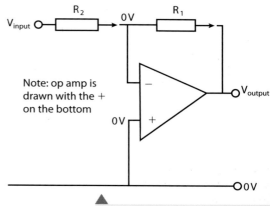

Note: op amp is drawn with the + on the bottom

Figure 11.27 The inverting amplifier.

Referring to the inverting amplifier in Figure 11.27 (the supply is 10 V):

22 If $R_1 = 5\,k\Omega$ and $R_2 = 1\,k\Omega$
  (a) Calculate the gain of the amplifier.
  (b) If the input is 1 V what will the output be?
  (c) Calculate the current through R_2.
  (d) Calculate the pd across R_2.

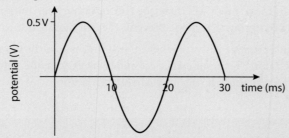

Figure 11.28

23 If the signal shown in Figure 11.28 is applied to the input of the amplifier in problem 22
  (a) What will the amplitude of the output be?
  (b) What will the frequency of the output be?

  (Remember frequency $= \dfrac{1}{\text{time for a complete cycle}}$.)

24 Draw the output obtained if the rising potential shown in Figure 11.29 is applied to the input of the amplifier in problem 22 .

25 If an inverting amplifier has a gain of 10, what will the value of R_2 be if $R_1 = 5\,k\Omega$?

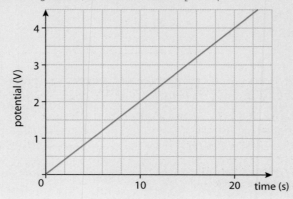

Figure 11.29

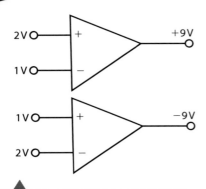

Figure 11.30 An op amp as a comparator

Figure 11.31 The circuit for a simple fire alarm includes a thermistor. This is a semi-conducting device with a resistance that goes down when its temperature increases. It also includes a diode which only allows current to flow in the direction of the arrow. ▶

Comparator

A comparator compares two potentials. If the potential on the + (positive) input is higher, then the output is +9 V and if the − (negative) is higher, the output is −9 V.

A simple fire alarm

Figure 11.31 shows a simple fire alarm that uses a thermistor to detect when the temperature goes above a certain value.

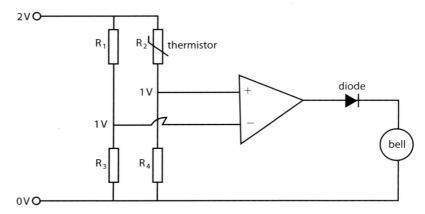

At normal room temperature all the resistances are equal ($R_1 = R_2 = R_3 = R_4$) so both inputs equal 1 V and the output is zero. If the temperature of the thermistor increases then its resistance gets less, resulting in a smaller pd across it. The potential to the + input will therefore rise, resulting in an output of 9 V. This will cause the bell to ring. The diode prevents the bell ringing if the thermistor gets cold.

This circuit is very sensitive, so the bell will ring even if the temperature rises only a small amount. The input can be set higher by varying the potential divider and so making make the bell ring only when there is a fire.

Remember
R_2 and R_4 are a potential divider so the potential divider equation
$$V_{out} = V_{in} \frac{R_4}{R_2 + R_4}$$
can be used.

Exercises

26 An op amp can be used to ring a bell if the temperature of a room falls below a certain value. The circuit is similar to the circuit in Figure 11.31 and uses a thermistor whose resistance varies with temp according to Table 7.

Temp (°C)	Resistance (Ω)
17	146.6
18	139.6
19	133.0
20	126.7
21	120.8
22	115.2
23	109.8

Table 7

(a) Suggest a way the circuit could be changed (involving the diode) so the circuit performs this task.
(b) What are the values of R_1, R_3 and R_4 so that the bell rings if the temperature drops below 18° C?
(c) If the temperature falls to 17° C, how much current will flow through the thermistor?
(d) At 17° C what will the potential at the + input be?
(e) At 17° C what will the output of the op amp be if the supply voltage is 9 V and the gain is 1 000 000?

Schmitt trigger

A Schmitt trigger is a type of comparator that switches to a high output when the input is above a given value (upper threshold) and only switches to a low output when the input gets lower than another low value (lower threshold). For example, if the thresholds are $+1\,V$ and $-1\,V$, then if the input is above $1\,V$ the output is $+9\,V$ until the input drops below $-1\,V$ when the output changes to $-9\,V$. When the input is between $+1\,V$ and $-1\,V$, the output is $+9\,V$ if it is on the way down and $-9\,V$ if on the way up. In this way the comparator remembers what its previous state was; this is called *hysteresis*.

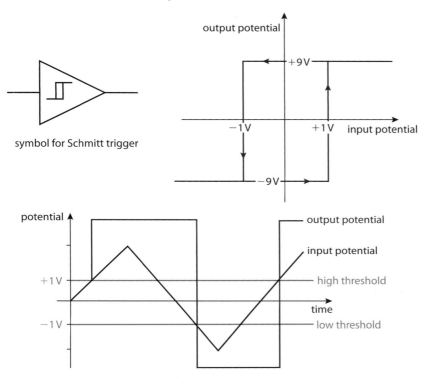

symbol for Schmitt trigger

◀ **Figure 11.32** The input and output of a Schmitt trigger and the relationship between these shown on the hysteresis curve.

Uses of the Schmitt trigger

One of the applications of a Schmitt trigger is for reshaping digital signals, especially to remove noise (see Figure 11.33).

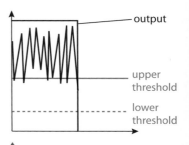

▲ **Figure 11.33** The noise on this digital signal is represented by the rapid variation on the signal. The Schmitt trigger switches the output to high when the input goes over the upper threshold and stays high until it goes below the lower threshold and so removes the noise.

Exercises

27 The potential in Figure 11.34 is connected to the input of a Schmidt trigger with an upper threshold of $+1\,V$ and a lower threshold of $-1\,V$.

Draw a graph of the output if the power supply to the op amp is $9\,V$.

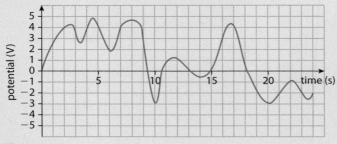

Figure 11.34

11.4 The mobile phone system

The mobile phone system

The mobile phone is a combination of two technologies: radio and telephone. These have been in use since the 1880s but the progress in the technologies is in the size and functionality of modern mobiles. For instance, a mobile can be a camera, an MP3 player, a calendar and an alarm clock as well as a phone. What are the developments that have made this possible?

The land phone system

The land-based telephone system today is very complicated and can perform many functions. However, the principle (and a lot of the wiring) is still the same as in the early days. In the early 20th century the phones in each town were connected to an operator and the operators in each town were connected to each other. When the phone was picked up a bulb would light up in a plug on the operators' switchboard and an operator would plug their headset into your line and ask who you wanted to speak to. If it was to someone in the same town then the operator would simply connect the two phone lines together but if it was further away then the operator would contact a second operator who would connect you. A long-distance call could involve many operators. Today the system has been replaced by electronic switches and when a number is dialled each digit is recognised and the caller is connected to the receiver. This can involve local, national and international exchanges. The complete system is called the *public switched telephone network* or PSTN.

Telephone operators routing calls at a local exchange in the early 20th century.

Radio telephone communication

Radio uses low frequency electromagnetic waves to transmit signals, rather than electric current in wires as used by telephone. Radio waves spread out in all directions, so caller and receiver cannot be connected together using switches and wires. Instead, each caller and receiver choose a certain frequency and the sound is then superimposed on this carrier frequency and transmitted. Some of the drawbacks with this system are that anyone may tune in to a conversation, and the transmission has a fairly short range unless you use a very big antenna and a powerful transmitter. In fact, it has been possible to connect a radio to the phone system in this way for many years. Each connected city had an antenna that could transmit and receive the signals from each radio phone and each phone had a selection of some 25 different frequency channels. So only 25 people could use the radio telephone system at any one time, and they had to be near a radio antenna! Also, the phones were huge as they had to have a powerful transmitter that needed a large battery.

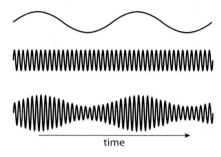

signal to be modified (e.g. speech or music)

carrier radio signal of higher frequency

carrier wave amplitude modulated by speech or music information

time

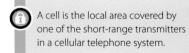

Figure 11.35 Sound can be superimposed on a carrier frequency by changing the amplitude of the carrier to match that of the sound. This is called amplitude modulation.

The cell phone

Modern mobile phones are radio transmitters in the same way as the old radio phone systems, but operate using *cells*, hence the name *cell phone*. As we have seen, the main problems with a radio telephone communication system are the need for a powerful transmitter and the limit on the number of users at any one time. If each city had 100 small antennae then this would increase the number of users and also take away the need for mobiles to have powerful transmitters. It would mean that if you were moving around across several cells whilst talking on the phone (the whole point of a mobile phone) you would need to be switched from one transmitter to another. To prevent a break in the conversation, this switching would need to be done quickly and automatically. It is only recently that computer technology has been able to perfect the switching process, enabling cell phones to become very much part of modern life.

How the cells are arranged

A city is split up into many small units, or cells, of hexagons each with an area of about 26 km² to enable a mobile phone to get coverage of the whole city. This is because a mobile has quite a weak transmitter and only has an operating distance of about 7 km (see Figure 11.36).

A mobile phone company is only allowed to use a limited range of frequencies (between 824 MHz and 894 MHz) so that phone calls don't interfere with radio transmission. This range will give the company about 800 channels that it can use.

A cell is the local area covered by one of the short-range transmitters in a cellular telephone system.

The original mobile phones received an analogue signal via a radio wave but the switching of the signal was digital. The modern phones use a higher frequency radio signal which has a digital signal superimposed on it. In this way many more channels can be opened enabling several hundred communications to take place simultaneously through the same antenna.

Each conversation must use two channels (full duplex); otherwise it would not be possible for the two people to talk at the same time. This limits the channels to 400. The seven cells that are closest to each other (the pink and yellow) cannot use the same bands, so the 400 available are split into 56 channels per cell. In this way the channels are organised so that no matter where you are, you cannot receive the same signal from two transmitters/antennae. The cells using the same channels (see Figure 11.36) are arranged so they are not next to each other. One advantage of this system is the ease with which it can be expanded to cater for more users. More channels can be added by simply reducing the size of the cells.

Receiving a call

When you switch on your mobile it sends out a signal, this isn't one of the 400 conversation bands but another band that has been reserved for this purpose. All the antennae in range in the cells will receive this signal but only the one that gets the strongest signal responds, and then only if you are a member of the right network. If you move to another cell then another antenna gets the strongest signal and knows to direct any calls to this new position.

Figure 11.36 In this arrangement of cells a phone in a pink cell is close enough to receive signals from all the transmitters (antennae) in the yellow cells but not the green ones. The pink and yellow cells cannot, therefore, use the same channels. The cells with the same number use the same channels and are arranged so they are not next to each other. If you start in position A you will receive a signal from pink cell 1 that will inform you that you are connected to the network. Any calls will be directed to pink 1 but if you now walk from A to B the signal to yellow 4 will become the strongest and the call will now be transferred to yellow 4.

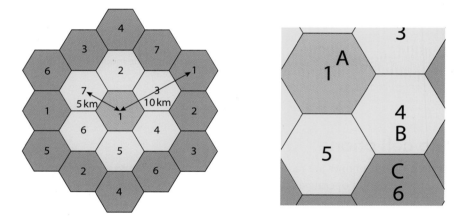

Tracking

For the digital switching system to operate, the transmission towers/antenna of the cell you are in and all the cells that you might go into need to be receiving your signal. The antenna with the strongest signal is the one which relays the phone call to you, but the others 'know you are there'. From the strength of the signal it is possible to calculate how far you are from each of the antennae and then some simple geometry will define your position.

Figure 11.37 If you are 4 km from A, 4 km from B and 6 km from C you must be at point X.

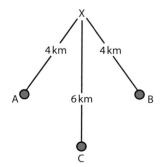

3G

The latest cell phones are known as third generation or 3G. These use not only digital switching but also a digital signal to enable the transfer of more than just conversations. 3G phones can open web pages, search the internet, download video files and pictures. Since the phone itself is a digital device, it can also process data and communicate with a computer – in fact it is closer to a computer than a telephone.

Advantages and disadvantages of the cell phone

Mobile communication

The obvious advantage of the cell phone is the possibility of communicating on the move. Before the introduction of the mobile phone you would have to be at home or in an office if you wanted to communicate with someone, unless you were one of the few people able to afford a radio phone (for conversations only, not text). When travelling, a phone box was the most common way to communicate (providing you had some coins in your pocket).

Not only can you talk whilst on the move, but digital technology has opened the doors for sending texts as a cheap and efficient way of communicating, or pictures, photos and video clips.

Tracking

It has been possible to track a mobile phone user's movements since the birth of cellular technology, but this was not the original purpose of the technology and so this facility has only been available to the police and emergency services until recently. Now it is available to the public and for a small fee you can receive information on the position of a mobile. It is easy to see how the police may have tracked criminals and how emergency services may have rescued lives. However it is not difficult to see how this can be abused.

The use of mobile phone tracking to catch criminals is often used in crime series on the television. This gives the impression that the police are doing it all the time. Maybe reality isn't quite the same.

Bringing people together

It is a relatively simple and cheap process to set up a cell phone network compared to running wires from house to house. This has meant that it has been possible to introduce mobile phones into areas that have not had communication before.

Mobile phone etiquette

Following close on the heels of the development of mobile phone technology has been the development of the social etiquette for its use. It has become accepted that there are places where the use of a mobile is not desirable and many stores, theatres and other public places now have signs asking the public to turn off their phones before entering. This avoids irritating ring tones, loud conversations, disturbances in hospitals, and interruptions to concert and theatre performances.

Social alienation

The mobile phone is a method of communication so it might seem strange that its use could lead to social alienation. However, there are certain things that are easier to say within a text message than face to face. Does the use of mobile phones and texting reduce the amount of time that people spend talking to each other?

It is very difficult to collect scientific data on the health effects of mobile phones. As it is not ethical to expose humans to higher and higher levels of high frequency radio waves until they develop symptoms, the data on health and mobiles comes from people who have become sick and have used mobile phones. It is difficult to say if the mobile phones have been the cause of the illness.

It is interesting to consider whether groups of young people sitting together and texting others rather than talking to each other has resulted in an increase in communication by including people who can't be there, or resulted in an decrease in communication between members of the group? Whatever the answer, the mobile phone has certainly changed the way we communicate.

Health

There has been a lot of talk in the media about the possible dangers of using a mobile phone. Reports mention possible links between exposure to electromagnetic radiation and cancer. However, concentrating on the physics, when the high frequency radio waves are absorbed by the human body, they will cause a slight rise in temperature, but the energy is not high enough to excite the atomic electrons that would be necessary to cause chemical changes.

The greatest health risks for mobile phone users are those related to the increased stress of being contactable 24 hours a day.

Environmental problems

To set up a cell phone network requires the building of antennae. This is not normally a problem in cities, where they can be put on top of existing buildings or even hidden inside church spires. However, in rural areas, the antennae are unsightly and often unwanted. Another environmental problem associated with this rapidly changing technology is the disposal of phones. Before the birth of mobile technology, when you bought a house, the phone came with it, and the life of the phone could be thirty or forty years. There were of course new styles of phone on the market but since few people would ever see your phone, it wasn't so popular to keep up with the new designs. The mobile is not just a phone but has become a fashion accessory and a status symbol. New models come out every week and old models look dated after a year. The life of a mobile is on average about 18 months, which means in a country the size of the UK around 15 million phones are discarded each year. Mobiles phones contain cadmium, rhodium, palladium, beryllium and lead solder, which are all highly toxic. For this reason, phones should be recycled and not thrown into the bin.

A mobile phone antenna shaped like a tree to make it blend into the environment!!

Practice questions

Note that as this is a new topic, the exam practice questions and answers are available online. Please visit www.heinemann.co.uk/hotlinks, enter the express code 4266 S and click on Weblink 11.1.

12 Relativity and particle physics (Option D)

12.1 Introduction to relativity

Assessment statements

D.1.1 Describe what is meant by a frame of reference.
D.1.2 Describe what is meant by a Galilean transformation.
D.1.3 Solve problems involving relative velocities using the Galilean transformation equations.

By the late 19th century, physicists believed that they had solved all the big problems.

Newton's laws explained the motion of bodies both on the Earth and beyond. Maxwell's equations beautifully linked electricity and magnetism; even showing mathematically that light has an electromagnetic nature.

At this time it was believed that light, like sound and other mechanical waves, required a medium or substance to pass through. It was hypothesized that something called the ether was the medium that surrounded the Earth and that light from the Sun reached us by passing through it. Nowadays we believe that space surrounds the Earth. Scientists tried very hard to detect the ether, but without success.

In one of the most famous negative experiments in the history of science, Michelson and Morley, two American physicists, measured the speed of light, very carefully, in different directions relative to the motion of the Earth through the ether. Everyone expected that light would move more slowly if it were going against the ether 'wind' - not surprisingly, because everyone knows it is easier to run with the wind than to run against it.

Albert Einstein (1879-1955) was born in Germany, lived for a while in Italy and finished school in Switzerland. It was while working in a patent office in Bern, Switzerland that he wrote the theory of special relativity. He later became a professor in Prague, Czechoslovakia before moving to the University of Berlin, Germany. With the rise of the Nazis in the early 1930s, Einstein, who was Jewish, decided to move to the US where he remained for much of the rest of his life.

 Can science ever really solve all the problems?

 How do we know that the Earth is surrounded by a vacuum, and not ether?

 Einstein wrote his paper on the theory of special relativity in 1905. This was called his *annus mirabilis*, or wonderful year, because he also wrote three other papers that year. One was on the photoelectric effect and eventually earned him a Nobel Prize. Another was about Brownian motion, supporting the kinetic theory of matter, and then there was a paper about the equivalence of mass and energy that included the most famous equation in the history of the world! To write any one of these papers would be a fantastic achievement for most scientists. The fact that Einstein wrote all four in one year is an indication of the level of his genius.

The fact that Michelson and Morley were unable to find any change in the speed of light, no matter how many times and how many ways they measured it, posed a problem for physics. It did not seem to make sense because everything else moved in a way that was relative. Think about the following example:

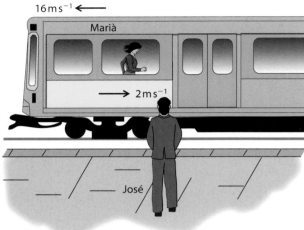

Figure 12.1 Simple relative motion. The train is moving to the left at a speed of 16 m s⁻¹. José is standing on the platform. Inside the train carriage Maria is walking to the right at a speed of 2m s⁻¹. Maria's motion relative to relative to José is 14 m s⁻¹ to the left.

$E = mc^2$
This is the most famous equation in the world. In the equation, E is energy, m is mass and c is the velocity of light. Since the velocity of light is such a large quantity, a small amount of mass multiplied by the square of the velocity of light is equivalent to a huge amount of energy.

What is a paradigm shift?
Can you think of an example of a paradigm shift in physics?
Can you think of an example of a paradigm shift in another area?

A frame of reference is a three-dimensional coordinate system.

Why is time called the fourth dimension?
Could there be other dimensions?

Before Galileo, motion in the y-direction was considered to be fundamentally different to motion in the x-and z-directions. One of Galileo's many achievements was to unite the three dimensions.

Clearly the way Maria moves depends on how you look at it. Her speed relative to José on the platform is different to his speed relative to someone standing next to her on the train. Any other situation you can think of would be the same, trains and boats and planes and rockets. Why should light be different to everything else and why was the ether not slowing down the light?

In 1905 Albert Einstein proposed a radical solution to these problems in his theory of special relativity. He suggested that light was different because it always travelled at a constant speed. If the speed of light was always constant, or absolute, this meant that the flow of time itself could not be absolute but must be relative, and would change if something was travelling very fast. Also it implied that the ether did not exist.

You are probably reading this book in a room somewhere, sitting down. Obviously your velocity relative to the floor of the room is zero; you are at rest. If someone were looking at you from the North Pole, however, then they would say you were rotating beneath them, once every day. There is another possibility; according to an observer out in space you would be orbiting the Sun once every year. All three of these positions are correct; it depends on the frame of reference.

This means that with three numbers, and a unit, one in each of the three dimensions x, y and z, it is possible to locate any place in the universe. You can describe where any point is in a room by stating how far it is from two mutually perpendicular walls and the ceiling. Similarly, it is possible to find any object in the solar system if you know exactly how far it is, at any given time, from the Sun, the Earth and the planet Jupiter.

As we have already seen with José and Maria, motion is relative. This kind of relative motion, at speeds well below the speed of light, is described by the Galilean transformation equations. These equations explain how position and velocity change from one frame of reference to another.

Think about a person who is trying to row a boat straight across a river with a speed v_1 when the river is flowing to the right with a speed v_2. The boat will move at an angle towards the right at a speed v and the angle will depend on the relative speeds of the boat and the river. There are two frames of reference; from the point of view of the person on the boat, and from the point of view of an observer on the bank of the river. The situation is shown in the diagrams below.

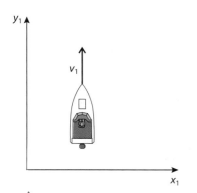

Figure 12.2 From the frame of reference of an observer on the boat, the speed is v_1 at 90° to the bank of the river.

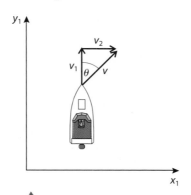

Figure 12.3 From the frame of reference of observer on the bank of the river, the speed is v at an angle θ.

Galileo Galilei (1564-1642). Galileo was apparently inspired to write his transformation equations by his famous experiments rolling a ball down a slope. These experiments also enabled him to obtain a value for the acceleration due to gravity and led directly to the idea we know as Newton's first law.

In general, these are the Galilean transformation equations:

If there is motion in the x-direction $\qquad x_1 = x + v_x t$

If there is motion in the y-direction $\qquad y_1 = y + v_y t$

If there is no motion in the z-direction $\qquad z_1 = z$

Since time is considered absolute $\qquad t_1 = t$

The velocity transformation is $\qquad v = v_1 + v_2$

Remember, velocity is a vector so these velocities must have a direction.

12.2 Concepts and postulates of special relativity

Assessment statements

D.2.1 Describe what is meant by an inertial frame of reference.
D.2.2 State the two postulates of the special theory of relativity.
D.2.3 Discuss the concept of simultaneity.

An inertial frame of reference is one where Newton's laws work. The first law is the law of inertia and is about the way things resist changes to their motion. A body will either remain at rest or move with a constant velocity (constant speed in a straight line) unless an unbalanced, or resultant, force acts on it. If an unbalanced force acts on a body, then it will accelerate according to the second law.

If you are not moving relative to your surroundings, then you are in an inertial frame of reference. If you are in a plane moving at constant velocity, you are also in an inertial frame of reference and this is why you can walk around inside the plane normally. If the plane accelerates, by changing speed or direction, then you should not walk around, but remain seated with your seatbelt fastened!

Einstein's theory of special relativity has two *postulates* or basic ideas.

- 1st postulate

The laws of physics are exactly the same in all inertial frames of reference.

This means that if you are in a car moving at constant velocity and drop a coin, then it will fall straight into your hand just as it would if you were sitting in a chair at home. Of course if the car is accelerating, by changing speed or direction, then the coin would not fall into your hand.

- 2nd postulate

The speed of light is constant and independent of the speed of the source of the light or the speed of the observer.

Although this follows logically from the work of Maxwell, and also Michelson and Morley, the implications are profound.

Simultaneity

As we saw earlier, if the speed of light is constant, then time must be relative, and this means we have to change the way we think about time. One change is that we are forced to realize that whether two events are simultaneous or not depends on the observer's frame of reference. If two events occur at the same point in space then there can be no doubt about their simultaneity. If the two events do not occur at the same point then everything changes, because the speed of light, though ultimate, is still finite, at approximately 3×10^8 m s^{-1}.

Think about the following thought experiment. Lightning strikes two poles by the side of a railroad track. Mehmet is standing in the middle and observes the lightning. He has no doubt that the two events are simultaneous.

A   Mehmet   B

Neslihan is on the train and travelling fast; she is in a moving frame of reference. When the lightning strikes she is looking out of the window at two mirrors joined together at an angle of 90°. According to Neslihan the lightning strikes are not simultaneous. From her frame of reference, the pole that she is travelling towards was struck before the other pole. Of course the difference in the timing of the strikes depends on the speed of the train, but there must be a difference because the speed of light is finite.

The success of Einstein's theory in correctly describing the motion of any particle does not mean that Newton was wrong. Far from it, in fact Newton's equations are contained inside Einstein's' equations. Newton's laws of motion work perfectly for any bodies moving at normal or everyday speeds.

Did time have a beginning? Will time have an end?

Figure 12.4 Simultaneous lightning strikes. Mehmet is stationary relative to the two lightning strikes. He sees them strike simultaneously.

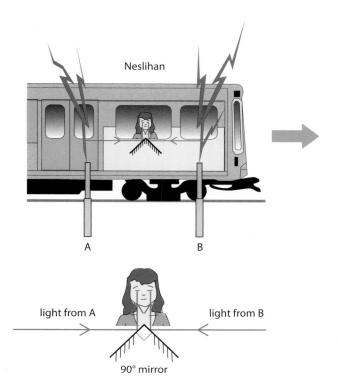

Neslihan

A   B

light from A   light from B

90° mirror

▲ **Figure 12.5** Non-simultaneous lightning strikes. Neslihan is on the train travelling towards pole B and away from pole A. She sees the reflection from B before the reflection from A. The light from B travels a shorter distance.

🔒 The concept of simultaneity states that two events occurring at different points in space will not be simultaneous for two observers in different frames of reference.

ⓘ One of the stranger ideas of Einstein's theory of special relativity is that time is not absolute but depends on the relative motion of the observer and what is being observed. Einstein later showed that time and space are different dimensions of the same thing, called space-time.

So who is right - Mehmet or Neslihan? In fact they are both right; time passes differently in separate frames of reference!

12.3 Relativistic kinematics

Assessment statements
D.3.1 Describe the concept of a light clock.
D.3.2 Define *proper time interval*.
D.3.3 Derive the time dilation formula.
D.3.4 Sketch and annotate a graph showing the variation with relative velocity of the Lorentz factor.
D.3.5 Solve problems involving time dilation.
D.3.6 Define *proper length*.
D.3.7 Describe the phenomenon of length contraction.
D.3.8 Solve problems involving length contraction.

Time dilation

As a result of Einstein's work, we were forced to reconsider our views about the nature of time. If time does not pass in the same way for different observers, then we need to label time in a new way. According to the theory of special relativity, there are two types of time, *dilated time* and *proper time*.

The proper time is the shortest possible time for an event to occur, but this is not the definition of proper time.

🔒 Proper time is the defined as the time taken for an event to occur as measured by an observer who is both stationary, relative to the event, and at the site of the event.

In theory, if light is reflected back and forth repeatedly between two parallel mirrors, the set up can be used to measure short intervals of time with great accuracy. This idea is called a *light clock*. It can be used to understand how proper time is related to dilated time by the time dilation formula.

Here is an 'easy' way to derive the time dilation formula. It also includes the derivation of the Lorentz factor.

At first, imagine an astronaut at rest in a spaceship observing a simple light clock as shown in the diagram. The light moves a distance D in a time Δt_o.

Figure 12.6 Light travels from the floor to the ceiling of the spaceship, a distance D, and then reflects from the mirror. Multiple reflections of this type can be used in a simple light clock.

The time here is the proper time (t_o) because the astronaut is stationary at the site of the event.

$$c = \frac{D}{\Delta t_o} \qquad D = c\Delta t_o$$

D is the height of the space ship and c is the speed of light.

In the second diagram, the astronaut is flying fast above the Earth and viewed by an observer on the ground.

Figure 12.7 The observer on the ground sees light leave the floor in position 1, and reflect from the mirror in position 2.

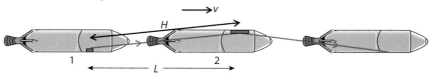

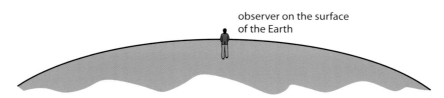

observer on the surface of the Earth

The speed of the space ship is v and it travels a distance L in time Δt as viewed by the observer on the ground. This is the dilated time because the observer is not stationary at the site of the event.

$$v = \frac{L}{\Delta t} \qquad L = v\Delta t$$

In the same time interval the light travels a distance H.

$$c = \frac{H}{\Delta t} \qquad H = c\Delta t$$

By Pythagoras:
$$H^2 = D^2 + L^2$$

Substituting from above gives us:
$$c^2\Delta t^2 = c^2\Delta t_o^2 + v^2\Delta t^2$$

Then dividing it all by c^2:
$$\Delta t^2 = \Delta t_o^2 + \frac{v^2\Delta t^2}{c^2}$$

Rearranging:
$$\Delta t_o^2 = \Delta t^2 - \frac{v^2\Delta t^2}{c^2}$$

Taking Δt^2 outside a bracket:

$$\Delta t_o^2 = \Delta t^2 \left(1 - \frac{v^2}{c^2}\right)$$

Taking the square root:

$$\Delta t_o = \Delta t \sqrt{1 - \frac{v^2}{c^2}}$$

Finally:

$$\Delta t = \gamma \Delta t_o$$

Where

$$\gamma = \frac{1}{\sqrt{1 - \frac{v^2}{c^2}}}$$

● **Examiner's hint:** Find these last two equations in the data booklet and make sure you know what each of the letters stands for.

γ is known as the *relativity factor* or the *Lorentz factor*; it is a ratio, so it has no unit.

It is essential that you practise calculations involving the Lorentz factor in order to understand how it varies with relative velocity. In particular, you should realize that relativistic effects are only significant at speeds approaching the speed of light.

Exercises

To fully appreciate how this all works, use your calculator to plug in the following velocities, v, into the formula and solve for γ, the Lorentz factor:

$$\gamma = \frac{1}{\sqrt{1 - \frac{v^2}{c^2}}}$$

1 $v = 1.00 \times 10^8 \text{ m s}^{-1}$ **2** $v = 1.50 \times 10^8 \text{ m s}^{-1}$
3 $v = 2.00 \times 10^8 \text{ m s}^{-1}$ **4** $v = 2.50 \times 10^8 \text{ m s}^{-1}$
5 $v = 2.80 \times 10^8 \text{ m s}^{-1}$ **6** $v = 2.90 \times 10^8 \text{ m s}^{-1}$
7 $v = 2.95 \times 10^8 \text{ m s}^{-1}$ **8** $v = 2.99 \times 10^8 \text{ m s}^{-1}$

Remember, c is the speed of light in a vacuum $= 3.00 \times 10^8 \text{ m s}^{-1}$.

● **Examiner's hint:** Please be sure to do this exercise for yourself; it will really help you to understand the ideas.

● **Examiner's hint:** Here are two ways of performing the final example on a calculator:

$$\frac{1}{\sqrt{1 - \frac{2.99^2}{3^2}}} = 12.26$$

$$\left[\sqrt{1 - \frac{2.99^2}{3^2}}\right]^{-1} = 12.26$$

 CERN is short for **C**onseil **E**uropéen pour la **R**echerche **N**ucléaire. It is the largest particle physics centre in the world. The countries involved with the work at CERN include Austria, Belgium, Bulgaria, the Czech Republic, Denmark, Finland, France, Germany, Greece, Hungary, Italy, The Netherlands, Norway, Poland, Portugal, the Slovak Republic, Spain, Sweden, Switzerland, the United Kingdom, India, Israel, Japan, the Russian Federation, Turkey, the USA, Algeria, Argentina, Armenia, Australia, Azerbaijan, Belarus, Brazil, Canada, China, Croatia, Cyprus, Estonia, Georgia, Iceland, India, Iran, Ireland, Mexico, Morocco, Pakistan, Peru, Romania, Serbia, Slovenia, South Africa, South Korea, Taiwan and the Ukraine.

 In the most powerful accelerators like the one at CERN, particle speeds of 0.99999999995 of the speed of light can be reached. At this speed the Lorentz factor is 140 000!

The circular tunnel of the main accelerator at CERN shown in this photograph is 27 km long and is buried 100 metres under the border between Switzerland and France. It contains the Large Hadron Collider which will probe deeper into matter than ever before.

 The World Wide Web was invented at CERN.

Here are the values for the Lorentz factor for the different speeds given in the exercises:

Velocity (m s^{-1} × 10^8)	1.00	1.50	2.00	2.50	2.80	2.90	2.95	2.99
Lorentz factor	1.06	1.15	1.34	1.81	2.79	3.91	5.50	12.3

● **Examiner's hint:** When solving problems using relativity equations, it is often easier to express the velocity as a fraction of c. For example, 2.7×10^8 is $0.9c$.

Now we calculate the relative values of v as a fraction of c.

For example, if $v = 1.50 \times 10^8$ m s^{-1} then the relative velocity, as a fraction of c, would be 0.50

Velocity (m s^{-1} × 10^8)	1.00	1.50	2.00	2.50	2.80	2.90	2.95	2.99
Relative velocity	0.333	0.500	0.667	0.833	0.933	0.967	0.983	.997

Finally, we sketch a graph of these relative values against the Lorentz factor.

Figure 12.8 This graph shows the variation with relative velocity of the Lorentz factor. The shape of the graph shows how relativistic effects are insignificant at low speeds and become increasingly dramatic as the speed of the body approaches the speed of light.

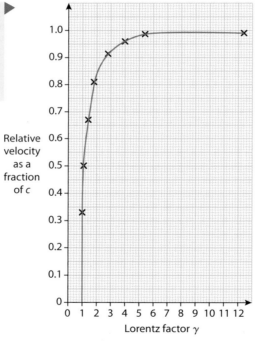

What this graph tells us is clear; firstly that relativistic effects are negligible at speeds below a certain value, a value that is already extremely fast! We find that at a speed of 100 000 m s^{-1} the Lorentz factor is 1.00000006, and Newton's laws will work perfectly well. However as the speed tends towards the speed of light, the Lorentz factor increases dramatically, tending to infinity, which is a sure sign that things are getting increasingly weird!

The equations show us that time would slow down to standstill at the speed of light, which is one reason that the 3×10^8 m s^{-1} is an upper limit for speed. Any speeds greater than this are either science fiction or mistakes in calculations!

Will it ever be possible to escape the solar system and explore new galaxies?

Worked example

A particle has a proper lifetime, when it is at rest, of 2.2 μs. Calculate its lifetime when it is accelerated to a velocity of 2.7×10^8 m s^{-1}.

Solution

The equation we need is:

$$\Delta t = \gamma \Delta t_o$$

Δt_o is the proper time = 2.2×10^{-6} s.

γ is the Lorentz factor.

Δt is the dilated time that we are trying to find.

$$v = 2.7 \times 10^8 \text{ m s}^{-1} = 0.9c$$

To calculate the Lorentz factor we will use the equation:

$$\gamma = \frac{1}{\sqrt{1 - \frac{v^2}{c^2}}}$$

$$\gamma = \frac{1}{\sqrt{1 - \frac{(0.9c)^2}{c^2}}}$$

$$\gamma = \frac{1}{\sqrt{(1 - 0.81)}}$$

$$\gamma = \frac{1}{\sqrt{0.19}}$$

$$\gamma = \frac{1}{0.44}$$

$$\gamma = 2.3$$

Now we can go back to the original equation to solve the problem:

$$\Delta t = \gamma \Delta t_o$$

$$\Delta t = 2.3 \times 2.2 \times 10^{-6} \, s$$

$$\mathbf{\Delta t = 5.1 \times 10^{-6} \, s}$$

The effects of time dilation mean that the Global Positioning System (GPS) must make ongoing corrections to clocks on satellites, or else it will not work accurately.

Exercises

9 The half-life of muons is 3.1×10^{-6} s as measured in a frame of reference that is stationary relative to the muons.

A pulse of muons is produced such that the muons have a speed of 2.8×10^8 m s^{-1} relative to a stationary observer.

Determine the distance travelled by the pulse, as measured by the observer, when half of the muons have decayed.

Length contraction

Remember from the second postulate that **the speed of light is constant and independent of the speed of the source of the light or the speed of the observer.**

If the speed of light is an absolute constant, and time is not fixed but relative, then there is a problem for our simple equation:

$$\text{constant speed} = \frac{\text{distance}}{\text{time}}$$

Unfortunately we have to let go of the concept of distance, or length, being fixed in order to balance the equation. If speed is fixed and time is changing, then distance has to change as well.

This idea is the called *length contraction* and means that at relativistic speeds things shrink in the direction of travel! We are not surprised to discover this because weirdness is built into the theory of relativity.

The proper length is the greatest distance we can measure for any object. Note that length contraction only occurs in the direction of travel.

The equation for problems involving length contraction is:

$$L = \frac{L_o}{\gamma}$$

where L_o is the proper length
L is the contracted length
γ is the relativistic factor

A body has a proper length, L_o, which is defined as the distance between two points measured, at the same time, by an observer at rest relative to the points.

Worked example

Imagine a spaceship travelling by the Earth at a speed of $1.50 \times 10^8 \text{ m s}^{-1}$.
If there is a computer screen in the spaceship 25.0 cm wide and 20.0 cm high, how would the screen appear to an observer on the Earth?

Solution

To calculate the Lorentz factor we will use the equation:

$$\gamma = \frac{1}{\sqrt{1 - \frac{v^2}{c^2}}}$$

$$= \frac{1}{\sqrt{1 - \frac{(0.50c)^2}{c^2}}} \qquad v = 1.5 \times 10^8 \text{ m s}^{-1} = 0.50c$$

$$= \frac{1}{\sqrt{0.75}}$$

$$= \frac{1}{0.866} = 1.15$$

Contracted length $\qquad L = \dfrac{L_o}{\gamma}$

$$L = \frac{25.0 \text{ cm}}{1.15}$$

$$\boldsymbol{L = 21.7 \text{ cm}}$$

The height would still appear to be 20.0 cm as there is no motion in that direction.

The theory of special relativity challenges fundamental ideas about space and time. However, it is important to realize that the theory is not science fiction, because it has been proved by repeatable experiments. Consequently it must be regarded as good science, and the concepts, however strange, have to be accepted as scientific fact.

Exercises

10 A super-fast spacecraft is moving at a speed of 0.80c with respect to observers on Earth. The spacecraft leaves Earth in May 2015 on its way to a distant solar system.
   (a) According to the observers in the spacecraft, 6.0 years have elapsed since leaving Earth. Calculate the time elapsed according to an observer on Earth.
   (b) Explain which time interval is the proper time interval.
   (c) Explain whether either measured time interval can be considered to be 'correct'.
   (d) Calculate the distance of the spacecraft from Earth according to an observer on Earth.
   (e) The observers in the spacecraft send a radio message to Earth to say that they have been travelling for 6.0 years. Determine how long it will take the message to get to Earth according to the spacecraft observers.

11 Muons are unstable particles that have an average lifetime of 2.2×10^{-6} s as measured in a reference frame in which they are at rest. Muons that are created at a height of 3.0 km above the Earth's surface move vertically downward with a speed of 0.98c as measured by an observer at rest on the Earth's surface.
   (a) Calculate the average lifetime of a muon as measured by the observer on Earth.
   (b) Calculate the distance travelled by a muon during a time equal to the average lifetime of the muon according to the observer at rest relative to the Earth's surface.
   (c) Calculate the distance travelled by the Earth during a time equal to the average lifetime of the muon according to an observer at rest relative to the muon.
   (d) Muons created at a height of 3.0 km above the Earth's surface are in fact detected on the surface of the Earth. Use your answers to (b) and (c) together with any other relevant calculations to explain this observation according to
      (i) the observer at rest on the surface of the Earth
      (ii) the observer at rest relative to the muon.

12.4 Description and classification of particles

Setting the scene

Modern particle physics can be said to have begun in the early 1930s. Before we can understand the development of particle physics, we must know something about what particles had been discovered and what theories had been proposed to describe their interactions at this time.

A very brief (and selective) history of discoveries

1898 Joseph Thomson measured the charge/mass ratio of the electron, leading to the 'plum pudding' model of the atom.

1905 Albert Einstein explained the photoelectric effect by proposing that light is made of photons.

1911 Ernest Rutherford suggested that the atom consists of a nucleus with surrounding electrons.

1931 James Chadwick found evidence for the neutron.

1930 Wolfgang Pauli explained why beta particles have a spread of energies, by proposing the existence of the neutrino.

1931 Paul Dirac proposed that every particle has an antiparticle with opposite charge.

In the 1930s physicists were developing the theories of quantum mechanics.

Particle	Antiparticle
electron	positron
proton	antiproton
neutron	antineutron
neutrino	antineutrino

◀ **Table 1** Particles and antiparticles.

Why do we think an electron is a particle?

In physics, when we talk about a particle, we mean a small ball. When we say an electron is a particle we don't mean it *is* a small ball we mean it *has the properties* of a small ball. What are those properties? If a ball is thrown forwards, it falls in a parabolic path due to the gravitational field of the Earth. When an electron is projected forwards in a uniform electric field, it also follows a parabolic path. When balls hit each other, momentum and energy are conserved. When two electrons hit each other, momentum and energy are conserved. So we say electrons have particle-like properties.

Particle nature of light

Light is electromagnetic radiation which has the wave-like properties of reflection, refraction, diffraction and interference. However, light is produced when an electron changes energy level and this results in a packet or quantum of energy. These packets are called *photons*. A photon has particle-like properties, for example it can bounce off an electron, resulting in a change of momentum.

Wave nature of particles

Electron diffraction: the pattern produced when electrons pass through a powder made of crystals.

We have seen that electrons have particle-like properties, but they also have wave-like properties. If electrons are passed through a crystal they land in a pattern that is very similar to the pattern formed when light passes through a diffraction grating. The electrons are being diffracted. The electrons are behaving like waves.

Probability waves

If one ball is travelling towards a stationary ball and we know the velocity of the moving one, then we can calculate exactly when they will hit. When two electrons travel towards each other, we cannot predict exactly when they will hit, but we can say when they are *most likely* to hit. We cannot write an exact (x, y, z) coordinate to give the position of an electron, but we can say where it is *most likely* to be. This leads to a probability distribution, and the equation for that probability distribution is similar to the equation for a wave. This is also the case for all sub-atomic particles.

Heisenberg's uncertainty principle

Since the position of a particle is defined by a probability distribution, it is not possible to define exactly where it is. Werner Heisenberg developed the idea that you cannot precisely know the position and momentum of a particle at the same time. To know where something is you must shine light on it, but if you do that you will change its momentum. This can be expresses in the equation:

$$\Delta p \Delta x \geqslant \frac{h}{4\pi} \qquad \left(\frac{h}{4\pi} = 5.28 \times 10^{-35}\,\text{J s}^{-1}\right)$$

where Δp = uncertainty in momemtum
Δx = uncertainty in position
h = Planck's constant

An alternative way of writing this is:

$$\Delta E \Delta t \geqslant \frac{h}{4\pi}$$

where ΔE = uncertainty in energy
$\quad\quad\Delta t$ = uncertainty in time

It is important to realize that this is not just about measurement; this is the way things are defined.

These balls will hit in 1s.

can't see electron but it's somewhere here

We can't say exactly when these electrons will collide.

Pauli exclusion principle

The Pauli exclusion principle is fundamental to the way particles interact; it says that two or more electrons cannot occupy the same quantum state at the same time. This means that when two electrons approach each other they will repel each other, unlike photons of light that pass through each other.

Mass/energy equivalence

Einstein's famous equation connected energy and mass. In particle physics, the mass of a particle is often given in MeV/c^2. In Chapter 7 we found that a unified mass unit of 1 U is equivalent to 931.5 MeV.

Worked example

An electron has a momentum between 1×10^{-24} Ns and 1.01×10^{-24} Ns. What is the uncertainty in its position?

Solution

The uncertainty in momentum is 0.01×10^{-24} Ns.

Applying Heisenberg's uncertainty principle $\left(\Delta p \Delta x \geqslant \frac{h}{4\pi}\right)$, the uncertainty in position is:

$$\Delta x \geqslant \frac{h/4\pi}{\Delta p} \geqslant \frac{5.28 \times 10^{-35}}{1.0 \times 10^{-16}} = 5.5 \times 10^{-8}\,\text{m}$$

Figure 12.9 Particles do not exist in exact locations.

Spin

Particles are said to have spin. This doesn't mean that they are spinning but they do have some similar properties to a spinning ball.

Particle	Spin
electron	$\frac{1}{2}$
proton	$\frac{1}{2}$
neutron	$\frac{1}{2}$
photon	1

Table 2 The exclusion principle applies to electrons, protons and neutrons (fermions) but not photons (bosons). This can be explained in terms of spin; particles with spin $\frac{1}{2}$ obey the principle but particles with spin 1 do not.

Mass

Particle	Mass $\left(\frac{\text{MeV}}{c^2}\right)$
Electron	0.5
Proton	938.3
Neutron	939.6
Neutrino	≈ 0

Table 3 Einstein established a relationship between energy and mass in his equation $E = mc^2$.

Exercises

12 If you know that an electron is somewhere near a nucleus, then its uncertainty in position would be about the size of the nucleus (10^{-15} m). Calculate the uncertainty in momentum of this particle.

13 A proton has a mass of 1.0078 U. If it were changed into energy, how much energy in eV would be produced?

Fundamental interactions

Assessment statements
D.4.7 List the fundamental interactions
D.4.8 Describe the fundamental interactions in terms of exchange particles.
D.4.9 Discuss the uncertainty principle for time and energy in the context of particle creation.

Interactions between particles

Two balls travelling towards the same point will bounce off each other; the bounce is called an *interaction*. Subatomic particles interact in four different ways.

Table 4 The four different types of interaction of sub-atomic particles.

Interaction	Relative size of forces
Strong	1
Electromagnetic	10^{-2}
Weak	10^{-6}
Gravity	10^{-39}

Strong

This is the interaction between the particles of the nucleus and also their antiparticles. This force is very strong and very short range.

Electromagnetic

The electromagnetic interaction takes place between two charged particles, e.g. two electrons. This interaction becomes stronger when the distances are small, but extends to infinity.

Weak

Neutrinos have no charge so do not take part in electromagnetic interactions. They are also not affected by the strong nuclear force. They do not interact very often but when they do, the interaction is termed a weak interaction.

Gravity

Gravity is a force that is only significant between large masses; it is generally ignored in particle physics.

Classification of particles

The fact that different particles take part in different interactions leads to a classification of the particles: hadrons take part in strong interactions but leptons don't.

Hadrons
Particles that take part in strong interactions
Proton
Neutron
(and their antiparticles)

Leptons
Particles that don't take part in strong interactions
Electron
Neutrino
(and their antiparticles)

Exchange forces

In 1933 Hideki Yukawa developed the theory of exchange forces. The idea is that every force is due to the exchange of a particle. Consider two canoes paddling parallel to each other. What happens if a heavy object is thrown from one canoe to the other as shown in Figure 12.10? When A throws the ball, A must exert a force on the ball, according to Newton's third law. A will experience an equal and opposite force causing A to move away from B. When B catches the ball, B must exert a force on the ball in order to stop it. B will therefore experience a force away from A. The canoes repel each other.

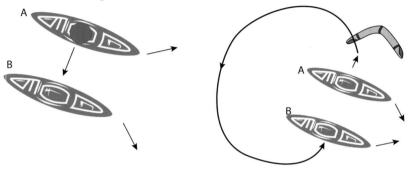

Figure 12.10 The exchange of particles leads to repulsive or attractive forces.

To explain an attractive force, imagine what would happen if A threw a boomerang in the opposite direction to B. The boomerang spins, following a path as shown in Figure 12.10. When B catches the boomerang, B will be pushed towards A.

This is not the way it happens with particles but it gives an idea that it is possible. The electric force, for example, is caused by a continual exchange of virtual photons; these interact with the charged particles to cause them to attract or repel.

Exchange particles

Yukawa linked the electromagnetic force with the photon. He explained the reason why the electromagnetic force decreases with distance $\left(F \propto \dfrac{1}{r^2} \right)$ in the following way: the size of the force is dependant on the number of photons that are exchanged between two particles; as photons move away from a particle they form a sphere. As the sphere gets bigger so the photons become more spread out and the force becomes weaker; since photons live for ever, they continue spreading for an infinite distance. This is why the electromagnetic force has an infinite range.

A short range force can be explained if the exchange particles disappear before they reach their objective, in other words they have a very short life. But if the particles keep disappearing, where does their energy go? Heisenberg's uncertainty principle gives the answer. Since $\Delta E \Delta t = \dfrac{h}{4\pi}$ if the exchange particles exist for a very short time they can have energy that doesn't have to be accounted for. Such short-lived particles are called *virtual particles*.

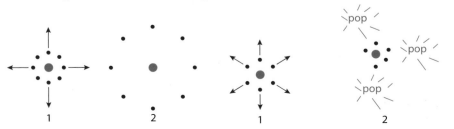

Figure 12.11 As photons spread out they cover a larger area, whereas 'short range' exchange particles disappear after a short distance.

From this it is possible to calculate the energy of the exchange particle. The force only extends within the nucleus, so the exchange particles only live long enough to travel across a small nucleus, about 1.0×10^{-15} m.

The time taken if they are travelling near to the speed of light will be

$$\frac{1.0 \times 10^{-15}}{3 \times 10^{-24}}\,s = 0.3 \times 10^{-24}\,s$$

Rearranging Heisenberg's equation gives $\Delta E = \dfrac{h}{4\pi\Delta t}$

So $\Delta E = \dfrac{5.28 \times 10^{-35}}{3 \times 10^{-24}} = 1.76 \times 10^{-11}\,J$

To convert this to eV divide by 1.6×10^{-19} C

$$\Delta E = 110\,\text{MeV}$$

According to Einstein, energy and mass are equivalent, which leads us to believe that the exchange particle has a rest mass of about $110\,\dfrac{\text{MeV}}{c^2}$. This particle is called a *pion*.

Using the same argument, if the electromagnetic force is infinite, the exchange particles must live forever.

According to Einstein $\Delta E = \Delta mc^2 = \dfrac{h}{2\pi\Delta t}$

So if Δt is infinite, $mc^2 = \dfrac{h}{2\pi\,\infty}$ which implies that the rest mass of a photon is zero.

Table 5 Summary of properties of exchange partiles.

The pion takes part in strong reactions but it has a much smaller mass than the proton and neutron. This leads to a further classification as shown in Table 6.

Interaction	Exchange particle	Range	Exchange particle mass
Strong force	pion	10^{-15} m	$120\,\dfrac{\text{MeV}}{c^2}$
Electromagnetic	photon	infinite	0
Weak	W and Z	10^{-18} m	$80\,\dfrac{\text{GeV}}{c^2}$

Table 6 The pion is a meson (medium), the proton and neutron are baryons (heavy) but both are hadrons (strong).

Hadrons	
Baryons	Mesons
proton	pion
neutron	

Exercise

14 Classify the particles in Table 7 as lepton, baryon or meson.

Particle	Interaction	Mass
Muon	Electromagnetic, weak, gravity	$106\,\dfrac{\text{MeV}}{c^2}$
Kaon	Strong, electromagnetic, weak, gravity	$494\,\dfrac{\text{MeV}}{c^2}$
Lambda	Strong, electromagnetic, weak, gravity	$1116\,\dfrac{\text{MeV}}{c^2}$
Tau	electromagnetic, weak, gravity	$1777\,\dfrac{\text{MeV}}{c^2}$

Table 7

Quantum numbers and conservation

In Chapter 7 we looked at some nuclear processes. When deciding whether a certain process can take place or not we made sure that the charge and mass were the same on each side of the equation. This is an example of a conservation principle, for example:

$$^{226}_{88}Ra \rightarrow \, ^{222}_{86}Rn + \, ^{4}_{2}He$$

The charge on the left is +88 and on the right is $86 + 2 = +88$
The mass on the left is 226 and on the right is $222 + 4 = 226$
Note: We don't use the actual charge and mass but whole numbers used to represent it; this makes it much easier to see whether charge and mass are conserved.

The same idea of conserving charge is used in particle physics. However, we find that charge and mass/energy is not enough, for example, it seems possible that:

$$\text{proton} \rightarrow \text{positron} + \text{gamma}$$

In this reaction, charge and energy/mass are conserved (if the gamma has enough energy) but it never happens. A baryon can't change into a lepton. After observing all the possible interactions, a set of numbers was allocated to each particle. These numbers, so-called quantum numbers, must be conserved in all interactions.

	Baryon number	Lepton number
Leptons	0	$^{+}1$
Antileptons	0	$^{-}1$
Baryons	$^{+}1$	0
Antibaryons	$^{-}1$	0

Table 8 The quantum numbers for baryons and leptons.

The allocation of numbers is quite straight forward and illustrated in Table 8. If we apply this principle to all the particles we have mentioned so far we get the data in shown Table 9.

Particle	Symbol	Charge	Baryon number	Lepton number
Photon	γ	0	0	0
Electron	e^-	$^{-}1$	0	$^{+}1$
Positron	e^+	$^{+}1$	0	$^{-}1$
Neutrino	ν	0	0	$^{+}1$
Antineutrino	$\bar{\nu}$	0	0	$^{-}1$
Proton	p	$^{+}1$	1	0
Antiproton	$\bar{p}$	$^{-}1$	$^{-}1$	0
Neutron	n	0	1	0
Antineutron	$\bar{n}$	0	$^{-}1$	0
Pion	π^+	$^{+}1$	0	0
Antipion	π^-	$^{-}1$	0	0
Pi zero	π°	0	0	0

Table 9 This can be used to predict possible interactions.

Examples

1 $p \rightarrow n + e^+ + \nu$

	p	$\rightarrow$	n	$+$	e^+	$+$	ν
Baryon number	1	$=$	1	$+$	0	$+$	0
Lepton number	0	$=$	0	$+$	$^-1$	$+$	1
Charge	1	$=$	0	$+$	1	$+$	0

Since all are conserved, this interaction seems to be possible.

2 $n \rightarrow p + e^- + \bar{\nu}$

	n	$\rightarrow$	p	$+$	e^-	$+$	$\bar{\nu}$
Baryon number	1	$=$	1	$+$	0	$+$	0
Lepton number	0	$=$	0	$+$	1	$+$	$^-1$
Charge	0	$=$	1	$+$	$^-1$	$+$	0

Again, all quantum numbers are conserved so the interaction is feasible.

3 $n + p \rightarrow e^+ + \bar{\nu}$

	n	$+$	p	$\rightarrow$	e^+	$+$	$\bar{\nu}$
Baryon number	1	$+$	1	$\neq$	0	$+$	0
Lepton number	0	$+$	0	$=$	1	$+$	$^-1$
Charge	0	$+$	1	$=$	1	$+$	0

Although charge and lepton number are conserved, the baryon number isn't. Therefore, this interaction is not possible.

Exercises

Use conservation principles to find out if the following are possible:

15 $p + e^- \rightarrow n + \nu$

16 $p + p \rightarrow p + p + \bar{p}$

17 $p + p \rightarrow p + p + \pi^0$

18 $p + \bar{p} \rightarrow \pi^0 + \pi^0$

19 $e^- + e^+ \rightarrow \gamma + \gamma$

20 $e^- + e^+ \rightarrow n + \gamma$

21 $p + \bar{p} \rightarrow n + \bar{\nu}$

Summary

The exchange particles we have discussed so far can be split into the following groups:

Leptons	Hadrons		Gauge bosons
	Baryons	**Mesons**	
electron	proton	pion	photon
neutrino	neutron		

Note: Gauge bosons are particles that can occupy the same energy state; they do not obey the Pauli exclusion principle. These are the exchange particles responsible for the fundamental forces.

Just as things were getting simple

In the 1930s the picture was looking very good, as all matter could be broken down into three particles: proton, neutron and electron. The forces between these particles had been explained in terms of the exchange of pions and photons and occasionally there was an interaction that involved a neutrino. Physicists are always looking for the simplest model and this one was quite simple. However, over the next 40 years things were to change.

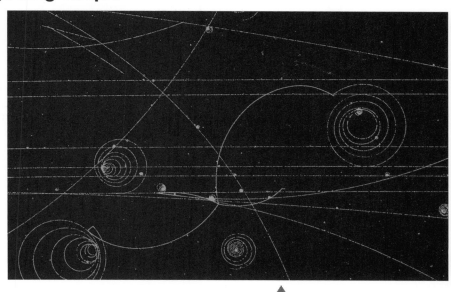

A bubble chamber photograph from the CERN accelerator. There is a magnetic field directed out of the chamber causing +ve particles to spiral clockwise.

Cosmic rays

The best way to find out if there are any other particles in the atomic nucleus is to smash it to bits and observe the result. To do this you either have to knock the nucleus apart with high energy particles, or find a place where this is happening naturally and catch what comes out. The Sun is a place where particles are moving so fast that when they collide they can knock each other apart, and the products fly off into the universe, some even landing on Earth. A very few landed in the detectors of experimental physicists in the 1930s and 40s, enough to lead to the discovery of a whole bunch of new particles.

Particle accelerators

A particle accelerator uses an electric field to accelerate charged particles. The earliest version was simply composed of a charged sphere and an evacuated tube for the particles to travel in. The problem with early versions was that it was impossible to create a potential higher than about 7 million volts without producing a huge electrical discharge (lightning). Using a pd of 7 MV it is possible to accelerate particles to a KE of 7 Mev.

To overcome this barrier, particles were accelerated in stages (either around a circle as in the cyclotron and synchrotron, or in a straight line as in the linear accelerator). The principle is a bit like surfing; even on a 2 m high wave a surfer can travel downwards for several hundred metres on a long ride. By the 1950s KEs in the order of several GeV had been achieved and by 2008, the Large Hadron Collider (LHC) at CERN is predicted to produce 7000 GeV collisions.

The bubble chamber

The bubble chamber is an example of one of the detectors used to discover new particles and analyse their interactions. The chamber contains liquid hydrogen, and when a particle passes through the liquid, it leaves a trail of small bubbles, as in the photo. By analysing these tracks it is possible to determine the properties of the particle.

22 How many joules of energy is 7000 GeV equivalent to?

23 If a bunch of particles contains 10^{12} protons, each with an energy of 7000 GeV, how much energy would the beam have?

24 If a 1 kg mass had the same amount of kinetic energy, how fast would it be moving?

25 If a bunch of particles hits a target every 10^{-29} seconds, what is the power of the beam?

26 Figure12.12 shows the tracks of an electron and a positron produced from a high energy gamma photon. (These are the spiralling tracks A and B, the other is an electron that has been knocked out of an atom of hydrogen.) The tracks are curved because there is a magnetic field into the plane of the page. From your knowledge of magnetic fields, deduce which particle is the electron and which is the position.

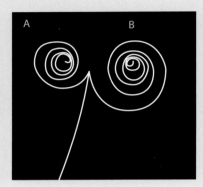

Figure12.12 A bubble chamber image of electron pair positron pair production.

The particle explosion

Once physicists started using the correct tools to look in the right places, they started to find the particles they were looking for; in fact they found hundreds of them. As each particle was discovered, they were classified according to their interactions. The following tables list some of these particles. Remember, each particle has an antiparticle with opposite charge.

Table 10 Many new hadrons have been discovered and this table includes some of the mesons.

Strangeness
Some particles do not interact as predicted by the conservation of charge and baryon number. This strange behaviour led to the introduction of a new quantum number 'strangeness'.
λ and Σ have strangeness of -1
Ξ have strangeness of -2
K has strangeness of $+1$
Strangeness is conserved in strong and electromagnetic interactions but not weak interactions. Strange!

Mesons			
Name	Symbol	Baryon	Strangeness
Pion	π^+	0	0
Pion	π^0	0	0
Kaon	κ^+	0	1
Kaon	κ^0	0	1
Eta	η	0	0
Rho	ρ^+	0	0
J/psi	ψ	0	0
Phi	ϕ	0	0
D	D	0	0

Baryons			
Name	Symbol	Baryon	Strangeness
Proton	p	1	0
Neutron	n	1	0
Delta	Δ^{++}	1	0
Delta	Δ^{+}	1	0
Delta	Δ°	1	0
Delta	Δ^{-}	1	0
Lambda	λ°	1	-1
Sigma	Σ^{+}	1	-1
Sigma	Σ°	1	-1
Sigma	Σ^{-}	1	-1
Xi	Ξ°	1	-2
Xi	Ξ^{-}	1	-2
Omega	Ω^{-}	1	-3

Table 11 Many new hadrons have been discovered and this table includes some of the baryons.

Leptons			
Charged lepton		Uncharged leptons	
Electron	e	Electron neutrino	ν_e
Muon	μ	Muon neutrino	ν_μ
Tau	τ	Tau neutrino	ν_τ

Table 12 Relatively few leptons have been discovered compared to the number of hadrons.

Lepton number
In any interaction there must be conservation of muon lepton number, electron lepton number and tau lepton number. Leptons have lepton number $+1$ and anti leptons have lepton number -1.

Exercises

27 Given the information that strangeness is not conserved in weak interactions, deduce which of the following interactions are weak:
(a) $\Sigma^{+} \rightarrow p + \pi^{\circ}$
(b) $\Sigma^{\circ} \rightarrow \lambda^{\circ} + \gamma$
(c) $K^{\circ} \rightarrow \pi^{+} + \pi^{\circ}$

28 Is the lepton number conserved in the following interactions?
(a) $n \rightarrow p + e^{-} + \bar{\nu}$
(b) $e^{-} \rightarrow \mu + \gamma$
(c) $\mu \rightarrow e^{+} + \bar{\nu}_e + \nu_\mu$

12.6 Quarks

Quarks

By 1960 the particle model was looking quite complex and rather untidy. It would simplify matters greatly if all the hadrons were made out of a few common particles. In 1964 Murray Gell-Mann proposed that all hadrons were made of combinations of fundamental particles called quarks.

Spin

As mentioned, particles have a property called spin. Baryons have spin $\frac{1}{2}$ or $1\frac{1}{2}$ and mesons 0 or 1. Spins can either add, if they are in the same direction, or cancel, if opposite. If quarks have spin $\frac{1}{2}$ then baryons can be made of 3 quarks and mesons can be made of 2, as shown.

$$\uparrow \quad \downarrow \quad \uparrow$$
$$+\tfrac{1}{2} - \tfrac{1}{2} + \tfrac{1}{2} =$$

$$\uparrow \quad \uparrow \quad \uparrow$$
$$+\tfrac{1}{2} + \tfrac{1}{2} + \tfrac{1}{2} = 1\tfrac{1}{2}$$

$$\uparrow \quad \downarrow$$
$$+\tfrac{1}{2} - \tfrac{1}{2} = 0$$

$$\uparrow \quad \uparrow$$
$$+\tfrac{1}{2} + \tfrac{1}{2} = 1$$

Neutron

A neutron is a baryon so contains 3 quarks. It has zero charge so the charges of the quarks must cancel e.g. $+\frac{2}{3} - \frac{1}{3} - \frac{1}{3}$

Proton

A proton also contains 3 quarks but has a charge of $+1$. Assuming these are the same types of quark that make up a neutron, we can achieve this with $+\frac{2}{3} + \frac{2}{3} - \frac{1}{3}$

So we can make the proton and the neutron from combinations of 2 different types of quark. The quarks are said to have different flavours, the $-\frac{1}{3}$ has flavour down and the $+\frac{2}{3}$ flavour up.

To make all known hadrons we need a total of 6 flavours.

Table 13 The six possible quarks that make up hadrons.
Note: To keep things simple, charm, bottom and top quarks will not be considered in the following examples.

Quark			Antiquark	
Flavour	Symbol	Charge	Symbol	Charge
Up	u	$+\frac{2}{3}$	$\bar{u}$	$-\frac{2}{3}$
Down	d	$-\frac{1}{3}$	$\bar{d}$	$+\frac{1}{3}$
Strange	s	$-\frac{1}{3}$	$\bar{s}$	$+\frac{1}{3}$
Charm	c	$+\frac{2}{3}$	$\bar{c}$	$-\frac{2}{3}$
Bottom	b	$-\frac{1}{3}$	$\bar{b}$	$+\frac{1}{3}$
Top	t	$+\frac{2}{3}$	$\bar{t}$	$-\frac{2}{3}$

Strangeness

Strange particles contain strange quarks. The strangeness number is calculated from the number of antistrange quarks – strange quarks.

Baryons

Baryons are made out of three quarks.

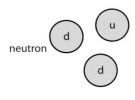

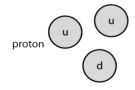

Delta minus

	Charge	Baryon number	Strangeness
Δ−	−1	1	0

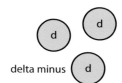

delta minus

Quark combination:

	d	d	d
Charge	$-\frac{1}{3}$	$-\frac{1}{3}$	$-\frac{1}{3}$

Lambda zero

	Charge	Baryon number	Strangeness
λ°	0	1	−1

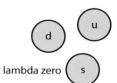

lambda zero

Strangeness −1 implies strange quark.

The combination *uds* has the correct charge and strangeness.

Quark combination:

	u	d	s
Charge	$\frac{2}{3}$	$-\frac{1}{3}$	$-\frac{1}{3}$

Mesons

Mesons are a combination of a quark and an antiquark.

Pion plus

	Charge	Baryon number	Strangeness
π^+	+1	0	0

pion plus

Quark combination:

Strangeness 0 implies no strange quarks.

The combination up, antidown will give a charge +1.

	u	$\bar{d}$
Charge	$+\frac{2}{3}$	$+\frac{1}{3}$

kaon plus

Kaon plus

	Charge	Baryon number	Strangeness
K⁺	+1	0	+1

Quark combination:

Strangeness +1 implies that the K+ has an antistrange quark.

To test your predictions, visit www.heinemann.co.uk/hotlinks, enter the express code 4266S and click on Weblink 12.3.

An antistrange quark has charge $+\frac{1}{3}$ so to give a total charge of +1 an up quark is needed so combination is $u\bar{s}$:

	u	$\bar{s}$
Charge	$+\frac{2}{3}$	$+\frac{1}{3}$

Exercise

29 Using the properties of the particles found in th above tables, deduce the quark content of the following particles:
 (a) π^-
 (b) Ω^-
 (c) Ξ^-
 (d) Ξ°

30 During β-decay a neutron changes to a proton. Which quark changes during this process?

Properties of quarks

Quark confinement

No one has ever detected a free quark; they only exist confined inside other particles. This phenomenon is called *quark confinement*. The reason for this is due to the nature of the force between quarks, which is very strong and constant with increasing distance (unlike electromagnetic force that gets less). As two quarks are separated, the energy transferred gets bigger and bigger (work done = force × distance). At a certain point the energy becomes big enough to create another quark or antiquark, so instead of a free quark you get a meson.

Since we can never detect a quark on its own, can we really say that they exist?

Gluon

We have seen that the forces between sub-atomic particles are exchange forces: electromagnetic force is due to the exchange of photons and the strong force is due to the exchange of pions. The force between quarks is also the strong force. However, the exchange particle in this case is the gluon rather than the pion. This is a bit confusing but we have come across a similar case when talking about the force between atoms. This is called the interatomic force, even though it is actually the electric force between the electron clouds of the different atoms. We call this a *residual force*. So the force between nucleons is due to the exchange of pions, but it is really the gluons that are exchanging between the pions and nucleons that transfer the force.

Colour charge

To explain the observation that two electrons repel each other we used the concept of charge – this is the name given to the property/thing that causes the force. The fact that some particles attract each other and some repel leads us to believe that there are two types of charge. This is very convenient because we also have two types of numbers + and – , so we use + and – to represent charge. Even more convenient is the way that opposite charges cancel in the same way that numbers do. If charge is the property that causes the electromagnetic interaction, what property of quarks causes the strong interaction? This time it isn't so simple, as there are three types of this property not two, so we can't use numbers. However, there are three primary colours on which the model can be based, and the property is called *colour charge*.

Quarks can be red, green or blue, and antiquarks are anti-red, anti-green and anti-blue. All particles must be white, so a baryon must contain a red, green and blue and a meson, for example, red and anti-red. Gluons, however, have two colours giving them colour charge and the ability to carry the strong force. The complete theory is called *Quantum Chromo Dynamics* (QCD).

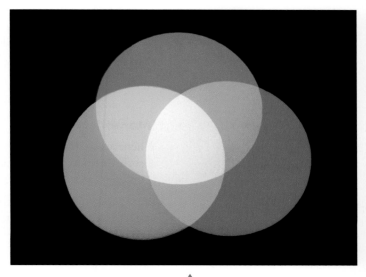

Red, green and blue light combine together to give white light.

QCD is an example where numbers cannot be used to model the physical property.

Fundamental particles

The standard model

A fundamental particle is one that cannot be broken down into anything smaller; a proton is therefore not fundamental but an electron is. The standard model of particle physics splits the fundamental particles into three groups: leptons, quarks and exchange particles (gauge bosons). Tables of these particles show a certain degree of symmetry. The particles are ordered in three groups according to mass (heaviest to the left) – these groups are called *generations*.

The standard model is very simple, you could say it is beautiful, but is the simplest model necessarily correct?
Why are we always trying to find the simplest solution?

Quarks

Charge	1st Generation	2nd Generation	3rd Generation
$+\frac{2}{3}$	up	charm	top
$-\frac{1}{3}$	down	strange	bottom

Table 14 Each of these fundamental particles has an anti-particle, which can also be arranged in a similar way.

Leptons

Charge	1st Generation	2nd Generation	3rd Generation
0	electron neutrino	muon neutrino	tau neutrino
−1	electron	muon	tau

Table 15 Each of these fundamental particles has an anti-particle, which can also be arranged in a similar way.

Gauge bosons

Table 16 These are the exchange particles that are responsible for the fundamental forces.
Note: it is now recognised that at high energies the electric and weak forces are one and the same thing. This is called the electroweak force.

Gluon	Strong
Photon	Electromagnetic
W and Z	Weak

Interactions

Whenever an interaction takes place an exchange particle is either emitted or absorbed. The type of particle absorbed determines the type of interaction (photon if electromagnetic).

Leptons can only interact with leptons in the same generation.
Quarks can only interact with quarks in the same generation or diagonal (e.g. up and strange).

Exercises

31 Can an electron neutrino interact with a tau?

32 Can a muon interact with a muon neutrino?

33 Can a charm quark interact with a down quark?

34 Can an up quark interact with a bottom quark?

35 Which exchange particle will be involved with an interaction between a top and a bottom quark?

36 Which exchange particle is involved in an interaction between an electron neutrino and an electron?

12.7 Feynman diagrams

Assessment statements
D.4.10 Describe what is meant by a *Feynman diagram*.
D.4.11 Discuss how a Feynman diagram may be used to calculate probabilities for fundamental processes.
D.4.12 Describe what is meant by *virtual particles*.
D.4.13 Apply the formula for the range *R* for interactions involving the exchange of a particle.
D.4.14 Describe pair annihilation and pair production through Feynman diagrams.
D.4.15 Predict particle processes using Feynman diagrams.

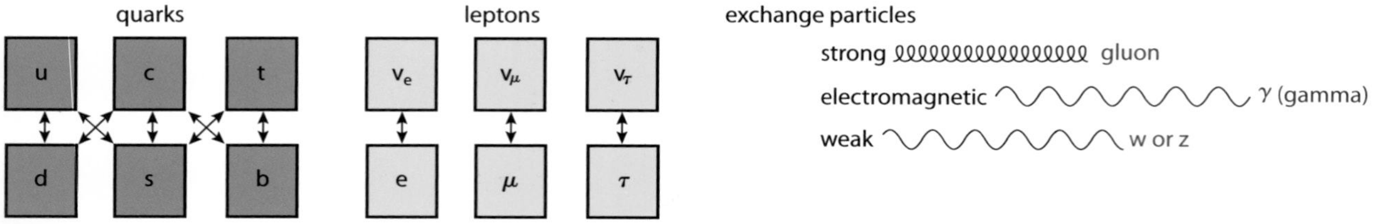

Figure 12.13 The standard model of possible particle interactions.

Feynman diagrams represent the particle interactions that are possible according to the standard model summarised in Figure 12.13.

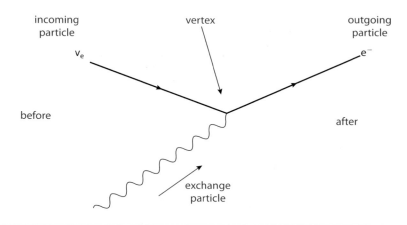

Figure 12.14 The Feynman diagram of an electron and an electron neutrino shows that a particle comes in, absorbs an exchange particle and a particle comes out. So, before the interaction there was a v_e and an exchange particle after was an e^-.

> **Feynman diagram interactions**
> It is important to realise that a Feynman diagram is not a drawing of the particle paths, it is just a representation of the interaction.
> - The vertex of the diagram is always made up of two particles and an exchange particle.
> - Particles have straight lines and exchange particles have wavy lines.
> - Time progresses from left to right.
> - The direction of the particles is given by the arrows, antiparticles travel in the opposite direction to the arrow.
>
> **Feynman diagram rules**
> - Each vertex has two arrows and one wavy/curly line.
> - Particle arrows point forwards in time and antiparticles backwards.
> - There's always one arrow entering and one leaving a vertex.
> - You can't mix leptons and quarks on one vertex.

According to the standard model, an electron should interact with an electron neutrino. The interaction will be a weak interaction since the neutrino can only take part in weak interactions (see Figure 12.14).

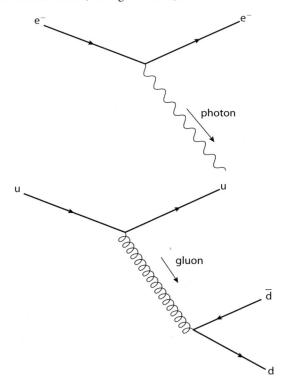

Figure 12.15 An electron emits a photon: notice the vertex has two arrows and one wavy/curly line.

Figure 12.16 An up quark emits a gluon that then forms a quark/anti-quark pair: notice the antiquark arrow points backwards in time.

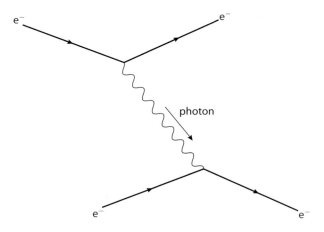

Figure 12.17 An electron emits a photon absorbed by another electron. This is the electromagnetic repulsion between two electrons.

Making predictions

Feynman diagrams are not just a nice way to represent interactions, they can also be used to make predictions. If we take a Feynman diagram and swing the arrows around it will give the diagram for another interaction – all such interactions are possible. For example, Figure 12.18 shows an electron emitting a photon. If we swing the arrows around (still following the rules) we can get another two possible interactions.

Figure 12.18 The first Feynman diagram shows an electron-positron pair production. Time progresses L to R so the arrows represent particles leaving. The arrow pointing to the vertex must therefore be an antiparticle. After an anticlockwise turn the diagram represents an electron emitting a photon. After a further turn the Feynman diagram represents an electron-positron annihilation. This time the arrow pointing away from the vertex is the anti-particle.

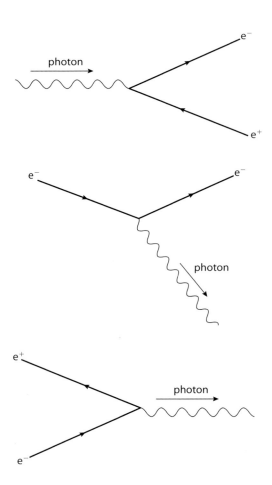

 Is there really any point in predicting whether events that we will never be able to see can happen or not?

37 Draw a Feynman diagram for:

a) a positron absorbing a photon

b) an electron absorbing a photon.

38 The following questions refer to the Feynman diagram in Figure 12.19.

(a) Which particle comes into the interaction?

(b) What kind of interaction is this?

(c) What particles come out of the interaction?

(d) What well-known decay does this interaction represent?

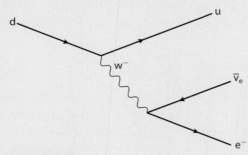

Figure 12.19

39 By swinging the vertices around predict

(a) what would be emitted if a down quark interacted with a positron?

(b) if an anti up quark interacted with a positron what would be emitted?

Practice questions

1 This question is based upon a thought experiment first proposed by Einstein.

(a) Define the terms *proper time* and *proper length*.

In the diagram below, Miguel is in a railway carriage that is travelling in a straight line with uniform speed relative to Carmen who is standing on the platform.

Miguel is midway between two people sitting at opposite ends A and B of the carriage.

At the moment that Miguel and Carmen are directly opposite each other, the person at end A of the carriage strikes a match as does the person at end B of the carriage. According to Miguel these two events take place simultaneously.

(b) (i)   Discuss whether the two events will appear to be simultaneous to Carmen.

   (ii)   Miguel measures the distance between A and B to be 20.0 m. However, Carmen measures this distance to be 10.0 m. Determine the speed of the carriage relative to Carmen.

   (iii) Explain which of the **two** observers, if either, measures the correct distance between A and B?

2 This question is about time dilation.

(a) State what is meant by an *inertial* frame of reference.

An observer S in a spacecraft sees a flash of light. The light is reflected from a mirror, distance D from the flash, and returns to the source of the flash as illustrated below. The speed of light is c.

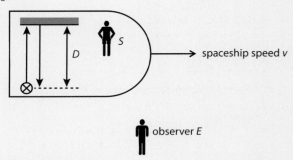

(b) Write down an expression, in terms of D and c, for the time T_0 for the flash of light to return to its original position, as measured by the observer S who is at rest relative to the spaceship.

The spaceship is moving at speed v relative to the observer labelled E in the diagram. The speed of light is c.

(c) (i)   Draw the path of the light as seen by observer E. Label the position F from where the light starts and the position R where the light returns to the source of the flash.

   (ii)   The time taken for the light to travel from F to R, as measured by observer E, is T. Write down an expression, in terms of the speed v of the spacecraft and T, for the distance FR.

   (iii) Using your answer in (ii), determine, in terms of v, T and D, the length L of the path of light as seen by observer E.

   (iv)   Hence derive an expression for T in terms of T_0, v and c.

3 This question is about frames of reference.

(a) Explain what is meant by a *reference frame*.

In the diagram below, Jasper regards his reference frame to be at rest and Morgan's reference frame to be moving away from him with constant speed v in the x-direction.

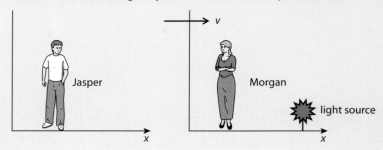

Morgan carries out an experiment to measure the speed of light from a source which is at rest in her reference frame. The value of the speed that she obtains is c.

(b) Applying a Galilean transformation to the situation, state the value that Jasper would be expected to obtain for the speed of light from the source.

(c) State the value that Jasper would be expected to obtain for the speed of light from the source based on Maxwell's theory of electromagnetic radiation.

In Morgan's experiment to measure the speed of light she uses a spark as the light source. According to her, the spark lasts for a time interval of 1.5 μs. In this particular situation, the time duration of the spark as measured by Morgan is known in the special theory of relativity as the proper time.

(d) **(i)** Explain what is meant by *proper time*.

(ii) According to Jasper, the spark lasts for a time interval of 3.0 μs. Calculate the relative velocity between Jasper and Morgan.

4 This question is about muon decay.

Muons, created in the upper atmosphere, travel towards the Earth's surface at a speed of 0.994c relative to an observer at rest on the Earth's surface.

A muon detector at a height above the Earth's surface of 4150 m, as measured by the observer, detects 2.80×10^4 muons per hour. A similar detector on the Earth's surface detects 1.40×10^4 muons per hour.

The half-life of muons as measured in a reference frame in which the muons are at rest is 1.52 μs.

(a) Calculate the half-life of the muons, as observed by the observer on the Earth's surface.

(b) Calculate, as measured in the reference frame in which the muons are at rest,

(i) the distance between the detectors

(ii) the time it takes for the detectors to pass an undecayed muon.

(b) Use your answers to (a) and (b) to explain the concepts of

(i) time dilation

(ii) length contraction.

5 This question is about particle physics.

(a) Possible particle reactions are given below. They cannot take place because they violate one or more conservation laws. For each reaction identify one conservation law that is violated.

(i) $\mu^- \rightarrow e^- + \gamma$

Conservation law: (1)

(ii) $p + n \rightarrow p + \pi^0$

Conservation law: (1)

(iii) $p \rightarrow \pi^+ + \pi^-$

Conservation law: (1)

(b) State the name of the exchange particle(s) involved in the strong interaction. (1)

(Total 4 marks)

6 This question is about deducing the quark structure of a nuclear particle.

When a K⁻ meson collides with a proton, the following reaction can take place.

$$K^- + p \rightarrow K^0 + K^+ + X$$

X is a particle whose quark structure is to be determined.

The quark structure of mesons is given below.

Particle	Quark structure
K⁻	$s\bar{u}$
K⁺	$u\bar{s}$
K⁰	$d\bar{s}$

(a) State and explain whether the original K⁻ particle is a hadron, a lepton or an exchange particle. (2)

(b) State the quark structure of the proton. (2)

(c) The quark structure of particle 3 is *sss*. Show that the reaction is consistent with the theory that hadrons are composed of quarks. (2)

(Total 6 marks)

13 Astrophysics (Option E)

13.1 Introduction to the universe

Assessment statements
E.1.1   Outline the general structure of the solar system.
E.1.2   Distinguish between a stellar cluster and a constellation.
E.1.3   Define the *light year*.
E.1.4   Compare the relative distances between stars within a galaxy and between galaxies, in terms of order of magnitude.
E.1.5   Describe the apparent motion of the stars/constellations over a period of a night and over a period of a year, and explain these observations in terms of the rotation and revolution of the Earth.

 If life does exist on other planets, would it have evolved in a similar way to life on Earth? How sure could we be about the answer to this question?

The solar system and beyond

In 2006 Pluto was officially reclassified as a dwarf planet, meaning that we now regard our solar system has having 8 planets rather than 9. At the same time many new planets have been discovered orbiting other stars, some of which have the conditions necessary for life to exist.

 Our solar system is made up of a collection of eight planets bound in elliptical orbits around a star we call the Sun.

The planetary orbits have the Sun at one of the two foci of an ellipse. The orbit of Earth is almost circular, a circle being a special kind of ellipse. All the planets revolve around the Sun in the same direction.

The following table shows some key facts for the planets in the solar system.

Figure 13.1 Planetary orbits in the solar system have the Sun as one of the two foci of an ellipse. The other focus is in space.

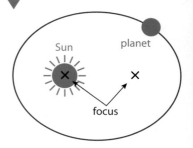

Planet	Mass relative to the Earth	Radius relative to the Earth	Mean distance from the Sun (AU)
Mercury	0.06	0.38	0.39
Venus	0.81	0.97	0.72
Earth	1.00	1.00	1.00
Mars	0.11	0.53	1.52
Jupiter	318	11.2	5.20
Saturn	92.0	9.50	9.54
Uranus	14.5	3.70	19.2
Neptune	17.1	3.50	30.0

 The distance from the Earth to the Sun is called an astronomical unit or AU.
1 astronomical unit (AU)
$= 1.50 \times 10^{11}$ m.

Our Moon is some 400 times smaller than Earth and orbits us about once a month. Some of the larger planets have many moons in orbit around them; one of Jupiter's moons, Ganymede, is bigger than Pluto.

To see a simulation of planetary orbits, visit www.heinemann.co.uk/ hotlinks, enter the express code 4266S and click on Weblink 13.1.

An asteroid is a small, minor planet that drifts in the solar system, orbiting the Sun. Many are located between Mars and Jupiter in a region known as the *asteroid belt*.

Comets are mixtures of rock and ice moving in highly elliptical orbits around the Sun. As they approach the Sun, the ice melts, leaving a bright trail of debris which can be millions of kilometres long, pointing away from the Sun. Typically comets are a few kilometres in diameter. The most famous is Halley's Comet which was last visible on Earth in 1986 and will reappear in 2061.

The comet Hale-Bopp seen at dawn from the Mauna Kea Observatory in Hawaii. ▶

1 light year is defined as the distance light travels in 1 year.

1 light year (ly)
$= 3.0 \times 10^8 \, \text{m s}^{-1} \times 365 \times 24 \times 60 \times 60$ seconds $= 9.46 \times 10^{15}$ m

A stellar or globular cluster is a group of stars that are physically close to each other in space, created by the collapse of the same gas cloud. Stellar clusters can contain between 100 000 and 1 000 000 stars crowded into a region 30–100 light years across.

M55 is a typical globular cluster consisting of a spherical collection of hundreds of thousands of stars orbiting a galaxy. M55 is about 17 300 light years from Earth. ▶

● **Examiner's hint:** The conversion factors between several of the astrophysics units can be found at the beginning of the Data Booklet.

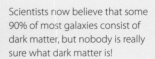 

In ancient times there were no computers, no television and no electric light. People used to spend a lot of time simply looking at the sky at night and trying to make sense of what they saw.

Some 88 different regions of the sky have been identified as constellations and given names; many familiar from astrology such as Taurus, Gemini, Leo and Pisces. From Earth they appear to be close to each other, but this is not in fact the case.

The Sun is part of a very large collection of stars called a *galaxy*. Our galaxy is called the Milky Way and consists of 100 billion stars.

The Sun orbits the galactic centre approximately once every 250 million years. At the galactic centre there is thought to be a giant black hole.

There are literally billions of galaxies in the universe. Galaxies are grouped together in galaxy clusters held together by their mutual gravitational attraction. Our local galaxy cluster is made up of around twenty galaxies including the Large Magellanic Cloud and the Andromeda galaxy.

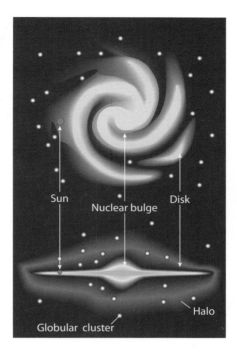

Sun   Nuclear bulge   Disk

Globular cluster   Halo

Figure 13.2 The Milky Way, from above and in cross-section. The halo consists of stars and globular clusters, which are some of the oldest stars in the galaxy. The bulge is very dense and contains young, hot stars.

All the ancient civilisations took a keen interest in the night sky. The stars were grouped into fixed patterns by the Babylonians and the Greeks. We now call these patterns *constellations*.

The Milky Way is a spiral galaxy containing our own solar system, located between the two arms near the centre at the bottom of the picture.

The galaxies in the local group, clustering around the two largest galaxies, our Milky Way (lower left) and Andromeda (upper right). The Milky Way is about 2.9×10^6 light years from Andromeda.

This map shows the large scale distribution of galaxies in a region of sky near the south galactic pole. The image shows the clumpy nature of the Universe. The map covers about 10% of the sky and shows the distribution of some 2 million galaxies.

The nearest galaxy cluster to us is the Virgo cluster at a distance of 5.9×10^7 ly. This is a cluster of possibly 2000 galaxies. Bigger galaxy clusters contain up to 10 000 galaxies.

Clusters are grouped into superclusters and can spread over a distances of 10^8 ly. Superclusters form into filaments, leaving vast voids of empty space in between.

The universe on a large scale is very uniform. When the Earth is viewed from space, the mountains are no longer visible and the surface appears to be smooth. In a similar way, the 'lumpiness' of the universe is smoothed out when seen on a larger scale.

Viewed for a whole night, the stars seem to rotate around one star, Polaris, also known as the Pole Star or North Star. This effect is because of the rotation of the Earth about its own axis. In addition, the night sky appears to change seasonally due to the rotation of the Earth around the Sun.

If has been shown from modern measurements that some stars appear to be moving relative to each other. This proper motion will affect the shape of constellations over periods of 100 000 years.

In ancient times people could see the constellations easily, but in the 21st century it is almost impossible to view the stars at night in populated areas, owing to light pollution.

This picture shows star tracks in the evening sky in northern California. Time lapse photography shows the stars as circles due to the rotation of the Earth.

Exercises

1 Four of the planets in the solar system are Jupiter, Earth, Mars and Neptune.
   (a) List these four planets in order of increasing distance from the Sun.

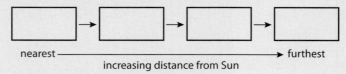

   nearest ⟶ furthest
   increasing distance from Sun

   (b) List these four planets in order of increasing diameter.

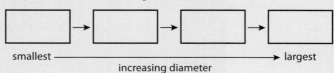

   smallest ⟶ largest
   increasing diameter

2. **(a)** Briefly describe the nature of a star.
   (b) Distinguish between a constellation and a galaxy.

13.2 Stellar radiation and stellar types

Energy source

A star such as our own Sun radiates an enormous amount of energy into space, estimated to be 10^{26} joules every second. The source of this energy is *nuclear fusion* in the interior of the star. The conditions inside a star are too extreme for atoms to hold together and stars consist of *plasma*, ions and electrons.

Inside the Sun, nuclei of hydrogen fuse together to form helium, releasing energy in the process. Because of the high pressures, the nuclei are sufficiently close to each other for collisions to occur. Owing to temperatures in excess of 10^8 K, the electrostatic repulsion between hydrogen nuclei (protons) can be overcome and they can fuse together.

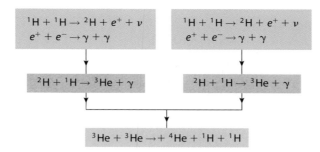

Figure 13.3 It would be impossible for four hydrogen nuclei to fuse together all at once. The process occurs in three steps.

H = Hydrogen nucleus
He = helium nucleus
e^+ = positron
ν = neutrino
γ = gamma ray photon.
e^- = electron

The energy produced is carried away by the gamma photons and neutrinos. As they move outwards, they collide with surrounding protons and electrons, transferring some of the energy.

As the kinetic energy of the particles inside the Sun increases, the *radiation pressure* increases. Radiation pressure is the force exerted by solar radiation on the surroundings. It acts to stabilize the Sun against gravitational collapse, creating a kind of equilibrium.

The overall equation for fusion in the Sun is:
$$4^1_1H \rightarrow {}^4_2He + 2e^+ + 2\nu + 2\gamma$$

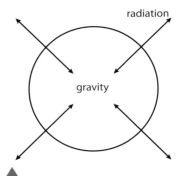

Figure 13.4 The equilibrium of a star is maintained by the balance between the outward radiation pressure from the hot expanding gases and the inward pull of gravity.

 The luminosity of a star is defined as the energy emitted per unit time.

 The apparent brightness of a star is defined as the power incident on Earth, perpendicular to unit area.

 In this equation, we are assuming that energy is conserved.

The Sun has been radiating energy for 4.6 billion years and will continue to do so for about the same length of time. More than 99% of the mass of the entire solar system is found in the Sun and it is estimated to be losing mass at the rate of 4.26×10^9 kg every second.

Worked example

If the Sun is losing mass at a rate of 4.26×10^9 kg s^{-1}, calculate the rate at which energy is being emitted.

Solution

To solve this we will use Einstein's mass-energy equivalence equation:

$\Delta E = \Delta mc^2$

$\quad = 4.26 \times 10^9 \text{ kg s}^{-1} \times (3.00 \times 10^8 \text{ m s}^{-1})^2$

$\quad = 3.83 \times 10^{26} \text{ Js}^{-1}$

$\quad = \mathbf{3.83 \times 10^{26} \text{ W}}$

This quantity is known as the *luminosity*.

Exercise

3   The luminosity of the star Rigel is 2.5×10^{31} W. Calculate the rate at which it is losing mass.

Luminosity and brightness

Luminosity is abbreviated to L and is measured in watts. It depends on both the surface temperature of the star and its radius or surface area. If the *radius* of two stars is the same, the one with the higher temperature will have the greater luminosity. If the *temperature* of two stars is the same, the one with the larger radius will have the greater luminosity.

Apparent brightness is related to the luminosity by the distance the star is from Earth. Clearly if two stars have the same luminosity, the one that is closer to us will have the greater apparent brightness.

The relationship between the apparent brightness and the distance is an inverse square:

$$b = \frac{L}{4\pi d^2}$$

b is the apparent brightness   W m^{-2}

L is the luminosity   W

d is the distance from the star to the Earth   m

To measure apparent brightness, the light reaching the Earth is collected with a telescope and detected using a charge-coupled device (CCD). The data is processed by a computer and the apparent brightness can then be worked out accurately.

Worked example

The apparent brightness of a star is 6.4×10^{-8} W m^{-2}. If its distance from Earth is 15 ly, find its luminosity.

Solution

$b = \dfrac{L}{4\pi d^2}$

$L = b4\pi d^2$

$\quad = 6.4 \times 10^{-8} \text{ W m}^{-2} \times 4\pi \times (15 \times 9.46 \times 10^{15} \text{ m})^2$

$\quad = \mathbf{1.62 \times 10^{28} \text{ W}}$

Exercise

4 The luminosity of a star is 5.0 × 10³¹ W and its apparent brightness is 1.4 × 10⁻⁹ W m⁻². Calculate the distance of the star from Earth.

Wien's law and the Stefan–Boltzmann law

Hot objects emit electromagnetic radiation and when the temperature approaches 1000° C, some of the radiation will be in the visible region of the spectrum.

The radiation from a perfect emitter is known as *black-body radiation*. In reality there is no such thing as a perfect emitter, but to a good approximation, stars fit the model.

A black body is defined as being a perfect absorber and emitter of radiation.

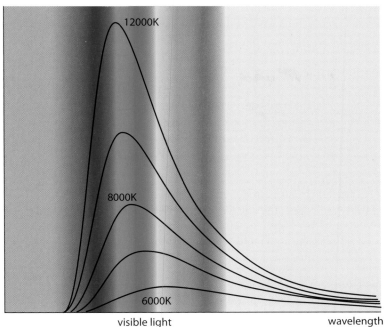

Figure 13.5 Our Sun has a surface temperature of about 5 000 K and so it looks yellow to us, because the wavelength of yellow light is the most intense at that temperature.

These graphs show the spectrum of radiation from black-body emitters at different temperatures. A hot object emits radiation across a broad range and there is a peak in intensity at a particular wavelength. For a hotter body the peak is at a higher intensity and a shorter wavelength.

The peak wavelength, at which the maximum amount of energy is radiated, is related to the surface temperature by *Wien's displacement law*.

Wien's displacement law states that the peak wavelength of the emission of a black body is inversely proportional to its temperature. This idea can be written as an equation:

$$\lambda_{max} = \frac{2.90 \times 10^{-3}}{T}$$

λ_{max}	is the peak wavelength	m
2.90×10^{-3}	is Wien's displacement constant	mK
T	is the temperature of the black-body	K

If the energy emitted from a star is analysed over a range of wavelengths and the peak wavelength is determined, then the surface temperature of the star can be determined.

As temperature increases, the total energy emitted increases. We can see this from the graphs because the area under the curves increases. This is not a linear relationship; the area does not increase evenly.

Stars with high surface temperatures will emit radiation over the full range of visible frequencies and so they will appear to be white. Wien's law tells us that stars with lower surface temperatures will emit more light of a higher wavelength and so appear to be red.

The Stefan–Boltzmann law relates the energy radiated per unit time to the temperature of a black body. The energy emitted per unit time is known in general as the *power* and here also known as the *luminosity*.

The Stefan–Boltzmann law states that the total energy radiated per unit surface area in unit time from a black body is directly proportional to the fourth power of the kelvin temperature of the body.
This can be written as:

$$L \propto T^4$$

The full equation is:

$$L = \sigma A T^4$$

L is the total energy radiated per unit time   W

σ is the Stefan–Boltzmann constant $= 5.67 \times 10^{-8}\,\mathrm{W\,m^{-2}\,K^{-4}}$

A is the surface area of the body

For a star, $A = 4\pi r^2$ where r is the radius of the star.

Worked example

A star in the Plough constellation has a surface temperature of 17 000 K and a luminosity of 6.1×10^{29} W.
(a) Find the peak wavelength in its spectrum.
(b) Find its radius.

Solution
(a) Use Wien's Law:

$$\lambda_{\max} = \frac{2.90 \times 10^{-3}}{T}\,\mathrm{m}$$

$$= \frac{2.90 \times 10^{-3}}{17\,000}\,\mathrm{m}$$

$$= \mathbf{1.7 \times 10^{-7}\,m}$$

(b) Use the Stefan-Boltzmann Law:

$$L = \sigma A T^4$$

$$= \sigma 4\pi r^2 T^4$$

$$r = \sqrt{\frac{L}{\sigma 4\pi T^4}}\,\mathrm{m}$$

$$= \sqrt{\frac{6.1 \times 10^{29}}{5.67 \times 10^{-8} \times 4\pi \times (17\,000)^4}}\,\mathrm{m}$$

$$= \mathbf{3.2 \times 10^9\,m}$$

Some of the stars we see no longer exist. They died a long time ago but their light is still reaching us.

Exercises

5 Estimate the surface temperature of the Sun if the peak wavelength of the light it emits is around 500 nm.

6 The star Betelgeuse has a radius of 3.1×10^{11} m and a surface temperature of 2800 K. Find its luminosity.

Stellar spectra

The radiation reaching us from stars does not form a continuous spectrum.
There is a series of black lines crossing the background. These lines correspond to
missing wavelengths of light that have been absorbed by the cooler, outer layers of
the star. This type of spectrum is called an *absorption spectrum.*

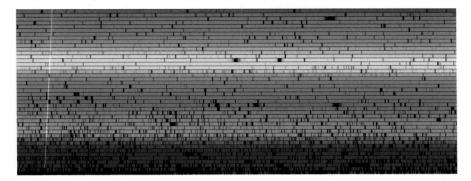

This is the spectrum of the star Arcturus.
It is so long that it has been cut into
many thin strips. The vertical black
lines are caused by the absorption
of different wavelengths of light by
elements in the atmosphere of the star.
Analysis of the position and strength of
the lines give us information about the
composition of the star.

The wavelengths absorbed are characteristic of the atoms present. Hence the
absorption spectrum can be used to identify the elements present in the outer
layers of the star. So we can deduce both chemical and physical data about stars
from their absorption spectra. We can use them to determine the chemical
composition and to find the surface temperature.

In addition we can gain information about the speed, and direction of motion, of
stars from an analysis of their spectra, using the Doppler effect.

In general if a source of waves is moving towards us, their frequency is shifted
upwards. This is commonly observed with as a car or train approaches while
emitting a sound wave. The reason is because the wavefronts bunch up and the
wavelength is shortened, increasing the frequency.

Conversely when a source of waves is moving away from us, the wavefronts are
more spaced out, the wavelength is increased and the frequency is shifted down.
You can read more about the Doppler effect in Chapter 9.

If a star is moving away from Earth, the light waves reaching us are more spaced
out and their absorption lines will shift to longer wavelengths. The red end of the
visible spectrum has the longest wavelengths so we say they are *red-shifted.*

If stars move towards us, their wavelengths appear shorter and the absorption lines
are said to be *blue-shifted*. The amount of red- or blue-shift is related to the speed
that the star, or galaxy, is moving relative to Earth.

Stars can be classified according to their spectra. The eight Harvard spectral classes
are assigned the letters O, B, A, F, G, K and M. Our Sun is in the G class.

Class	Temperature/K	Colour	Mass relative to the Sun
O	30 000–60 000	blue	60
B	10 000–30 000	blue	18
A	7500–10 000	blue-white	3.1
F	6000–7500	white	1.7
G	5000–6000	yellow-white	1.1
K	3500–5000	orange	0.8
M	2000–3500	red	0.3

● **Examiner's hint:** A sentence starting
with a particular sequence of letters
is called a mnemonic and can act as a
powerful memory aid. Make up your
own sentence starting with these letters
to help you remember the sequence.

Types of star

Some stars like our own Sun exist by themselves as single stars, but many have a partner. These *binary stars* rotate about their common centre of mass.

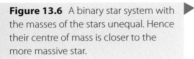

Figure 13.6 A binary star system with the masses of the stars unequal. Hence their centre of mass is closer to the more massive star.

To view a simulation, visit www.heinemann.co.uk/hotlinks, enter the express code 4266S and click on Weblink 13.3.

Our Sun will eventually become a red giant and engulf the inner planets, including the Earth. Do not worry about this too much because it will not happen for about 5 000 000 000 years!

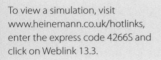

By analysing their orbital period and separation, the mass of each star in the binary system can be found.

Red giants are extremely large stars with high luminosity but with relatively low temperature, evidenced by their reddish colour. A few stars become *red supergiants*, like red giants only cooler, more luminous and bigger. These stars are the largest structures in the universe, although they are not the most massive.

This picture shows the relative sizes of some stars. Antares is a red supergiant while Rigel is a blue giant. Sirius A is a white star, hotter and younger than our Sun and 2.3 times more massive.

Sirius A, the large star on the left, is only 8.6 light years from Earth. It has a very small companion, Sirius B, visible as a dot in the centre to the right.

White dwarf stars are small and have low luminosity. Their white colour tells us that they are relatively hot. They are usually composed of oxygen and carbon in an extremely dense form.

Cepheids are stars with a luminosity that varies periodically over time. The internal structure of the star changes, causing it to grow and shrink in size. This variation in surface area, as well as temperature, causes its luminosity to vary.

Binary stars, like Sirius A, that can be seen with the naked eye or with a telescope are called *visual binaries*. When the stars are further away from us, or closer together, visual resolution becomes more difficult.

In some cases, stellar spectra can be used to deduce the presence of the two stars. These are called *spectroscopic binary stars*. As the stars move around their common centre of mass, one star will be approaching as the other is receding.

Sirius B is a well known white dwarf star, but it is difficult to detect, being very faint. Ironically Sirius B is part of a binary system and its partner, Sirius A, is the brightest star in the night sky.

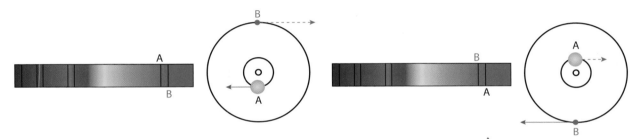

In the left hand diagram, star A is approaching us and so its spectral lines are shifted towards the blue end of the spectrum. At the same time light from star B is red-shifted. In the right-hand diagram, because the stars are moving in the opposite direction, the shift is reversed.

Figure 13.7 This shows a spectroscopic binary system. As star A approaches and B recedes from our line of sight, the absorption lines of A are blue-shifted and those of B red-shifted by the Doppler effect.

Eclipsing binary stars show a periodic variation in the brightness of light emitted from the star system. This occurs because, during their rotation, one star periodically obscures, or eclipses, the other.

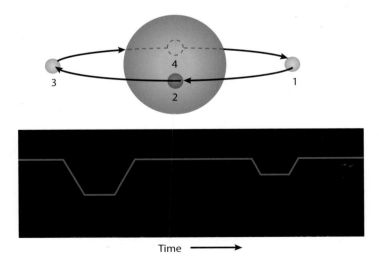

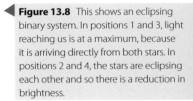
Figure 13.8 This shows an eclipsing binary system. In positions 1 and 3, light reaching us is at a maximum, because it is arriving directly from both stars. In positions 2 and 4, the stars are eclipsing each other and so there is a reduction in brightness.

Time

When one star blocks the light coming from the other star, the intensity drops. The pattern repeats periodically with time as the stars orbit their common centre of mass.

The European Space Agency is made up of seventeen member states. They are Austria, Belgium, Denmark, Finland, France, Germany, Greece, Ireland, Italy, Luxembourg, The Netherlands, Norway, Portugal, Spain, Sweden, Switzerland and the United Kingdom. By coordinating the financial and intellectual resources of its members, it can undertake programmes and activities far beyond the scope of any single European country.

The H-R diagram is an attempt to look for patterns in the stars rather in the same way as the periodic table was constructed to look for patterns in the elements.

Figure 13.9 The Hertzprung-Russell diagram. The fact that most stars lie close to the main sequence implies that this represents some kind of stability.

The Hertzsprung–Russell diagram

An important astronomical discovery, made around 1910, by Hertzsprung and Russell, was that for most stars there was a relationship between surface temperature and luminosity.

The dots on the diagrams represent stars and the scales are not linear. The temperature scale runs backwards, high temperatures being on the left. Some 90% of stars fall on a diagonal band known as the *main sequence*. It can be shown using the Stefan–Boltzmann law that the stars increase in size as we move up the main sequence.

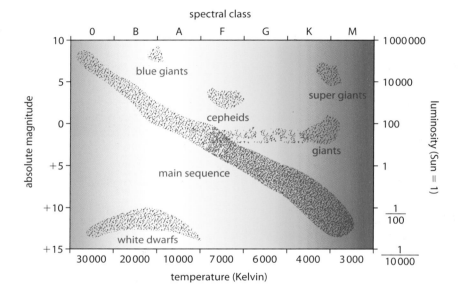

Starting at the lower right we find the coolest stars, reddish in colour. Further up towards the left we find hotter and more luminous stars that are yellow and white. Still further up, we find more luminous blue stars.

The mass of a star increases moving up the main sequence. The gravitational pressure increases with mass, so to maintain equilibrium, fusion reactions in the core must generate a greater radiation pressure. The star has to 'burn' at a higher temperature, giving it greater luminosity.

About 9% of stars are red giants and supergiants. We can see from the Stefan–Boltzmann law that their high luminosity and low temperature means they must have a very large area. This is why they are giants. The white dwarfs are very hot and not luminous. Using the same reasoning, they must be much smaller than their counterparts on the main sequence.

A final group of stars, the cepheids, congregate in a great band of instability that appears between the main sequence and the red giants.

Exercises

7 Explain the equilibrium that exists in a stable star such as our Sun.

8 Outline how atomic spectra may be used to deduce chemical and physical data for stars.

9 Distinguish between the characteristics of spectroscopic binary stars and eclipsing binary stars.

13.3 Stellar distances

Assessment statements

E.3.1   Define the parsec.

E.3.2   Describe the stellar parallax method of determining the distance to a star.

E.3.3   Explain why the method of stellar parallax is limited to measuring stellar distances less than several hundred parsecs.

E.3.4   Solve problems involving stellar parallax.

E.3.5   Describe the apparent magnitude scale.

E.3.6   Define absolute magnitude.

E.3.7   Solve problems involving apparent magnitude, absolute magnitude and distance.

E.3.8   Solve problems involving apparent brightness and apparent magnitude.

E.3.9   State that the luminosity of a star may be estimated from its spectrum.

E.3.10 Explain how stellar distance may be determined using apparent brightness and luminosity.

E.3.11 State that the method of spectroscopic parallax is limited to measuring stellar distances less than about 10 Mpc.

E.3.12 Solve problems involving stellar distances, apparent brightness and luminosity.

E.3.13 Outline the nature of a Cepheid variable.

E.3.14 State the relationship between period and absolute magnitude for Cepheid variables.

E.3.15 Explain how Cepheid variables may be used as "standard candles".

E.3.16 Determine the distance to a Cepheid variable using the luminosity–period relationship.

Various methods are used to determine the distances to stars and galaxies depending upon the distances involved. In order of increasing distances, the four methods we will describe are *stellar parallax, absolute and apparent magnitudes, spectroscopic parallax* and *Cepheid variables*.

Parallax method

If you walk across the room looking out of the window at a house across the street, an object on the windowsill will appear to move relative to the house. The apparent movement of the object is called *parallax*.

A star is viewed from Earth in January, and then again six months later in July against a fixed background of other stars. The star appears to have moved slightly to the right owing to the change in position of the Earth as it orbits the Sun. All the stars are a long way from Earth so the apparent movement will only be slight.

 Stellar parallax is the apparent shifting of a star against a background of very distant fixed stars, when viewed from two different points.

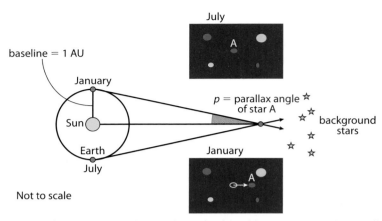

Figure 13.10 Star A appears to move relative to the fixed background of stars as viewed from the Earth at two different times during the year.

The distance of the star from the Earth can be found by measuring the parallax angle and using trigonometry. Of course the angle will be extremely small and is measured in seconds or arc-seconds. One degree is equal to sixty minutes of arc, and one minute is equal to sixty seconds of arc.

The word *parsec* comes from one *par*allax *sec*ond and it is abbreviated to *pc*. SI prefixes are sometimes used to give units like kpc and Mpc.

Using the small angle approximation and the right units we can obtain a simple equation:

$$d(\text{parsec}) = \frac{1}{p} \text{ (arc-second)}$$

d is the distance from Earth to the star   parsec
p is the parallax angle   arc-second or seconds of arc

To view a simulation, visit www.heinemann.co.uk/hotlinks, enter the express code 4266S and click on Weblink 13.5.

Worked example

The nearest star to Earth is Alpha Centauri, which is at a distance of 4.37 ly. Calculate the parallax angle that must be measured to determine this.

Solution
First change the light years into parsec:

$$4.37 \text{ ly} = \frac{4.37}{3.26} = 1.34 \text{ pc}$$

$$d = \frac{1}{p} \qquad p = \frac{1}{d}$$

$$p = \frac{1}{1.34 \; pc}$$

$$= \textbf{0.746 arc-second}$$

The parsec is defined as the distance from Earth of a star that has a parallax angle of one second. Calculations show that 1 parsec (pc) = 3.26 light years (ly).

The more distant a star is from Earth, the smaller its parallax angle becomes. Using photographic techniques with the most accurate equipment, the smallest parallax angle that can be currently measured is about 0.01 arc-second.

The limit on our ability to measure small angles means that the stellar parallax method can only be used to measure the distances of the closest stars, less than a few hundred parsecs from Earth. Orbiting telescopes can extend this distance but for more remote stars, different methods are used.

Exercise

10 A star called Fomalhaut has a parallax angle of 0.148 arc-seconds. Find its distance from the Earth in light years.

Absolute and apparent magnitudes

Stars were first classified according to their brightness by the ancient Greeks. The brightest stars were classified as being magnitude 1, the dimmest as magnitude 6. The apparent magnitude is abbreviated to m, so in the ancient system for a magnitude 1 star, $m = 1$.

A magnitude 1 star was considered to be twice as bright as a magnitude 2 star, which was in turn twice as bright as magnitude 3 and so on. This gave a simple logarithmic scale.

During the 19th century a typical magnitude 1 star was *defined* as being 100 times brighter than a typical magnitude 6 star.

Given that a magnitude 1 star is 100 times brighter than magnitude 6, a difference of 5 magnitudes corresponds to a ratio of 100 in the measured intensity of light. On a logarithmic scale this means that a magnitude 1 star is a factor of the fifth root of 100 times as bright as a magnitude 2 star.

So a magnitude 1 star is $2.51^5 = 100$ times brighter than a magnitude 6 star.

Under the modern magnitude scale, a star of apparent brightness of 2.52×10^{-8} W m^{-2} is given an apparent magnitude of zero. Note that apparent brightness has a unit while apparent magnitude is a ratio, just a number, and so has no unit.

The apparent magnitude of a star depends on two things; the luminosity of the star and its distance from Earth. The scale is back to front; the brightest objects have more negative values not more positive.

In the table you can see the apparent magnitude of some common objects:

Worked example

It can be shown that the ratio of the apparent brightness of two stars A and B is related to their apparent magnitudes by the formula

$$\frac{b_A}{b_B} = 2.51^{M_B - M_A}$$

If the apparent magnitudes of A and B are -1.5 and 9.5 respectively, find the ratio of their apparent brightness.

Solution

Here we simply substitute the exponents checking for their signs:

$$\frac{b_A}{b_B} = 2.51^{9.5 - (-1.5)}$$
$$= 2.51^{11}$$
$$= 2.49 \times 10^4$$

The apparent magnitude of a celestial body is defined as its apparent brightness viewed by an observer on Earth.

It is not surprising that the magnitude scale is logarithmic because the eye is a logarithmic detector. Otherwise if you could see clearly in bright sunlight, you would be blind in the shade!

Each magnitude is 2.51 times brighter than the next.

Object	Apparent magnitude
Sun	−26.8
Full Moon	−12.5
Venus at brightest	−4.4
Jupiter at brightest	−2.7
Sirius	−1.47
Vega	0.04
Betelgeuse	0.41
Polaris	1.99
Naked eye limit	6 0
Pluto	15.1
Hubble Space Telescope	31

Exercise

11 Given that two stars are equidistant from the observer, explain why a star with an apparent magnitude 6 radiates approximately 2.5 times more power than one with an apparent magnitude of 7.

Absolute magnitude

A star which appears to be bright could be either a star with low luminosity not too far away from Earth, or a very much brighter more distant star. To be able to compare the actual brightness of stars, clearly we must take into account their distance.

To determine the *absolute magnitude* of stars, the standard distance is taken as 10 parsec. This is equal to 32.6 light years or 3.08×10^{17} metres.

Most stars are farther than 10 pc from the Earth; they would appear brighter if they were only 10 pc away. What this means is that for *most* stars their absolute magnitudes are more negative than their apparent magnitudes. The absolute magnitude range is from -10 to $+15$.

It can be shown that:

$$m - M = 5 \log\left(\frac{d}{10}\right)$$

m is the apparent magnitude
M is the absolute magnitude
$\log$ is log to the base 10
d is the distance from Earth   parsec

> Astronomers define the absolute magnitude (M) of a star as the apparent magnitude it would have if it were 10 pc from Earth.

Worked example

Alpha Centauri has an apparent magnitude of 0.10 and is at a distance of 1.34 pc. Calculate its absolute magnitude.

Solution

First write the equation and change the subject:

$$m - M = 5 \log\left(\frac{d}{10}\right)$$

$$M = m - 5 \log\left(\frac{d}{10}\right)$$

$$M = 0.10 - 5 \log\left(\frac{1.34}{10}\right)$$

$$= \mathbf{4.5}$$

Exercises

12 The following data is for the star Arcturus.

Distance from Earth/m	Apparent magnitude	Absolute magnitude	Spectral type	Luminosity / W
3.39×10^{17}	-0.1	-0.3	K	3.8×10^{28}

(a) Explain the difference between *apparent magnitude* and *absolute magnitude*.
(b) State and explain, with reference to the data, whether Arcturus would be visible without the aid of a telescope on a clear night.
   Techniques for determining stellar distances include the use of stellar parallax, spectroscopic parallax and Cepheid variables.
(c)   (i)   Calculate the distance, in pc, of Arcturus from the Earth.
      (ii)   State and explain which technique would be most suitable for determining the distance to Arcturus.
      (iii)   Outline the method you have chosen in your answer to (c) (ii).
(d) State how it may be deduced from the data that the surface temperature of Arcturus is lower than that of the Sun.
   The temperature of Arcturus is 4000 K.
(e) Calculate
      (i)   the surface area of Arcturus
      (ii)   the radius of Arcturus
      (iii)   the wavelength at which the light from Arcturus has its maximum intensity.
(f) Using your answers to (e) deduce the stellar type to which Arcturus belongs.

Spectroscopic parallax

Stellar parallax is limited by our ability to detect small changes in the position of distant stars as the Earth moves in its orbit. The H–R diagram provides a powerful alternative method for measuring the distance to more remote stars, using a technique known as *spectroscopic parallax*.

The name is misleading since no use of parallax is being made. It refers to a method that involves the luminosity and apparent brightness of a star. We can use analysis of spectra and Wien's displacement law to find the surface temperature of the star:

$$\lambda_{max} = \frac{2.90 \times 10^{-3}}{T}$$

Assuming the star is a main sequence star, we can use the H–R diagram to find its luminosity. Then if its apparent brightness is known, the distance to the star can be found using the relationship between the apparent brightness and the distance:

$$b = \frac{L}{4\pi d^2}$$

This method can be used to measure distances up to about 10 Mpc. At distances greater than this, the uncertainty in the luminosity and apparent brightness becomes too great.

Worked example

A detailed study of a certain star suggests that it fits on the main sequence of the H-R diagram. Its measured apparent brightness is 1.0×10^{-12} W m^{-2} and the peak wavelength of its spectrum is 600 nm.

(a) Find the surface temperature of the star.

(b) If this temperature corresponds to a luminosity of 1.0×10^{26} W, calculate its distance from us in light years.

Solution

(a) Change the subject of Wien's displacement law:

$$T = \frac{2.90 \times 10^{-3}}{\lambda_{max}} \text{ K}$$

$$= \frac{2.90 \times 10^{-3}}{600 \times 10^{-9}} \text{ K}$$

$$= \mathbf{4.8 \times 10^3 \text{ K}}$$

(b) Use the inverse square relationship, changing the subject:

$$d = \sqrt{\frac{L}{4\pi b}} \text{ m}$$

$$= \sqrt{\frac{1.0 \times 10^{26}}{4\pi \times 1.0 \times 10^{-12}}} \text{ m}$$

$$= 2.8 \times 10^{18} \text{ m}$$

Now change into light years:

$$d = \frac{2.8 \times 10^{18}}{9.46 \times 10^{15}}$$

$$= \mathbf{300 \text{ ly}}$$

Cepheid variables

The main problem with trying to measure the distance of stars farther than 10 Mpc away, is that we cannot easily distinguish between a brighter, more distant star and a dimmer star that is closer to us.

To determine the distance to a galaxy, we need a star of known luminosity in the galaxy, and then we can make comparisons with other stars. The star of known luminosity is sometimes called a *standard candle*.

Earlier in this chapter we mentioned that a Cepheid or Cepheid variable star has a luminosity that varies periodically with time. This is because the outer layers of the star undergo periodic expansion and contraction, causing variations in surface area and temperature. During expansion the luminosity increases.

The Stefan–Boltzmann Law tells us that:

$$L = \sigma A T^4$$

If the surface area and temperature are changing, then the luminosity of the star must also change. Leavitt discovered a relationship between the maximum luminosity or absolute magnitude and the log of the period and was able to represent this graphically.

Figure 13.11 The diagram on the left shows a typical 'shark fin' curve for a Cepheid variable; the periodic nature of the *apparent* magnitude can clearly be seen.

The diagram on the right shows the linear relationship of *absolute* magnitude with period, but note that scale of the horizontal axis is not linear.

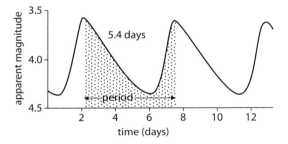

There is a linear relationship between the absolute brightness and the log of the period.

Some Cepheid variables were discovered that were close enough for their distances to be measured using stellar parallax. Knowing the apparent magnitude and the distance, the absolute magnitude could be found from

$$m - M = 5 \log \left(\frac{d}{10} \right)$$

● **Examiner's hint:** Often in questions about Cepheid variables, you are expected to read information from a graph before using the equation.

When observing a Cepheid variable far away it became possible to calculate its absolute magnitude from the period. Then the distance to the galaxy could be calculated. The Cepheid is acting like a standard candle.

Exercise

13 (a) Define
  (i) luminosity
  (ii) apparent brightness.
(b) State the mechanism for the variation in the luminosity of the Cepheid variable.
The variation with time t, of the apparent brightness b, of a Cepheid variable is shown opposite.

$b \times 10^{-10}$ (W m^{-2})

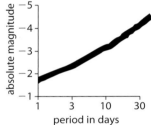

Figure 13.12

(c) (i) Assuming that the surface temperature of the star stays constant, deduce whether the star has a larger radius after two days or after six days.

(ii) Explain the importance of Cepheid variables for estimating distances to galaxies.

(d) (i) The maximum luminosity of this Cepheid variable is 7.2×10^{29} W. Use data from the graph to determine the distance of the Cepheid variable.

(ii) Cepheids are sometimes referred to as 'standard candles'. Explain what is meant by this.

13.4 Cosmology

Assessment statements

E.4.1   Describe Newton's model of the universe.

E.4.2   Explain Olbers' paradox.

E.4.3   Suggest that the red-shift of light from galaxies indicates that the universe is expanding.

E.4.4   Describe both space and time as originating with the Big Bang.

E.4.5   Describe the discovery of cosmic microwave background (CMB) radiation by Penzias and Wilson.

E.4.6   Explain how cosmic radiation in the microwave region is consistent with the Big Bang model.

E.4.7   Suggest how the Big Bang model provides a resolution to Olbers' paradox.

E.4.8   Distinguish between the terms *open*, *flat* and *closed* when used to describe the development of the universe.

E.4.9   Define the term *critical density* by reference to a flat model of the development of the universe.

E.4.10 Discuss how the density of the universe determines the development of the universe.

E.4.11 Discuss problems associated with determining the density of the universe.

E.4.12 State that current scientific evidence suggests that the universe is open.

E.4.13 Discuss an example of the international nature of recent astrophysics research.

E.4.14 Evaluate arguments related to investing significant resources into researching the nature of the universe.

Olbers' paradox

Newton's view of the universe was that it was infinite in space and time, uniform and static (otherwise it would collapse under its own gravitational force). This implied that the universe was unchanging, and contained an infinite number of stars spreading out to infinity.

In 1823 the German astronomer Heinrich Olbers described an apparent paradox. If Newton's model were right, and there were an infinite number of stationary stars, no matter which direction you looked in the night sky, you would see a star.

This meant that the sky at night should be bright, whereas we all know perfectly well that in fact it is dark!

This contradiction is known as *Olbers' paradox*.

There is a quantitative explanation of the paradox. Let us assume that the stars are evenly distributed in an infinite number of thin shells, spreading out like the layers of an onion.

Each star has the same luminosity L related to the apparent brightness b and the distance d by the inverse square law:

$$b = \frac{L}{4\pi d^2}$$

Imagine a thin shell of stars of thickness T at distance d.

The volume of the thin shell will be the surface area × the thickness $= 4\pi d^2 T$.

If there are n stars per unit volume in the shell, then the total number of stars in the shell N will be given by:

$$N = n \times 4\pi d^2 T$$

This means that the total number of stars in the shell is directly proportional to d^2.

If we move out to a shell at a greater distance the stars in the shell will be dimmer according to the inverse square law:

$$b \propto \frac{1}{d^2}$$

Clearly in the more distant shell there will be more stars. Since the number of stars is directly proportional to the distance squared and the brightness is inversely proportional to the same quantity there is an interesting implication; the amount of light we receive from the shell should not depend upon the distance!

If there were a billion shells we would simply have to multiply the energy received from one shell by a billion to find the total energy. What this means is that if the universe were infinite, the night sky should be infinitely bright!

The Big Bang model

In 1929 Edwin Hubble proposed a law that in essence states that the universe is not static, but is expanding. He made detailed measurements of many observed galaxies and found that the absorption lines in their spectra were usually shifted towards the red end of the spectrum.

The red-shift of light was explained in terms of the Doppler effect; the increase in the wavelength of the spectral lines meaning that the galaxies were moving away from us.

The logical extension to this idea is that all galaxies are moving away from each other. There is no scientific reason to suppose that we are at the centre of the universe; presumably the same measurements made in another galaxy would lead to the same conclusion.

If the galaxies are moving away from each other, then they must have been much closer to each other in the past.

The logical extension to this idea is that at some time in the past everything in the universe must have all been located at one point, called a *singularity*.

This is the basis for the idea that the universe began at a certain time in the past, put at about 13.7 billion years ago, by most modern measurements, with an explosion known as the *Big Bang*.

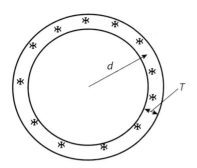

Figure 13.13 A thin shell of stars of thickness T at a distance d from Earth. The apparent brightness of all such shells at increasing distance will be the same.

Our senses clearly tell us that the sky at night is dark. How can this be a paradox?

The Hubble Space Telescope was named after Edwin Hubble. Since its launch in 1990, it has become one of the most important instruments in the history of astronomy.

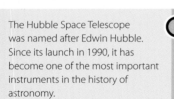

Religions sometimes propose that we were created at the centre of the universe. How can this be reconciled with the Big Bang Model?
The Big Bang Model proposes the instantaneous creation of light, space and time. How can this be reconciled with religion?

From a state of infinitely high density and temperature, space and time were created, into which the universe we know today has expanded. The universe continues to expand, but is not expanding into a void.

A major piece of evidence supporting the Big Bang model is the cosmic microwave background (CMB) radiation. It was first observed inadvertently in 1965 by Penzias and Wilson. The radiation was acting as a source of excess noise in a radio receiver they were building.

The cosmic microwave background radiation is a kind of echo of the original Big Bang still resonating around the universe.

Penzias and Wilson found that the intensity of the radiation they received, from all directions, had a wavelength in the microwave region. When they plugged this wavelength into the Wien's displacement law equation it gave a temperature of 2.7 K.

The Big Bang model resolves Olbers' paradox. If the galaxies are moving away from us in all directions then the radiation reaching us from them will be red-shifted owing to the Doppler effect. This explains why the sky appears dark at night; the light from receding stars has been shifted into the infra-red region of the electromagnetic spectrum and so is no longer visible to us.

The Big Bang is the huge explosion that is believed to have created the universe 13.7 billion years ago. Evidence supporting this theory includes the continued expansion of the universe and the presence of background microwave radiation thought to be an afterglow of the explosion.

Initially the radiation was thought to be some sort of contamination and they tried to remove it by cleaning the receiver.

We know that 2.7 K is the ambient temperature of the universe, and so CMB radiation provides excellent evidence in support of the Big Bang model. The universe has cooled down to this temperature from its extremely hot origin.

Scientists still do not know what happened in the time $0-10^{-42}$ s after the Big Bang.
How could pure energy have been produced from nothing?

Exercise

14 (a) Describe what is meant by *cosmic background radiation*.

(b) The graph shows the spectrum of the cosmic background radiation i.e. the variation, with wavelength, of the intensity of the cosmic background radiation.

There is evidence to suggest that the universe will expand forever. On the same axes, sketch a graph to show the spectrum of the background radiation for the universe many millions of years from now.

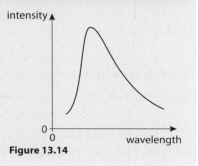

Figure 13.14

The development of the universe

There are three proposed outcomes for the development of the universe:
An *open universe* is one that continues to expand. Gravity slows the rate of expansion but is not strong enough to stop it.

A *closed universe* is one that will eventually collapse back on itself. This would result in a *big crunch*, the reverse of a big bang.

A *flat universe* is somewhere in between the other two possibilities. The force of gravity keeps on slowing the expansion, but theoretically it takes an infinite time to come to rest.

The outcome depends upon the *mass density*, the amount of matter per unit volume available to provide gravitational attraction.

Figure 13.15 The possible futures of the universe. Most recent opinion would suggest that the universe is open.

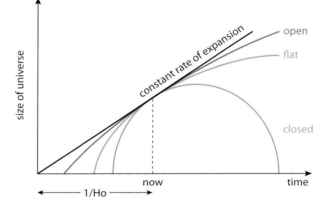

The critical density ρ_0 is defined as the theoretical value of the density that would create a flat universe. The value of the critical density has been measured as 4.5×10^{-27} kg m^{-3} but this value is not certain.

An open universe would occur if the mass density were greater than the critical density; $\rho > \rho_0$. A closed universe would result if the critical density was greater than the mass density.

Exercise

15 (a) Explain the significance of the critical density of matter in the universe with respect to the possible fate of the universe.
The critical density ρ_0 of matter in the universe is given by the expression

$$\rho_0 = \frac{3H_0^2}{8\pi G}$$

where H_0 is the Hubble constant and G is the gravitational constant.
An estimate of H_0 is 2.7×10^{-18} s^{-1}

(b) (i) Calculate a value for ρ_0.
(ii) Hence determine the equivalent number of nucleons per unit volume at this critical density.

The future of the universe

In order to determine the fate of the universe we have to know how much mass it contains. Working out the mass of all the galaxies in the universe should be relatively straightforward, but in fact we can only 'see' about 10% of the universe.

Most of the mass is in the universe is made up of dark matter; so called because it is too cool for its radiation to be detected.

Some of the dark matter may be contained in Massive Astronomical Compact Halo Objects or MACHOs. Weakly Interacting Massive Particles, or WIMPs, are hypothetical particles serving as another possible solution to the problem of dark matter.

In 1997 cosmologists made a surprising discovery. Supernova explosions in distant galaxies showed that instead of the expected deceleration in the rate of the expansion of the universe, it appeared that the expansion was in fact accelerating!

So the universe appears to be more open than expected. There must be some other, previously unknown force, acting in opposition to gravity, which is pushing the universe apart. This new phenomenon is called *dark energy* and will occupy the minds of scientists for many years to come.

Can we justify the expense of sending astronauts on a mission to Mars?

Should funds spent on space exploration be allocated to other areas of scientific research?

Exercises

16 Outline an astrophysics project that is funded internationally. Include details of the aims of the project, the research involved and the countries or organisations providing the funding.

Practice questions

1. The diagram below shows the grid of a Hertzsprung–Russell (H–R) diagram on which the positions of the Sun and four other stars A, B, C and D are shown.

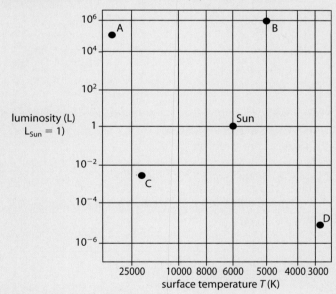

(a) State an alternative labelling of the axes
   (i) x-axis
   (ii) y-axis.
(b) Complete the table below.

Star	Type of star
A	
B	
C	
D	

(c) Explain, using information from the H-R diagram, and without making any calculations, how astronomers can deduce that star **B** is larger than star **A**.

(d) Using the following data and information from the H-R diagram, show that star **B** is at a distance of about 700 pc from Earth.

Apparent visual brightness of the Sun $= 1.4 \times 10^3 \, \text{W m}^{-2}$

Apparent visual brightness of star B $= 7.0 \times 10^{-8} \, \text{W m}^{-2}$

Mean distance of the Sun from Earth $= 1.0 \, \text{AU}$

1 parsec $= 2.1 \times 10^5 \, \text{AU}$

(e) Explain why the distance of star **B** from Earth cannot be determined by the method of stellar parallax.

2 This question is about the possible evolution of the universe.

The diagram below is a sketch graph that shows three possible ways in which the size of the universe might change with time.

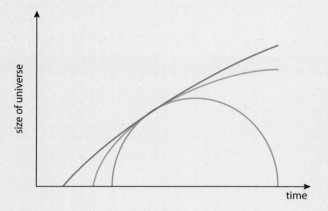

Depending on which way the size of the universe changes with time, the universe is referred to either being *open* or *flat* or *closed*.

(a) On the diagram, identify each type of universe.

(b) Complete the table below to show how the mean density of each type of universe is related to the critical density.

Type of universe	Relation between ρ and ρ_0
Open	
Flat	
Closed	

3 Barnard's star, in the constellation Ophiuchus, has a *parallax angle* of 0.549 arc-second as measured from Earth.

(a) With the aid of a suitable diagram, explain what is meant by *parallax angle* and outline how it is measured.

(b) Deduce that the distance of Barnard's star from the Sun is 5.94 ly.

(c) The ratio $\dfrac{\text{apparent brightness of Barnard's star}}{\text{apparent brightness of the Sun}}$ is 2.6×10^{-14}.

    (i) Define the term *apparent brightness*.

    (ii) Determine the value of the ratio $\dfrac{\text{luminosity of Barnard's star}}{\text{luminosity of the Sun}}$

    (1 ly $= 6.3 \times 10^4 \, \text{AU}$).

(d) The surface temperature of Barnard's star is about 3 500 K. Using this information and information about its luminosity, explain why Barnard's star cannot be

    (i) a white dwarf

    (ii) a red giant.

4 (a) Describe what is meant by *cosmic background radiation*.

(b) Explain how cosmic background radiation is evidence in support of the Big Bang model of the universe.

(c) State *one* other piece of evidence in support of the Big Bang model.

(d) A student makes the statement that "*as a result of the Big Bang, the universe is expanding into a vacuum*". Discuss whether the student's statement is correct.

5 This question is about eclipsing binary stars.

(a) In a particular binary star system, star A has apparent brightness 8.0×10^{-13} W m^{-2} and star B has apparent brightness 2.0×10^{-14} W m^{-2}.

    (i) Explain how it is possible to deduce that star A has a higher luminosity than star B.

    (ii) The surface area of star B is 10 000 times smaller than that of star A. Calculate the ratio

$$\frac{\text{surface temperature of star B}}{\text{surface temperature of star A}}$$

(b) The graph below shows the variation with time of the intensity of light received on Earth from the two stars.

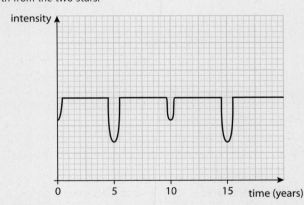

    (i) The diagrams below each show the orbits of the two stars. Star A is in the inner orbit. Annotate the diagrams to show the relative positions of stars A and B as seen from Earth, that correspond to the intensity-time graph above at times of 5 and 10 years.

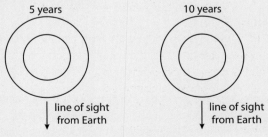

    (ii) State the period of this binary star system.

    (iii) State what can be deduced from knowing the period of the binary and the separation of the stars.

6 The characteristics of a Cepheid variable were first observed in 1784.

(a) **(i)** Describe the characteristic by which a Cepheid variable may be identified from Earth.

(ii) Outline the cause of this characteristic.

A particular Cepheid variable is found to have an average value of apparent magnitude of 5.2 and a time period of pulsation of 50 days. Apparent magnitude m is related to absolute magnitude M and distance d (measured in parsec) by the expression

$$m - M = 5 \log d - 5$$

(b) **(i)** Distinguish between *apparent magnitude* and *absolute magnitude*.

The graph below shows how the absolute magnitude M of some Cepheid variables varies with time period T of pulsation.

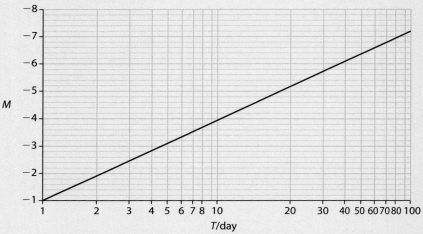

(ii) Use the graph to obtain a value for the absolute magnitude of this Cepheid variable and hence determine its distance from Earth.

7 **(a)** Explain the term *black-body radiation*.

The diagram below is a sketch graph of the black-body radiation spectrum of a certain star.

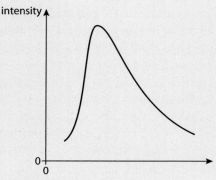

(b) Label the x-axis of the graph.

(c) On the graph, sketch the black-body radiation spectrum of a star that has a lower surface temperature and lower apparent brightness than this star.

The star Betelgeuse in the Orion constellation emits black-body radiation that has a maximum intensity at a wavelength of 0.97 μm.

(d) Deduce that the surface temperature of Betelgeuse is about 3000 K.

14 Communications
(Option F)

Radio communication

Assessment statements

F.1.1 Describe what is meant by the modulation of a wave.
F.1.2 Distinguish between a carrier wave and a signal wave.
F.1.3 Describe the nature of amplitude modulation (AM) and frequency modulation (FM).
F.1.4 Solve problems based on the modulation of the carrier wave in order to determine the frequency and amplitude of the information signal.
F.1.5 Sketch and analyse graphs of the power spectrum of a carrier wave that is amplitude-modulated by a single frequency signal.
F.1.6 Define what is meant by sideband frequencies and bandwidth.
F.1.7 Solve problems involving sideband frequencies and bandwidth.
F.1.8 Describe the relative advantages and disadvantages of AM and FM for radio transmission and reception.
F.1.9 Describe, by means of a block diagram, an AM radio receiver.

Communication between people

People communicate by speaking to each other. This is an analogue form of communication since the amplitude and frequency of the voice changes smoothly rather than in steps.

Radio communication

Radio communication includes not only broadcast radio stations but many other forms of communication that rely on radio signals to transfer information, such as mobile phones, wireless internet and television.

Radio waves

Radio waves are electromagnetic waves that originate from an alternating current. The changing electric field that causes the electrons to move up and down the wire spreads out in all directions. The changing electric field also causes a magnetic field, hence the name electromagnetic wave. The two fields are perpendicular to each other (remember the grip rule).

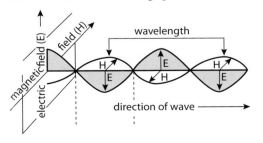

Figure 14.1 A radio wave is an electromagnetic wave.

The phone and the computer use radio communication (but not the cat!).

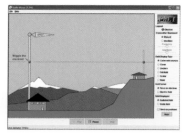

To see how the electric field spreads out, visit www.heinemann.co.uk/hotlinks, enter the express code 4266S and click on Weblink 14.1.

The radio spectrum

The frequency of the oscillating electrons is the same as the frequency of the wave. This can be anything from a few times a second up to several billion times a second: these frequencies are known as radio frequencies or RF. Different ranges of frequency have different names (see Table 1).

Name	Frequency	Wavelength	Use
Very low frequency	3–30 kHz	100 km–10 km	avalanche beacons
Low frequency	30–300 kHz	10 km–1 km	Longwave radio
Medium frequency	300 kHz–3 MHz	1 km–100 m	AM radio
High frequency	3–30 MHz	100 m–10 m	Shortwave radio
Very high frequency	30–300 MHz	10 m–1 m	FM radio
Ultra high frequency	300–3000 MHz	1 m–100 mm	TV, Bluetooth, LAN, mobiles

Table 1 The complete radio spectrum.

The principle of radio communication

The transmitter

Figure 14.2 A simple radio transmitter and receiver.

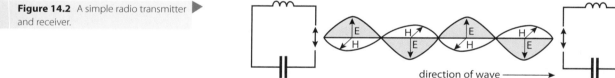

A changing electric field must be created in order to produce a radio wave. This can be done using an oscillating circuit, which in its simplest form comprises a coil of wire and a pair of parallel plates (a capacitor). The tuned circuit causes the electrons to oscillate at a single frequency given by the number of turns on the coil and the size of the capacitor, rather like a pendulum whose frequency is fixed by its length. When electrons oscillate in the circuit, a radio wave will radiate in all directions. This circuit is called the *transmitter*.

The receiver

If a second oscillator circuit is placed at a distance from the transmitter it will be in a region of changing electric and magnetic field. Electrons in the circuit will be caused to oscillate due to the changing field. The amplitude of this oscillation is however very small, especially if the transmitter is a long distance away. However, if the frequency of the second oscillator is the same as the first, then resonance occurs, resulting in a much larger amplitude, enough to be detected.

Communication

So we have communication between the two circuits but all we have communicated is a single frequency. A single frequency of sound would be a continuous whistle. When communicating with sound we change the frequency of the sound to make different words, but if we changed the frequency of a radio wave then the receiver wouldn't be able to receive it, since it is tuned in to one specific frequency. The simplest way to communicate would be to repeatedly switch the current on and off. This is how early communication was carried out. Morse Code is a way of representing each letter and number by a series of dots and dashes (a dot is a short pulse and a dash is a long one). In this way text messages can be sent: *dot dot dot, dash dash dash, dot dot dot* is still an internationally recognized distress signal standing for SOS (save our souls). Changing a wave to carry a signal is called *modulation*. If many people in the same area want to communicate by radio waves then each one needs to choose a different frequency; this is called a *channel*.

There are two common forms of modulation used to broadcast radio programmes, these are *frequency modulation* and *amplitude modulation*; this is what the letters FM and AM stand for on a radio tuner.

Amplitude modulation

Amplitude modulation is when the amplitude of the carrier wave (the radio wave) is varied at the same rate as a signal (see Figure 14.3).

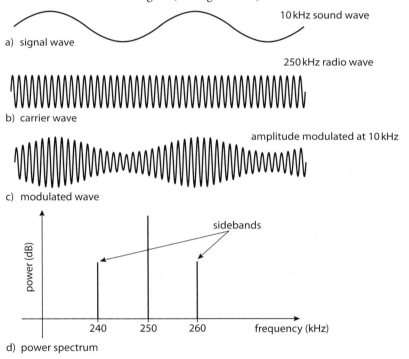

Figure 14.3 A carrier wave modulated by a signal wave. In this example the 250 kHz carrier will have two sidebands 260 kHz (250 + 10) and 240 kHz (250 − 10). The sidebands can be represented on a power spectrum as shown here.

Sidebands

You may remember that when a body oscillates with SHM its displacement can be described by the formula:

$x = x_o \sin\omega_1 t$ where x_o is the amplitude and ω_1 is the angular frequency, $2\pi f$

If x_o also varies sinusoidally then we can write $x_o = A \sin\omega_2 t$

The resultant amplitude is then $x = A \sin\omega_2 t.\sin\omega_1 t$

Now, $\sin A \sin B = \frac{1}{2}(\cos(A-B) - \cos(A+B))$

So $x = \frac{1}{2}A(\cos(\omega_2 t - \omega_1 t) - \cos(\omega_2 t + \omega_1 t))$

In other words, the oscillation is made up of two components: one with angular frequency $(\omega_2 + \omega_1)$ the other with angular frequency $(\omega_2 - \omega_1)$.

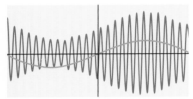

modulation index = 0.5

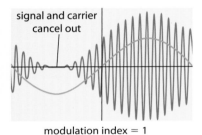

signal and carrier cancel out

modulation index = 1

Figure 14.4 With modulation index 1 the signal and carrier wave can completely cancel each other out.

Figure 14.5 The power spectrum for a signal modulated by a band of frequencies.

A similar thing happens with the wave, modulating the amplitude causes the carrier frequency to split into two components, these are called *sidebands*. The sidebands do not affect the ability of the receiver to resonate with the signal but it does mean that radio channel frequencies cannot be too close to each other.

Power spectrum

A power spectrum (see Figure 14.3d)) is a chart showing the relative powers of the different frequencies that make up a signal. This is like the frequency analyser found on many music systems. The power scale is in decibels, which is a logarithmic scale. An increase of 1 bel means that the power has increased by a factor of 10. The central line in the spectrum shown in Figure 14.3d) therefore represents a much bigger power than the sidebands.

Modulation index

The modulation factor is the ratio of the signal amplitude to the carrier amplitude. A high modulation factor will cause the final signal to vary greatly.

Bandwidth

In the previous example a single frequency sound of 10 kHz was transmitted. More than just one frequency needs to be used to transmit complex sounds such as music. The complete range of frequencies that humans can hear is from 20 Hz to 20 kHz. Modulating the carrier between these two frequencies would result in a wide band of frequencies from 230 kHz to 280 kHz as in Figure 14.5.

So the signal will occupy a band of frequencies from 230 to 280 kHz. This means that there can't be any other radio channels in this range. It is however possible to reduce the bandwidth by cutting out the highest and lowest frequency notes from the music, but this will result in a loss in quality. Medium wave radio channels are allocated a 9 kHz band width. Telephone uses a narrower bandwidth of 3 kHz since only the human voice is transmitted. An analogue TV signal, on the other hand, has a bandwidth of 6 MHz since information about both pictures and sound needs to be transmitted. Greater bandwidth implies more information can be transmitted.

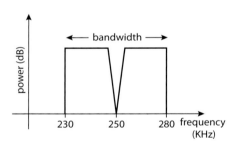

Exercises

1   If the amplitude of a signal of frequency 500 kHz is modulated by a frequency of 15 kHz, what will the frequency of the sidebands be?

2   Refer to the graph of the modulated signal shown in Figure 14.6.
    (a) What is the frequency of the carrier signal?
    (b) What is the frequency of the signal wave?
    (c) What sidebands will be present in this signal?

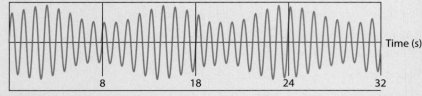

Figure 14.6

Frequency modulation

Frequency modulation also superimposes a signal onto a carrier radio wave but instead of varying the amplitude of the carrier, the frequency is varied between two values either side of the carrier frequency (see Figure 14.7).

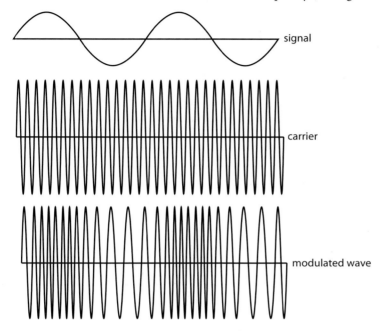

signal

carrier

modulated wave

Figure 14.7 In a FM signal the frequency of the carrier, f is modulated by the signal so that its frequency varies continuously between two values, f_1 and f_2.

Peak frequency deviation

In an FM signal, the carrier wave deviates from its original frequency f by an amount Δf. This is known as the *peak frequency deviation*. Therefore the maximum frequency $f_2 = f + \Delta f$ and the minimum $f_1 = f - \Delta f$

Modulation index

If the carrier frequency, f is modulated between f_1 and f_2 then the modulation

$$\text{index} = \frac{(f_2 - f_1)}{f}$$

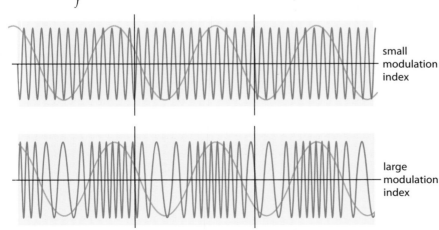

small modulation index

large modulation index

Figure 14.8 FM signals with a large and a small modulation index and the frequency spectrum and power spectrum respectively.

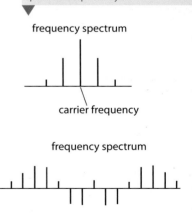

frequency spectrum

carrier frequency

frequency spectrum

Sidebands

As in AM, the addition of the modulated wave can be split into components. These components can be displayed on a frequency spectrum (see Figure 14.8).

Bandwidth

As can be seen from these examples, FM signals occupy a bandwidth of frequencies. The width of this band is actually infinite. However, as you can see from the frequency spectrum in Figure 14.8, the power of the bands gets smaller and smaller, until after a certain point they are so small that they can be ignored. The effective bandwidth can be calculated using Carson's Rule.

Bandwidth = 2 × (peak deviation + highest modulating frequency)

Example

If a carrier signal of 100 MHz is modulated between with a peak deviation of 50 kHz to carry an audio signal with a maximum frequency of 20 kHz Then the band width = 2 × (50 + 20) = 140 kHz

Frequency modulation
You can try varying the carrier and signal frequencies to see what happens to the side bands. To try this, visit www.heinemann.co.uk/hotlinks, enter the express code 4266S and click on Weblink 14.3

Exercises

3 A 150 MHz signal is modulated between 149.9 MHz and 150.1 MHz to carry a signal ranging from 100 Hz to 20 kHz. Calculate:
  (a) the peak frequency deviation
  (b) the modulation index
  (c) the band width.

4 For the signal in Figure 14.9 calculate:
  (a) the highest and lowest modulation frequencies
  (b) the signal frequency.

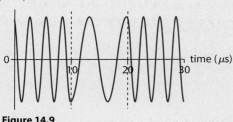

Figure 14.9

Comparing AM and FM

Bandwidth

The bandwidth allocated to AM radio is 9 kHz, just enough to transmit a reasonable quality audio signal. FM uses a bandwidth of 200 kHz. This means that when you tune into FM radio channels they are further apart than AM. This is also why FM uses a higher frequency, although the actual frequencies used by FM and AM are decided by international agreement, not the laws of physics. To use a frequency band, a radio station must pay a sum of money to the controlling body in that country. Two stations can use the same band but they must be geographically far enough apart so that their signals don't interfere.

Range

The range of an AM signal is much longer than an FM signal. This isn't because of the modulation but because the frequencies used by AM are much lower than those used by FM. Low frequency radio waves have two ways of travelling from A to B, either along the ground, or reflected off an atmospheric layer called the *ionosphere*. The latter enables the waves to travel long distances, so two AM radio stations using the same bandwith must be a long way apart. On the other hand, high frequency waves travel in straight lines and don't reflect off the ionosphere. Rather than travelling round the Earth they shoot off into space. This means that to receive FM you have to be able to have direct contact with the transmitter. Satellite TV also uses high frequency radiation, and this is why a receiving dish has to be pointed straight at the satellite: this is called *line of sight*. The good thing about this is that FM stations using the same frequency can be close together, and this is why local radio stations tend to use FM.

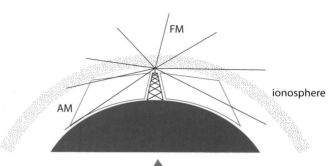

Figure 14.10 AM waves reflect off ionosphere and travel along the ground whereas FM waves travel in straight lines.

Quality

Radio channels are not the only source of radio waves, as any movement of charge will cause EM radiation, e.g. lightning. These signals will interact with the radio signal causing a change in amplitude but not frequency. These disturbances (noise) affect the signal carried by an AM channel but not an FM channel. This is the main problem with AM, it is very susceptible to noise. This is why high quality music channels tend to use FM not AM.

Cost

A simple AM radio receiver can be built for very little money out of a crystal diode, a capacitor and a coil of wire. An FM receiver is rather more complicated and therefore costs more.

The AM radio receiver

In this course you do not have to know how each component in a radio receiver works but you do have to understand the stages. These can be represented in a block diagram as shown in Figure 14.11.

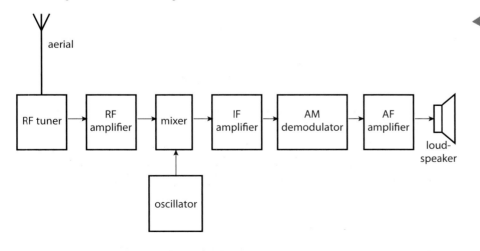

Figure 14.11 The AM radio receiver and its component parts.

Aerial

The aerial is a long conducting rod. Radio waves passing through it cause a changing electric and magnetic field in it.

RF tuner

Anywhere on Earth there will be radio waves from many different sources, each of different frequency and all of which will cause a changing field in the aerial. The radio frequency tuner is manually set to resonate with just one of those frequencies. This is what you do when you tune your radio.

RF amplifier

The signal from the tuner is very small so needs to be amplified before the signal is passed onto the mixer. The reason for this initial amplification is because the mixing stage can add noise to the signal. In other words, it can mess it up a bit. Making the signal bigger reduces the effect of the noise.

Mixer/oscillator

The tuner and RF amplifier receive different frequency signals depending on the radio channel that the receiver is tuned in to. The next stage of the process is to demodulate the signal and recover the original audio frequency. This would need a different circuit for each received channel, so to simplify things all carrier signals are changed into the same frequency by mixing with an intermediate frequency in the mixer.

Figure 14.12 Signal before and after mixing, and after demodulation.

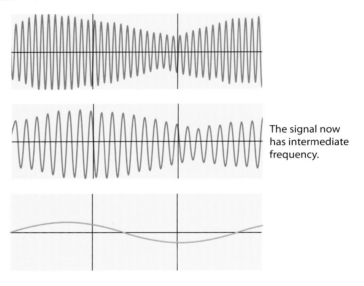

The signal now has intermediate frequency.

IF amplifier

This increases the amplitude of the intermediate frequency signal.

AM demodulator

The demodulator splits the audio signal from the carrier signal. Only the audio signal continues to the next stage, the RF signal is discarded.

AF amplifier

This increases the amplitude of the audio frequency signal.

Loudspeaker

This turns the signal into music and/or speech.

14.2 Digital signals

Assessment statements
F.2.1 Solve problems involving the conversion between binary numbers and decimal numbers.
F.2.2 Distinguish between analogue and digital signals.
F.2.3 State the advantages of the digital transmission, as compared to the analogue transmission, of information.
F.2.4 Describe, using block diagrams, the principles of the transmission and reception of digital signals.
F.2.5 Explain the significance of the number of bits and the bit-rate on the production of a transmitted signal.
F.2.6 Describe what is meant by time-division multiplexing
F.2.7 Solve problems involving analogue-to-digital conversion.
F.2.8 Describe the consequences of digital communication and multiplexing on worldwide communications.
F.2.9 Discuss thee moral, ethical, economic and environmental issues from access to the Internet.

Communication between computers

A computer is a digital device, everything it does is coded from a sequence of 1s and 0s. It is not obvious how 1s and 0s can be used to communicate information, until you understand the binary system.

The binary system

Our normal system of numbers is called the decimal system. In this system we can represent any number by using 10 symbols (0123456789). The way it works is that we group units, tens, hundreds and so on. So 365 is 3 hundreds, 6 tens and 5 units. Units, tens and hundreds are all powers of 10. 10^0, 10^1, 10^2 etc. This is called *base 10* (see Table 2).

Power of 10	3	2	1	0
	1000	100	10	1
	Thousands	Hundreds	tens	units

Table 2 The decimal system of numbers.

Power of 2	3	2	1	0
	8	4	2	1
	eights	fours	twos	ones

Table 3 The binary system of numbers.

The base of our number system doesn't have to be10. We can use any number. If we use 2 this is called the binary system, as represented in Table 3. With 4 digits we can count from 0 to 15, with 8 digits we can count to 255 (see Table 4).

Decimal	Binary
1	00000001
2	00000010
3	00000011
4	00000100
5	00000101
6	00000110
7	00000111
8	00001000
9	00001001
10	00001010

Exercises

5 Convert the following numbers into binary form:
   (a) 12   **(b)** 26   **(c)** 33

6 Convert the following binary numbers into base 10:
   (a) 00110   **(b)** 11001   **(c)** 11110

7 What are the most significant bits for the numbers in Exercise 6?

Sending the data

When computers communicate, binary numbers are sent as a series of high and low electrical potentials (see Figure 14.13). When receiving a series of 1s and 0s it is impossible to know what numbers they represent unless you know how many bits there are per number. So digital devices are standardized by the number of bits they use; this is usually a multiple of 8.

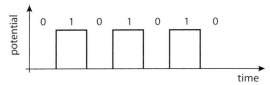

Timing

A digital signal is easy enough to read if the sequence is 0101010 as in Figure 14.13. Often it's as complicated as the sequence in Figure 14.14. This could be 011111010 or 00111111111100110 depending on how long each pulse is. A computer uses a very fast clock to read the signal each time it expects a pulse. If information is sent at 20 kb/s then each pulse lasts 1/20000 s, so the computer needs to know when to start reading and it must read the signal every 50 μs. If the pulses don't come at exactly the right time or if the clock isn't exact then the computer will start to read the wrong information.

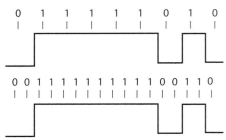

Synchronous transmission

In synchronous transmission the sender and receiver clocks are set at the same rate so the transmission of the pulses is regular. A clock signal is sent with the data in order to synchronise the clocks. No clock is 100% accurate, so information is sent in 'blocks'. There is, however, some room for error since the computer doesn't have to take its reading exactly in the centre of each block.

Asynchronous transmission

If the clocks are not synchronised then the signal must contain information to inform the receiver how often to take readings. There is more chance of error in this system so the block lengths must be much smaller. This system can only be used for slow transfer of data. All fast transfer is synchronous.

Time division multiplexing

Because digital information is sent in blocks, it is a relatively simple process to send different pieces of information in different blocks. In this way many signals can be sent along the same cable. All that has to be added is some code before each block to say which blocks go together and where they should go.

Figure 14.15 Three time division multiplexed signals.

Compression

If the time duration of each pulse is reduced then it is possible to transmit the signal in less time; this is called *compression*.

Figure 14.16 A signal and its compressed version. The minimum size of a pulse depends on the speed of the transmitter and receiver.

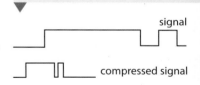

Exercises

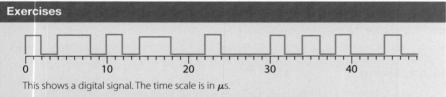

This shows a digital signal. The time scale is in μs.

8 What is the binary data in this signal if it is read at a rate of 500 kHz.

9 If the signal contains two multiplexed signals each 6 μs long, work out the binary data in each of the signals.

10 Convert each of the 3-bit binary numbers in Exercise 9 to base 10.

MP3
An MP3 file is a compressed file. A piece of music recorded onto a CD takes up 10 times more space that it does when compressed into MP3 format.

Difference between analogue and digital

We have considered two different forms of communication, people communicating via radio waves and computers communicating through wires. The signals sent in these examples are fundamentally different; the radio signal carrying music changes continuously from one amplitude to another (AM) or one frequency to another (FM). This continuous variation is called *analogue*. On the other hand, a digital signal is either high or low, there is no variation between the two.

Advantages of digital signals

Noise

When an electrical signal travels from A to B it is affected by changes in electric field that take place between A and B. This could be caused by lightning, electric machinery etc. When an analogue signal is changed by noise, it changes the signal, so music that is affected by noise will sound different. When a digital signal is affected by noise, the information carried is unaltered. Figure 14.17 shows the effect of noise on the signals shown. The analogue signal can be seen to be quite different whereas the digital on is just the same.

Figure 14.17 The effect of noise on an analogue signal and digital signal.

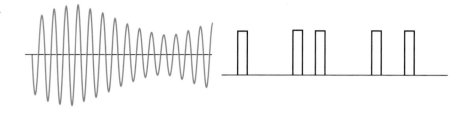

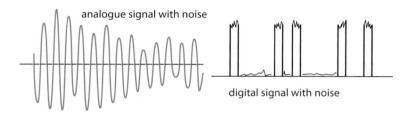

analogue signal with noise

digital signal with noise

Compression

If a music signal were to be compressed, the pitch of the music would become higher. Compressing a digital signal does not change the information, it just enables it to be transmitted more quickly.

Multiplexing

It is much simpler to multiplex digital signals than analogue ones.

Source independence

A digital signal is always a series of pulses independent of what type of information is being transmitted. This means speech, text, music and video can all be transmitted on the same signal.

Coding

By changing the sequence of the 1s and 0s in a predetermined way, a digital signal can be coded to prevent anyone not knowing the information (spies) from reading the message.

Data manipulation

A computer is a powerful tool that can only accept digital data. An advantage of using a digital signal is that we can use the computer to manipulate our data.

For these reasons it is very useful to convert analogue signals into data signals. A device designed to do this is called an *analogue to digital converter* (ADC).

The analogue to digital converter (ADC)

When a sound is converted into an electrical signal, a continuously varying pd is created. This can be transmitted through a wire and is an analogue signal.

Sampling

To convert an analogue signal into a digital one, it must be changed from a continuously changing pd to one that changes in steps. This is done by measuring the pd at regular intervals (sampling) then rounding those pds to the nearest whole number (quantizing).

Decimal	Binary
1	00000001
2	00000010
3	00000011
4	00000100
5	00000101
6	00000110

Table 5 The numbers 1–6 in binary.

By sampling the signal in Figure 14.18 once each second, it can be represented by the following numbers: 0,1,4,5,5,2,0,2,4,1. These can then be converted into binary form. Since the highest number is only 5 these can be represented by just 3 bits. So the first four numbers would therefore be 000 001 100 101.

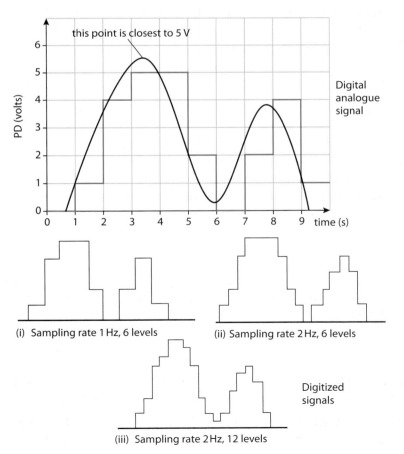

(i) Sampling rate 1 Hz, 6 levels

(ii) Sampling rate 2 Hz, 6 levels

(iii) Sampling rate 2 Hz, 12 levels

Figure 14.18 Converting an analogue signal into quantized levels.

Sampling rate

When this data is received, the original signal can be reconstructed. This is not exactly the same as the original signal. However it could be improved by increasing the sampling rate as in Figure 14.19 (ii).

Number of bits

It is also possible to reduce the gap between the steps by creating more levels to each volt. The representation of each volt by one digit can be increased to 2 digits per volt giving 12 quantized levels as in Figure 14.18 (iii). Increasing the number of quantized levels means that we need to increase the number of bits to 4. By increasing the sampling rate and using sufficient quantized levels, the signal can be quite close to the original. This system is used in digital sound recording.

Digital music (44.1kHz 16bit)

Digitally recorded music is very close to the original because the signal is sampled 44 100 times each second and the quantized levels are stored as 16-bit binary numbers. With 16 bits you can make 65 536 different numbers and so the equivalent number of quantized levels.

Exercises

11 Using a sampling rate of 1 Hz and 8 quantized levels, convert the analogue data shown in Figure 14.19 to a digital signal (you don't need to turn the signal into binary form, just give the answer as a list of base 10 numbers).

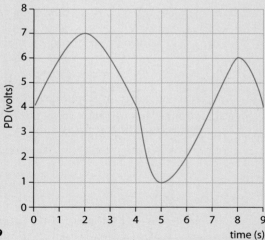

Figure 14.19

12 Convert the first 4s of data into 4-bit binary.

13 If a 5 minute piece of stereo music is recorded on a 16-bit 44 kHz MP3 player, how many bits of information will be recorded? How many bytes is that?

14 Use your answer to Exercise 13 to calculate how many hours of music can be recorded with 1 Gbyte of storage. If this is changed to MP3 format and it is compressed by a factor of 10, how many hours of music can you store on a 1 Gbyte MP3 player?

The complete system

The complete digital communication system can be represented by a block diagram.

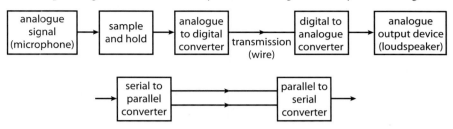

Figure 14.20 A block diagram for a digital communications system and its component parts.

Analogue signal

The original information to be communicated often starts off as an analogue signal, e.g. music. This must first be converted to an electrical signal by a microphone.

Sample and hold

The ADC works by comparing the instantaneous potential with a set number of predetermined quantized levels. This process cannot be performed instantaneously so the signal needs to be held for a short time. The sample and hold stage involves sampling the potential and holding the information so the ADC has time to process it. The time of the hold depends on the sampling rate of the ADC; if it is 44.1 kHz then the signal will be held for 20 μs.

Analogue to digital converter

The ADC takes the steady potential from the sample and hold stage and converts this to the nearest number of quantized levels. This is then converted to a binary number. The number of binary digits depends on how many quantized levels there are, but it is generally a multiple of 8 bits. The clock rate is also included in this data or sent on a separate cable, this is the rate at which the bits are sent. If the sampling is done at 44 kHz and converted to 32 bits then the clock rate would be 32×44 kHz = 1.4 MHz.

Transmission

The digital signal can now be transmitted to the receiver. This can be through a single wire, optical fibre or radio wave (more about this in the next section). The signal is said to be serial since all the information is in a line. However it can be sent along parallel wires if first changed into a parallel signal with a serial to parallel converter.

Digital to analogue converter

The DAC decodes the binary information and clock data to convert the series of 1s and 0s to a changing potential. If the receiver is a digital device such as a computer this stage is not needed.

Exercise

15 If an ADC converts an analogue signal to 16 bits at a rate of 1 MHz
    (a) for how long must the signal be held in the sample and hold stage?
    (b) what is the clock rate of the ADC?

The use of the interface in physical measurements

It is likely that you have used a computer interface or data logger during the practical part of your physics course. This is a device that takes a signal from a sensor and passes it on to a computer. The information coming in to the interface is always a potential; the interface converts this to a binary code so a computer can process it.

A data logger.

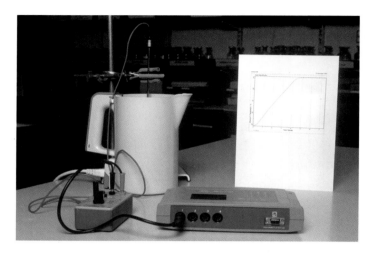

A photo gate is a digital sensor.

Digital sensors

A photo gate is an example of a digital sensor. This is because the photo gate has only two outputs: high or low and nothing in between. The photo gate consists of an IR beam and a detector. When the detector receives the beam, a 5 V potential is created, and if the beam is blocked the potential is 0 V. The interface records the time of a change, converts this into binary code and sends the signal to a computer.

Analogue sensor

Most sensors used in physics experiments are analogue sensors. These produce a continually varying potential. An example of an analogue sensor is a temperature sensor. This gives out a potential that is proportional to the temperature. The interface samples this potential, converts it to a binary code and sends it to the computer.

A temperature sensor is an analogue sensor.

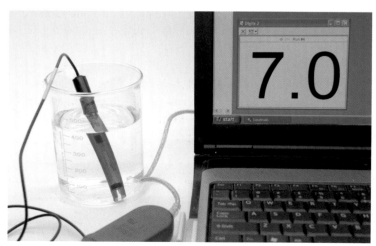

Sampling rate

The sampling rate of the ADC is set by the computer software. A rapidly changing quantity will need to be sampled often; a typical school interface will be able to sample up to 250 000 times a second. If the signal is alternating then the sampling rate must be more than twice the frequency of the signal. You can get some very strange results if you don't sample fast enough, as shown in Figure 14.21.

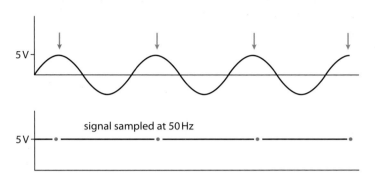

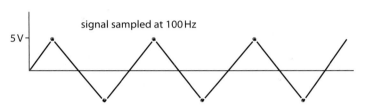

Figure 14.21 A potential alternating at 50 Hz is sampled at 50 Hz and 100 Hz.

Exercises

16 If a data logger can sample at a maximum rate of 10 kHz, what is the highest frequency signal that it can measure?

Optic fibre transmission

Assessment statements

F.3.1 Explain what is meant by critical angle and total internal reflection.

F.3.2 Solve problems involving refractive index and critical angle.

F.3.3 Apply the concept of total internal reflection to the transmission of light along fibres.

F.3.4 Describe the effects of material dispersion and modal dispersion.

F.3.5 Explain what is meant by attenuation and solve problems involving attenuation measured in decibels (dB).

F.3.6 Describe the variation with wavelength of the attenuation of radiation in the core of a monomode fibre.

F.3.7 State what is meant by noise in an optic fibre.

F.3.8 Describe the role of amplifiers and reshapers in optic fibre transmission.

F.3.9 Solve problems involving optic fibres.

The light emitted from the ends of the fibres make a nice pattern.

Figure 14.22 ▶

Refraction of light

Light has different speeds in different materials. If light passes from one material to another, the change in speed causes the light to change direction. If the speed of the light increases, it is deflected towards the boundary between the two materials as in Figure 14.22.

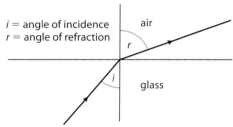

i = angle of incidence
r = angle of refraction

air

glass

(i) Light refracted from glass to air.

Snells law tells us that

$$\frac{\sin i}{\sin r} = \text{the refractive index from glass to air}$$

The critical angle

If the angle of incidence increases, a point will be reached where the refracted ray is refracted along the boundary. The angle at which this happens is called the *critical angle*.

C = critical angle   air

glass

(ii) Light refracted at 90°.

Applying Snell's law to this situation:

$$\frac{\sin C}{\sin 90} = \text{refractive index from glass to air}$$

$\sin C$ = refractive index from glass to air

Refractive index is usually measured from air to glass, but

$$\text{Refractive index (air-glass)} = \frac{1}{\text{Refractive index (glass-air)}}$$

$$\text{So } \sin C = \frac{1}{\text{Refractive index (air-glass)}}$$

Refractive index(air-glass) = 1.5

$$\text{So } \sin C = \frac{1}{1.5}$$

$$C = 42°$$

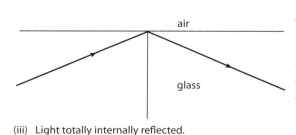

air

glass

(iii) Light totally internally reflected.

Total internal reflection

If the critical angle is exceeded, all of the light is reflected. This is known as *total internal reflection*. Since all the light is reflected none is transmitted. This is not the case when light is reflected off a mirror when some is absorbed.

Optical fibre

An optical fibre is a thin strand of glass or clear plastic. If a ray of light enters its end at a small angle, the ray will be total internally reflected when it meets the side. Since the sides are parallel, the ray will be reflected back and forth until it reaches the other end as in Figure 14.23. Optical fibres are used extensively in communication.

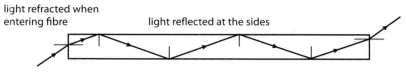

light refracted when entering fibre

light reflected at the sides

Figure 14.23 Light reflected along a fibre.

Step indexed

Actual fibres have two layers. The light reflects at the boundary between the layers, this is so fibres can be bundled together. This is called *step indexed* since there is a step in refractive index between the core and sheath.

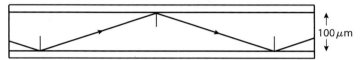

$100\,\mu m$

Figure 14.24 A step-indexed multimode fibre.

Modal dispersion

Not all rays of light enter one end of the fibre and come out of the other, only certain waves make it. The possible paths are called *modes*.

The more direct modes reach the end first. This can cause problems with data transfer as bits of data might not arrive in the correct order. It is possible to make very thin fibres that only allow one mode; these are called *mono-mode fibres*.

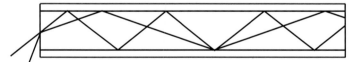

Figure 14.25 There are different possible paths along a fibre.

Material dispersion

When light passes through a prism, different frequencies are refracted by different amounts, causing the colours to disperse. When light travels down a fibre, different frequencies have different paths, as in Figure 14.26.

This will cause a problem if different bits of data arrive at the wrong time.

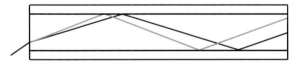

Figure 14.26 Different frequencies have different paths.

Exercises

17 Light enters a glass block of refractive index 1.5 at an angle 70° as shown in Figure 14.27.
   (a) Use Snells Law to calculate the angle of refraction θ_1.
   (b) Use geometry to find the angle θ_2.
   (c) Calculate the critical angle for glass.
   (d) Will the ray be totally internally reflected?
   (e) Calculate length D.

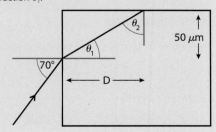

θ_2

$50\,\mu m$

θ_1

70°

D

Figure 14.27

Attenuation

Attenuation is the opposite of amplification. If a signal is attenuated its power gets less. Attenuation is measured in decibels (dB).

The decibel

A decibel is a measurement of power with relation to some fixed value. The scale is logarithmic rather than linear; in other words, a change from 1 dB to 2 dB is not the same as a change from 2 dB to 3 dB.

When we use dB to measure attenuation, it gives a measure of how much the power of a signal has been reduced.

The way it is calculated is with the formula:

Table 6 Remember $\log_{10}x$ is the power you would have to raise 10 to in order to make x.

$\log_{10}(1) = 0$	$10^0 = 1$
$\log_{10}(10) = 1$	$10^1 = 10$
$\log_{10}(100) = 2$	$10^2 = 100$
$\log_{10}(1000) = 3$	$10^3 = 1000$

$$\text{Attenuation} = 10\log_{10}\left(\frac{P_{in}}{P_{out}}\right)$$

Where P_{in} is the original power and P_{out} the power after attenuation. The factor 10 is to convert from bels to decibels.

Table 7 Attenuation table

Power in (mW)	Power out (mW)	Attenuation (dB)
1	0.9	0.46
1	0.8	0.97
1	0.7	1.55
1	0.6	2.22

Fibre type	Attenuation
Multimode	0.8 dB/km
Monomode	0.3 dB/km

Worked example

If the power in to a fibre is 1 mW and the power out is 0.01 mW, calculate the attenuation.

Solution

$$\text{Attenuation} = 10\log_{10}(\frac{1}{0.01}) = \mathbf{20\ dB}$$

Attenuation in fibres

The attenuation of an optical fibre is related to its length, so when calculating the attenuation of a fibre, attenuation per km is calculated.

Worked example

If the attenuation of a fibre is 0.3 dB/km what is the power of a 1 mW signal after 5 km?

Solution

If attenuation is 0.3 dB/km then attenuation in 5 km is 1.5 dB

From the definition of dB, $1.5 = 10 \log_{10}\left(\dfrac{1}{P_{out}}\right)$

$0.15 = \log_{10}\left(\dfrac{1}{P_{out}}\right)$

$10^{0.15} = \dfrac{1}{P_{out}}$ 10^x is the inverse of $\log 10^x$.

$1.41 = \dfrac{1}{P_{out}}$

$P_{out} = \mathbf{0.71\ mW}$

Attenuation and wavelength

The attenuation of light in an optical fibre is different for different wavelengths. To minimize attenuation, wavelengths with low attenuation should be used.

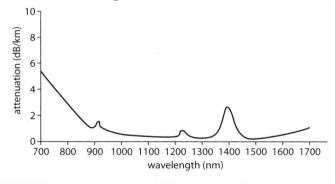

Figure 14.28 This shows attenuation against wavelength for an optical fibre.

Exercises

18 The power into a fibre is 1 mW. Calculate the attenuation if the power out is;
  (a) 0.1 mW   **(b)** 0.2 mW   **(c)** 0.01 mW

19 The attenuation of light in a given fibre is 2 dB/km.
  (a) What is the attenuation after 5 km of fibre?
  (b) If a signal of 1 mW is sent into 5 km of fibre, what is the power of the signal that comes out?

20 By looking at the graph in Figure 14.28, decide if a wavelength of 1400 nm would be a good choice for sending a signal along this fibre.

Amplification in optical fibres

As light travels along a fibre its power becomes less. For long-distance communication the signal therefore needs to be amplified. Amplification can be achieved by inserting a length of fibre that has the addition of atoms that give out light when the signal passes. This is called *stimulated emission* and is used in the operation of lasers. The added (doped) atoms are selected so that the light they emit is the same wavelength as the signal. They are first excited (pumped) by a laser, and then when the signal passes they give out light in the same direction and in phase.

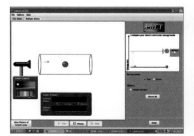

This simulation from PhET shows how a laser works. To view, visit www.heinemann.co.uk/hotlinks, enter the express code 4266S and click on Weblink 14.4.

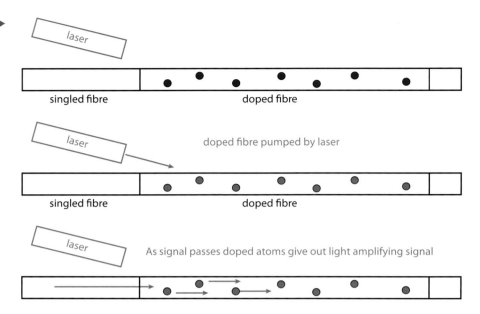

Figure 14.29 A doped fibre used to amplify the signal. The doped atoms are excited by a laser. The signal causes the doped atoms to emit radiation.

laser

singled fibre   doped fibre

laser   doped fibre pumped by laser

singled fibre   doped fibre

laser   As signal passes doped atoms give out light amplifying signal

Noise

Since light is not a radio frequency it is not affected by interference with RF sources, however there is some noise created on amplification. Some of the atoms pumped can give out light before the signal arrives. The effect of this noise can be reduced by reshaping the signal.

Comparing optical fibres to copper cables

Compared to copper coaxial cables, optical fibres:
- have much greater bandwidth due to higher frequencies used
- have less attenuation
- have greater security since it is very difficult to tap into an optical fibre
- have no noise due to RF interference
- are lighter and thinner
- are more expensive.

 14.4 # Channels of communication

Assessment statements

F.4.1   Outline different channels of communication, including wire pairs, coaxial cables, optic fibres, radio waves and satellite communication.

F.4.2   Discuss the uses and the relative advantages and disadvantages of wire pairs, coaxial cables, optic fibres and radio waves.

F.4.3   State what is meant by a geostationary satellite.

F.4.4   State the order of magnitude of the frequencies used for communication with geostationary satellites, and explain why the up-link frequency and the down-link frequency are different.

F.4.5   Discuss the relative advantages and disadvantages of the use of geostationary and of polar-orbiting satellites for communication.

F.4.6   Discuss the moral, ethical, economic and environmental issues arising from satellite communication.

A digital signal is a varying potential which can be sent from A to B by connecting a conducting wire between A and B. The wire is called a *communication channel*. Applying a changing potential to one end of the wire causes a changing potential at the other. Alternatively, the signal can be changed into electromagnetic radiation and sent as a radio signal.

Types of cable

Wire pairs

Wire pairs are the cheapest form of cable, consisting of two insulated wires that can either be parallel or twisted. The main problem with this form of cable is that the strength of the signal gets less as the length of the cable increases. This is attenuation. There are several reasons for this:

- Resistance: the resistance of a wire is proportional to its length. The resistance of the wire causes energy to be lost in the form of heat. This can be minimized by making the wires out of a material with low resistivity.
- Radiation losses: the changing electric field in the wire creates a changing electric and magnetic field that radiates from the wire This can also lead to interference between the wires or 'cross talk'.

Attenuation also increases with frequency so wire pairs can only be used for long range low frequency signals such as telephone or short range high frequency signals as in the communication between computers. Wire pairs can transfer data at a rate of several Mb/s over short distances.

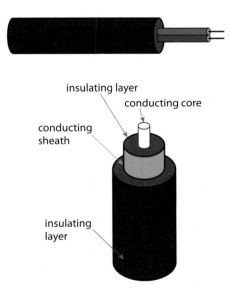

insulating layer

conducting core

conducting sheath

insulating layer

Figure 14.30 Comparison of a cable pair and coaxial cable.

Coaxial cables

The two conductors in coaxial cables consist of a core surrounded by a sheath; the two are separated by an insulator.

The attenuation in a coaxial cable is much less a wire pair because the outer sheath prevents the loss of signal by radiation. It also prevents disturbance of the signal from outside sources. Coaxial cables are use for transmission of the TV signal from the aerial to the TV set and also for long range internet connections. It is possible to transfer data at a rate of several Gb/s over short distances with a coaxial cable.

Using radio waves to transmit digital information

Radio waves are a continuous variation of electric and magnetic fields so they are themselves analogue signals. However, they can be used to transmit a digital signal in the same way as they are used to transmit an analogue signal. This is done by modulating the wave.

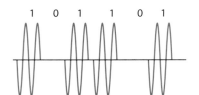 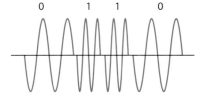

Amplitude modulation

The amplitude is modulated between two values as in Figure 14.31. This is different from AM radio where the amplitude varies continuously.

Frequency modulation

The frequency of the carrier wave is modulated between two frequencies, one representing 1 and the other 0. Computers can communicate with each other via wireless internet connections by using modulated radio waves.

Bandwidth

Remember that when a wave is modulated the wave changes from having one frequency to being made up of many frequencies, all added together to give the final wave shape. The digitally modulated waves have a wide bandwidth. This becomes is a problem when using radio frequencies to transmit digital signals, since all the available bands are already used by radio stations.

Microwave

Microwaves are high frequency electromagnetic waves that when modulated enable a high rate of data transfer. Microwaves do not travel very far in the atmosphere and will not pass through concrete buildings. It is for this reason that the 'point to point' communication is necessary: the receiver must be in the 'line of sight' of the transmitter. The advantage is that no cables need to be laid. Microwaves are commonly used for wireless connections at home and in public places and in long range situations where there is a line of sight.

Note: The radio wave is always analogue, it is the information that is digital.

Light

Light has a frequency in the order of 10^{14} Hz. With such a high frequency a very high rate of data transfer is possible. Light can undergo amplitude modulation, in simplest terms, by switching on and off. The speed at which this can be done is currently the limiting factor to the maximum speed of data transfer using light. Other factors affecting the use of light is that the signal must be point to point, and it is affected by weather and other atmospherics. One way round this is to transmit the light signal in an optical fibre.

Satellite communication

Using high frequency modulated radio waves to transmit digital information would be an attractive possibility if it were not for the fact that the transmitter and receiver must be in direct line of contact with each other (line of sight). Therefore, to communicate over long distances, a chain of transmitters and receivers must be constructed. An alternative is to use a satellite to transfer the signal as in Figure 14.32.

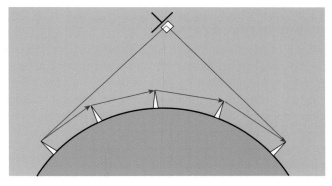

◀ **Figure 14.32** Signal transmitted from antenna to antenna and the alternative route via a satellite.

Geostationary satellites

A satellite is an object that travels around the centre of the Earth in a circular path. They are only useful for communication purposes if they stay in the same place. The Earth completes a full rotation once a day and, in order to stay above the same point on the Earth, a satellite must circle the Earth at the same rate and have the same axis of rotation. To make this possible the satellites are positioned above the equator. These are called *geostationary satellites*.

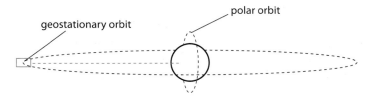

◀ **Figure 14.33** Comparison of a polar and geostationary orbits. Polar satellites can orbit the Earth at a height of only 1000 km with a period of 2 hours. Geostationary satellites are always above the same point and orbit the Earth once a day at a height of 35 786 km.

Satellite TV

Geostationary satellites are used to transmit satellite TV stations. A TV broadcasting company transmits a microwave signal at a chosen uplink frequency (12–14 GHz) from a transmitter on Earth. The satellite receives the signal and sends it back to Earth at a different frequency, the downlink frequency. The reason for the change in frequency is to avoid interference with the uplink signal. On reaching the Earth, the signal is focused using a parabolic dish and decoded with a receiver. Since the satellite is far from the Earth, the signal will cover a large area. Satellite TV uses a compressed digital signal; the high frequency (12–14 GHz) gives a broad bandwidth, allowing a rapid transfer of data. The signal from one satellite can transmit up to 200 TV channels.

 Kepler's Law
The square of the time for the satellite to complete one orbit (time period) is proportional to the cube of the orbit radius.
$$T^2 \propto R^3$$
This means that satellites in low orbits go around the Earth in less time than satellites in high orbits.

Polar satellites

A polar satellite orbits the North or South Poles. These satellites have a much lower orbit than geostationary ones and travel much faster. Using these satellites it is possible to take a signal from one place on the Earth and transfer it to another, this information could be stored and used later: every two hours you would receive the

When a satellite is in polar orbit, it is possible to synchronize the orbit with the Sun, so that the satellite is always on the sunny side of the Earth. This is an advantage if the satellite is used for taking photos.

The Outer Space Treaty: Signed by 98 countries, this is a legal framework set up to control the use of outer space. To find more information, visit www.heinemann.co.uk/hotlinks, enter the express code 4266Sand click on Website 14.5.

information for the next hour of TV programmes. Alternatively, if several satellites are used, then the orbits can be arranged so that there is always one in view. This system is used to provide satellite TV for some areas of Russia that are too far north to be in line with geostationary satellites positioned over the equator.

Since these satellites are much closer to the Earth they are much cheaper to put in orbit and do not need to transmit such a powerful signal as the geostationary satellites.

Communication in remote areas

One of the benefits of satellite communication is that it is possible to reach parts of the world that are inaccessible with land-based systems. After a major earthquake or other natural disaster the ground-based communication systems, such as telephone wires and radio antennae, are often destroyed making communication impossible. Satellite systems are unaffected by such disasters and are invaluable to rescue teams working in the area.

International understanding

Land-based TV systems lie within national boundaries whereas satellite systems do not. Satellite systems, therefore, give many possibilities for cross cultural exchange. Viewers can watch news programmes with different perspectives, entertainment from other countries, or foreign language programmes that can aid language education. Communication leads to understanding and international communication leads to international understanding.

Environmental concerns

Using satellites for communication reduces the need to lay cables and/or build many transmitter aerials on the ground. In this way it can be seen as an environmentally friendly means of communication. However, to put a satellite into orbit requires large amounts of fuel and so creates a large amount of pollution. In addition, launch pads have to be built in places away from large cities and may be in environmentally sensitive areas.

Colonizing space

There are ethical questions that need to be taken into consideration when using satellites for communication. Who owns space? Is space owned by the first country that put its flag there? Can anyone take over a piece of space for their satellite? What if two countries want to use the same piece of space, who decides who can use it?

Exercises

21 If the radius of a geostationary satellite is 42 000 km, what is the radius of a satellite with an orbit of 2 hours?

22 What is the speed of the satellite in Exercise 21?

23 If the radius of the Earth is 6400 km, what is the height of the satellite above the Earth?

Digitalizing everything

Most of the information we gain from our surroundings using our senses is analogue information; that is it continuously varies rather than happening in discrete steps. For example, when we use our sight to look at a scene, we see a continuous variation of colour and intensity, or when we listen to music we hear a continuous variation of frequency and loudness. We have seen in this chapter how it is possible to convert analogue to digital signals and how it is then possible to send this information with great speed along wires, optical fibres or via radio waves from one place to another. So it is possible to take pictures and sounds, digitalize them, process them with a computer then send them from one place to another at the speed of light. This is the basis of the Internet.

The internet

From the early days of computing in the 1950s it was possible to send data from one computer to another, through a system called a *network*. The internet is far more extensive than this, for every computer can communicate with all the other computers that are connected. You may say this is just like the phone system. However, when you use the phone, the wires are connected by a system of switches called the telephone exchange. Once connected, your wires stay connected until you put the phone down; this is called a *circuit switching network*. The internet became a reality when *packet switching networks* became possible in the 1960s. Since the signal between computers is digital it can be split into packets, compressed and transmitted. When received it can be reassembled. As long as the bits are put back in the correct order, the signal can be mixed up with other data and even sent along different routes. So, unlike a telephone conversation where information is directed from one person to another, the information on the internet can be transmitted in bits. This packet switching system was developed by the military, so that vital information could be easily spread accross different locations rather than being stored on one vulnerable computer.

Tim Berners-Lee, inventor of the World Wide Web, who made his idea freely available, with no patent and no royalties due.

Advantages of the internet

Multiple communications

One of the main advantages of the internet is that you can communicate with many people at the same time. For example, sending an email to all the people on your address list, or posting an article for sale on eBay so anyone in the world can buy it.

Sharing information

With the internet came web pages which could be opened using a browser and contained information in the form of text and pictures. This has made web-based research, weblogs and social networking sites (such as Facebook and MySpace) accessible to everyone with an internet connection.

Business

It wasn't long after the initial development of the internet that businesses started to see the possible benefits. With its own internet site even a small business can advertise its products to the whole world. This is not only beneficial to the owners of the business but also to the consumers who can now find products, compare prices and even read consumer reports before deciding to buy something. The buying process can take place online, with Paypal for instance, and then a check on a bank balance can also take place online. With the advent of digitalizing and encoding signals, it has been possible for the internet to handle secure information such as credit card numbers and bank account details.

The internet was made possible by rapid advancement of technology but with its development have come many unforeseen problems. Are there some technologies that are best left undeveloped and who should decide whether to develop a new technology or not?

Global perspective
Since the Internet had no central place or point of control, anyone could make a web page and share their experiences, knowledge, ideas and opinions. A certain knowledge of the programming language HTML was required but soon many individuals were mastering the procedure and making their own web pages. In recent years the process has been simplified so that any computer-literate individual can make their own webpage or write a blog.

Some problems

One of the great things about the internet is the freedom it offers, for it isn't owned by anybody or run by anybody and anyone can use it. This of course, isn't quite true, since individuals must abide by the laws of the country they live in. However, the web is worldwide and different countries have different laws. Needless to say, this freedom of expression has brought its own problems, some of which are outlined below.

Copyright infringement

As the speed of the signal increased it became possible to send not only pictures and text but also sound and video files. This made it possible to share the latest music and video; all it needed was for one person to buy a CD or DVD, copy it onto their computer and allow the world to copy it. Although this is illegal, it can be difficult to stop.

Pornography

In some countries around the world pornography is illegal. In the days before the internet, pornographic material would have to be smuggled from country to country. The internet opened up a whole new way of distributing pornography that was instantly exploited. Apart from the problem of monitoring the legality of content in different countries, there also came the problem of ensuring that the material was not viewed by young children. The 'Do not enter if under 18' signs probably did little to solve this problem.

Extreme views

An individual with extreme views living in a small community may not find many people who share those views. However, with the world as an audience through the internet it is very likely that groups of like-minded people will be able to come together.

Gambling

The ability to exchange money online opened up the possibility of online gambling. Here there is often no regulation, no doormen who check identity and refuse entry to those who are under age or have had too much to drink. Gambling online at home can take place 24/7 with no restrictions.

Plagiarism

Students writing essays (and authors writing books) have instant access to millions of sources of information; they also have access to completed essays. Plagiarism is nothing new but has become a bigger problem through the internet.

Spam

The ability to send emails to millions of people at the same time is open to abuse by those pushing material and information on to people who don't want it.

1 This question is about refractive index and critical angle.

The diagram right shows the boundary between glass and air.

(a) On the diagram, draw a ray of light to illustrate what is meant by critical angle. Mark the critical angle with the letter "c". (3)

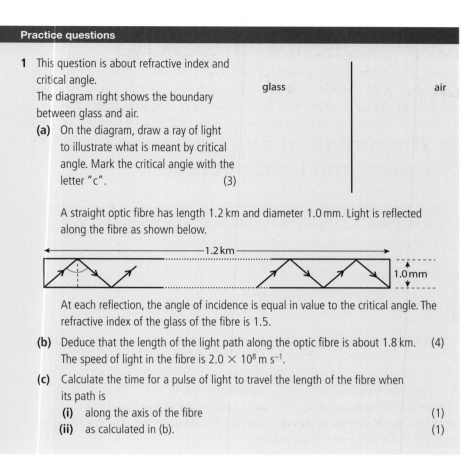

A straight optic fibre has length 1.2 km and diameter 1.0 mm. Light is reflected along the fibre as shown below.

At each reflection, the angle of incidence is equal in value to the critical angle. The refractive index of the glass of the fibre is 1.5.

(b) Deduce that the length of the light path along the optic fibre is about 1.8 km. (4)

The speed of light in the fibre is 2.0×10^8 m s^{-1}.

(c) Calculate the time for a pulse of light to travel the length of the fibre when its path is

    (i) along the axis of the fibre (1)

    (ii) as calculated in (b). (1)

For additional practice questions and answers, please visit www.heinemann.co.uk/hotlinks, enter the express code 4266 S and click on Weblink 14.6.

Electromagnetic waves (Option G)

The nature of electromagnetic (EM) waves and light sources

Assessment statements

G.1.1 Outline the nature of EM radiation.
G.1.2 Describe the different regions of the EM spectrum.
G.1.3 Describe what is meant by the dispersion of EM waves.
G.1.4 Describe the dispersion of EM waves in terms of the dependence of refractive index on wavelength.
G.1.5 Distinguish between transmission, absorption and scattering of radiation.
G.1.6 Discuss examples of the transmission, absorption and scattering of EM radiation.
G.1.7 Explain the terms *monochromatic* and *coherent*.
G.1.8 Identify laser light as a source of coherent light.
G.1.9 Outline the mechanism for the production of laser light.
G.1.10 Outline an application of the use of a laser.

Scottish physicist James Clerk Maxwell (1831–1879) who discovered the magnetic field associated with a changing electric field.

The origin of EM radiation

If your physics teacher were to bring a charged object into class, it would make your hair stand on end, not because it is frightening but because your hairs would be repelling each other. The way we explain how this can happen, even though the object is not touching you, is by defining an electric field. This is a region of space where we feel the effect of electric charge. Students at the back of the room wouldn't feel such a large effect since the field gets less with distance. If the charge is now moved away from the students everyone will feel a change, the field will be weaker and everyone's hair will go down. This spreading out of disturbance is like the spreading out of a water wave when a stone is dropped into a pool of water, except the disturbance is of an electric field not the surface of water.

When a charge is moved, a second field is created, a magnetic field. (This is what happens when a current flows through a wire). The direction of the magnetic field is perpendicular to the electric field. The result is that when a charge is moved, a changing electric and magnetic field spreads out. If this disturbance meets a different medium we find that it is reflected and refracted. When it passes through a small opening, it is diffracted and two different disturbances interfere. These are the properties of a wave and this is called an *electromagnetic wave*.

Creating an electromagnetic wave

An electromagnetic wave can be created by passing an alternating current through a wire as shown in Figure 15.2. Waves created in this way are called *radio waves*. James Maxwell found that it was not the moving charge that caused the magnetic field but the changing electric field that caused the charge to move. This explains how electromagnetic waves can travel through a vacuum: the changing fields induce each other. Maxwell also calculated that the speed of the wave in a vacuum was approximately $3 \times 10^8 \, \text{m s}^{-1}$. This value was about the same as the measured value for the speed of light, so close in fact, that Maxwell concluded that light was an electromagnetic wave.

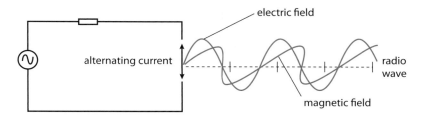

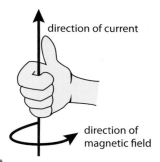

Figure 15.1 The right-hand grip rule. If a wire is gripped as shown, the fingers show the direction of the magnetic field and the thumb shows the current direction.

Figure 15.2 An alternating current produces a radio wave.

How light is produced

The difference between light and radio waves is the frequency. Light waves have a much higher frequency than radio waves. However, it is not possible to produce light by simply moving a charge up and down very fast, as it is not possible to change the direction of charge quickly enough.

Light comes from the individual atom. Atoms contain electrons that can exist in different energy levels. When an electron changes from a high energy level to a low one it gives out energy in the form of electromagnetic radiation. The frequency of the light, f, is related to the change in energy ΔE by the equation:

$$\Delta E = hf$$

where h = Planck's constant $6.6 \times 10^{-34} \, \text{m}^2 \, \text{kg s}^{-1}$

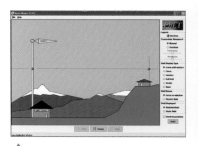

The PhET simulation 'Radio Waves' shows the components of a wave. To view, visit www.heineman.co.uk/hotlinks, enter the express code 4266S and click on Weblink 15.1.

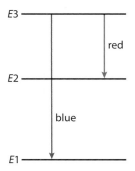

Figure 15.3 Since there are many electron energy levels in an atom this leads to the emission of light with many different frequencies, each frequency corresponding to a different colour.

Even higher frequencies

Electron energy levels are in the order of 10 eV. This is $10 \times 1.6 \times 10^{-19}$ J.

Using the formula $\Delta E = hf$, an energy change of 10 eV will give rise to light with a frequency of 2.42×10^{15} Hz. However, EM radiation with much higher frequency, over 10^{20} Hz, does exist. This would need an energy change in the order of MeV, much greater than electron energies. Radiation with such high energy comes from the nucleus.

1. Calculate the frequency of light emitted when an electron changes from an energy of 10 eV to 6 eV

2. An atom has electrons that can exist in 4 different energy levels, 10 eV, 9 eV, 7 eV and 2 eV. Calculate:
   (a) the highest frequency radiation that can be produced
   (b) the lowest frequency radiation.

3. What energy change would be required to produce EM radiation with a frequency of 1×10^{18} Hz?

The electromagnetic spectrum (EM spectrum)

Wavelength

The frequency of electromagnetic waves can range from almost 0 Hz up to 10^{20} Hz. The speed of all electromagnetic radiation is $3 \times 10^8 \, \text{m s}^{-1}$. Using the formula $v = f\lambda$ we can calculate the wavelength of the waves.

Figure 15.4 The electromagnetic spectrum. Waves can be classified in terms of their wavelength. Each range of wavelength has a different name, different mode of production and different uses.

● **Examiner's hint:** Note that the regions are not clearly separated, For example, there is considerable overlap between X-rays and gamma rays.

Why do humans use the visible range of frequencies to see? With all these different types of EM radiation you may wonder why we use the frequencies we do. Well, most of the light we use to see comes from the Sun. This contains many more frequencies than just the visible light; however most of the frequencies are absorbed when the radiation passes through the atmosphere. It's also true that if we used radio to see then we would have to have antennae instead of eyes and that wouldn't look very attractive!

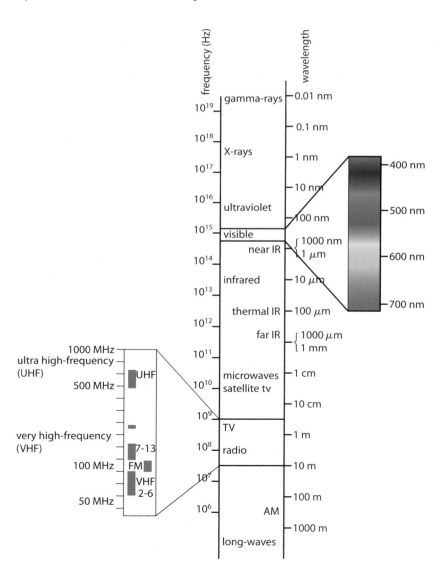

Worked example

What is the wavelength of green light with a frequency of 6×10^{14} Hz?

Solution

Rearranging $v = f\lambda$ gives $\lambda = \dfrac{v}{f}$

so the wavelength of green light $= \dfrac{3 \times 10^8}{6 \times 10^{14}}$ m

$\lambda = 500 \times 10^{-9}$ m

Radio waves

Radio waves are produced from an alternating current in a tuned electrical circuit. Radio waves are used in communication; they are split into smaller subdivisions according to frequency. High frequency waves can carry more information per unit time than low frequency waves, so they are used for the rapid transfer of information required by satellite TV and the internet. Low frequency radio is used by the traditional radio stations.

Microwaves

Microwaves are produced by oscillations of electrons in a vacuum. The EM wave produced resonates in a hollow metal tube to produce a beam. Microwaves are also emitted when certain semiconductors are excited. Microwaves of frequency 2450 MHz resonate with water molecules, the molecules vibrate and the increased kinetic energy implies an increase in temperature. Microwaves of this frequency are used in cooking. Since microwaves have a high frequency they can be used to transfer data at the speed required for satellite TV broadcasts and short-range internet links.

Infrared

When a body is given heat, the internal energy of the body increases; in other words the atoms gain energy. Atoms can lose this energy in the form of electromagnetic radiation. The frequency of the radiation depends on the temperature of the body. Bodies at room temperature give out radiation at around 10^{13} Hz. This is classified as infrared. Infrared is used in TV remote controls and optical communications. It is also used in night vision binoculars to see warm objects in the absence of visible light.

Visible light

Visible light is in the range of frequencies that our eyes are sensitive to. Our brains respond to different frequencies by seeing them as different colours: red is the lowest frequency and blue the highest.

Colour	Wavelength
violet	380–450 nm
blue	450–495 nm
green	495–570 nm
yellow	570–590 nm
orange	590–620 nm
red	620–750 nm

◀ **Table 1** The visible spectrum.

Ultraviolet

Ultraviolet radiation is produced by high energy electron transitions. Ultraviolet cannot be seen but does cause the emission of visible light from some substances. This is why white clothes glow when illuminated by ultraviolet disco lights.

X-rays

X-ray radiation is high frequency radiation emitted when high energy electrons collide with a metal target. X-rays affect photographic film and can pass through matter. A photograph taken with X-radiation will therefore reveal the inside of an object. This has many applications in medicine.

Gamma radiation (γ)

Gamma radiation is emitted when a nucleus loses energy after a nuclear reaction. These energies are typically in the order of MeVs resulting in radiation with a frequency in the region of 10^{20} Hz. Gamma radiation is even more penetrating than X-rays.

Exercises

Use the spectrum in Figure 15.4 to find out what type of radiation the following wavelengths would be and calculate their frequency:

4 430 nm

5 3.75 m

6 10 μm

7 1 nm

Radio waves spread out in a sphere centred on the source.

The interaction of EM radiation with matter

Transmission/absorption

When EM radiation is produced, changing electric and magnetic fields spread out in three dimensions from the source: we say that the wave is transmitted through the medium. The intensity of a wave is the power per unit area, as the wave becomes more spread out its intensity becomes less.

If the power in the whole wave is P then at a distance r this power is spread over a sphere of area $4\pi r^2$. The intensity, I, at a distance, r, is therefore $I = \dfrac{P}{4\pi r^2}$. In other words $I \propto \dfrac{1}{r^2}$. This is called an *inverse square relationship*.

As the wave spreads out it interacts with atoms of the medium. If an interaction takes place the radiation is absorbed. This can only happen if the energy given up ($\Delta E = hf$) is the correct amount to excite the medium. This is why: microwaves are absorbed by water molecules; IR radiation is absorbed by atoms in solids; and UV radiation is absorbed by the ozone layer. However, the energy in an X-ray is too high to excite an atomic electron and it can pass through most solids.

Reflection

When EM radiation lands on an object it will either be absorbed or transmitted. On absorption the radiation can be re-emitted and this is called reflection. The colour of objects can be explained in terms of reflection and absorption of different wavelengths of light. If a mixture of red, blue and green light is shone onto a blue object the red and green is absorbed but the blue is reflected.

Refraction

EM radiation travels at different speeds in different mediums. When a wave passes from one medium to another the change in speed causes its direction to change. This explains why a ray of light bends when it passes through a block of glass.

Dispersion

The angle of refraction is dependent on the wavelength of the radiation. If red light and blue light both pass into a block of glass the blue light bends more than the red. This is why rainbows are produced when white light passes through a prism.

Dispersion of light by a prism.

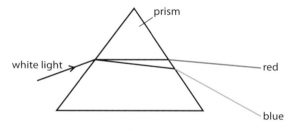

Figure 15.5 When white light is passed through a prism then blue light is refracted more than red light.

Exercises

8   If a light bulb emits 50 W of light what will its intensity be at a distance of 10 m?

9   If intensity of the radiation from the Sun reaching the Earth's atmosphere is 1400 W m^{-2} and the Sun is 146×10^9 m from the Earth, calculate the power of the Sun.

Scattering

When light interacts with small particles such as air molecules or water droplets, it is re-emitted at a different angle, and this causes the light to be scattered. The angle of scattering is dependant on the wavelength of light. Blue light is scattered more than red, this is why the sky and glacier ice look blue.

You can see this glacier because light from the Sun (above) is scattered sideways by the ice. The blue colour is because blue light is scattered most.

EM radiation and health

When electromagnetic radiation is absorbed by human tissue the effect is dependent on the wavelength.

Radio – microwave

When radio waves are absorbed by the body, they cause a slight heating, but do not change the structure of the cells. There seems to be no physical reason why they should cause illness, but cases of illness have been attributed to closeness to a powerful source of radio waves such as a radio antenna. The higher frequency of microwaves used in mobile phone communication means that the heating effects are greater but the power of the signal is weak. There is some evidence that a mobile phone held close to the brain for a long period of time might cause some damage. There is however, significant risk for people dependent on electronic devices such as pacemakers, that interference from strong sources of radio signals can result in malfunction.

IR

The heating effect caused by infrared radiation is significant: exposure to IR can result in burns but low levels of IR cause no harm.

Light

High powered sources of visible light, such as lasers, can damage the eyes and burn the skin.

UV

Exposure to ultraviolet radiation triggers the release of chemicals in the skin that cause redness and swelling. The effect is rather like a burn, hence the name sunburn. UV radiation can also change the structure of the skin's DNA leading to skin cancer.

Ouch!

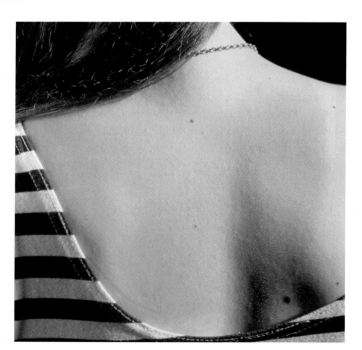

X-ray and γ ray

Both X-rays and γ (gamma) rays have enough energy to remove electrons from atoms; this is called ionization. When radiation ionizes atoms that are part of a living cell it can affect the ability of the cell to carry out its function or even cause the cell wall to be ruptured. If a large number of cells that are part of a vital organ are affected then this can lead to death. To prevent this there are strict limits to the exposure of individuals to these forms of radiation.

Sources of light

Light is produced when atomic electrons change from a high energy level to a low one. Electrons must first be given energy to reach the high energy level. This can be achieved in a variety of ways.

The light bulb

A light bulb consists of a thin wire filament enclosed in a glass ball. When an electric current flows through the filament, energy is transferred to the filament. This causes the filament to get hot and electrons to become excited (lifted to a higher energy level). Each time an excited electron falls back down to its low energy level a pulse of light is emitted, and these pulses are called *photons*.

The glowing filament of a light bulb.

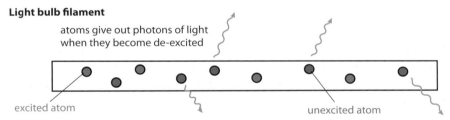

Figure 15.6a An incandescent light bulb

The discharge tube

A discharge tube is a glass tube containing a low pressure gas. A high potential difference created between the ends of the tube causes charged particles in the gas to be accelerated. When these fast moving particles interact with the other gas atoms they excite atomic electrons into high energy levels. When the electrons become de-excited light is emitted.

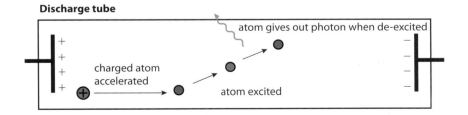

Figure 15.6b A discharge tube

The fluorescent tube

As you can see from the photograph of the discharge tube containing mercury vapour, it does not produce much light. However, a large amount of radiation

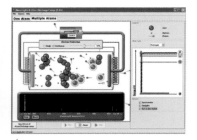

To view this simulation of a discharge tube, visit www.heinemann.co.uk/hotlinks, enter the express code 4266S and click on Weblink 15.3.

W

The amount of light from a discharge tube containing mercury vapour is low but the UV radiation is high.

in the UV region is emitted. This is invisible to the human eye, but if the inside of the tube is coated with a substance that absorbs UV radiation and gives out visible light (fluorescence) then this invisible radiation is converted to light. The result is a much brighter light. This is the principle behind the common strip light, properly called a fluorescent light.

Figure 15.6c A fluorescent tube. ▶

Fluorescent tube

UV absorbed by atom of fluorescent coating which gives out visible radiation when de-excited

UV photon given out by mercury atom

The laser

The laser uses a material with atoms that are able to stay excited for a short time after excitation, e.g. ruby. Electrons are first pumped up to the higher level by a flash of light. This is called population inversion, since there are more excited atoms than non-excited. The excited ruby atoms then start to de-excite, giving out photons of light. This happens in all directions, but some will be emitted along the length of the crystal. These photons will travel past ruby atoms that are still excited causing them to de-excite. The result is an amplification of the light, hence the name LASER (Light Amplification by the Stimulated Emission of Radiation). The amplification can be increased by half silvering the ends so that light is reflected up and down the crystal.

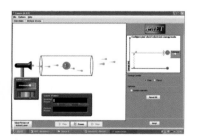

To view this simulation of a discharge tube, visit www.heinemann.co.uk/hotlinks, enter the express code 4266S and click on Weblink 15.4.

W

Figure 15.7 The tube flashes, ▶ pumping the ruby atoms into the high level. As each photon passes an excited ruby atom it de-excites and another photon is emitted. This is called *stimulated emission of radiation* because the atoms are being stimulated to give out radiation by the passing photon.

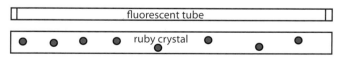
fluorescent tube
ruby crystal

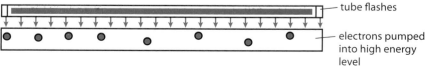
tube flashes

electrons pumped into high energy level

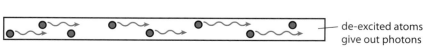
de-excited atoms give out photons

Monochromatic

Unlike other light sources, each photon of laser light has the same wavelength; this means the laser is a single colour or *monochromatic*. Light sources giving many wavelengths are white.

Coherence

When a *light bulb* emits photons, they are emitted randomly in different directions and with different phase. Each *laser* photon is emitted in the same direction and phase; this is called *coherence*.

Use of lasers

Laser light consists of a parallel beam of coherent light. This means if the beam is split into two parts then, when those two parts are brought together, the interference effects are stable. This property of laser light makes it ideal for the following applications:

- bar code reader
- CD/DVD reader
- production of holograms.

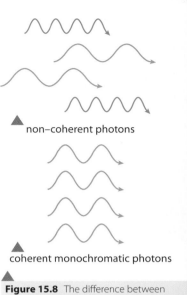

non–coherent photons

coherent monochromatic photons

Figure 15.8 The difference between coherent an non-coherent light.

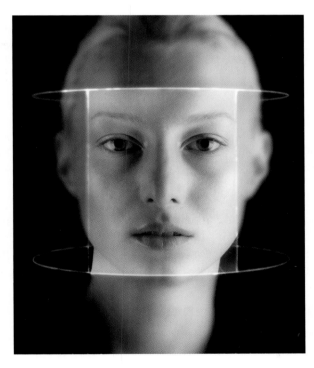

A laser used to scan a face.

The beam can also be made very intense and the fact that it is parallel means that the intensity does not decrease significantly with distance. This makes it possible to use the laser for:

- surgery
- welding
- communications
- measuring devices.

Two-source interference of waves

Assessment statements

G.3.1 State the conditions necessary to observe interference between two sources.
G.3.2 Explain, by means of the principle of superposition, the interference pattern produced by waves from two coherent point sources.
G.3.3 Outline a double-slit experiment for light and draw the intensity distribution of the observed fringe pattern.
G.3.4 Solve problems involving two-source interference.

Superposition

When two waves of the same type are incident at the same place they add together to give one resultant wave, this is called superposition. The resultant is dependent on the relative phase of the two waves as shown in Figure 15.9.

Figure 15.9 Constructive and destructive interference. This effect occurs when two light beams overlap but it can only be observed if the beams are coherent.

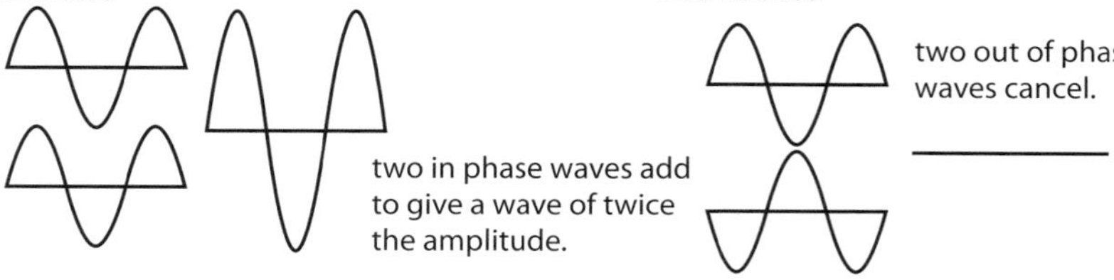

constructive interference

two in phase waves add to give a wave of twice the amplitude.

destructive interference

two out of phase waves cancel.

Coherence

Waves that have the same frequency, similar amplitude and constant phase relationship are said to be coherent. As we have seen, the light from a light bulb is emitted randomly so two light bulbs will not be coherent. However, we can make two coherent sources by splitting one source in two, but first we must make one light source as illustrated in Figure 15.10. Different parts of a filament give out light of different wavelength and phase, but using a narrow slit we can select just one part of the filament. This doesn't make the source monochromatic but all parts are in phase.

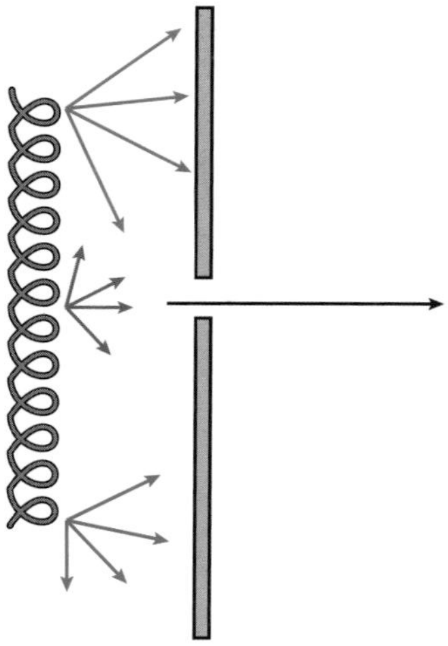

Figure 15.10 A filament bulb is turned into a single source using a narrow slit.

The double-slit experiment

When the light passes through the narrow slit it spreads out due to diffraction; this makes it possible to pass the light through two more slits.

light spreads out due to diffraction

in the overlapping region the waves superpose

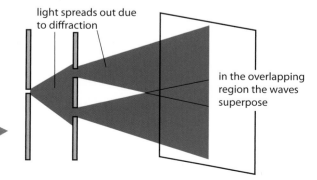

Figure 15.11 Light passing through two narrow slits overlaps due to diffraction.

Note: If laser light is used it is already coherent so the first slit is not necessary.

Phase difference and path difference

Figure 15.12 shows how two waves starting a journey in phase will remain in phase as if they travel the same distance. However, if one wave travels further than the other, they may no longer be in phase.

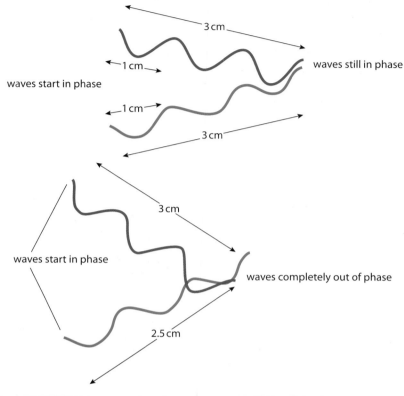

waves start in phase

3 cm
1 cm
waves still in phase

1 cm
3 cm

waves start in phase

3 cm
waves completely out of phase

2.5 cm

Figure 15.12 Two waves with no path difference and two waves with a path difference of $\frac{1}{2}$ wavelength. In the latter, the blue wave has travelled an extra 0.5 cm, this is the same as $\frac{1}{2}$ a wavelength so at the meeting point a blue peak meets a red trough resulting in destructive interference. This will also happen if the path difference is $1\frac{1}{2}\lambda$, $2\frac{1}{2}\lambda$, $3\frac{1}{2}\lambda$ etc. If the path difference is a whole number of wavelengths then the interference is constructive.

Exercises

10 Two sources of radio waves separated by a distance of 3 km produce coherent waves of wavelength l00 m. As you walk along a straight line from one station to the other, the signal on your radio is sometimes strong and sometimes weak. This is caused by interference. Calculate whether the signal is strong or weak after walking:
   (a) 100 m
   (b) 125 m
   (c) 250 m.

11 X and Y in Figure 15.13 are coherent sources of 2 cm waves. Will they interfere constructively or destructively at:
   (a) A
   (b) B
   (c) C?

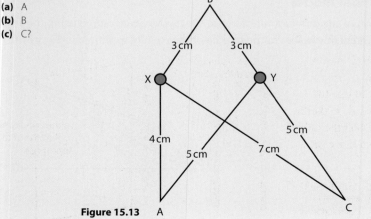

B

X 3 cm   3 cm Y

4 cm   5 cm

5 cm   7 cm

Figure 15.13   A   C

Interference of waves from two point sources

When waves from two point sources interfere, the path difference is different at different places; this causes an interference pattern consisting of regions where the waves add and other areas where they cancel.

In Figure 15.14, the 1 cm wavelength waves are interfering and at point O waves can be seen. This means constructive interference is taking place. Both waves have travelled a distance of 5 cm. At point X there are no waves, so destructive interference is taking place. However at point C, there are waves again, so there is constructive interference. The path difference is now one complete wavelength.

Figure 15.14 The interference pattern from two dripping taps and the radial lines showing the interference effect.

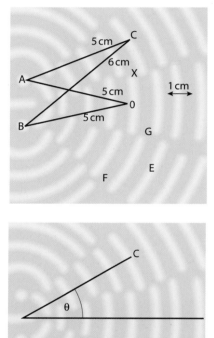

Geometrical model

The position of the different interference effects can be measured using the angle θ that the radial line makes to the middle of the sources as shown in Figures 15.14 and 15.15.

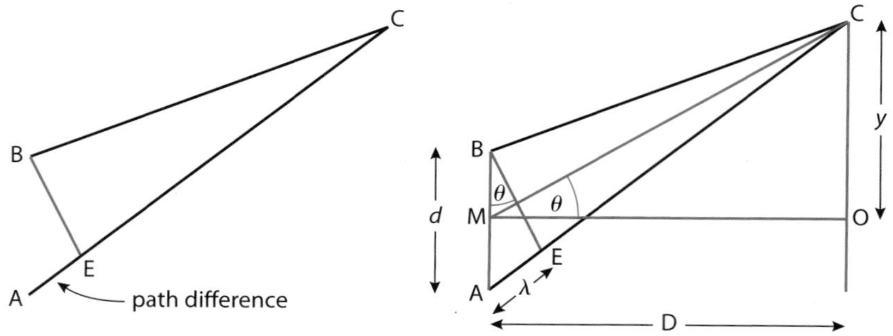

Figure 15.15 Considering point C in Fig 15.14, the path difference is found by drawing the line B-E. This splits the two paths into equal lengths B-C and E-C, the bit left over (A-E) is the path difference. Calculations for two-slit interference can be made with additional construction lines.

C is the position where the path difference is 1λ.

So AE = λ

If we use light then λ is very small, so the angle θ will be small also.

The angle AEB is almost 90° so $\sin\theta = \dfrac{\lambda}{d}$

From triangle MCO we see that $\tan\theta = \dfrac{y}{D}$

Since θ is very small,

$\tan\theta = \sin\theta$, so

$\sin\theta = \dfrac{y}{D}$

Therefore $\dfrac{\lambda}{d} = \dfrac{y}{D}$

The spacing of the interference bands $y = \dfrac{\lambda D}{d}$

In light, this distance is called the *fringe spacing*.

From this equation we can see that if you make *d* smaller then *y* gets bigger. The effect is therefore more visible with sources that are close together.

Exercises

12 Referring to Figure 15.14, what is the path difference at the following points:
  (a) E
  (b) F
  (c) G?

13 Referring to Figure 15.14, two taps separated by 5 cm are dripping into a square tank of water creating waves of wavelength 1.5 cm. The distance to the far side is 1.5 m (D). How far apart will the positions of constructive interference be (*y*) if measured on the far side of the tank?

14 Calculate *y* if the taps are moved together so they are now 4 cm apart.

Two slit interference with light

When two coherent sources of light interfere, destructive interference results in a dark region; constructive interference gives a bright region. Unlike water waves, you can't see light waves interfering as they travel but you can see the effect when they land on a screen. Figure 15.16 shows an example of an interference pattern caused when light passes through two slits. The pattern is a faint series of dots. They are so faint because for diffraction to take place at the slits they must be very narrow.

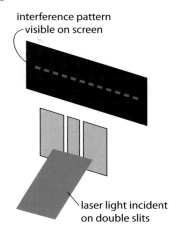
interference pattern visible on screen

laser light incident on double slits

Figure 15.16 An interference pattern

Exercises

15 Two narrow slits 0.01 mm apart (*d*) are illuminated by a laser of wavelength 600 nm. Calculate the fringe spacing (*y*) on a screen 1.5 m (D) from the slits.

16 Calculate the fringe spacing if the laser is replaced by one of wavelength 400 nm.

Graphical representation

Using a light sensor it is possible to measure the intensity of light across a diffraction pattern. In this way we can produce a graph of intensity against position as shown in Figure 15.17.

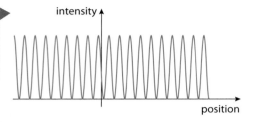

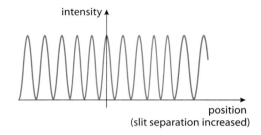

15.3 Diffraction grating

Assessment statements

G.4.1 Describe the effect on the double-slit intensity distribution of increasing the number of slits.

G.4.2 Derive the diffraction grating formula for normal incidence.

G.4.3 Outline the use of a diffraction grating to measure wavelengths.

G.4.4 Solve problems involving a diffraction grating.

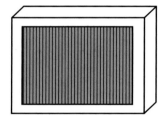

Multiple-slit diffraction

The intensity of double-slit interference patterns is very low but can be increased by using more than two slits. A diffraction grating is a series of very fine parallel slits mounted on a glass plate.

Diffraction at the slits

When light is incident on the grating it is diffracted at each slit. The slits are very narrow so the diffraction causes the light to propagate as if coming from a point source.

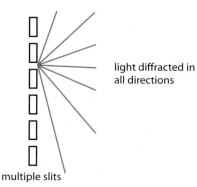

light diffracted in all directions

multiple slits

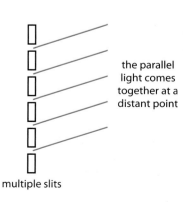

the parallel light comes together at a distant point

multiple slits

Interference between slits

To make the geometry simpler we will consider what would happen if the light passing through the grating were observed from a long distance. This means that we can consider the light rays to be almost parallel. So the parallel light rays diffracted through each slit will come together at a distant point. When they come together they will interfere.

Geometrical model

Let us consider waves that have been diffracted at an angle θ as shown in Figure 15.20 (remember light is diffracted at all angles – this is just one angle that we have chosen to consider).

We can see that when these rays meet, the ray from A will have travelled a distance x further than the ray from B. The ray from D has travelled the same distance further than C, and so on. If the path difference between neighbours is λ then they will interfere constructively, if $\frac{1}{2}\lambda$ then the interference will be destructive.

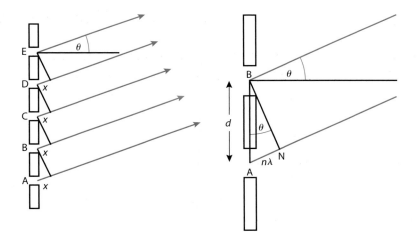

Figure 15.20 Parallel light travels through the grating and some is diffracted at an angle θ. The expansion shows just slits A and B, if the path difference is $n\lambda$ then constructive interference takes place.

The line BN is drawn perpendicular to both rays so angle N is 90°

Therefore from triangle ABN we see that $\sin\theta = \dfrac{n\lambda}{d}$

Rearranging gives $d\sin\theta = n\lambda$

If you look at a light source through a diffraction grating and move your head around, bright lines will be seen every time $\sin\theta = \dfrac{n\lambda}{d}$.

Producing spectra

If white light is viewed through a diffraction grating, each wavelength undergoes constructive interference at different angles. This results in a spectrum. The individual wavelengths can be calculated from the angle using the formula $d\sin\theta = n\lambda$.

Worked example

If blue light of wavelength 450 nm and red light wavelength 700 nm are viewed through a grating with 600 lines/mm, at what angle will the first bright blue and red lines be seen?

Solution

Figure 15.21 Bright lines appear at angles when $\sin\theta = \frac{n\lambda}{d}$. Red and blue lines appear at different angles.

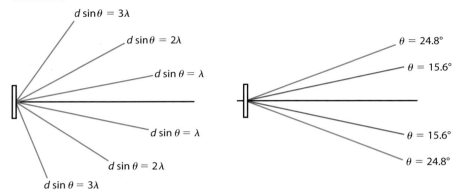

$$d\sin\theta = 3\lambda$$
$$d\sin\theta = 2\lambda$$
$$d\sin\theta = \lambda$$
$$d\sin\theta = \lambda$$
$$d\sin\theta = 2\lambda$$
$$d\sin\theta = 3\lambda$$

$\theta = 24.8°$
$\theta = 15.6°$
$\theta = 15.6°$
$\theta = 24.8°$

If there are 600 lines/mm, $d = \dfrac{1}{600}$ mm $= 0.001\,67$ mm

For the first lines, $n = 1$

For blue light, $\sin\theta = \dfrac{450 \times 10^{-9}}{0.001\,67 \times 10^{-3}} = 0.269$

Therefore $\theta_{\text{blue}} = \textbf{15.6°}$

$\sin\theta = \dfrac{n\lambda}{d}$

For red light, $\sin\theta = \dfrac{700 \times 10^{-9}}{0.001\,67 \times 10^{-3}} = 0.419$

Therefore $\theta_{\text{red}} = \textbf{24.8°}$

Figure 15.22 A hydrogen lamp viewed through a grating.

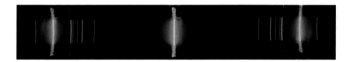

Exercises

17 Red light ($\lambda = 700$ nm) is shone through a grating with 300 lines/mm. Calculate:
    (a) the separation of the lines on the grating
    (b) the diffraction angle of the first red line.

15.4 Lenses and image formation

Assessment statements
G.2.1   Define the terms *principal axis*, *focal point*, *focal length* and *linear magnification* as applied to a converging (convex) lens.
G.2.2   Define the *power* of a *convex lens* and the *dioptre*.
G.2.3   Define *linear magnification*.
G.2.4   Construct ray diagrams to locate the image formed by a convex lens.
G.2.5   Distinguish between a real image and a virtual image.
G.2.6   Apply the convention 'real is positive, virtual is negative' to the thin lens formula.
G.2.7   Solve problems for a single convex lens using the thin lens formula.

Lenses

A lens is a glass disc that refracts light. If the faces of the disc are curved inwards then the light is caused to spread out (diverge). If the faces curve out then the light is made to focus inwards (converge).

Convex lens

Rays of light parallel to the axis converge at the principal focus when they pass through a convex lens as in Figure 15.23 (a).

Power of a lens

Lenses with greater curvature bend the light more, resulting in a shorter focal length. Fat lenses are more powerful.

The concave lens

Rays of parallel light are diverged away from the principal focus as in Figure 15.23(b).

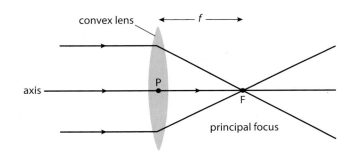

(a)

◀ **Figure 15.23** The focal length (f) is the distance from the centre of the lens, P (the pole) to the principal focus, F. The optical power of a lens is equal to 1/focal length (units are dioptres).

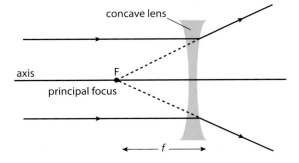

(b)

Exercises

18 Parallel light is focused 15 cm from the a convex lens, what is:
  (a) the focal length of the lens
  (b) the power of the lens?

Image formation

Point object

A point object gives out light rays in all directions. When viewed, some of those rays will pass into the eye enabling the observer to see the object. The observer knows that the object is where the rays are coming from. If the light from a point object passes through a lens then the observer will see the light coming from somewhere else, and this is called an *image*. There are two types of image: *real* and *virtual* (see Figure 15.24)

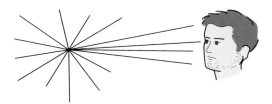

Real image

A real image is an image where the rays come from the image. In a convex lens the observer will see the light coming from a point much nearer than the actual object. A real image can be projected onto a screen.

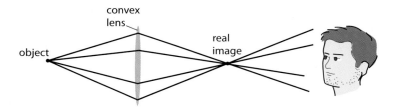

Virtual image

An image is called a virtual image when the rays only *appear* to come from a point. The rays are coming from the image just the other side of the concave lens.

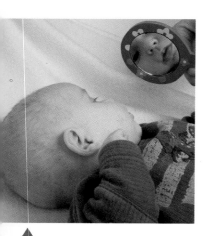

A good example of a virtual image is the image you see when you look into a mirror. It looks like the light is coming from the other side of the mirror but it isn't. This baby doesn't realise that it's just a virtual image.

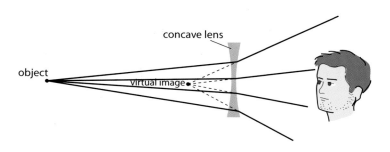

Extended object

Except when we are looking at stars we rarely look at single point object. Objects normally have size; we call an object with size an extended object. An *extended object* is represented with an arrow and can be treated like two points, one at the top and one at the bottom.

Image formation in convex lenses

The image of an extended object in a convex lens can be found by carefully drawing the path of two rays from the top of the object, the image will be formed where these rays cross or appear to cross.

The nature of the image

We describe the nature of an image according to whether it is:

- real or virtual
- bigger or smaller
- closer or further away
- upright or upside down.

The nature of the image is different for different object positions (see Figure 15.26).

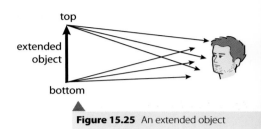

Figure 15.25 An extended object

Object further than 2 × focal length

How to draw a ray diagram:

- Draw the axis and lens.
- Choose an appropriate scale and mark the principal foci on either side of the lens.
- Measure and draw the object position. This will be given in the question, in this case it is 'more than 2F'.
- Draw a ray from the top of the object parallel to the axis. This ray will be refracted so that it passes through the principal focus (the red ray in Figure 15.26). Refraction takes place at the lens surfaces but for ray diagrams the light can bend at the central line.
- Draw a ray that passes through the centre of the lens. Since the centre of the lens has parallel sides this ray will pass straight through (the blue ray in Figure 15.26).
- The top of the image is the point where the rays cross, and the bottom of the image is on the axis (we don't need to draw rays to find this). Draw the image arrow from the axis to the crossing point.
- The position of the image can now be measured with a rule and scaled up to find the actual image distance.
- The nature of the image can also be determined.

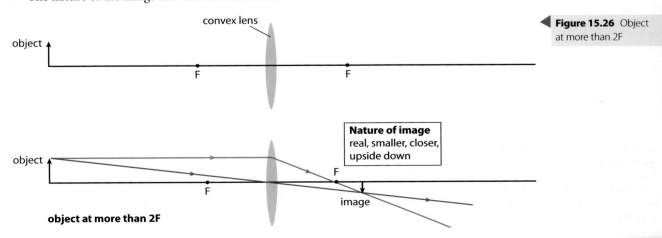

Figure 15.26 Object at more than 2F

Nature of image
real, smaller, closer, upside down

object at more than 2F

Figure 15.27

Objects between 2F and the lens

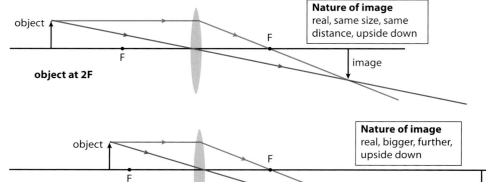

object

object at 2F

Nature of image
real, same size, same distance, upside down

image

object

object between F and 2F

Nature of image
real, bigger, further, upside down

image

● **Examiner's hint:** In this case it looks like there isn't an image but if you were to look at the light coming through the lens your eyes would focus the light like they do when you look at a star. We can say that the light appears to come from infinity.

object

object at F

Nature of image
virtual, bigger, at infinity, upright

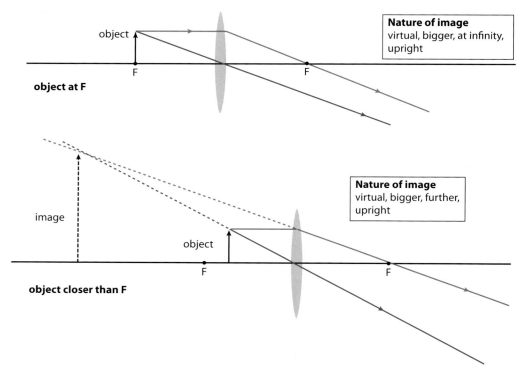

image

object

object closer than F

Nature of image
virtual, bigger, further, upright

Linear magnification

Linear magnification is the ratio of image height/object height. For example, if the object is 2 cm high and the image is 6 cm high the magnification is $\frac{6}{2} = 3$

The lens formula

A simulation draws ray diagrams for lenses. To try this, visit www.heinemann.co.uk/hotlinks, enter the express code 4266S and click on Website 15.6.

An alternative way of finding the image position is to use the lens formula:

$$\frac{1}{f} = \frac{1}{u} + \frac{1}{v}$$

f = focal length
u = object distance
v = image distance

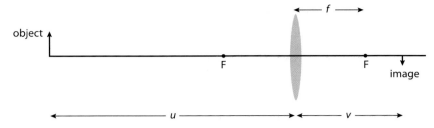

Figure 15.28 Defining the lengths u, v and f.

Worked examples

1 An object is placed 24 cm from a convex lens of focal length 6 cm. Find the image position.

2 An object is placed 3 cm from a convex lens of focal length 6 cm. Find the image position.

Solution

● **Examiner's hint:** Always draw a sketch of the relative positions of the object, image and lens. This will help you to see what the problem involves. Then use the formula to find the thing you are asked to calculate.

1 From the question:

$u = 24$ cm

$f = 6$ cm

rearranging: $\frac{1}{f} = \frac{1}{u} + \frac{1}{v}$ gives $\frac{1}{v} = \frac{1}{f} - \frac{1}{u}$

substituting values: $\frac{1}{v} = \frac{1}{6} - \frac{1}{24} = \frac{4}{24} - \frac{1}{24} = \frac{3}{24}$

so $v = \frac{24}{3} = 8$ cm

2 From the question:

$u = 24$ cm

f $= 6$ cm

rearranging: $\frac{1}{f} = \frac{1}{u} + \frac{1}{v}$ gives $\frac{1}{v} = \frac{1}{f} - \frac{1}{u}$

substituting values: $\frac{1}{v} = \frac{1}{6} - \frac{1}{3} = \frac{1}{6} - \frac{2}{6} = \frac{-1}{6}$

so $v = \frac{-6}{1} = -6$ cm

Sign convention

We know from the ray diagrams that the image in Worked example 1 is real and the one in Worked example 2 is virtual. We can see that the images are different by looking at the sign of the answer.

REAL IS POSITIVE
VIRTUAL IS NEGATIVE

This convention applies to focal lengths and object distances too.

Linear magnification

From the definition the linear magnification of the image in Figure 15.29 is $\frac{h_i}{h_o}$

But we can see that the blue ray makes two triangles with the same angle,

therefore $\frac{h_i}{h_o} = \frac{v}{u}$

Linear magnification, $M = \frac{v}{u}$

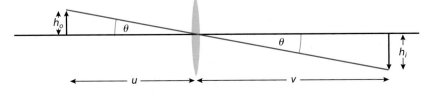

Figure 15.29 Linear magnification.

Exercises

Use the lens formula to solve the following problems. You can check your answers by drawing ray diagrams too.

19 A 25 cm focal length lens is used to focus an image of the sun onto a piece of paper. What will the distance between the lens and the paper be?

20 An object is placed 30 cm from a convex lens of focal length 10 cm.

    (a) Calculate the image distance.

    (b) Is the image real or virtual?

    (c) Calculate the magnification of the image.

21 A real image is formed 20 cm from a convex lens of focal length 5 cm. Calculate the object distance.

22 An object is placed 5 cm from a lens of focal length 15 cm,

    (a) Calculate the image distance.

    (b) Is the image real or virtual?

    (c) Calculate the magnification of the image.

23 A camera with a single lens of focal length 5 cm is used to take a photograph of a bush 5 m away. A simple camera uses a convex lens.

    (a) What is the object distance?

    (b) Calculate the distance from the lens to the film (v).

    (c) What is the linear magnification of the camera?

    (d) If the bush were 1 m high how high will the image be?

24 The camera of Question 23 is used to take a picture of a flower on the bush so the photographer moves towards the bush until he is 20 cm from the flower.

    (a) Calculate the image distance.

    (b) What is the linear magnification?

(15.5) Optical instruments

Assessment statements

G.2.8 Define the terms *far point* and *near point* for the unaided eye.

G.2.9 Define *angular magnification*.

G.2.10 Derive an expression for the angular magnification of a simple magnifying glass for an image formed at the near point and at infinity.

G.2.11 Construct a ray diagram for a compound microscope with final image formed close to the near point of the eye (normal adjustment).

G.2.12 Construct a ray diagram for an astronomical telescope with the final image at infinity (normal adjustment).

G.2.13 State the equation relating angular magnification to the focal lengths of the lenses in an astronomical telescope in normal adjustment.

G.2.14 Solve problems involving the compound microscope and the astronomical telescope.

In this section, we are going to investigate three optical instruments: the magnifying glass, the telescope and the microscope. All three instruments enable us to see an object more clearly, but first we should see how well we can do with the unaided eye.

The human eye

Inside the eye there is a convex lens. This, together with the front part of the eye, focuses light onto the retina, where millions of light sensitive cells sense the light and send electrical signals to the brain.

The eye lens is made of a rubbery substance that can be squashed; squashing the lens makes it fatter and therefore more powerful. In this way the eye can be adapted to focus on objects that are close or far away as illustrated in Figure 15.31. There is a limit to how fat the lens can get. If an object is too close to the eye, then it can't focus the rays on the retina, and the image is 'out of focus'. The average closest distance is 25 cm, but this tends to get longer with age.

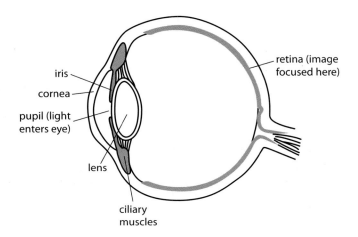

iris

cornea

pupil (light enters eye)

lens

ciliary muscles

retina (image focused here)

◀ **Figure 15.30** Parts of the human eye.

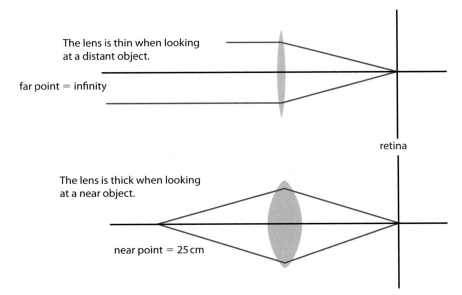

The lens is thin when looking at a distant object.

far point = infinity

retina

The lens is thick when looking at a near object.

near point = 25 cm

An object that is too close is focused behind the retina.

◀ **Figure 15.31** The eye lens changes shape to view different objects.

 Short sight
Short sighted people have a near point that is closer to the eye than normal. This means they can read things that are much closer. Unfortunately it also means that they cannot see things that are far away.

Although the wind turbines are all the same size the nearest one looks bigger.

How big does an object appear?

We are all familiar with the fact that objects that are far away seem smaller than objects that are close. We can measure how big something appears using the angle that rays make when they enter the eye. In Figure 15.32 a) we can see how the object subtends a bigger angle when viewed from a short distance. If we want to make an object appear as big as possible then we should view it as near as possible. This means at a distance of 25 cm.

Figure 15.32 a) A close object appears bigger.

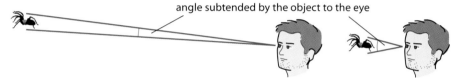

angle subtended by the object to the eye

The magnifying glass

We use a magnifying glass to make things look bigger; this is done by putting the object closer than the principal focus of a convex lens. Without a magnifying glass the best we can do is to put an object at our near point (25 cm in average eyes). The best we can do with a magnifying glass is with the *image* at the near point.

Figure 15.32 b) Using a magnifying glass with the image at 25 cm.

←25 cm→

←25 cm→

object at 25 cm

image at 25 cm with magnifying glass

The problem with looking at something so close is that it can be a bit tiring, since your eye muscles have to squash the lens.

It is more relaxing to view the image at a distance, and then the eye is relaxed. This however doesn't give such a magnified image. If the final image is far away (we could say an infinite distance) the rays coming to the observer should be parallel. In the previous section we saw that this means the object must be at the focal point. In both cases the angle subtended when using the magnifying glass is bigger than without (see Figure 15.32 c).

Figure 15.32 c) Using a magnifying glass with the image 'at infinity'.

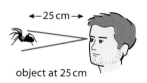
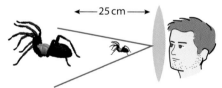

← 25 cm→

‹ f ›

object at 25 cm

image at infinity with magnifying glass

Angular magnification(M)

The angular magnification tells us how much bigger an object looks.

$$\text{Angular magnification} = \frac{\text{angle subtended by image at eye } (\beta)}{\text{angle subtended by object at unaided eye } (\alpha)}$$

Angular magnification for a magnifying glass

1. Image at infinty

When the final image is an infinite distance away the object must be placed at the focal point. Looking at Figure 15.34, you can see why this image looks bigger than the image in the unaided eye.

If the angles are small (for the original object with the image at infinity) and measured in radians then

$$\alpha = \frac{h_o}{25}$$

$$\beta = \frac{h_o}{f}$$

Since angular magnification $M = \frac{\beta}{\alpha} = \frac{h_o}{f} \times \frac{25}{h_o}$

So $M = \frac{25}{f}$

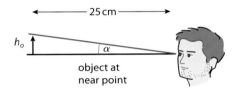
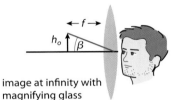

object at
near point

image at infinity with
magnifying glass

2. Image at the near point (normal adjustment)

Figure 15.34 b) compares an object as close as possible to the unaided eye to the same object viewed with a magnifying glass. So that the final image is also as close as possible, the object must be placed close to the lens.

This can be shown to give an angular magnification of $1 + \frac{25}{f}$. (One more than the previous example.)

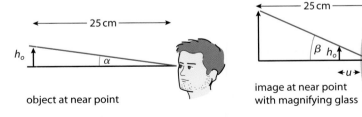

object at near point

image at near point
with magnifying glass

Derivation of $M = 1 + \frac{25}{f}$

Referring to Figure 15.34 b), if the angles are small then the angles expressed in radians are:

$$\alpha = \frac{h_o}{25}$$

$$\beta = \frac{h_o}{u}$$

so $M = \frac{\beta}{\alpha} = M = \frac{\beta}{\alpha} = \frac{h_o}{u} \times \frac{25}{h_o}$

$M = \frac{25}{u}$ (1)

but $\frac{1}{f} = \frac{1}{u} + \frac{1}{v}$ so $\frac{1}{u} = \frac{1}{f} - \frac{1}{v}$

but $v = -25$ cm so $\frac{1}{u} = \frac{1}{f} + \frac{1}{25}$

Rearranging gives $u = \frac{25f}{25 + f}$

Substituting for u in equation (1)

gives $M = \left(\frac{25 + f}{f}\right) = 1 + \frac{25}{f}$

So $M = 1 + \frac{25}{f}$

Figure 15.34 a) Angular magnification for an original object with image at infinity and viewed with a magnifying glass.

Remember the radian $= \frac{s}{r}$
If the angle is very small then the arc, s can be taken as a straight line.

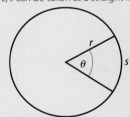

Figure 15.33

Figure 15.34 b)

Exercises

25 The Moon is about 3500 km in diameter and about 400 000 km away from the Earth. Estimate the angle subtended by the Moon to an observer on the Earth.

26 If a small insect 1 mm long is viewed at a distance of 25 cm from the eye, what angle will it subtend to the eye?

27 How close to a lens of focal length 5 cm should the insect of Exercise 26 be placed so that an image is formed 25 cm from the eye?

28 Use the formula to calculate the angular magnification of the insect viewed with a lens of focal length 5 cm if the final image is at the near point.

● **Examiner's hint:** If you draw the object before you draw the first ray you often end up with a final image that doesn't fit on the page (try it).

However, if the position of the object is given in the exam question you have to use it. The examiner will have made sure that everything will fit okay, so draw the ray in Step 1 from the top of the object and continue through the steps.

The microscope

The microscope is used to produce an enlarged image of a close object. The microscope consists of two convex lenses: the one closest to the object is called the *objective*; and the one you look through is the *eyepiece*. To give maximum magnification, the final image is at the near point of the eye. Figure 15.35 shows the ray diagram for a point object. This is called *normal adjustment*.

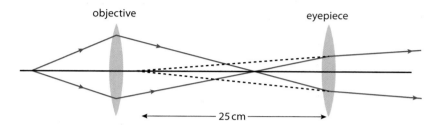

Figure 15.35 Simple ray diagram for a microscope.

Drawing the ray diagram with an extended object

Drawing the ray diagram for an extended object is a bit more difficult, but you need to know how to do it for the exam.

1. Draw the lenses and axis then a ray through the centre of the objective to a point half way down the eyepiece. Then draw an object a short distance from the objective.
2. Draw a ray from the object parallel to the axis. Continue this ray so that it hits the bottom of the eyepiece. Now mark F_o, it is the point where this ray crosses the axis.
3. To find the position of the final image draw a construction line (black) from the top of the first image through the middle of the eyepiece. The top of the image will lie on this line. Choose a point on this line beyond the objective and draw the rays coming from this point. Now add arrows to all the rays.

Figure 15.36 The steps in drawing a ray diagram with an extended object.

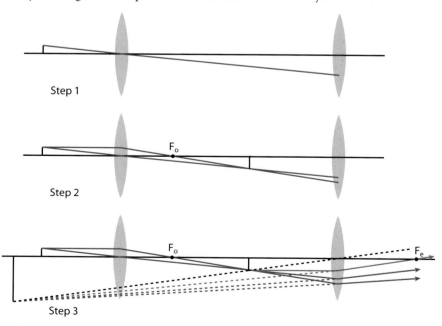

To find the focal point of the eyepiece, the red construction line can be drawn. This comes from the top of the first image and goes parallel to the axis. When it passes through the lens it appears to come from the top of the final image. The ray will pass through the focal point.

The astronomical telescope

The astronomical telescope is used to view stars and planets. It has no use for looking at things on Earth since the image is upside down. The simple telescope consists of two convex lenses that are used to produce a virtual image of a distant object at infinity (see Figure 15.38) The final image could be produced anywhere but in normal adjustment it is at infinity, in other words the rays come out parallel.

The objective lens forms an image of a distant object at its principal focus. This image is at the principal focus of the eyepiece, so the final image is at infinity (the rays are parallel).

How to draw the ray diagram

This diagram looks difficult to draw but is okay if done in stages.

1. Draw the lenses and axis but don't draw the foci yet.
2. Draw a ray passing through the centre of the objective hitting the eyepiece about half way down.
3. Draw two more rays entering the objective at the same angle as the first. Then draw the top ray hitting the bottom of the eyepiece.
4. The bottom ray will cross the other two at the same place; this is just below the principal focus. You can now mark this on the axis and draw in the first image (F_o).
5. The rays emerge from the eyepiece parallel. To find the angle, draw a construction line (dotted) from the top of the image straight through the centre of the eyepiece. All the rays will be parallel to this. Add arrows to all the rays.

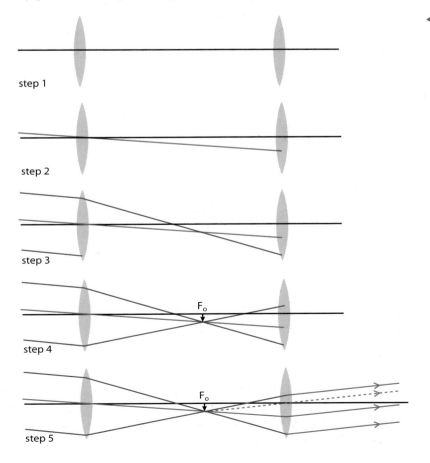

Figure 15.37 Steps in drawing the ray diagram for an astronomical telescope.

step 1

step 2

step 3

step 4

F_o

step 5

F_o

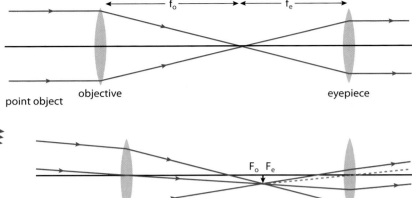

Figure 15.38 The astronomical telescope (point object and extended object).

To see how this produces a magnified image we must use an extended object. In the case in Figure 15.38 the object is the Moon. The three blue rays are coming from the top of the Moon and the bottom of the Moon is in line with the axis. By the time the rays reach the Earth they are very nearly parallel.

Angular magnification

Since the object is very far away, the image subtended to the unaided eye is the same as the image subtended to the telescope. The angles subtended by the object and the image are as shown in Figure 15.39.

Figure 15.39 Angles subtended at the lenses in an astronomical telescope.

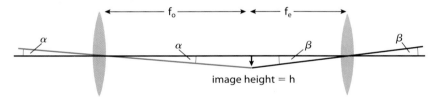

If the angles are small and measured in radians then:

$$\alpha = \frac{h}{f_o}$$

$$\beta = \frac{h}{f_e}$$

$$\text{angular magnification} = \frac{\beta}{\alpha} = \frac{h}{f_e} \times \frac{f_o}{h} = \frac{f_o}{f_e}$$

A telescope with a large angular magnification is very long. The problem then is that not much light can travel through it; this means that lenses with a large diameter should be used. These are difficult to make, so most high powered telescopes use mirrors not lenses.

● **Examiner's hint:** Before starting the calculation, draw a sketch showing the different positions of the lenses and object. Don't try to draw the rays, the sketch is just to help you see the relative positions.

To access a virtual optics lab, visit www.heinemann.co.uk/hotlinks, enter the express code 4266S and click on Weblink 15.7.

Exercises

29 A microscope is constructed from an objective of focal length 1 cm and an eyepiece of focal length 5 cm. An object is placed 1.5 cm from the objective.
   (a) Calculate the distance from the objective to the first image.
   (b) If the final image is a virtual image 25 cm from the eyepiece, calculate the distance between the first image and the eyepiece.
   (c) Calculate the distance between the lenses.

30 A telescope is constructed from two lenses: an objective of focal length 100 cm and an eyepiece of focal length 10 cm. The telescope is used in normal adjustment (final image at infinity):
   (a) Calculate the angular magnification.
   (b) What is the distance between the lenses?

31 A telescope has an objective of focal length 50 cm. What focal length eyepiece should be used to give a magnification of 10?

15.6 Aberrations

Assessment statements

G.2.15 Explain the meaning of spherical aberration and of chromatic aberration as produced by a single lens.

G.2.16 Describe how spherical aberration in a lens may be reduced.

G.2.17 Describe how chromatic aberration in a lens may be reduced.

We have assumed in all the previous examples that parallel rays of light are brought to a point when they shine through a convex lens. However, this is not the case with a real lens.

Spherical aberration

Because of the spherical curvature of a lens, the rays hitting the outer part are deviated more than the ones on the inside (see Figure 15.40).

The result is that if the image is projected onto a screen there will be a spot instead of a point. If such a lens were used to take a photograph then the picture would be blurred. To reduce this effect, the outer rays are removed by placing a card with a hole in it over the lens. This is called *stopping*.

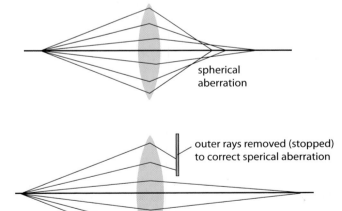

spherical
aberration

outer rays removed (stopped)
to correct sperical aberration

Figure 15.40 Spherical and chromatic aberration in a convex lens.

Chromatic aberration

It has been mentioned before that different wavelengths of light are refracted by different amounts. If white light is focused with a convex lens the different colours are focused at different points. This also causes the image to be blurred. It can be corrected by making the lens out of two lenses of different refractive index stuck together. This is called an *achromatic doublet*. The blue light is most converged by the convex lens and most diverged by the concave one. These two effects cancel each other out.

Figure 15.41 Chromatic aberration ▶

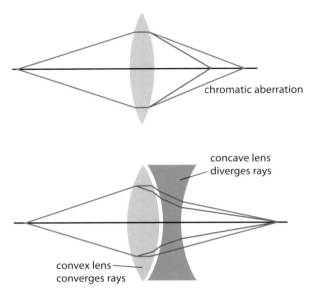

chromatic aberration

concave lens
diverges rays

convex lens
converges rays

Practice questions

1 This question is about converging lenses.
    (a) The diagram shows a small object O represented by an arrow placed in front of a *converging* lens L. The focal points of the lens are labelled F.

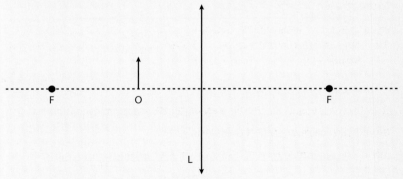

F   O   F

L

    (i)   Define the *focal point* of a converging lens.   (2)
    (ii) On the diagram above, draw rays to locate the position of the image of the
              object formed by the lens.   (3)
    (iii) Explain whether the image is real or virtual.   (1)

    (b) A convex lens of focal length 6.25 cm is used to view an ant of length 0.80 cm that
            is crawling on a table. The lens is held 5.0 cm above the table.
    (i)   Calculate the distance of the image from the lens.   (2)
    (ii) Calculate the length of the image of the ant.   (2)
                                                                         (Total 10 marks)

2 This question is about an astronomical telescope.

(a) Define the focal point of a convex (converging) lens. (2)

The diagram below shows two rays of light from a distant star incident on the objective lens of an astronomical telescope. The paths of the rays are also shown after they pass through the objective lens and are incident on the eyepiece lens of the telescope.

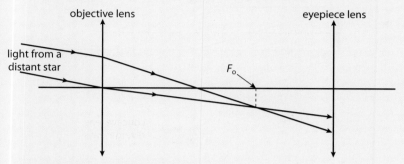

The principal focus of the objective lens is F_0

(b) On the diagram above, mark
  (i) the position of principal focus of the eyepiece lens (label this F_E). (1)
  (ii) the position of the image of the star formed by the objective lens (label this I). (1)

(c) State where the final image is formed when the telescope is in normal adjustment. (1)

(d) Complete the diagram above to show the direction in which the final image of the star is formed for the telescope in normal adjustment. (2)

The eye ring of an astronomical telescope is a device that is placed outside the eyepiece lens of the telescope at the position where the image of the objective lens is formed by the eyepiece lens. The diameter of the eye ring is the same as the diameter of the image of the objective lens. This ensures that all the light passing through the telescope passes through the eye ring.

(e) A particular astronomical telescope has an objective lens of focal length 98.0 cm and an eyepiece lens of focal length 2.00 cm (i.e. $f_0 = 98.0$ cm, $f_e = 20.0$ cm). Determine the position of the eye ring. (4)

(Total 11 marks)

3 This question is about light and the electromagnetic spectrum.

(a) Outline the electromagnetic nature of light. (2)

(b) The diagram below is a representation of the electromagnetic spectrum.

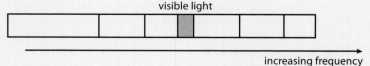

In the diagram the region of visible light has been indicated. Indicate on the diagram above the approximate position occupied by
  (i) infrared waves (label this I). (1)
  (ii) microwaves (label this M). (1)
  (iii) gamma rays (label this G). (1)

(Total 5 marks)

4 This question is about a concave (diverging) lens.

The diagram below shows four rays of light from an object O that are incident on a thin concave (diverging) lens. The *focal points* of the lens are shown labelled F. The lens is represented by the straight line XY.

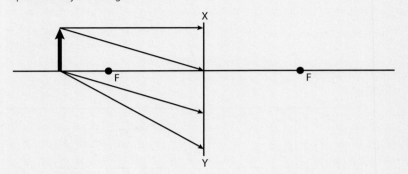

(a) Define the term *focal point*. (2)

(b) On the diagram,

   (i) complete the paths of the four rays in order to locate the position of the image formed by the lens (4)

   (ii) show where the eye must be placed in order to view the image. (1)

(c) State and explain whether the image is real or virtual. (2)

(d) The focal length of the lens is 50.0 cm. Determine the linear magnification of an object placed 75.0 cm from the lens. (3)

(e) Half of the lens is now covered such that only rays on one side of the principal axis are incident on the lens. Describe the effects, if any, that this will have on the linear magnification and the appearance of the image. (2)

(Total 14 marks)

5 This question is about the wave properties of light.

The diagram below (not to scale) is an arrangement for observing the interference pattern produced on a screen when the light from two narrow slits S_1 and S_2 overlaps. A beam of light from a laser is incident on the slits and after passing through the slits, the light is incident on a screen. The separation between the slits is large compared to the width of the slits and the distance between the slits and the screen is large compared to the slit separation.

The point X on the screen is equidistant from S_1 and S_2.

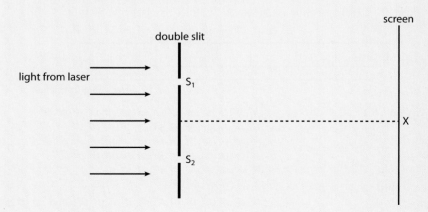

(a) Explain why an interference pattern will not be observed on the screen if the laser is replaced with a tungsten filament lamp.(2)

(b) On the axes below, draw a sketch-graph to show how the intensity of the observed interference pattern varies with distance along the screen. (2)

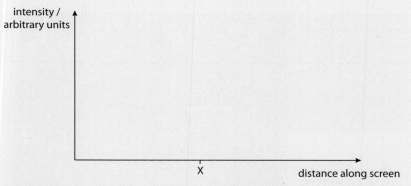

(c) The wavelength of the light from the laser is 633 nm and the angular separation of the bright fringes on the screen is 4.00×10^{-4} rad. Calculate the distance between S_1 and S_2. (3)

16 Theory of knowledge

> "The task is not to see what has never been seen before, but to think what has never been thought before about what you see everyday."
>
> *Erwin Schrodinger*

Introduction

In the *Theory of knowledge* course you will be asked to analyze and discuss the different ways of knowing and areas of knowledge. Physics is one of the areas of knowledge that you have been introduced to, but what makes it different from other subjects such as art or languages? In this chapter we will look at the way that you gain knowledge in physics, so that you can compare this with the ways of knowing in your other subjects.

What is the role of imagination in physics? Can physics be beautiful? Is physics all logic and maths or is there a place for feelings?

▲ Are these particle physics equations beautiful?
Can you use your imagination to work out what they represent?

Is this sunset more beautiful to people who ▶
understand Einstein's theory of general relativity?

Is this what an ▶
atom looks like?

> "If we knew what it was we were doing, it would not be called research, would it?"
>
> *Albert Einstein*

> "The secret of genius is to carry the spirit of childhood into maturity."
>
> *T. H. Huxley*

The scientific method

The scientific method is the way that physicists work to invent new theories and to discover new laws, and it is also the way that you will have been working in the practical program. There are actually many variations to this process and many exceptions, where new theories have come about without following any strict procedure. However, to make things simple, we will consider just one four-step version.

1 Observation

Physics is all about making models to help us understand the universe. Before we can make a model, we must observe what is happening. In physics, the observations are often of the form "How does one thing affect another?"

▲ Galileo makes observations using a telescope.

2 Hypothesis

Having made an observation, the next step is to use your knowledge to develop an idea of what is causing the event you have observed. What factors cause this thing to happen and what factors are not involved? Having made a hypothesis, it is possible to predict the outcome of a change in one of the variables.

3 Experiment

All experiments are ▶ conducted to test hypotheses.

The experiment is designed to test the hypothesis. It is important to change only the quantity that you think is responsible for the event – you must keep the other variables constant.

If the experiment does not prove the hypothesis then you must go back to the observations and think of a new one (this is often helped by the outcome of the experiment). If the experiment supports the hypothesis then you can go on to the next step.

4 Theory

If experiment supports the hypothesis, you can make a theory that relates the variables involved. A theory is a set of related statements that can be used to make predictions and explain observations.

▲ Franklin's lightning experiment. If Franklin had had a full understanding of electricity, he wouldn't have done this. He was lucky that the kite did not get struck by lightning, and in fact many people died repeating this experiment.

Example - the simple pendulum

Observation

A student watches a simple pendulum swinging and wonders what factors affect the frequency of the swing.

Hypothesis

The student hadn't studied the motion of the pendulum so used his intuition to come up with an idea related to the mass of the bob. He thought that since the bigger mass had more weight, then the force pulling it down would be greater, causing it to swing faster. So the hypothesis was that the frequency of the bob was proportional to the mass of the bob.

Experiment

An experiment was carried out measuring the frequency of bobs with different mass. The length of the string, the height of release and all other variables were kept constant. The result showed that there was no change; the hypothesis was therefore wrong.

Back to observations

On observing the pendulum further, the student noticed that if its length were increased, it appeared to swing more slowly. This led to a second hypothesis and the process continued.

"There are children playing in the street who could solve some of my top problems in physics, because they have modes of sensory perception that I lost long ago."
Robert Oppenheimer

Theories must be falsifiable

For a theory to be accepted it must be possible to think of a way that it can be proved wrong. For example; Newton's gravitational theory would be proved wrong if an object with mass was seen to be repelled from the Earth.

However, the theory that the Earth is inhabited by invisible creatures with eyes on each finger is not falsifiable since you cannot see the creatures to tell if they have eyes on their fingers or not.

Occam's razor

A razor is a strange name for a principle. Its name arises because it states that a theory should not contain any unnecessary assumptions – it should be *shaved* down to its bare essentials.

This is the same as the KIS principle "keep it simple".

For example, a theory for gravitational force could be that there is a force between all masses that is proportional to the product of their mass and is caused by invisible creatures with very long arms. The last bit about the invisible creatures is unnecessary so can be cut out of the theory (using Occam's razor).

"Just a theory"

If someone says "The theory of special relativity is just a theory", what do they mean?

The use of the word *theory* in the English language can cause some problems for scientists. The word is sometimes used to mean that something isn't based on fact. For instance, you could say that you have a theory as to why your friend was annoyed with you last night. In physics, a theory is based on strong experimental evidence.

Serendipity

Discoveries aren't always made by following a rigorous scientific method - sometimes luck plays a part. Serendipity is the act of finding something when you were looking for something else. For example, someone could be looking for their car keys but find their sunglasses. There are some famous examples of this in physics.

Hans Christian Oersted discovered the relationship between electricity and magnetism when he noticed the needle of a compass moving, during a lecture on electric current.

Arno A. Penzias and Robert Woodrow Wilson discovered radiation left over from the Big Bang, whilst measuring the microwave radiation from the Milky Way. They at first thought their big discovery was just annoying interference.

These serendipitous discoveries were all made by people who had enough knowledge to know that they had found something interesting. If they weren't expert physicists, would they have realized that they had discovered something new?

Previous knowledge

When you do practical work for the IB diploma, is the principle behind what you are doing the same as that used by leading physicists working in research departments of universities around the world?

What you are doing is using the knowledge learnt in class to develop your hypothesis. You should find out that, if you apply your knowledge correctly, your experiment will support your hypothesis. At the cutting edge of science, the scientists are developing new theories so the experiment is used to test the theory, not to test if they have applied accepted theory correctly. To find a new way of relating quantities requires imagination, but what you are being asked to do in your physics lab is to use accepted theory and not to use imagination. How can students trained to apply strict physical laws be expected to make imaginative new theories?

Hans Christian Oersted experimenting with magnets and current after a chance observation.

Paradigm shifts

A paradigm is a set of rules that make up a theory that is accepted by the scientific community. Having completed this course, you will have accepted certain paradigms. We see and interpret the world by virtue of paradigms and theories. Newtonian mechanics is a paradigm - we apply Newton's laws of motion to balls, electrons, planes and cars. The theory works well and is accepted by the scientific community. The way we treat almost everything as a particle is another paradigm. This paradigm is so entrenched in the way that we think that it is almost impossible to think of matter not being made of particles. How could you have a gas that was continuous? Before anyone thought of matter being made of particles, this wouldn't have been a problem, but now it is. To change your way of thinking requires a big leap of imagination, and this is called a paradigm shift. Throughout the development of physics there have been many paradigm shifts.

Copernicus

In 1543, when Copernicus suggested that the Sun was the centre of the solar system, it went against a theory that had been accepted for over a thousand years. Furthermore, it not only went against scientific theory it went against common sense, for how can we be going around the Sun when we are quite obviously standing still? It required a totally new way of thinking to accept this new idea. At the time the evidence was not strong enough to be convincing and the old paradigm remained. It was not until Galileo provided more evidence and later Newton developed an explanation, that the shift took place.

Einstein's theory of relativity

Before Einstein, it was accepted that time is the same everywhere, the length of a body is the same as measured by everyone and the mass of a body is constant. Einstein showed that time, length and mass all depend on the relative velocity of two observers. After this discovery it wasn't possible to carry on as if nothing had happened; what was required was a new way of thinking and a new set of laws. However, when a paradigm shift takes place, the old laws don't suddenly become obsolete – they just obtain limits. Newtonian mechanics is still fine when relative velocities are much less than the speed of light, and that is why it is still included in physics courses such as this.

The next paradigm shift

Will there be another paradigm shift? Can physics advance without one? Because there have been paradigm shifts in the past, does that mean that there has to be another one to advance physics further? In 1900 Lord Kelvin famously said "There is nothing new to be discovered in physics now, all that remains is more and more precise measurement". He was certainly wrong. Does that mean that if someone said the same thing today they'd also be wrong? One problem is that, as students go through the process of education, they get entrenched in the ways of thinking of their teachers, so the leap in imagination to make that new paradigm shift becomes bigger and bigger as time goes on.

Use of language

In physics, we use language in a very precise way; every time a quantity is named, it is given a specific definition. For example *velocity* means one thing and one thing only, the rate of change of displacement. In normal use of language, words can mean more than one thing; this is often used in jokes, poems and literature but not in physics.

"You feel awkward? You're the one who said we ought to hunt ba[...]"

Sometimes the other meanings of a word can lead to confusion. *Potential energy* sounds like a body could possibly have energy but it actually means the energy a body has owing to its position. *Electron spin* sounds like the electron is actually a little ball spinning; a spinning charge would indeed have the properties exhibited by the electron; however these properties do not arise because it's spinning. To get around this problem, physicists sometimes use words that can't be confused with other meanings, who would think that a charm quark was actually charming, for instance?

The battleship and a bucket of water

Can a battleship float in a bucket of water? To solve this problem, you use Archimedes' principle that tells you that a body will float if it displaces it own weight of water. You might therefore conclude that the ship can't float in a bucket of water, because it has to displace (move out of the way) it own weight of water and there isn't that much water in the bucket. However, this is a misinterpretation of the theory. What Archimedes meant is that, when a boat is floating, if you filled the space in the water taken up by the boat with water, then it would be the same weight as the boat. This still might not make sense - that's why physicists use so many diagrams.

This demonstrates again how important it is to understand the language.

Opinions

If you see a painting, read a book or watch the news on the television, you will probably formulate some opinion about it. In many subjects that you study you are actively encouraged to formulate opinions and discuss them in class. For example, you could think the painting here is beautiful or you could think that it is horrible. Either way is fine, because it's your opinion and you can have whatever opinion you like when it comes to such things.

Can you have an opinion in physics? Is it OK to say that in your opinion Newton was wrong when he said that force was proportional to rate of change momentum and that you think that they are independent? In physics, opinions don't count for much, although they can sometimes be the beginning of the formulation of a testable hypothesis.

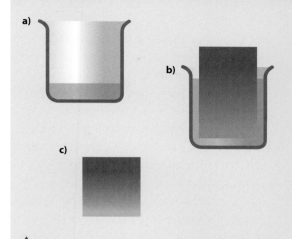

▲ **Figure 16.1** a) Bucket with a bit of water. b) Large object floating in bucket. The bucket is now almost full because the object is taking the place of the water. The object displaces the water. c) Archimedes says that the weight of fluid displaced equals the weight of the object. So this amount of water will have the same weight as the object.

> **"All truths are easy to understand once they are discovered; the point is to discover them."**
> *Galileo Galilei*

How much water do you need to float this huge oil tanker?
▼

Laws

In Physics we use the term *law* quite a lot; for example, Newton's laws of motion, the law of conservation of energy and Ohm's law. The laws are generalized descriptions of observations that are used to solve problems and make predictions. If we want to know what height a ball will reach when thrown upwards, then we can use the law of conservation of energy to find the answer. When you use a law to solve a problem, you have a solid foundation for your solution. If someone were to disagree with your solution then they are disagreeing not only with you, but the law (assuming you applied it correctly). Laws sometimes give easy answers to difficult problems. If someone comes to you with a design of a machine that is 100% efficient, you don't need to study the details, because you can simply apply the second law of thermodynamics and say it won't work.

Universal laws

Some of the laws in physics are called universal laws; for example, Newton's universal law of gravitation. A universal law applies to the whole universe, but it is possibly naïve (or arrogant) to think that we can write laws that apply to the whole universe, when we can only make measurements from one very small part of it. Today, scientists are more modest in their claims and accept that there are probably parts of the universe that do not behave in the same way as things in our solar system.

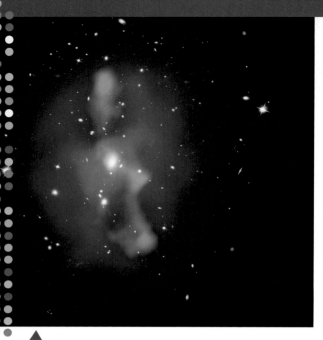

▲ Galaxy cluster MS0735.6+7421 The red part of this image is radio, the blue X-ray and the yellow is light. You could never see this.

Seeing is believing?

▲ Can you see a hidden face in this picture? Apparently those with "physical brains" take a long time. See below for a hint.

During the IB physics course you will have been asked to make observations and devise research questions; is this easier when you have studied the topic already or when it's something totally new? When you already know what you are supposed to be looking for, it is often easier to get started. However, if you have no preconceived ideas, you might have more chance of spotting something new.

Hint: look between 3 o'clock and 5 o'clock.

Sense and perception

Physics is based on observation and observations are made with our senses. This was certainly true hundreds of years ago but today, although the information finally arrives into our brain via our senses, the observation itself is often done via some instrument. Copernicus had difficulty convincing anyone about his theory that the planets orbited the Sun, because he didn't have any convincing observations. He had predicted that Venus would have phases like the Moon, but couldn't observe this. Galileo used the telescope to observe that Venus did indeed have phases like the Moon. At first, this was still not accepted, since people didn't trust the telescope - they wanted to "see it with their own eyes".

Deceptive pictures

A camera operates on the same physical principle as the human eye. Visible light is reflected from an object and focused by a lens onto a screen. It is reasonable to think that a picture is a good record of what we see. Using digital technology, it is now possible to recreate pictures from light that we can't see. Is this seeing? Can we say that we have seen a distant galaxy when we look at a picture constructed from radio waves? Can we say that we have seen the face of a flea when the picture was constructed from the diffraction pattern of electrons?

The face of a flea. Can you really say that this is what it looks like since you can never see it directly?
▼

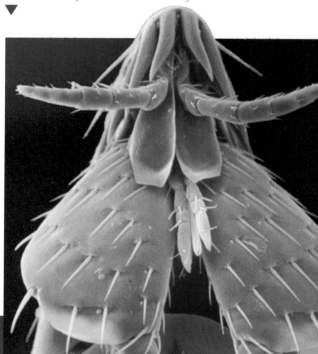

The Moon illusion

Have you ever noticed that the Moon looks bigger when it's close to the horizon? If you know some physics, you might have thought of an explanation. Maybe it's due to the refraction of the light by the atmosphere, or the elliptical orbit of the Moon causing it to sometimes be closer to the Earth. These theories would be based on the observation that you have made using your senses. However, if you were actually to measure the size of the Moon you'd find that it doesn't change as it moves from overhead to the horizon; it's an illusion. Physical theories are based on measurement not perception.

Imagination

Have you made use of your imagination during this course? Maybe not, but it is important that physicists have imagination, as Einstein famously said;

"I am enough of an artist to draw freely upon my imagination. Imagination is more important than knowledge. Knowledge is limited. Imagination encircles the world".

Without imagination, the huge leaps that have brought about the paradigm shifts in the way we perceive the world would never have been made. In learning basic physics, following rules tends to be emphasized more than using imagination, but at the cutting edge it is imagination that enables scientists to forge their way forward.

Children use their imagination all the time when playing. What happens to this skill in later life?
▼

Physics or intuition?

One of the problems with studying physics is that we all live in the physical world and have all seen how bodies interact. We all know that if you drop something it falls to Earth and if you push someone on a swing they will move back and forth. These observations give us a feeling for what is going to happen in other instances; we call this feeling *intuition*, the ability to sense or know what is going to happen without reasoning. In physics, we create models to help give a reason for what is happening. This all works fine until intuition gives us a different answer to the laws of physics. Here's an example: Consider a metal bar floating in space, where the gravitational field strength is zero. If you apply two forces to the bar as shown in Figure 16.2, what happens?

Intuition will probably tell you that the bar will rotate about point A. This is because if you do this yourself that is what will happen. However that answer is wrong. Let's now apply Newton's laws of motion to the problem.

Newton's 1st law states that a body will remain at rest or with uniform motion in a straight line unless acted upon by an unbalanced force. The forces in this example are balanced, so the centre of mass of the bar (B) will not move.

We can see however that the turning effect (torque) of these forces are *not* balanced, so the rod will turn.

If the rod turns but point B doesn't move, then the rod must turn about B. And that is what happens.

The reason for the difference in these two predictions is that this rod is not in a gravitational field. When we try to do this with a rod on Earth, there are other forces acting.

Intuition was wrong; physics was right. The laws of physics can tell you what happens even if you can't do it or see it yourself.

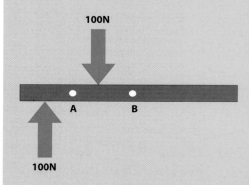

Figure 16.2 What happens when the bar experiences these forces?

Peer review

One of the strengths of modern scientific practice is that every new discovery goes through a rigorous process of peer review. Before a theory is published, it is sent to other scientists working in the same field. They give feedback to the research team before the theory is published. In this way mistakes can be spotted and problems ironed out. It also gives the possibility for other groups working in the same field to think of experiments that could be conducted to prove the theory wrong. Scientists are continually looking for ways to prove theories wrong, so when a theory is accepted by the scientific community one can be sure that it has been rigorously tested.

"It doesn't matter how beautiful your theory is, it doesn't matter how smart you are. If it doesn't agree with experiment, it's wrong."
Richard Feynman

"There are many hypotheses in science which are wrong. That's perfectly all right; they're the aperture to finding out what's right.
Carl Sagan

"The most exciting phrase to hear in science, the one that heralds new discoveries, is not 'Eureka!' (I found it!) but 'That's funny...' "
Isaac Asimov

Ethics and physics

Ethics is the study of right and wrong. It is sometimes not easy to decide when a course of action is right or wrong, and in these cases, it is useful to have a moral code or set of guidelines to refer to. In physics, there are two areas where ethical considerations are important;

1 The way physicists work in relation to other physicists; for example, they shouldn't copy each other's work or make up data.

2 The way their actions affect society; for example, physicists shouldn't work on projects that will endanger human life.

Whether a particular piece of research is ethical or not can be difficult to determine, especially when you do not know what the results of the experiment might lead to.

Should Rutherford have performed his experiments in nuclear physics, since the discovery of the nucleus led to the discovery of the atom bomb?

Can it be ethical to work in the weapons industry?

Who should decide whether a piece of research is carried out, physicists or governments?

If you left your body to science, would it be OK if it were used to test car seat belts? How about if it were used to test how far different types of bullets penetrate flesh?

Is it ethical to spend billions to carry out an experiment to test someone's hypothesis?

Internal assessment

Internal Assessment or IA counts for 24% of your final IB grade; if you work hard and do the IA properly you are already half way to passing physics. It will be assessed by your teacher but their grades will be **moderated**. What this means is that samples of your work will be sent to an IB moderator who may adjust the grades to bring them into line with the required standards.

The Internal Assessment criteria have been changed and the new system started in August 2007. It is essential that you follow the **new programme** and that you do not use the ideas from the old system.

If you are studying HL Physics you will need to complete 60 hours of IA, and for SL 40 hours. For everybody these totals include 10 hours for the **Group 4 Project**. The Group 4 Project does not mean that you work in groups of four; it refers to the number of the science group in the IB hexagon. You have to do the Group 4 Project; it is not an option.

The most important thing to understand about IA is that you will be assessed, first, last, and **only against the criteria**. It does not matter how much time or effort you put in to the lab reports; if they do not meet the criteria then the teachers and moderators cannot give you top grades.

There are five criteria: **Design, Data collection and processing, Conclusion and evaluation, Manipulative skills and Personal skills**. Each criterion is divided into three aspects and for each aspect you will get a grade of either:

Complete   2 marks

Partial   1 mark

Not at all   0 marks.

The maximum score for each criterion is *Complete* for each of the three aspects, which would be 3×2 marks $= 6$ marks. The first three criteria will each be assessed (at least) twice which gives a possible total of $3 \times 2 \times 6$ marks $= 36$ marks. The other two criteria will be assessed once each to give a further possible 12 marks. So for IA the maximum total score would be $36 + 12 = 48$ marks, which is then scaled down to give the number out of 24.

The first three criteria are the most heavily weighted because they are each assessed twice. They can be assessed any time through the course but do not be disappointed, or even surprised, if your grades are low to start with. There will be plenty of opportunities for you to improve later in the course.

On the following page, the criteria are given in detail with some advice on how you can score high grades for each one.

Design

Levels/marks	Aspect 1 Defining the problem and selecting variables	Aspect 2 Controlling variables	Aspect 3 Developing a method for collection of data
Complete/2	Formulates a focused problem/research question and identifies the relevant variables.	Designs a method for the effective control of the variables.	Develops a method that allows for the collection of sufficient relevant data.
Partial/1	Formulates a problem/research question that is incomplete or identifies only some relevant variables.	Designs a method that makes some attempt to control the variables.	Develops a method that allows for the collection of insufficient relevant data.
Not at all/0	Does not identify a problem/research question **and** does not identify any relevant variables.	Designs a method that does not control the variables.	Develops a method that does not allow for any relevant data to be collected.

Although this is the first criterion, it will probably not be the first one you will be assessed against during the course. Most people find the skills needed here to be quite difficult.

When assessing this criterion, your teacher will not give you detailed instructions about what you should do. Instead you will be given an open-ended task which might ask you to investigate the factors affecting a particular situation or concept.

The first aspect requires you to do two things; state a focused problem or research question and identify relevant variables.

For the research question you must not simply repeat the aim given by the teacher. For example, let us say the instructions are 'Investigate the factors affecting the simple pendulum'. It is not sufficient for you to simply say 'What are the main factors that affect the motion of the simple pendulum?' What is expected is something more like 'How does the time period of the simple pendulum depend on the length of the string?'

The variables, the things that can change during the experiment, come in three categories:
dependent or measured variables
independent or manipulated variables
controlled or constant variables

To obtain *Complete* here you must identify each of them clearly.

In the pendulum example, the dependent variable would be the time, the independent variable would be the length of the string and the controlled variables would include the weight of the pendulum bob and the angle at which it was released.

For the aspects 2 and 3, you have to design a method. This will involve selecting the best apparatus to perform the experiment. Clear **labelled diagrams** are extremely useful here and are highly recommended.

For aspect 2, your method must explain how you are going to control the variables. This refers particularly to how your experimental design will keep the controlled variables you identified from changing. For example, how you will ensure that the pendulum is always released from the same angle.

For aspect 3, your method must allow you to collect sufficient data to draw a valid conclusion about your research question. Be specific about details of repetitions and the range and amount of data to be collected.

To measure the time period of the pendulum it is better to time ten swings and divide by ten, rather than trying to measure just one swing. The length of the string should be as long as is practical, maybe 1.5 m or more and not just 30 cm. The length should be varied several times, maybe at intervals of 10 cm, to give a good range. If you took just three readings you would not obtain *Complete* here.

Data collection and processing

Levels/ marks	Aspect 1 Recording raw data	Aspect 2 Processing raw data	Aspect 3 Presenting processed data
Complete/2	Records appropriate quantitative and associated qualitative raw data, including units and uncertainties where relevant.	Processes the quantitative raw data correctly.	Presents processed data appropriately and, where relevant, includes errors and uncertainties.
Partial/1	Records appropriate quantitative and associated qualitative raw data, but with some mistakes or omissions.	Processes quantitative raw data, but with some mistakes and/or omissions.	Presents processed data appropriately, but with some mistakes and/or omissions.
Not at all/0	Does not record any appropriate quantitative raw data **or** raw data is incomprehensible.	No processing of quantitative raw data is carried out **or** major mistakes are made in processing.	Presents processed data inappropriately **or** incomprehensibly.

All the same criteria are used for biology, chemistry and physics. In a biology experiment the data might be qualitative, without any numbers. In a physics experiment the **data will be quantitative.** Also in a physics experiment, **errors and uncertainties are always relevant**.

For aspect 1 your data should be recorded in tables; the best thing is to include the handwritten data as well as the word-processed tables.

The tables should have headings at the top with the units and **uncertainty or ± values**. The uncertainty values will depend on what is being measured but should be sensible. For example, if you time ten swings of a pendulum with a stopwatch there will be an uncertainty due to your reaction time. Reasonable values would be in the range ± 0.1 s to ± 0.5 s. Values of ± 0.01 s or ± 2.0 s would not be accepted as sensible.

To obtain *Complete* in aspect 1 your data must have consistent numbers of significant figures and decimal places.

Aspect 2 includes any calculations based on the raw data and also changing the data round to get it in the correct form to draw a graph. Usually there will be a graph plotted showing the relationship between the independent and dependent variables. Typically you will draw a best-fit line and measure the gradient.

For presenting the data in aspect 3, you must make sure that your graph has good scales, the axes are labelled with units and the points are accurately plotted. To get *Complete* you need error bars and maximum and minimum lines to find the uncertainty in the best-fit line.

For *Complete* in aspect 3 you also need **numerical error analysis**. Uncertainties from the raw data must be combined, manipulated and worked through equations here. It is not enough to simply find the percentage error between your result and the accepted value.

Conclusion and evaluation

Levels/ marks	Aspect 1 Concluding	Aspect 2 Evaluating procedure(s)	Aspect 3 Improving the investigation
Complete/2	States a conclusion, with justification, based on a reasonable interpretation of the data.	Evaluates weaknesses and limitations.	Suggests realistic improvements in respect of identified weaknesses and limitations.
Partial/1	States a conclusion based on a reasonable interpretation of the data.	Identifies some weaknesses and limitations, but the evaluation is weak or missing.	Suggests only superficial improvements.
Not at all/0	States no conclusion or the conclusion is based on an unreasonable interpretation of the data.	Identifies irrelevant weaknesses and limitations.	Suggests unrealistic improvements.

When drawing a conclusion in aspect 1, if you find a value for a constant, like the acceleration due to gravity, you should compare your result and the accepted value. When you do this you should reference the source of the accepted value. You should discuss systematic and random errors and uncertainties, and compare the percentage error with the total random error.

In aspect 2 you should identify any problems with the apparatus or method and comment on how significant they are. Comment also on the precision and accuracy of the measurements.

The suggestions for improvements in aspect 3 should be based on the weaknesses identified in aspect 2. You should discuss improvements to the method and apparatus, and suggest ways to reduce random errors and remove systematic errors.

The modifications must be specific and realistic. Do not suggest doing the experiment in a vacuum and do not say things such as you will be more careful next time. Do not simply state that better apparatus should be used; rather describe exactly what kind of apparatus would improve the investigation.

Manipulative skills (assessed summatively)

Levels/ marks	Aspect 1 Following instructions*	Aspect 2 Carrying out techniques	Aspect 3 Working safely
Complete/2	Follows instructions accurately, adapting to new circumstances (seeking assistance when required).	Competent and methodical in the use of a range of techniques and equipment.	Pays attention to safety issues.
Partial/1	Follows instructions but requires assistance.	Usually competent and methodical in the use of a range of techniques and equipment.	Usually pays attention to safety issues.
Not at all/0	Rarely follows instructions or requires constant supervision.	Rarely competent and methodical in the use of a range of techniques and equipment.	Rarely pays attention to safety issues.

Manipulative skills will be assessed summatively at the end of the course. What this means is that your teacher will base your grade on your performance throughout the experimental programme and not just on one experiment.

You should ensure that your teacher knows you can follow both written and verbal instructions without too much assistance. You should always check with your teacher whether there are any safety issues; behaving safely at all times is a key factor in this criterion.

Personal skills (for group 4 project assessment only)

Levels/ marks	Aspect 1 Self-motivation and perseverance	Aspect 2 Working within a team	Aspect 3 Self-reflection
Complete/2	Approaches the project with self-motivation and follows it through to completion.	Collaborates and communicates in a group situation and integrates the views of others.	Shows a thorough awareness of their own strengths and weaknesses and gives thoughtful consideration to their learning experience.
Partial/1	Completes the project but sometimes lacks self-motivation.	Exchanges some views but requires guidance to collaborate with others.	Shows limited awareness of their own strengths and weaknesses and gives some consideration to their learning experience.
Not at all/0	Lacks perseverance and motivation.	Makes little or no attempt to collaborate in a group situation.	Shows no awareness of their own strengths and weaknesses and gives no consideration to their learning experience.

One of the IA changes is that you can now **only** be assessed for Personal skills during the Group 4 project; you cannot be assessed for any of the other criteria. Also this is now the only time during the course when you **can** be assessed for Personal skills and it only happens once.

The means of assessment will vary from school to school, but in addition to using their own judgment many teachers may use peer assessment and self assessment. This means you will be asked for your opinion, usually confidentially, on the participation of your fellow students and on your own contributions to the project. You should simply be as honest as you can in this type of exercise; ultimately your teacher will make the final decisions.

During the project make sure that you listen to the other students in your group and do not exclude anybody. Try to put any negative personal feelings to one side; it is only going to last for ten hours. Make sure that you follow through and do not shirk your share of the tasks. Take a full part in any brainstorming exercise and in the final presentations.

Most students enjoy the Group 4 project; often it is identified as one of the highlights of the year. The more you put into it, the more you will get from it and this includes your Personal skills grade.

Extended essays

These notes are intended to give you some help with writing an Extended Essay in Physics. They are not a substitute for the most important person who will be involved in assisting you with the project; that will be your Extended Essay Supervisor. Choose your Supervisor wisely; ideally it will be a person with some prior experience and someone with whom you can easily maintain a good working relationship.

- The Extended Essay is a requirement for IB Diploma candidates; you have to write one or you do not get a Diploma.

- It is an independent research project of some 4000 words in length so is the longest assignment you will write during your two years of IB study.

- The Extended Essay shares with TOK a concern with interpreting and evaluating evidence and constructing reasoned arguments.

- You should choose a topic that interests you because you will clearly be spending a considerable amount of time working on this project.

- Complex topics like black holes, gravity or the fate of the universe are not suitable because you will not be able to produce an in-depth personal analysis.

- Avoid crossing into metaphysics or bad science. Examples of this would be the unknown forces of the pyramids, the physics of the existence of God or investigations into extrasensory perception.

- Read some previous essays to identify strengths and weaknesses. There will probably be some available for you in school, otherwise you can look online.

- You will need to find a supervisor; normally a physics teacher. There is a limit to the number of essays each teacher can supervise so you should try and approach the teacher early.

- After you have a topic and supervisor you need to formulate a Research Question. This should be sharply focused and it is crucially important to your essay.

- You should ask your supervisor or IB coordinator for a copy of subject specific details for Physics Extended Essays which is in the Extended Essay Guide.

- Now you are ready to start your research. You will need a bibliography at the end of your essay so keep a record of all your sources.

- Do not do all your research online; use other sources like the school and local university libraries.

- Make sure that your work is backed up properly; you will probably need to submit an electronic version and at least two hard copies when it is finished.

- Although it is not a requirement, most good Physics Extended Essays are experimentally based.

- You should not attempt anything too complicated or difficult. Listen to the advice of your physics teacher about what will, or will not, work in the lab.

- You will usually need to be supervised while working in the lab and you will have to finish your experimental work to the school deadlines.
- In most schools, students start their Extended Essay in the second half of Grade 11 and finish by the middle of Grade 12. Ideally, you should have all experimental work finished by the end of the summer.
- Safety is of primary importance. Do not even consider doing anything in the lab which may put you, or anyone else, at any sort of risk.
- You will need to submit drafts of your essay to your supervisor, meeting all the school deadlines. One reason for this is so that the supervisor, having seen the development of your essay, can guarantee that the final draft is all your own work.
- Your supervisor will comment on your first draft but will not edit it or make detailed corrections. Typically you should expect to spend 3-4 hours with your supervisor overall.
- When the essay is finished, it should include the following elements in the order listed:
  Title page
  Abstract
  Contents page
  Introduction
  Body (development/methods/results)
  Conclusion
  References and bibliography
  Appendices
- There must be some physics theory in the body of your essay. Carry out research to find out what other physicists have discovered in your chosen area.
- The upper limit is 4000 words; longer essays are subject to penalties. There is no lower limit, but clearly a very short essay is unlikely to achieve a good grade.
- The following are not included in the 4000 word limit:
  the abstract
  acknowledgments
  the contents page
  diagrams and tables
  equations, formulae and calculations
  references and footnotes
  the bibliography
  appendices
- For the new programme, which will be examined for the first time in 2009, all Extended Essays will be graded using the same criteria. They are:

A:	research question	2 marks
B:	introduction	2 marks
C:	investigation	4 marks
D:	knowledge and understanding	4 marks
E:	reasoned argument	4 marks
F:	analytical and evaluative skills	4 marks
G:	use of language	4 marks
H:	conclusion	2 marks
I:	formal presentation	4 marks
J:	abstract	2 marks
K:	holistic judgement	4 marks

- You should ask your supervisor or IB coordinator for a copy of the details of the new criteria and read them very carefully. Your essay will be graded solely on the basis of how well it meets these criteria.

- Do not confuse the extended essay with the IA criteria; your essay will not be graded against the IA criteria.

- When you have finished writing the essay, you will write the abstract. Your supervisor will probably help you with that. When the whole thing is finished proofread it carefully and check it against all the criteria.

- Although 4000 words sounds like a lot, initially many students end up having to cut back because they have written too much. Writing an Extended Essay is an excellent preparation of university; you will be proud of your essay, and yourself, when it is completed. Good luck!

Answers

Chapter 1

1. B
2. A
3. B
4. 2.36×10^6 J or 2.36 MJ
5. 1.09×10^6 Hz or 1.09 MHz
6. 500 nm
7. 0.01 μs
8. D
9. A
10. C
11. C
12. 20 N

Practice questions

1. C
2. D
3. B
4. C

Chapter 2

1. (a) 0.43 s   (b) 0.02 s
2. 18 m
3.

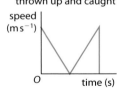

4.

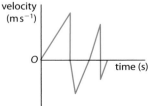

5. (a) 3.2 m s^{-2} (b) 4.8×10^5 N
6. (a) zero   (b) 131 N   (c) 1.03 m s^{-2}
7. (a) 5.0 m s^{-1} (b) 4×10^4 N

8. (a) (i) 1.35×10^4 J   (ii) 6.5×10^5 J
   (b) 15 kW
9. (a) 321 m   (b) 100 MJ   (c) (i) 130 kN
10. 0.22 m s^{-2}

Practice questions

1. A
2. D
3. C
4. B
5. B
6. B
7. C
8. B
9. A
10. B
11. B
12. B
13. C
14. B
15. C
16. B
17. C
18. D
19. D
20. A
21. B
22. (a) (i) 3.2 m   (ii) 0.80 s
    (b) 21 m
23. (b) (i) 2.0 m s^{-1} (ii) 6000 J
24. (a) 1.6 m s^{-2} (b) 9.2 m
    (c) 23 kJ   (d) 1.9 kW
    (e) 38%
25. (f) $5.4 \times 10^3 \text{ m s}^{-1}$
    (g) 4.2 years

Chapter 3

1. (a) $7.12 \times 10^{-6} \text{ m}^3$ (b) 6.022×10^{23} molecules
   (c) $1.2 \times 10^{-29} \text{m}^3$
2. 27 g
3. (a) 3.92×10^3 J   (b) 3.92×10^3 J
4. 1.8×10^6 J
5. 420 kJ
6. (a) 3.6×10^6 J   (b) $3.6 \times 10^5 \text{ J °C}^{-1}$
   (c) Some is lost to the outside.

7. 1.33×10^4 J
8. (a) 1kg (b) 3.36×10^5 J (c) 336 s
9. (a) 3×10^5 J (b) 686.7 °C
10. (a) 3×10^5 J (b) 2.25×10^5 J
    (c) 51°C
11. (a) 80 kg (b) 1.34×10^7 J
12. 3.35×10^{11} J
13. 1.135×10^3 s
14. (a) 1.84×10^4 kg (b) 6.16×10^9 J
    (c) 3.42×10^5 W (d) 342 W m^{-2}

Practice questions

1. (c) (ii) 2.1×10^3 J kg^{-1} K^{-1}
       (iii) 3.3×10^5 J kg^{-1}
2. 1800 s
4. (a) (i) 120 J kg^{-1} K^{-1} (ii) 5.4×10^5 J kg^{-1}
5. (b) (ii) 7.3 K (d) (ii) 490 g
6. D
7. C
8. A
9. A

Chapter 4

1. (b)
2. (a) 1.67 Hz (b) 10.5 Hz
3. 1.1 cm down
4. displacement

5. 1.67s
6. -0.5 m s^{-1}
7. (a) 2.5 m s^{-1} (b) 3.16 m s^{-2}
8. 0.62 m s^{-2}
9. 0.318m
10. 29°
11. 15°
12. 2×10^8 m s^{-1}

Practice questions

1. (b) (i) 0.5 m (ii) 0.5 mm (iii) 330 m s^{-1}
2. (c) (ii) 333 Hz (iv) 4.5×10^{-3} m
3. (c) (i) 9.6 km s^{-1} (ii) 5.7 km s^{-1}
   (d) (iv) L$_1$: 1060 km $\pm$ 20; L$_2$: 650 km $\pm$ 20;
            L$_3$: 420 km $\pm$ 20

Chapter 5

1. 3 kΩ
2. 0.3 V
3. 0.02 A
4. 100 kΩ, 100 kΩ, 25 kΩ
5. 1 Ω
6. 11.5 V
7. (a) 500 J (b) 3×10^4 J
8. 0.03125 W
9. 0.5 W
10. (a) 450 kJ (b) 37.5 kW
    (c) 125 A (d) No other losses
11. (a) 0.45 A (b) 20 J
12. (a) 4.5 A (b) 1.8×10^7 J
13. 16/3 Ω
14. 8 Ω
15. 28 Ω
16. 16/7 Ω
17. 5 V, 0.5 A
18. 3 V, 3 A
19. 6 V, 1.5 A
20. 6 V, 3 A
21. 714 Ω

Practice questions

1. (i) 1.4 V (ii) 1.0 Ω (iii) 6.9×10^3 J
   (c) (i) 50 Ω (ii) R = 2.0 Ω
2. (a) (ii) 0.20 A (b) (ii) r = 2.0 Ω
   (c) (i) 3.3 Ω (ii) 13 Ω
   (f) 0.60 V
4. (a) (i) EI (ii) I^2r (iii) VI
   (d) E = 1.5 V (ii) 1.3 ($\pm$0.1) A
   (e) 0.47 W or 0.48 W

Chapter 6

1. 1.62 m s^{-2}
2. 24.7 m s^{-2}
3. 7.34 m s^{-2}
4. 6.69×10^{-8} N kg^{-1}
5. 0 N kg^{-1}
6. (a) 1.8×10^6 N C^{-1} (b) 4.5×10^5 N C^{-1}
   (c) 0.045 N
7. (a) 1×10^{-7} N (b) 1×10^{-5} m s^{-2}
8. (a) 2×10^{-5} N (b) East
9. (a) 5×10^{-6} N (b) West

Practice questions

1. (d) g = 5.6 N kg^{-1}
3. (b) (ii) M = 1.9×10^{27} kg

Chapter 7

1. 10
2. 13.06 eV, 3.17×10^{15} Hz
3. 0.31 eV
4. 13.6 eV, 3.29×10^{15} Hz
5. (a) 17p, 18n   (b) 28p, 30n
   (c) 82p, 122n
6. 4.16×10^{-18} C, 9×10^{-26} kg
7. $^{235}_{92}$U
8. 92 protons, 146 neutrons
9. (a) 92p, 141n   (b) 234.9405u
   (c) 1.901u   (d) 1771 MeV
   (e) 7.60 MeV
10.

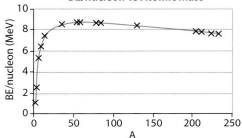

11. 21p, 24n
12. 55p, 82n
13. (a) α (b) α (c) β
14. (a) 5.24 MeV   (b) 4.67 MeV
    (c) 0.39 MeV   (d) 0.04 MeV
15. 12.5g
16. 12.5 s^{-1}
17. 20 000 years
18. (a) $^{18}_{9}$F, $^{1}_{1}$H   (b) $^{123}_{53}$I
    (c) $^{17}_{7}$N, $^{18}_{8}$O   (d) $^{30}_{15}$P
19. (a) $^{-}1.017375$ U   (b) 948 MeV
20. (a) 3.27 MeV   (b) 4.03 MeV
    (c) 18.3 MeV
21. 10n, 133.9 MeV
22. 135.7 MeV

Practice questions

1. (b) (i) $^{4}_{2}$He/$^{4}_{2}\alpha$ $^{222}_{86}$Rn
       (ii) 7.77×10^{-13} J or 4.86 MeV
2. (a) (ii) $^{235}_{92}$U + $^{1}_{0}$n $\rightarrow$ $^{98}_{38}$Sr + $^{142}_{54}$Xe + 4 $^{1}_{0}$n
       (iii) mass number unchanged;
             atomic number increases by $+1$
   (b) (i) 2.2×10^{-18} N s
   (c) (i) 7.9×10^{-12} J   (ii) 8.4×10^{4} J
       (iv) 4.1×10^{-9} kg

Chapter 8

1.

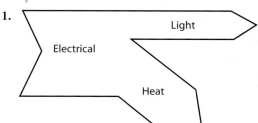

2.

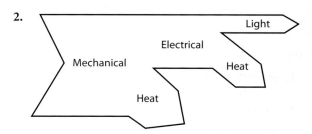

3. (a) 80 km   (b) 1.44×10^{8} J
   (c) 1.92×10^{8} J   (d) 4.2 kg
   (e) 4.7 litres   (f) 0.06 ltr/km
4. (a) 8.64×10^{13} J   (b) 2.16×10^{14} J
   (c) 6.65×10^{6} kg   (d) 67 truck loads
5. (a) $^{238}_{92}$U $\rightarrow$ $^{0}_{1}n$ $\rightarrow$ $^{239}_{92}$U
   (b) $^{239}_{92}$Np $\rightarrow$ $^{239}_{93}$Np + β^{-} + $\bar{v}$
   (c) $^{239}_{93}$U + $^{239}_{94}$Pu + β^{-} + $\bar{v}$
6. (a) $^{142}_{56}$Ba $\rightarrow$ $^{142}_{57}$La + β^{-} + $\bar{v}$
   (b) 9 years
7. (a) 7
   (b) $^{239}_{94}$Pu $\rightarrow$ $^{136}_{54}$Xe + $^{96}_{40}$Zr + 7n^{0}
   (c) 164 MeV   (d) 239 g
   (e) 2.5×10^{24} atoms (f) 4.13×10^{26} MeV
   (g) 6.6×10^{13} J
8. 2.7×10^{12} J
9. (a) 3.6×10^{10} J   (b) 13g
10. (a) 4000 W   (b) 2000 J
    (c) 28.6 °C
11. (a) 0.015 W   (b) 0.03 A
    (c) 5 V   (d) 0.3 A
    (e) 6667
12.

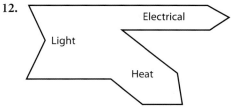

13. (a) 1.5×10^{14} kg   (b) 1.6×10^{17} J
    (c) 1.9×10^{9} J   (d) 1.7×10^{6} kg
14. (a) 3.2 kW   (b) 64 kg
15. (a) 5.5 MW   (b) 1.1 MW
    (c) 3.7 MW

16. (a) $10 \, \text{m s}^{-1}$
  (b) $2 \times 10^6 \, \text{W}$
  (c) $4 \times 10^9 \, \text{W}$
17. (a) $9552 \, \text{W m}^{-2}$
  (b) $51.3 \, \text{W m}^{-2}$
18. $3.3 \times 10^{-19} \, \text{J}$ (2eV)
19. $4.8 \times 10^{-7} \, \text{m}$
20. $7.35 \times 10^7 \, \text{W m}^{-2}$
21. $4.52 \times 10^{26} \, \text{W}$

Practice questions

2. (b) (i) $0.91 \, \text{m}^2$ **(ii)** 33%
4. (b) $12 \, \text{m}$
5. (a) (i) fission   **(ii)** kinetic energy
6. (a) (i) kinetic energy of the fission products/
     neutrons/photons
   (iii) the moderator
   (iv) 984 or $9.8 \times 10^2 \, \text{kg yr}^{-1}$
  (b) (i) 800 MW   **(ii)** 200 MW
   (iii) 1600 MW
   (iv) the second law of the thermodynamics
   (v) $\eta = \dfrac{800}{2400}$ or 33%
   (vi) 450 K
7. (a) (i) 120 kW

Chapter 9

4. (a) 48 cm
  (b) $120 \, \text{m s}^{-1}$
5. (b) $330 \, \text{m s}^{-1}$
6. (a) $\dfrac{c}{f}$
  (b) $c + v$
7. (a) (i) $0.75 \, \text{m}$ **(ii)** $440 \, \text{Hz}$ **(b)** $330 \, \text{m s}^{-1}$
  (c) (i) $0.732 \, \text{m}$ **(ii)** $451 \, \text{Hz}$
8. $5.0 \times 10^{-10} \, \text{m}$
9. $2.2 \times 10^{-5} \, \text{m}$
10. (b) 2 mm – 5 mm is acceptable
   (c) $2.4 \times 10^{-4} \, \text{rad}$ (calculated with 3 mm) so
      resolved.
12. 45°

Practice questions

1. (b) (i) $0.317 \, \text{m}$
2. (b) $2000 \, \text{m s}^{-1}$
3. (c) $2.0 \times 10^{11} \, \text{m}$
4. (a) 0.25 rad 0.50 rad
6. (b) $9.8 \approx 10 \, \text{cm}$

7. (b) 52°

Chapter 10

1. (b) (i) $6.9 \, (\pm 0.3) \times 10^{-34} \, \text{Js}$
     (ii) $3.3 \, (\pm 0.5) \times 10^{-19} \, \text{J}$
2. (b) (ii) $6.4 \times 10^{-20} \, \text{J}$
3. (b) $1.7 \times 10^{-11} \, \text{m}$
4. (a) $1.4 \times 10^{-10} \, \text{m}$
6. (c) $4 \times 10^{16} \, \text{s}$
7. (b) $0.23 \, \text{min}^{-1}$ **(c)** 10 min

Practice questions

2. (b) (i) $3.8 \, (\pm 0.2) \times 10^{14} \, \text{Hz}$
     (ii) $6.5 \, (\pm 0.2) \times 10^{-34} \, \text{Js}$
     (ii) $1.5 \, (\pm 0.1) \, \text{eV}$
3. (b) (ii) $1.7 \, \text{eV}$
4. (b) $22 \, \text{u}$
  (c) 15 cm path: 10 protons 10 neutrons
       16.5 cm path: 10 protons 12 neutrons
5. (b) $0.13 \, y^{-1}$ **(c)** $8.4 \, y$
6. (b) $8.2 \times 10^{-6} \, \text{g}$
  (c) (i) $5.3 \times 10^{-10} \, y^{-1}$ **(ii)** $3.6 \times 10^9 \, y$

Chapter 11

1. (a) 00000111   **(b)** 00001110
  (c) 00010000   **(d)** 01000011
  (e) 01111101
2. (a) 7   **(b)** 36   **(c)** 51   **(d)** 63
3. 01000010 01000001 01000100
4. 6 333 years
5.

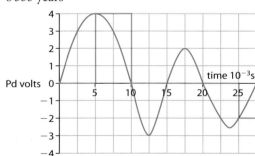

6.

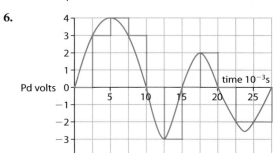

7. 100 Hz

8.

Time	No.	Binary
0.0	6	0110
0.5	10	1010
1.0	11	1011
1.5	9	1001
2.0	6	0110
2.5	3	0011
3.0	1	0001
3.5	3	0011
4.0	6	0110

9.

Time	No.	Binary
0.0	3	011
0.5	4	100
1.0	5	101
1.5	4	100
2.0	3	011
2.5	0	000

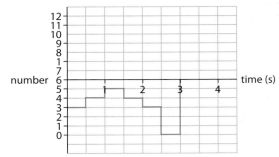

10. (a) 3×10^9 bits   (b) 6×10^9 bits
     (c) 753 MB
11. (a) 3.1×10^9 bits   (b) 6.2×10^9 bits
     (c) 781 MB
12. 0.33 V
13. 100 μC
14. 8×10^{-18} V 8×10^{-11} V
15. 4.24 mm 1.8×10^5 pixels
16. 4.24×10^{-4}
17. (a) 2×10^4 photons   (b) 1.4×10^4 electrons
18. 0.2s
19. 1.7×10^5 pixels
20. (a) 5V   (b) 9V   (c) ⁻9V
21. (a) 11   (b) 5.5 V
     (c) 0.5 mA   (d) 5 V
22. (a) 5   (b) ⁻5V   (c) 1 mA
     (d) 1 mA   (e) 1 V
23. (a) 2.5 V   (b) 50 Hz

24.

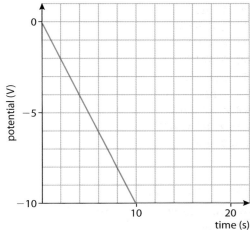

26. (a) Reverse diode   (b) 139.6 Ω
     (c) 7 mA   (d) 0.976 V
     (e) ⁻9 V

27.

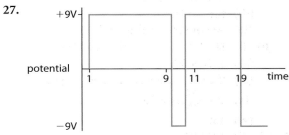

Chapter 12

1. 1.06
2. 1.15
3. 1.34
4. 1.81
5. 2.79
6. 3.91
7. 5.50
8. 12.26
9. 2.4×10^3 m
10. (a) 10 years
     (d) 8 light years = 7.6×10^{16} m
     (e) 24 years
11. (a) 1.1×10^{-5} s
     (b) 3200 m
     (c) 650 m
12. 5.3×10^{-20} N s
13. 938 MeV
14. Lepton
     Meson
     Baryon
     Lepton
15. yes

16. no
17. no
18. yes
19. yes
20. no
21. no
22. 1.12×10^{-6} J
23. 1.12×10^{6} J
24. $1500 \, \mathrm{m \, s^{-1}}$
25. 1.12×10^{15} W
26. B – positron
    A – electron
27. (a) weak   (b) not weak   (c) weak
28. (a) yes   (b) yes   (c) no
29. (a) $d\bar{u}$ (b) sss (c) ssd (d) ssu
30. $d \rightarrow u$
31. no
32. yes
33. yes
34. no
35. gluon
36. W
37. (a)

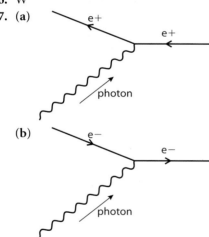

(b)

38. (a) down quark
    (b) weak
    (c) up quark
    (d) up quark, antineutrino, electron
    (e) beta decay
39. (a) up antineutrino

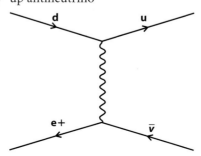

(b) anti down, antineutrino

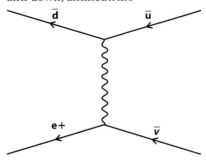

Practice questions

1. (b) (ii) $0.87c = 2.6 \times 10^{8} \, \mathrm{m \, s^{-1}}$
3. (b) $c\text{-}v$ (c) c
   (d) (ii) $0.87c = 2.6 \times 10^{8} \, \mathrm{m \, s^{-1}}$
4. (a) $13.9 \, \mu s$
   (b) (i) 454 m   (ii) 1.52 μs

Chapter 13

1. (a) Earth $\rightarrow$ Mars $\rightarrow$ Jupiter $\rightarrow$ Pluto
   (b) Pluto $\rightarrow$ Mars $\rightarrow$ Earth $\rightarrow$ Jupiter
3. $2.8 \times 10^{14} \, \mathrm{kg \, s^{-1}}$
4. 5.3×10^{19} m
5. 6000 K
6. 4.1×10^{30} W
10. 22.1 ly
12. (c) (i) 11.0 pc
    (e) (i) 2.62×10^{21} m^2
        (ii) 1.44×10^{10} m
        (iii) 730 nm
    (f) red giant
13. (c) (i) 2 days
    (d) (i) 2.14×10^{19} m
15. (b) (i) $1.3 \times 10^{-26} \, \mathrm{kg \, m^{-3}}$ (ii) 7 or 8 m^{-3}

Practice questions

1. (a) (i) spectral class   (ii) absolute magnitude
   (b) A = main sequence   B = red supergiant
       C = white dwarf   D = main sequence
2. Open $\rho > \rho_0$ Flat $\rho = \rho_0$ Closed $\rho < \rho_0$
3. (c) (ii) 3.8×10^{-3}
5. (a) (ii) 4.0
   (b) (ii) 10 years
6. (b) (ii) 1900 pc
7. (b) wavelength

Chapter 14

1. 515 kHz, 485 kHz
2. **(a)** 1 Hz **(b)** 0.09 Hz
   (c) 0.91 Hz, 1.09 Hz
3. **(a)** 0.1 MHz **(b)** 0.001
   (c) 240 kHz
4. **(a)** 0.33 MHz, 0.15 MHz **(b)** 0.05 MHz
5. **(a)** 001100 **(b)** 011010
   (c) 100001
6. **(a)** 6 **(b)** 25 **(c)** 30
7. **(a)** 0 **(b)** 1 **(c)** 1
8. 101 101 011 001 000 101 010 010
9. 101 011 000 010
   101 001 101 010
10. 5 3 0 2
    5 1 5 2
11. 4, 6, 7, 6, 4, 1, 2, 4, 6, 4
12. 0100, 0110, 0111, 0110, 0100
13. 4.22×10^8 bits, 52.8MB
14. 94.5 min, 15.8 hours
15. **(a)** 1×10^{-6} s **(b)** 16 MHz
16. 5kHz
17. **(a)** 38.8° **(b)** 51.2°
    (c) 41.8° **(d)** yes
    (e) 62.2μm
18. **(a)** 10 dB **(b)** 7 dB
    (c) 20 dB
19. **(a)** 10 dB **(b)** 0.1 mW
20. No, attenuation too high
21. 8000 km
22. 25 000 km/hr
23. **(a)** 1600km

Practice question

1. **(c)** **(i)** 6 μs **(ii)** 9 μs

Chapter 15

1. 9.7×10^{14} Hz
2. **(a)** 1.9×10^{15} Hz **(b)** 2.42×10^{14} Hz
3. 4.13 keV

4. visible 6.98×10^{14} Hz
5. radio 8.00×10^7 Hz
6. infrared 3.00×10^{13} Hz
7. X ray 3.00×10^{17} Hz
8. 3.98×10^{-2} W m^{-2}
9. 3.75×10^{26} W
10. **(a)** strong **(b)** weak
    (c) strong
11. **(a)** destructive **(b)** constructive
    (c) constructive
12. **(a)** 1cm **(b)** 1.5 cm **(c)** 0.5 cm
13. 450 cm
14. 562.5 cm
15. 9 cm
16. 6 cm
17. **(a)** 3.3 μm **(b)** 12.2°
18. **(a)** 15 cm **(b)** 6.67 dioptres
19. 25 cm
20. **(a)** 15 cm **(b)** real
    (c) 0.5
21. 6.67 cm
22. **(a)** $^-$7.5 cm **(b)** virtual
    (c) 1.5
23. **(a)** 5 m **(b)** 5.05 cm
    (c) 0.01 **(d)** 0.01m
24. **(a)** 6.67 cm **(b)** 0.33
25. 8.75×10^{-3} rads
26. 4×10^{-3} rads
27. 4.16 cm
28. 6
29. **(a)** 3 cm **(b)** 4.17 cm
    (c) 7.17 cm
30. **(a)** 10 **(b)** 110 cm
31. 5 cm

Practice questions

1. **(b)** **(i)** $v = -25$ cm, so distance is 25 cm
       (ii) 4.0 cm
2. **(c)** at infinity
   (e) $v = 2.04$ cm; beyond eyepiece lens/between eyepiece lens and eye
4. **(d)** $m = \dfrac{-30}{75} = -0.4$
5. **(c)** 1.58 mm

Index

A

aberrations   409
absolute zero   65–6
absorption lines   247
absorption spectroscopy   202–3
absorption spectrum   247, 333
acceleration
    centripetal   40–1
    definition   16
    uniformly accelerated motion   16–20
accommodation   215
achromatic doublet   409
albedo   200, 210
Alkemade, Nicholas   20
alpha emission   187
alpha energy   155
alpha particles   144–5, 154–5
alpha radiation   154–7
ampere   4
amplifier   282–5
    gain   284
    inverting   285
    non-inverting   284
amplitude   71
    damped harmonic motion   81
    light waves   98
    sound waves   99
amplitude modulation   289, 353–4
analogue and digital storage
    accessing data   273–4
    corruption of data   274
    damaged data retrieval   274
    home entertainment   274
    personal information   275
    processing data   273
    social implications   274–5
    storing text   274
analogue sensor   366
analogue signals   263–75
    Nyquist frequency   268
    recording   264–5
    sampling   267–8
    sampling rate   267
analogue to digital conversion   267
analogue to digital converter   363–4
    sampling   363–4, 367
AND gate signal   265
Andromeda galaxy   327
anechoic chamber   99
angular frequency   71
angular magnification   405, 408
answers to exercises and practice
    questions   427–33
antimatter   157
antiparticles   157, 303, 312, 314
antiquarks   314
    colour charge   317
APPCDC   211

Aristotle   28
ASCII code   267
asteroid   326
astronomical telescope   407–8
astrophysics   325–50
    introduction   325–8
atom bomb   184
atomic energy states   247–50
atomic physics   144–68
atomic spectra   247–50
atomic theory
    alpha particles   144–5
    Bohr's model   145–6
    energy level model   147
    history   144–6
    ionization   149
    light absorption   149
    modern model   147–9
    photon   147–8
    raisin bun theory   144
    Rutherford's model   144–5
attenuation   370–1
audio tapes   265
Aurora Borealis   148
automatic light switch   122
Avogadro's number   51

B

B field   139
balanced forces   26–7
bandwidth   354, 356
baryons   308, 313, 314–15
battery   103–6
    conservation of energy   104
    energy transformation   105
    potential difference   105
beat track   156
becquerel   162, 258
Becquerel, Henri   259
Berners-Lee, Tim   377
beta decay   257
beta minus particles   156
Big Bang model   344–5
binary numbers   266
binary star system   334
binary stars   335
binary system   359
binding energy   151–3
binding energy curve   152–3
biomass   174
bits   266, 268–9, 360
black-body radiation   200, 331
blue-shifted wavelengths   333
Bohr's model   145–6, 248, 249
Bohr, Niels   145, 252
boiling   58–9
Brewster's law   232
bubble chamber   311–12
bytes   266, 272, 360

C

cable types   373
calculations, practical hints   28–9
candela   233
capacity   61
carbon dating   162, 257
CDs   230
celsius – kelvin   54
centripetal acceleration   40–1
centripetal force   41–2
cepheids   335, 336
CERN accelerator   299, 311
Chadwick, James   303
change of phase   57
changing state   57–9
charge   132
charge coupled device (CCD)
    astronomy   281
    flash card   276, 277
    X-ray machines   281
charge-coupled device (CCD)   330
Chinese characters   267
chromatic aberration   409
circular motion
    acceleration   76
    displacement   76
    simple harmonic motion   76–7
    velocity   76
circular wavefront   93
coal   173–4
    history   177–9
coal-fired power station   179–80
coastal winds   194
coldness   53
collisions
    elastic   37
    inelastic   37
    momentum   37
colour blind   217
communications   351–79
compact discs (CDs)   270–2
    construction   270
    lands   270
    pits   270
    reading   270–1
    tracking   271–2
comparator   286–7
compounds   51
compression waves   87
computer to computer
    communication   359–61
concave lens   397
conductors   106
    graphs   109
cones   216–17
conservation of charge   133
conservation of energy   36–7
    battery   104
    electric circuit   111

conservation of momentum   30
constant velocity   28
constellations   327
convex lens   397
    image formation   399–400
cooling towers   179
copper coaxial cables   372, 373
cosmic microwave background
        radiation   345
cosmic rays   311
cosmology   343–7
critical damping   81
Curie, Marie   259

D

damped harmonic motion   81
    amplitude   81
    frequency   81
damping   80–1
dark energy   347
dark matter   326, 347
data capture   275–81
de Broglie hypothesis   243–4
de Broglie wavelength   243
de Broglie, Louis   243
decay chains   158
decay constant   258, 259
decibel   370
delta minus   315
Denmark, wind power   195
depth of vision   216
derived units   4–6
deuterium   183
diffraction   226–7
    light waves   97
    overlapping   229
    single slit   226–7
    sound waves   99
    waves   86, 96
diffraction grating
    multiple-slit diffraction   394–6
digital camera
    capacitance   276
    charge coupled device (CCD)   276, 277
    data reading   278
    flash card   276, 277
    photodiode   277
    pixels   277
    serial register   278
    thermionic emissions   277
digital communications system
    diagram   365
digital devices   265
digital electronics   265–6
digital imaging   175–81
    colour   280
    digital photography vs film   280
    lenslets   278
    magnification   278
    quantum efficiency   278
    resolution of images   279–80
    terms and quantities   278–9
    video   280
digital sensors   366
digital signals   263–75, 359–67

advantages   361–2
analogue-digital difference   361
asynchronous transmission   361
binary system   359
coding   362
compression   361, 362
computer to computer
        communication   359–61
data manipulation   362
data transmission   360
MP3 file   361
multiplexing   362
noise   361–2
source independence   362
synchronous transmission   361
time division multiplexing   361
timing   360
digital storage   270
digital technology   263–92
digital to binary conversion   268–9
digital video discs (DVDs)
    laser wavelength   272
    layers   272
    track   272
dilated time   297
dipoles   137
Dirac, Paul   303
discharge tube   386
displacement, definition   15
Doppler effect   223–5, 333
double-slit experiment   390–1
DVDs   230
dwarf planet   325
dynamics
    forces   25–32

E

$E=mc^2$ 294
Earth
    atmosphere   201–3
    emmisivity   202
    gravitational field   131
    Sun   129
    temperature if no atmosphere   201
earthquake waves   89
eclipsing binary stars   335
efficiency   38–9
Einstein, Albert   151, 240, 241, 252, 273,
        293–4, 303
elastic collisions   37
elastic limit   34
electric cells, internal resistance   111–12
electric circuit
    energy changes   110–11
    shopping centre analogy   111–12
electric field
    addition   136
    Coulomb's law   134
    field lines   133–6
    strength   134–5
    strength close to a sphere of charge   136
    strength in a uniform field   135
electric force   132–3
    charge   132
electric force and field   132–6

electric kettle   114
electric motor   115
electric transformer   38
electrical currents   103–23
electrical measurement
    current   119–20
    multimeter   119
    potential difference   119
electrical power   113–15
    cells in series   118
    components combined   115–18
    electric motor   115
    kettle   114
    kilowatt-hours   113
    light bulb   114–15
    power delivered   113
    power dissipated   113–14
    resistor combinations   117
    resistors in parallel   116–17
    resistors in series   116
electrical sensors   121–3
    automatic light switch   122
    fire alarm   123
    light dependent resistor (LDR)   121
    light sensor   121
    potential divider   121–3
    strain gauge   121, 123
    thermistor   121
    uses   121–2
electrical signals   263
electricity
    alternating current   172
    circuits   110–23
    generation   172, 179
    resistance   106–7
    water analogy   104–6
    water waves   197–8
electromagnetic radiation
    cancer   385
    health   385
    matter   384–5
    origin   380
    transmission absorption   384
electromagnetic spectrum   382
    wavelength   382–4
electromagnetic waves   380–412
    creating   381–2
electron clouds   251
electron energy   148
electron energy levels   248
electron in a box model   250–1
electron microscope   230, 246
electronics   281–7
    amplifier   282–5
    comparator   286–7
    op amp   282–3
    operational amplifier   282–3
electrons   105
            excited   199
    particles   303
electronvolts   148, 248
elements   51
emf   111
emission spectrum   247
emmisivity   202
energy   33–9

energy

changes during simple harmonic motion 78–80

conservation 36–7

dark 347

degradation 170–1

density 173

derived but not from Sun 176

derived from Sun 175–6

electrical, world consumption 177

electron 148

fuels 169–70, 173–5

geothermal 176

hydroelectric power 175

internal 52–3

kinetic 34–5

lowest possible 152

potential 35

solar 175

steam train 178

Sun 190

tidal power 176

transfer by waves 87

transfer, examples 171

water power 191–4

wave power 176

wave transfer 87

wind power 175

wind turbine 195

work 34

world consumption 176–7

world sources 173–7

equilibrium

pendulum 71

thermal 54

translating 26

error bar 9

ethics 423

European Space Agency 335–6

evaporation 58–9

exchange forces 307

exchange particles 307–8, 310

extended essays 430–32

extension of spring 34

eye, the 215–19, 403

accommodation 215

angular magnification 405

colour blind 217

colour mixing 218–19

colour vision 216–17

cones 216–17

depth of vision 216

humours 215

magnifying glass 404–5

object size 404

perception 219

rods 216

sense perception 219

short sight 403

F

Feynman diagrams 318–21

interactions 319

predictions using 320–1

'rules' 319

field lines

electric field 133–6

gravitational field 130–1

magnetic field 138

fields and forces 127–43

film 276

film camera 275–6

fire alarm 123, 286

fission benefits

no CO_2 187

plutonium 187

sustainability 187

fission bomb 184

fission reaction 181–3

flash card 276, 277

Fleming's left hand rule 141, 142

fluorescent tube 386–7

force 25–6

balanced 26–7

dynamics 25–32

electrical 132–3

sensor 84

total effective 12

translating 26

types 132

forced oscillations 80–4, 82

fossil fuel power 177–81

coal-fired power station 179–80

electricity generation 179

gas-fired power station 180–1

industrial revolution 178

oil 178–9

oil-fired power station 180

petroleum 178–9

steam engine 178

steam train 178

free body diagrams 11–13

frequency, oscillations 71

frequency modulation 355–6

frequency of sound waves 99

fuels

biomass 174

coal 173–4

energy 169–70, 173–5

fossil fuel 177–81

fusion fuel 175

gas 174

nuclear 183–4

nuclear fuel 174

oil 174

wood 174

fundamental frequency 220–1

fundamental particles 317–18

fusion 187–8

fusion

burning plasma 188

fusion bomb 188

fusion reactor 188

heating plasma 188

hydrogen bomb 188

magnetic confinement 188

plasma 188

tokamak 188

fusion bomb 188

fusion fuel 175

fusion reactor 188

G

galaxy 327

Gallileo Galilei 28, 35, 294, 295

gamma energy 157

gamma radiation 157–8

gamma rays 382, 384

gas 174

gas, ideal 63–4

doing work on 65

gas doing work 65

kinetic model 62–6

pressure 64

pressure and temperature 65

pressure and volume 64

properties 64–5

temperature 63, 65

volume 64

gas-fired power stations 180–1

gauge bosons 318

Gell-Mann, Murray 314

geostationary satellites 375

geothermal energy 176

glaciers 209

Global Positioning System (GPS) 301

global warming 205–9

causes 207

CO_2 208–9

enhanced greenhouse effect 207

future possibilities 209–11

future possible solutions 210–11

glaciers 209

greenhouse gases 207

ice cores 207–8

international problem 211

models and modelling 205–6

sand analogy 205–6

sea level rising 210

weather changes 210

globular cluster 326

gluons 316–17

graphs

acceleration vs time 22–3

acceleration vs time, simple harmonic motion 75

amplitude vs frequency, damping 82

binding energy curve 152–3

binding energy per nucleon vs nucleon number 152, 164, 165

conductors 109

displacement vs position, longditudinal waves 91

displacement vs position, waves 90

displacement vs time 20–1, 83

displacement vs time, longditudinal waves 91

displacement vs time, simple harmonic motion 73–4

displacement vs time, waves 90

distance vs time 20–1

error bar 9

heat loss 61

heating 60–1

kinetic energy, simple harmonic motion 79

load vs time, sand analogy 206

motion 20–3
non-ohmic conductor 109
ohmic conductor 109
oscillations 73–5
outlier 9, 10
potential energy, simple harmonic
    motion 79
practical hints 24
relative velocity vs Lorentz factor 300
temperature vs time 60
tension vs time 84
total energy, simple harmonic
    motion 79
velocity vs time 21–2
velocity vs time, simple harmonic
    motion 74
waves 90
gravitational field
    addition of fields 131
    around a spherical object 130
    Earth 131
    field lines 130–1
    strength 130
gravitational force and field 127–31
greenhouse effect 198–204
    albedo 200
    black body radiation 200
    electrons excited 199
    energy flow 204
    global warming 207
    ionization 199
    light-matter interaction 199–201
    molecules excited 199
    radiation from Sun 201–3
    Sankey diagrams 204
    solar radiation 198–9
    solids interaction 200
    Stefan-Boltzmann law 201
greenhouse gases 207
ground state 248

H

hadrons 306, 308, 312–13
half-life 160–2, 258, 259
Halley's Comet 326
Hallwach's electroscope 239
Hallwachs, Wilhelm 239
Harvard spectral classes 333
health
    electromagnetic radiation 385
    nuclear radiation 158–9
heat
    graphical representation 60–1
    hotness 53
    latent 59
    loss 61
    lost 59
    'red hot' 200
    transfer 54
Heisenberg uncertainty principle 252–3
    particles 304–5
Heisenberg, Werner 252, 253, 304
Hertz, Heinrich 239–40
Hertzsprung-Russell diagram 336
Hideki Yukawa 307

hot air balloon engine 169–70
hotness 53
Hubble, Edwin 344
humours 215
hydroelectric power 175, 191–4
    energy from water 191–4
    pumped storage schemes 193
    run-of-the-river power stations 193
    small scale advantages 193
    tidal power 193
hydrogen, line spectrum 146
hydrogen bomb 188

I

ice cores 207–8
image formation 398–402
    convex lens 399–400
    extended object 398
    lens formula 400–1
    linear magnification 401–2
    point object 398
    real image 398
    virtual image 398
impulse 29, 31–2
industrial revolution, fossil fuel power 178
inelastic collision 37
inertial frame of reference 295–6
infrared 383
instantaneous velocity 21, 40
insulator 106
interference
    sound waves 99
    waves 86, 87, 89, 96–7
internal assessment
    conclusion and evaluation 427
    data collection and processing 426–7
    design 425–26
    manipulative skills 428
    overview 424
    personal skills 428–9
internal energy 52–3
internet 377
    advantages 377
        broadband 354
    problems 378
inverting amplifier 285
ionization 199
IPCC 211
iris 215

K

katabatic wind 195
kelvin 4, 65–6
    celsius 54
Kepler's law 375
kilowatt-hours 113
kinematics 15–24
    air resistance 19
    instantaneous velocity 21
    relative velocity 23–4
    simple harmonic motion 70–99
    terminal velocity 19
    waves 70–99
kinetic energy 34–5
    simple harmonic motion 78, 79

knowledge, theory of 414–24
Kyoto Protocol 211

L

lambda zero 315
lands 270
Large Hadron Collider 299
Large Magellanic Cloud 327
laser 388, 389
latent heat 59
    water vaporization 62
laws
    Brewster's law 232
    Coulomb's law 134
    Kepler's law 375
    Malus' law 233
    Newton's first law of motion 26, 28, 295
    Newton's laws of motion and Einstein's
        equations 296
    Newton's second law of motion 28
    Newton's third law of motion 32
    Newton's universal law of
        gravitation 127–8
    Ohm's law 108–9
    radioactivity decay law 258
    reflection, laws of 94
    second law of thermodynamics 170
    Snell's law 95
    Stefan-Boltzmann law 201, 331–2
    Wien's displacement law 331–2
Leavitt, Henrietta 342
lenses 275, 397
    aberrations 409
    astronomical telescope 407–8
    chromatic aberration 409
    formula 400–1
    magnifying glass 404–5
    microscope 406
            power 397
    spherical aberration 409
lenslets 278
lepton number 313
leptons 306, 313, 317
light
    candela 233
    colour mixing 218–19
    diffraction 226–7
    dispersion 218
    dual nature 231, 243
    electromagnetic nature 231
    liquid-crystal displays (LCDs) 234–5
    optically active substances 234
    particle nature 231, 240
    particles 304
    plane-ploarized 231
    polarization 89, 231–5
    polarized 231
    primary colours 218
    production 381
    refraction 368
    sources 386–8
    transverse wave 231
light bulb 114–15, 387
light damping 81
light dependent resistor (LDR) 121

light pollution   328
light sensor   121
light waves   97–8, 381, 383
light year   326
linear momentum   29
liquid-crystal displays (LCDs)   234–5
logic gates   265–6
longitudinal waves   89, 89, 91
Lorentz factor   299–300
lowest possible energy   152
lsb (least significant bit)   360
luminosity   330–1, 332, 342

M

MACHOs (Massive Astronomical Compact
    Objects)   347
magnetic confinement   188
magnetic field   138–9
   B field   139
   charges in   142
   field caused by currents   139–40
   field inside a coil   140
   field inside a solenoid   140
   field lines   138
   grip rule   140
   magnetic flux density   139
magnetic flux density   139
magnetic force, current-carrying
    conductor   140–1
magnetic force and field   137–42
magnetic poles   137–8
   dipoles   137
   unlike attract   138
magnifying glass   404–5
magnitude
   order of   2
   quantities   1–3
Malus' law   233
mass   25–6
   spheres of   128
mass on a spring   72–3
mass spectrometer   255–6
matter
   gas   51–2
   liquid   51–2
   particle model   50
   solid   51–2
   thermal properties   55–62
   three states   51–2
   wave nature   243–6
Maxwell, James Clerk   380
measurement
   accuracy   7–8
   electrical   119–20
   errors   7–8
   oscillations, experimental   84
   physical, interface use   366–7
   precision   7–8
   significant figures   8–9
   uncertainties   3, 7–8
mechanics   15–49
meltdown   186
mesons   308, 312–13, 314, 315–16
metal, specific heat   61
microscope   406

microscopic models
   battery   105
   resistance   107
microwave   383
Milky Way   327
Millikan, Robert   242
mnemonics
   Harvard spectral classes   333
   suvat equations   16–20
mobile phones
   environment   292
   health   292
modulation factor   354
modulation index   354, 355
mole   51
molecules   58
molecules excited   199
momentum
   collisions   37
   conservation   30
   linear   29
Moon
 size   404
illusion   421
motion
   centripetal acceleration   40–1
   graphing   20–3
   in a circle   40–2
MP3 file   361
msb (most significant bit)   360
multiple-slit diffraction   394–6

N

natural frequency   82
neutrino   156, 257
neutron mass   150
neutrons   314
Newton's laws of motion
   first law   26, 28, 295
   second law   28
   third law   32
Newton's laws of motion and Einstein's
    equations   296
Newton's universal law of gravitation   127–8
Newton, Sir Isaac   27
non-inverting amplifier   284
non-ohmic conductor   109
nuclear energy levels   256
nuclear energy problems
   meltdown   186
   reactor efficiency   185
   uranium extraction   185
   waste   186
nuclear fission   165–6
nuclear force
   binding energy   151–3
   mass defect   152
   strong force   150–1
nuclear fuel   174, 183–4
   fuel bundle   183
   plutonium   184
   reaction rate control   184
   uranium enrichment   183
nuclear fusion   163–5
   Sun   329

nuclear masses   150, 153
nuclear physics   144–68, 254–60
nuclear power   181–91
   chain reaction   182
   critical mass   183
   deuterium   183
   fission reaction   181–3
   neutrons moderation   183
nuclear power station   184–5
nuclear radiation
   health   158–9
   protection against   159
nuclear reactions   162–5
   transmutation, nitrogen into
    carbon   162–3
nuclear reactor fuel   184
nuclear structure   149–54
   charge of the nucleus   150
   exponential decay curve   160
   half-life   160–2
   mass of the nucleus   149
   terms and quantities   150
nuclear submarines   185
nuclear weapons   186
nuclides   153
Nyquist frequency   268

O

Occam's razor 416
Ohm's law   108–9
ohmic conductor   109
oil   174, 178–9
oil, history   177–9
oil-fired power stations   180
Olbers' paradox   343–4
Olbers, Heinrich   343
one-dimensional waves   86–7
   superposition   92
op amp   282–3 and see operational amplifier
operational amplifier
   ideal   283
   input impedance   283
   open loop gain   282
   output impedance   283
optic fibre transmission   367–72
   amplification   371–2
   attenuation   371
   copper coaxial cables   372, 373
   light refraction   368
   material dispersion   369
   modal dispersion   369
   step indexed   369
optical instruments   402–8
optical resolution   228–30
OR gate symbol   265
orbitals   251
order of magnitude   2
oscillating water column   197
oscillations   70–1
   amplitude   71
   analysing   72–3
   angular frequency   71
   critical damping   81
   cycle   71
   damping   80–1

equilibrium position   71
forced   80–4, 82
frequency   71
graphs   73–5
light damping   81
mass on a spring   72–3
measurement, experimental   84
natural frequency   82
pendulum   72
radio tuner   82
resonance   80–4, 82
time period   71
Outer Space Treaty   376
outlier   9, 10
overlapping diffraction   229

P

packet switching networks   377
paradigm shift 417–8
parsec   338
particle model, matter   50
particle physics   303–24
history   303
particles
accelerators   311
antiparticles   303, 312, 314
baryons   308, 313
bubble chamber   311–12
classification   306
conserving charges   308–9
cosmic rays   311
electrons   303
exchange   307–8, 310
exchange forces   307
explosion   312–13
fundamental   317–18
gauge bosons   310, 318
generations   317
hadrons   306, 308, 312–13
Heisenberg uncertainty principle   304–5
interaction between   306
interactions   318
leptons   306, 313, 317
light   304
mass-energy equivalence   305
mesons   308, 312–13
Pauli exclusion principle   305, 310
pions   308
probability waves   304
quarks   314–18, 317
spin   305
standard model   317
strangeness   312
virtual   307
wave nature   304
particles wavelength   243
path difference   96
Pauli exclusion principle   305, 310
Pauli, Wolfgang   303
peer review 422
pelamis   197
pendulum
definitions of terms   70–1
equilibrium   71
perception 420

petroleum   178–9
phase   83
difference   83, 96
horse riding   83
phone systems
cell   289–91
cell phone advantages-
disadvantages   291–2
land   288
mobile   288–92
public switched telephone network
(PSTN)   288
radio telephone communication   289
receiving a call   290
3G system   291
tracking   290–1
photo gate   84
photodiode   277
photoelectric effect   239–42
photoelectric effect experiment
(Mllikan)   242
photoelectric equation (Einstein)   241
photoelectrons   240
photoemission   240
photovoltaic cell   191
physical work   33
pion plus   315
pions   308
pipes, waves   221–2
pits   270
pixels   277
Planck length   2
Planck, Max   240, 241
plane wavefront   93
plane-polarized light   231
plutonium   184
polar satellites   375–6
Polaris   328
polarization   231–5
analyser   233
light   89
polarizer   233
stress analysis   234
waves   89
polarization by reflection   231–2
polarized light   231
polaroid combinations   233
polaroid sunglasses   232
position sensor   84
potential difference   105
measuring   119
Ohm's law   108–9
potential energy   35
simple harmonic motion   78, 79
power   33–9, 37–8
power spectrum   354
power stations
coal-fired   179–80
gas-fired   180–1
nuclear   184–5
oil-fired   180
run-of-the-river   193
practical hints
calculations   28–9
extended essays   430–2
graphs   24

perception   219
predictions using Feynman diagrams   320–1
primary colours   218
probability waves   304
proper time   297
proton mass   150
protons   315
pumped storage schemes   193

Q

quantities
estimating approximately   3, 14
magnitude   1–3
quantum chromo dynamics (QCD)   317
quantum efficiency   278
quantum numbers   248
spin   314
quantum physics   239–53
photoelectric effect   239–42
radiation   239–43
quarks   2
antiquarks   314
baryons   314–15
colour charge   317
confinement   316
delta minus   315
gluons   316–17
kaon plus   316
lambda zero   315
mesons   314, 315–16
neutrons   314
particles   314–18, 317
pion plus   315
properties   316–18
protons   315
strange   315
strangeness   314, 315

R

radiation, quantum nature   239–43
radio communication
aerial   357
AF amplifier   358
AM and FM compared   356–7
AM demodulator   358
AM receiver   357–8
amplitude modulation   353–4
bandwidth   354, 356
cost   357
FM and AM compared   356–7
frequencies   352–3
frequency modulation   355–6
IF amplifier   358
loudspeaker   358
mixer/oscillator   358
modulation factor   354
modulation index   354, 355
peak frequency deviation   355
power spectrum   354
principle   352–3
quality   357
radio spectrum   352
radio waves   351
radio waves transmitting digital
information   374

range 356–7
receiver 352
RF Amplifier 358
RF tuner 358
sidebands 353–4, 355
transmitter 352
radio waves 351, 383
radioactive decay 257–60
alpha energy 155
alpha particles 154–5
alpha radiation 154–7
antimatter 157
antiparticle 157
beta minus particles 156
beta track 156
decay chains 158
gamma energy 157
gamma radiation 157–8
neutrino 156
radioactivity decay law 258
raisin bun theory 144
ray diagrams 406–8
Rayleigh criterion 228–30
red giant stars 334
red supergiant stars 334
red-shifted wavelengths 333
reflection
sound waves 98
waves 85, 93–4
reflection, laws of 94
refraction
sound waves 99
waves 86, 94–5
refraction index 95
relative velocity 23–4
relativistic kinematics 297–302
relativity 293–302
introduction 293–5
length contraction 301–2
simple relative motion 294
simultaneity 296–7
space-time 297
theory of special relativity 294
relativity factor 299–300
relativity, special
concepts and postulates 295–7
resolution
modern technology 230
optical 228–30
resolution of images 279–80
magnification 279
quantum efficiency 280
resonance 80–4, 82
resonance curve 82
resultant, vectors 12
right-hand grip rule 140, 381
rods 216
Rutherford's model 144–5
Rutherford, Ernest (later Lord) 144, 254, 303

S

Sankey diagrams
car engine 171
electric motor 171

greenhouse effect 204
satellite communication 375
satellite television 375
scalars 10–11
Schmit trigger 287
Schrödinger equation 251
Schrödinger model 251
Schrödinger, Erwin 243, 251
scientific method 415
sense perception 219
serendipity 416
short sight 403
SI (Système International) units 4–6
sidebands 355
sight *see* the eye
significant figures 8–9
simple harmonic motion 70–99
simple harmonic motion
acceleration 76
circular motion 76–7
displacement 76
energy changes during 78–80
equations 77
kinetic energy 78, 79
potential energy 78, 79
total energy 78, 79
velocity 76
simultaneity 296–7
Sirius A 334
slinky 88
Snell's law 95
solar cell 191
solar constant 190
solar energy 175
solar heating panel 190–1
solar power 189–91
solar radiation 198–9, 201–3
solar spectrum 202
solar system 325–8
sound transmission 264
specific heat, metal 61
specific heat capacity 56–7
specific latent heat 59
spectrometer 247, 248–9
spectroscope 247, 248–9
spectroscopic binary stars 335
spheres of mass 128
spherical aberration 409
spring, waves in 88–9
spring extension 34
standard candle 342
standing waves 219–22
stars
binary 335
binary star system 334
blue-shifted wavelengths 333
brightness 330–1
cepheids 335, 336
eclipsing binary 335
energy source 329–30
Hertzsprung-Russell diagram 336
luminosity 330–1, 332, 342
red giants 334
red supergiants 334
red-shifted wavelengths 333
Sirius A 334

spectroscopic binary 335
Stefan-Boltzmann law 331–2
stellar distances 337–43
stellar spectra 333
types 334–5
visual binary 335
white dwarf 335
Wien's displacement law 331–2
State, change of 57–9
stationary waves 219–22
Stefan-Boltzmann law 201, 331–2
stellar cluster 326
stellar distances
absolute magnitude 339–40
apparent magnitude 339
cepheid variables 342
parallax method 337–8
spectroscopic parallax 341
stellar radiation 329–36
stellar spectra 333
stellar types 329–36
stopping potential 242
strain gauge 121, 123
strange quarks 314, 315
stress analysis 234
string, polarized waves 89
stringed instruments 88
stringed instruments, waves 220–1
Sun
astronomical unit 325
core 189
Earth 129
energy from 190
energy sources derived from 175–6
nuclear fusion 329
overview 189–91
photovoltaic cell 191
radiation 207
radiation from 201–3
radiation pressure 329
solar cell 191
solar constant 190
solar flares 207
solar heating panel 190–1
Solar power 189–91
solar spectrum 202
temperature 189
sunspots 207
superclusters 328
surface heat capacity 203
suvat equations 16–20

T

temperature 53–4
absolute zero 65–6
an earth with no atmosphere 201
emmisivity 202
gas, ideal 63, 65
Kelvin scale 65–6
particle model 54
perception 53
'red hot' 200
Sun 189
surface heat capacity 203
thermal

capacity   55–6
concepts   50–4
equilibrium   54
properties of matter   55–62
quantities measured by mixtures   61–2
thermal physics   50–66
thermistor   121, 286
thermodynamics, second law   170
Thomson, J J   144, 240
Thomson, Joseph   303
threshold frequency   240
tidal power   176, 193
time
dilation   297–301
proper   297
time period, oscillations   71
tokamak   188
total effective force   12
total energy, simple harmonic motion   78, 79
translating equilibrium   26
transverse waves   87, 88, 89
travelling waves   222
two-dimensional waves   92–3
two-source interference of waves
coherence   390
double-slit experiment   390–1
geometrical model   392–3
path difference   391
phase difference   391
superposition   390
two slit interference with light   393–4
waves from two point sources   392–3

U

ultraviolet radiation   384
uncertainties
calculated results   9
graphs   9–10
measurement   3, 7–8
uniform circular motion   40–2
units
derived   4–6
fundamental   4–6
prefixes   6
SI system   4–6
universal laws 419
universe
dark energy   347
dark matter   347
development of   346–7, 347
future   346–7
MACHOs (Massive Astronomical Compact Objects)   347
WIMPSs (Weakly Interacting Massive Particles)   347
up quark   2
uranium enrichment   183
uranium extraction   185

V

vectors   10–11
resultant   12
velocity
constant   28

instantaneous   21, 40
relative   23–4
vibrating body   70
vinyl records (LPs)   264
Virgo cluster   328
virtual particles   307
visual binary stars   335
volume of ideal gas   64

W

water vaporization, latent heat   62
water waves   96
Watt, James   38
wave power   196–8
electricity from water waves   197–8
oscillating water column   197
pelamis   197
power in water wave   196–7
water waves   196–7
wavelength of light waves   98
waves   85–99
amplitude of light   98
amplitude of sound   99
antinode   220
characteristics   85–92
circular wavefront   93
compression   87
continuous in a string   87–8
definition   85
diffraction   86, 96
diffraction of light   97–8
diffraction of sound   99
Doppler effect   223–5
earthquake   89
electromagnetic   380–412
energy transfer   87
examples   97–9
first harmonic   221
frequency of sound   99
fundamental frequency   220–1
graphs   90
in a spring   88–9
infrared   383
interference   86, 87, 89, 96–7
interference of sound   99
light   97–8, 381, 383
longditudinal   89, 89, 91
matter waves   243–4
medium, change of   94
microwave   383
node   220
one-dimensional   86–7
one-dimensional, superposition   92
path difference   96
phase difference   96
pipes   221–2
plane wavefront   93
polarization   89
power   176
probability   304
properties   92–9
pulses interference   87
radio   351, 383
rays   93
reflection   85, 93–4

reflection in a spring   89
reflection of sound   98
refraction   86, 94–5
refraction of sound   99
Snell's law   95
sound   98–9
standing   219–22
stationary   219–22
string, polarized   89
stringed instruments   88
strings   220–1
transverse   87, 88, 89, 231
travelling   222
two-dimensional   92–3
two-source interference   390–4
water   96, 196–7
wave power   196–8
wave pulse in a string   86
wave pulse reflection   86
wavefront   92
wavelength of light   98
waves from two point sources   392–3
weight   25–6
white dwarf stars   335
Wien's displacement law   331–2
WIMPSs (Weakly Interacting Massive Particles)   347
wind power   175, 194–6
coastal winds   194
Denmark   195
katabatic wind   195
wind farms   195
wind turbine   195–6
windy places   195
wind turbine   195–6
windmill   194
wire pairs   373
wood   174
work   33–9
energy   34
physical   33
work function   241
world
electrical energy consumption   177
energy consumption   176–7
energy sources   173–7

X

X-ray machines   281
X-ray radiation   382, 384

Y

Young's two slits   239–43
Young, Thomas   239